CONTENTS

The BOYS™

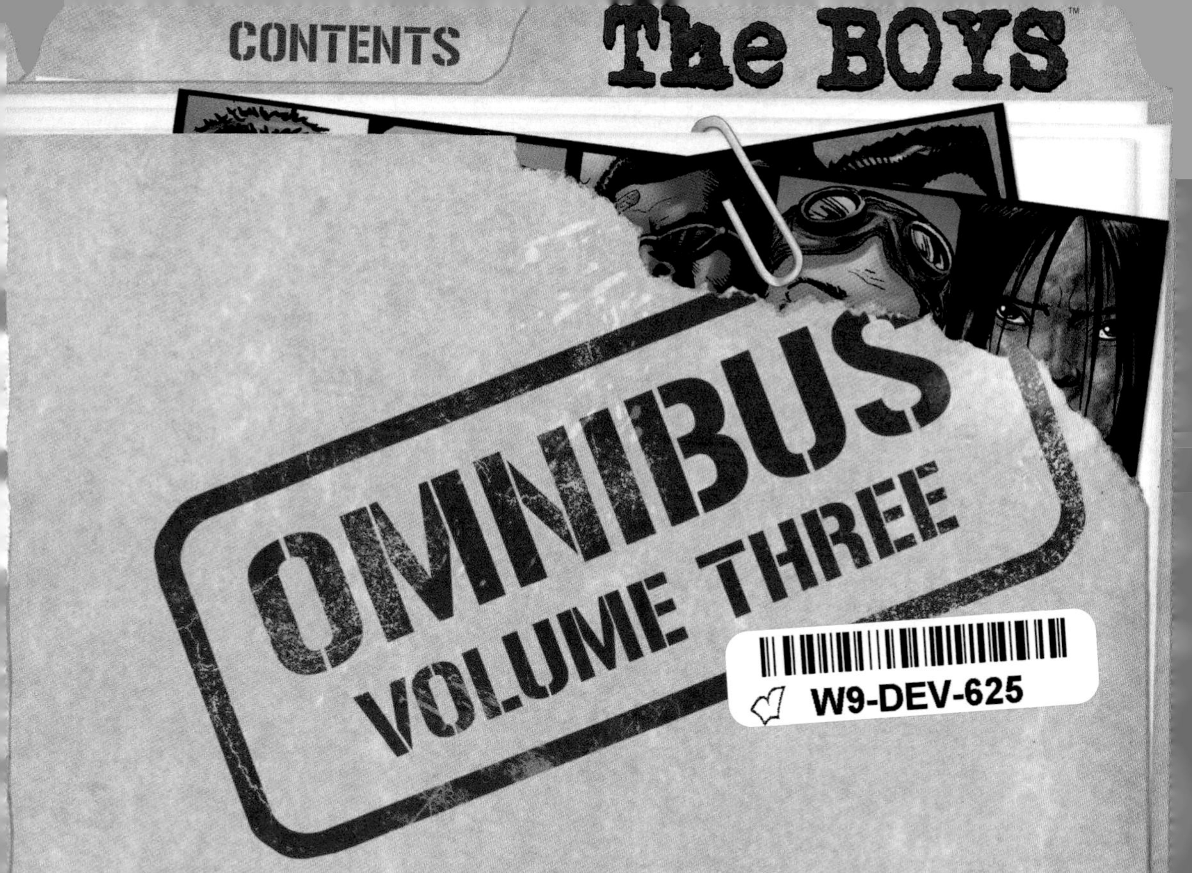

OMNIBUS
VOLUME THREE

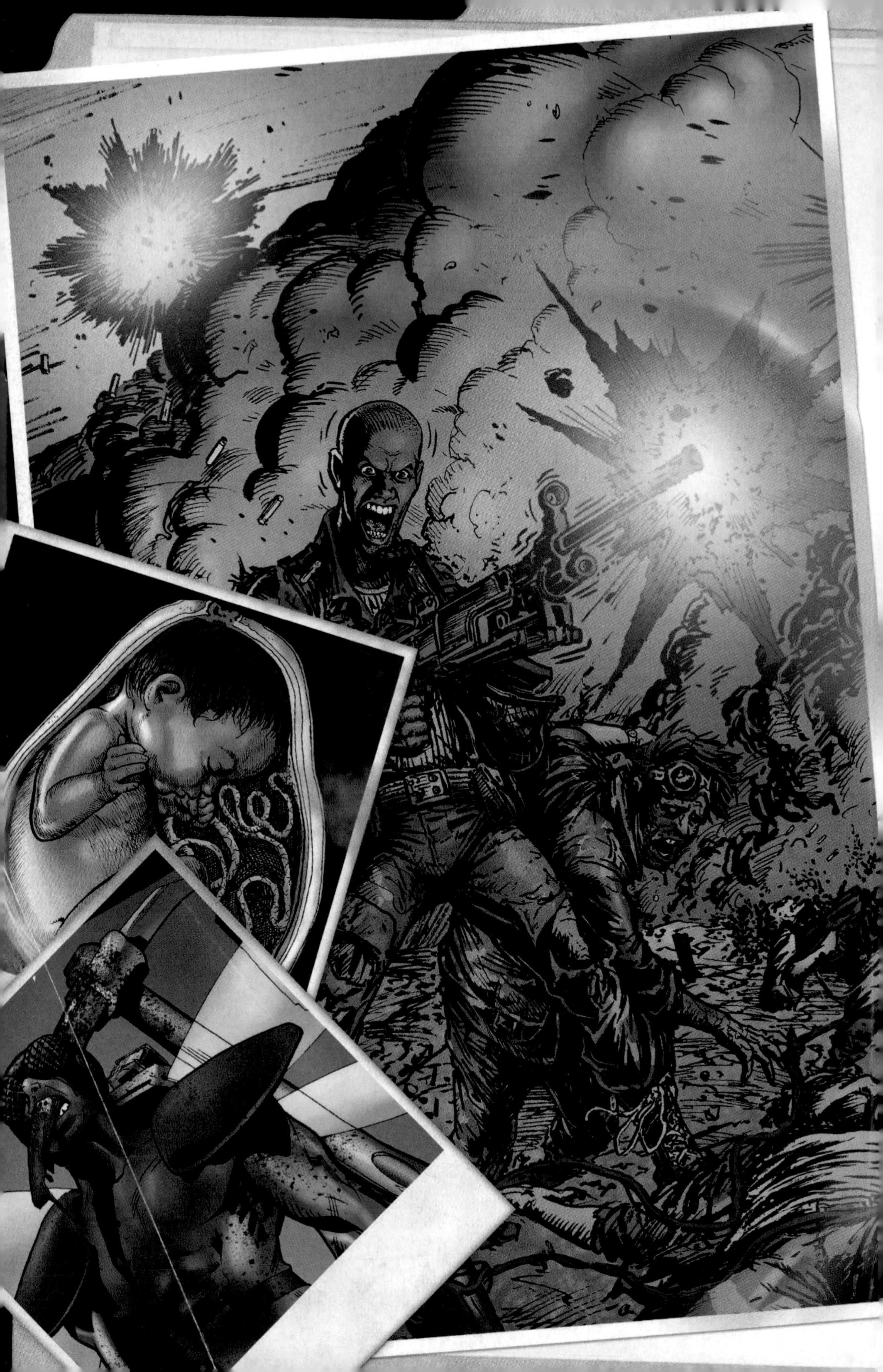

The BOYS™

OMNIBUS VOLUME THREE

The Boys created by: GARTH ENNIS & DARICK ROBERTSON

Written by:
GARTH ENNIS

Illustrated by:
JOHN McCREA w/ KEITH BURNS Herogasm #1-6, The Boys #33
CARLOS EZQUERRA The Boys #31, 32-34
DARICK ROBERTSON The Boys #35-38

Additional inks by:
KEITH BURNS w/ JOHN McCREA Herogasm #1-6
and **HECTOR EZQUERRA** The Boys #31, 32-34

Colored by:
TONY AVIÑA

Lettered by:
SIMON BOWLAND

Series covers by:
DARICK ROBERTSON & TONY AVIÑA

Book design by:
JASON ULLMEYER

Editor:
JOE RYBANDT

Collects issues one through six of The Boys: Herogasm
and thirty-one through thirty-eight of The Boys published
by Dynamite.

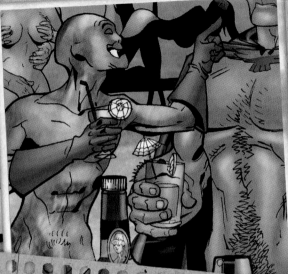

DYNAMITE®

Nick Barrucci, CEO / Publisher

Juan Collado, President / COO

Brandon Dante Primavera, V.P. of IT and Operations

Joe Rybandt, Executive Editor

Matt Idelson, Senior Editor

Kevin Ketner, Editor

Cathleen Heard, Art Director

Rachel Kilbury, Digital Multimedia Assistant

Alexis Persson, Graphic Designer

Katie Hidalgo, Graphic Designer

Alan Payne, V.P. of Sales and Marketing

Rex Wang, Director of Consumer Sales

Pat O'Connell, Sales Manager

Vincent Faust, Marketing Coordinator

Jay Spence, Director of Product Development

Mariano Nicieza, Marketing Manager

Amy Jackson, Administrative Coordinator

www.DYNAMITE.com

Facebook: /Dynamitecomics

Instagram: /Dynamitecomics

Twitter: @dynamitecomics

Standard ISBN: 978-1-5241-1003-1

Media Tie-In ISBN: 978-1-5241-1346-9

Second Printing   10 9 8 7 6 5 4 3 2 1

Printed in Canada

For information regarding press, media rights, foreign rights, licensing, promotions, and advertising e-mail: marketing@dynamite.com

CONTENTS

- INTRODUCTION BY JASON AARON
  (FROM BOYS DEFINITIVE EDITION VOLUME THREE)
- HEROGASM
- THE SELF-PRESERVATION SOCIETY
- NOTHING LIKE IT IN THE WORLD
- LA PLUM DE MA TANTE ESTE SUR LA TABLE
- THE INSTANT WHITE-HOT WILD

BONUS MATERIALS

- THE COMIC THAT GOT THE LEGEND FIRED
- SCRIPT TO ISSUE #37 BY GARTH ENNIS
  (FEATURING B/W ART BY DARICK ROBERTSON)
- DARICK ROBRETSON - SKETCHBOOK
- JOHN McCREA - SKETCHBOOK
- CARLOS EZQUERRA - SKETCHBOOK
- CREATOR BIOGRAPHIES

WAIT A MINUTE, THEY DID FUCKING WHAT?

Faces ripped off? Golden showers? Orgies? Gerbils up the ass?

You're shitting me. They've been doing all that shit with fucking super heroes? For how long? 40 issues! And a fucking spin-off mini-series? You're shitting me. You are totally fucking shitting me.

I love superheroes, man. Have since I was a kid. Right now I'm even making my living off superheroes. Superheroes feed my children. Put a roof over my head. Put lollipops in my mouth and butter in my ass. What kind of sick fucking psycho would do that sort of depraved awful shit to my beloved American superheroes?

Gotta be a fucking foreigner, right? Ain't no way it's a...

That dude over there? You're saying that dude sitting at that table right fucking over there is the one responsible for this fucking depravity? That big guy drinking the Guinness?

Let me just go talk to this fucking guy.

No, let me go, don't hold me back! I'm gonna talk to this motherfucker!

Hey! You! Yeah, you, dude! I got something I wanna...

Oh.

Hey, Garth.

I didn't know it was...

Nah, what? No, I was just... I was just playing, man. Chill. No no no, don't get up, don't get up. No, man, no that was just, I was just kidding around, you know. Like fucking...

Nah, nobody needs to get their ass kicked. Not at all. No, sir. No, sir, I don't...

Hey, let me get you another beer, okay? You need another beer? Guinness right? I'll be right back.

...

Dude, you didn't fucking tell me it was Garth fucking Ennis you were talking about! Goddamnit, he's gonna kick my fucking ass now! Jesus Christ. C'mon, have you ever read that guy's stuff? It's fucking genius, I mean, PREACHER and PUNISHER and everything, right, but c'mon, the guy fucking scares me, man. He fucking scares me. The shit that comes outta that dude's head... Jesus Christ, is he looking over here?

Beer's on the way, Garth! Coming right up!

Fuck, I am so fucking dead.*

Maybe I could... I gotta ask him if I can write the intro to his book or something. Like a gesture of good will or something, you know. Yeah, that's it, I'll write an intro and talk about how much I love *The Boys*. I mean, c'mon, nobody deserves to be fucked with more than superheroes, right? They've had it coming for a long fucking time.

And look at this, man, look at this, this is Garth being Garth. Billy Butcher. That's a quintessential Garth Ennis character if there ever was one. That guy could outfight, outdrink and definitely outfuck Punisher any day of the fucking week. And the rest of these bastards, Mother's Milk and The Frenchman and The Female? Jesus, they make the cast of *Preacher* look like a fucking Saturday night church social. And Wee Hughie, c'mon, you can't help but like that poor fucking guy, right?

And hey, Darick Robertson's art is awesome. He draws scenes of fucked-up, cringe-worthy violence as well as anyone in the biz. And John McCrea. I've loved everything he's ever done with Garth.

And it's funny. I mean seriously fucking funny. I hate that phrase "laugh out loud funny," but that's what this is, you know, it's laugh out loud funny. You fucking laugh when you're reading this. If you're a, you know, person with a completely fucked-up sense of humor. Which I totally am.

No, I'm not kissing Garth's ass, I'm not, I'm just saying. *The Boys* is a ballsy book. It's one of the ballsiest books on the market today. It's got balls to fucking spare. It's got balls coming out its ears and shit.

I don't know, you think he'll fucking buy it?

Here comes that beer Garth!

Here ya go, pal.

Wait a second, what's that? What's so funny? I don't...

What's that you're holding there... is that a...

Is that a gerbil?

AAAAAAAAAAAAAAAAAAARRRRGGHHH!!!!

Jason Aaron
Kansas City
2011 (for *The Boys Definitive Edition Vol. 3*)

Jason Aaron is an award-winning comic book writer best known for his work with Marvel Comics, including the creation of the headline-grabbing female version of *Thor* and the launch of an acclaimed new *Star Wars* series in 2015, the first issue of which became the best-selling American comic book in more than 20 years. Aaron is also the current writer on Marvel's flagship *Avengers* series. His critically acclaimed creator-owned work includes the Eisner Award-winning *Southern Bastards* from Image Comics and the *New York Times* best-selling crime series *Scalped* from Vertigo Comics. Aaron was born and raised in Alabama and currently resides in Kansas City.

* The real Garth Ennis in no way resembles the figure described here. He believes in kindness, harmony, understanding and the peaceful settling of differences through the exploration of common ground. He also believes in hiding under the table or climbing out the nearest window. His book on conflict resolution, No Please Not The Face, *will soon be available from Amazon.com.*

HEROGASM #1
cover

by DARICK ROBERTSON
and TONY AVIÑA

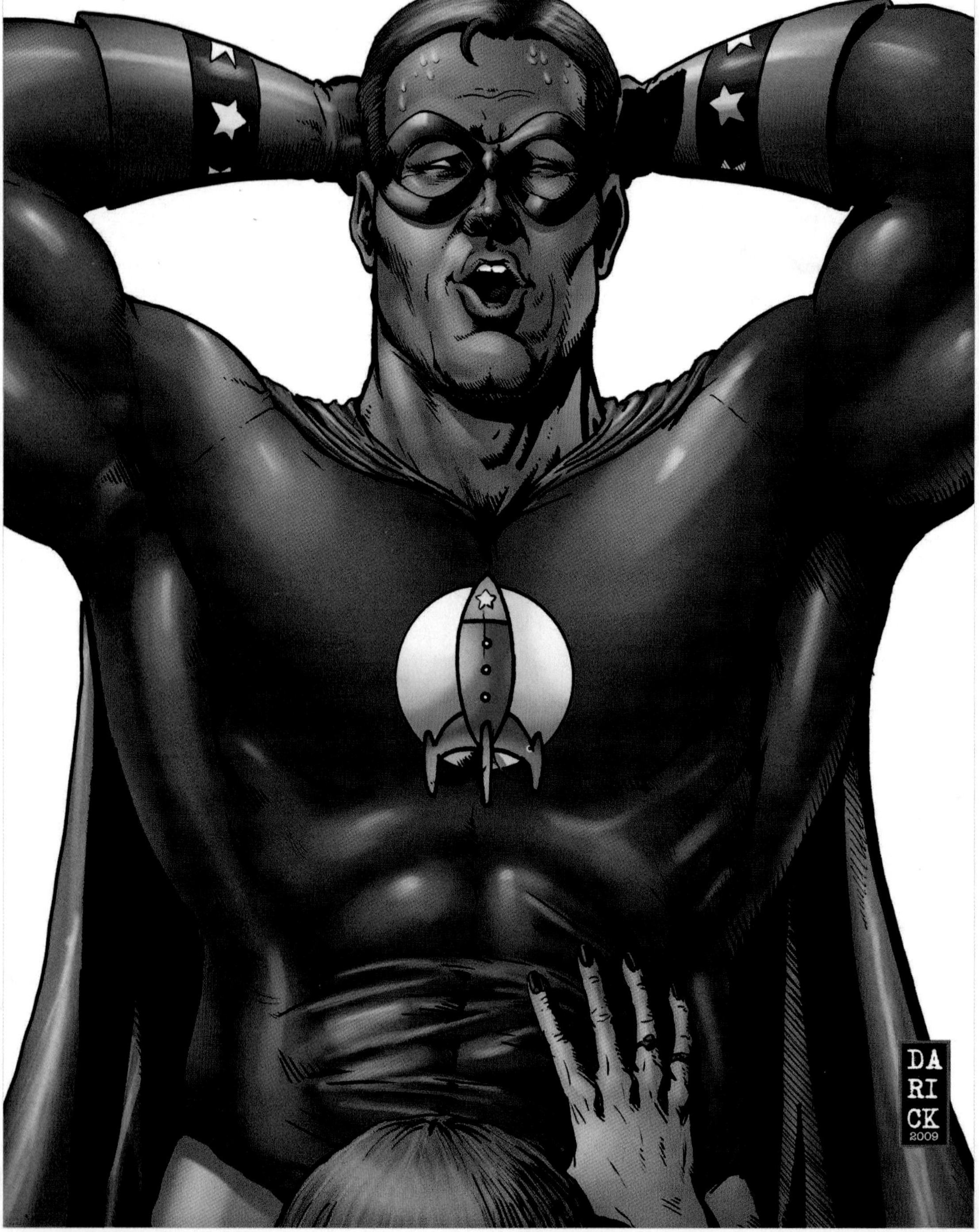
DARICK
2009

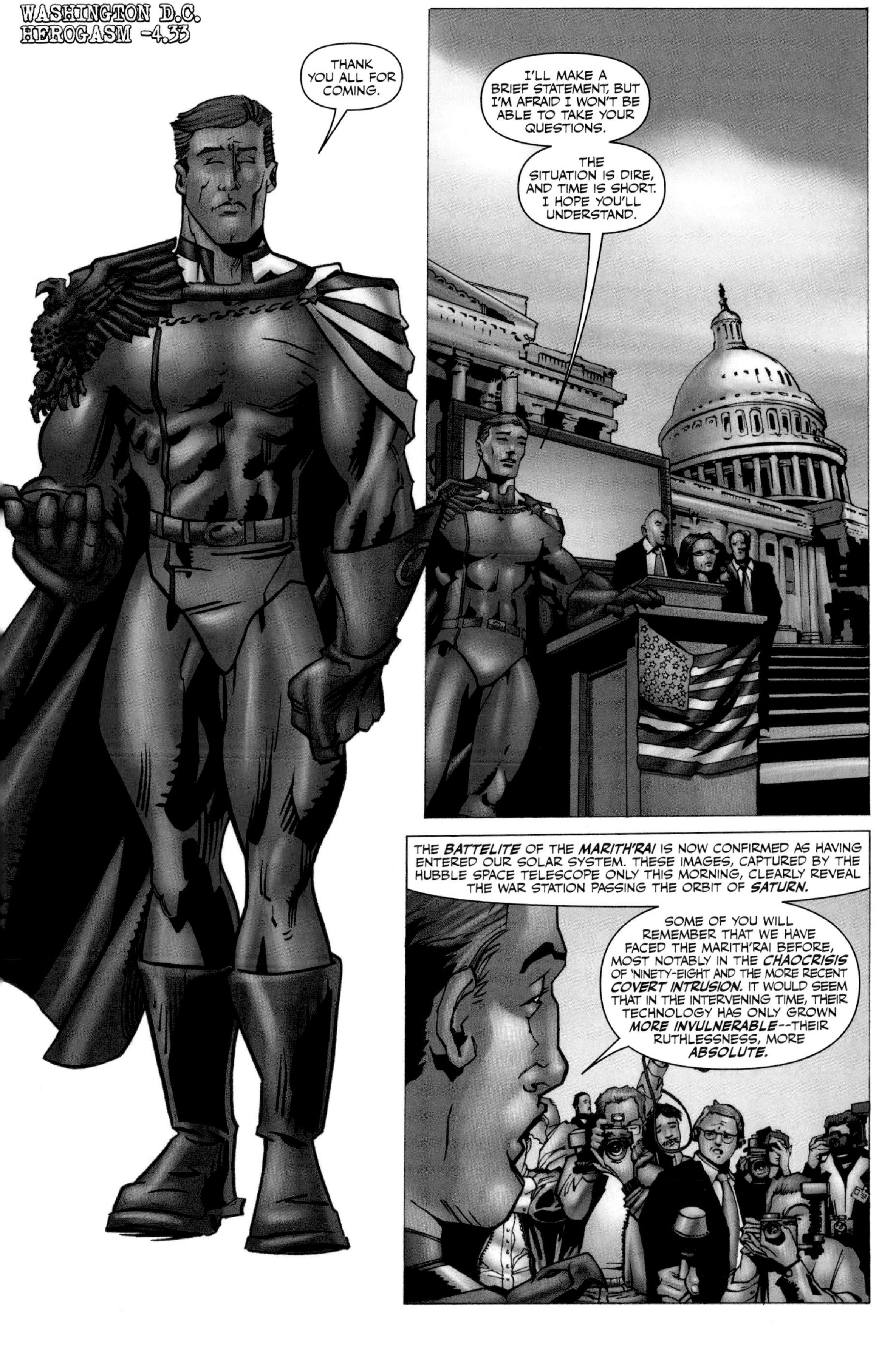
WASHINGTON D.C.
HEROGASM -4.33
THANK YOU ALL FOR COMING.
I'LL MAKE A BRIEF STATEMENT, BUT I'M AFRAID I WON'T BE ABLE TO TAKE YOUR QUESTIONS.
THE SITUATION IS DIRE, AND TIME IS SHORT. I HOPE YOU'LL UNDERSTAND.
THE *BATTELITE* OF THE *MARITH'RAI* IS NOW CONFIRMED AS HAVING ENTERED OUR SOLAR SYSTEM. THESE IMAGES, CAPTURED BY THE HUBBLE SPACE TELESCOPE ONLY THIS MORNING, CLEARLY REVEAL THE WAR STATION PASSING THE ORBIT OF *SATURN.*
SOME OF YOU WILL REMEMBER THAT WE HAVE FACED THE MARITH'RAI BEFORE, MOST NOTABLY IN THE *CHAOCRISIS* OF 'NINETY-EIGHT AND THE MORE RECENT *COVERT INTRUSION.* IT WOULD SEEM THAT IN THE INTERVENING TIME, THEIR TECHNOLOGY HAS ONLY GROWN *MORE INVULNERABLE*--THEIR RUTHLESSNESS, MORE *ABSOLUTE.*

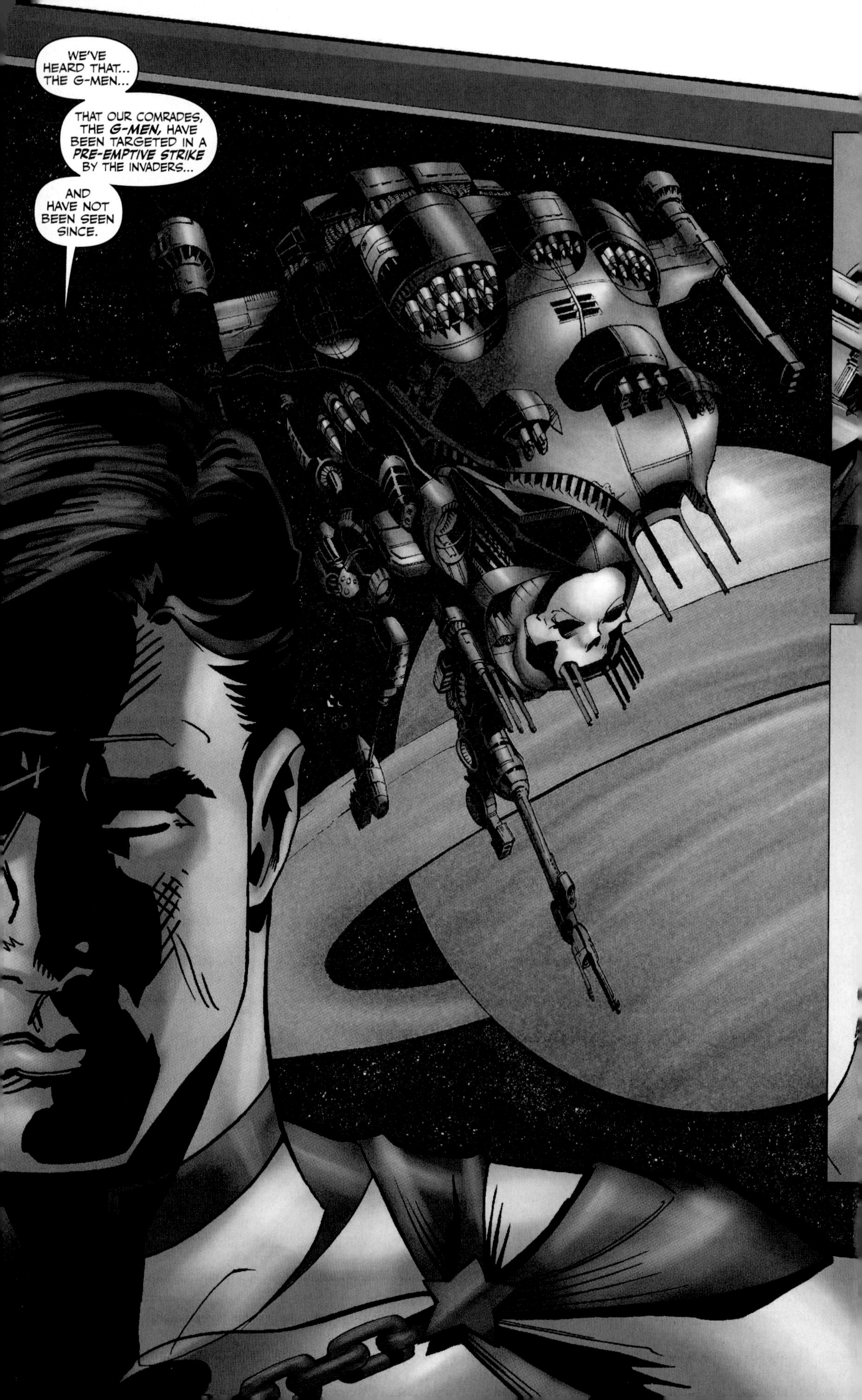
WE'VE HEARD THAT... THE G-MEN...
THAT OUR COMRADES, THE *G-MEN,* HAVE BEEN TARGETED IN A *PRE-EMPTIVE STRIKE* BY THE INVADERS...
AND HAVE NOT BEEN SEEN SINCE.

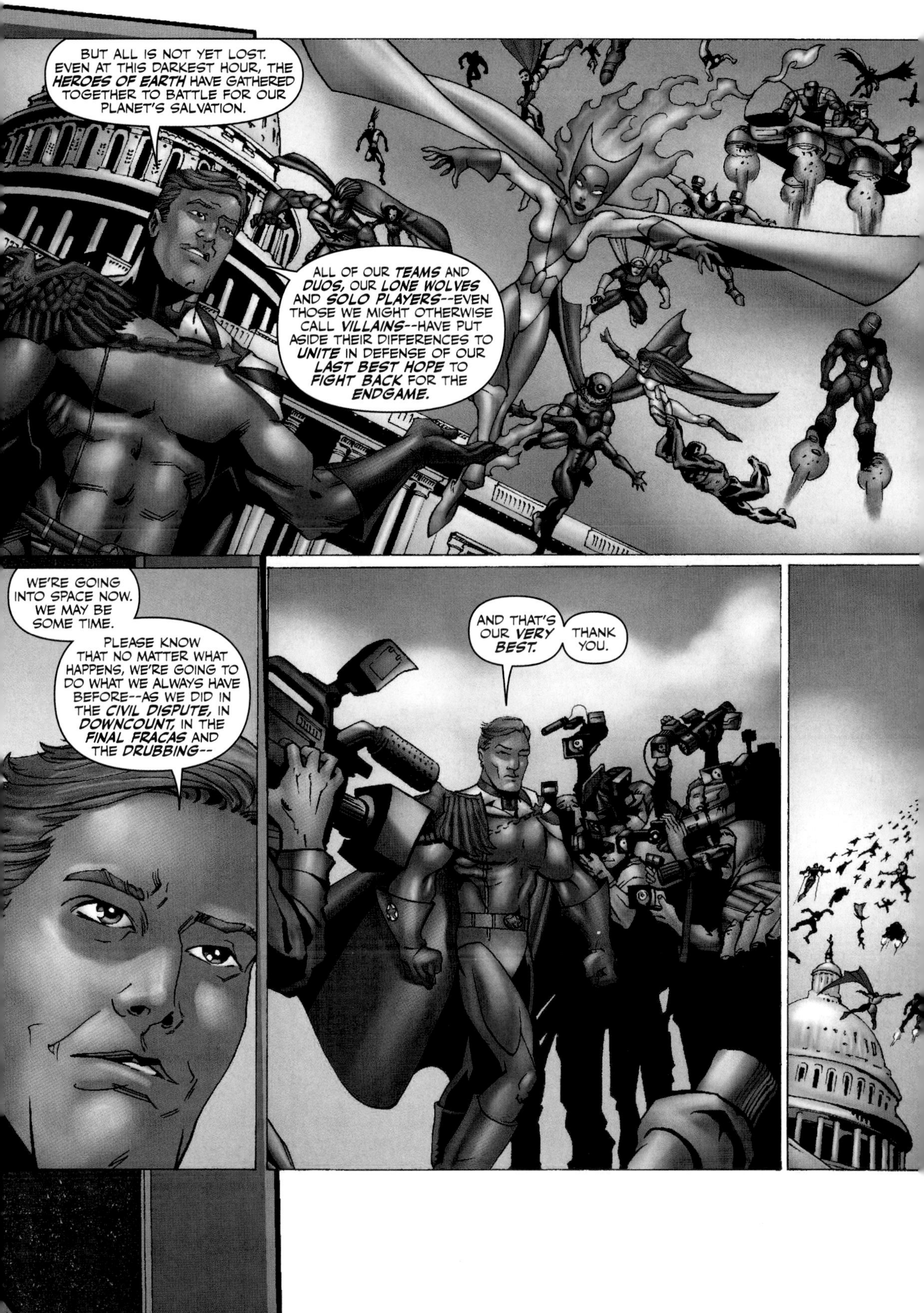
BUT ALL IS NOT YET LOST. EVEN AT THIS DARKEST HOUR, THE HEROES OF EARTH HAVE GATHERED TOGETHER TO BATTLE FOR OUR PLANET'S SALVATION.
ALL OF OUR TEAMS AND DUOS, OUR LONE WOLVES AND SOLO PLAYERS--EVEN THOSE WE MIGHT OTHERWISE CALL VILLAINS--HAVE PUT ASIDE THEIR DIFFERENCES TO UNITE IN DEFENSE OF OUR LAST BEST HOPE TO FIGHT BACK FOR THE ENDGAME.
WE'RE GOING INTO SPACE NOW. WE MAY BE SOME TIME.
PLEASE KNOW THAT NO MATTER WHAT HAPPENS, WE'RE GOING TO DO WHAT WE ALWAYS HAVE BEFORE--AS WE DID IN THE CIVIL DISPUTE, IN DOWNCOUNT, IN THE FINAL FRACAS AND THE DRUBBING--
AND THAT'S OUR VERY BEST.
THANK YOU.

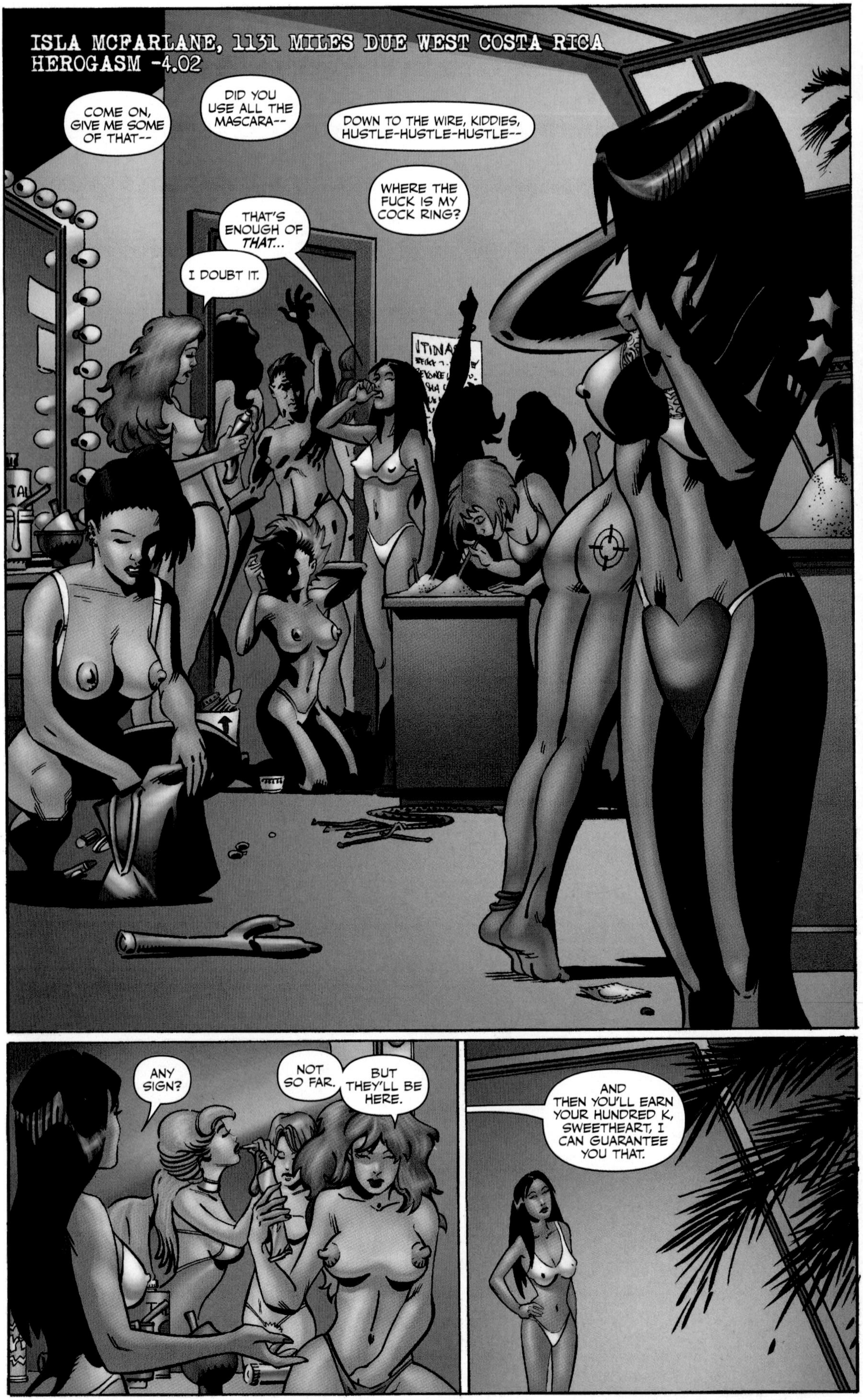
ISLA MCFARLANE, 1131 MILES DUE WEST COSTA RICA
HEROGASM -4.02
COME ON, GIVE ME SOME OF THAT--
DID YOU USE ALL THE MASCARA--
DOWN TO THE WIRE, KIDDIES, HUSTLE-HUSTLE-HUSTLE--
WHERE THE FUCK IS MY COCK RING?
THAT'S ENOUGH OF *THAT*...
I DOUBT IT.
ANY SIGN?
NOT SO FAR.
BUT THEY'LL BE HERE.
AND THEN YOU'LL EARN YOUR HUNDRED K, SWEETHEART, I CAN GUARANTEE YOU THAT.

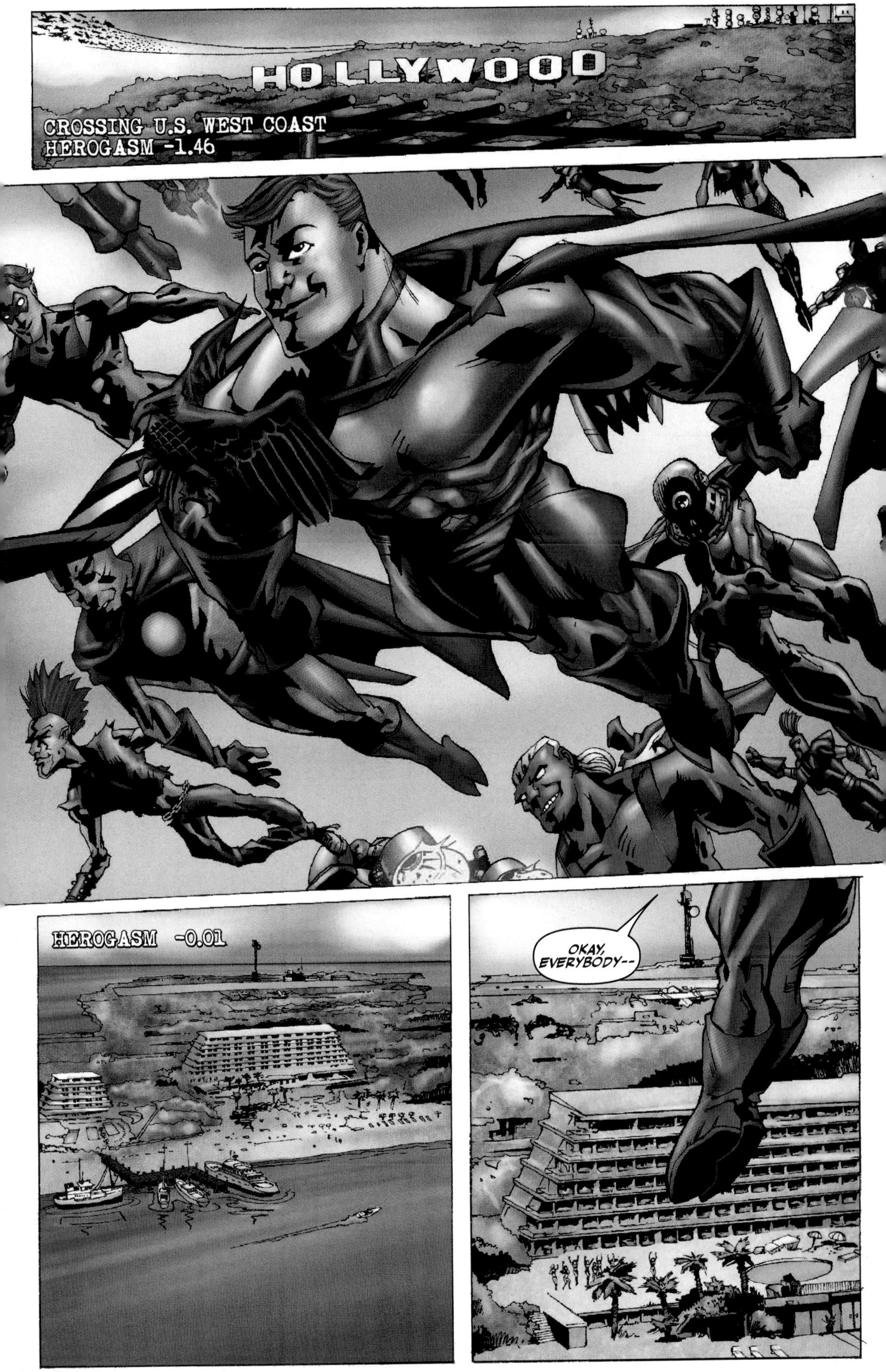
HOLLYWOOD
CROSSING U.S. WEST COAST
HEROGASM -1.46
HEROGASM -0.01
OKAY, EVERYBODY--

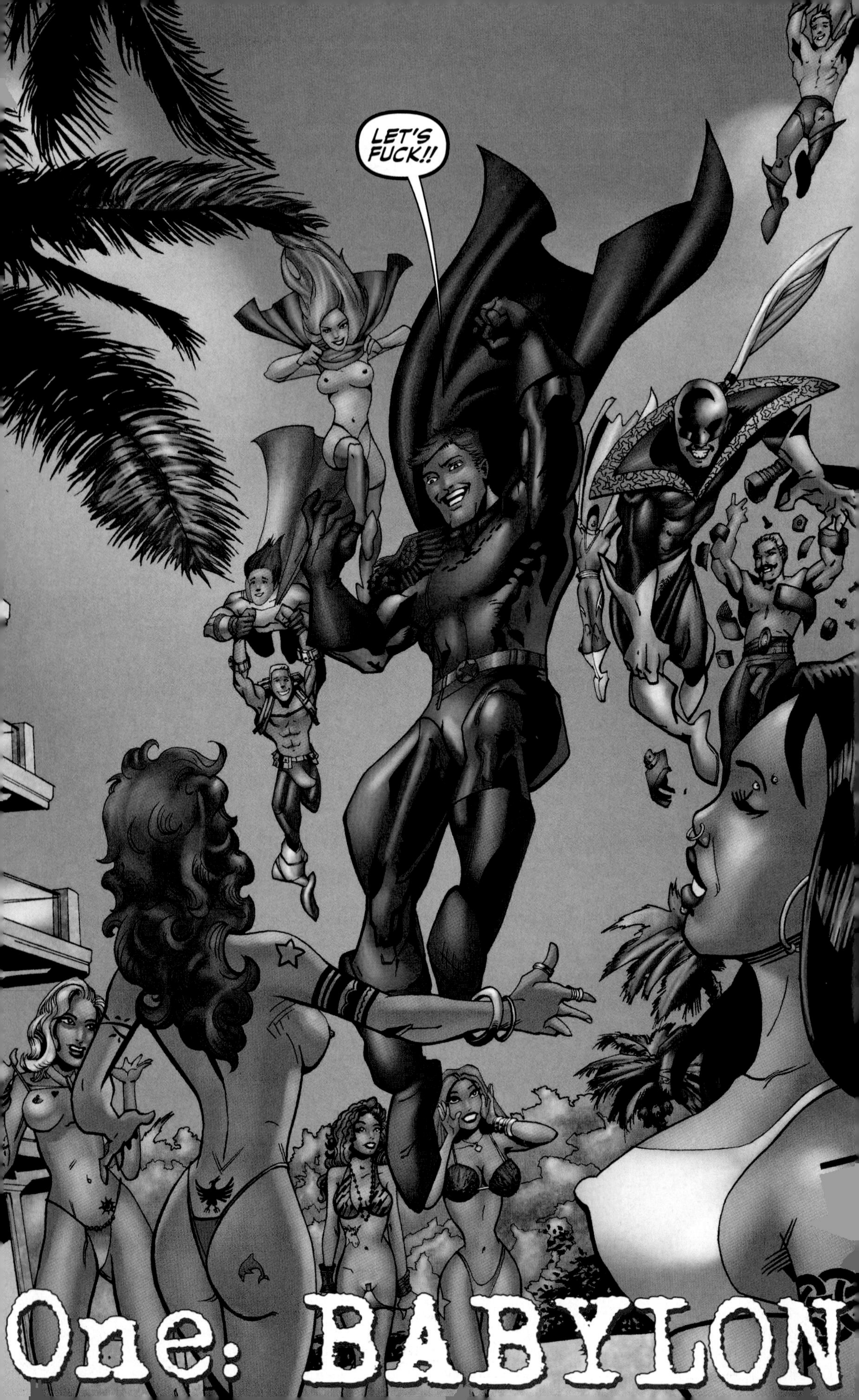
LET'S FUCK!!

One: BABYLON

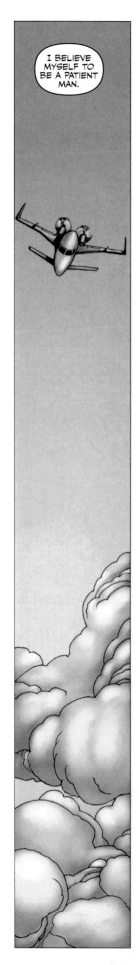

I BELIEVE MYSELF TO BE A PATIENT MAN.

I'D SAY THAT WAS THE UNDERSTATEMENT OF THE--

PLEASE LET ME FINISH.

I DEAL WITH THE SEVEN ON A REGULAR BASIS, SO I'M MORE THAN FAMILIAR WITH EXTREMES OF EGO. THE HOMELANDER IN PARTICULAR IS A TANGLED WEB OF CONCEIT AND INSECURITY THAT WOULD TRY THE PATIENCE OF A SAINT, AND YET I SOMEHOW PREVAIL.

NEITHER AM I ANY STRANGER TO THE NOTION OF LOW INTELLECT. IT WAS ME, AFTER ALL, WHO CONVINCED SOLDIER BOY TO REFORM PAYBACK AFTER THE HUGO QUEER INCIDENT-- A CONVERSATION NOT WITHOUT ITS PITFALLS, I ASSURE YOU.

I KNOW WHAT YOU'RE SAYING. I UNDERSTAND YOUR FRUSTRATION.

BUT IT SIMPLY HAS TO BE YOU...

THANK YOU.

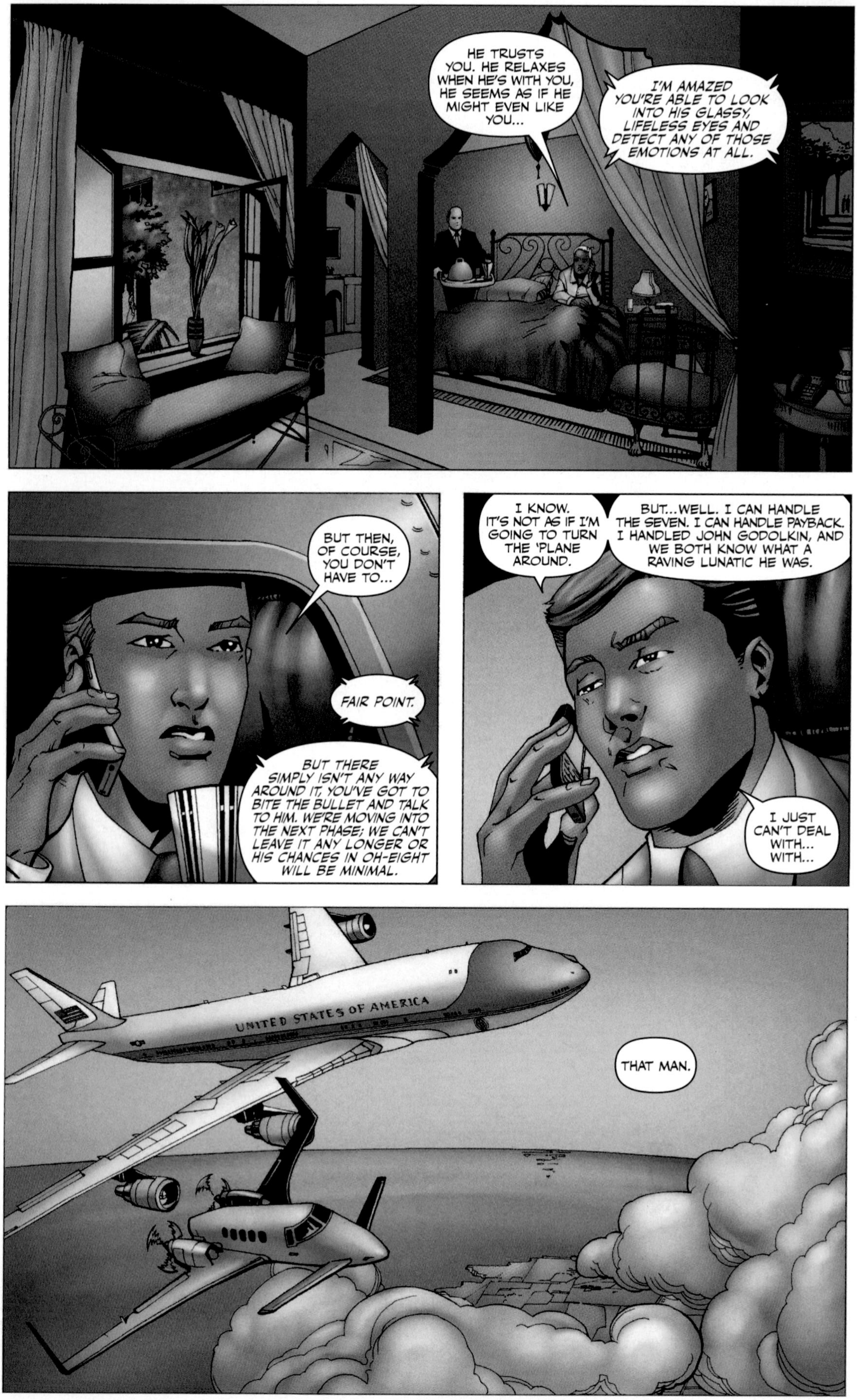
HE TRUSTS YOU. HE RELAXES WHEN HE'S WITH YOU, HE SEEMS AS IF HE MIGHT EVEN LIKE YOU...
I'M AMAZED YOU'RE ABLE TO LOOK INTO HIS GLASSY, LIFELESS EYES AND DETECT ANY OF THOSE EMOTIONS AT ALL.
BUT THEN, OF COURSE, YOU DON'T HAVE TO...
FAIR POINT.
BUT THERE SIMPLY ISN'T ANY WAY AROUND IT, YOU'VE GOT TO BITE THE BULLET AND TALK TO HIM. WE'RE MOVING INTO THE NEXT PHASE; WE CAN'T LEAVE IT ANY LONGER OR HIS CHANCES IN OH-EIGHT WILL BE MINIMAL.
I KNOW. IT'S NOT AS IF I'M GOING TO TURN THE 'PLANE AROUND.
BUT...WELL. I CAN HANDLE THE SEVEN. I CAN HANDLE PAYBACK. I HANDLED JOHN GODOLKIN, AND WE BOTH KNOW WHAT A RAVING LUNATIC HE WAS.
I JUST CAN'T DEAL WITH... WITH...
UNITED STATES OF AMERICA
THAT MAN.

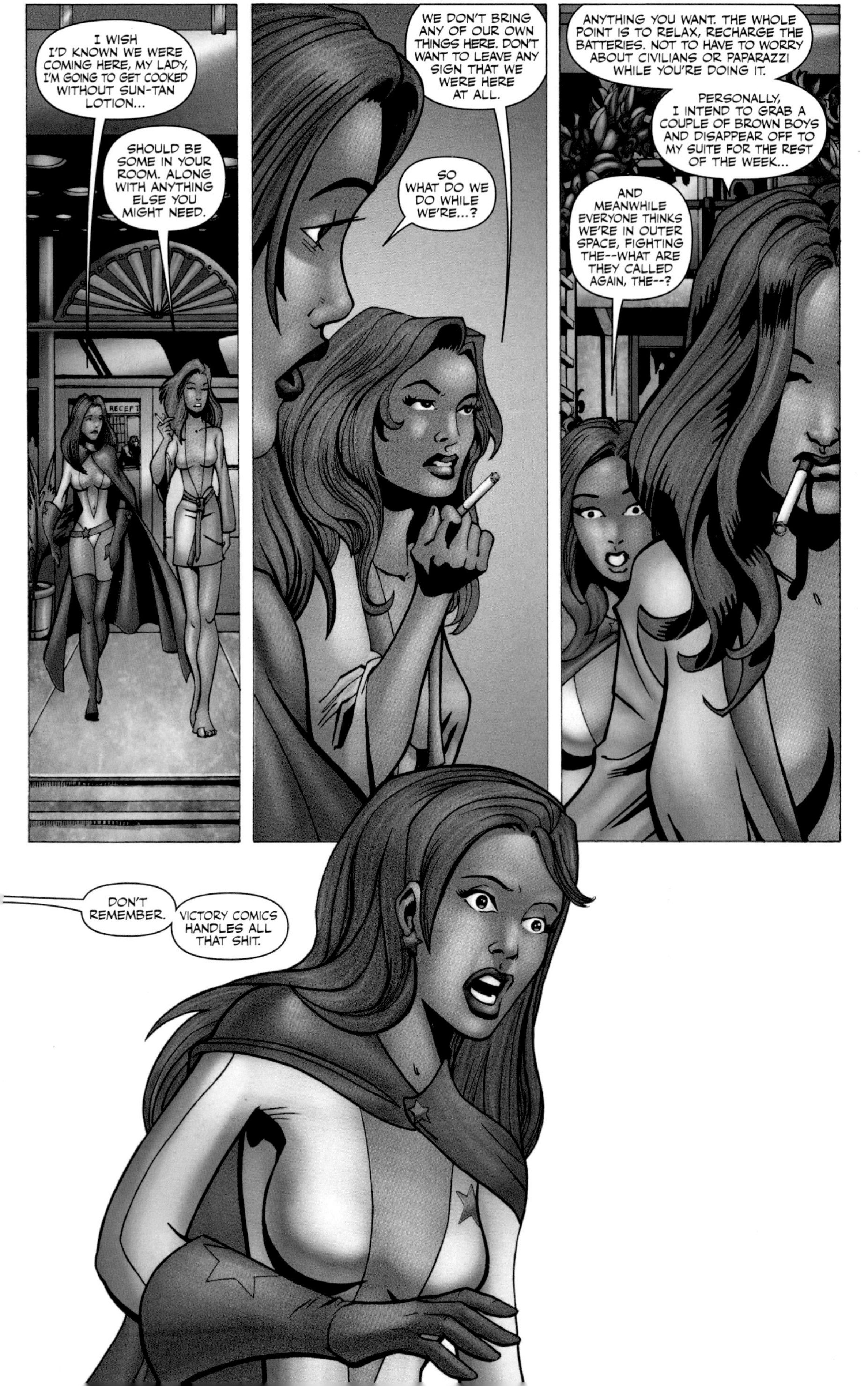
I WISH I'D KNOWN WE WERE COMING HERE, MY LADY, I'M GOING TO GET COOKED WITHOUT SUN-TAN LOTION...
SHOULD BE SOME IN YOUR ROOM. ALONG WITH ANYTHING ELSE YOU MIGHT NEED.
WE DON'T BRING ANY OF OUR OWN THINGS HERE. DON'T WANT TO LEAVE ANY SIGN THAT WE WERE HERE AT ALL.
SO WHAT DO WE DO WHILE WE'RE...?
ANYTHING YOU WANT. THE WHOLE POINT IS TO RELAX, RECHARGE THE BATTERIES. NOT TO HAVE TO WORRY ABOUT CIVILIANS OR PAPARAZZI WHILE YOU'RE DOING IT.
PERSONALLY, I INTEND TO GRAB A COUPLE OF BROWN BOYS AND DISAPPEAR OFF TO MY SUITE FOR THE REST OF THE WEEK...
AND MEANWHILE EVERYONE THINKS WE'RE IN OUTER SPACE, FIGHTING THE--WHAT ARE THEY CALLED AGAIN, THE--?
RECEPT
DON'T REMEMBER.
VICTORY COMICS HANDLES ALL THAT SHIT.

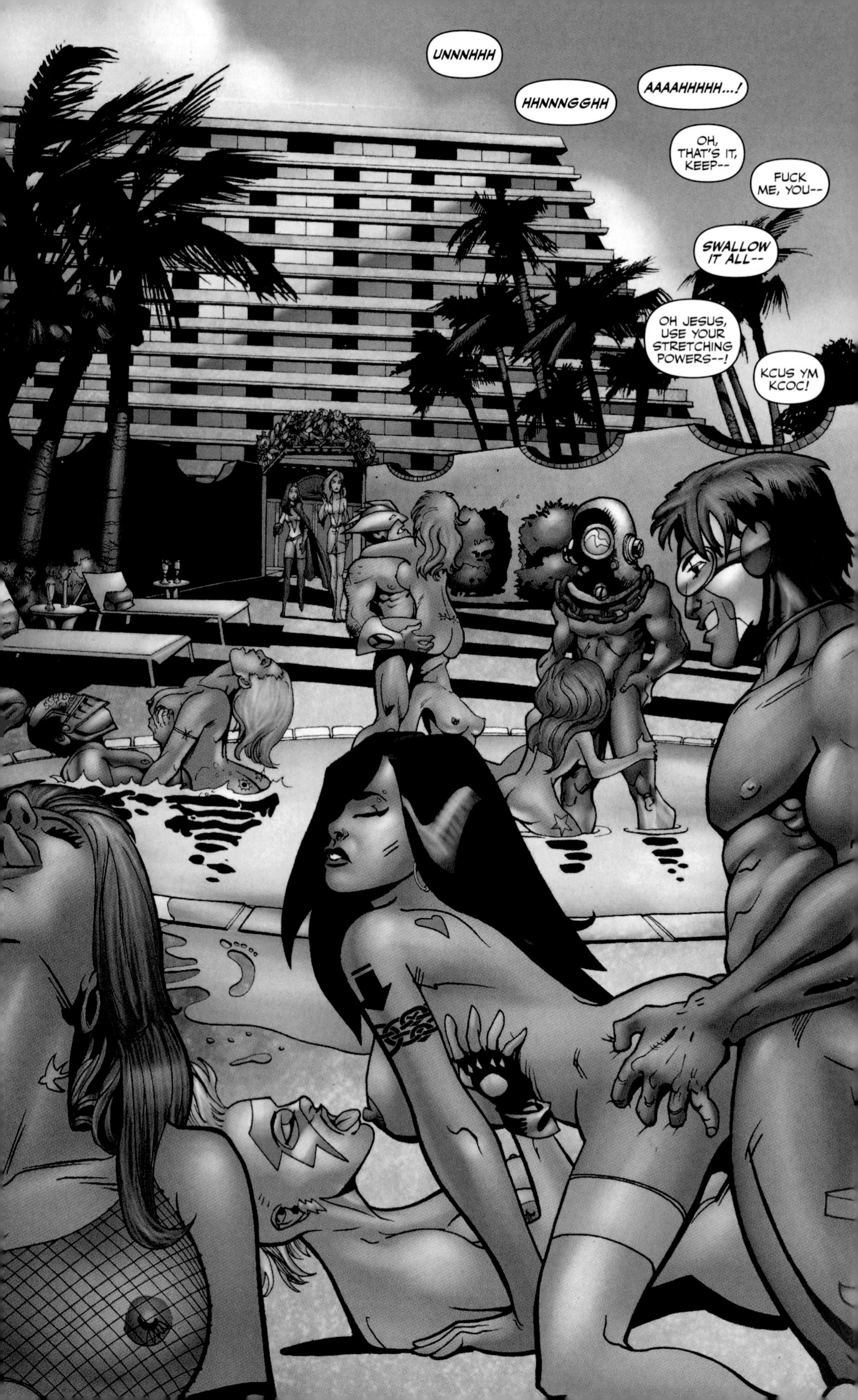
UNNNHHH
HHNNNGGHH
AAAAHHHHH...!
OH, THAT'S IT, KEEP--
FUCK ME, YOU--
SWALLOW IT ALL--
OH JESUS, USE YOUR STRETCHING POWERS--!
KCUS YM KCOC!

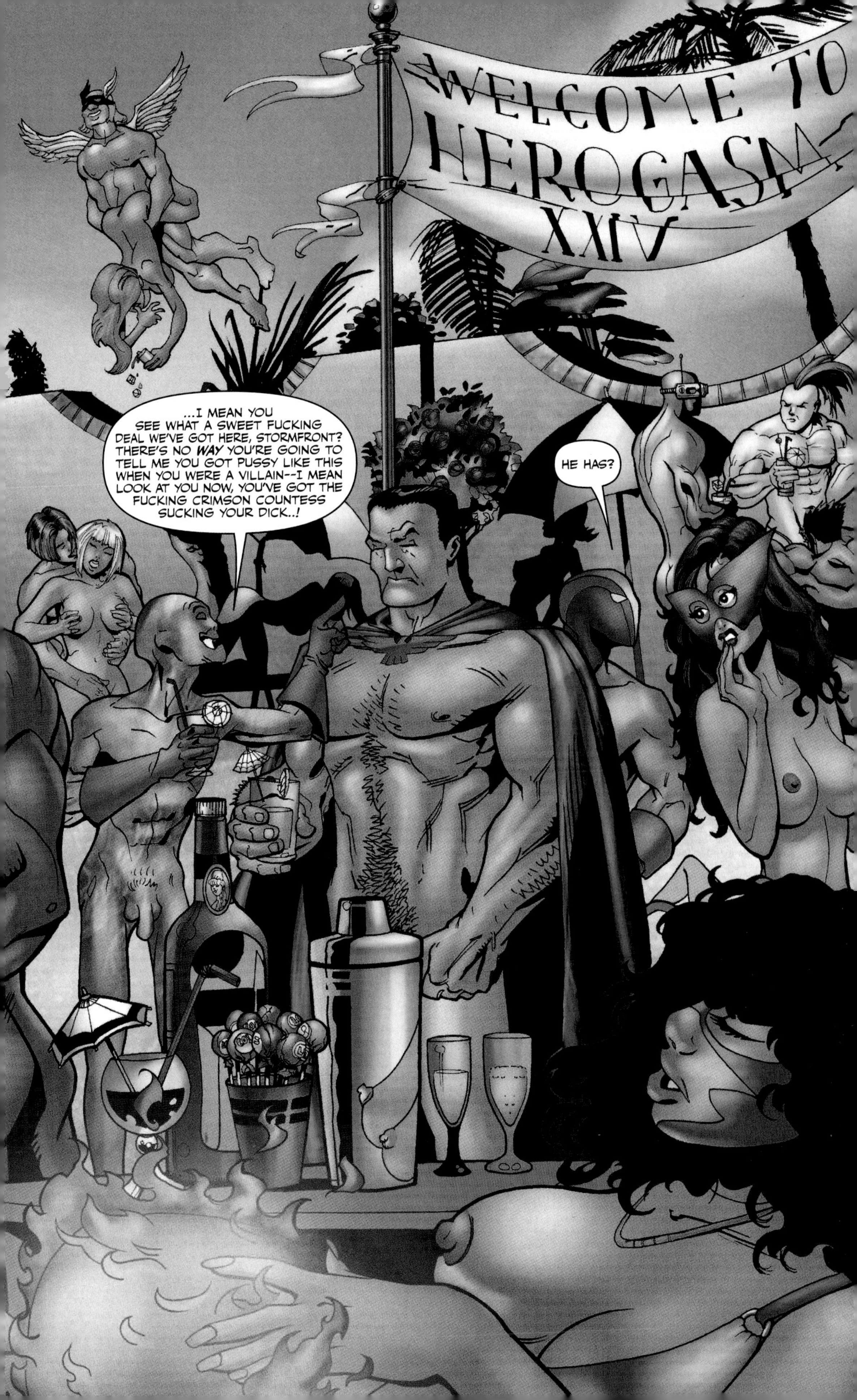
WELCOME TO HEROGASM XXIV
...I MEAN YOU SEE WHAT A SWEET FUCKING DEAL WE'VE GOT HERE, STORMFRONT? THERE'S NO WAY YOU'RE GOING TO TELL ME YOU GOT PUSSY LIKE THIS WHEN YOU WERE A VILLAIN--I MEAN LOOK AT YOU NOW, YOU'VE GOT THE FUCKING CRIMSON COUNTESS SUCKING YOUR DICK..!
HE HAS?

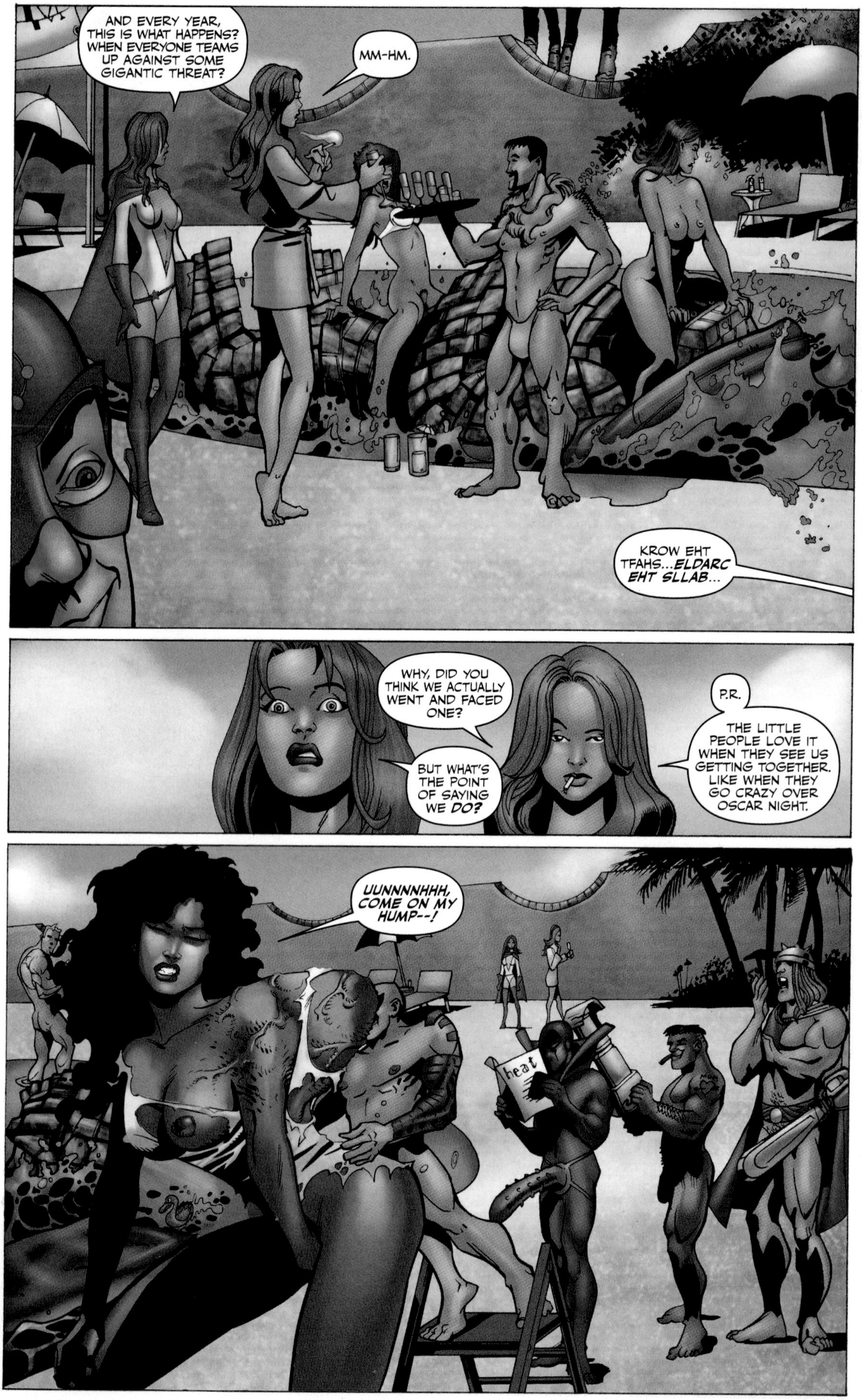
AND EVERY YEAR, THIS IS WHAT HAPPENS? WHEN EVERYONE TEAMS UP AGAINST SOME GIGANTIC THREAT?
MM-HM.
KROW EHT TFAHS...ELDARC EHT SLLAB...
WHY, DID YOU THINK WE ACTUALLY WENT AND FACED ONE?
BUT WHAT'S THE POINT OF SAYING WE DO?
P.R.
THE LITTLE PEOPLE LOVE IT WHEN THEY SEE US GETTING TOGETHER. LIKE WHEN THEY GO CRAZY OVER OSCAR NIGHT.
UUNNNNHHH, COME ON MY HUMP--!
heat

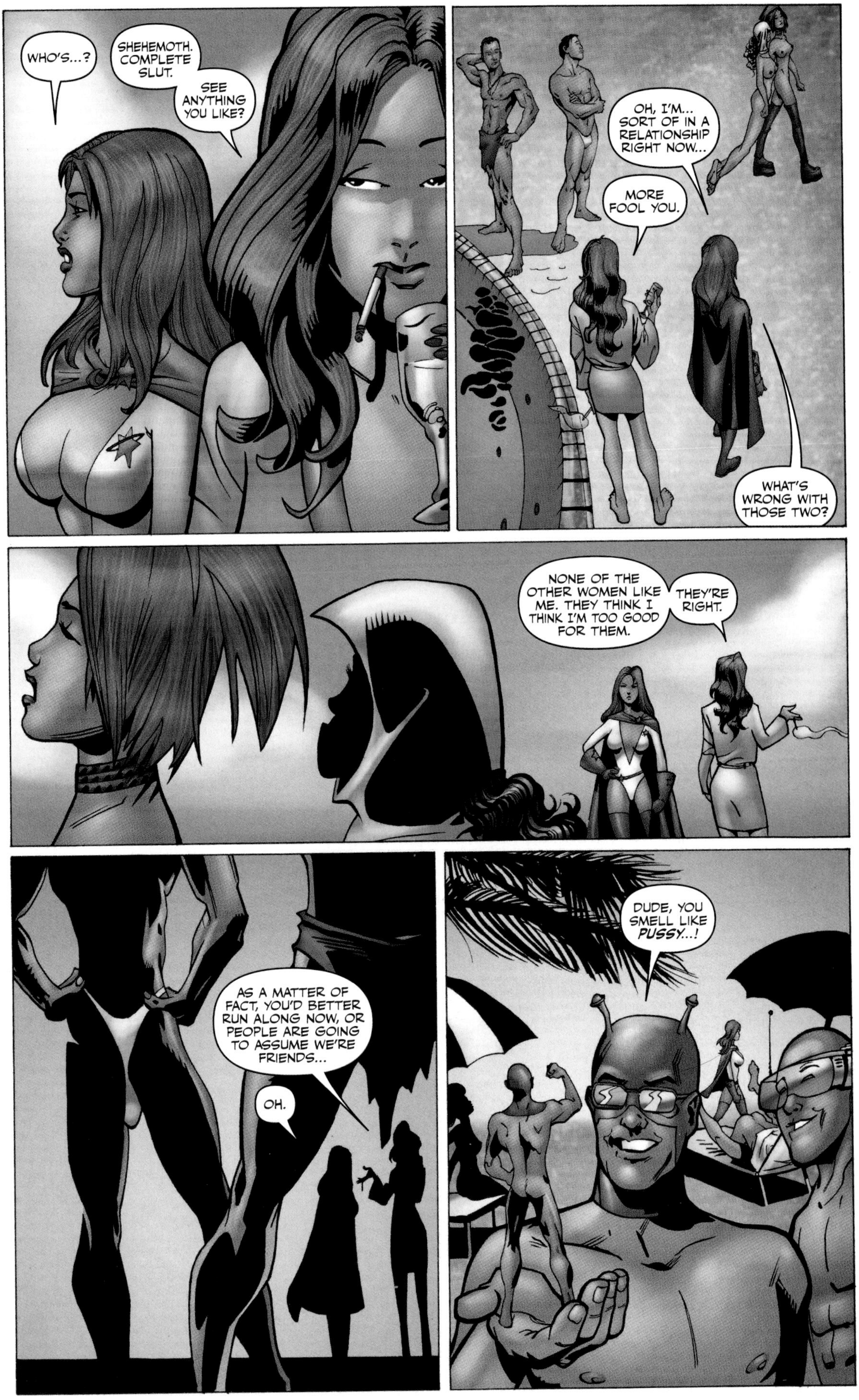
WHO'S...?
SHEHEMOTH. COMPLETE SLUT.
SEE ANYTHING YOU LIKE?
OH, I'M... SORT OF IN A RELATIONSHIP RIGHT NOW...
MORE FOOL YOU.
WHAT'S WRONG WITH THOSE TWO?
NONE OF THE OTHER WOMEN LIKE ME. THEY THINK I THINK I'M TOO GOOD FOR THEM.
THEY'RE RIGHT.
AS A MATTER OF FACT, YOU'D BETTER RUN ALONG NOW, OR PEOPLE ARE GOING TO ASSUME WE'RE FRIENDS...
OH.
DUDE, YOU SMELL LIKE *PUSSY*...!

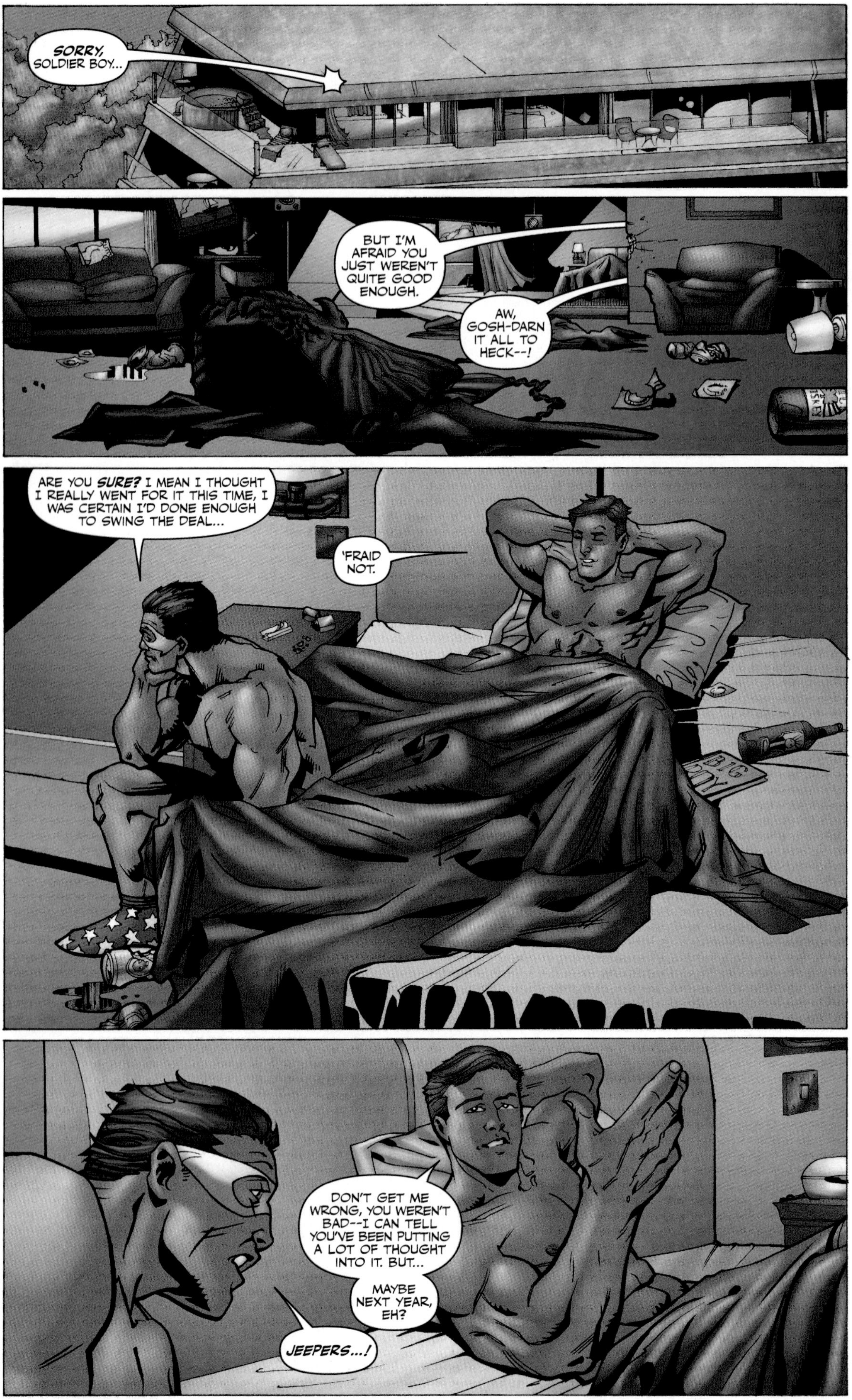
SORRY, SOLDIER BOY...
BUT I'M AFRAID YOU JUST WEREN'T QUITE GOOD ENOUGH.
AW, GOSH-DARN IT ALL TO HECK--!
ARE YOU SURE? I MEAN I THOUGHT I REALLY WENT FOR IT THIS TIME, I WAS CERTAIN I'D DONE ENOUGH TO SWING THE DEAL...
'FRAID NOT.
DON'T GET ME WRONG, YOU WEREN'T BAD--I CAN TELL YOU'VE BEEN PUTTING A LOT OF THOUGHT INTO IT. BUT...
MAYBE NEXT YEAR, EH?
JEEPERS...!

ANOTHER YEAR IN PAYBACK, I DON'T KNOW IF I CAN STAND IT... TEK-KNIGHT AND EAGLE WERE THE ONLY ONES WHO WERE NICE TO ME, AND EVER SINCE THEY DIED IT'S LIKE THE OTHERS HAVE GOTTEN EVEN MEANER...

SWATTO'S NO USE, HE JUST SITS AROUND MAKING THAT NUTTY BUZZING SOUND. MIND-DROID AND THE CRIMSON COUNTESS FIGHT ALL THE TIME, AND STORMFRONT KEEPS CALLING ME *SCHWEINER AMERIKANER*. IT'S ALL JUST SO LAME, YOU KNOW?

SO... SECOND BEST.

HOMELANDER, I WANT TO BE IN THE *SEVEN*...!

AND YOU WILL BE, OLD COMRADE, YOU WILL BE. THERE'S A PLACE READY AND WAITING FOR YOU.

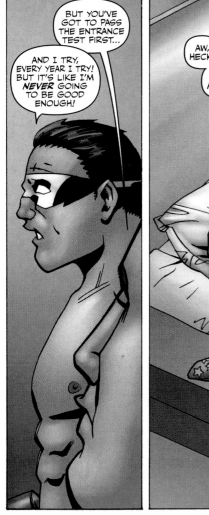

BUT YOU'VE GOT TO PASS THE ENTRANCE TEST FIRST...

AND I TRY, EVERY YEAR I TRY! BUT IT'S LIKE I'M *NEVER* GOING TO BE GOOD ENOUGH!

AW, HECK.

JUST *HECK*.

I GUESS I'LL SEE YOU LATER, THEN.

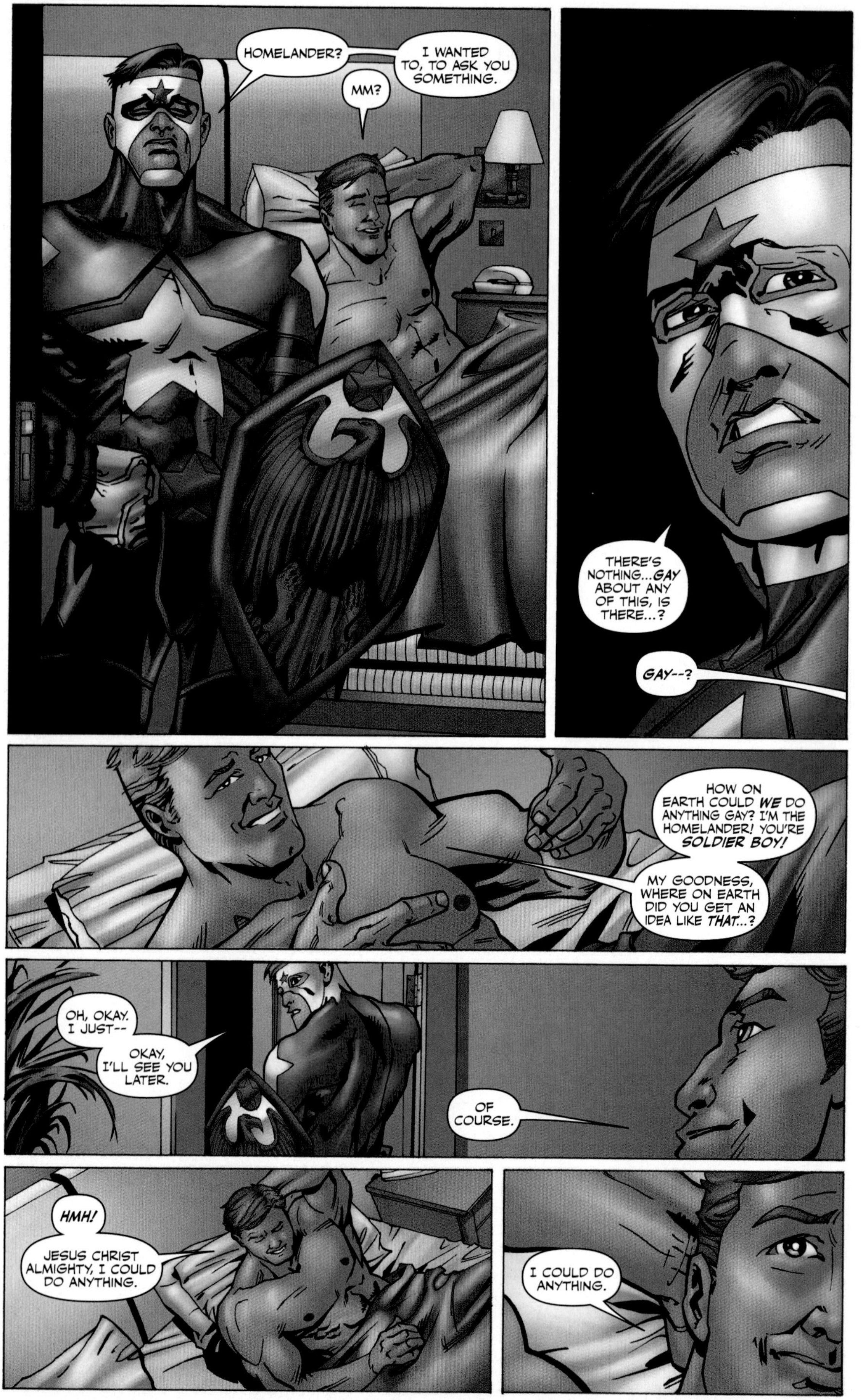
HOMELANDER?
I WANTED TO, TO ASK YOU SOMETHING.
MM?
THERE'S NOTHING...GAY ABOUT ANY OF THIS, IS THERE...?
GAY--?
HOW ON EARTH COULD WE DO ANYTHING GAY? I'M THE HOMELANDER! YOU'RE SOLDIER BOY!
MY GOODNESS, WHERE ON EARTH DID YOU GET AN IDEA LIKE THAT...?
OH, OKAY. I JUST--
OKAY, I'LL SEE YOU LATER.
OF COURSE.
HMH!
JESUS CHRIST ALMIGHTY, I COULD DO ANYTHING.
I COULD DO ANYTHING.

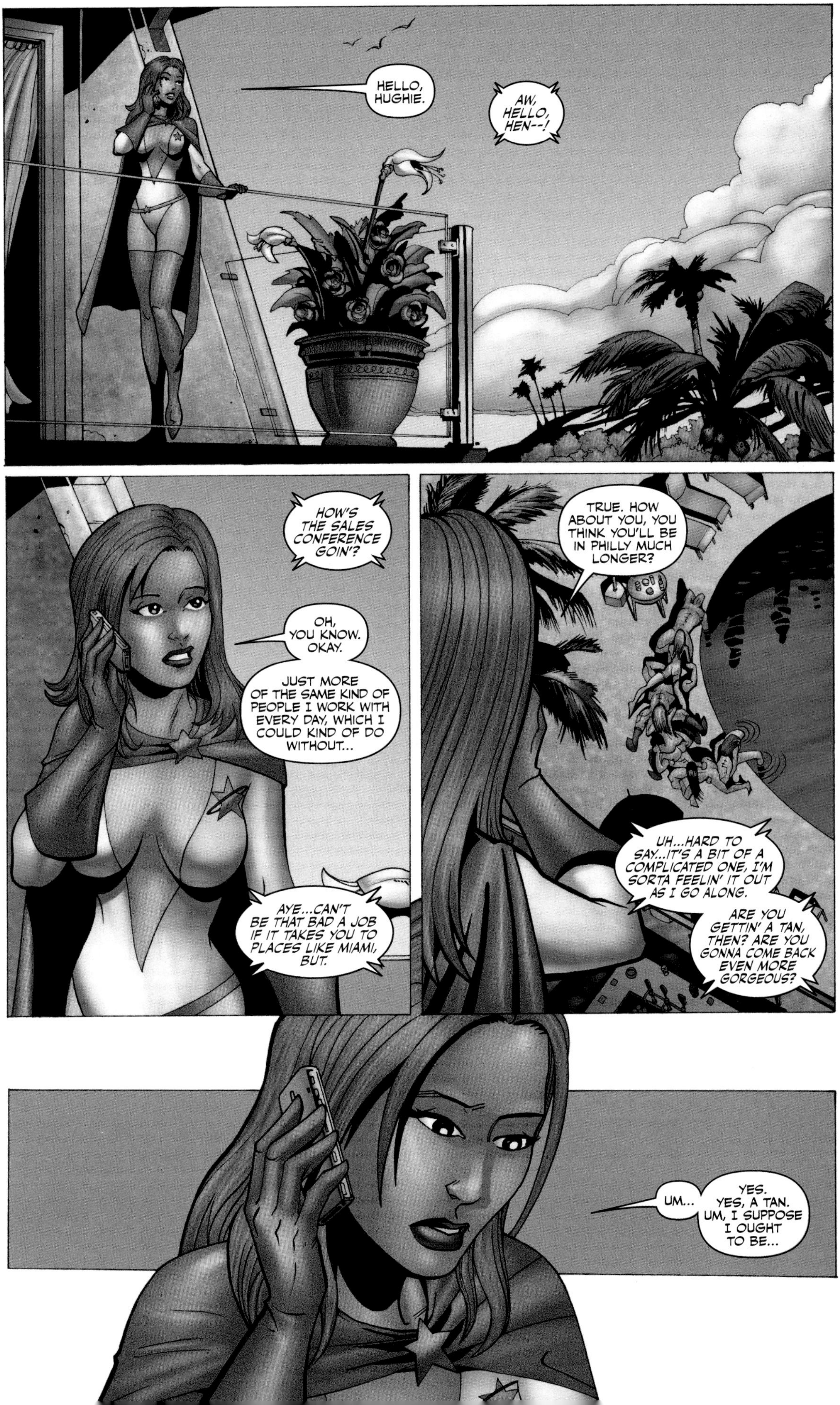
HELLO, HUGHIE.
AW, HELLO, HEN--!
HOW'S THE SALES CONFERENCE GOIN'?
OH, YOU KNOW. OKAY.
JUST MORE OF THE SAME KIND OF PEOPLE I WORK WITH EVERY DAY, WHICH I COULD KIND OF DO WITHOUT...
AYE...CAN'T BE THAT BAD A JOB IF IT TAKES YOU TO PLACES LIKE MIAMI, BUT.
TRUE. HOW ABOUT YOU, YOU THINK YOU'LL BE IN PHILLY MUCH LONGER?
UH...HARD TO SAY...IT'S A BIT OF A COMPLICATED ONE, I'M SORTA FEELIN' IT OUT AS I GO ALONG.
ARE YOU GETTIN' A TAN, THEN? ARE YOU GONNA COME BACK EVEN MORE GORGEOUS?
UM...
YES. YES, A TAN. UM, I SUPPOSE I OUGHT TO BE...

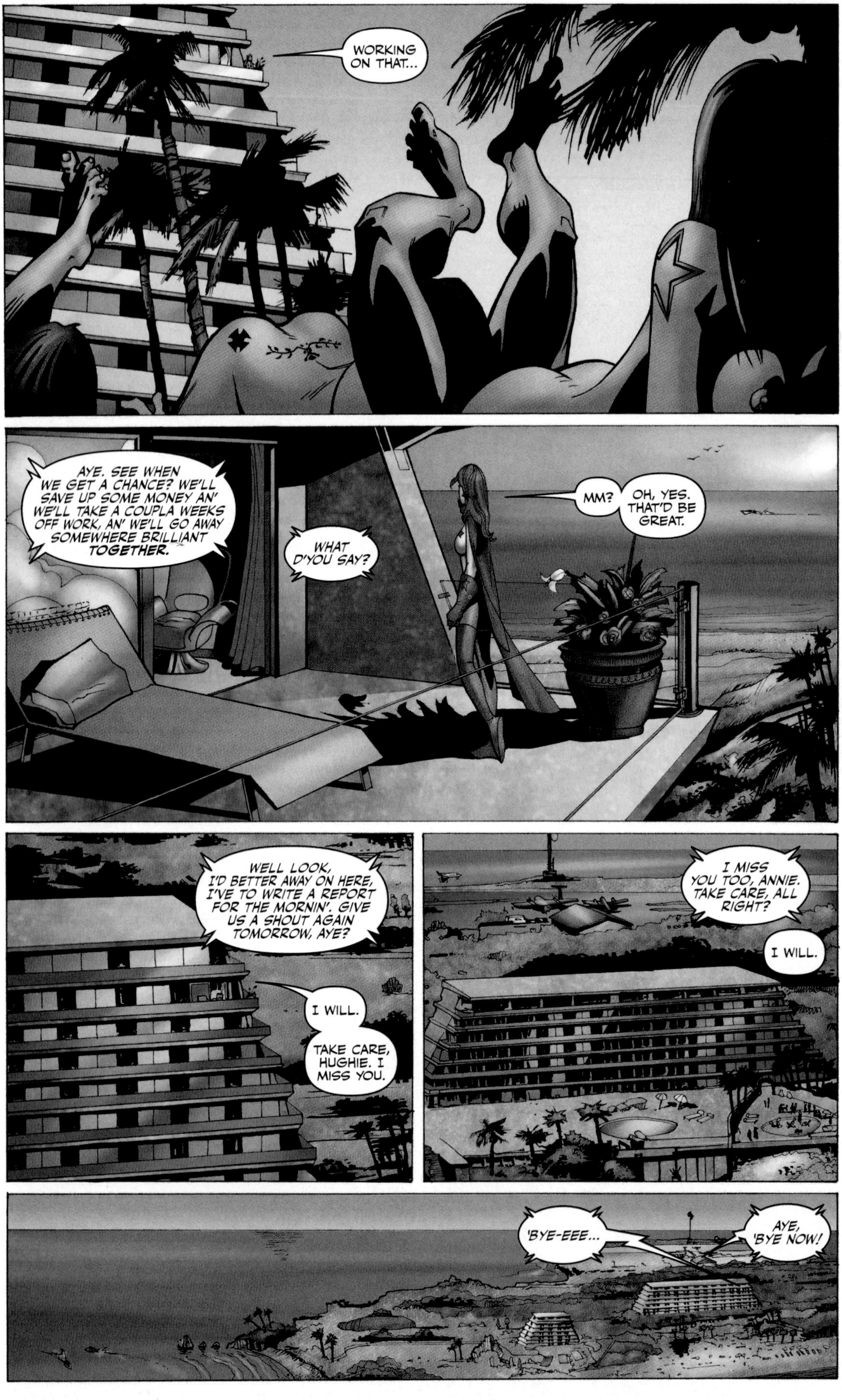
WORKING ON THAT...
AYE. SEE WHEN WE GET A CHANCE? WE'LL SAVE UP SOME MONEY AN' WE'LL TAKE A COUPLA WEEKS OFF WORK, AN' WE'LL GO AWAY SOMEWHERE BRILLIANT TOGETHER.
MM?
WHAT D'YOU SAY?
OH, YES. THAT'D BE GREAT.
WELL LOOK, I'D BETTER AWAY ON HERE, I'VE TO WRITE A REPORT FOR THE MORNIN'. GIVE US A SHOUT AGAIN TOMORROW, AYE?
I WILL.
TAKE CARE, HUGHIE. I MISS YOU.
I MISS YOU TOO, ANNIE. TAKE CARE, ALL RIGHT?
I WILL.
'BYE-EEE...
AYE, 'BYE NOW!

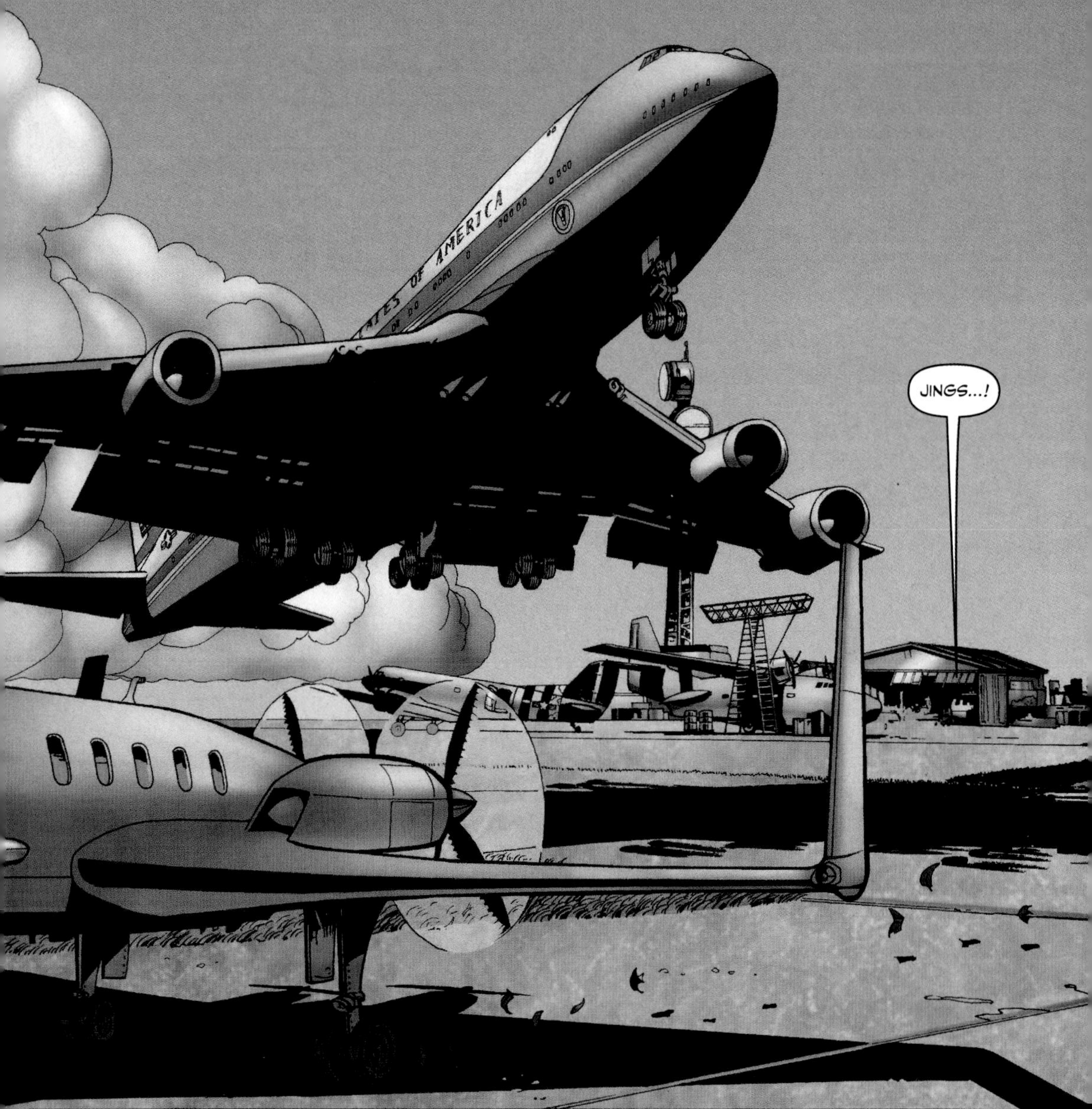
ATES OF AMERICA
JINGS...!

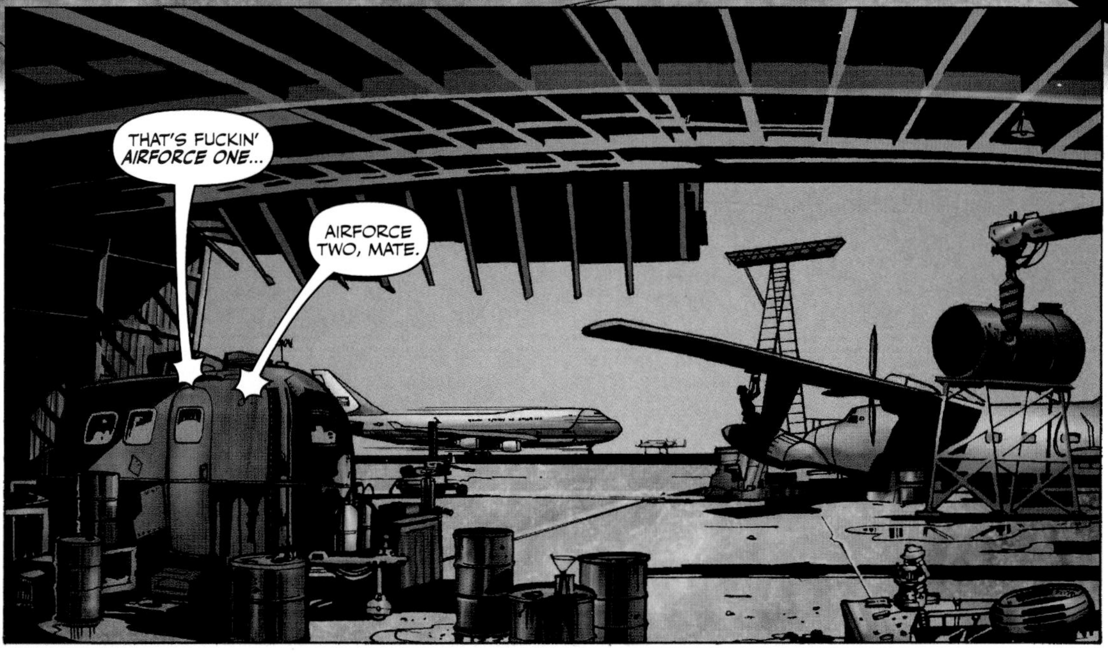
THAT'S FUCKIN' *AIRFORCE ONE*...
AIRFORCE TWO, MATE.

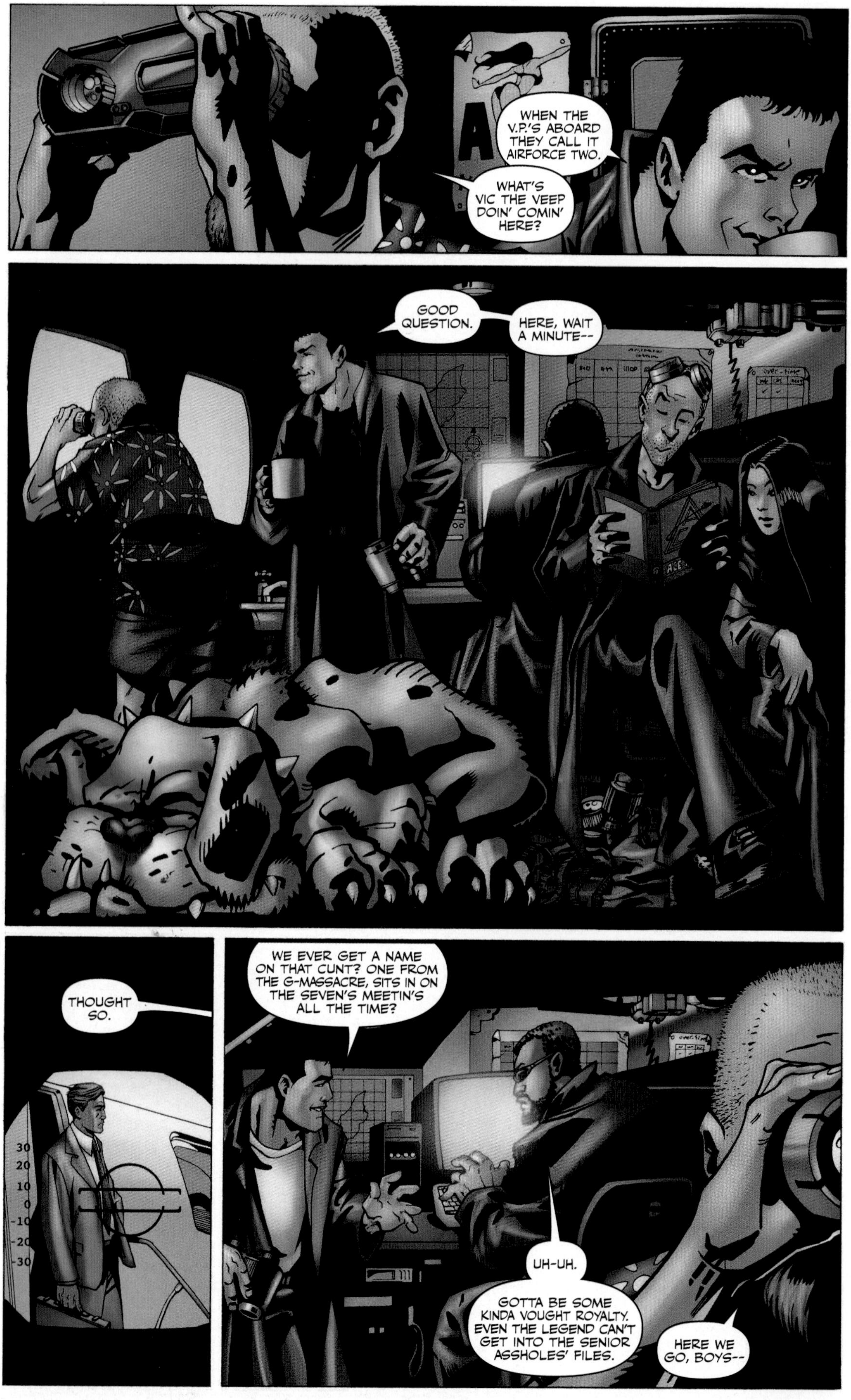
WHEN THE V.P.'S ABOARD THEY CALL IT AIRFORCE TWO.
WHAT'S VIC THE VEEP DOIN' COMIN' HERE?
GOOD QUESTION.
HERE, WAIT A MINUTE--
THOUGHT SO.
WE EVER GET A NAME ON THAT CUNT? ONE FROM THE G-MASSACRE, SITS IN ON THE SEVEN'S MEETIN'S ALL THE TIME?
UH-UH.
GOTTA BE SOME KINDA VOUGHT ROYALTY. EVEN THE LEGEND CAN'T GET INTO THE SENIOR ASSHOLES' FILES.
HERE WE GO, BOYS--

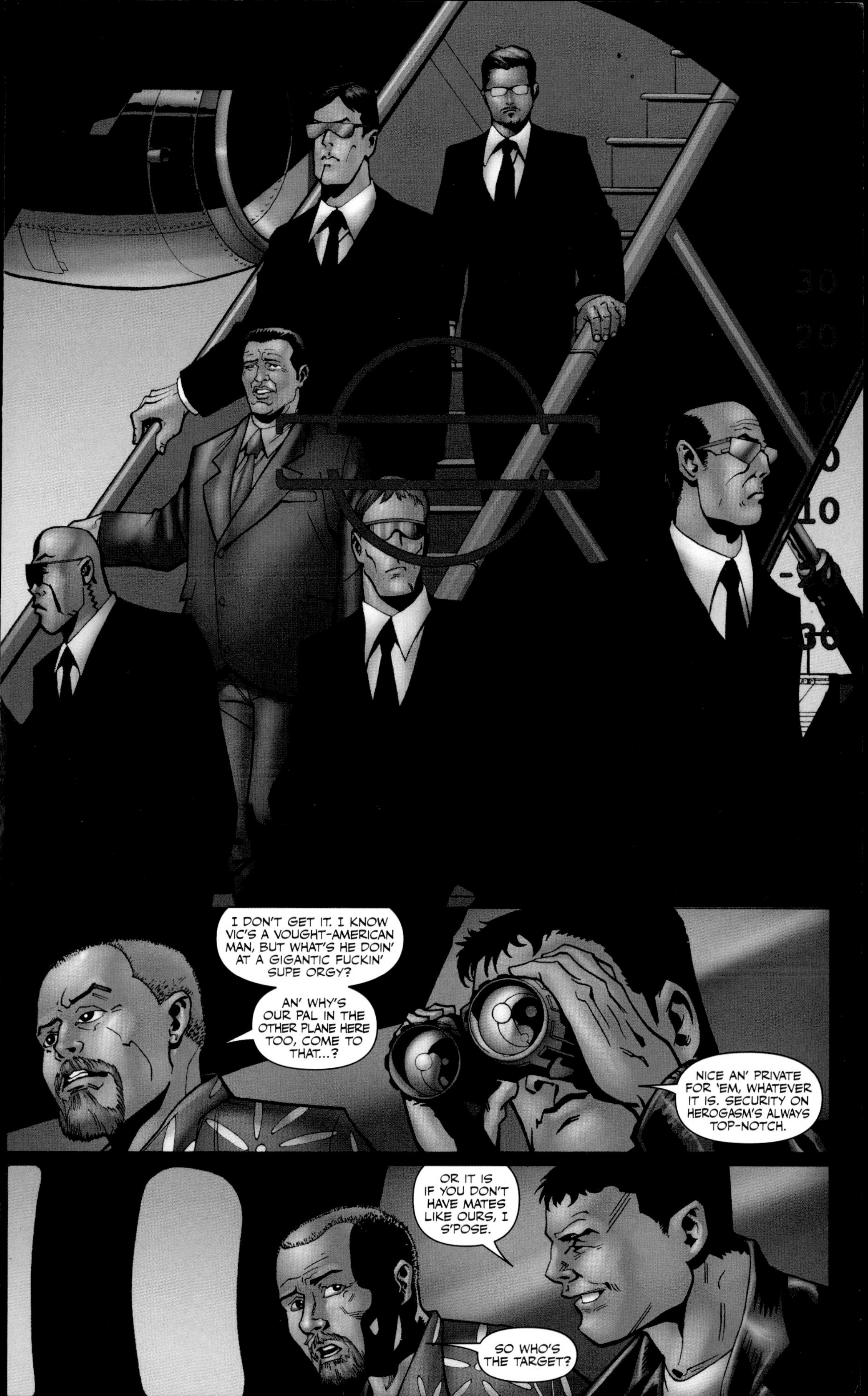
I DON'T GET IT. I KNOW VIC'S A VOUGHT-AMERICAN MAN, BUT WHAT'S HE DOIN' AT A GIGANTIC FUCKIN' SUPE ORGY?
AN' WHY'S OUR PAL IN THE OTHER PLANE HERE TOO, COME TO THAT...?
NICE AN' PRIVATE FOR 'EM, WHATEVER IT IS. SECURITY ON HEROGASM'S ALWAYS TOP-NOTCH.
OR IT IS IF YOU DON'T HAVE MATES LIKE OURS, I S'POSE.
SO WHO'S THE TARGET?

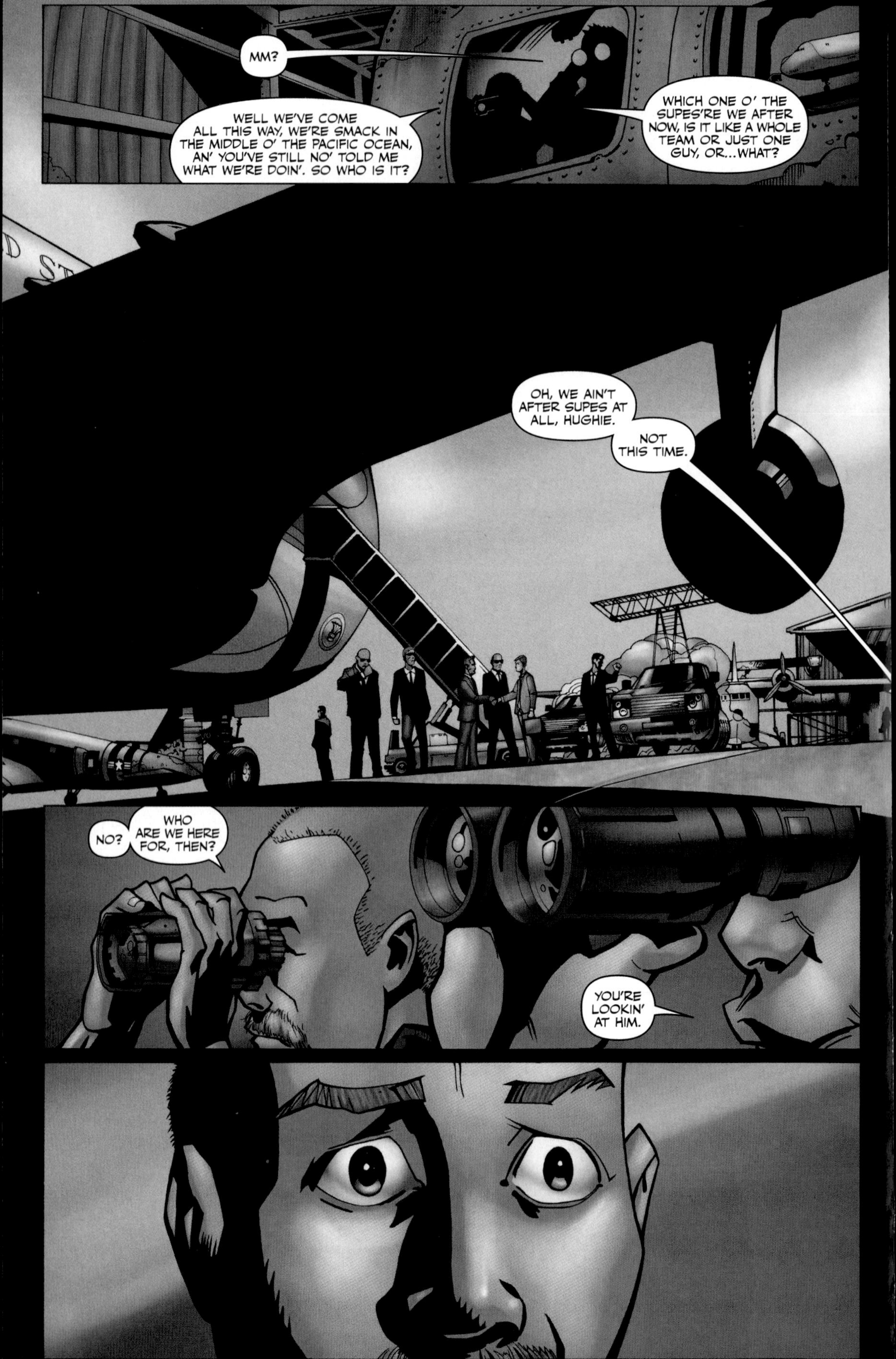
MM?
WELL WE'VE COME ALL THIS WAY, WE'RE SMACK IN THE MIDDLE O' THE PACIFIC OCEAN, AN' YOU'VE STILL NO' TOLD ME WHAT WE'RE DOIN'. SO WHO IS IT?
WHICH ONE O' THE SUPES'RE WE AFTER NOW, IS IT LIKE A WHOLE TEAM OR JUST ONE GUY, OR...WHAT?
OH, WE AIN'T AFTER SUPES AT ALL, HUGHIE.
NOT THIS TIME.
NO?
WHO ARE WE HERE FOR, THEN?
YOU'RE LOOKIN' AT HIM.

HEROGASM #2
cover

by DARICK ROBERTSON
and TONY AVIÑA

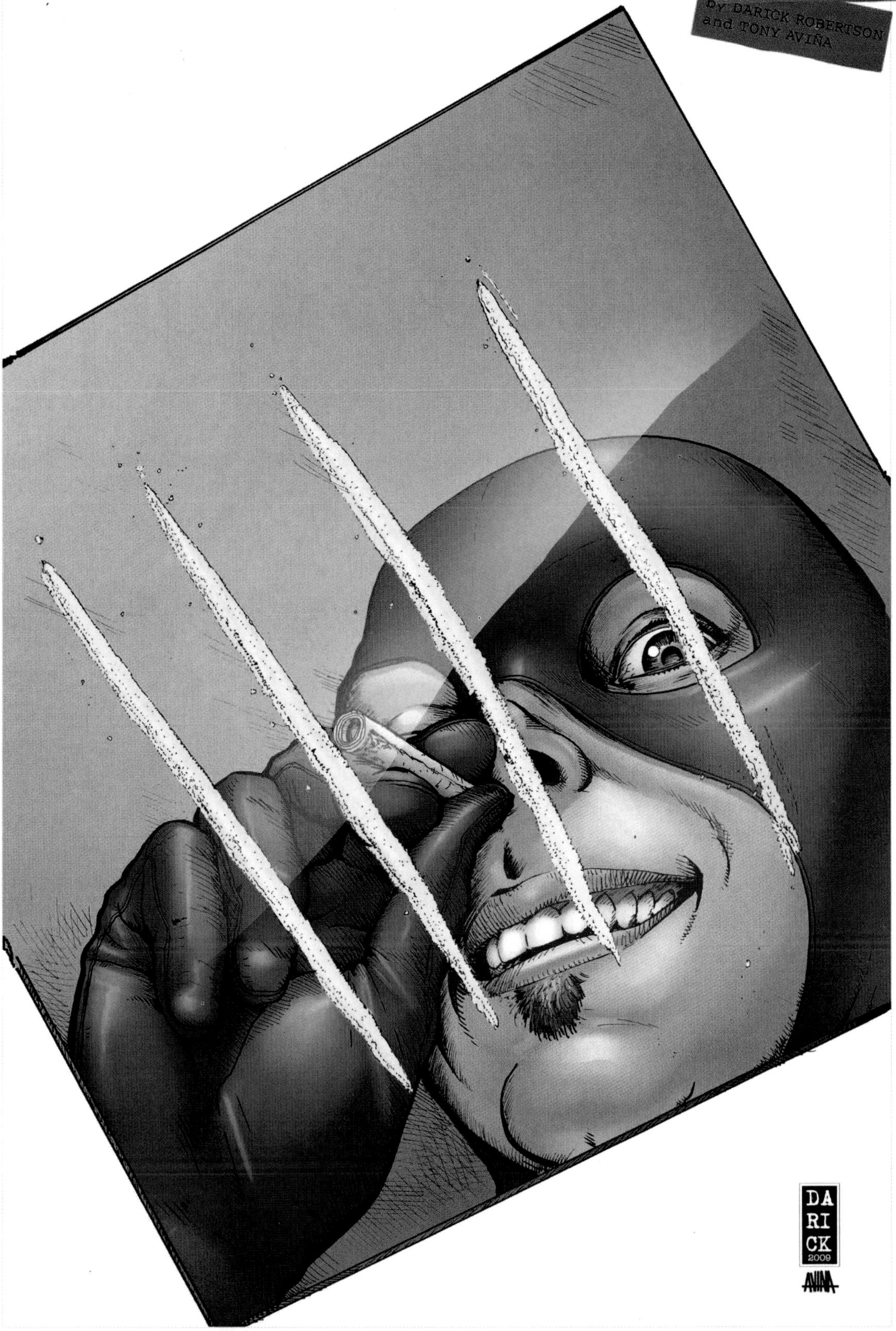
DA
RI
CK
2009
AVIÑA

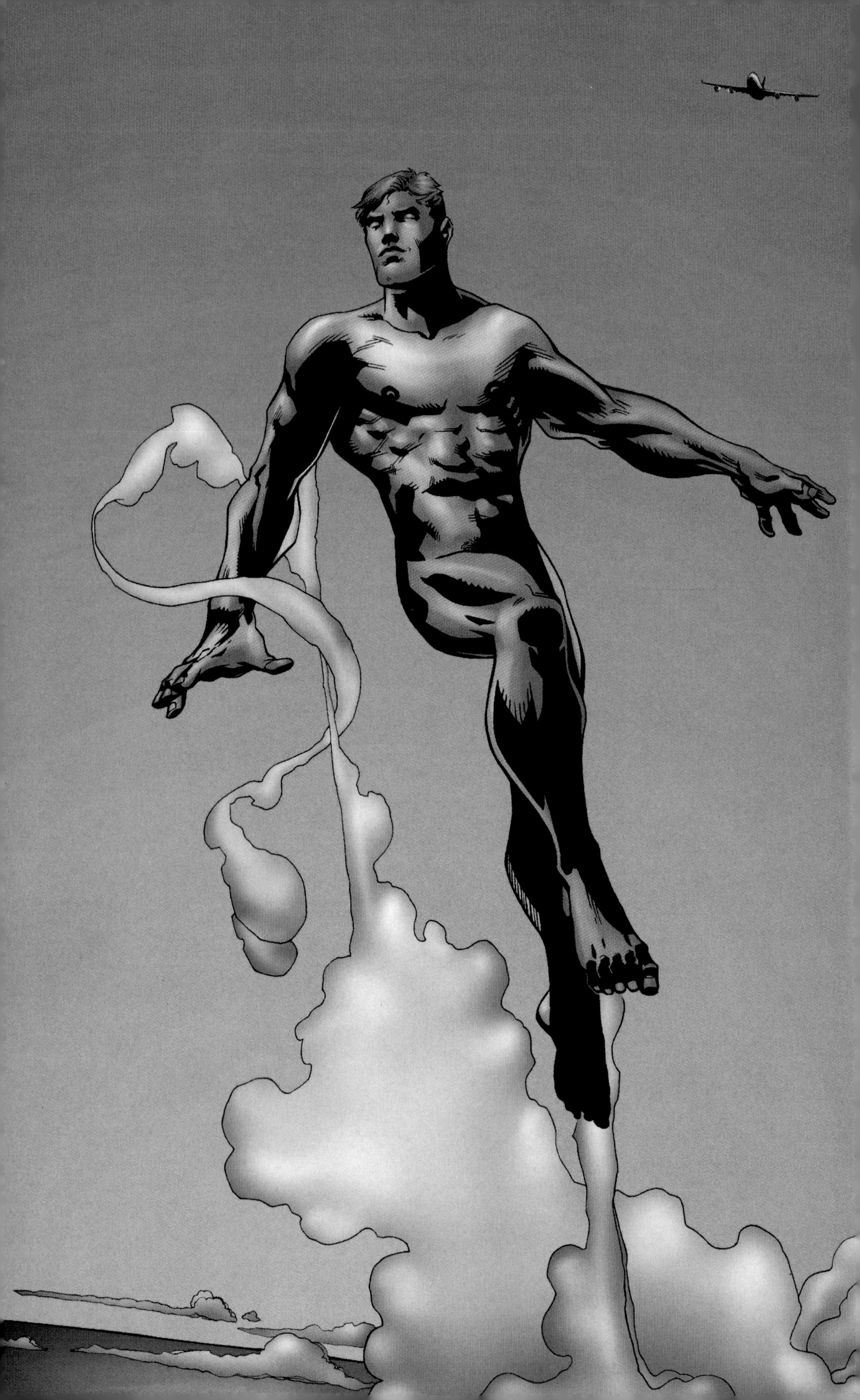

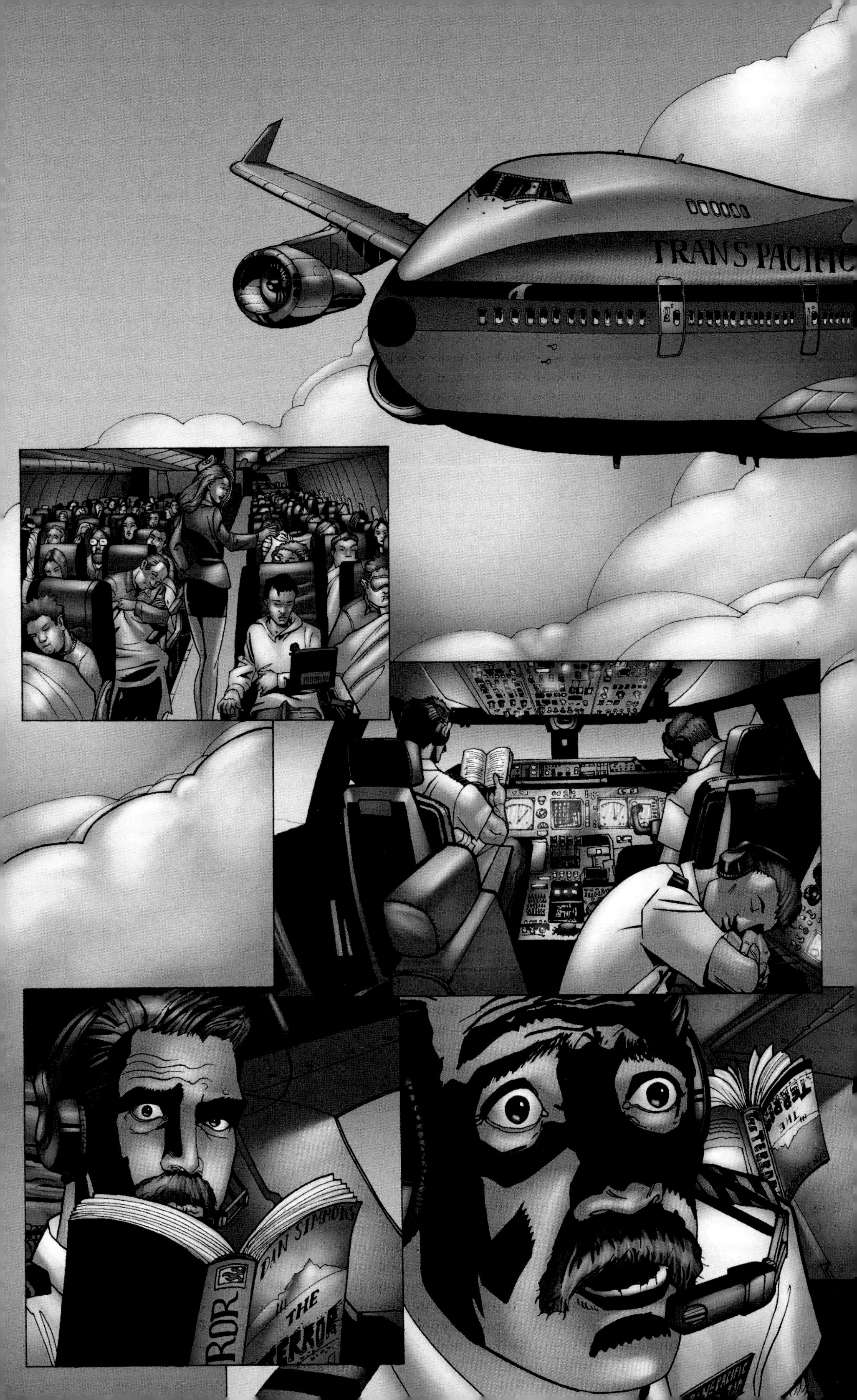
DAN SIMMONS
THE TERROR

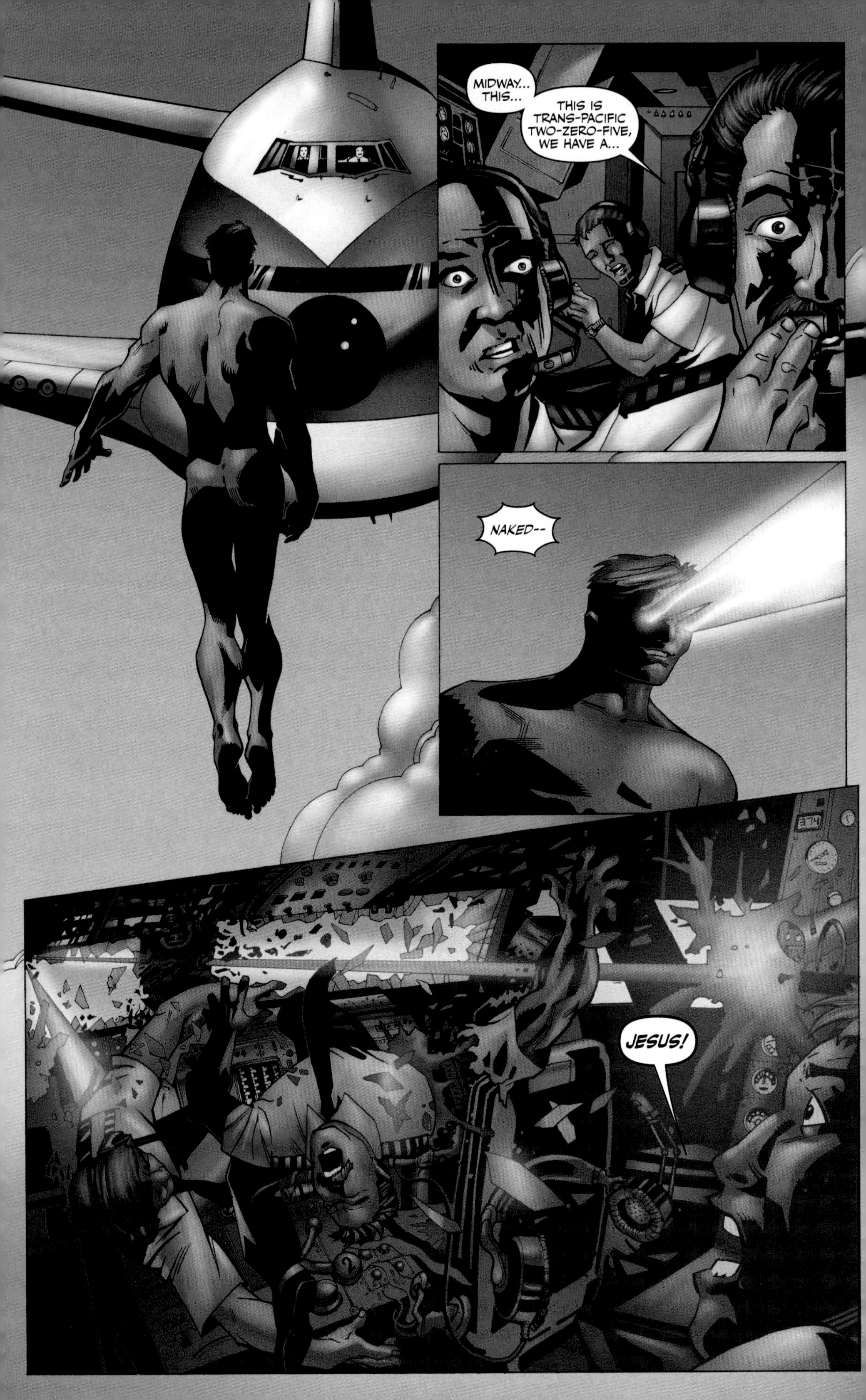
MIDWAY... THIS...
THIS IS TRANS-PACIFIC TWO-ZERO-FIVE, WE HAVE A...
NAKED--
JESUS!

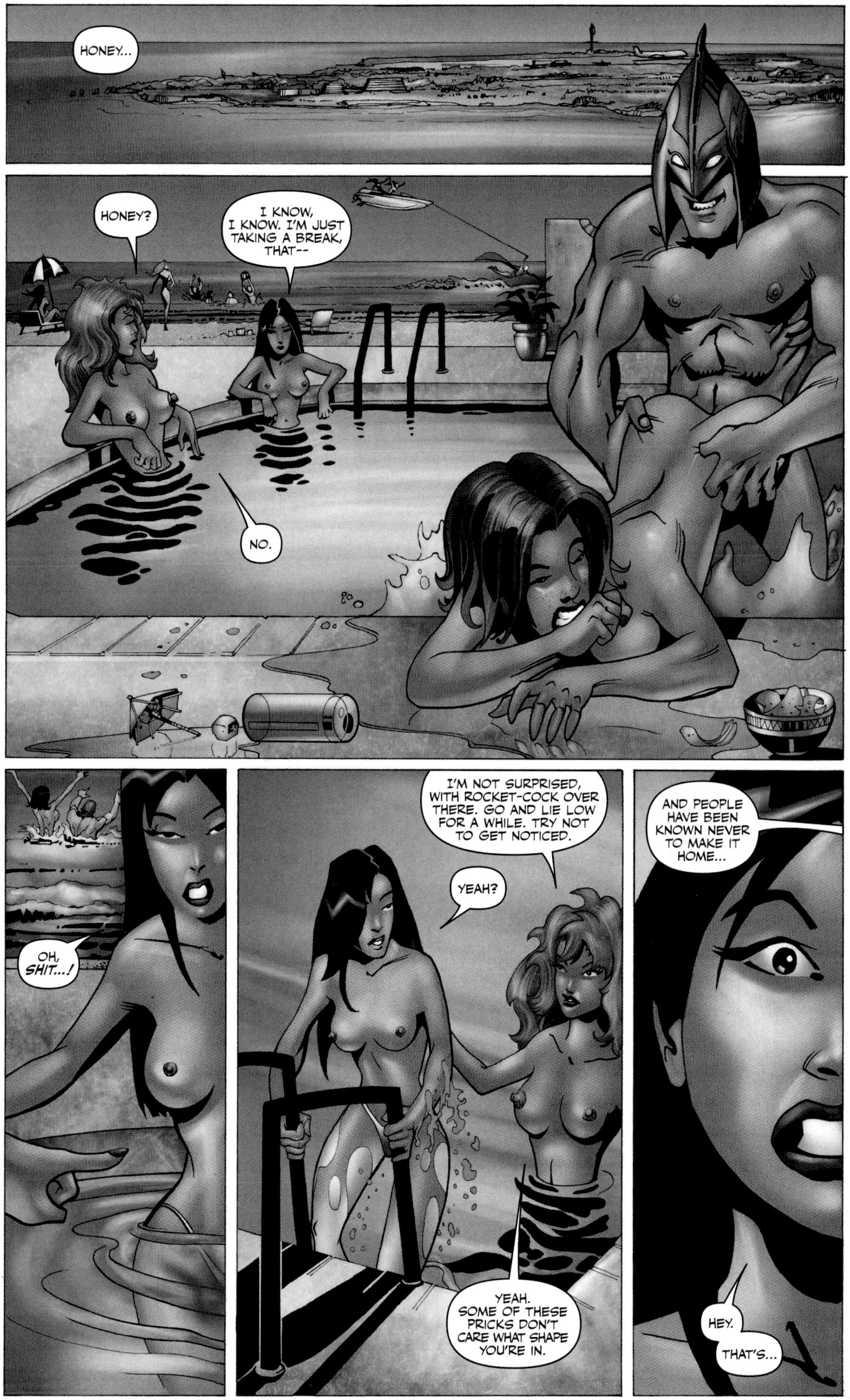
HONEY...
HONEY?
I KNOW, I KNOW. I'M JUST TAKING A BREAK, THAT--
NO.
OH, SHIT...!
I'M NOT SURPRISED, WITH ROCKET-COCK OVER THERE. GO AND LIE LOW FOR A WHILE. TRY NOT TO GET NOTICED.
YEAH?
YEAH. SOME OF THESE PRICKS DON'T CARE WHAT SHAPE YOU'RE IN.
AND PEOPLE HAVE BEEN KNOWN NEVER TO MAKE IT HOME...
HEY.
THAT'S...

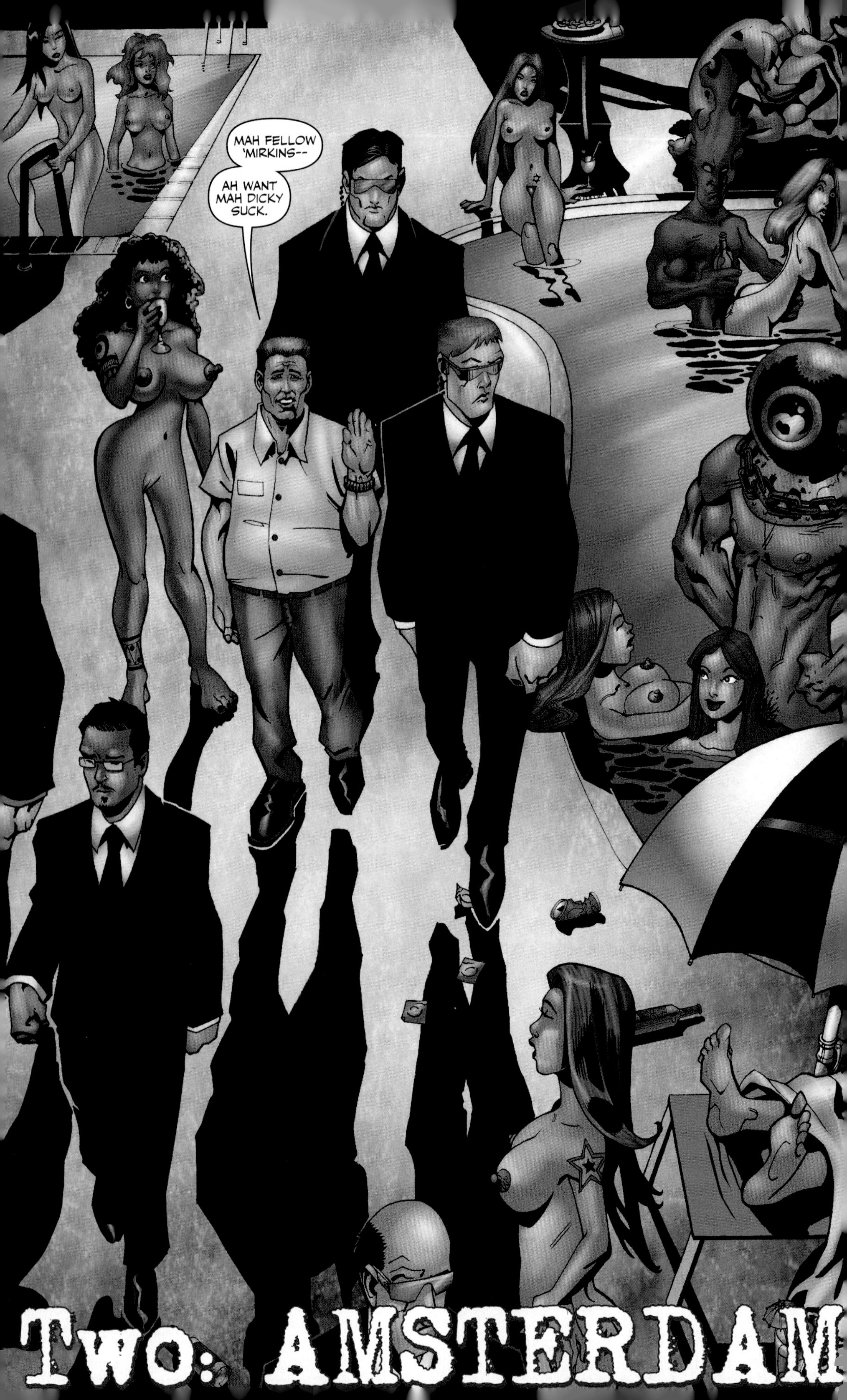
MAH FELLOW 'MIRKINS--
AH WANT MAH DICKY SUCK.
Two: AMSTERDAM

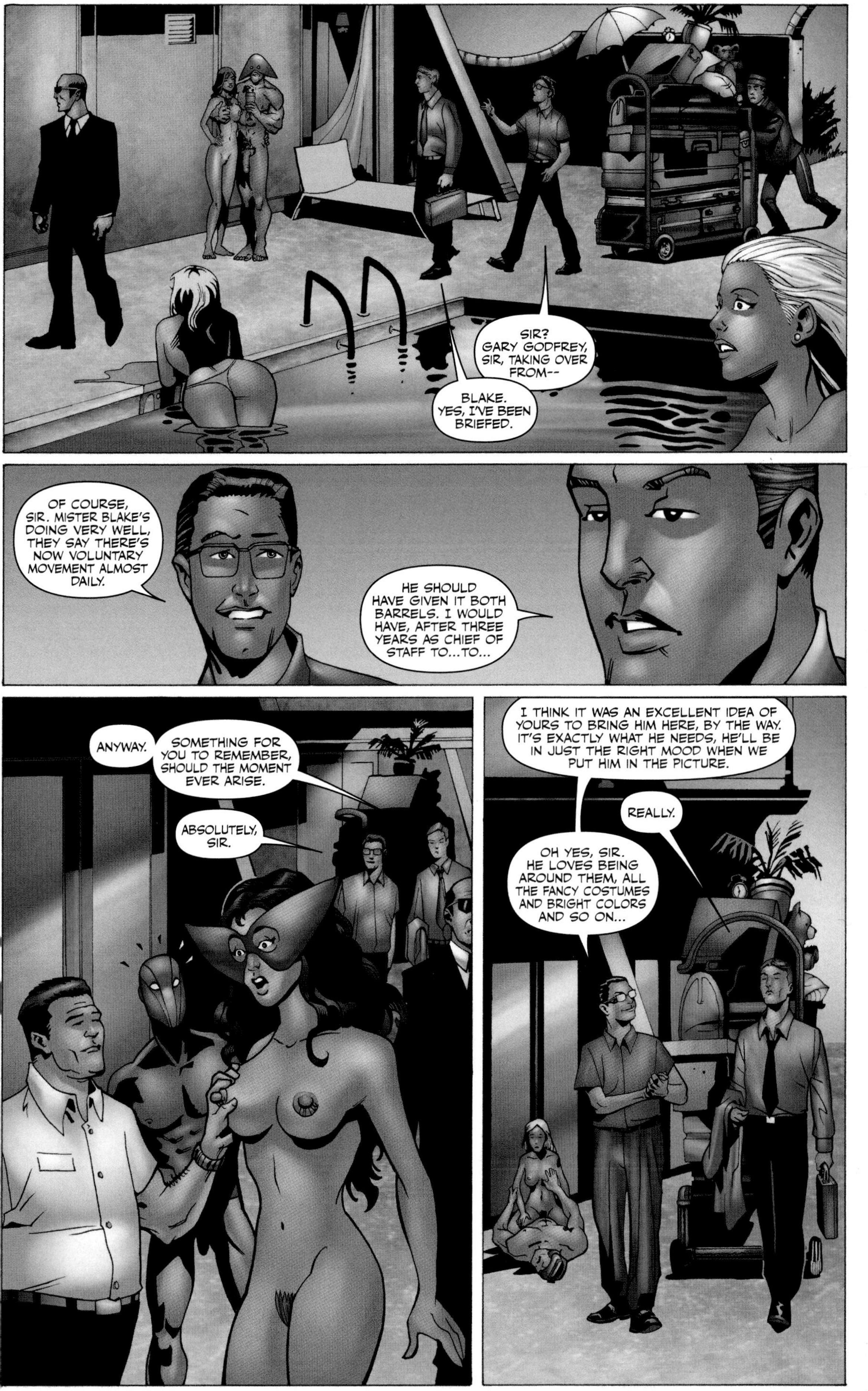
SIR? GARY GODFREY, SIR, TAKING OVER FROM--
BLAKE. YES, I'VE BEEN BRIEFED.
OF COURSE, SIR. MISTER BLAKE'S DOING VERY WELL, THEY SAY THERE'S NOW VOLUNTARY MOVEMENT ALMOST DAILY.
HE SHOULD HAVE GIVEN IT BOTH BARRELS. I WOULD HAVE, AFTER THREE YEARS AS CHIEF OF STAFF TO...TO...
ANYWAY.
SOMETHING FOR YOU TO REMEMBER, SHOULD THE MOMENT EVER ARISE.
ABSOLUTELY, SIR.
I THINK IT WAS AN EXCELLENT IDEA OF YOURS TO BRING HIM HERE, BY THE WAY. IT'S EXACTLY WHAT HE NEEDS, HE'LL BE IN JUST THE RIGHT MOOD WHEN WE PUT HIM IN THE PICTURE.
REALLY.
OH YES, SIR. HE LOVES BEING AROUND THEM, ALL THE FANCY COSTUMES AND BRIGHT COLORS AND SO ON...

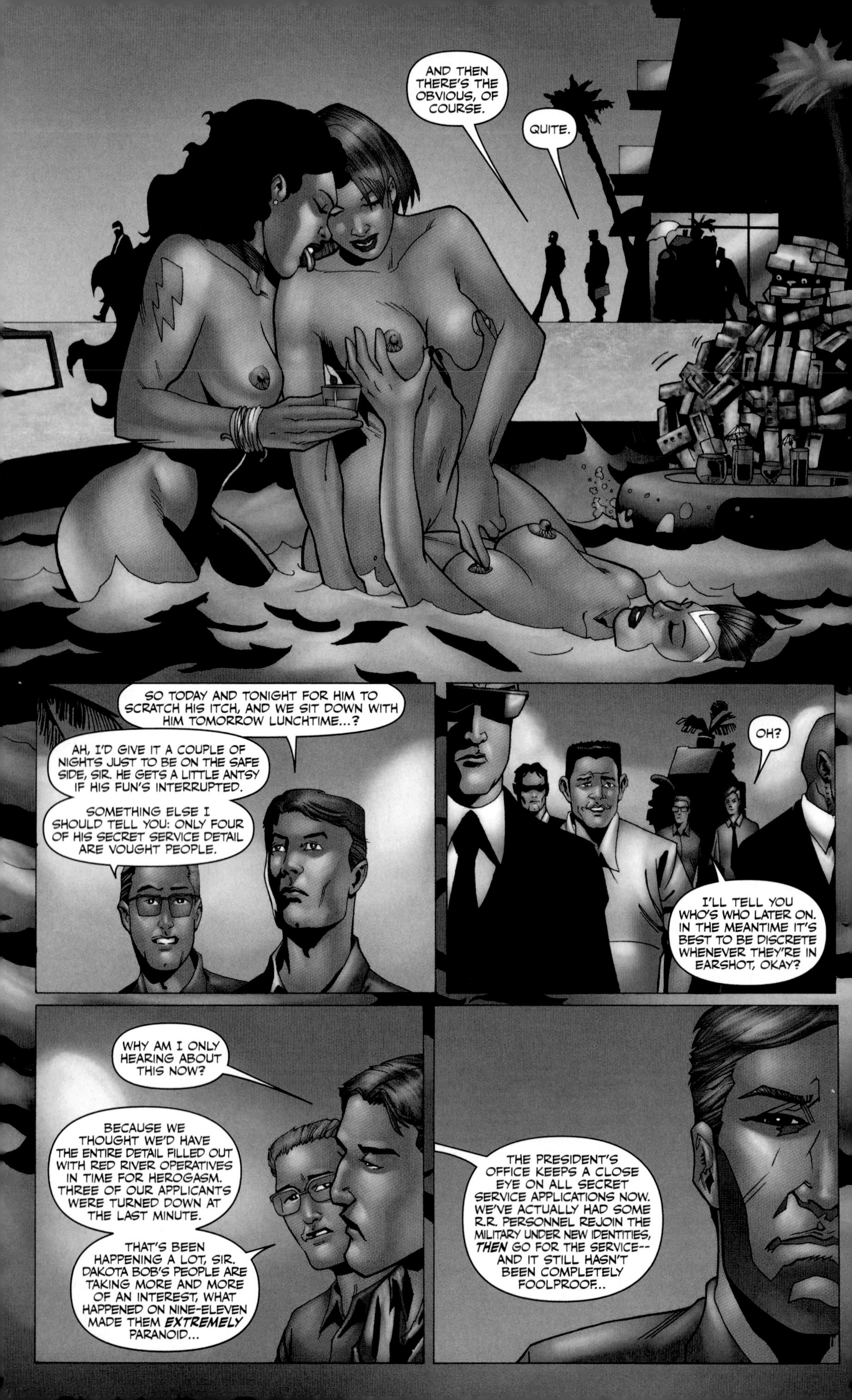
AND THEN THERE'S THE OBVIOUS, OF COURSE.
QUITE.
SO TODAY AND TONIGHT FOR HIM TO SCRATCH HIS ITCH, AND WE SIT DOWN WITH HIM TOMORROW LUNCHTIME...?
AH, I'D GIVE IT A COUPLE OF NIGHTS JUST TO BE ON THE SAFE SIDE, SIR. HE GETS A LITTLE ANTSY IF HIS FUN'S INTERRUPTED.
SOMETHING ELSE I SHOULD TELL YOU: ONLY FOUR OF HIS SECRET SERVICE DETAIL ARE VOUGHT PEOPLE.
OH?
I'LL TELL YOU WHO'S WHO LATER ON. IN THE MEANTIME IT'S BEST TO BE DISCRETE WHENEVER THEY'RE IN EARSHOT, OKAY?
WHY AM I ONLY HEARING ABOUT THIS NOW?
BECAUSE WE THOUGHT WE'D HAVE THE ENTIRE DETAIL FILLED OUT WITH RED RIVER OPERATIVES IN TIME FOR HEROGASM. THREE OF OUR APPLICANTS WERE TURNED DOWN AT THE LAST MINUTE.
THAT'S BEEN HAPPENING A LOT, SIR. DAKOTA BOB'S PEOPLE ARE TAKING MORE AND MORE OF AN INTEREST, WHAT HAPPENED ON NINE-ELEVEN MADE THEM EXTREMELY PARANOID...
THE PRESIDENT'S OFFICE KEEPS A CLOSE EYE ON ALL SECRET SERVICE APPLICATIONS NOW. WE'VE ACTUALLY HAD SOME R.R. PERSONNEL REJOIN THE MILITARY UNDER NEW IDENTITIES, THEN GO FOR THE SERVICE-- AND IT STILL HASN'T BEEN COMPLETELY FOOLPROOF...

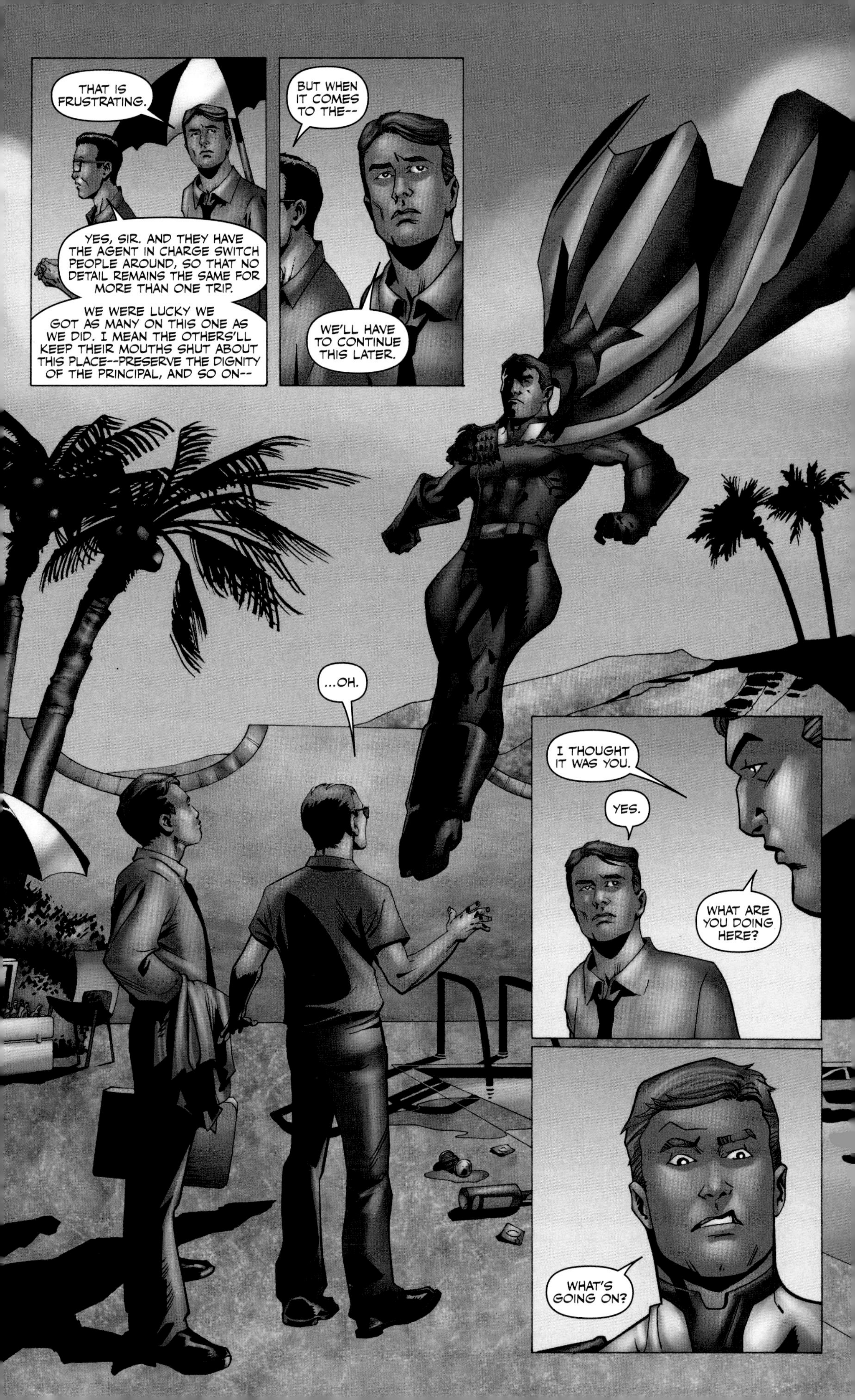
THAT IS FRUSTRATING.
YES, SIR. AND THEY HAVE THE AGENT IN CHARGE SWITCH PEOPLE AROUND, SO THAT NO DETAIL REMAINS THE SAME FOR MORE THAN ONE TRIP.
WE WERE LUCKY WE GOT AS MANY ON THIS ONE AS WE DID. I MEAN THE OTHERS'LL KEEP THEIR MOUTHS SHUT ABOUT THIS PLACE--PRESERVE THE DIGNITY OF THE PRINCIPAL, AND SO ON--
BUT WHEN IT COMES TO THE--
WE'LL HAVE TO CONTINUE THIS LATER.
...OH.
I THOUGHT IT WAS YOU.
YES.
WHAT ARE YOU DOING HERE?
WHAT'S GOING ON?

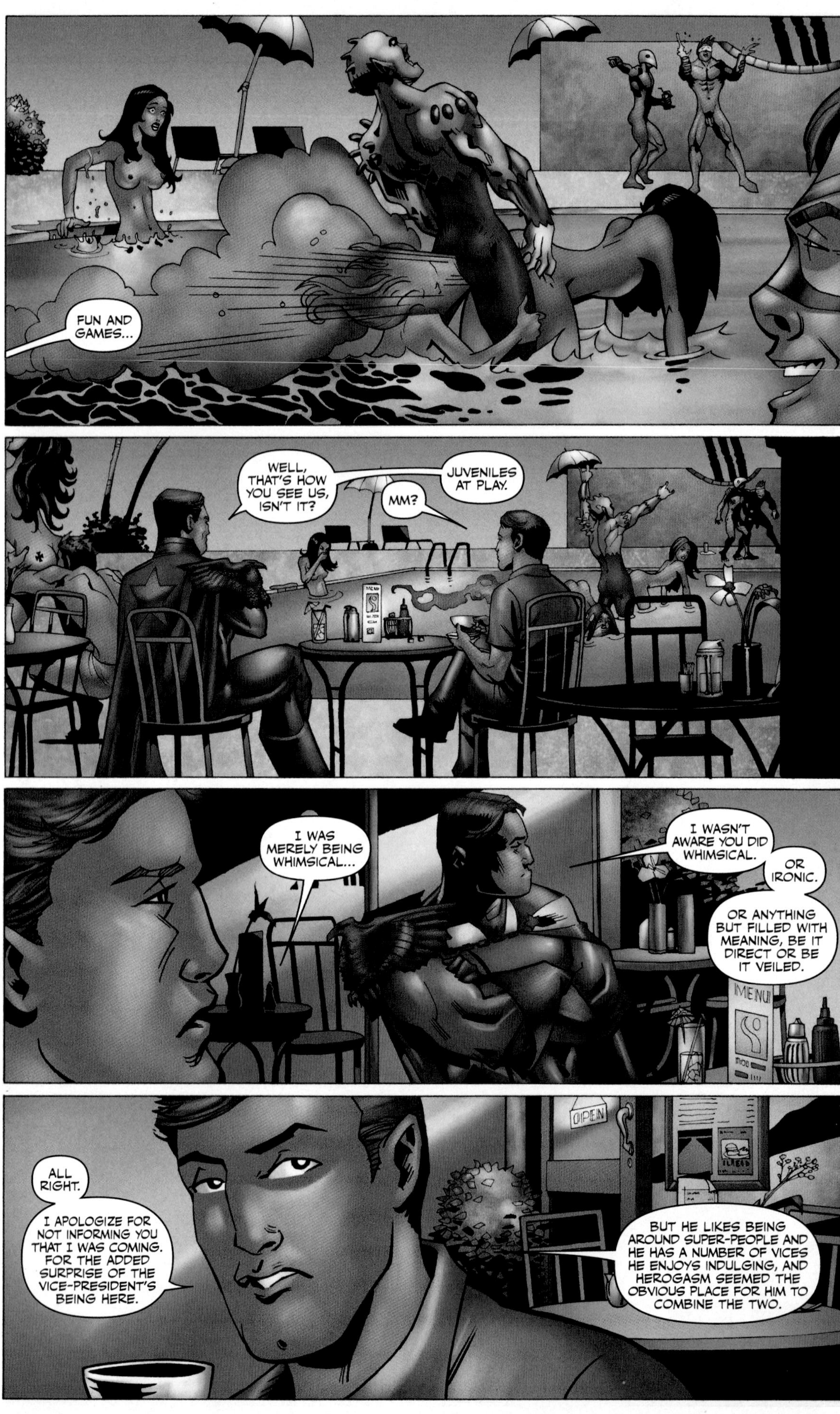
FUN AND GAMES...
WELL, THAT'S HOW YOU SEE US, ISN'T IT?
MM?
JUVENILES AT PLAY.
I WAS MERELY BEING WHIMSICAL...
I WASN'T AWARE YOU DID WHIMSICAL.
OR IRONIC.
OR ANYTHING BUT FILLED WITH MEANING, BE IT DIRECT OR BE IT VEILED.
MENU
ALL RIGHT.
I APOLOGIZE FOR NOT INFORMING YOU THAT I WAS COMING. FOR THE ADDED SURPRISE OF THE VICE-PRESIDENT'S BEING HERE.
OPEN
BUT HE LIKES BEING AROUND SUPER-PEOPLE AND HE HAS A NUMBER OF VICES HE ENJOYS INDULGING, AND HEROGASM SEEMED THE OBVIOUS PLACE FOR HIM TO COMBINE THE TWO.

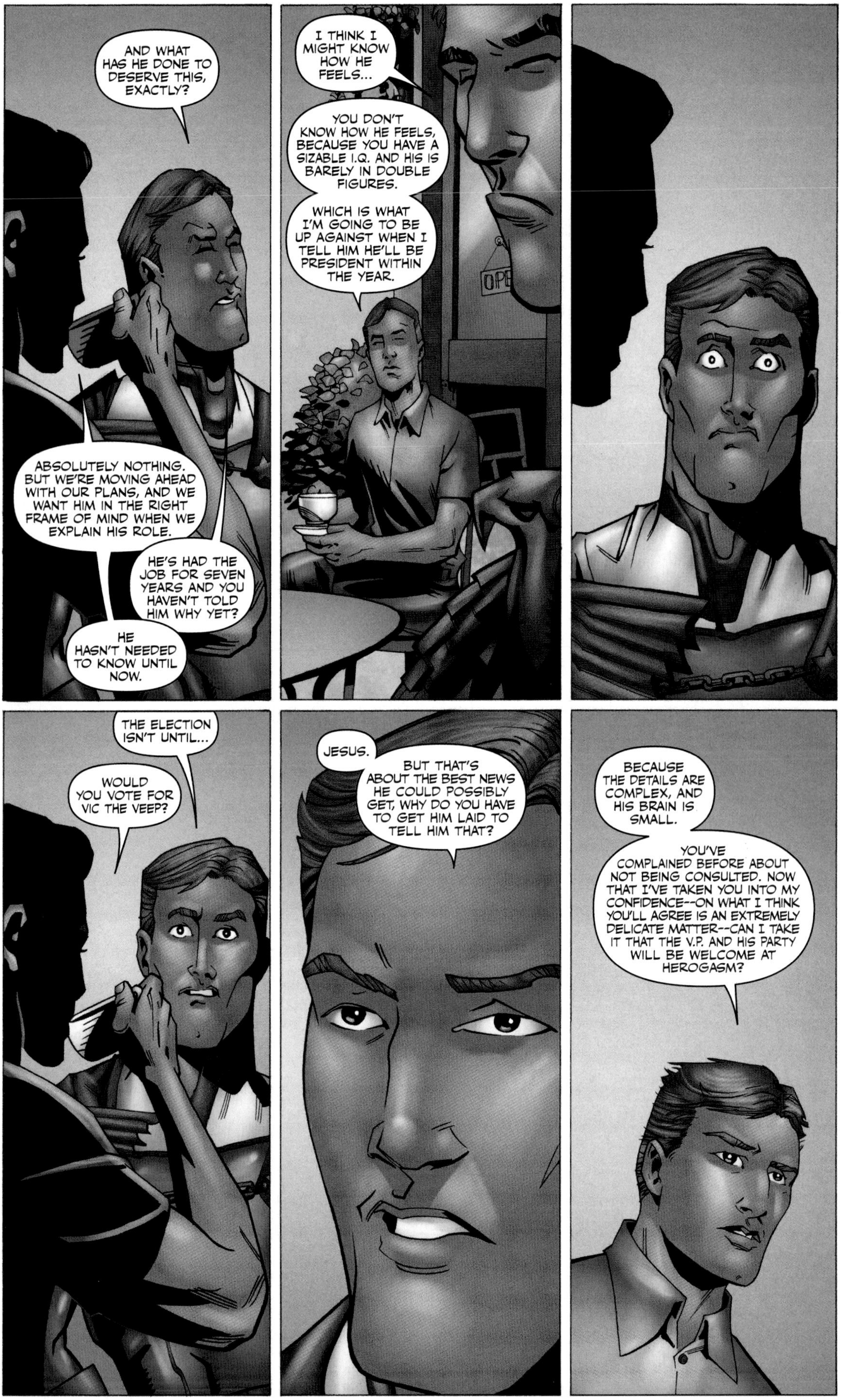
AND WHAT HAS HE DONE TO DESERVE THIS, EXACTLY?
ABSOLUTELY NOTHING. BUT WE'RE MOVING AHEAD WITH OUR PLANS, AND WE WANT HIM IN THE RIGHT FRAME OF MIND WHEN WE EXPLAIN HIS ROLE.
HE'S HAD THE JOB FOR SEVEN YEARS AND YOU HAVEN'T TOLD HIM WHY YET?
HE HASN'T NEEDED TO KNOW UNTIL NOW.
I THINK I MIGHT KNOW HOW HE FEELS...
YOU DON'T KNOW HOW HE FEELS, BECAUSE YOU HAVE A SIZABLE I.Q. AND HIS IS BARELY IN DOUBLE FIGURES.
WHICH IS WHAT I'M GOING TO BE UP AGAINST WHEN I TELL HIM HE'LL BE PRESIDENT WITHIN THE YEAR.
THE ELECTION ISN'T UNTIL...
WOULD YOU VOTE FOR VIC THE VEEP?
JESUS.
BUT THAT'S ABOUT THE BEST NEWS HE COULD POSSIBLY GET, WHY DO YOU HAVE TO GET HIM LAID TO TELL HIM THAT?
BECAUSE THE DETAILS ARE COMPLEX, AND HIS BRAIN IS SMALL.
YOU'VE COMPLAINED BEFORE ABOUT NOT BEING CONSULTED. NOW THAT I'VE TAKEN YOU INTO MY CONFIDENCE--ON WHAT I THINK YOU'LL AGREE IS AN EXTREMELY DELICATE MATTER--CAN I TAKE IT THAT THE V.P. AND HIS PARTY WILL BE WELCOME AT HEROGASM?

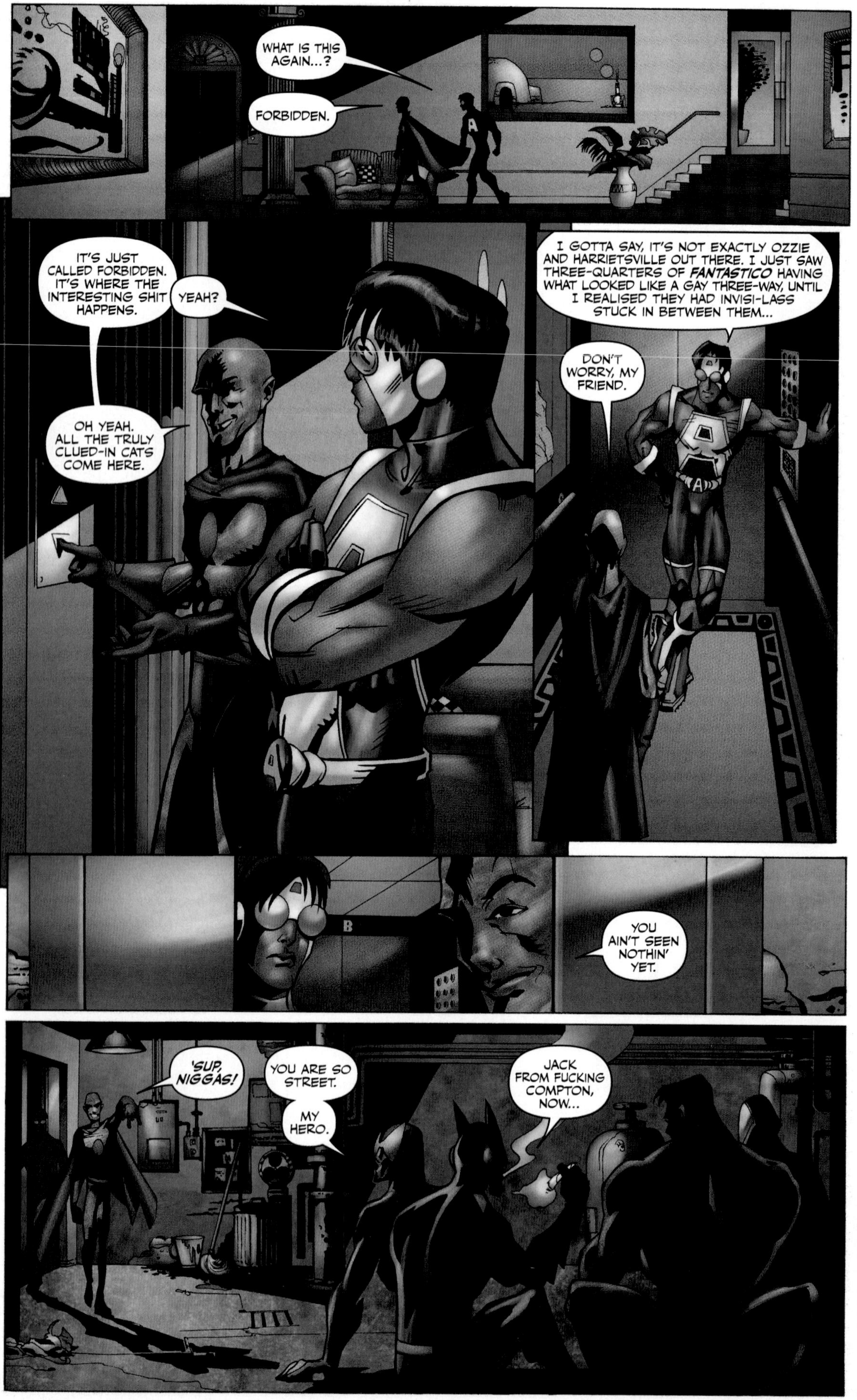
WHAT IS THIS AGAIN...?
FORBIDDEN.
IT'S JUST CALLED FORBIDDEN. IT'S WHERE THE INTERESTING SHIT HAPPENS.
YEAH?
OH YEAH. ALL THE TRULY CLUED-IN CATS COME HERE.
I GOTTA SAY, IT'S NOT EXACTLY OZZIE AND HARRIETSVILLE OUT THERE. I JUST SAW THREE-QUARTERS OF FANTASTICO HAVING WHAT LOOKED LIKE A GAY THREE-WAY, UNTIL I REALISED THEY HAD INVISI-LASS STUCK IN BETWEEN THEM...
DON'T WORRY, MY FRIEND.
YOU AIN'T SEEN NOTHIN' YET.
'SUP, NIGGAS!
YOU ARE SO STREET.
MY HERO.
JACK FROM FUCKING COMPTON, NOW...

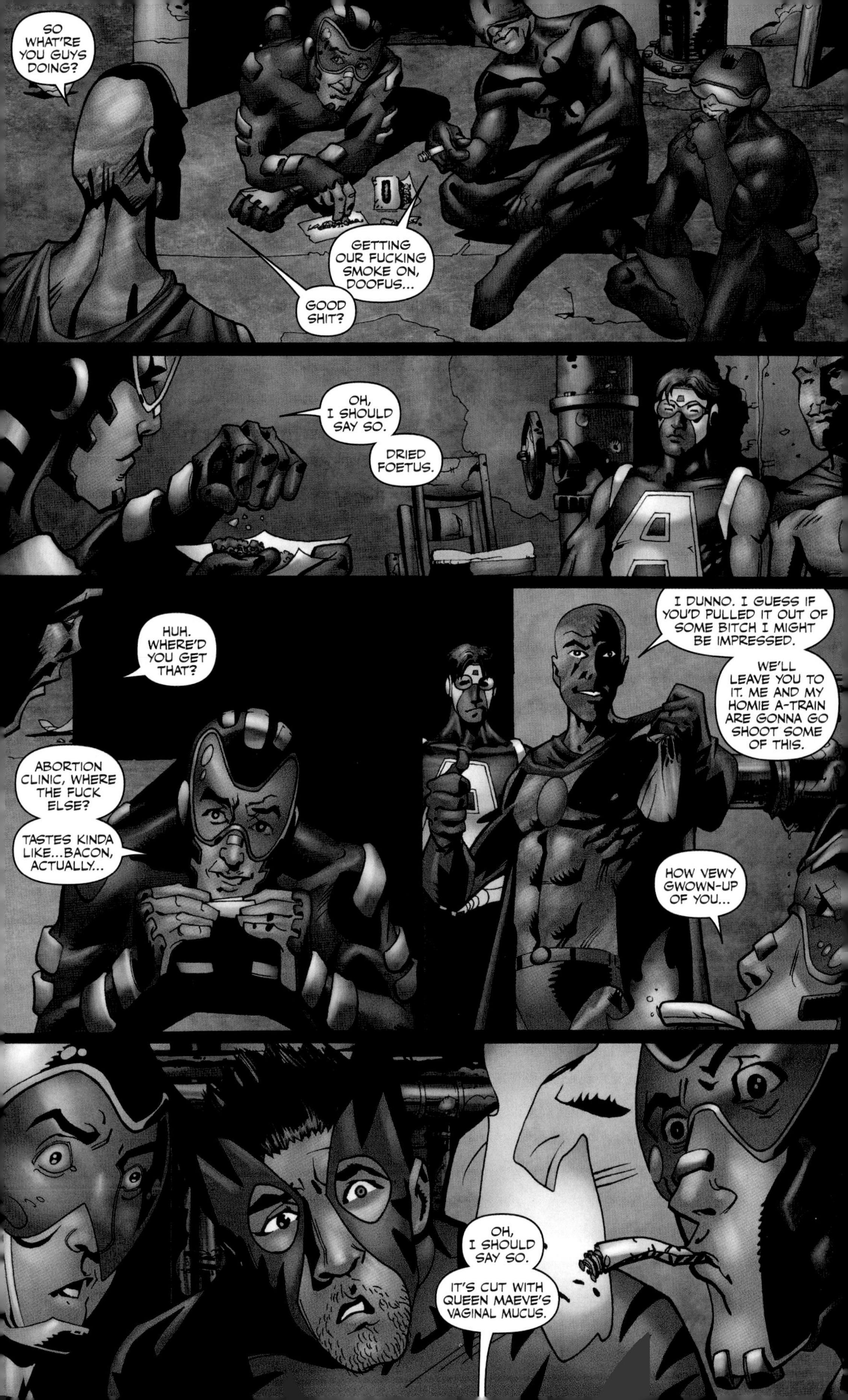
SO WHAT'RE YOU GUYS DOING?
GETTING OUR FUCKING SMOKE ON, DOOFUS...
GOOD SHIT?
OH, I SHOULD SAY SO.
DRIED FOETUS.
HUH. WHERE'D YOU GET THAT?
ABORTION CLINIC, WHERE THE FUCK ELSE?
TASTES KINDA LIKE...BACON, ACTUALLY...
I DUNNO. I GUESS IF YOU'D PULLED IT OUT OF SOME BITCH I MIGHT BE IMPRESSED.
WE'LL LEAVE YOU TO IT. ME AND MY HOMIE A-TRAIN ARE GONNA GO SHOOT SOME OF THIS.
HOW VEWY GWOWN-UP OF YOU...
OH, I SHOULD SAY SO.
IT'S CUT WITH QUEEN MAEVE'S VAGINAL MUCUS.

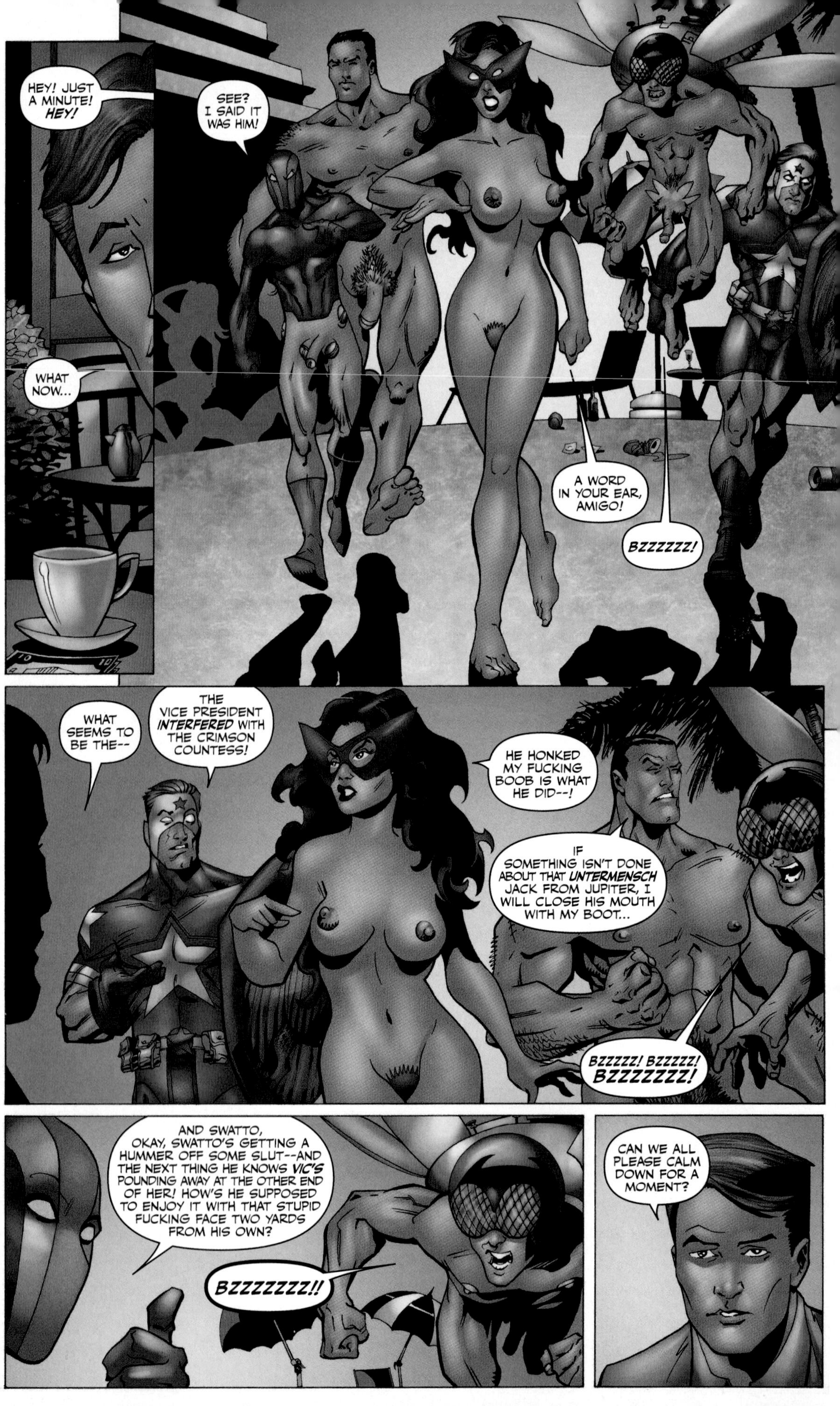
HEY! JUST A MINUTE! HEY!
SEE? I SAID IT WAS HIM!
WHAT NOW...
A WORD IN YOUR EAR, AMIGO!
BZZZZZZ!
WHAT SEEMS TO BE THE--
THE VICE PRESIDENT INTERFERED WITH THE CRIMSON COUNTESS!
HE HONKED MY FUCKING BOOB IS WHAT HE DID--!
IF SOMETHING ISN'T DONE ABOUT THAT UNTERMENSCH JACK FROM JUPITER, I WILL CLOSE HIS MOUTH WITH MY BOOT...
BZZZZZ! BZZZZZ! BZZZZZZZ!
AND SWATTO, OKAY, SWATTO'S GETTING A HUMMER OFF SOME SLUT--AND THE NEXT THING HE KNOWS VIC'S POUNDING AWAY AT THE OTHER END OF HER! HOW'S HE SUPPOSED TO ENJOY IT WITH THAT STUPID FUCKING FACE TWO YARDS FROM HIS OWN?
BZZZZZZZ!!
CAN WE ALL PLEASE CALM DOWN FOR A MOMENT?

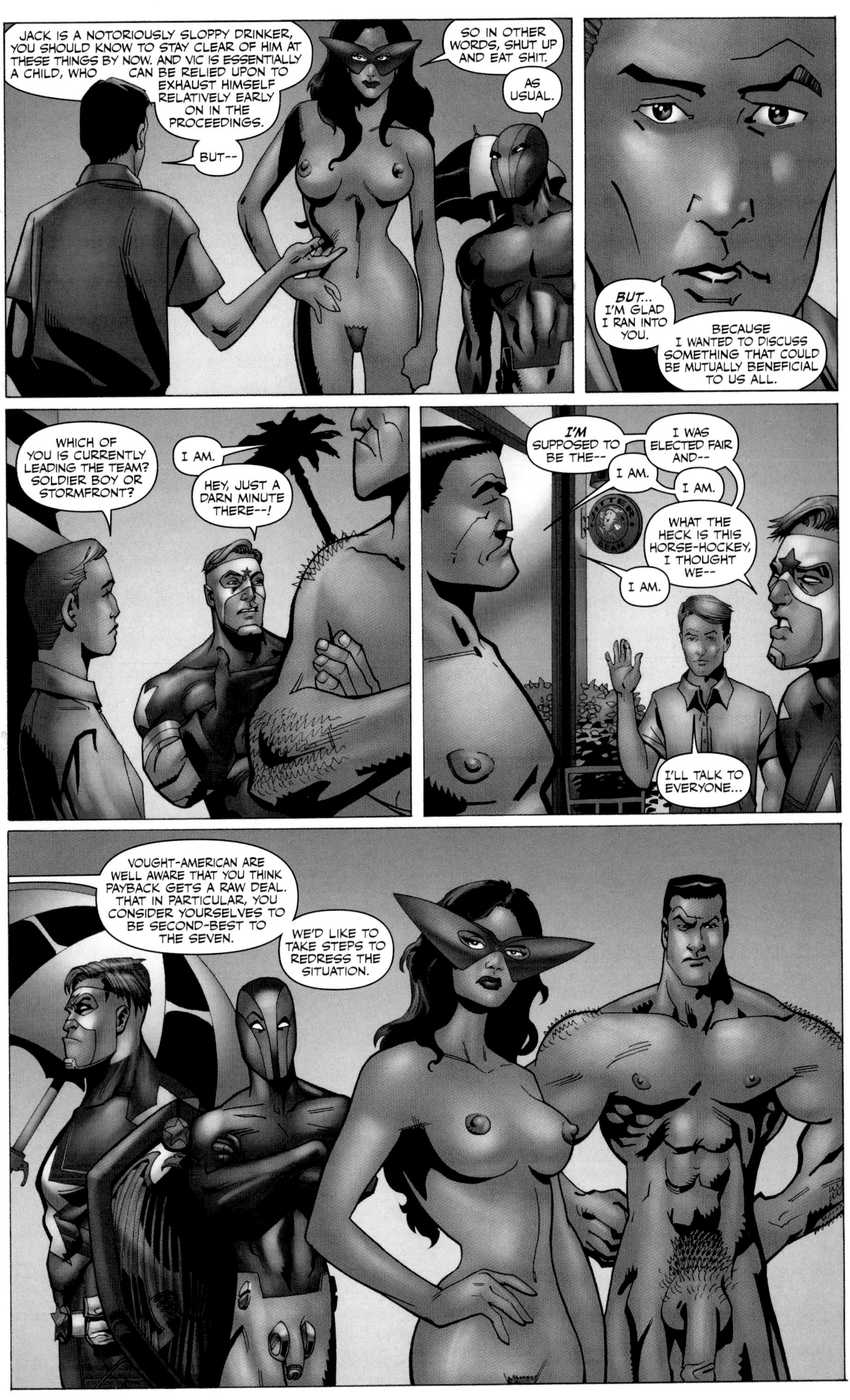
JACK IS A NOTORIOUSLY SLOPPY DRINKER, YOU SHOULD KNOW TO STAY CLEAR OF HIM AT THESE THINGS BY NOW. AND VIC IS ESSENTIALLY A CHILD, WHO CAN BE RELIED UPON TO EXHAUST HIMSELF RELATIVELY EARLY ON IN THE PROCEEDINGS.
SO IN OTHER WORDS, SHUT UP AND EAT SHIT.
AS USUAL.
BUT--
BUT... I'M GLAD I RAN INTO YOU.
BECAUSE I WANTED TO DISCUSS SOMETHING THAT COULD BE MUTUALLY BENEFICIAL TO US ALL.
WHICH OF YOU IS CURRENTLY LEADING THE TEAM? SOLDIER BOY OR STORMFRONT?
I AM.
HEY, JUST A DARN MINUTE THERE--!
I'M SUPPOSED TO BE THE--
I WAS ELECTED FAIR AND--
I AM.
I AM.
WHAT THE HECK IS THIS HORSE-HOCKEY, I THOUGHT WE--
I AM.
I'LL TALK TO EVERYONE...
VOUGHT-AMERICAN ARE WELL AWARE THAT YOU THINK PAYBACK GETS A RAW DEAL. THAT IN PARTICULAR, YOU CONSIDER YOURSELVES TO BE SECOND-BEST TO THE SEVEN.
WE'D LIKE TO TAKE STEPS TO REDRESS THE SITUATION.

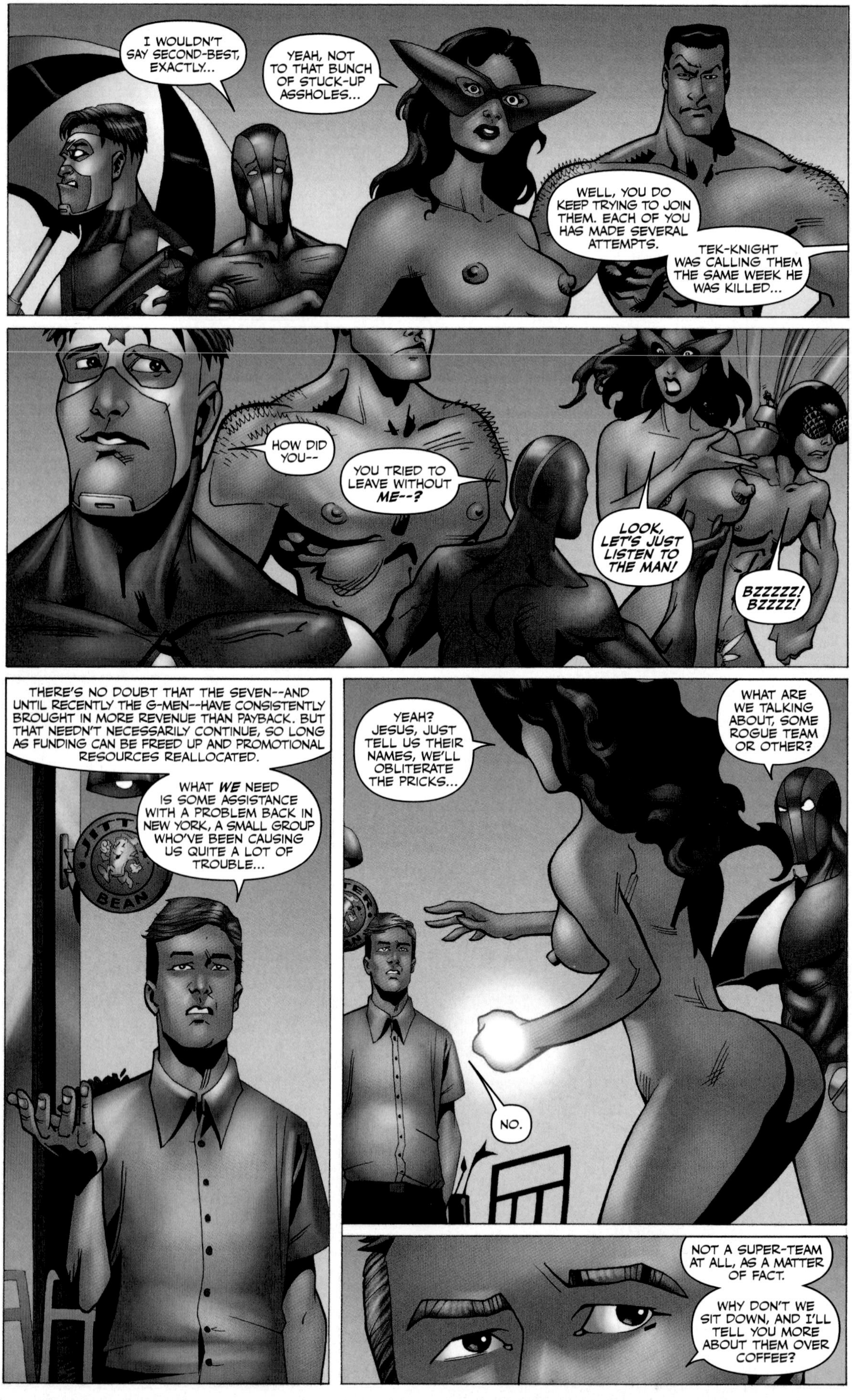
I WOULDN'T SAY SECOND-BEST, EXACTLY...
YEAH, NOT TO THAT BUNCH OF STUCK-UP ASSHOLES...
WELL, YOU DO KEEP TRYING TO JOIN THEM. EACH OF YOU HAS MADE SEVERAL ATTEMPTS.
TEK-KNIGHT WAS CALLING THEM THE SAME WEEK HE WAS KILLED...
HOW DID YOU--
YOU TRIED TO LEAVE WITHOUT *ME--?*
LOOK, LET'S JUST LISTEN TO THE MAN!
BZZZZZ! BZZZZ!
THERE'S NO DOUBT THAT THE SEVEN--AND UNTIL RECENTLY THE G-MEN--HAVE CONSISTENTLY BROUGHT IN MORE REVENUE THAN PAYBACK. BUT THAT NEEDN'T NECESSARILY CONTINUE, SO LONG AS FUNDING CAN BE FREED UP AND PROMOTIONAL RESOURCES REALLOCATED.
WHAT *WE* NEED IS SOME ASSISTANCE WITH A PROBLEM BACK IN NEW YORK, A SMALL GROUP WHO'VE BEEN CAUSING US QUITE A LOT OF TROUBLE...
BEAN
YEAH? JESUS, JUST TELL US THEIR NAMES, WE'LL OBLITERATE THE PRICKS...
WHAT ARE WE TALKING ABOUT, SOME ROGUE TEAM OR OTHER?
NO.
NOT A SUPER-TEAM AT ALL, AS A MATTER OF FACT.
WHY DON'T WE SIT DOWN, AND I'LL TELL YOU MORE ABOUT THEM OVER COFFEE?

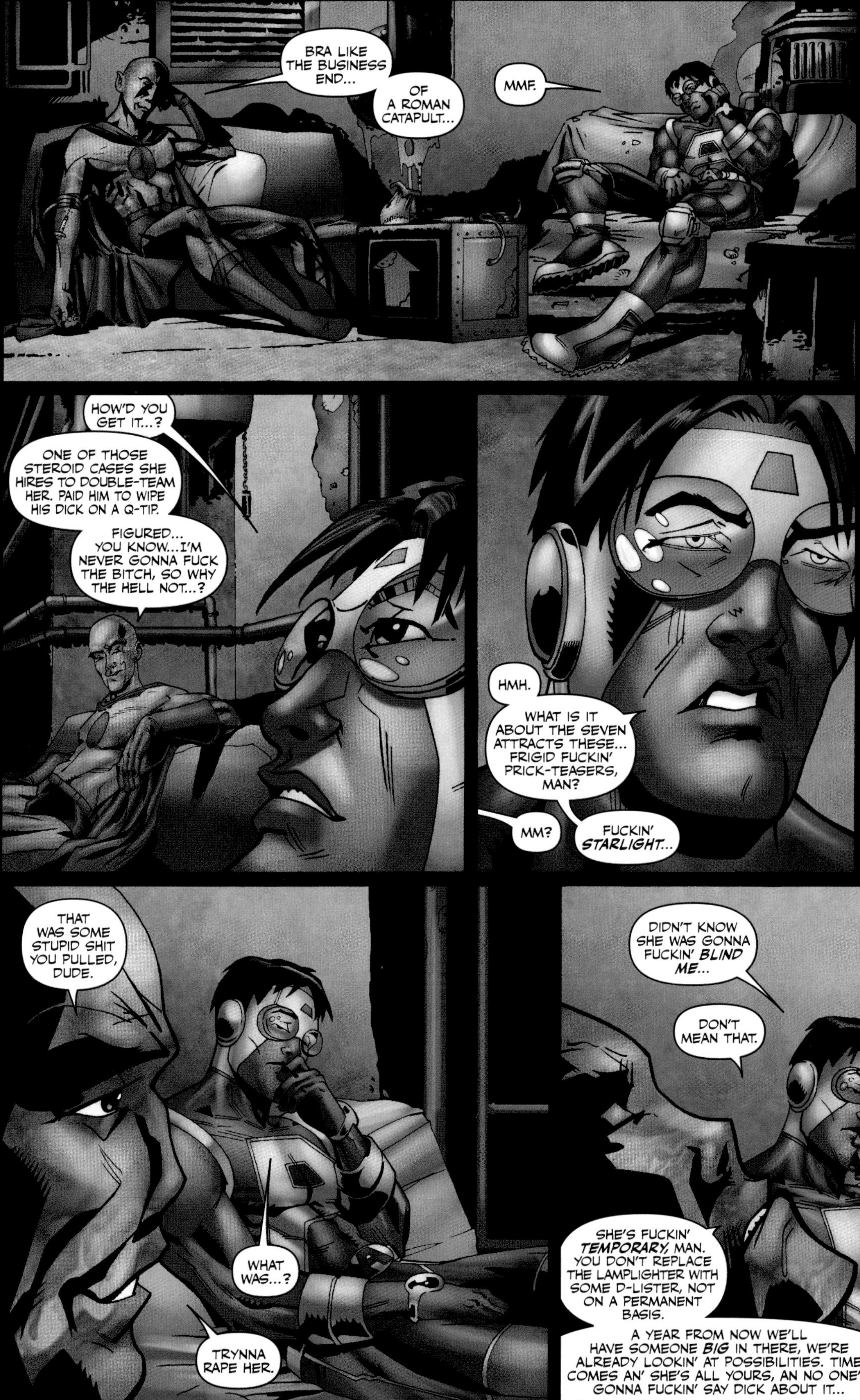
BRA LIKE THE BUSINESS END...
OF A ROMAN CATAPULT...
MMF.
HOW'D YOU GET IT...?
ONE OF THOSE STEROID CASES SHE HIRES TO DOUBLE-TEAM HER. PAID HIM TO WIPE HIS DICK ON A Q-TIP.
FIGURED... YOU KNOW...I'M NEVER GONNA FUCK THE BITCH, SO WHY THE HELL NOT...?
HMH.
WHAT IS IT ABOUT THE SEVEN ATTRACTS THESE... FRIGID FUCKIN' PRICK-TEASERS, MAN?
MM?
FUCKIN' STARLIGHT...
THAT WAS SOME STUPID SHIT YOU PULLED, DUDE.
WHAT WAS...?
TRYNNA RAPE HER.
DIDN'T KNOW SHE WAS GONNA FUCKIN' BLIND ME...
DON'T MEAN THAT.
SHE'S FUCKIN' TEMPORARY, MAN. YOU DON'T REPLACE THE LAMPLIGHTER WITH SOME D-LISTER, NOT ON A PERMANENT BASIS.
A YEAR FROM NOW WE'LL HAVE SOMEONE BIG IN THERE, WE'RE ALREADY LOOKIN' AT POSSIBILITIES. TIME COMES AN' SHE'S ALL YOURS, AN NO ONE'S GONNA FUCKIN' SAY DICK ABOUT IT...

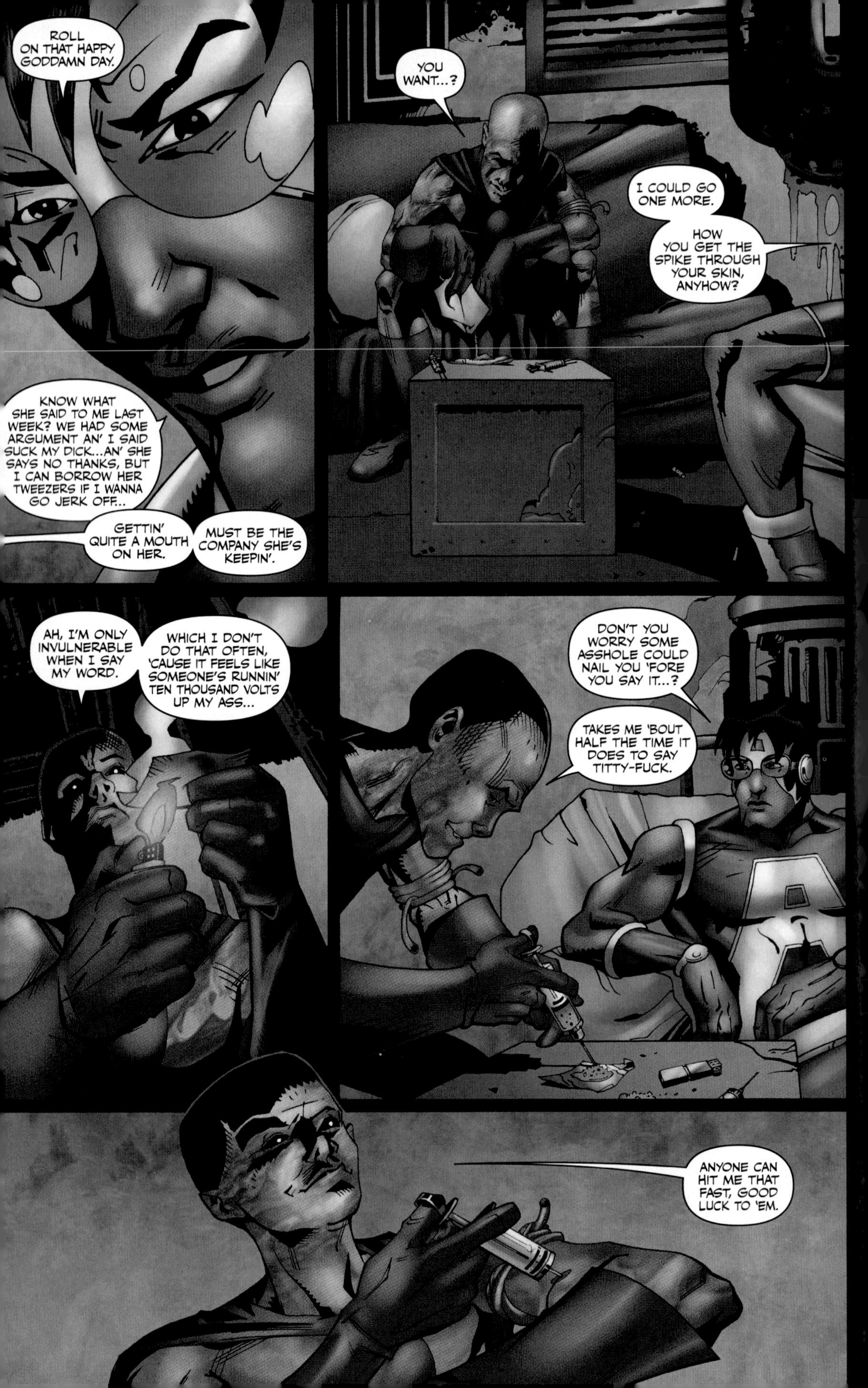

ROLL ON THAT HAPPY GODDAMN DAY.
YOU WANT...?
I COULD GO ONE MORE.
HOW YOU GET THE SPIKE THROUGH YOUR SKIN, ANYHOW?
KNOW WHAT SHE SAID TO ME LAST WEEK? WE HAD SOME ARGUMENT AN' I SAID SUCK MY DICK...AN' SHE SAYS NO THANKS, BUT I CAN BORROW HER TWEEZERS IF I WANNA GO JERK OFF...
GETTIN' QUITE A MOUTH ON HER.
MUST BE THE COMPANY SHE'S KEEPIN'.
AH, I'M ONLY INVULNERABLE WHEN I SAY MY WORD.
WHICH I DON'T DO THAT OFTEN, 'CAUSE IT FEELS LIKE SOMEONE'S RUNNIN' TEN THOUSAND VOLTS UP MY ASS...
DON'T YOU WORRY SOME ASSHOLE COULD NAIL YOU 'FORE YOU SAY IT...?
TAKES ME 'BOUT HALF THE TIME IT DOES TO SAY TITTY-FUCK.
ANYONE CAN HIT ME THAT FAST, GOOD LUCK TO 'EM.

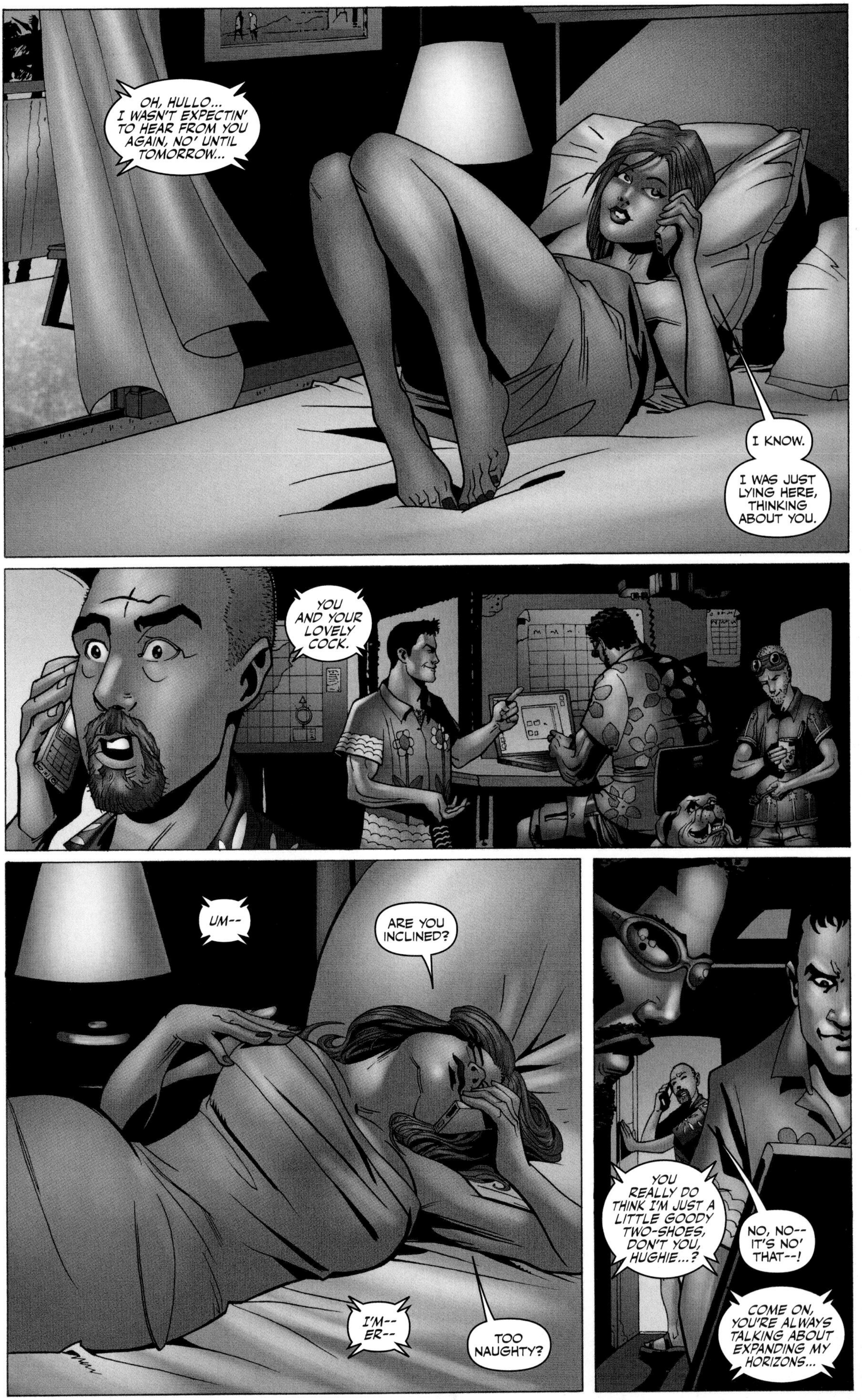
OH, HULLO... I WASN'T EXPECTIN' TO HEAR FROM YOU AGAIN, NO' UNTIL TOMORROW...
I KNOW.
I WAS JUST LYING HERE, THINKING ABOUT YOU.
YOU AND YOUR LOVELY COCK.
UM--
ARE YOU INCLINED?
I'M-- ER--
TOO NAUGHTY?
YOU REALLY DO THINK I'M JUST A LITTLE GOODY TWO-SHOES, DON'T YOU, HUGHIE...?
NO, NO-- IT'S NO' THAT--!
COME ON, YOU'RE ALWAYS TALKING ABOUT EXPANDING MY HORIZONS...

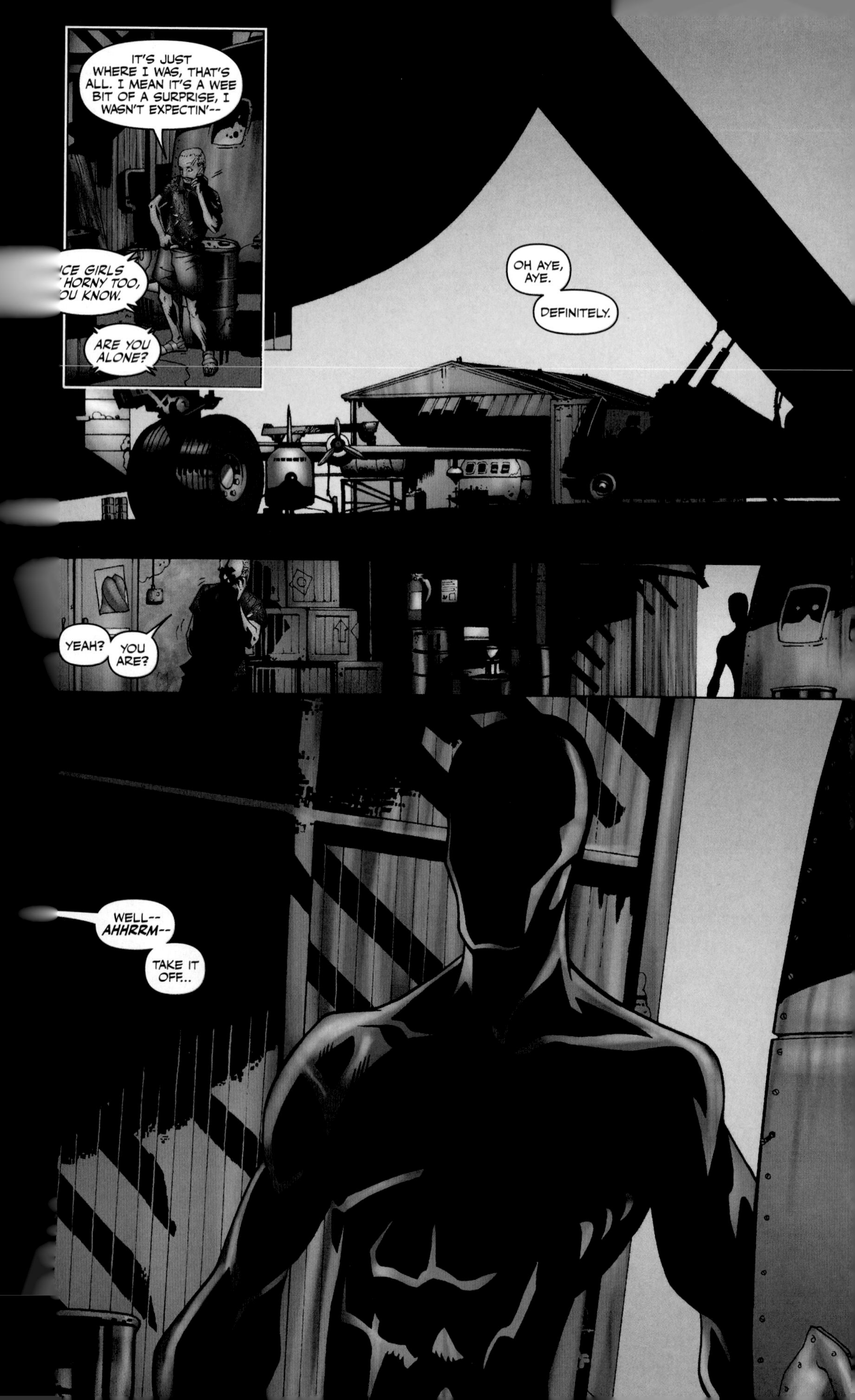
IT'S JUST WHERE I WAS, THAT'S ALL. I MEAN IT'S A WEE BIT OF A SURPRISE, I WASN'T EXPECTIN'--
ICE GIRLS HORNY TOO, OU KNOW.
ARE YOU ALONE?
OH AYE, AYE.
DEFINITELY.
YEAH?
YOU ARE?
WELL-- AHHRRM--
TAKE IT OFF...

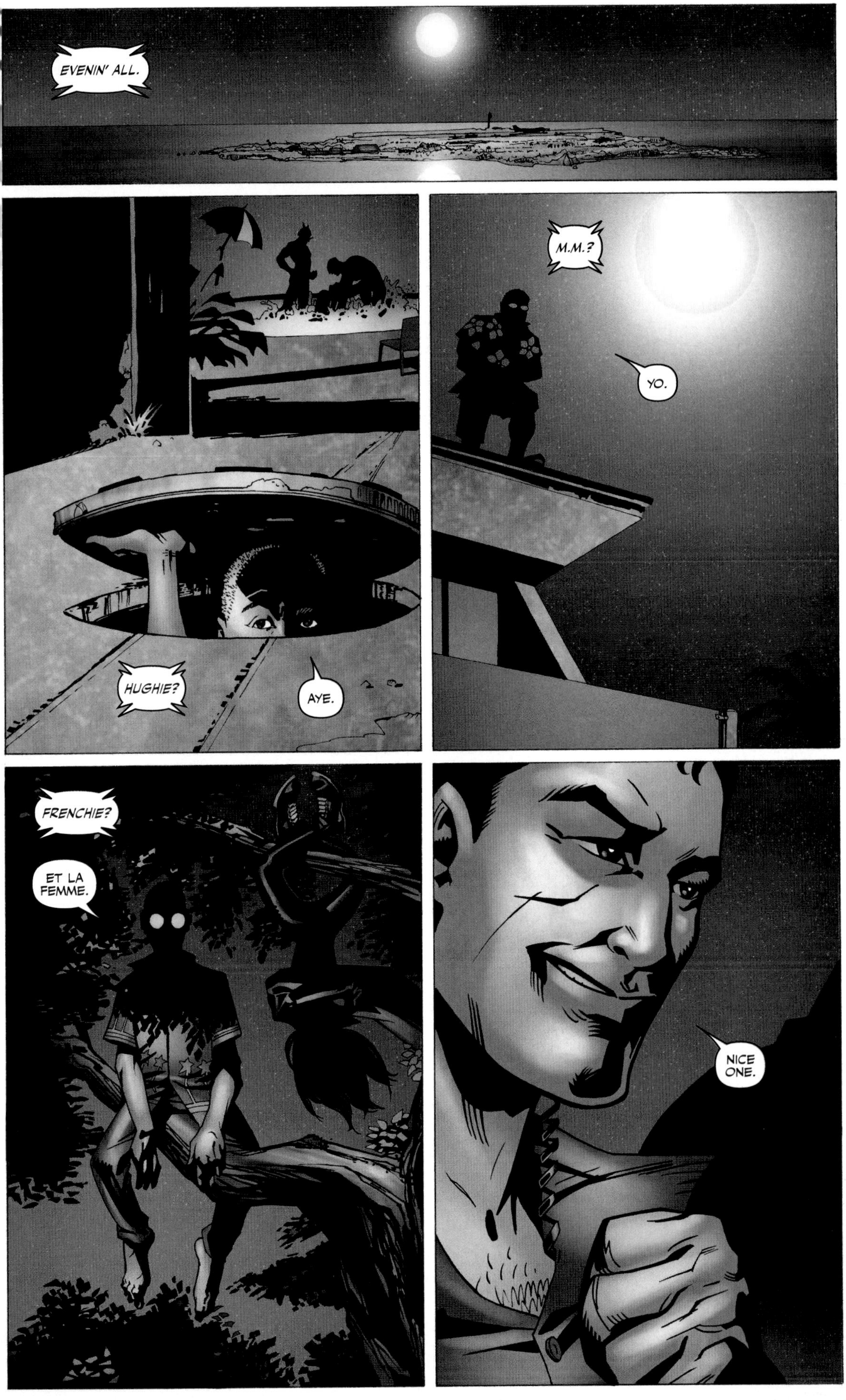
EVENIN' ALL.
HUGHIE?
AYE.
M.M.?
YO.
FRENCHIE?
ET LA FEMME.
NICE ONE.

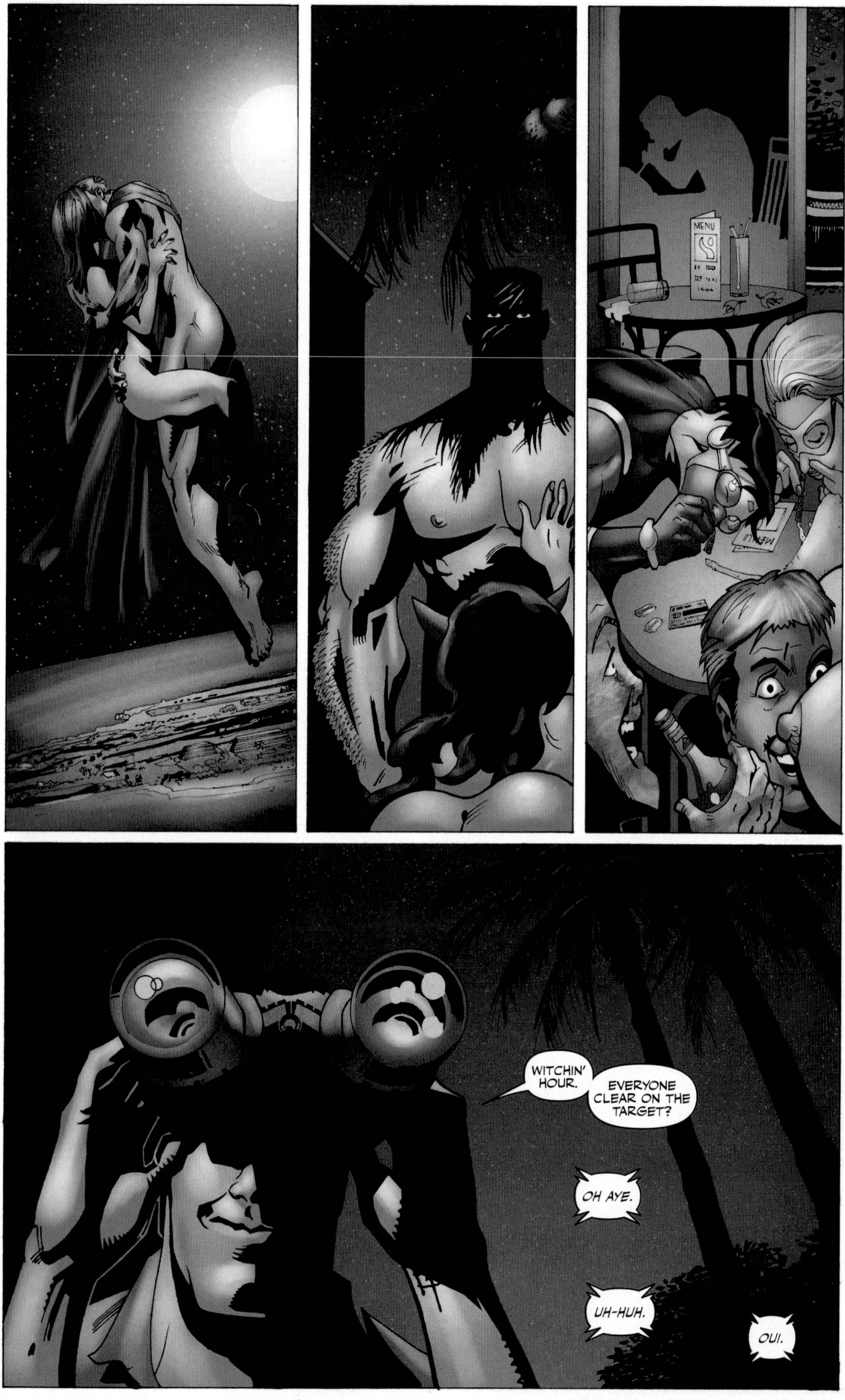
MENU
MENU
WITCHIN' HOUR.
EVERYONE CLEAR ON THE TARGET?
OH AYE.
UH-HUH.
OUI.

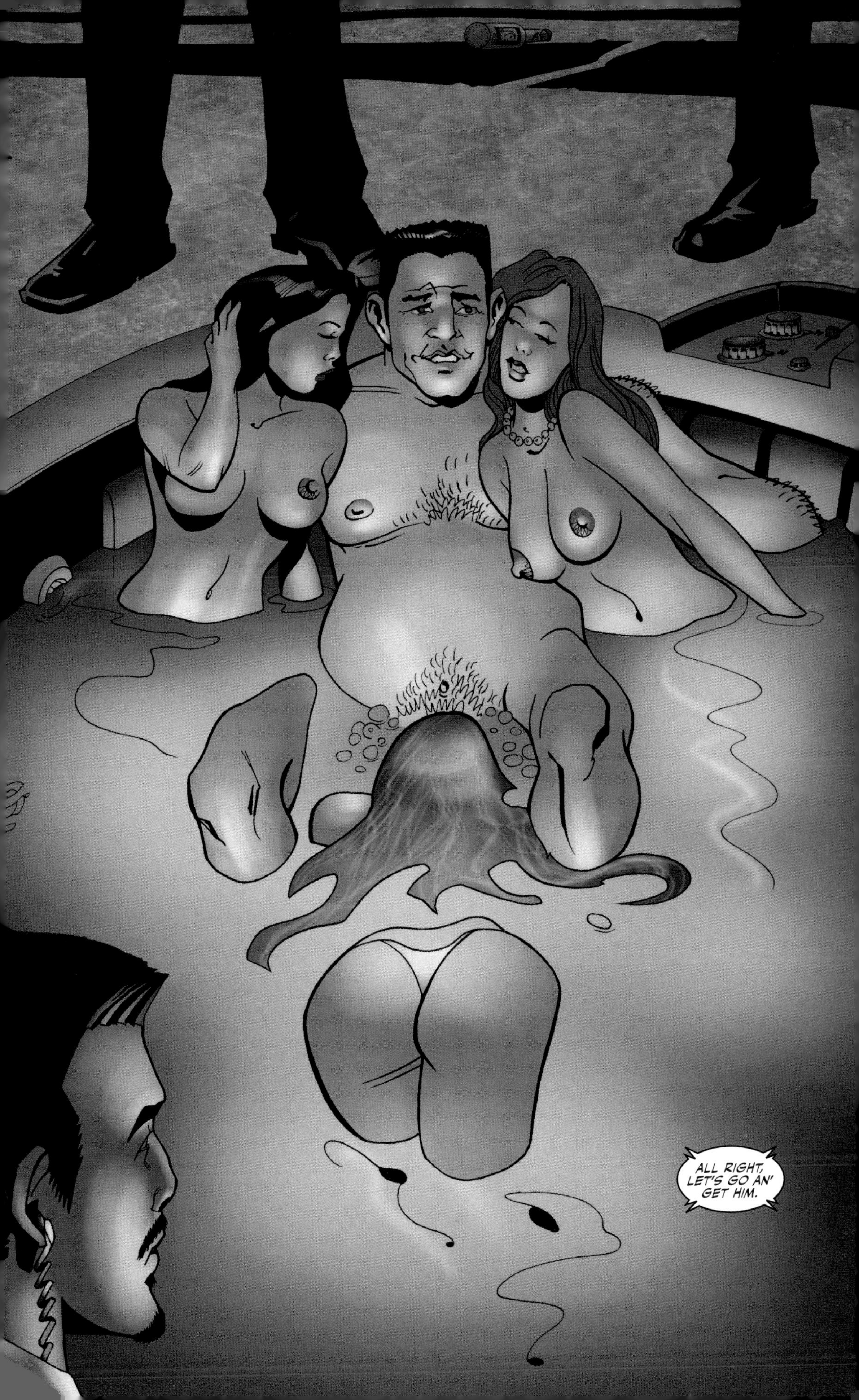
ALL RIGHT, LET'S GO AN' GET HIM.

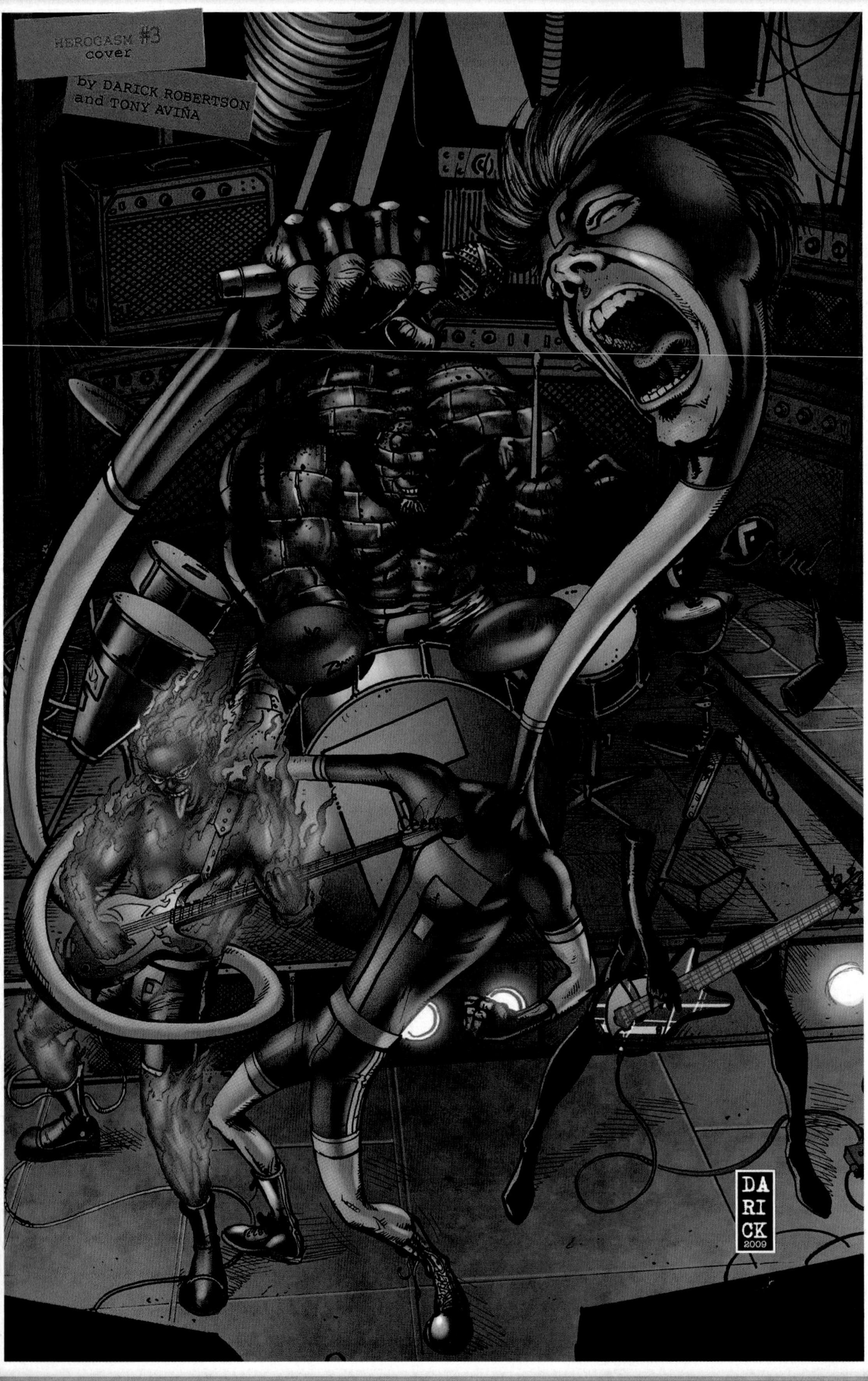
DA
RI
CK
2009

HEROGASM #3
cover

by DARICK ROBERTSON
and TONY AVIÑA

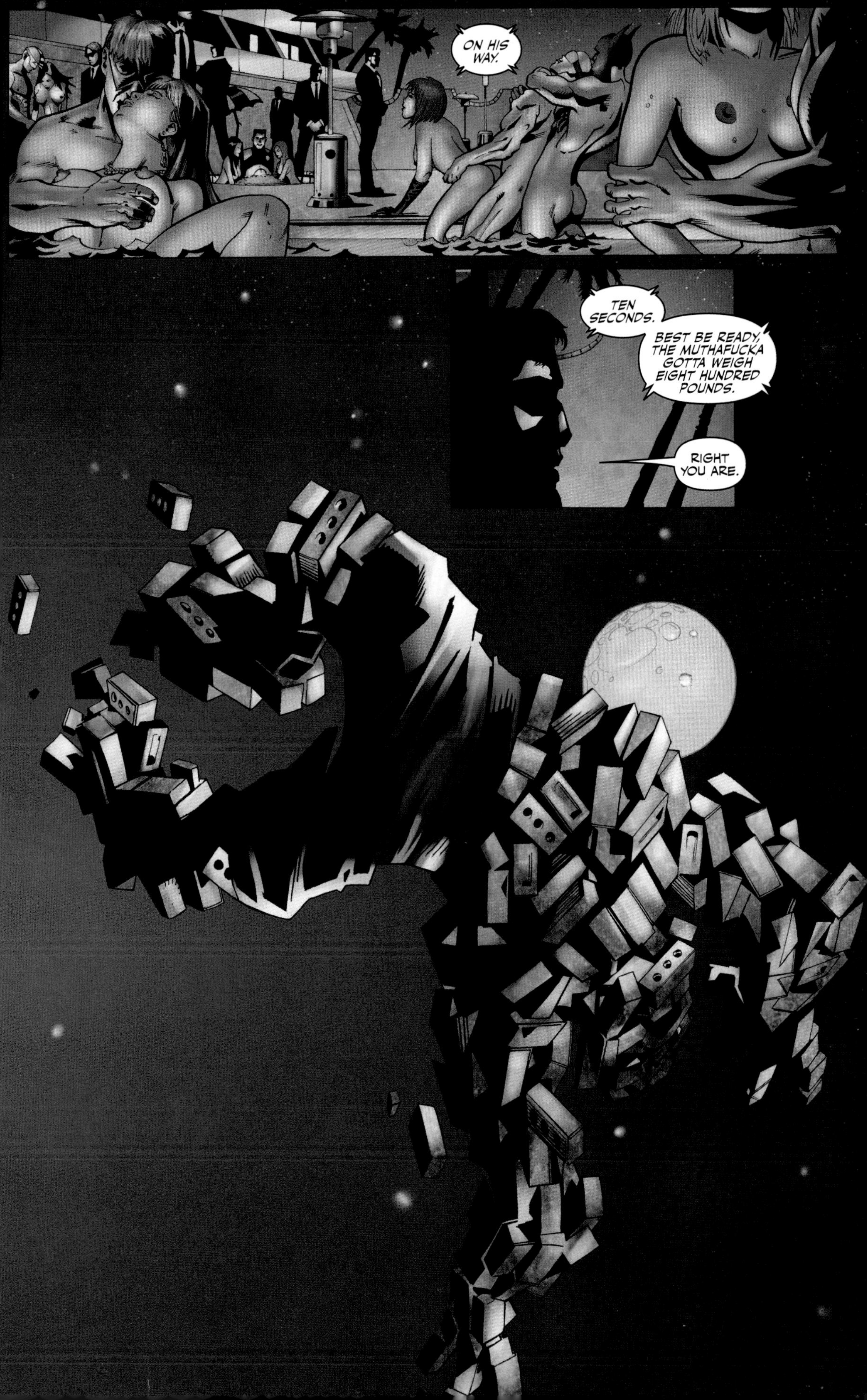
ON HIS WAY.
TEN SECONDS.
BEST BE READY, THE MUTHAFUCKA GOTTA WEIGH EIGHT HUNDRED POUNDS.
RIGHT YOU ARE.

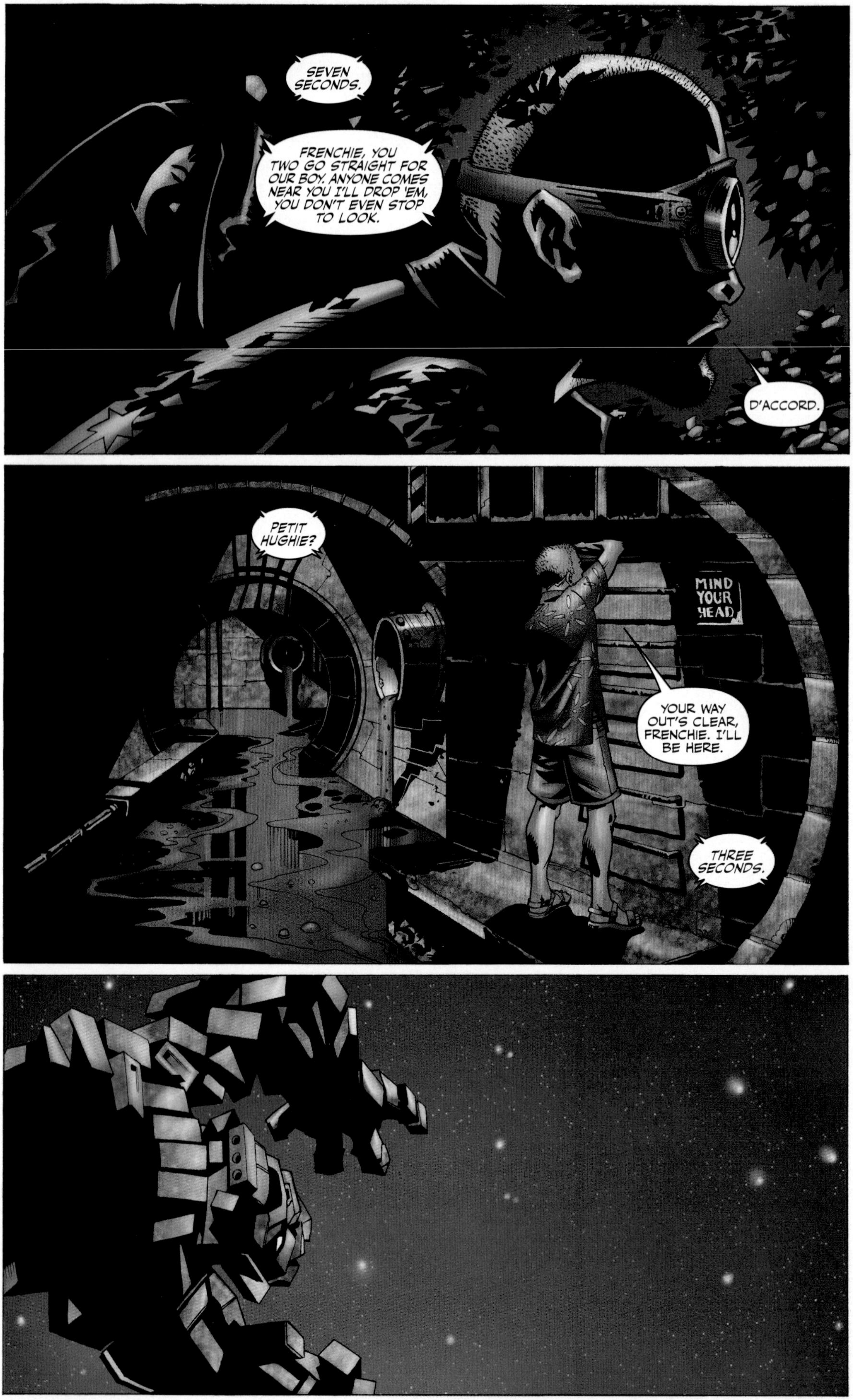
SEVEN SECONDS.
FRENCHIE, YOU TWO GO STRAIGHT FOR OUR BOY. ANYONE COMES NEAR YOU I'LL DROP 'EM, YOU DON'T EVEN STOP TO LOOK.
D'ACCORD.
PETIT HUGHIE?
MIND YOUR HEAD
YOUR WAY OUT'S CLEAR, FRENCHIE. I'LL BE HERE.
THREE SECONDS.

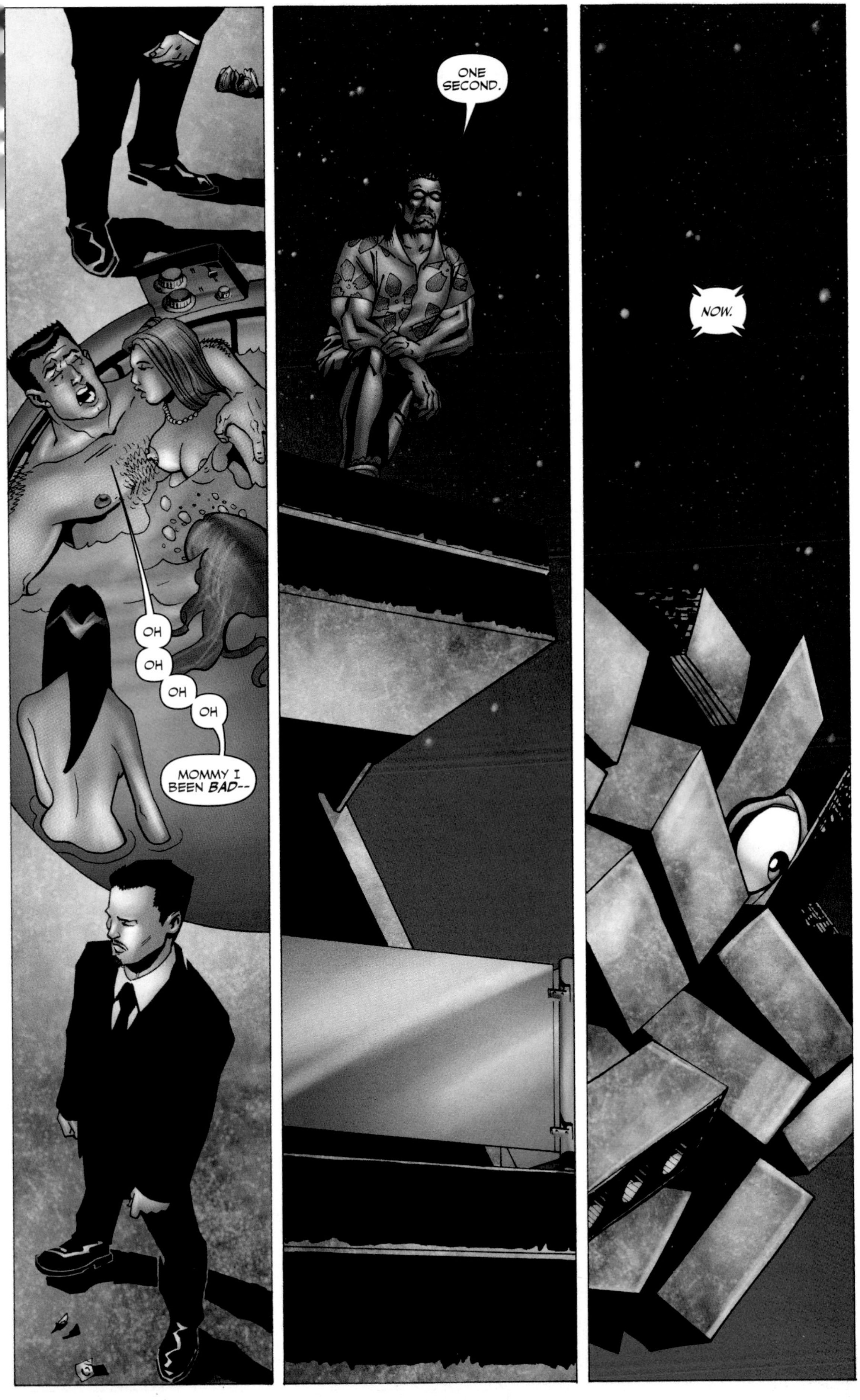
OH
OH
OH
OH
MOMMY I BEEN BAD--
ONE SECOND.
NOW.

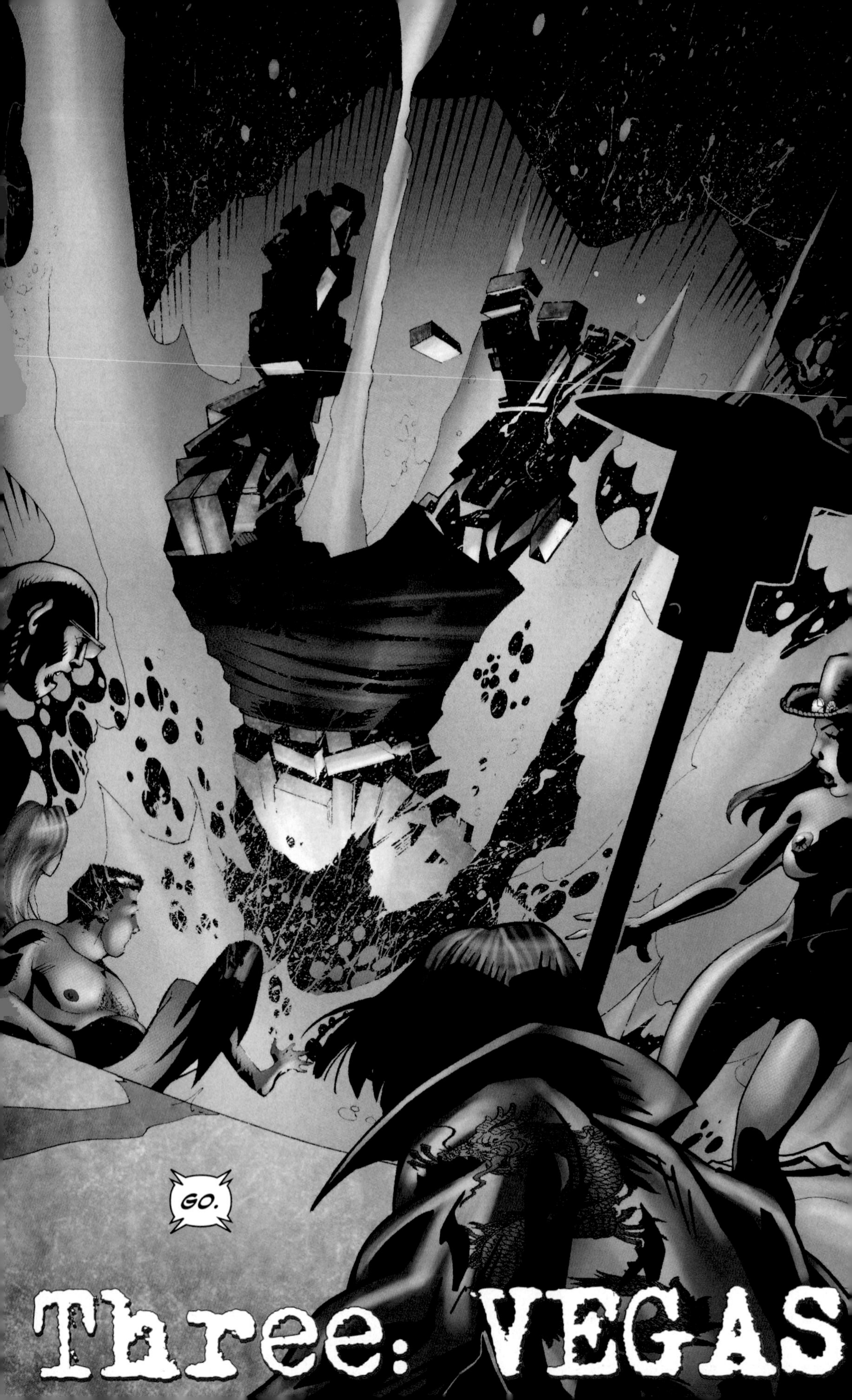
GO.
Three: VEGAS

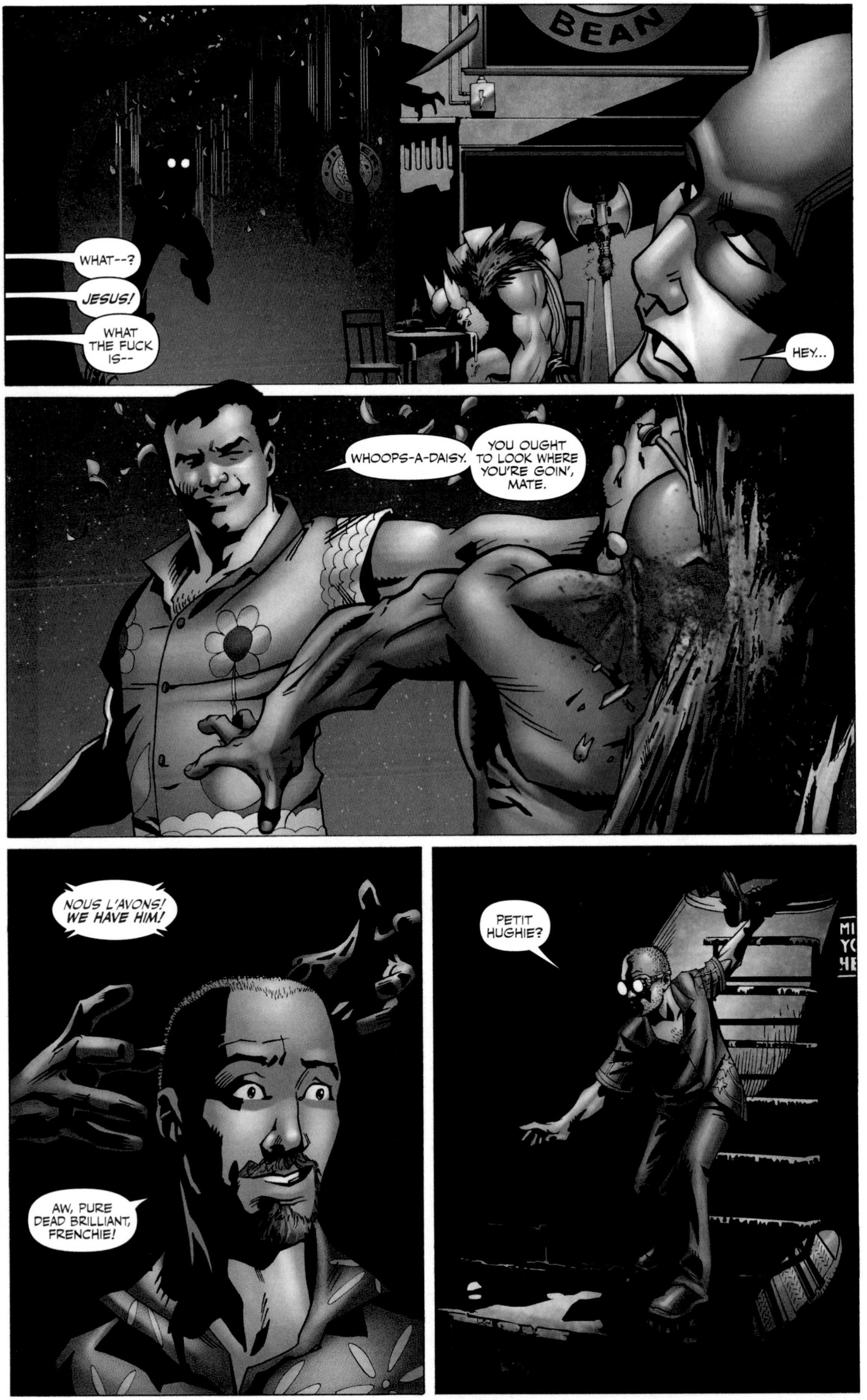
BEAN
WHAT--?
JESUS!
WHAT THE FUCK IS--
HEY...
WHOOPS-A-DAISY.
YOU OUGHT TO LOOK WHERE YOU'RE GOIN', MATE.
NOUS L'AVONS! WE HAVE HIM!
AW, PURE DEAD BRILLIANT, FRENCHIE!
PETIT HUGHIE?

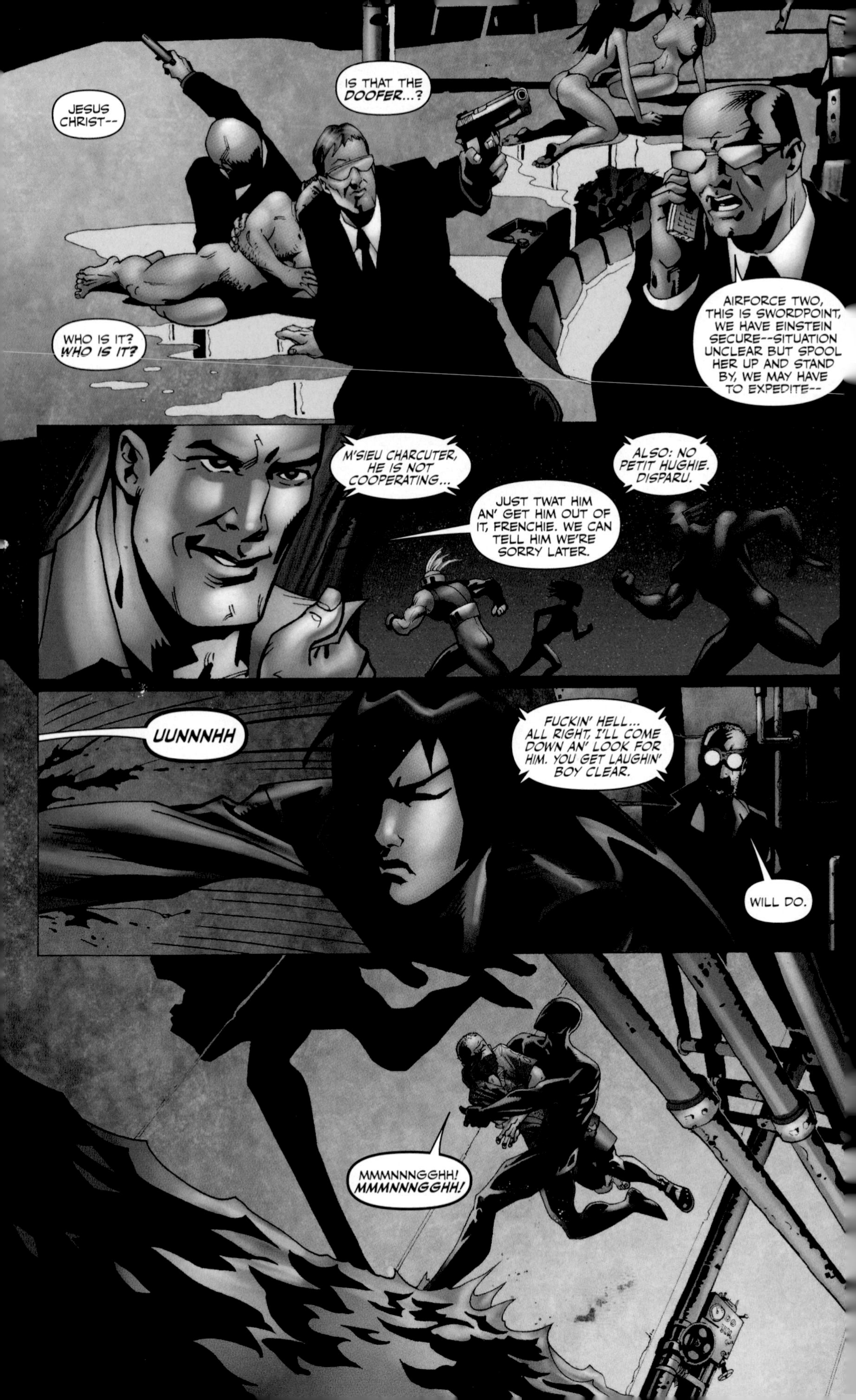

JESUS CHRIST--
IS THAT THE DOOFER...?
AIRFORCE TWO, THIS IS SWORDPOINT, WE HAVE EINSTEIN SECURE--SITUATION UNCLEAR BUT SPOOL HER UP AND STAND BY, WE MAY HAVE TO EXPEDITE--
WHO IS IT? WHO IS IT?
M'SIEU CHARCUTER, HE IS NOT COOPERATING...
JUST TWAT HIM AN' GET HIM OUT OF IT, FRENCHIE. WE CAN TELL HIM WE'RE SORRY LATER.
ALSO: NO PETIT HUGHIE. DISPARU.
UUNNNHH
FUCKIN' HELL... ALL RIGHT, I'LL COME DOWN AN' LOOK FOR HIM. YOU GET LAUGHIN' BOY CLEAR.
WILL DO.
MMMNNNGGHH! MMMNNNGGHH!

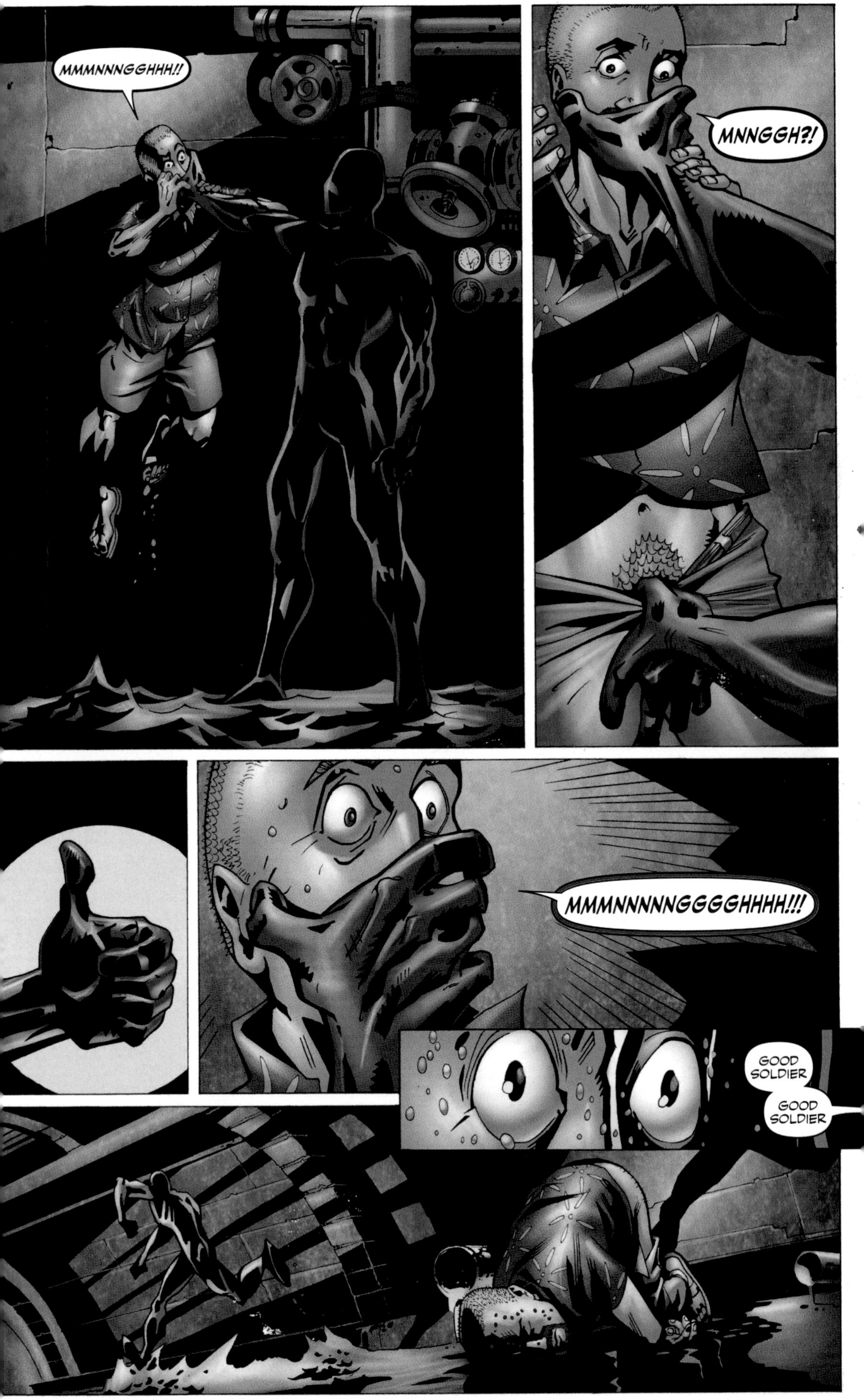
MMMNNNNGGHHH!!
MNNGGH?!
MMMNNNNNGGGGHHHH!!!
GOOD SOLDIER
GOOD SOLDIER

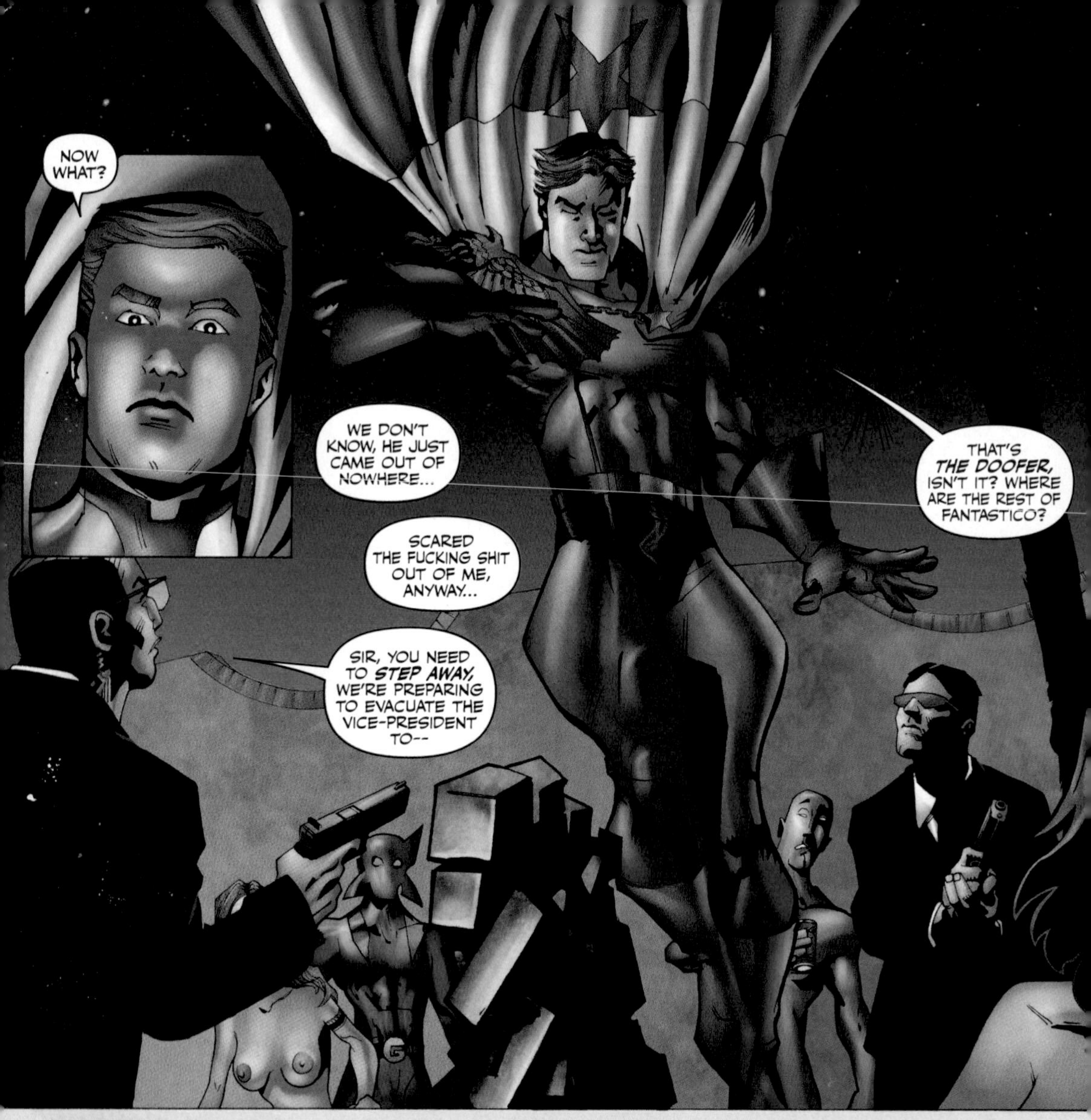
NOW WHAT?
WE DON'T KNOW, HE JUST CAME OUT OF NOWHERE...
SCARED THE FUCKING SHIT OUT OF ME, ANYWAY...
THAT'S THE DOOFER, ISN'T IT? WHERE ARE THE REST OF FANTASTICO?
SIR, YOU NEED TO STEP AWAY, WE'RE PREPARING TO EVACUATE THE VICE-PRESIDENT TO--

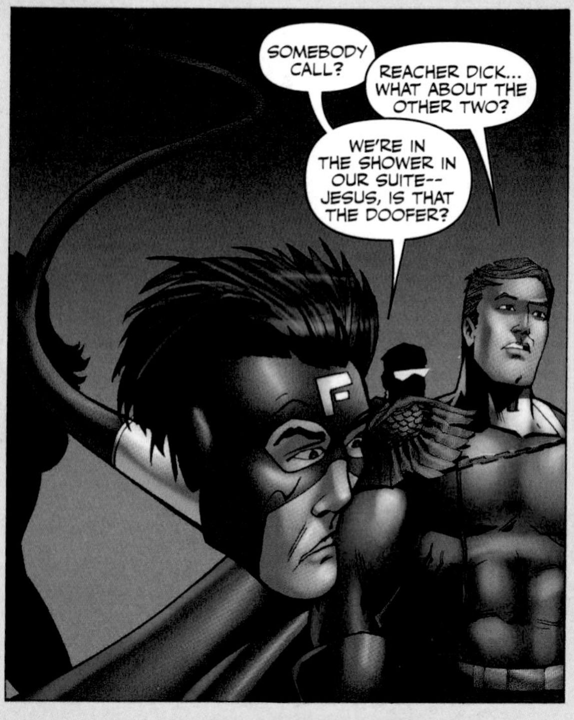
SOMEBODY CALL?
REACHER DICK... WHAT ABOUT THE OTHER TWO?
WE'RE IN THE SHOWER IN OUR SUITE-- JESUS, IS THAT THE DOOFER?

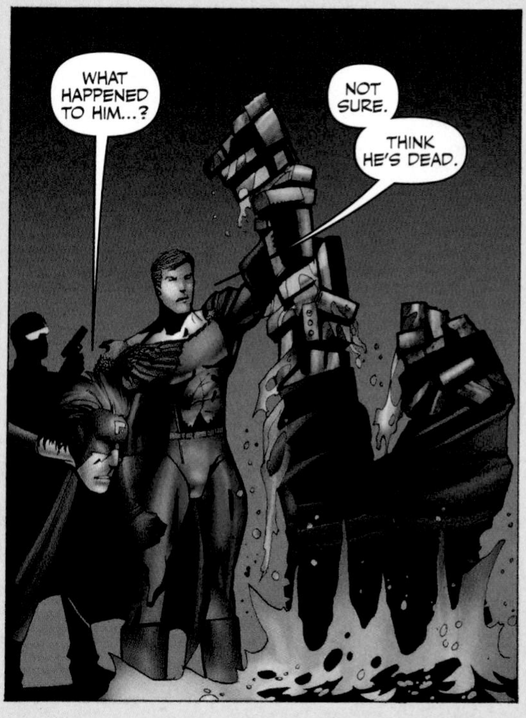
WHAT HAPPENED TO HIM...?
NOT SURE.
THINK HE'S DEAD.

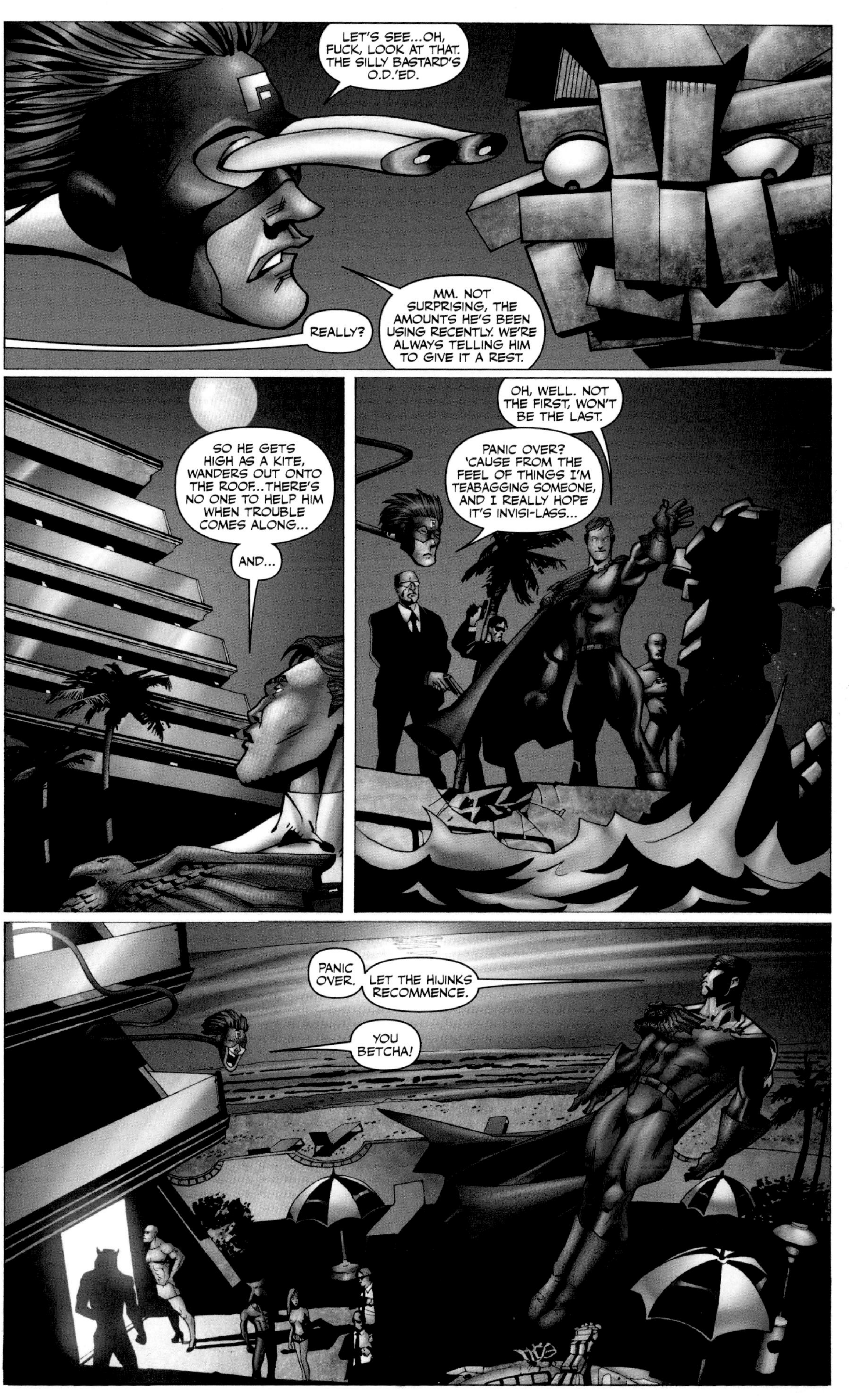
LET'S SEE...OH, FUCK, LOOK AT THAT. THE SILLY BASTARD'S O.D.'ED.
REALLY?
MM. NOT SURPRISING, THE AMOUNTS HE'S BEEN USING RECENTLY. WE'RE ALWAYS TELLING HIM TO GIVE IT A REST.
SO HE GETS HIGH AS A KITE, WANDERS OUT ONTO THE ROOF...THERE'S NO ONE TO HELP HIM WHEN TROUBLE COMES ALONG...
AND...
OH, WELL. NOT THE FIRST, WON'T BE THE LAST.
PANIC OVER? 'CAUSE FROM THE FEEL OF THINGS I'M TEABAGGING SOMEONE, AND I REALLY HOPE IT'S INVISI-LASS...
PANIC OVER.
LET THE HIJINKS RECOMMENCE.
YOU BETCHA!

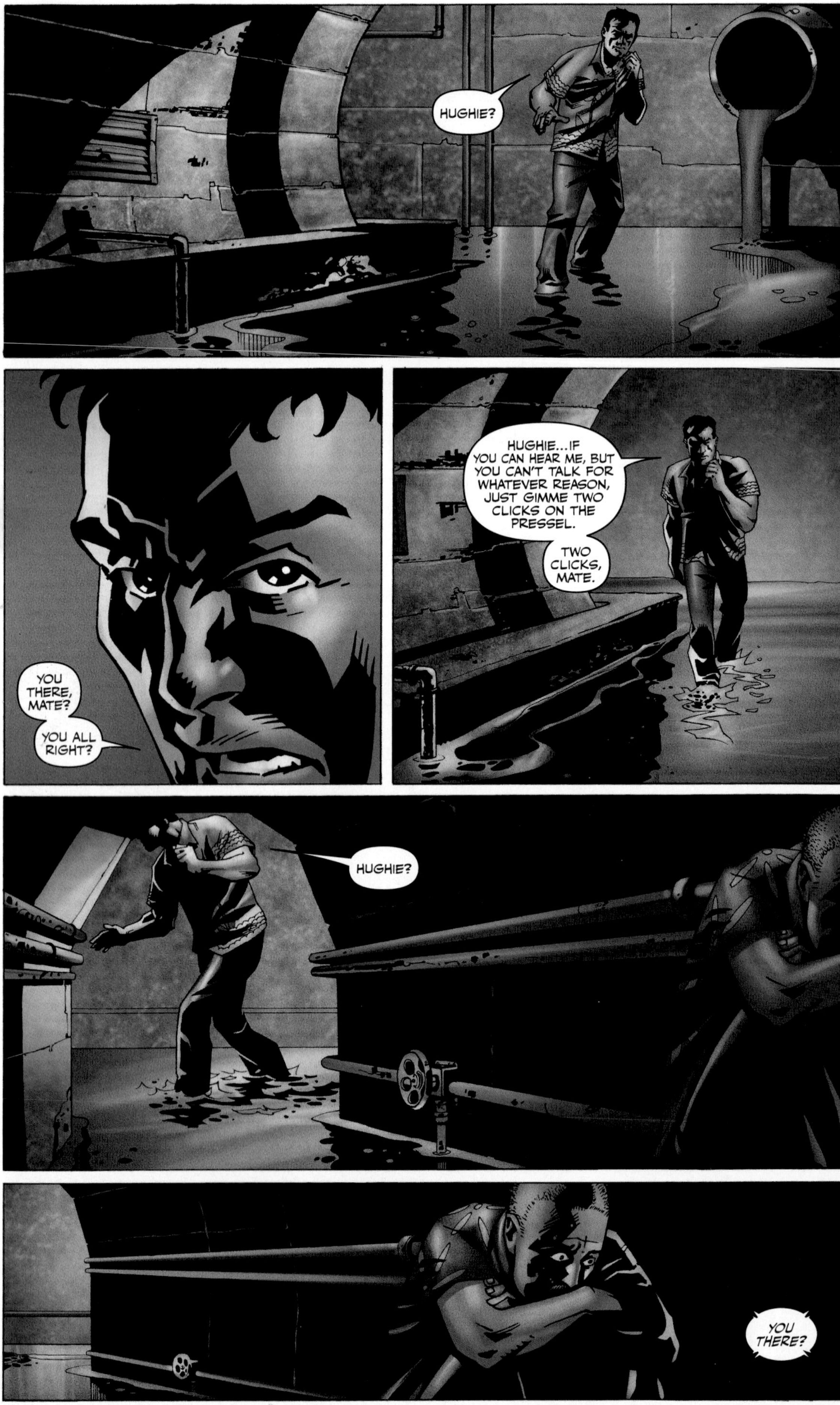
HUGHIE?
YOU THERE, MATE?
YOU ALL RIGHT?
HUGHIE...IF YOU CAN HEAR ME, BUT YOU CAN'T TALK FOR WHATEVER REASON, JUST GIMME TWO CLICKS ON THE PRESSEL.
TWO CLICKS, MATE.
HUGHIE?
YOU THERE?

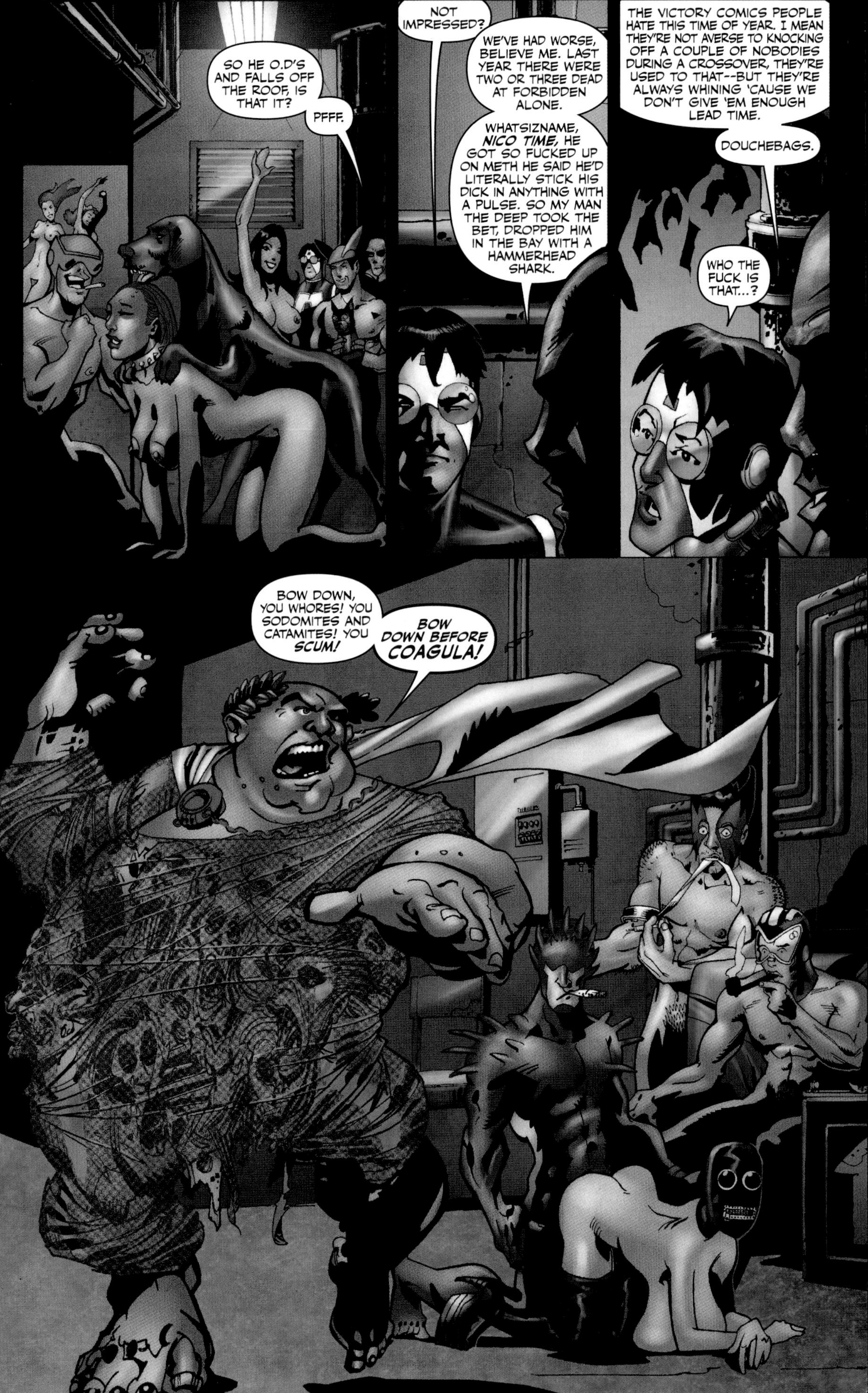

SO HE O.D'S AND FALLS OFF THE ROOF, IS THAT IT?
PFFF.
NOT IMPRESSED?
WE'VE HAD WORSE, BELIEVE ME. LAST YEAR THERE WERE TWO OR THREE DEAD AT FORBIDDEN ALONE.
WHATSIZNAME, NICO TIME, HE GOT SO FUCKED UP ON METH HE SAID HE'D LITERALLY STICK HIS DICK IN ANYTHING WITH A PULSE. SO MY MAN THE DEEP TOOK THE BET, DROPPED HIM IN THE BAY WITH A HAMMERHEAD SHARK.
THE VICTORY COMICS PEOPLE HATE THIS TIME OF YEAR. I MEAN THEY'RE NOT AVERSE TO KNOCKING OFF A COUPLE OF NOBODIES DURING A CROSSOVER, THEY'RE USED TO THAT--BUT THEY'RE ALWAYS WHINING 'CAUSE WE DON'T GIVE 'EM ENOUGH LEAD TIME.
DOUCHEBAGS.
WHO THE FUCK IS THAT...?
BOW DOWN, YOU WHORES! YOU SODOMITES AND CATAMITES! YOU SCUM!
BOW DOWN BEFORE COAGULA!

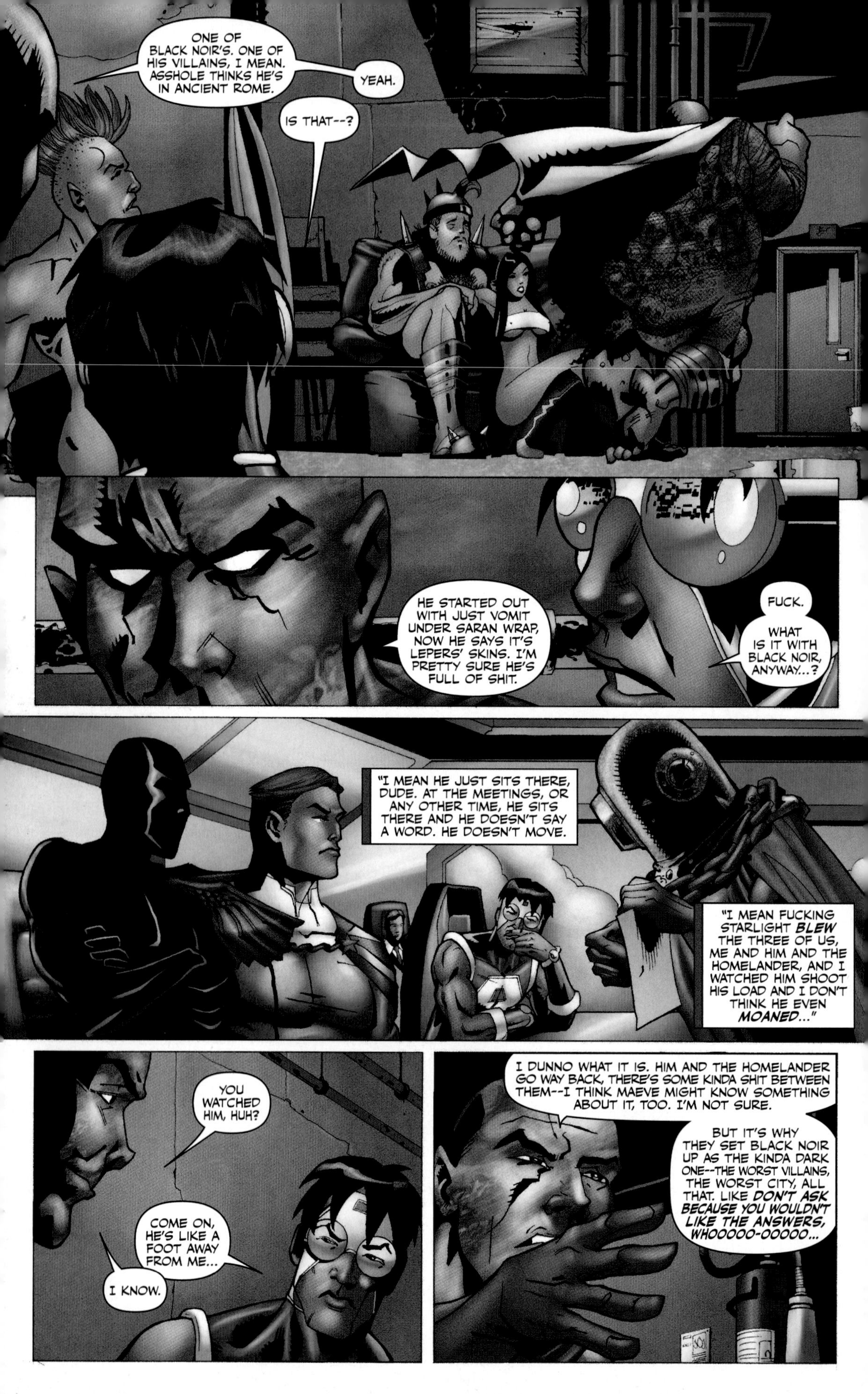
ONE OF BLACK NOIR'S. ONE OF HIS VILLAINS, I MEAN. ASSHOLE THINKS HE'S IN ANCIENT ROME.
YEAH.
IS THAT--?
HE STARTED OUT WITH JUST VOMIT UNDER SARAN WRAP, NOW HE SAYS IT'S LEPERS' SKINS. I'M PRETTY SURE HE'S FULL OF SHIT.
FUCK.
WHAT IS IT WITH BLACK NOIR, ANYWAY...?
"I MEAN HE JUST SITS THERE, DUDE. AT THE MEETINGS, OR ANY OTHER TIME, HE SITS THERE AND HE DOESN'T SAY A WORD. HE DOESN'T MOVE.
"I MEAN FUCKING STARLIGHT BLEW THE THREE OF US, ME AND HIM AND THE HOMELANDER, AND I WATCHED HIM SHOOT HIS LOAD AND I DON'T THINK HE EVEN MOANED..."
YOU WATCHED HIM, HUH?
COME ON, HE'S LIKE A FOOT AWAY FROM ME...
I KNOW.
I DUNNO WHAT IT IS. HIM AND THE HOMELANDER GO WAY BACK, THERE'S SOME KINDA SHIT BETWEEN THEM--I THINK MAEVE MIGHT KNOW SOMETHING ABOUT IT, TOO. I'M NOT SURE.
BUT IT'S WHY THEY SET BLACK NOIR UP AS THE KINDA DARK ONE--THE WORST VILLAINS, THE WORST CITY, ALL THAT. LIKE DON'T ASK BECAUSE YOU WOULDN'T LIKE THE ANSWERS, WHOOOOO-OOOOO...

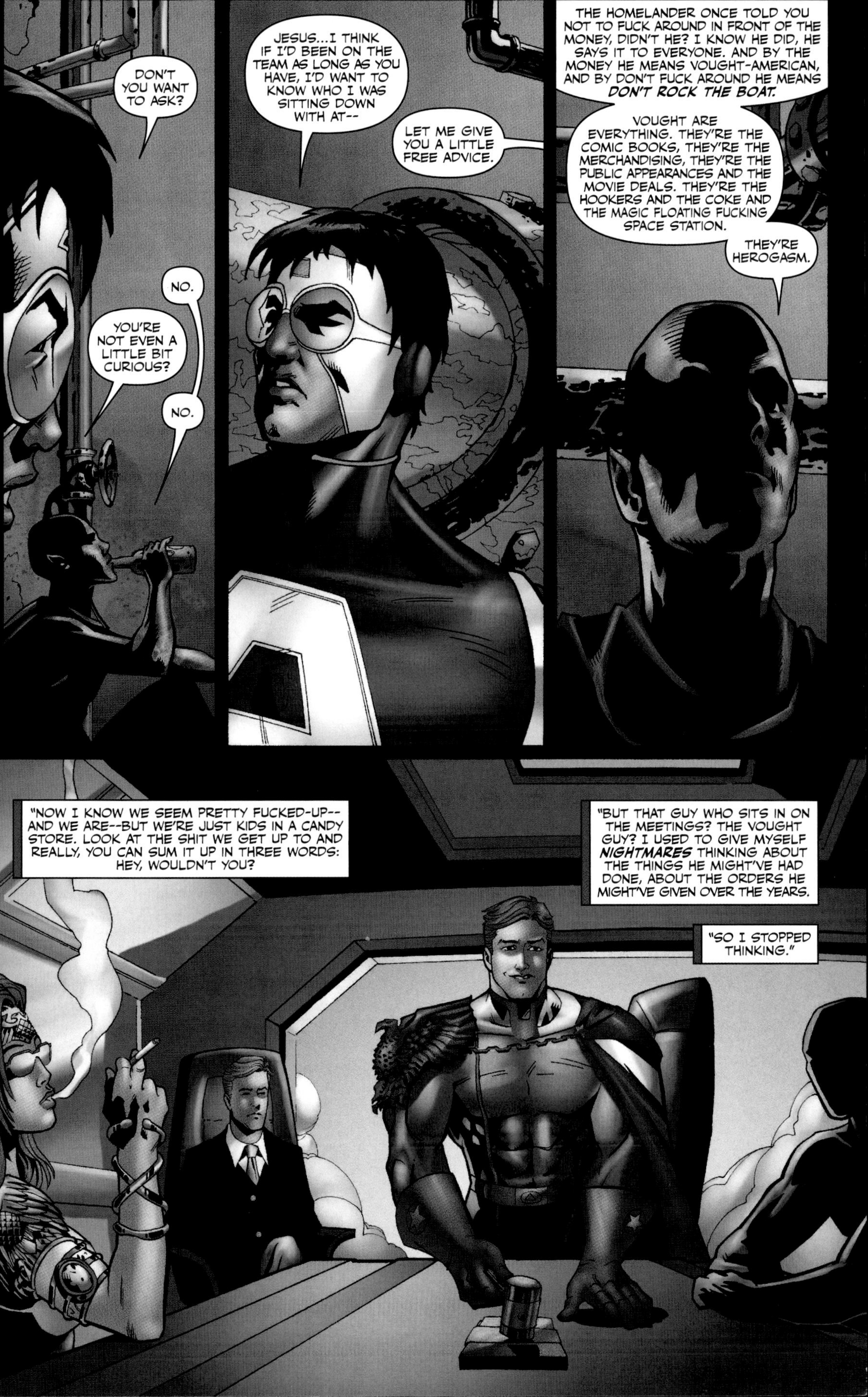
DON'T YOU WANT TO ASK?
JESUS...I THINK IF I'D BEEN ON THE TEAM AS LONG AS YOU HAVE, I'D WANT TO KNOW WHO I WAS SITTING DOWN WITH AT--
LET ME GIVE YOU A LITTLE FREE ADVICE.
THE HOMELANDER ONCE TOLD YOU NOT TO FUCK AROUND IN FRONT OF THE MONEY, DIDN'T HE? I KNOW HE DID, HE SAYS IT TO EVERYONE. AND BY THE MONEY HE MEANS VOUGHT-AMERICAN, AND BY DON'T FUCK AROUND HE MEANS *DON'T ROCK THE BOAT.*
VOUGHT ARE EVERYTHING. THEY'RE THE COMIC BOOKS, THEY'RE THE MERCHANDISING, THEY'RE THE PUBLIC APPEARANCES AND THE MOVIE DEALS. THEY'RE THE HOOKERS AND THE COKE AND THE MAGIC FLOATING FUCKING SPACE STATION.
THEY'RE HEROGASM.
NO.
YOU'RE NOT EVEN A LITTLE BIT CURIOUS?
NO.
"NOW I KNOW WE SEEM PRETTY FUCKED-UP-- AND WE ARE--BUT WE'RE JUST KIDS IN A CANDY STORE. LOOK AT THE SHIT WE GET UP TO AND REALLY, YOU CAN SUM IT UP IN THREE WORDS: HEY, WOULDN'T YOU?
"BUT THAT GUY WHO SITS IN ON THE MEETINGS? THE VOUGHT GUY? I USED TO GIVE MYSELF *NIGHTMARES* THINKING ABOUT THE THINGS HE MIGHT'VE HAD DONE, ABOUT THE ORDERS HE MIGHT'VE GIVEN OVER THE YEARS.
"SO I STOPPED THINKING."

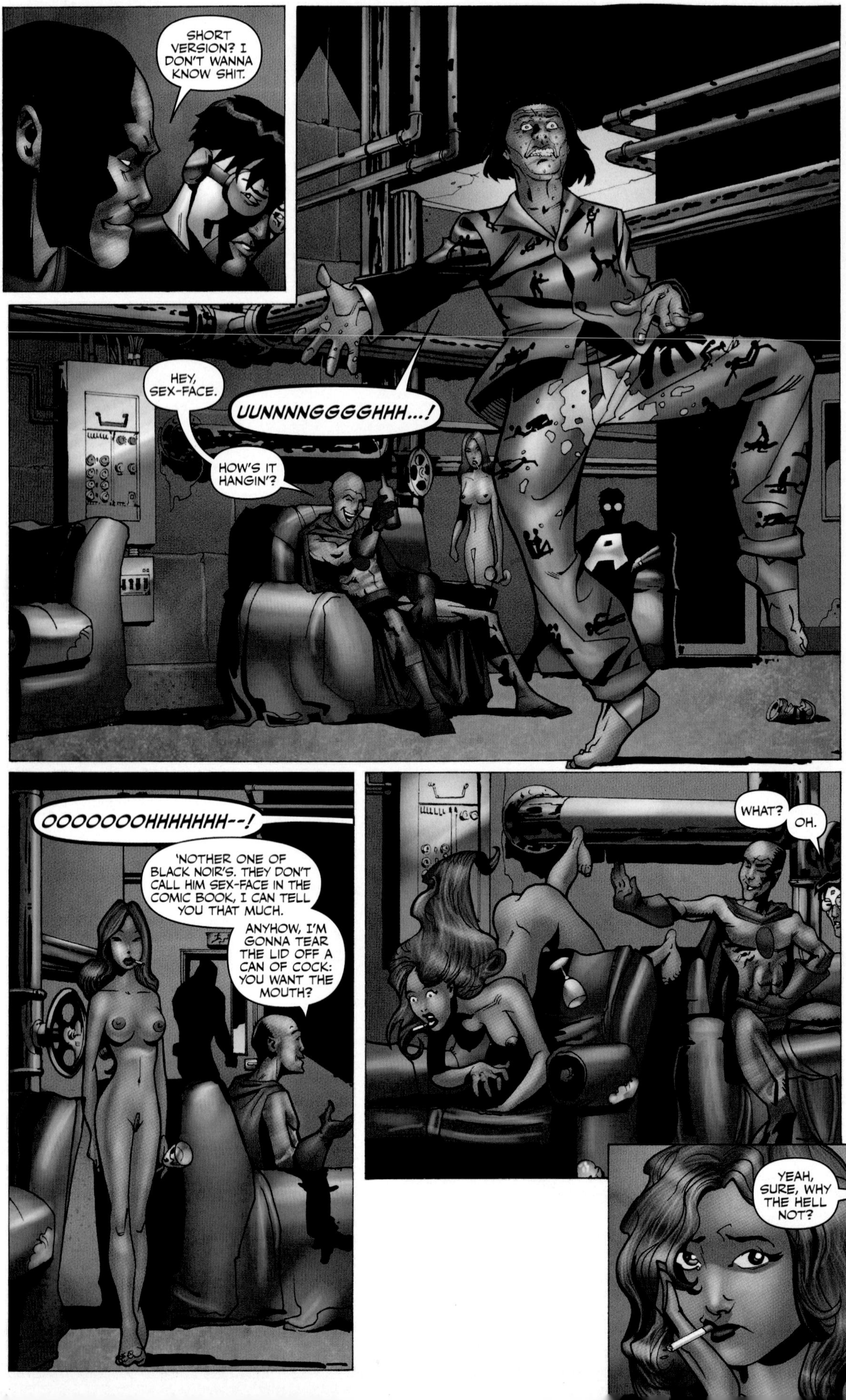
SHORT VERSION? I DON'T WANNA KNOW SHIT.
HEY, SEX-FACE.
UUNNNNGGGGHHH...!
HOW'S IT HANGIN'?
OOOOOOOHHHHHHH--!
'NOTHER ONE OF BLACK NOIR'S. THEY DON'T CALL HIM SEX-FACE IN THE COMIC BOOK, I CAN TELL YOU THAT MUCH.
ANYHOW, I'M GONNA TEAR THE LID OFF A CAN OF COCK: YOU WANT THE MOUTH?
WHAT?
OH.
YEAH, SURE, WHY THE HELL NOT?

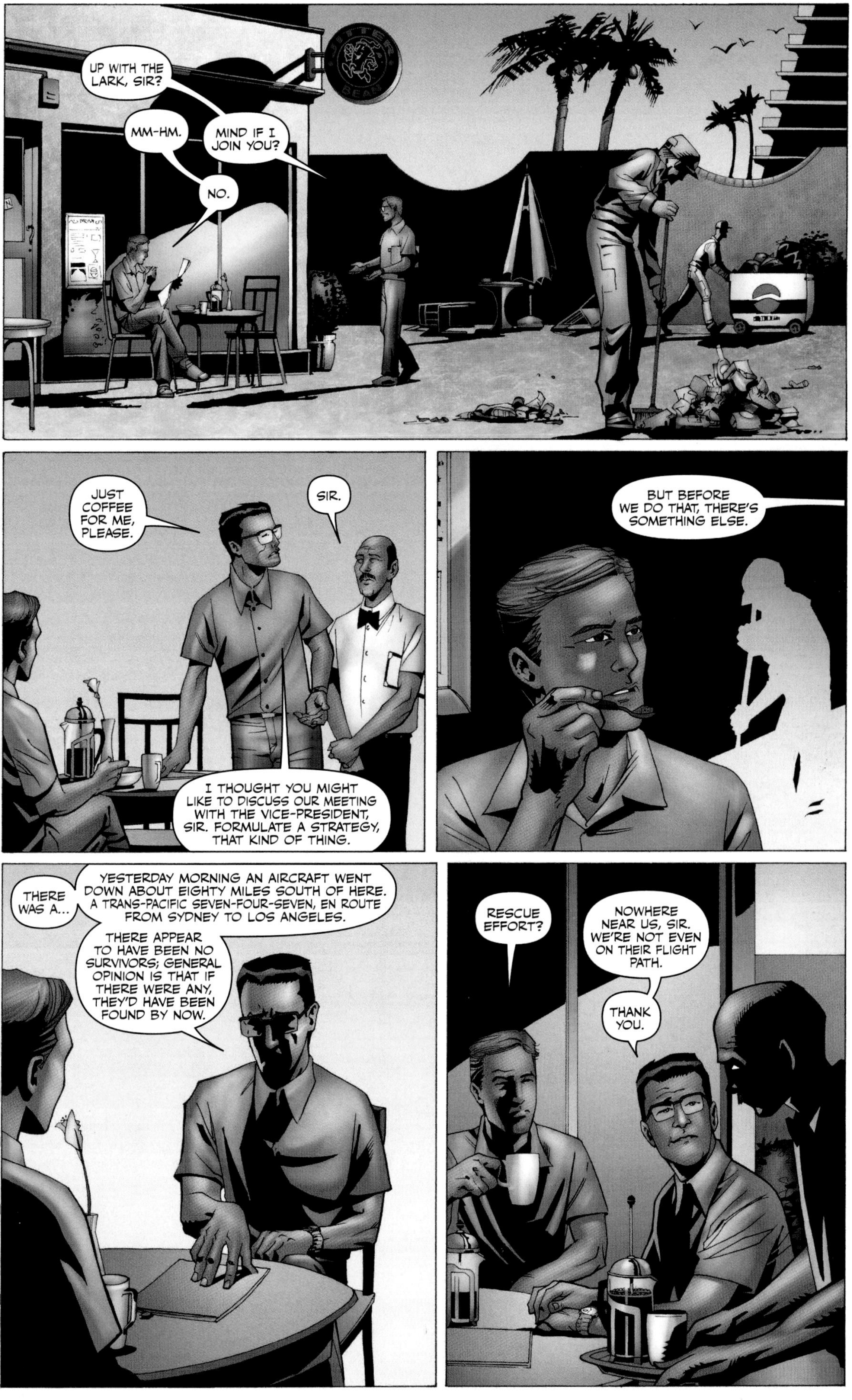
UP WITH THE LARK, SIR?
MM-HM.
MIND IF I JOIN YOU?
NO.
JUST COFFEE FOR ME, PLEASE.
SIR.
I THOUGHT YOU MIGHT LIKE TO DISCUSS OUR MEETING WITH THE VICE-PRESIDENT, SIR. FORMULATE A STRATEGY, THAT KIND OF THING.
BUT BEFORE WE DO THAT, THERE'S SOMETHING ELSE.
THERE WAS A...
YESTERDAY MORNING AN AIRCRAFT WENT DOWN ABOUT EIGHTY MILES SOUTH OF HERE. A TRANS-PACIFIC SEVEN-FOUR-SEVEN, EN ROUTE FROM SYDNEY TO LOS ANGELES.
THERE APPEAR TO HAVE BEEN NO SURVIVORS; GENERAL OPINION IS THAT IF THERE WERE ANY, THEY'D HAVE BEEN FOUND BY NOW.
RESCUE EFFORT?
NOWHERE NEAR US, SIR. WE'RE NOT EVEN ON THEIR FLIGHT PATH.
THANK YOU.

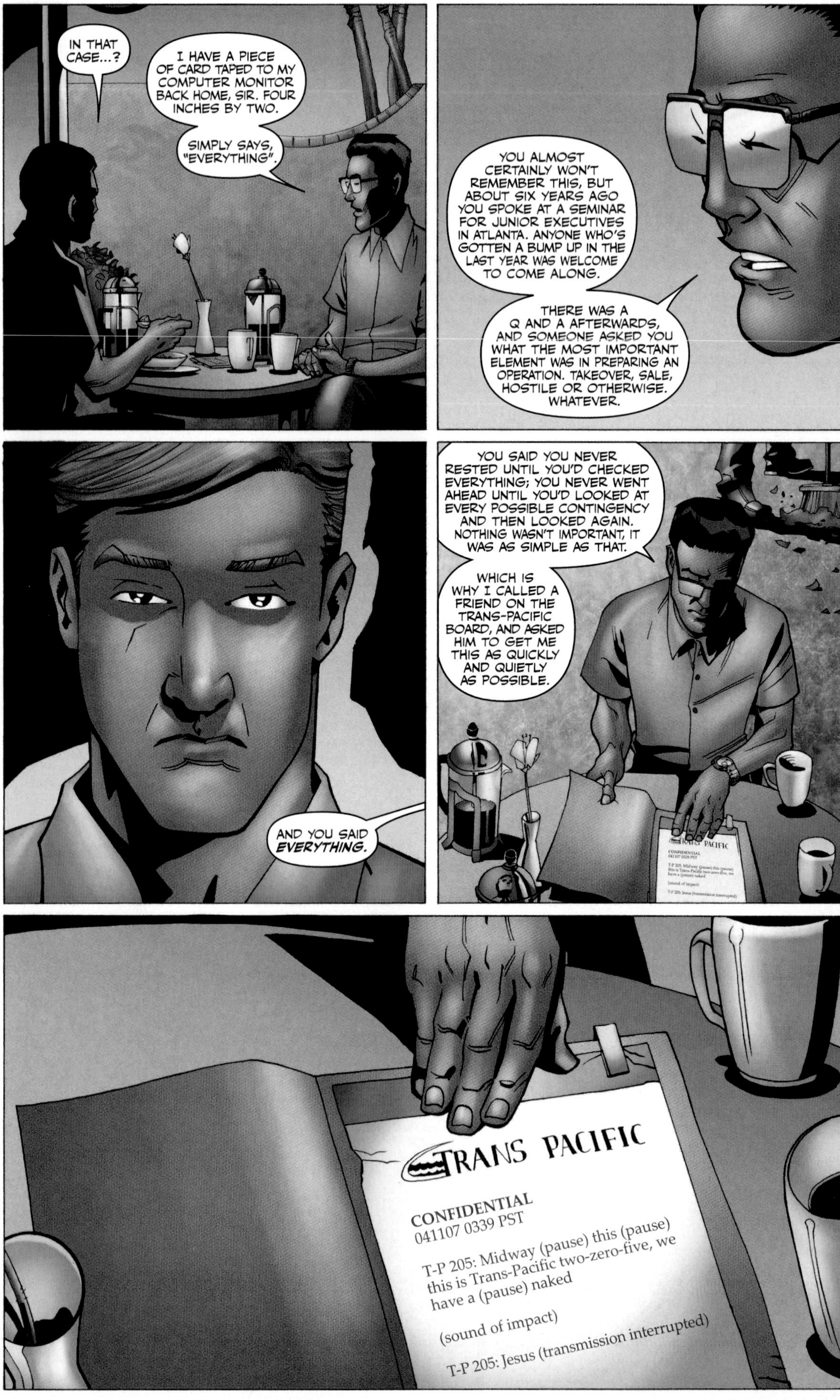
IN THAT CASE...?
I HAVE A PIECE OF CARD TAPED TO MY COMPUTER MONITOR BACK HOME, SIR. FOUR INCHES BY TWO.
SIMPLY SAYS, "EVERYTHING".
YOU ALMOST CERTAINLY WON'T REMEMBER THIS, BUT ABOUT SIX YEARS AGO YOU SPOKE AT A SEMINAR FOR JUNIOR EXECUTIVES IN ATLANTA. ANYONE WHO'S GOTTEN A BUMP UP IN THE LAST YEAR WAS WELCOME TO COME ALONG.
THERE WAS A Q AND A AFTERWARDS, AND SOMEONE ASKED YOU WHAT THE MOST IMPORTANT ELEMENT WAS IN PREPARING AN OPERATION. TAKEOVER, SALE, HOSTILE OR OTHERWISE. WHATEVER.
AND YOU SAID *EVERYTHING.*
YOU SAID YOU NEVER RESTED UNTIL YOU'D CHECKED EVERYTHING; YOU NEVER WENT AHEAD UNTIL YOU'D LOOKED AT EVERY POSSIBLE CONTINGENCY AND THEN LOOKED AGAIN. NOTHING WASN'T IMPORTANT, IT WAS AS SIMPLE AS THAT.
WHICH IS WHY I CALLED A FRIEND ON THE TRANS-PACIFIC BOARD, AND ASKED HIM TO GET ME THIS AS QUICKLY AND QUIETLY AS POSSIBLE.
TRANS PACIFIC
CONFIDENTIAL
041107 0339 PST
T-P 205: Midway (pause) this (pause) this is Trans-Pacific two-zero-five, we have a (pause) naked
(sound of impact)
T-P 205: Jesus (transmission interrupted)

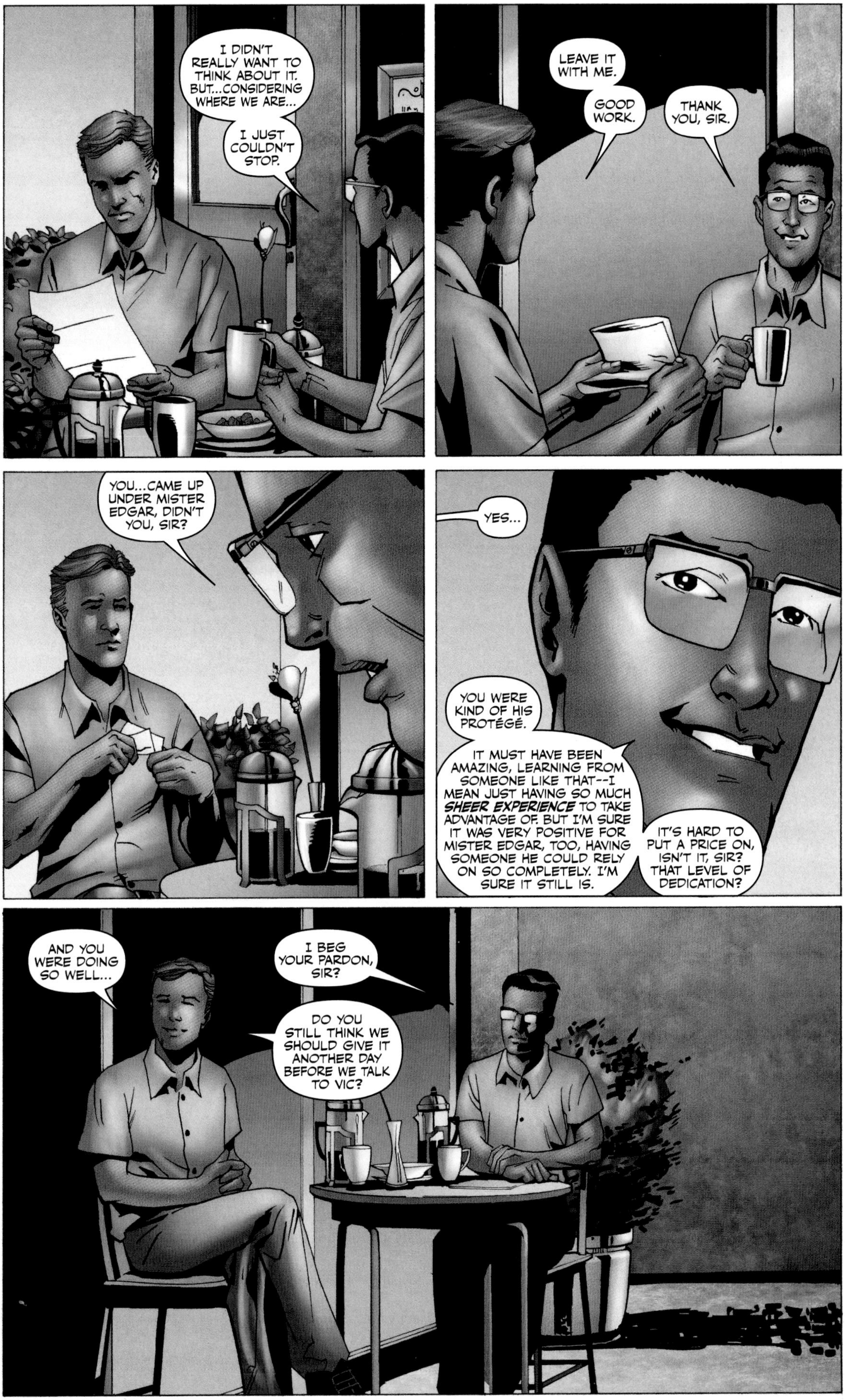
I DIDN'T REALLY WANT TO THINK ABOUT IT. BUT...CONSIDERING WHERE WE ARE...
I JUST COULDN'T STOP.
LEAVE IT WITH ME.
GOOD WORK.
THANK YOU, SIR.
YOU...CAME UP UNDER MISTER EDGAR, DIDN'T YOU, SIR?
YES...
YOU WERE KIND OF HIS PROTÉGÉ.
IT MUST HAVE BEEN AMAZING, LEARNING FROM SOMEONE LIKE THAT--I MEAN JUST HAVING SO MUCH SHEER EXPERIENCE TO TAKE ADVANTAGE OF. BUT I'M SURE IT WAS VERY POSITIVE FOR MISTER EDGAR, TOO, HAVING SOMEONE HE COULD RELY ON SO COMPLETELY. I'M SURE IT STILL IS.
IT'S HARD TO PUT A PRICE ON, ISN'T IT, SIR? THAT LEVEL OF DEDICATION?
AND YOU WERE DOING SO WELL...
I BEG YOUR PARDON, SIR?
DO YOU STILL THINK WE SHOULD GIVE IT ANOTHER DAY BEFORE WE TALK TO VIC?

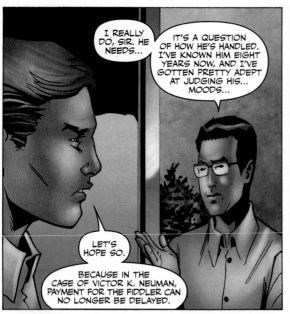

I REALLY DO, SIR. HE NEEDS...

IT'S A QUESTION OF HOW HE'S HANDLED. I'VE KNOWN HIM EIGHT YEARS NOW, AND I'VE GOTTEN PRETTY ADEPT AT JUDGING HIS... MOODS...

LET'S HOPE SO.

BECAUSE IN THE CASE OF VICTOR K. NEUMAN, PAYMENT FOR THE FIDDLER CAN NO LONGER BE DELAYED.

REALLY?

REALLY.

DAKOTA BOB HAS BEEN GOOD TO HIS PEOPLE. FROM HALLIBURTON ALL THE WAY DOWN TO BLACKWATER, HE'S COME THROUGH FOR THEM AGAIN AND AGAIN.

HE SOLD OFF MOST OF THE FEDERAL GOVERNMENT, AND ON TOP OF THAT HE DELIVERED PAKISTAN-- THE C.I.A. SAID HUNT BIN LADEN IN AFGHANISTAN, BUT BOB CAME THROUGH WITH A REAL WAR. CAN YOU IMAGINE WHAT THOSE CONTRACTORS MUST BE MAKING, DOING HALF THE WORK BADLY AND CHARGING TWICE THE GOING RATE?

THAT MAN IS A TEAM PLAYER.

WELL: NOW IT'S OUR TURN.

OUR AGENDA.

OUR MAN IN THE OVAL OFFICE.

WE'LL SPLIT THE DIFFERENCE. DINNER TONIGHT, NOT LUNCH TOMORROW.

UH...

THAT'S SETTLED, THEN.

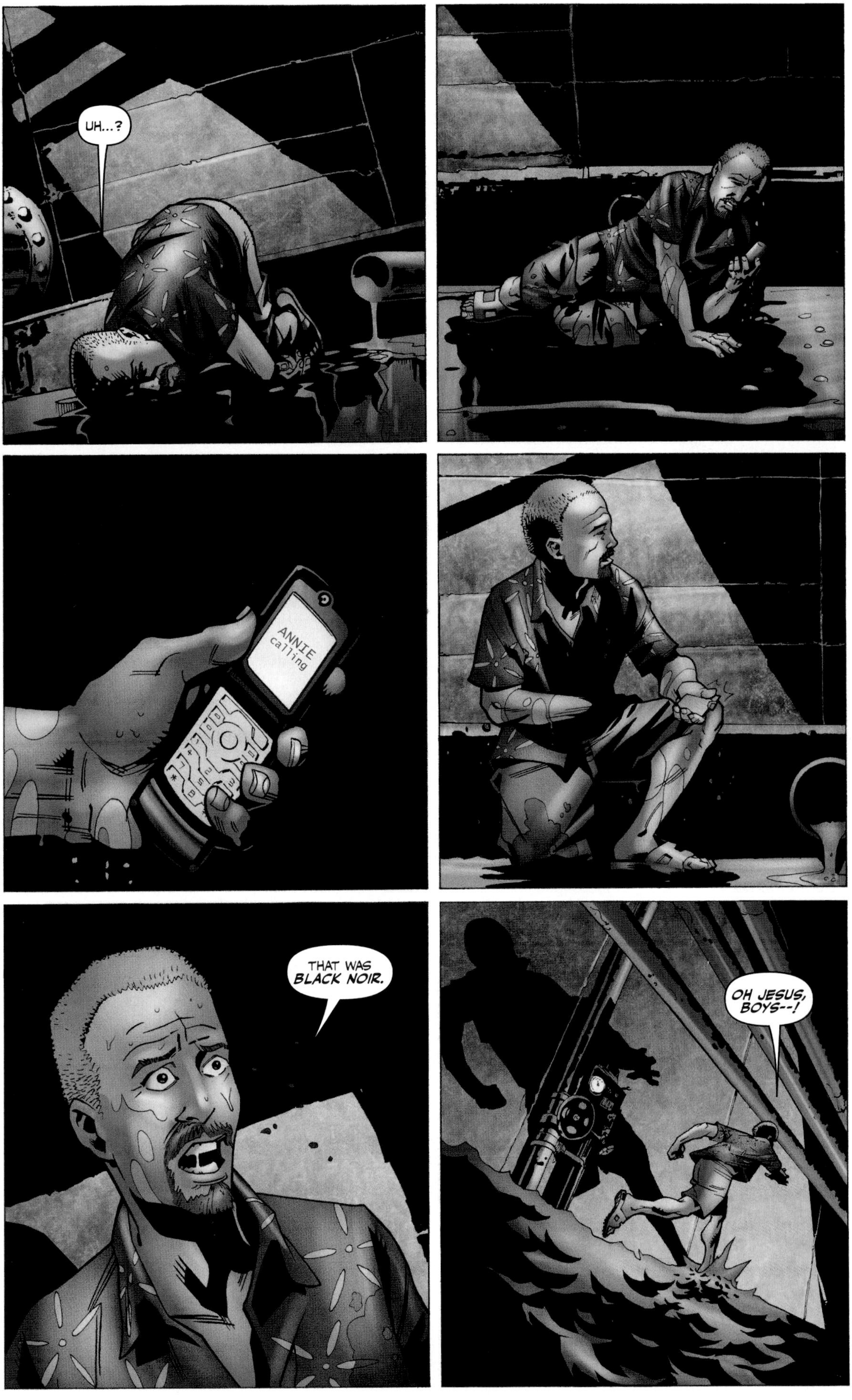
UH...?
ANNIE
calling
THAT WAS BLACK NOIR.
OH JESUS, BOYS--!

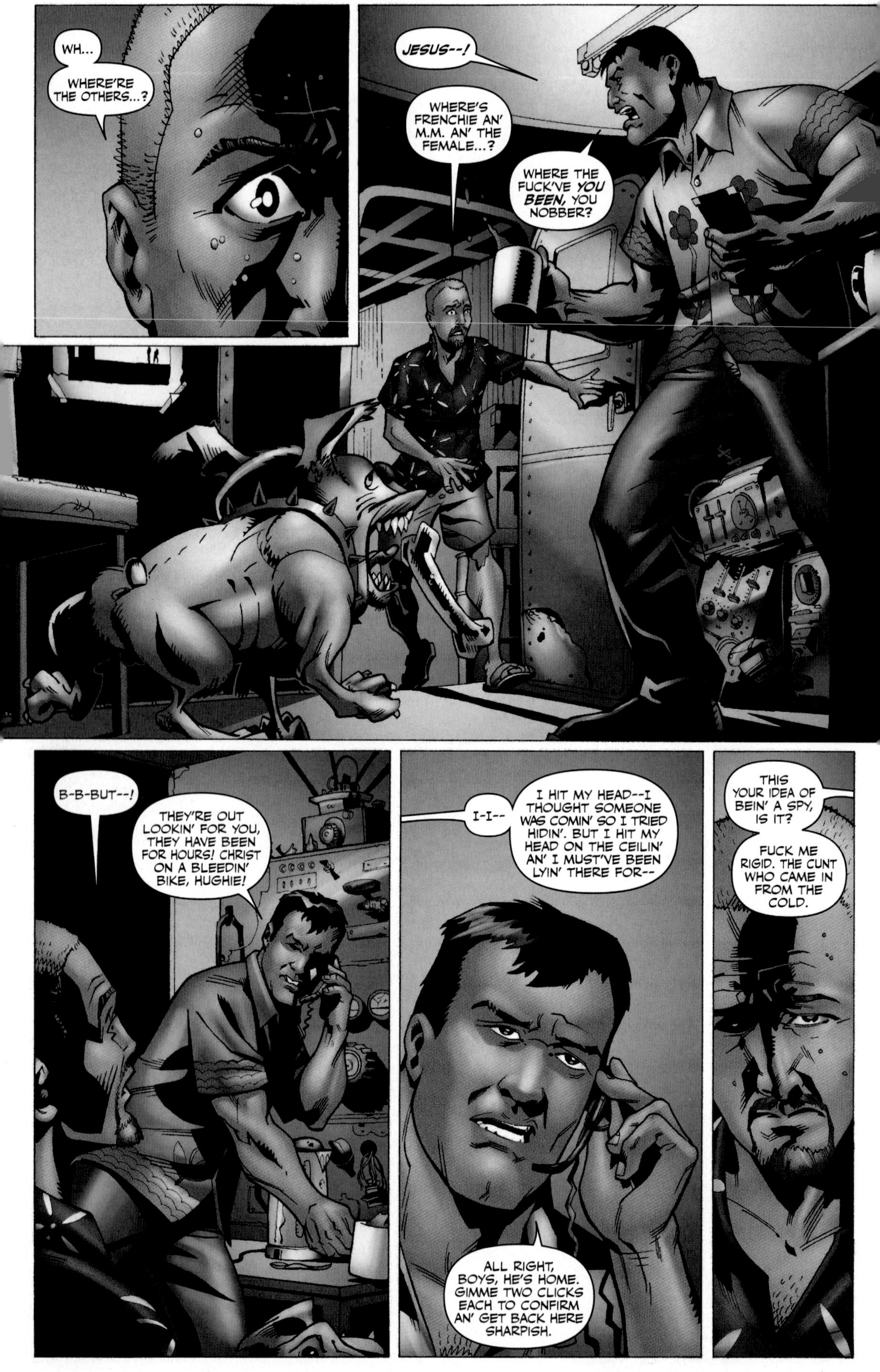
WH...
WHERE'RE THE OTHERS...?
JESUS--!
WHERE'S FRENCHIE AN' M.M. AN' THE FEMALE...?
WHERE THE FUCK'VE YOU BEEN, YOU NOBBER?
B-B-BUT--!
THEY'RE OUT LOOKIN' FOR YOU, THEY HAVE BEEN FOR HOURS! CHRIST ON A BLEEDIN' BIKE, HUGHIE!
I-I--
I HIT MY HEAD--I THOUGHT SOMEONE WAS COMIN' SO I TRIED HIDIN'. BUT I HIT MY HEAD ON THE CEILIN' AN' I MUST'VE BEEN LYIN' THERE FOR--
ALL RIGHT, BOYS, HE'S HOME. GIMME TWO CLICKS EACH TO CONFIRM AN' GET BACK HERE SHARPISH.
THIS YOUR IDEA OF BEIN' A SPY, IS IT?
FUCK ME RIGID. THE CUNT WHO CAME IN FROM THE COLD.

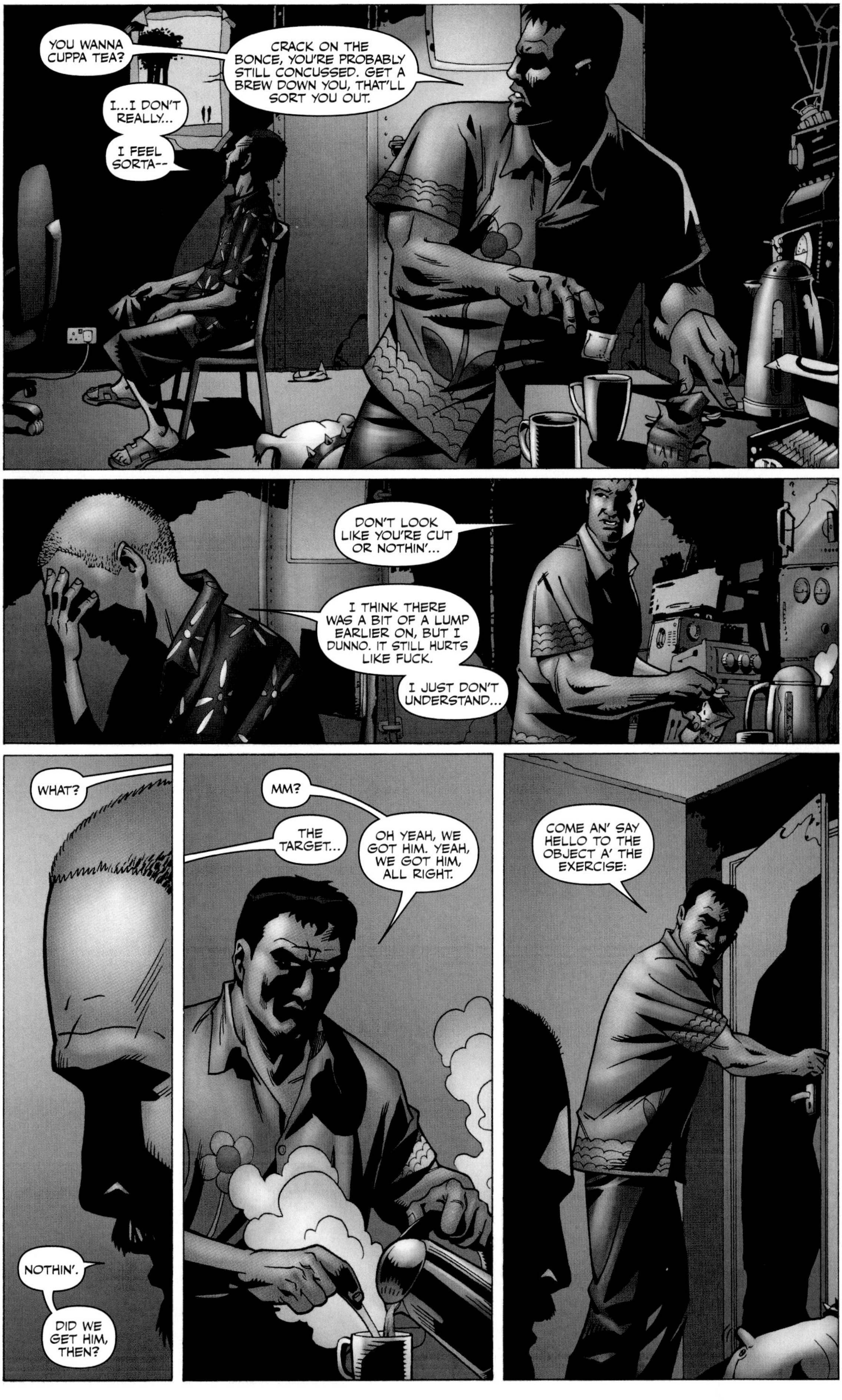

YOU WANNA CUPPA TEA?
CRACK ON THE BONCE, YOU'RE PROBABLY STILL CONCUSSED. GET A BREW DOWN YOU, THAT'LL SORT YOU OUT.
I...I DON'T REALLY...
I FEEL SORTA--
DON'T LOOK LIKE YOU'RE CUT OR NOTHIN'...
I THINK THERE WAS A BIT OF A LUMP EARLIER ON, BUT I DUNNO. IT STILL HURTS LIKE FUCK.
I JUST DON'T UNDERSTAND...
WHAT?
NOTHIN'.
DID WE GET HIM, THEN?
MM?
THE TARGET...
OH YEAH, WE GOT HIM. YEAH, WE GOT HIM, ALL RIGHT.
COME AN' SAY HELLO TO THE OBJECT A' THE EXERCISE:

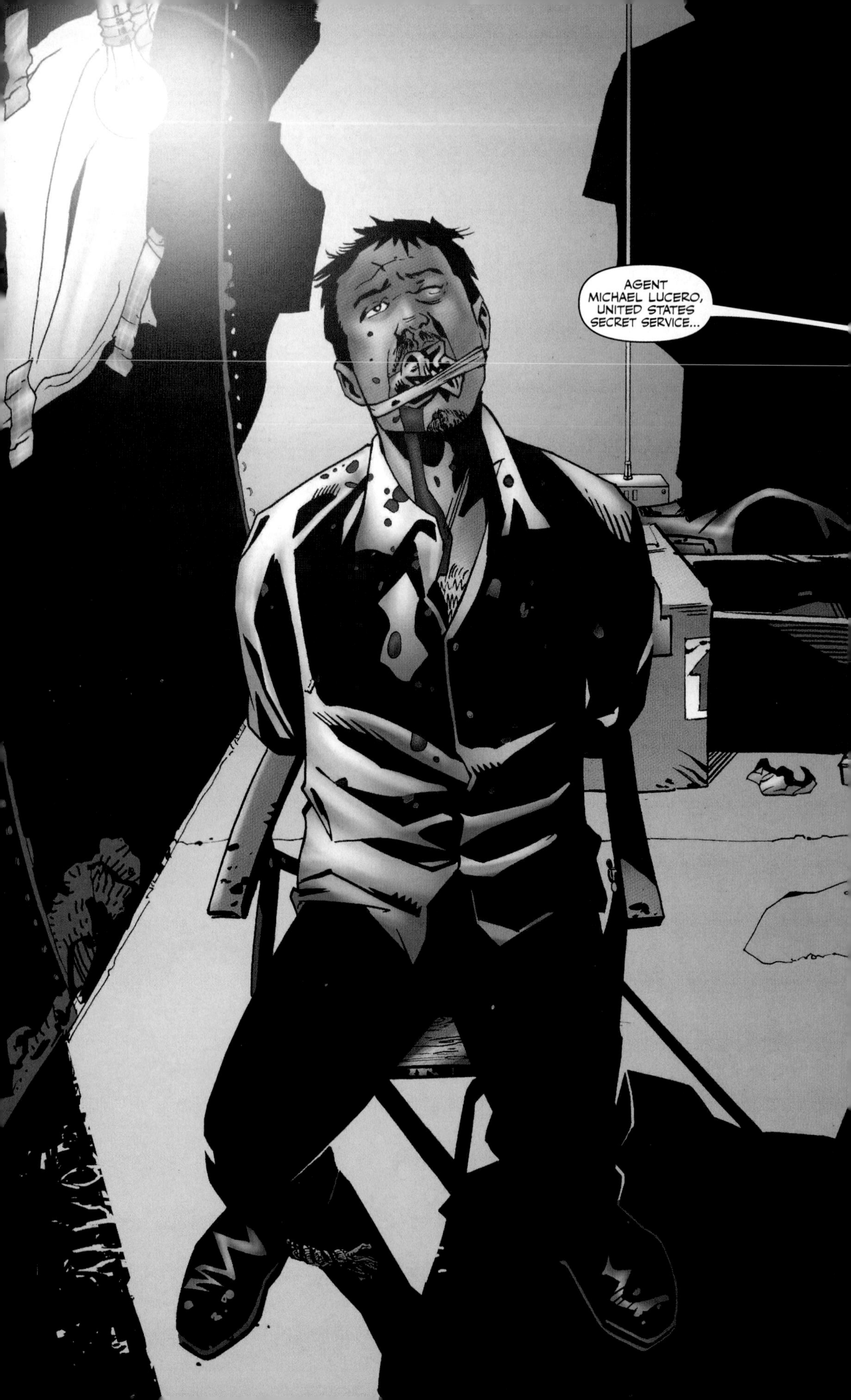
AGENT MICHAEL LUCERO, UNITED STATES SECRET SERVICE...

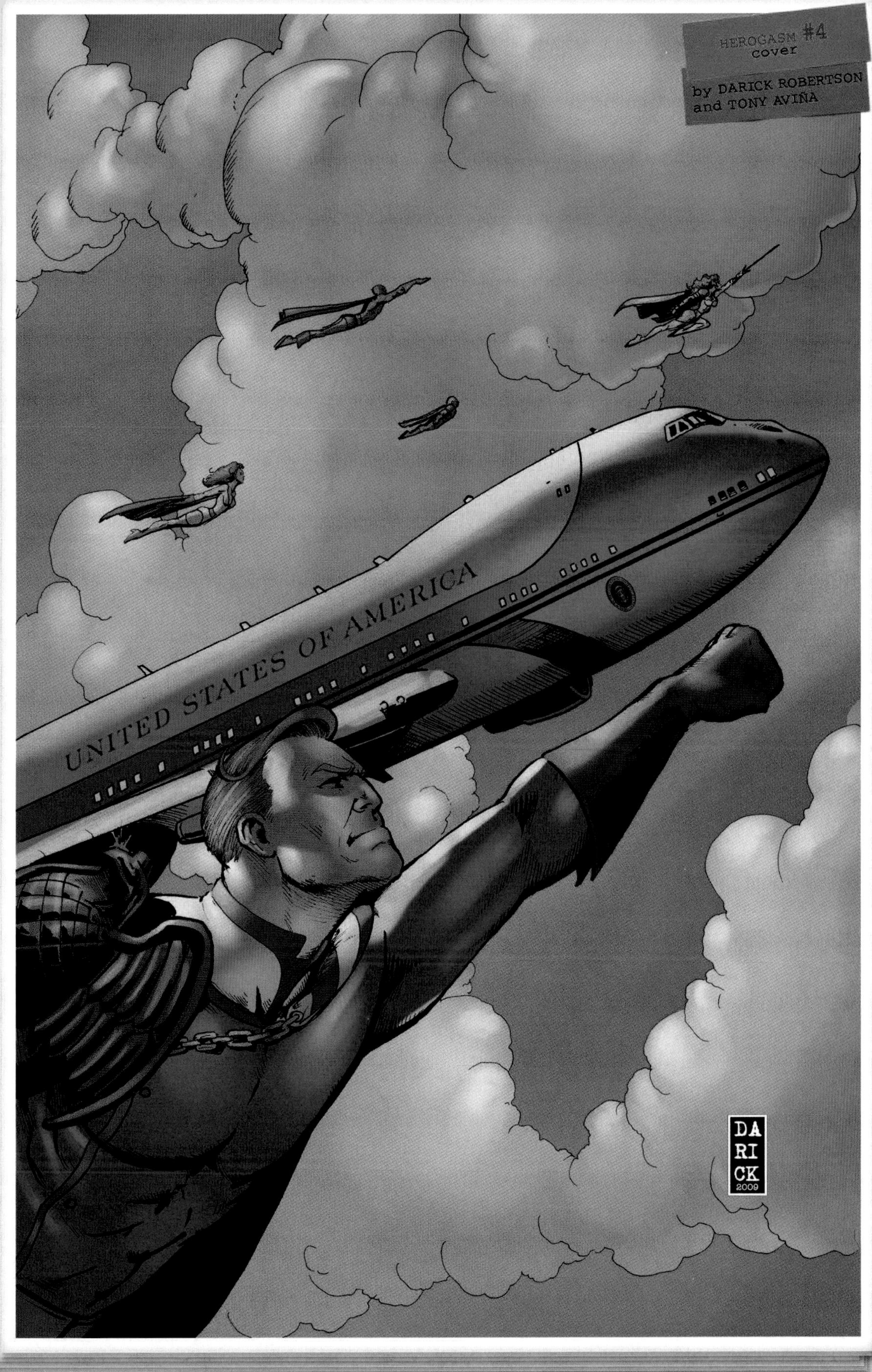
HEROGASM #4
cover
by DARICK ROBERTSON
and TONY AVIÑA
UNITED STATES OF AMERICA
DA
RI
CK
2009

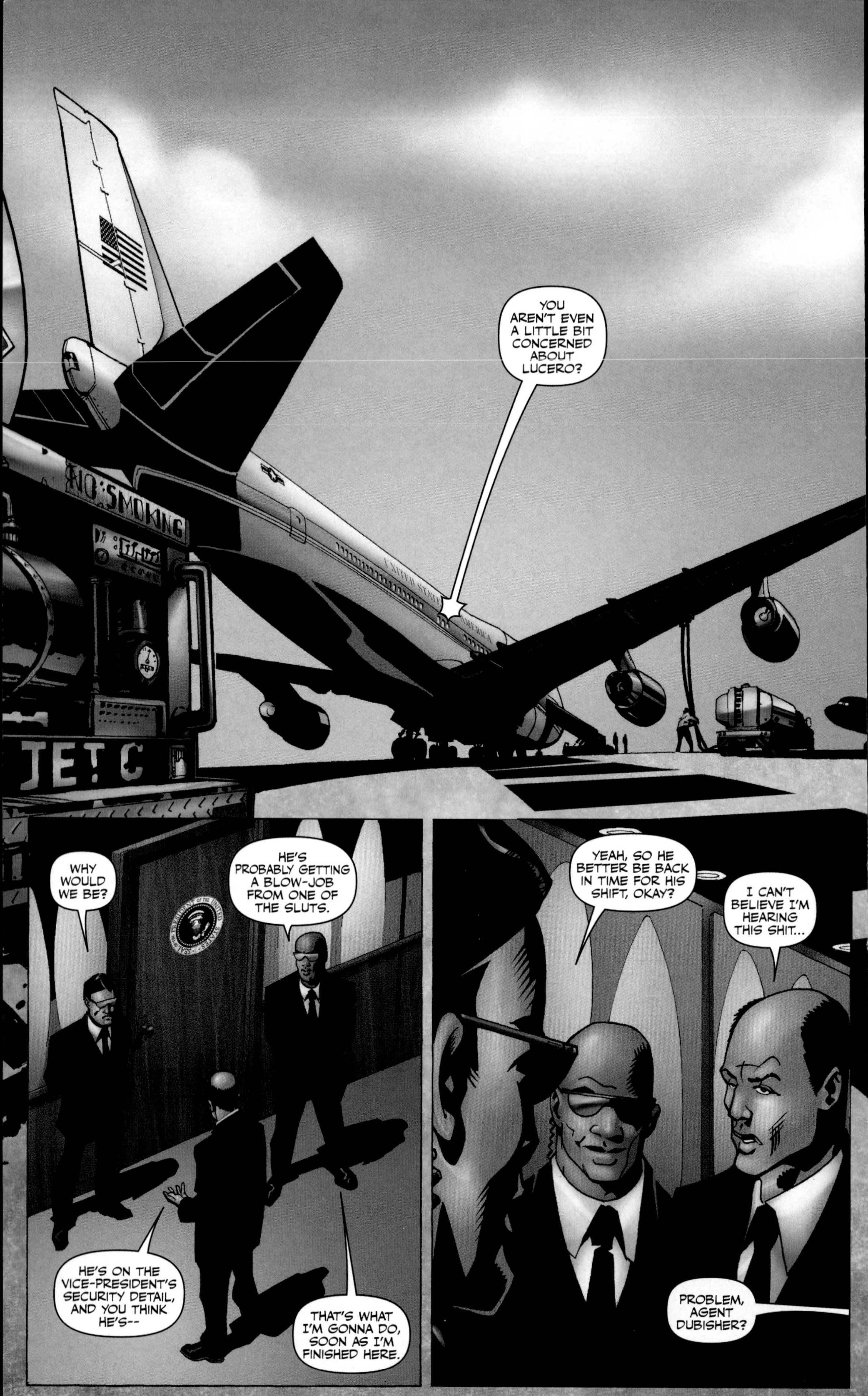
NO SMOKING
JET C
YOU AREN'T EVEN A LITTLE BIT CONCERNED ABOUT LUCERO?
WHY WOULD WE BE?
HE'S PROBABLY GETTING A BLOW-JOB FROM ONE OF THE SLUTS.
HE'S ON THE VICE-PRESIDENT'S SECURITY DETAIL, AND YOU THINK HE'S--
THAT'S WHAT I'M GONNA DO, SOON AS I'M FINISHED HERE.
YEAH, SO HE BETTER BE BACK IN TIME FOR HIS SHIFT, OKAY?
I CAN'T BELIEVE I'M HEARING THIS SHIT...
PROBLEM, AGENT DUBISHER?

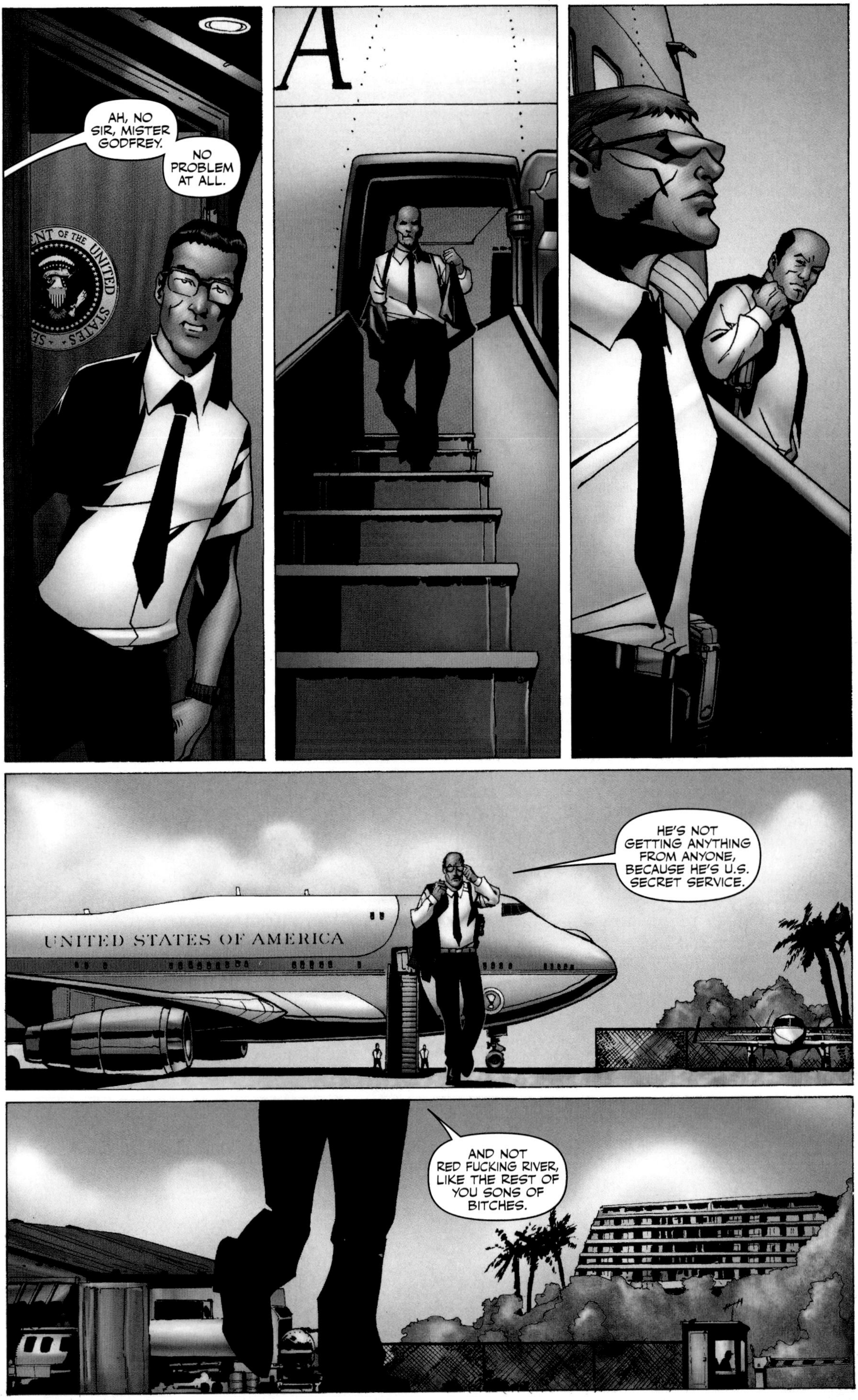
AH, NO SIR, MISTER GODFREY.
NO PROBLEM AT ALL.
UNITED STATES OF AMERICA
HE'S NOT GETTING ANYTHING FROM ANYONE, BECAUSE HE'S U.S. SECRET SERVICE.
AND NOT RED FUCKING RIVER, LIKE THE REST OF YOU SONS OF BITCHES.

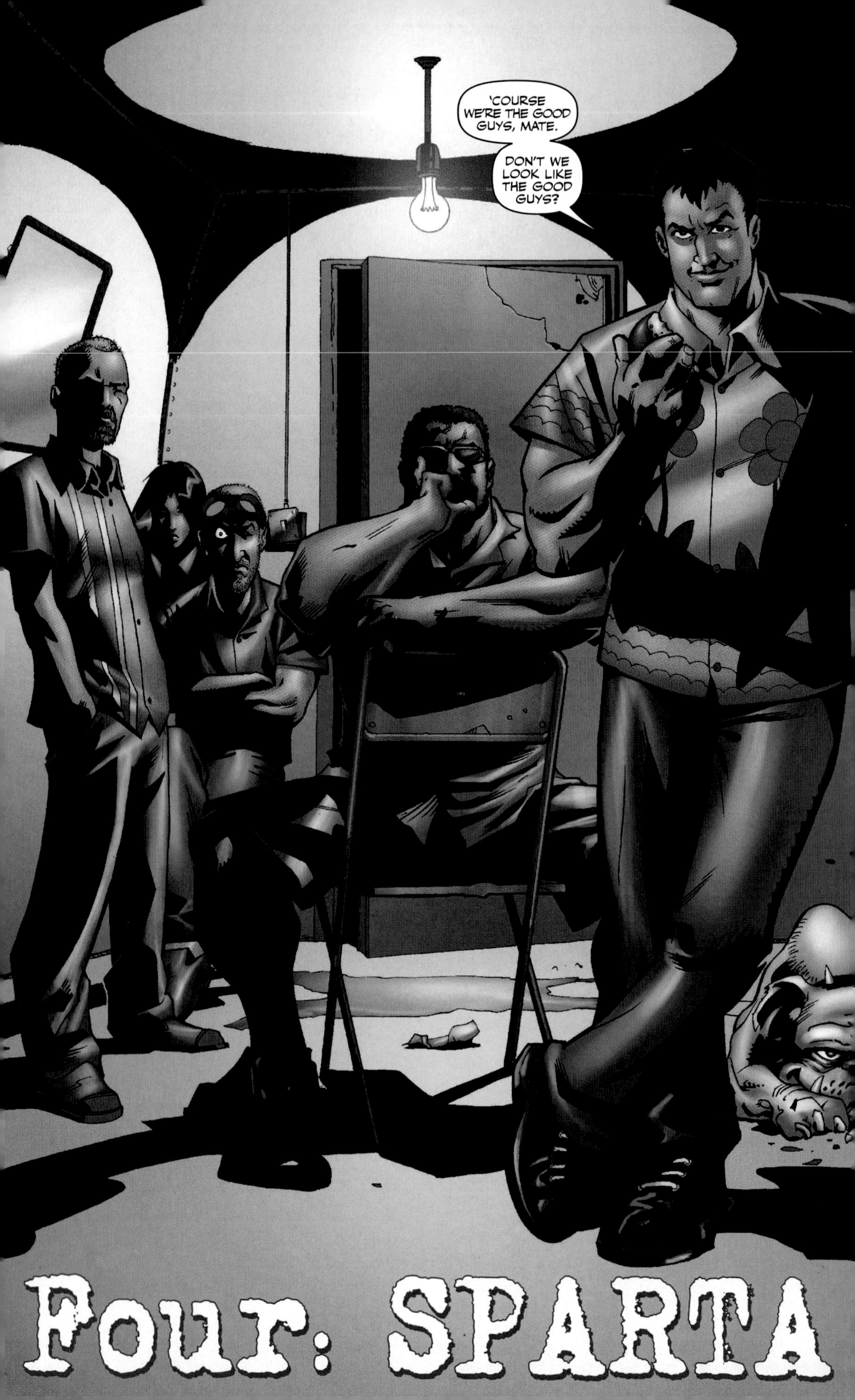
'COURSE WE'RE THE GOOD GUYS, MATE.
DON'T WE LOOK LIKE THE GOOD GUYS?
Four: SPARTA

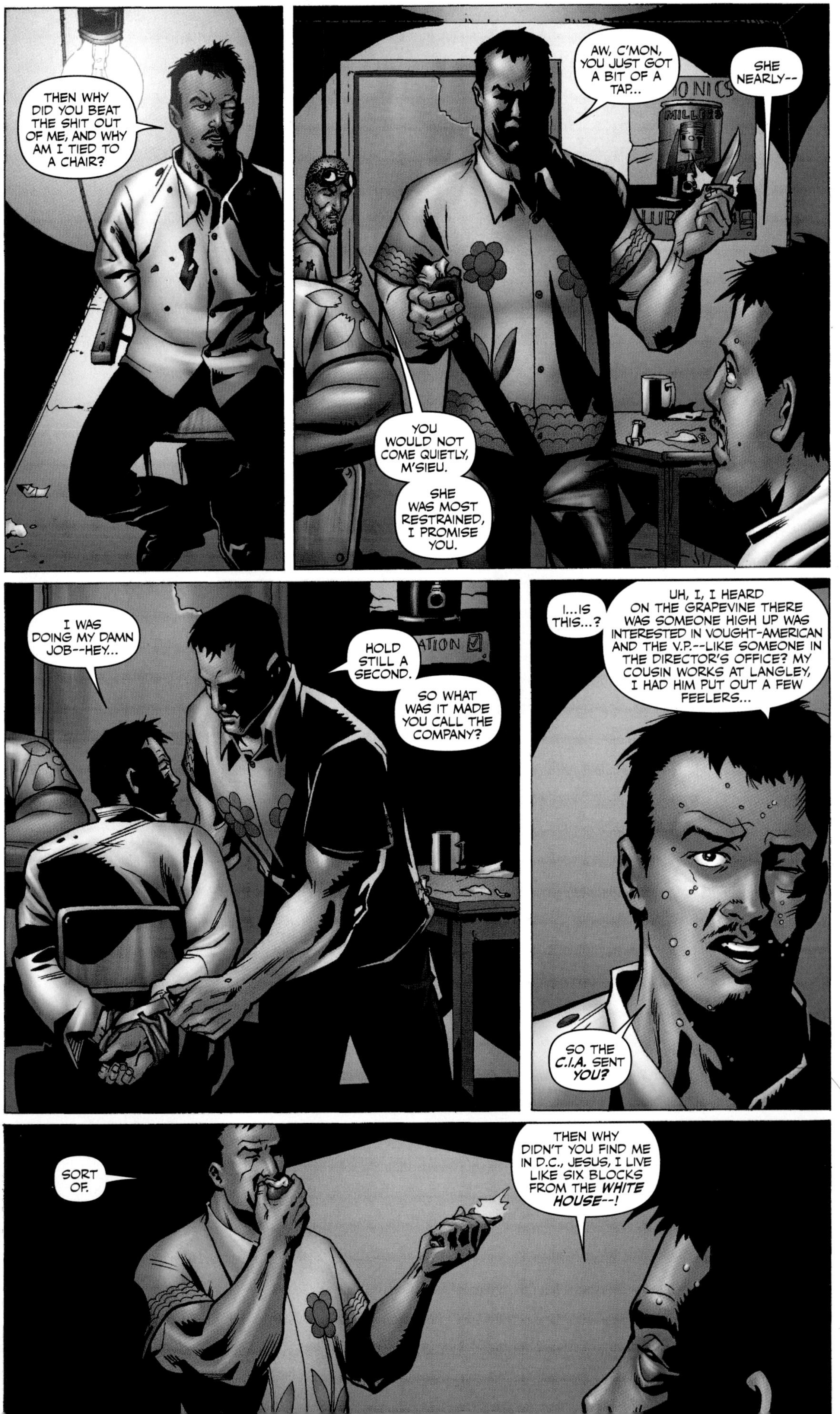
THEN WHY DID YOU BEAT THE SHIT OUT OF ME, AND WHY AM I TIED TO A CHAIR?
AW, C'MON, YOU JUST GOT A BIT OF A TAP...
SHE NEARLY--
YOU WOULD NOT COME QUIETLY, M'SIEU.
SHE WAS MOST RESTRAINED, I PROMISE YOU.
I WAS DOING MY DAMN JOB--HEY...
HOLD STILL A SECOND.
SO WHAT WAS IT MADE YOU CALL THE COMPANY?
I...IS THIS...?
UH, I, I HEARD ON THE GRAPEVINE THERE WAS SOMEONE HIGH UP WAS INTERESTED IN VOUGHT-AMERICAN AND THE V.P.--LIKE SOMEONE IN THE DIRECTOR'S OFFICE? MY COUSIN WORKS AT LANGLEY, I HAD HIM PUT OUT A FEW FEELERS...
SO THE *C.I.A.* SENT *YOU?*
SORT OF.
THEN WHY DIDN'T YOU FIND ME IN D.C., JESUS, I LIVE LIKE SIX BLOCKS FROM THE *WHITE HOUSE*--!

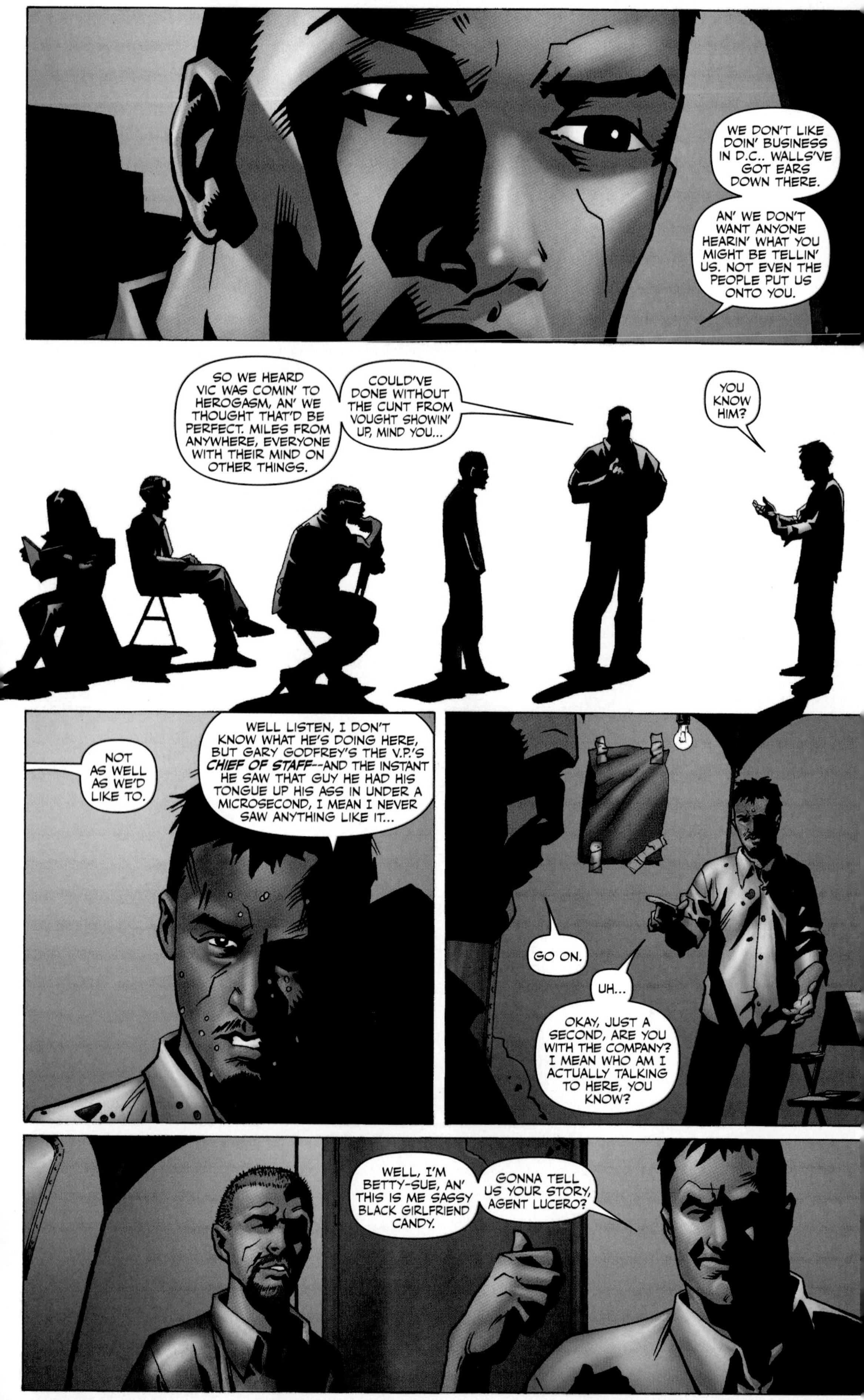
WE DON'T LIKE DOIN' BUSINESS IN D.C.. WALLS'VE GOT EARS DOWN THERE.
AN' WE DON'T WANT ANYONE HEARIN' WHAT YOU MIGHT BE TELLIN' US. NOT EVEN THE PEOPLE PUT US ONTO YOU.
SO WE HEARD VIC WAS COMIN' TO HEROGASM, AN' WE THOUGHT THAT'D BE PERFECT. MILES FROM ANYWHERE, EVERYONE WITH THEIR MIND ON OTHER THINGS.
COULD'VE DONE WITHOUT THE CUNT FROM VOUGHT SHOWIN' UP, MIND YOU...
YOU KNOW HIM?
NOT AS WELL AS WE'D LIKE TO.
WELL LISTEN, I DON'T KNOW WHAT HE'S DOING HERE, BUT GARY GODFREY'S THE V.P.'S *CHIEF OF STAFF*--AND THE INSTANT HE SAW THAT GUY HE HAD HIS TONGUE UP HIS ASS IN UNDER A MICROSECOND, I MEAN I NEVER SAW ANYTHING LIKE IT...
GO ON.
UH...
OKAY, JUST A SECOND, ARE YOU WITH THE COMPANY? I MEAN WHO AM I ACTUALLY TALKING TO HERE, YOU KNOW?
WELL, I'M BETTY-SUE, AN' THIS IS ME SASSY BLACK GIRLFRIEND CANDY.
GONNA TELL US YOUR STORY, AGENT LUCERO?

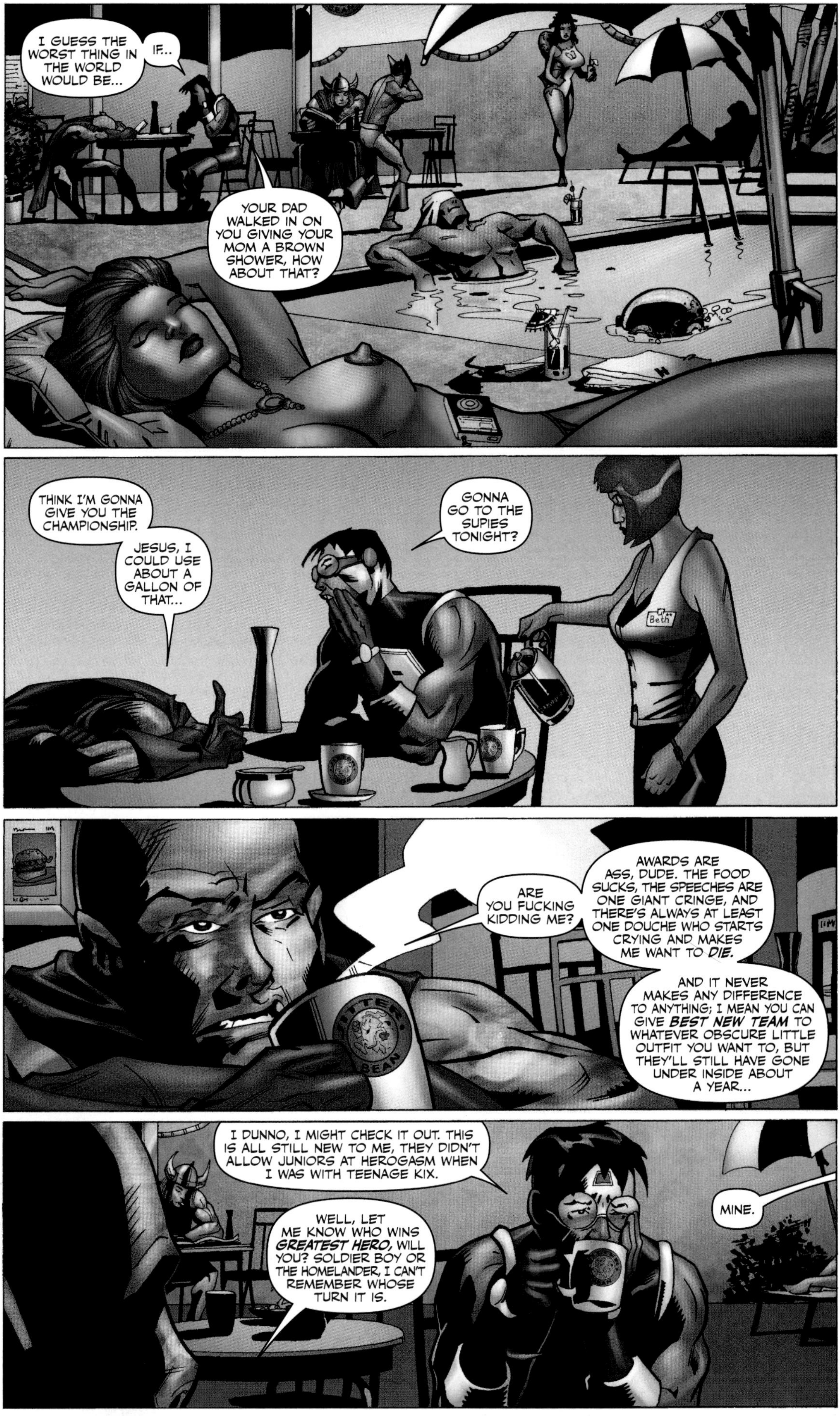
I GUESS THE WORST THING IN THE WORLD WOULD BE...
IF...
YOUR DAD WALKED IN ON YOU GIVING YOUR MOM A BROWN SHOWER, HOW ABOUT THAT?
THINK I'M GONNA GIVE YOU THE CHAMPIONSHIP.
JESUS, I COULD USE ABOUT A GALLON OF THAT...
GONNA GO TO THE SUPIES TONIGHT?
Beth
ARE YOU FUCKING KIDDING ME?
AWARDS ARE ASS, DUDE. THE FOOD SUCKS, THE SPEECHES ARE ONE GIANT CRINGE, AND THERE'S ALWAYS AT LEAST ONE DOUCHE WHO STARTS CRYING AND MAKES ME WANT TO *DIE.*
AND IT NEVER MAKES ANY DIFFERENCE TO ANYTHING; I MEAN YOU CAN GIVE *BEST NEW TEAM* TO WHATEVER OBSCURE LITTLE OUTFIT YOU WANT TO, BUT THEY'LL STILL HAVE GONE UNDER INSIDE ABOUT A YEAR...
I DUNNO, I MIGHT CHECK IT OUT. THIS IS ALL STILL NEW TO ME, THEY DIDN'T ALLOW JUNIORS AT HEROGASM WHEN I WAS WITH TEENAGE KIX.
WELL, LET ME KNOW WHO WINS *GREATEST HERO,* WILL YOU? SOLDIER BOY OR THE HOMELANDER, I CAN'T REMEMBER WHOSE TURN IT IS.
MINE.

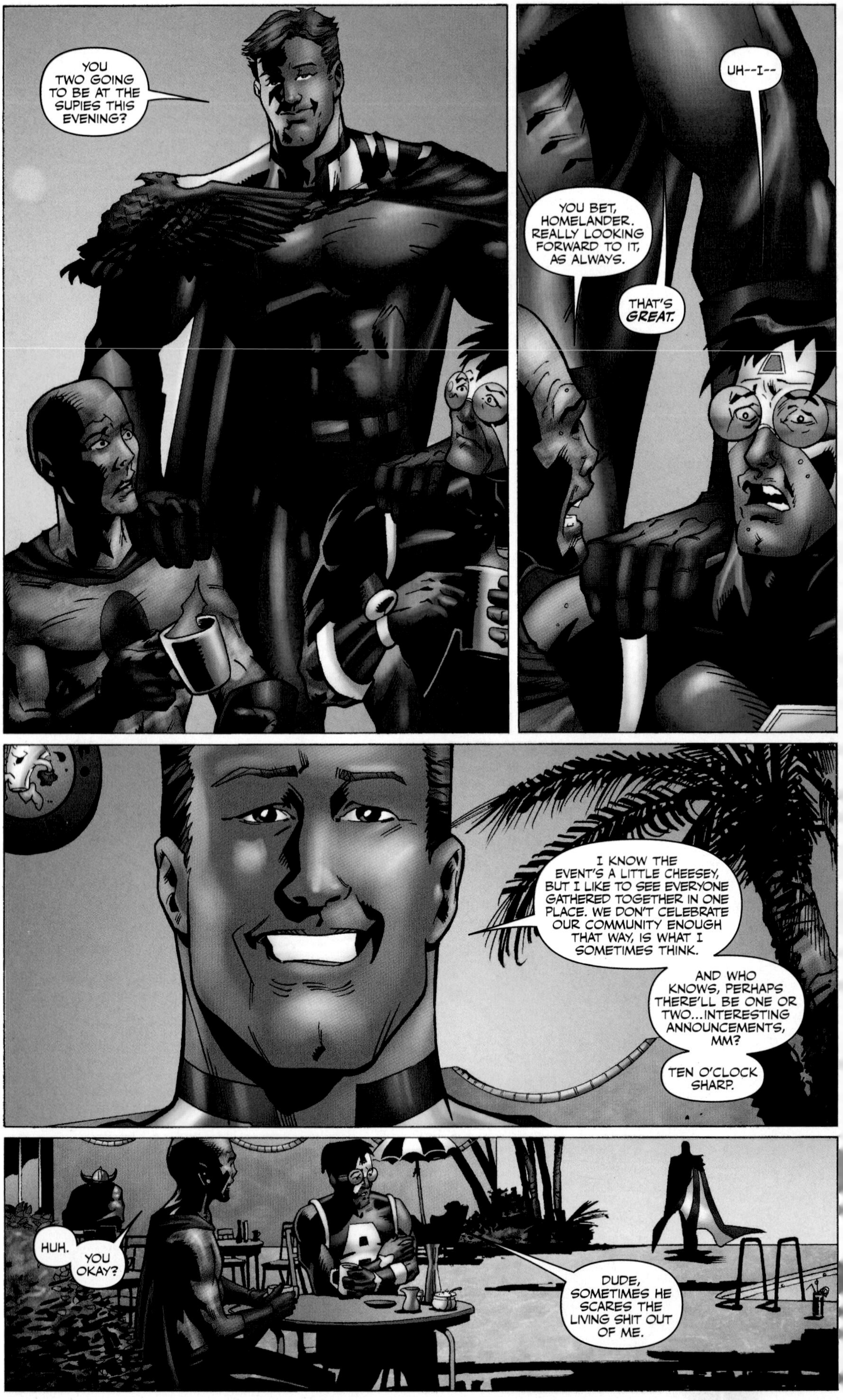
YOU TWO GOING TO BE AT THE SUPIES THIS EVENING?
UH--I--
YOU BET, HOMELANDER. REALLY LOOKING FORWARD TO IT, AS ALWAYS.
THAT'S GREAT.
I KNOW THE EVENT'S A LITTLE CHEESEY, BUT I LIKE TO SEE EVERYONE GATHERED TOGETHER IN ONE PLACE. WE DON'T CELEBRATE OUR COMMUNITY ENOUGH THAT WAY, IS WHAT I SOMETIMES THINK.
AND WHO KNOWS, PERHAPS THERE'LL BE ONE OR TWO...INTERESTING ANNOUNCEMENTS, MM?
TEN O'CLOCK SHARP.
HUH.
YOU OKAY?
DUDE, SOMETIMES HE SCARES THE LIVING SHIT OUT OF ME.

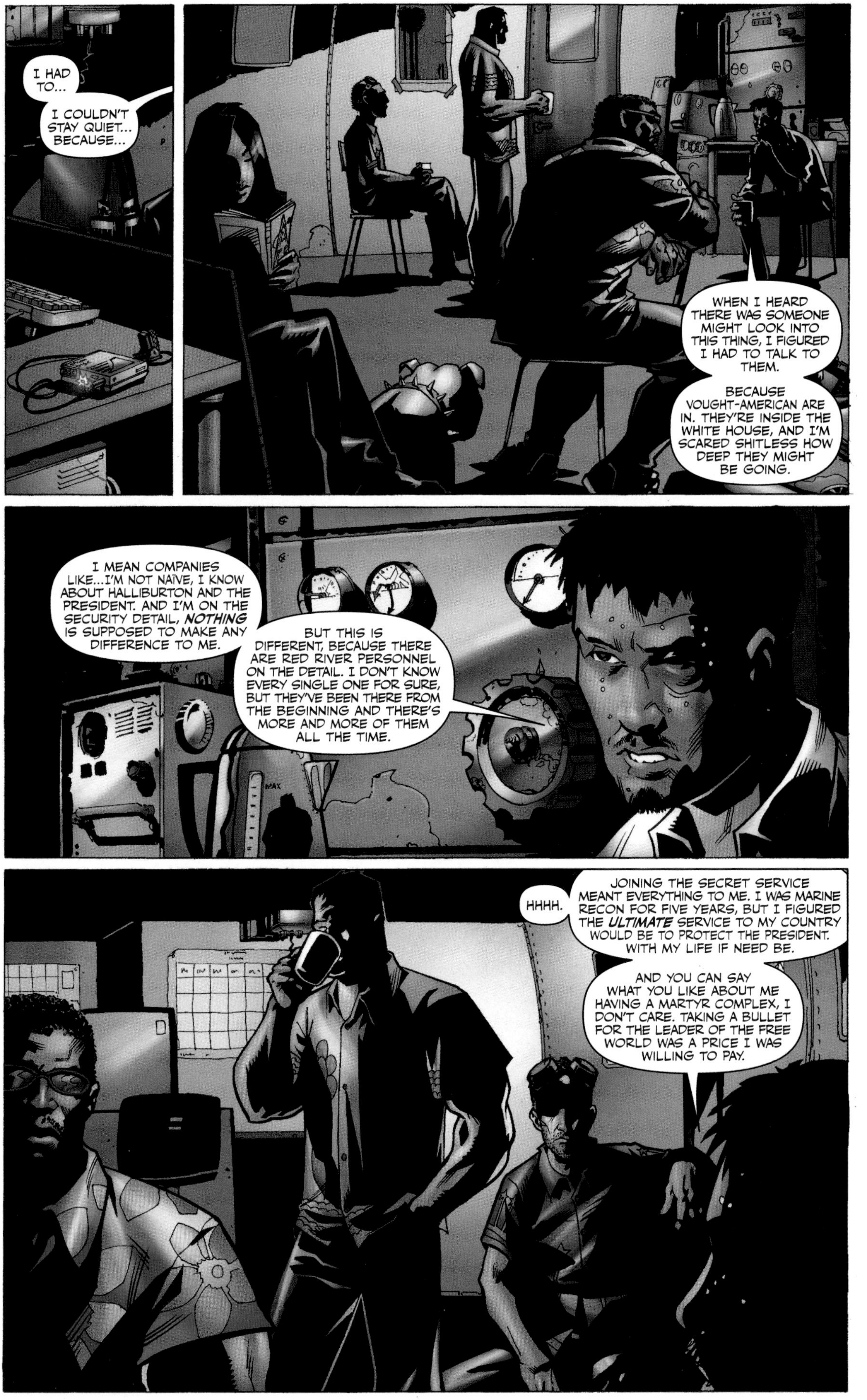
I HAD TO...
I COULDN'T STAY QUIET... BECAUSE...
WHEN I HEARD THERE WAS SOMEONE MIGHT LOOK INTO THIS THING, I FIGURED I HAD TO TALK TO THEM.
BECAUSE VOUGHT-AMERICAN ARE IN. THEY'RE INSIDE THE WHITE HOUSE, AND I'M SCARED SHITLESS HOW DEEP THEY MIGHT BE GOING.
I MEAN COMPANIES LIKE...I'M NOT NAÏVE, I KNOW ABOUT HALLIBURTON AND THE PRESIDENT. AND I'M ON THE SECURITY DETAIL, ***NOTHING*** IS SUPPOSED TO MAKE ANY DIFFERENCE TO ME.
BUT THIS IS DIFFERENT, BECAUSE THERE ARE RED RIVER PERSONNEL ON THE DETAIL. I DON'T KNOW EVERY SINGLE ONE FOR SURE, BUT THEY'VE BEEN THERE FROM THE BEGINNING AND THERE'S MORE AND MORE OF THEM ALL THE TIME.
HHHH.
JOINING THE SECRET SERVICE MEANT EVERYTHING TO ME. I WAS MARINE RECON FOR FIVE YEARS, BUT I FIGURED THE ***ULTIMATE*** SERVICE TO MY COUNTRY WOULD BE TO PROTECT THE PRESIDENT. WITH MY LIFE IF NEED BE.
AND YOU CAN SAY WHAT YOU LIKE ABOUT ME HAVING A MARTYR COMPLEX, I DON'T CARE. TAKING A BULLET FOR THE LEADER OF THE FREE WORLD WAS A PRICE I WAS WILLING TO PAY.

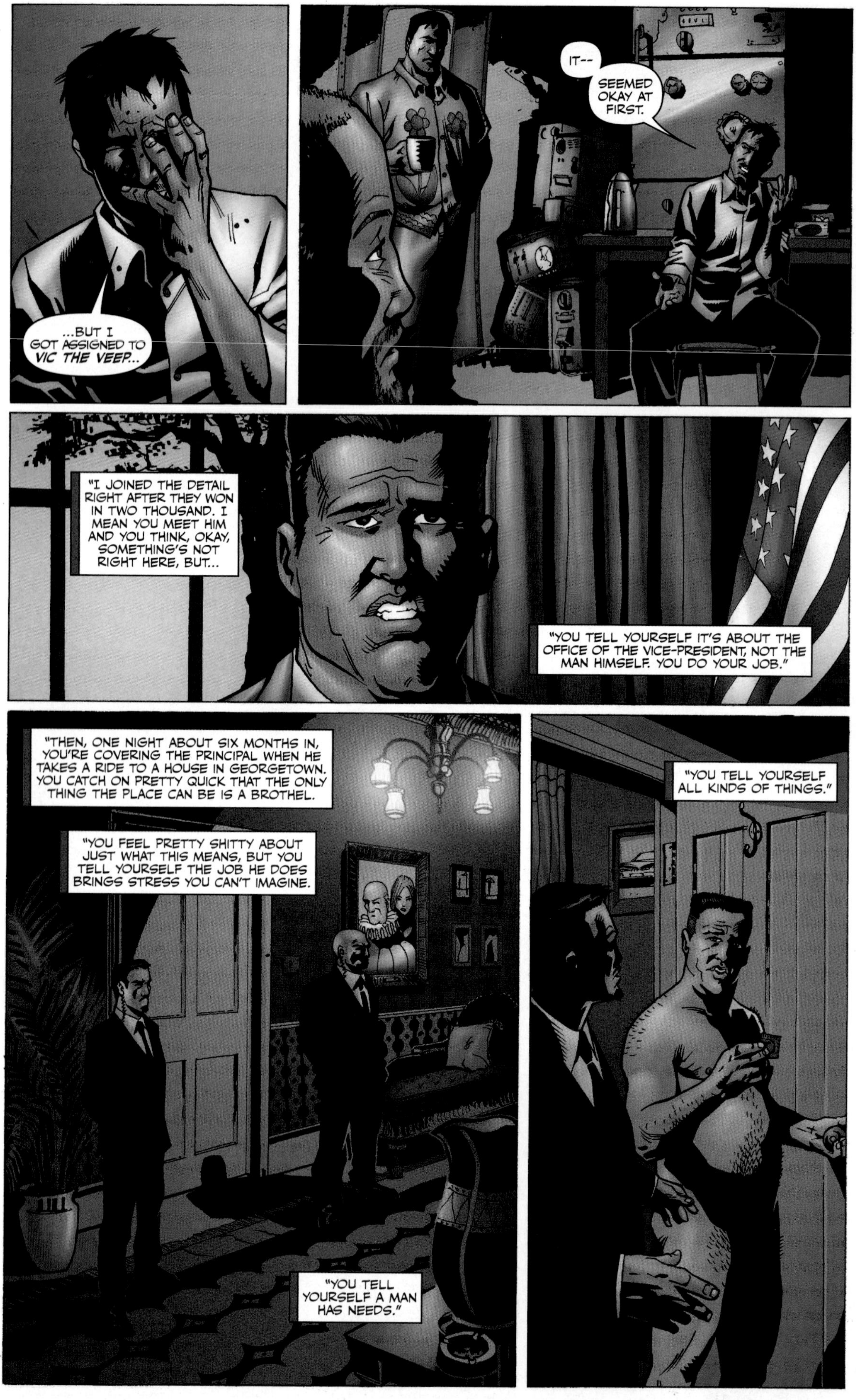
...BUT I
GOT ASSIGNED TO
VIC THE VEEP...
IT--
SEEMED OKAY AT FIRST.
"I JOINED THE DETAIL RIGHT AFTER THEY WON IN TWO THOUSAND. I MEAN YOU MEET HIM AND YOU THINK, OKAY, SOMETHING'S NOT RIGHT HERE, BUT...
"YOU TELL YOURSELF IT'S ABOUT THE OFFICE OF THE VICE-PRESIDENT, NOT THE MAN HIMSELF. YOU DO YOUR JOB."
"THEN, ONE NIGHT ABOUT SIX MONTHS IN, YOU'RE COVERING THE PRINCIPAL WHEN HE TAKES A RIDE TO A HOUSE IN GEORGETOWN. YOU CATCH ON PRETTY QUICK THAT THE ONLY THING THE PLACE CAN BE IS A BROTHEL.
"YOU FEEL PRETTY SHITTY ABOUT JUST WHAT THIS MEANS, BUT YOU TELL YOURSELF THE JOB HE DOES BRINGS STRESS YOU CAN'T IMAGINE.
"YOU TELL YOURSELF A MAN HAS NEEDS."
"YOU TELL YOURSELF ALL KINDS OF THINGS."

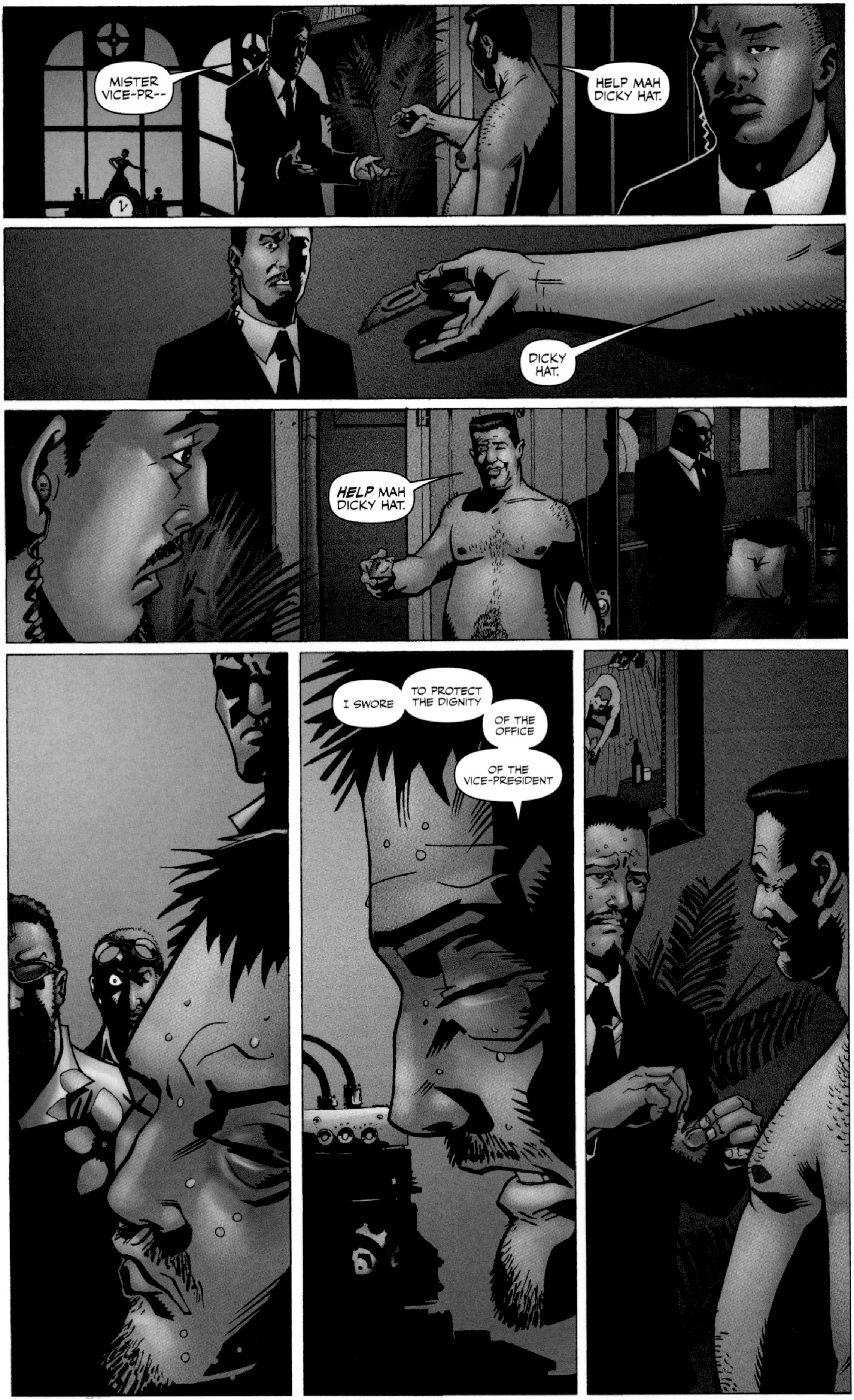
MISTER VICE-PR--
HELP MAH DICKY HAT.
DICKY HAT.
HELP MAH DICKY HAT.
I SWORE
TO PROTECT THE DIGNITY
OF THE OFFICE
OF THE VICE-PRESIDENT

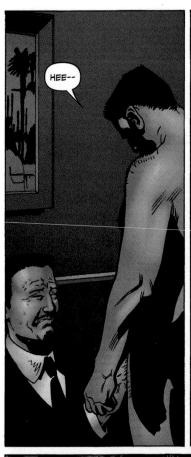

HEE--

HEE!!

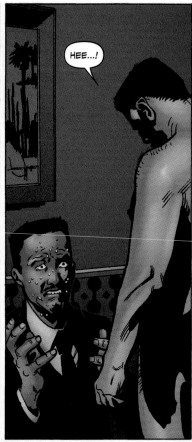

HEE...!

"GO AHEAD.

"LAUGH IT UP."

ALL MY FUCKING *LIFE* I DREAMED OF-- OF--

I WAS GOING TO QUIT. DUTY, OR-- SOMETHING--KEPT ME FROM FACING IT, BUT STILL I WAS A CUNT HAIR AWAY FROM QUITTING...

BUT IF I'D DONE THAT I WOULDN'T BE HERE NOW. TELLING YOU WHAT HAPPENED THREE MONTHS LATER, ON NINE-ELEVEN-OH-ONE.

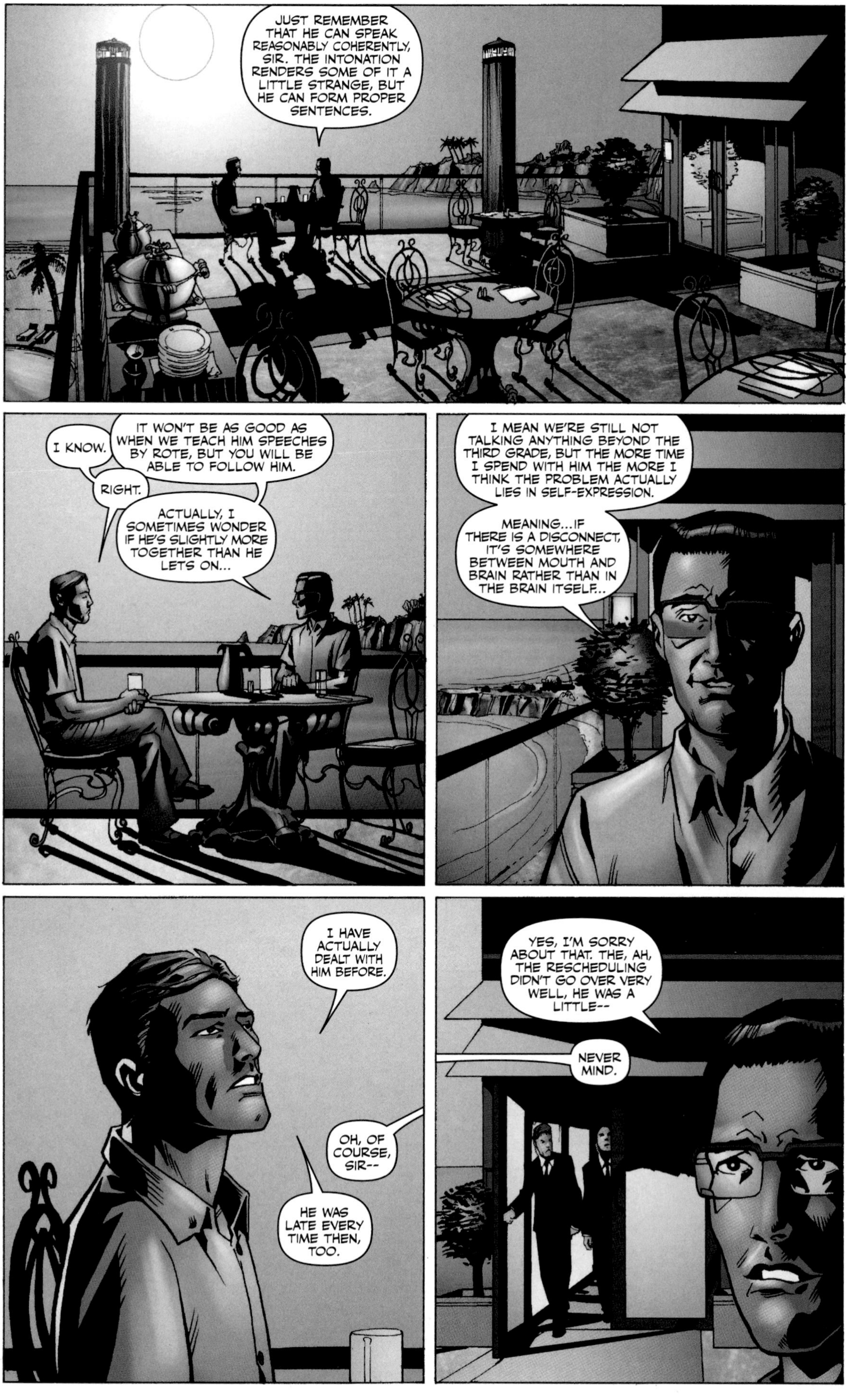
JUST REMEMBER THAT HE CAN SPEAK REASONABLY COHERENTLY, SIR. THE INTONATION RENDERS SOME OF IT A LITTLE STRANGE, BUT HE CAN FORM PROPER SENTENCES.
I KNOW.
IT WON'T BE AS GOOD AS WHEN WE TEACH HIM SPEECHES BY ROTE, BUT YOU WILL BE ABLE TO FOLLOW HIM.
RIGHT.
ACTUALLY, I SOMETIMES WONDER IF HE'S SLIGHTLY MORE TOGETHER THAN HE LETS ON...
I MEAN WE'RE STILL NOT TALKING ANYTHING BEYOND THE THIRD GRADE, BUT THE MORE TIME I SPEND WITH HIM THE MORE I THINK THE PROBLEM ACTUALLY LIES IN SELF-EXPRESSION.
MEANING...IF THERE IS A DISCONNECT, IT'S SOMEWHERE BETWEEN MOUTH AND BRAIN RATHER THAN IN THE BRAIN ITSELF...
I HAVE ACTUALLY DEALT WITH HIM BEFORE.
OH, OF COURSE, SIR--
HE WAS LATE EVERY TIME THEN, TOO.
YES, I'M SORRY ABOUT THAT. THE, AH, THE RESCHEDULING DIDN'T GO OVER VERY WELL, HE WAS A LITTLE--
NEVER MIND.

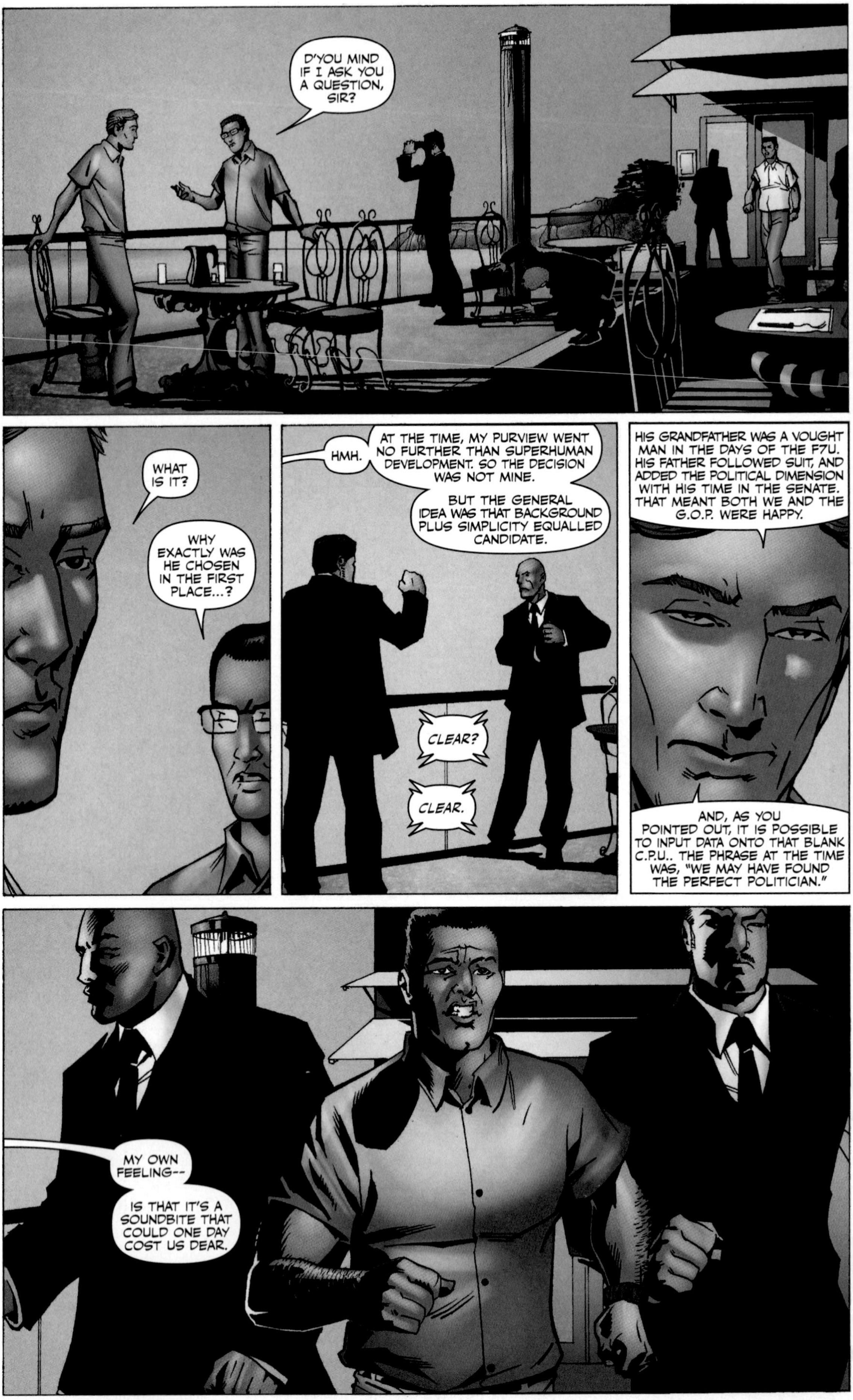
D'YOU MIND IF I ASK YOU A QUESTION, SIR?
WHAT IS IT?
WHY EXACTLY WAS HE CHOSEN IN THE FIRST PLACE...?
HMH.
AT THE TIME, MY PURVIEW WENT NO FURTHER THAN SUPERHUMAN DEVELOPMENT. SO THE DECISION WAS NOT MINE.
BUT THE GENERAL IDEA WAS THAT BACKGROUND PLUS SIMPLICITY EQUALLED CANDIDATE.
CLEAR?
CLEAR.
HIS GRANDFATHER WAS A VOUGHT MAN IN THE DAYS OF THE F7U. HIS FATHER FOLLOWED SUIT, AND ADDED THE POLITICAL DIMENSION WITH HIS TIME IN THE SENATE. THAT MEANT BOTH WE AND THE G.O.P. WERE HAPPY.
AND, AS YOU POINTED OUT, IT IS POSSIBLE TO INPUT DATA ONTO THAT BLANK C.P.U.. THE PHRASE AT THE TIME WAS, "WE MAY HAVE FOUND THE PERFECT POLITICIAN."
MY OWN FEELING--
IS THAT IT'S A SOUNDBITE THAT COULD ONE DAY COST US DEAR.

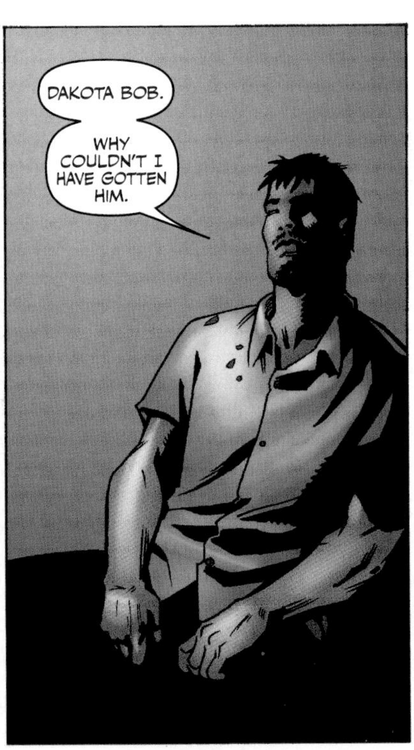
DAKOTA BOB.
WHY COULDN'T I HAVE GOTTEN HIM.

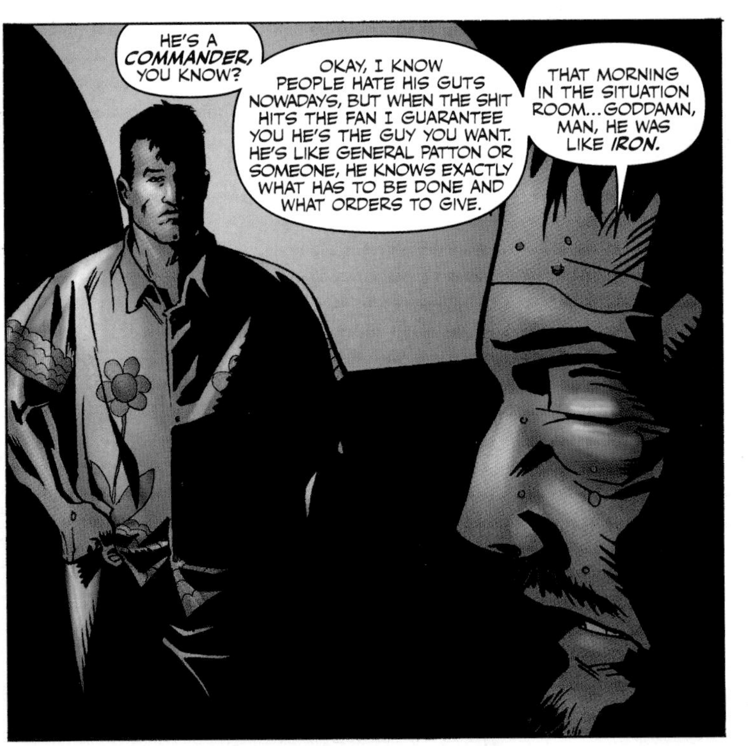
HE'S A *COMMANDER,* YOU KNOW?
OKAY, I KNOW PEOPLE HATE HIS GUTS NOWADAYS, BUT WHEN THE SHIT HITS THE FAN I GUARANTEE YOU HE'S THE GUY YOU WANT. HE'S LIKE GENERAL PATTON OR SOMEONE, HE KNOWS EXACTLY WHAT HAS TO BE DONE AND WHAT ORDERS TO GIVE.
THAT MORNING IN THE SITUATION ROOM...GODDAMN, MAN, HE WAS LIKE *IRON.*

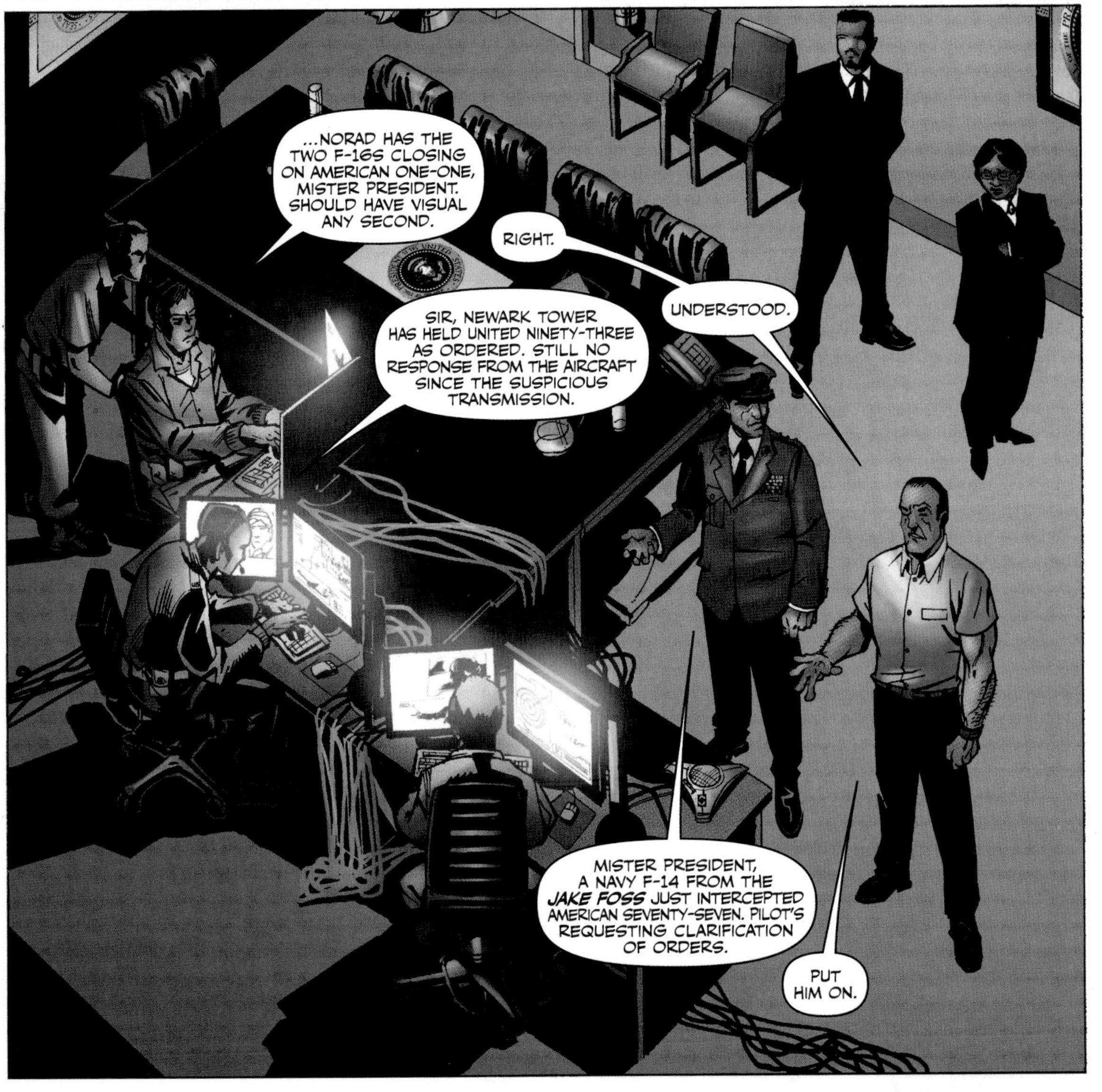
...NORAD HAS THE TWO F-16S CLOSING ON AMERICAN ONE-ONE, MISTER PRESIDENT. SHOULD HAVE VISUAL ANY SECOND.
RIGHT.
UNDERSTOOD.
SIR, NEWARK TOWER HAS HELD UNITED NINETY-THREE AS ORDERED. STILL NO RESPONSE FROM THE AIRCRAFT SINCE THE SUSPICIOUS TRANSMISSION.
MISTER PRESIDENT, A NAVY F-14 FROM THE *JAKE FOSS* JUST INTERCEPTED AMERICAN SEVENTY-SEVEN. PILOT'S REQUESTING CLARIFICATION OF ORDERS.
PUT HIM ON.

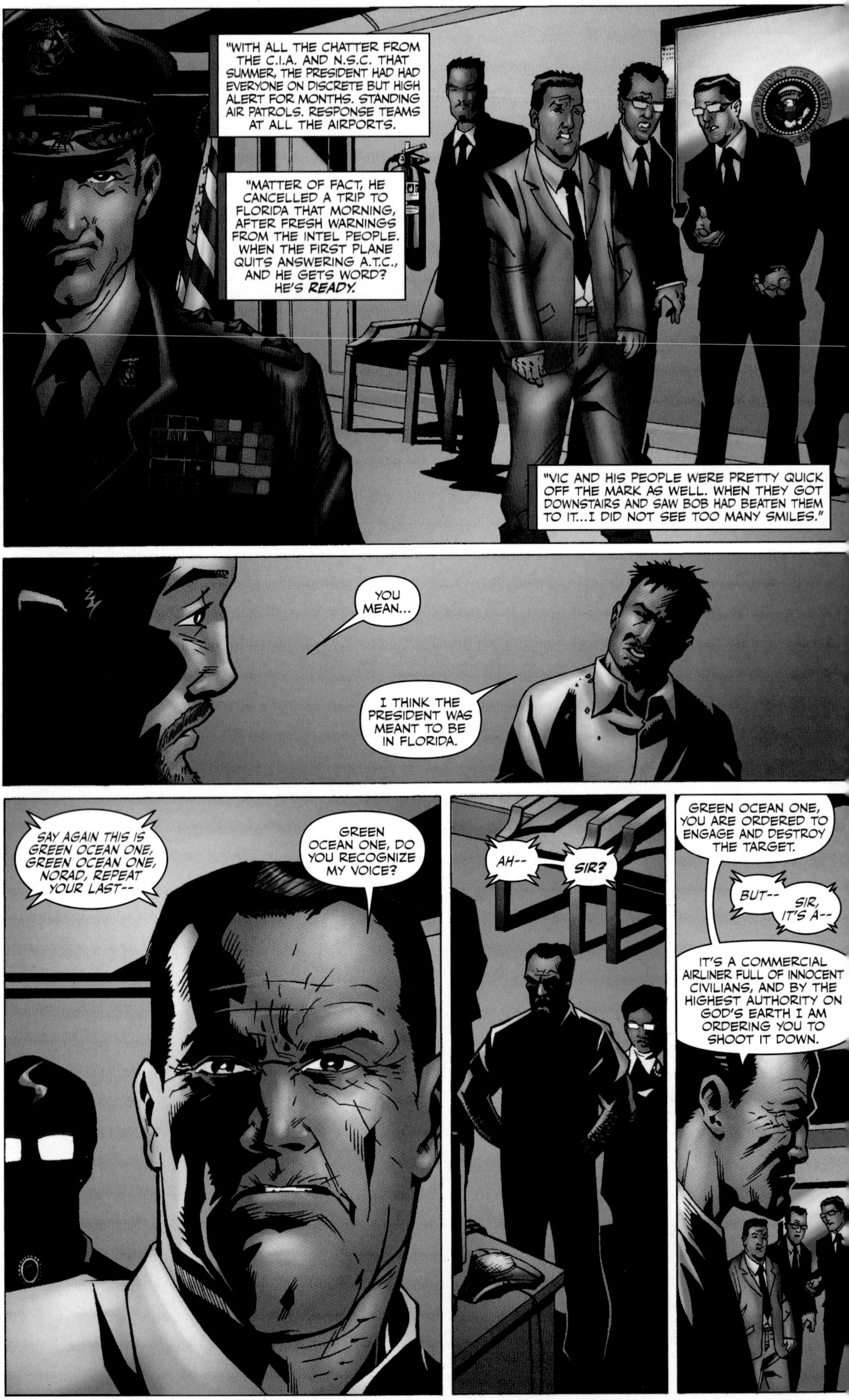
"WITH ALL THE CHATTER FROM THE C.I.A. AND N.S.C. THAT SUMMER, THE PRESIDENT HAD HAD EVERYONE ON DISCRETE BUT HIGH ALERT FOR MONTHS. STANDING AIR PATROLS. RESPONSE TEAMS AT ALL THE AIRPORTS.
"MATTER OF FACT, HE CANCELLED A TRIP TO FLORIDA THAT MORNING, AFTER FRESH WARNINGS FROM THE INTEL PEOPLE. WHEN THE FIRST PLANE QUITS ANSWERING A.T.C., AND HE GETS WORD? HE'S *READY.*
"VIC AND HIS PEOPLE WERE PRETTY QUICK OFF THE MARK AS WELL. WHEN THEY GOT DOWNSTAIRS AND SAW BOB HAD BEATEN THEM TO IT...I DID NOT SEE TOO MANY SMILES."
YOU MEAN...
I THINK THE PRESIDENT WAS MEANT TO BE IN FLORIDA.
SAY AGAIN THIS IS GREEN OCEAN ONE, GREEN OCEAN ONE, NORAD, REPEAT YOUR LAST--
GREEN OCEAN ONE, DO YOU RECOGNIZE MY VOICE?
AH--
SIR?
GREEN OCEAN ONE, YOU ARE ORDERED TO ENGAGE AND DESTROY THE TARGET.
BUT--
SIR, IT'S A--
IT'S A COMMERCIAL AIRLINER FULL OF INNOCENT CIVILIANS, AND BY THE HIGHEST AUTHORITY ON GOD'S EARTH I AM ORDERING YOU TO SHOOT IT DOWN.

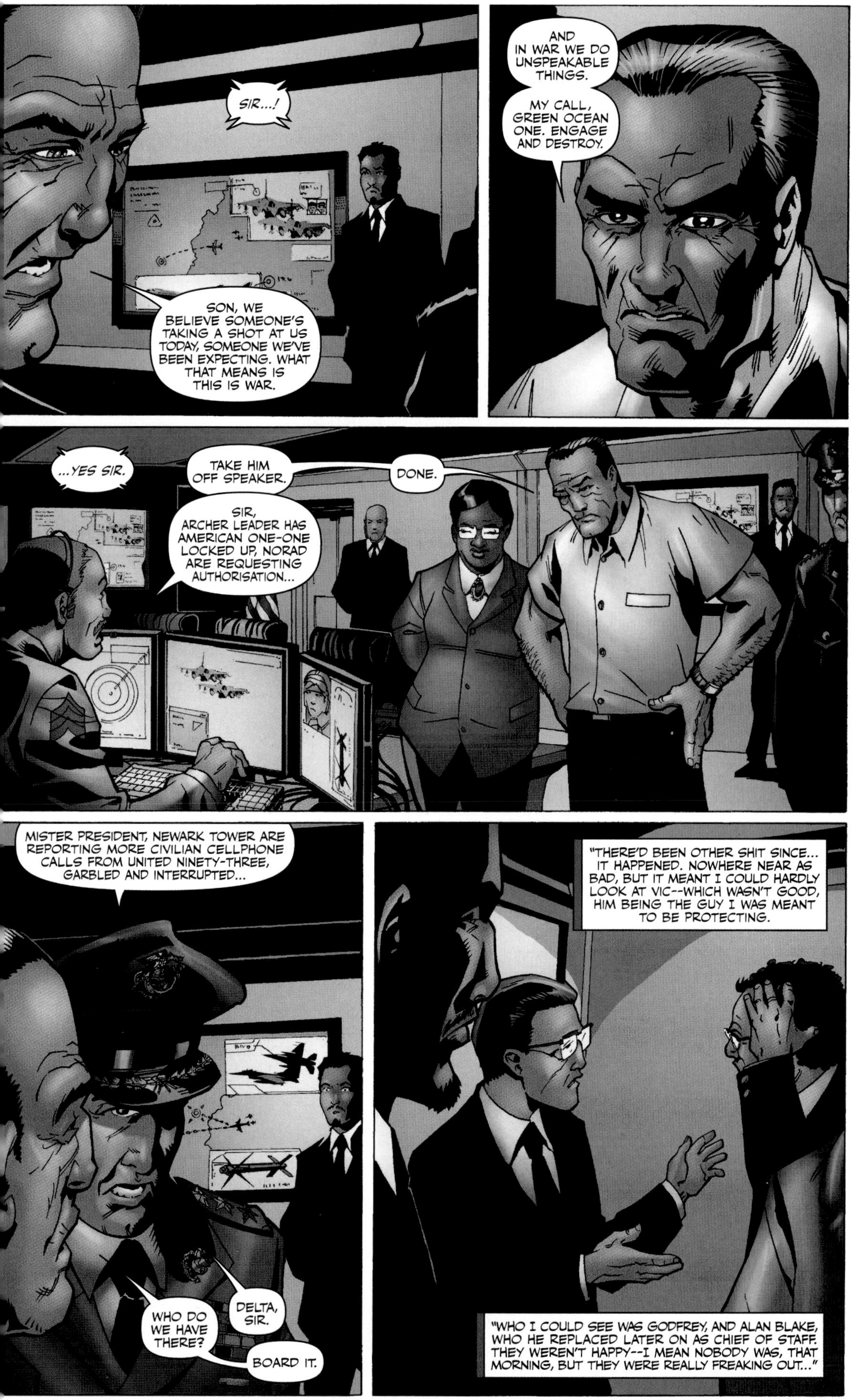

SIR...!
SON, WE BELIEVE SOMEONE'S TAKING A SHOT AT US TODAY, SOMEONE WE'VE BEEN EXPECTING. WHAT THAT MEANS IS THIS IS WAR.
AND IN WAR WE DO UNSPEAKABLE THINGS.
MY CALL, GREEN OCEAN ONE. ENGAGE AND DESTROY.
...YES SIR.
TAKE HIM OFF SPEAKER.
DONE.
SIR, ARCHER LEADER HAS AMERICAN ONE-ONE LOCKED UP, NORAD ARE REQUESTING AUTHORISATION...
MISTER PRESIDENT, NEWARK TOWER ARE REPORTING MORE CIVILIAN CELLPHONE CALLS FROM UNITED NINETY-THREE, GARBLED AND INTERRUPTED...
WHO DO WE HAVE THERE?
DELTA, SIR.
BOARD IT.
"THERE'D BEEN OTHER SHIT SINCE... IT HAPPENED. NOWHERE NEAR AS BAD, BUT IT MEANT I COULD HARDLY LOOK AT VIC--WHICH WASN'T GOOD, HIM BEING THE GUY I WAS MEANT TO BE PROTECTING.
"WHO I COULD SEE WAS GODFREY, AND ALAN BLAKE, WHO HE REPLACED LATER ON AS CHIEF OF STAFF. THEY WEREN'T HAPPY--I MEAN NOBODY WAS, THAT MORNING, BUT THEY WERE REALLY FREAKING OUT..."

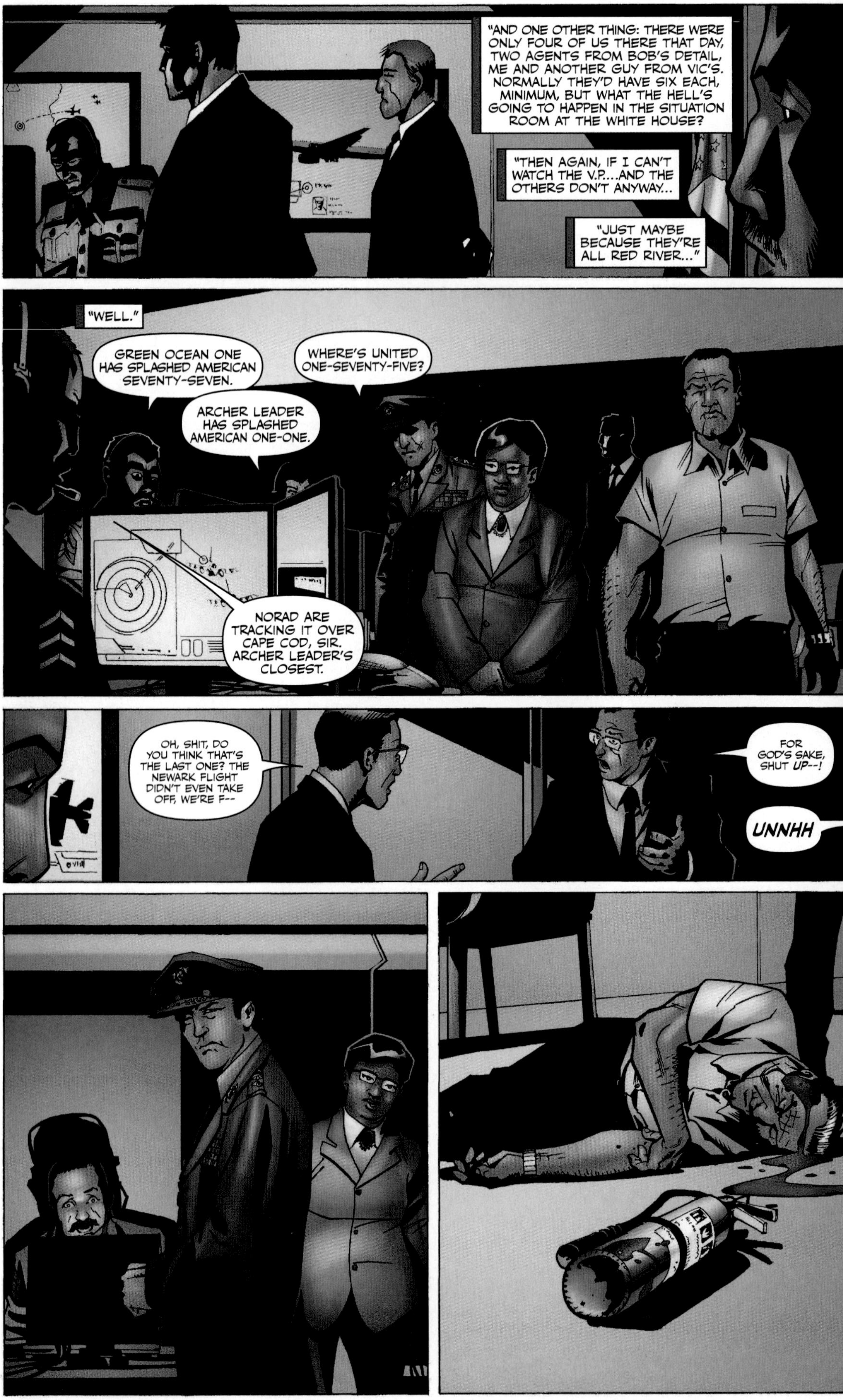
"AND ONE OTHER THING: THERE WERE ONLY FOUR OF US THERE THAT DAY, TWO AGENTS FROM BOB'S DETAIL, ME AND ANOTHER GUY FROM VIC'S. NORMALLY THEY'D HAVE SIX EACH, MINIMUM, BUT WHAT THE HELL'S GOING TO HAPPEN IN THE SITUATION ROOM AT THE WHITE HOUSE?
"THEN AGAIN, IF I CAN'T WATCH THE V.P.…AND THE OTHERS DON'T ANYWAY…
"JUST MAYBE BECAUSE THEY'RE ALL RED RIVER…"
"WELL."
GREEN OCEAN ONE HAS SPLASHED AMERICAN SEVENTY-SEVEN.
WHERE'S UNITED ONE-SEVENTY-FIVE?
ARCHER LEADER HAS SPLASHED AMERICAN ONE-ONE.
NORAD ARE TRACKING IT OVER CAPE COD, SIR. ARCHER LEADER'S CLOSEST.
OH, SHIT, DO YOU THINK THAT'S THE LAST ONE? THE NEWARK FLIGHT DIDN'T EVEN TAKE OFF, WE'RE F--
FOR GOD'S SAKE, SHUT UP--!
UNNHH

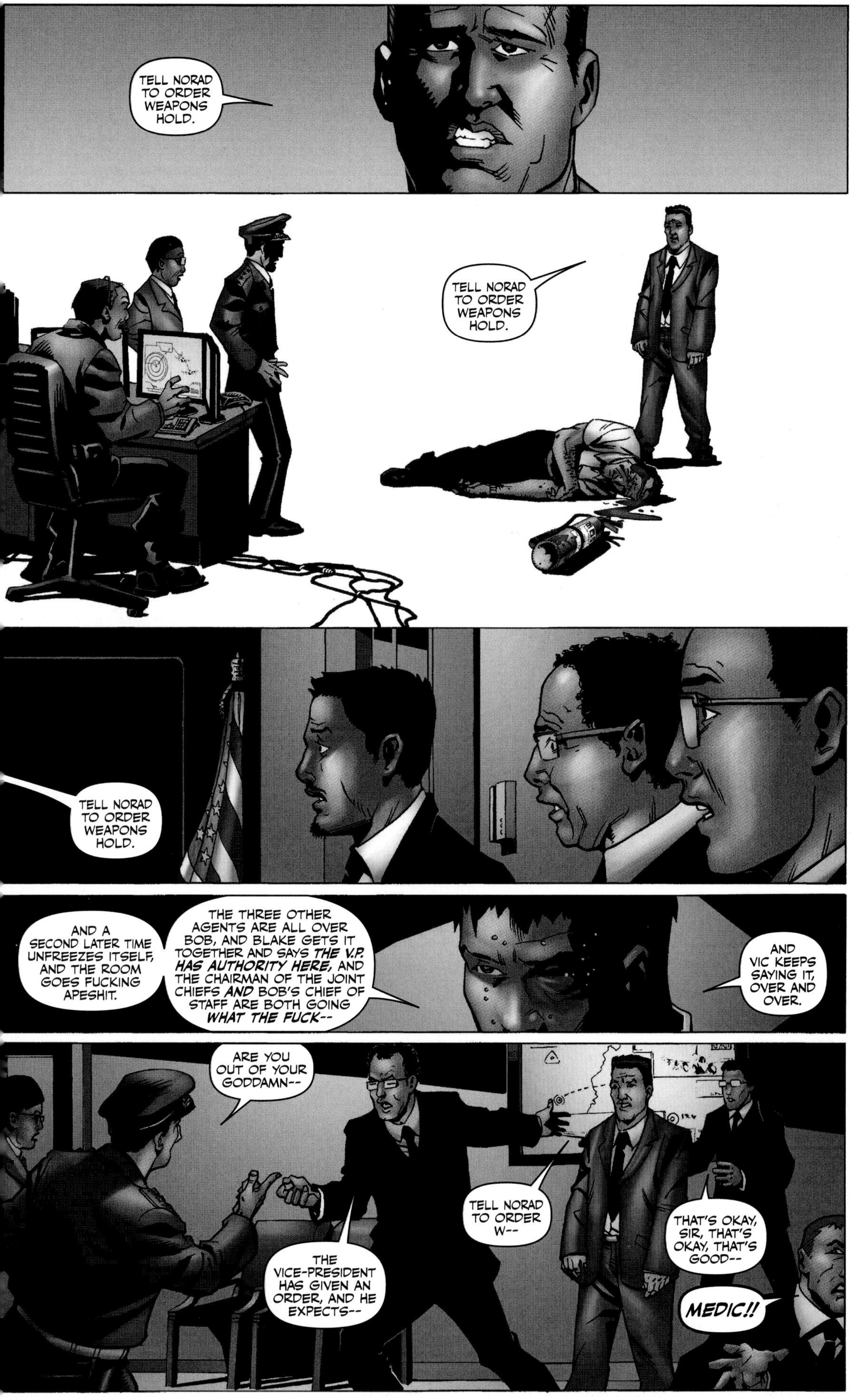
TELL NORAD TO ORDER WEAPONS HOLD.
TELL NORAD TO ORDER WEAPONS HOLD.
TELL NORAD TO ORDER WEAPONS HOLD.
AND A SECOND LATER TIME UNFREEZES ITSELF, AND THE ROOM GOES FUCKING APESHIT.
THE THREE OTHER AGENTS ARE ALL OVER BOB, AND BLAKE GETS IT TOGETHER AND SAYS THE V.P. HAS AUTHORITY HERE, AND THE CHAIRMAN OF THE JOINT CHIEFS AND BOB'S CHIEF OF STAFF ARE BOTH GOING WHAT THE FUCK--
AND VIC KEEPS SAYING IT, OVER AND OVER.
ARE YOU OUT OF YOUR GODDAMN--
THE VICE-PRESIDENT HAS GIVEN AN ORDER, AND HE EXPECTS--
TELL NORAD TO ORDER W--
THAT'S OKAY, SIR, THAT'S OKAY, THAT'S GOOD--
MEDIC!!

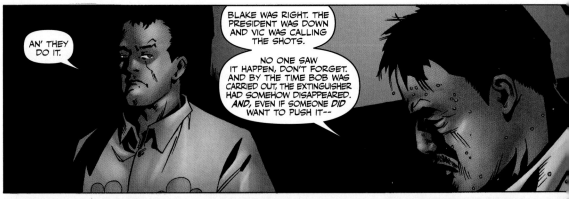

AN' THEY DO IT.

BLAKE WAS RIGHT. THE PRESIDENT WAS DOWN AND VIC WAS CALLING THE SHOTS.

NO ONE SAW IT HAPPEN, DON'T FORGET. AND BY THE TIME BOB WAS CARRIED OUT, THE EXTINGUISHER HAD SOMEHOW DISAPPEARED. *AND*, EVEN IF SOMEONE *DID* WANT TO PUSH IT--

"THERE WAS THE LITTLE MATTER OF AN ONGOING TERRORIST ATTACK."

...STRAIGHT FOR NEW YORK! NORAD, I JUST BLEW A PLANE-LOAD OF AMERICANS OUT OF THE SKY, IF WE LET THIS ONE THROUGH IT WAS FOR NOTHING! *PLEASE!*

ARCHER LEADER, THIS IS A DIRECT ORDER. DISENGAGE. RETURN TO BASE.

BUT--

ACKNOWLEDGE

OH, JESUS.

JESUS CHRIST.

ARCHER TWO, BREAK LEFT.

YES--

WAIT.

WHAT THE HELL--

ARCHER LEADER?

I THOUGHT I SAW...

NOTHING.

FUCK IT.

"LET'S GO HOME."

AND YOU COULD TELL THE GUY WAS CRYING LIKE A KID.

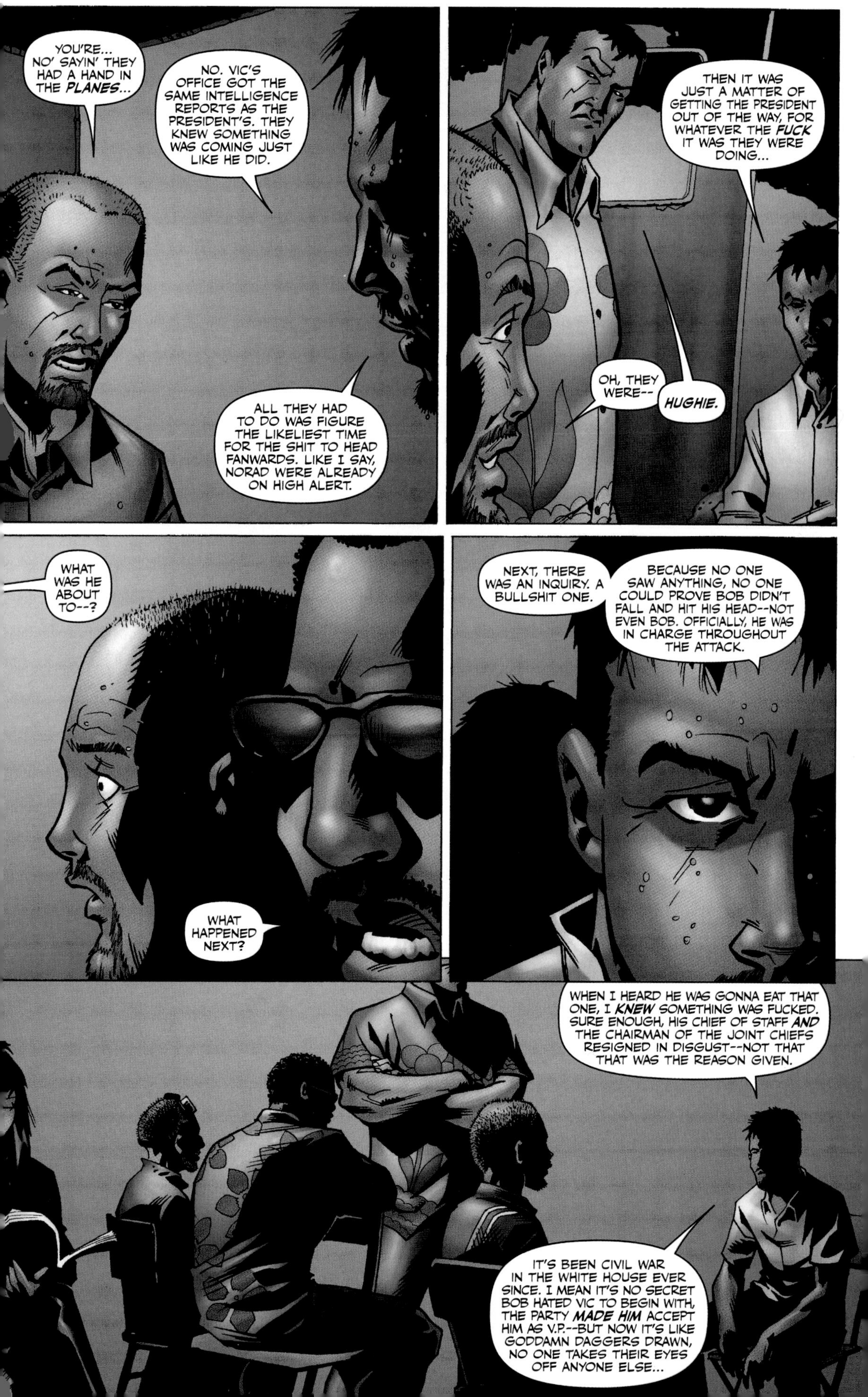

YOU'RE... NO' SAYIN' THEY HAD A HAND IN THE PLANES...
NO. VIC'S OFFICE GOT THE SAME INTELLIGENCE REPORTS AS THE PRESIDENT'S. THEY KNEW SOMETHING WAS COMING JUST LIKE HE DID.
ALL THEY HAD TO DO WAS FIGURE THE LIKELIEST TIME FOR THE SHIT TO HEAD FANWARDS. LIKE I SAY, NORAD WERE ALREADY ON HIGH ALERT.
THEN IT WAS JUST A MATTER OF GETTING THE PRESIDENT OUT OF THE WAY, FOR WHATEVER THE FUCK IT WAS THEY WERE DOING...
OH, THEY WERE--
HUGHIE.
WHAT WAS HE ABOUT TO--?
WHAT HAPPENED NEXT?
NEXT, THERE WAS AN INQUIRY. A BULLSHIT ONE.
BECAUSE NO ONE SAW ANYTHING, NO ONE COULD PROVE BOB DIDN'T FALL AND HIT HIS HEAD--NOT EVEN BOB. OFFICIALLY, HE WAS IN CHARGE THROUGHOUT THE ATTACK.
WHEN I HEARD HE WAS GONNA EAT THAT ONE, I KNEW SOMETHING WAS FUCKED. SURE ENOUGH, HIS CHIEF OF STAFF AND THE CHAIRMAN OF THE JOINT CHIEFS RESIGNED IN DISGUST--NOT THAT THAT WAS THE REASON GIVEN.
IT'S BEEN CIVIL WAR IN THE WHITE HOUSE EVER SINCE. I MEAN IT'S NO SECRET BOB HATED VIC TO BEGIN WITH, THE PARTY MADE HIM ACCEPT HIM AS V.P.--BUT NOW IT'S LIKE GODDAMN DAGGERS DRAWN, NO ONE TAKES THEIR EYES OFF ANYONE ELSE...

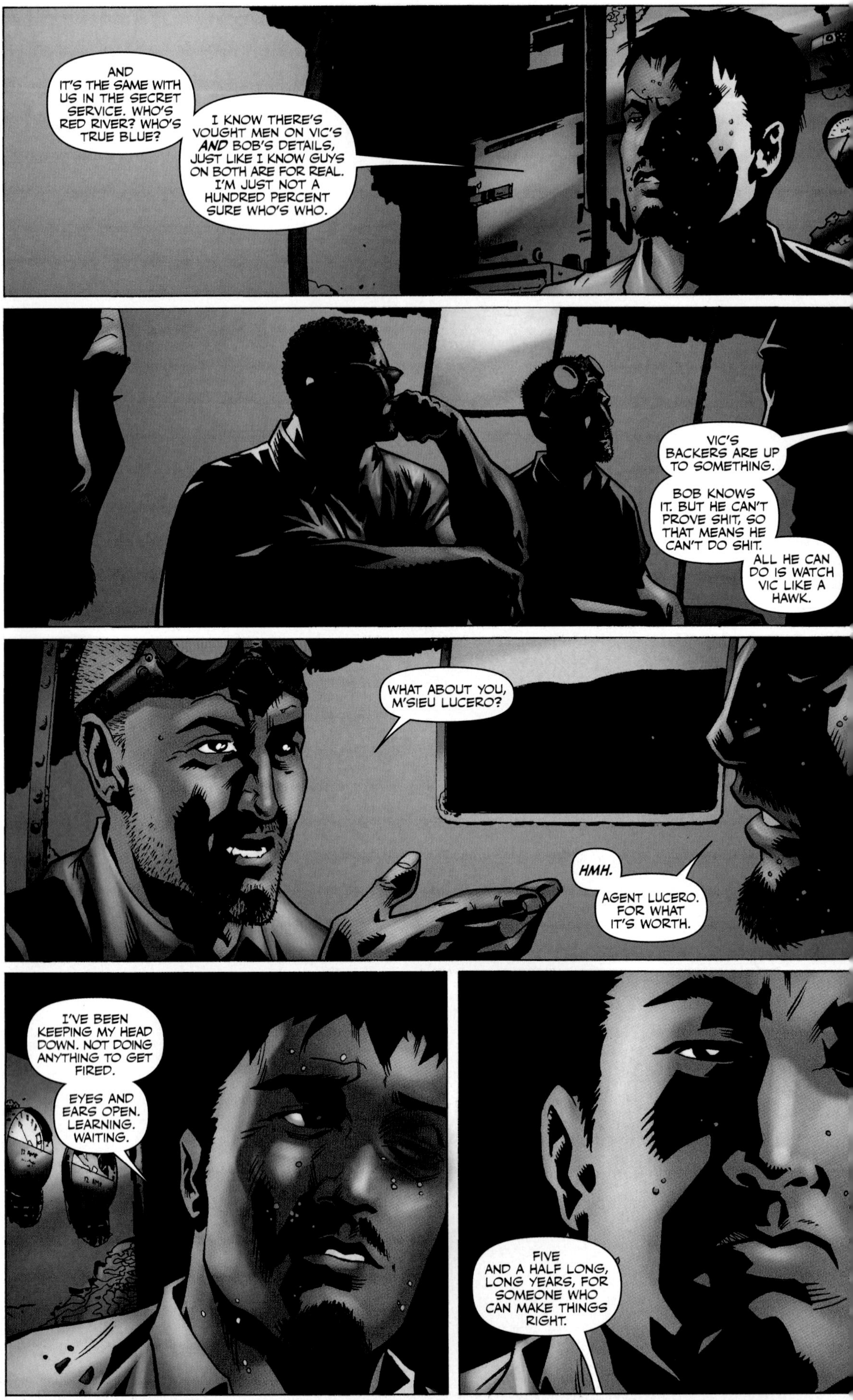
AND IT'S THE SAME WITH US IN THE SECRET SERVICE. WHO'S RED RIVER? WHO'S TRUE BLUE?
I KNOW THERE'S VOUGHT MEN ON VIC'S *AND* BOB'S DETAILS, JUST LIKE I KNOW GUYS ON BOTH ARE FOR REAL. I'M JUST NOT A HUNDRED PERCENT SURE WHO'S WHO.
VIC'S BACKERS ARE UP TO SOMETHING.
BOB KNOWS IT. BUT HE CAN'T PROVE SHIT, SO THAT MEANS HE CAN'T DO SHIT.
ALL HE CAN DO IS WATCH VIC LIKE A HAWK.
WHAT ABOUT YOU, M'SIEU LUCERO?
HMH.
AGENT LUCERO. FOR WHAT IT'S WORTH.
I'VE BEEN KEEPING MY HEAD DOWN. NOT DOING ANYTHING TO GET FIRED.
EYES AND EARS OPEN. LEARNING. WAITING.
FIVE AND A HALF LONG, LONG YEARS, FOR SOMEONE WHO CAN MAKE THINGS RIGHT.

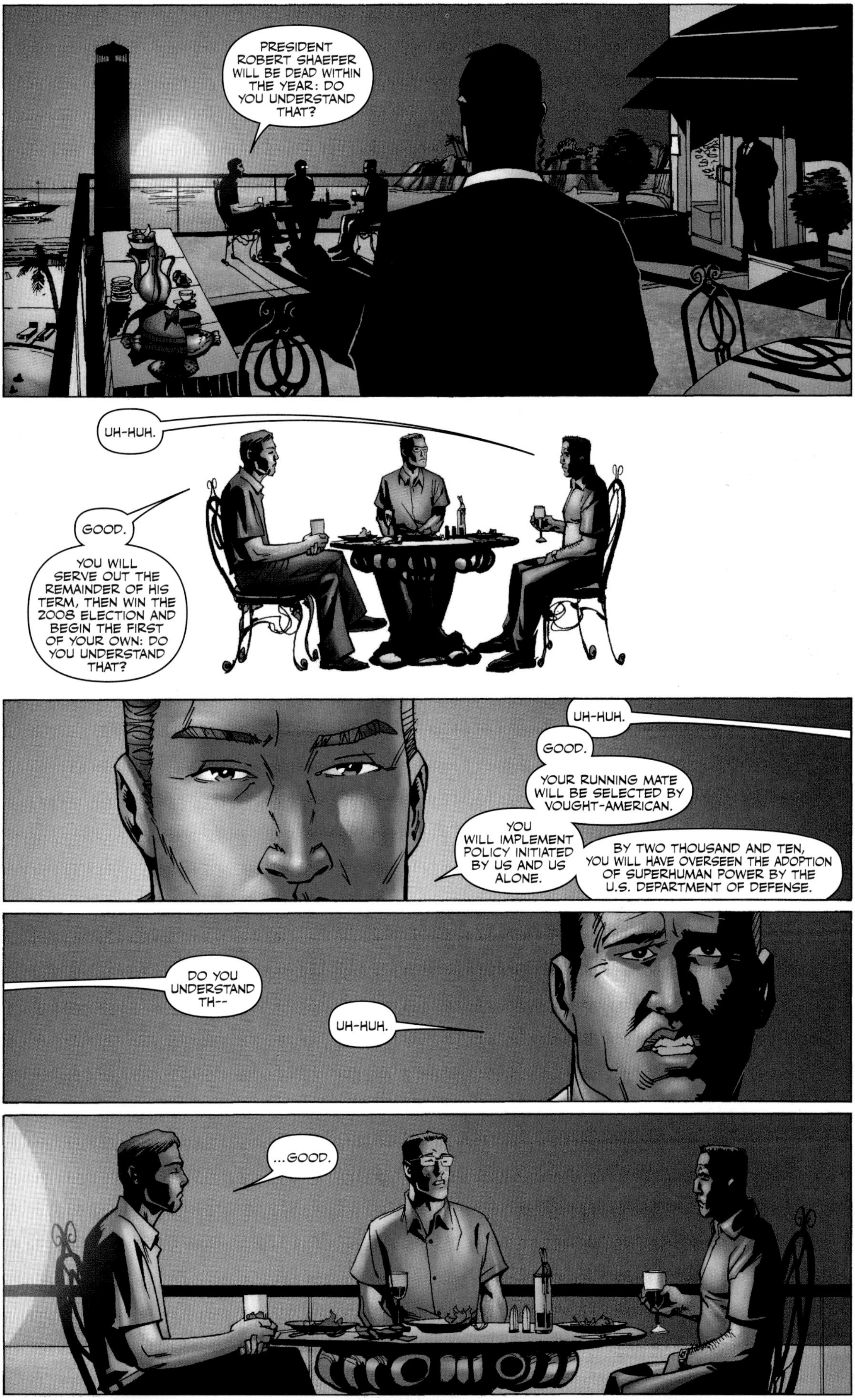
PRESIDENT ROBERT SHAEFER WILL BE DEAD WITHIN THE YEAR: DO YOU UNDERSTAND THAT?
UH-HUH.
GOOD.
YOU WILL SERVE OUT THE REMAINDER OF HIS TERM, THEN WIN THE 2008 ELECTION AND BEGIN THE FIRST OF YOUR OWN: DO YOU UNDERSTAND THAT?
UH-HUH.
GOOD.
YOUR RUNNING MATE WILL BE SELECTED BY VOUGHT-AMERICAN.
YOU WILL IMPLEMENT POLICY INITIATED BY US AND US ALONE.
BY TWO THOUSAND AND TEN, YOU WILL HAVE OVERSEEN THE ADOPTION OF SUPERHUMAN POWER BY THE U.S. DEPARTMENT OF DEFENSE.
DO YOU UNDERSTAND TH--
UH-HUH.
...GOOD.

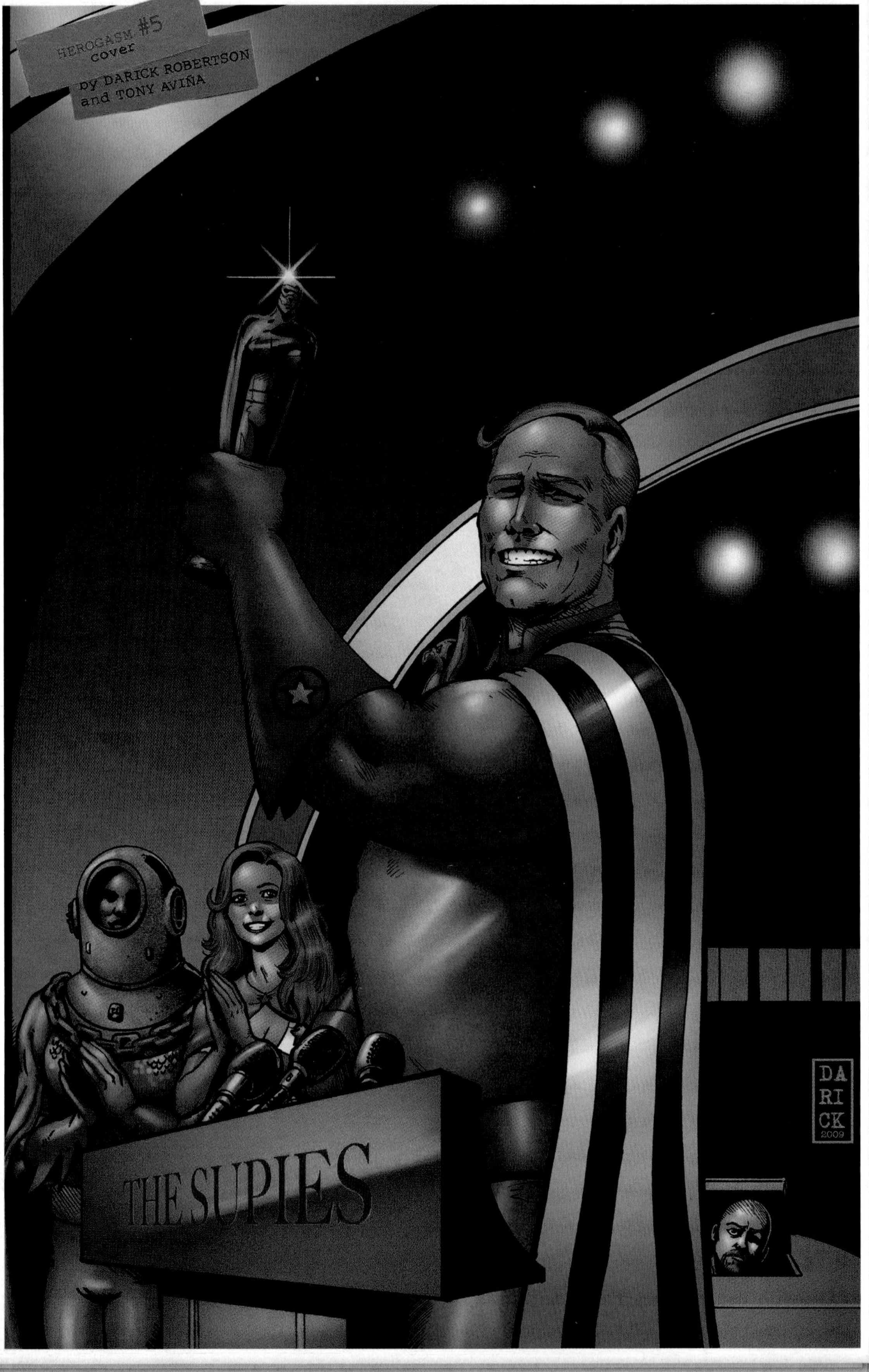

HEROGASM #5 cover
by DARICK ROBERTSON and TONY AVIÑA
THE SUPIES
DA RI CK 2009

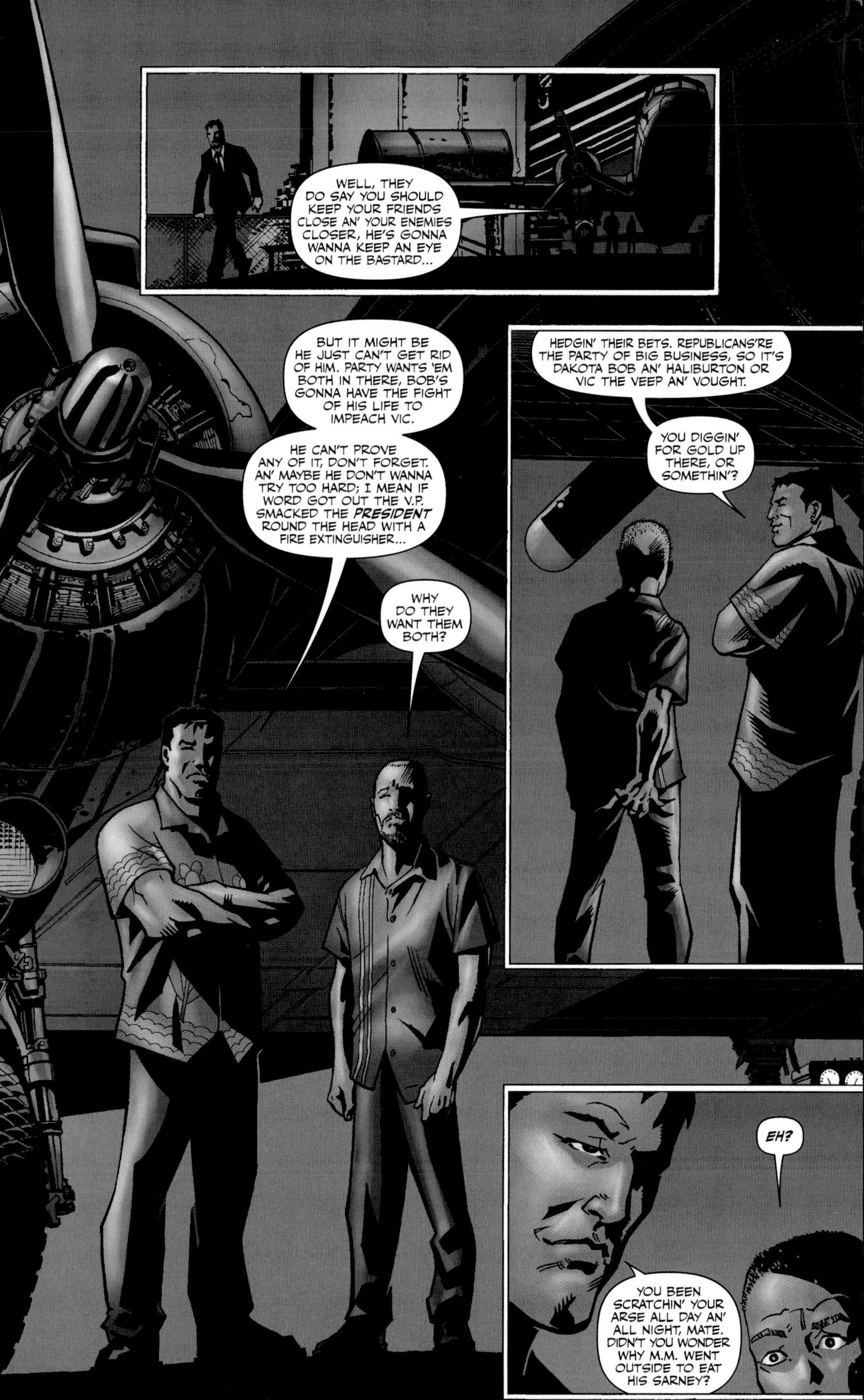
WELL, THEY DO SAY YOU SHOULD KEEP YOUR FRIENDS CLOSE AN' YOUR ENEMIES CLOSER, HE'S GONNA WANNA KEEP AN EYE ON THE BASTARD...
BUT IT MIGHT BE HE JUST CAN'T GET RID OF HIM. PARTY WANTS 'EM BOTH IN THERE, BOB'S GONNA HAVE THE FIGHT OF HIS LIFE TO IMPEACH VIC.
HE CAN'T PROVE ANY OF IT, DON'T FORGET. AN' MAYBE HE DON'T WANNA TRY TOO HARD; I MEAN IF WORD GOT OUT THE V.P. SMACKED THE *PRESIDENT* ROUND THE HEAD WITH A FIRE EXTINGUISHER...
WHY DO THEY WANT THEM BOTH?
HEDGIN' THEIR BETS. REPUBLICANS'RE THE PARTY OF BIG BUSINESS, SO IT'S DAKOTA BOB AN' HALIBURTON OR VIC THE VEEP AN' VOUGHT.
YOU DIGGIN' FOR GOLD UP THERE, OR SOMETHIN'?
EH?
YOU BEEN SCRATCHIN' YOUR ARSE ALL DAY AN' ALL NIGHT, MATE. DIDN'T YOU WONDER WHY M.M. WENT OUTSIDE TO EAT HIS SARNEY?

KEEP YOUR HAIR ON...

I'M SICKA BEIN' JUST A FUCKIN' STANDIN' JOKE AROUND HERE, THAT'S ALL.

I'M JUST A BIT ITCHY, I DIDN'T KNOW IT WAS THAT OBVIOUS...

WHAT, YOU STANDIN' THERE DOIN' YOUR BEST TO FIST YOURSELF? NAH, NOT A BIT OF IT.

LOOK, WHY THE FUCK'RE WE EVEN TALKIN' ABOUT THIS? JESUS *CHRIST*--!

IS HE GONNA BE ALL RIGHT...?

LUCERO?

AYE, I MEAN ARE THEY NO' GONNA HAVE MISSED HIM?

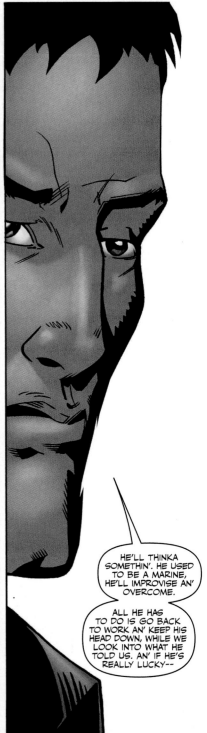

HE'LL THINKA SOMETHIN'. HE USED TO BE A MARINE, HE'LL IMPROVISE AN' OVERCOME.

ALL HE HAS TO DO IS GO BACK TO WORK AN' KEEP HIS HEAD DOWN, WHILE WE LOOK INTO WHAT HE TOLD US. AN' IF HE'S REALLY LUCKY--

HE'LL NEVER HEAR FROM US AGAIN.

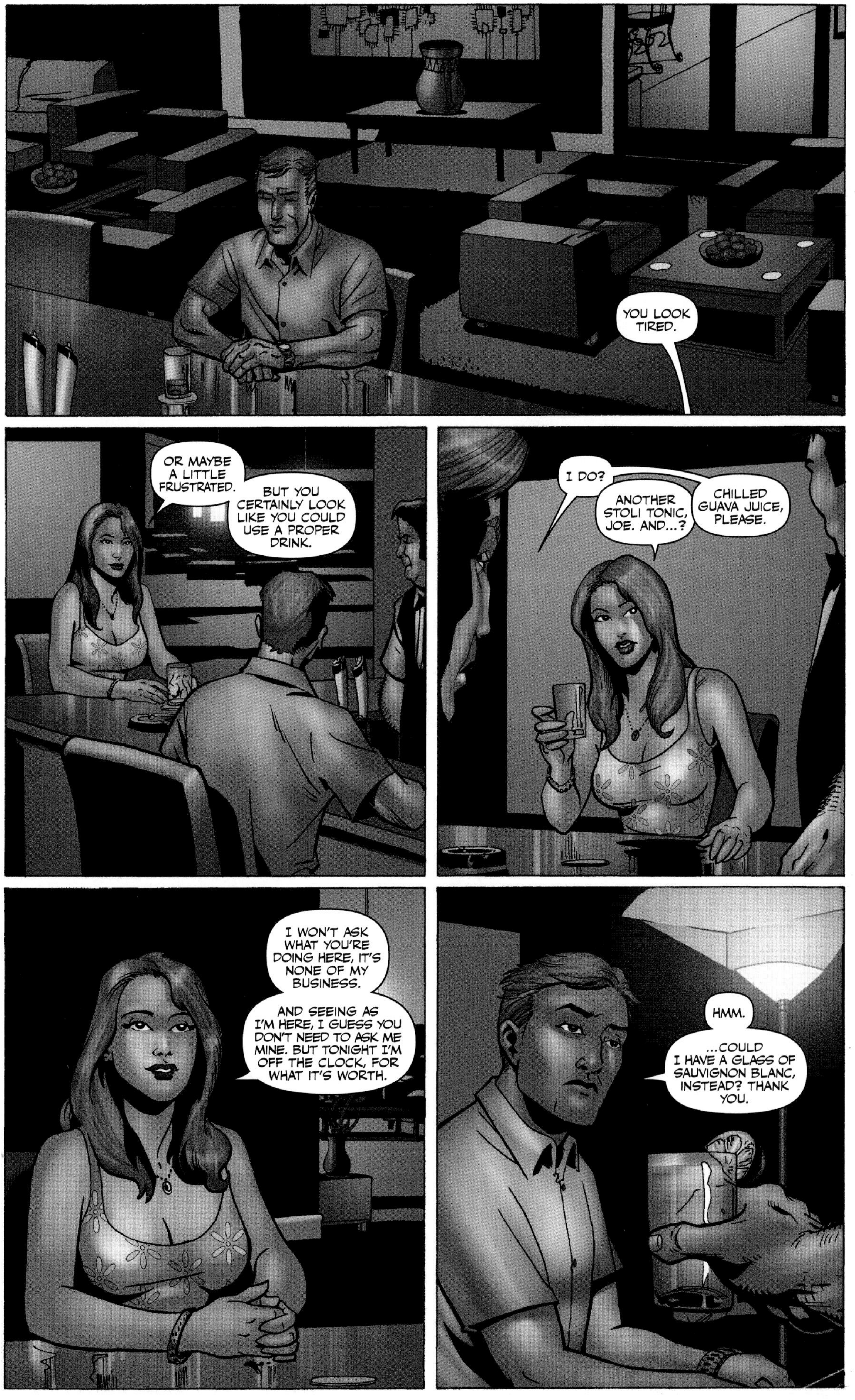
YOU LOOK TIRED.
OR MAYBE A LITTLE FRUSTRATED.
BUT YOU CERTAINLY LOOK LIKE YOU COULD USE A PROPER DRINK.
I DO?
ANOTHER STOLI TONIC, JOE. AND...?
CHILLED GUAVA JUICE, PLEASE.
I WON'T ASK WHAT YOU'RE DOING HERE, IT'S NONE OF MY BUSINESS.
AND SEEING AS I'M HERE, I GUESS YOU DON'T NEED TO ASK ME MINE. BUT TONIGHT I'M OFF THE CLOCK, FOR WHAT IT'S WORTH.
HMM.
...COULD I HAVE A GLASS OF SAUVIGNON BLANC, INSTEAD? THANK YOU.

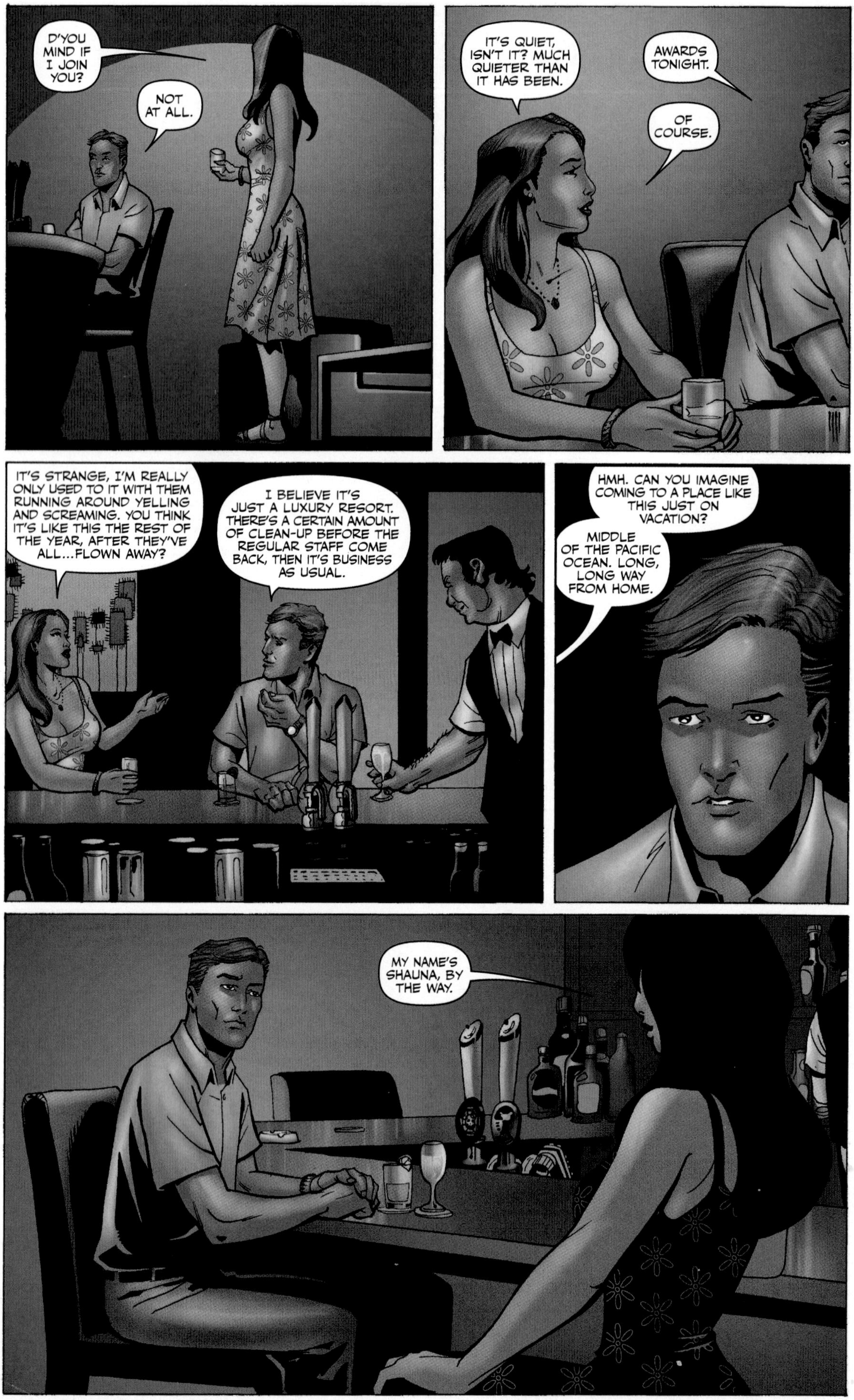
D'YOU MIND IF I JOIN YOU?
NOT AT ALL.
IT'S QUIET, ISN'T IT? MUCH QUIETER THAN IT HAS BEEN.
AWARDS TONIGHT.
OF COURSE.
IT'S STRANGE, I'M REALLY ONLY USED TO IT WITH THEM RUNNING AROUND YELLING AND SCREAMING. YOU THINK IT'S LIKE THIS THE REST OF THE YEAR, AFTER THEY'VE ALL...FLOWN AWAY?
I BELIEVE IT'S JUST A LUXURY RESORT. THERE'S A CERTAIN AMOUNT OF CLEAN-UP BEFORE THE REGULAR STAFF COME BACK, THEN IT'S BUSINESS AS USUAL.
HMH. CAN YOU IMAGINE COMING TO A PLACE LIKE THIS JUST ON VACATION?
MIDDLE OF THE PACIFIC OCEAN. LONG, LONG WAY FROM HOME.
MY NAME'S SHAUNA, BY THE WAY.

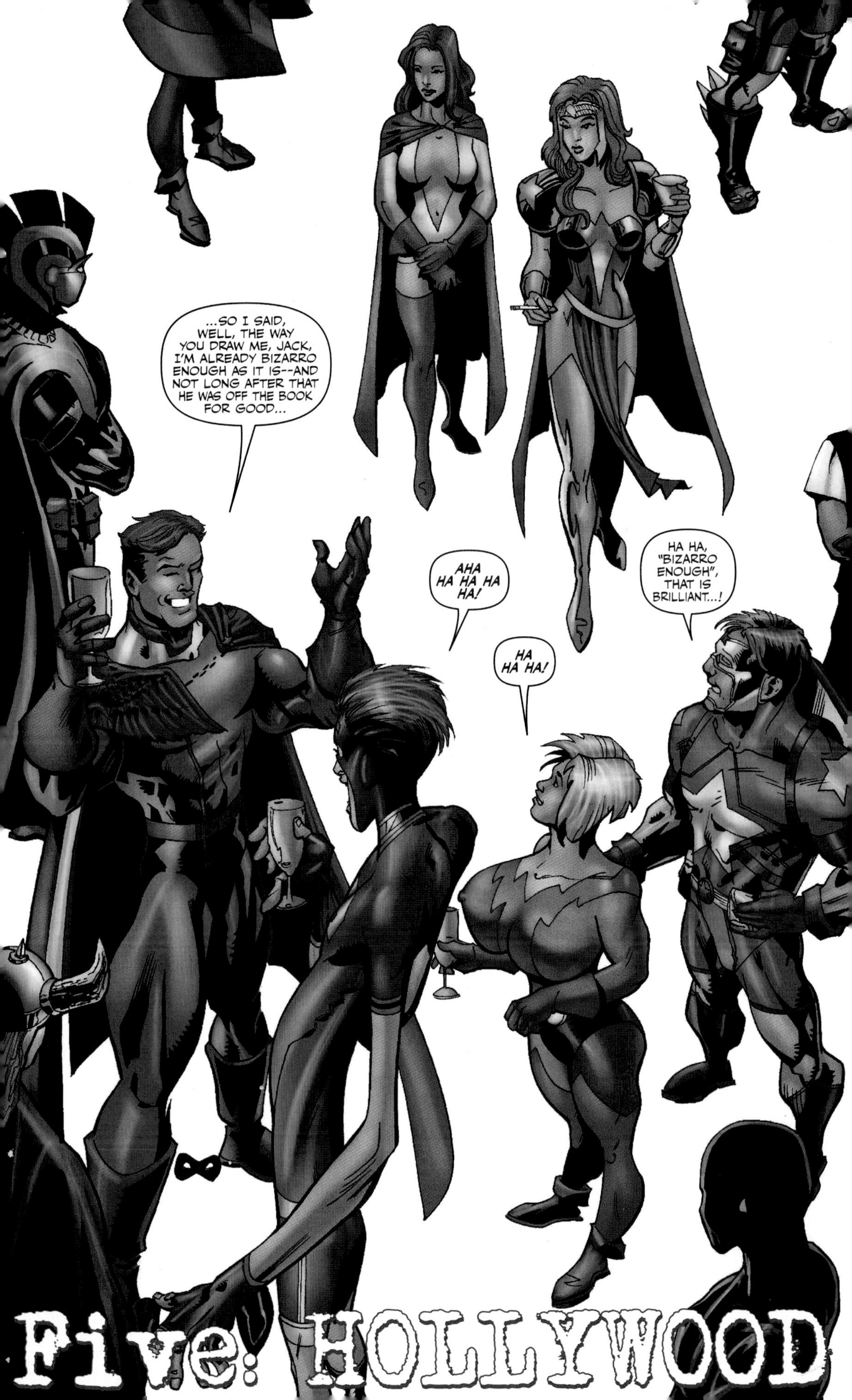
...SO I SAID, WELL, THE WAY YOU DRAW ME, JACK, I'M ALREADY BIZARRO ENOUGH AS IT IS--AND NOT LONG AFTER THAT HE WAS OFF THE BOOK FOR GOOD...
AHA HA HA HA HA!
HA HA HA!
HA HA, "BIZARRO ENOUGH", THAT IS BRILLIANT...!
Five: HOLLYWOOD

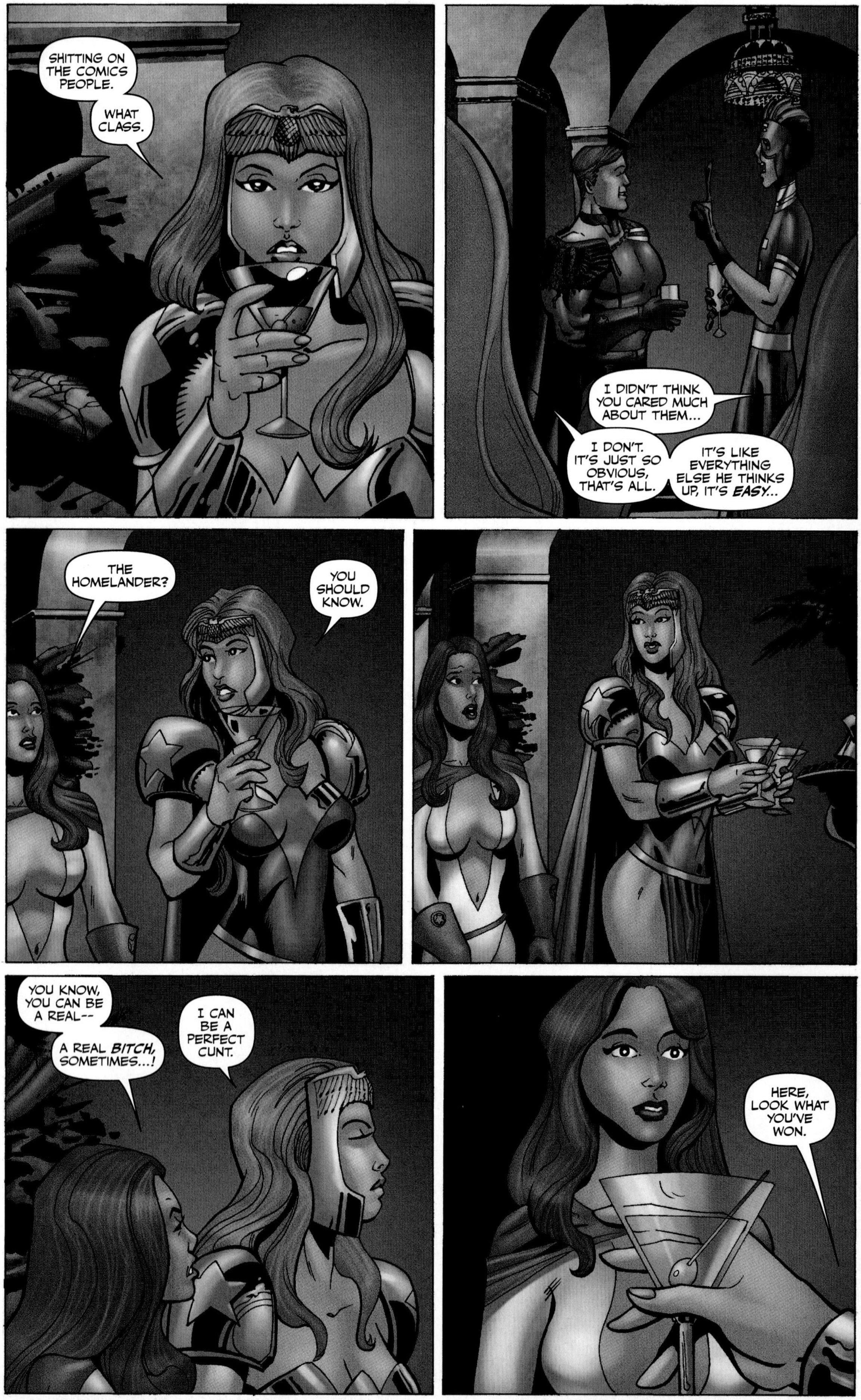
SHITTING ON THE COMICS PEOPLE.
WHAT CLASS.
I DIDN'T THINK YOU CARED MUCH ABOUT THEM...
I DON'T. IT'S JUST SO OBVIOUS, THAT'S ALL.
IT'S LIKE EVERYTHING ELSE HE THINKS UP, IT'S *EASY*...
THE HOMELANDER?
YOU SHOULD KNOW.
YOU KNOW, YOU CAN BE A REAL--
A REAL *BITCH*, SOMETIMES...!
I CAN BE A PERFECT CUNT.
HERE, LOOK WHAT YOU'VE WON.

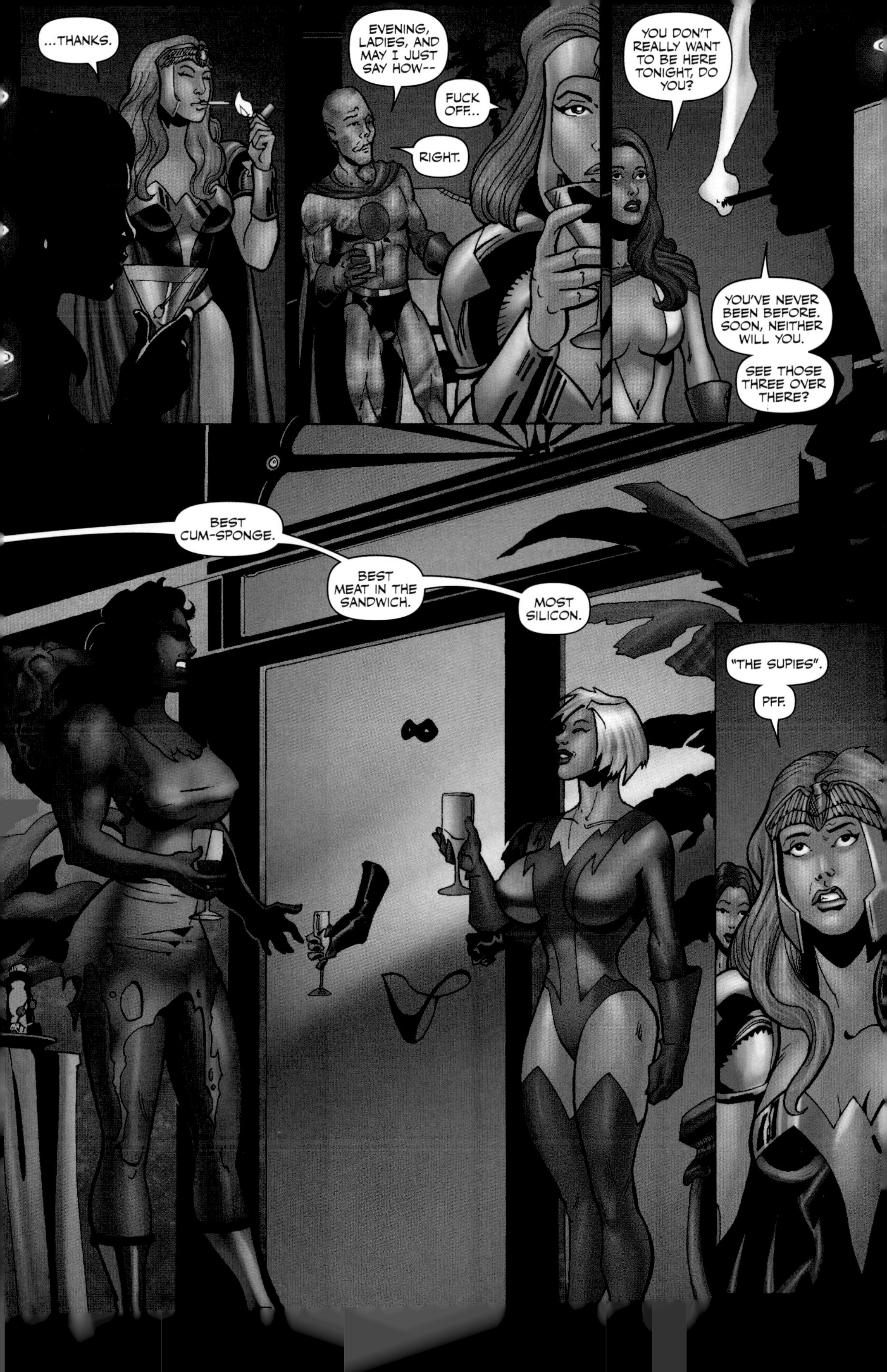
...THANKS.
EVENING, LADIES, AND MAY I JUST SAY HOW--
FUCK OFF...
RIGHT.
YOU DON'T REALLY WANT TO BE HERE TONIGHT, DO YOU?
YOU'VE NEVER BEEN BEFORE. SOON, NEITHER WILL YOU.
SEE THOSE THREE OVER THERE?
BEST CUM-SPONGE.
BEST MEAT IN THE SANDWICH.
MOST SILICON.
"THE SUPIES".
PFF.

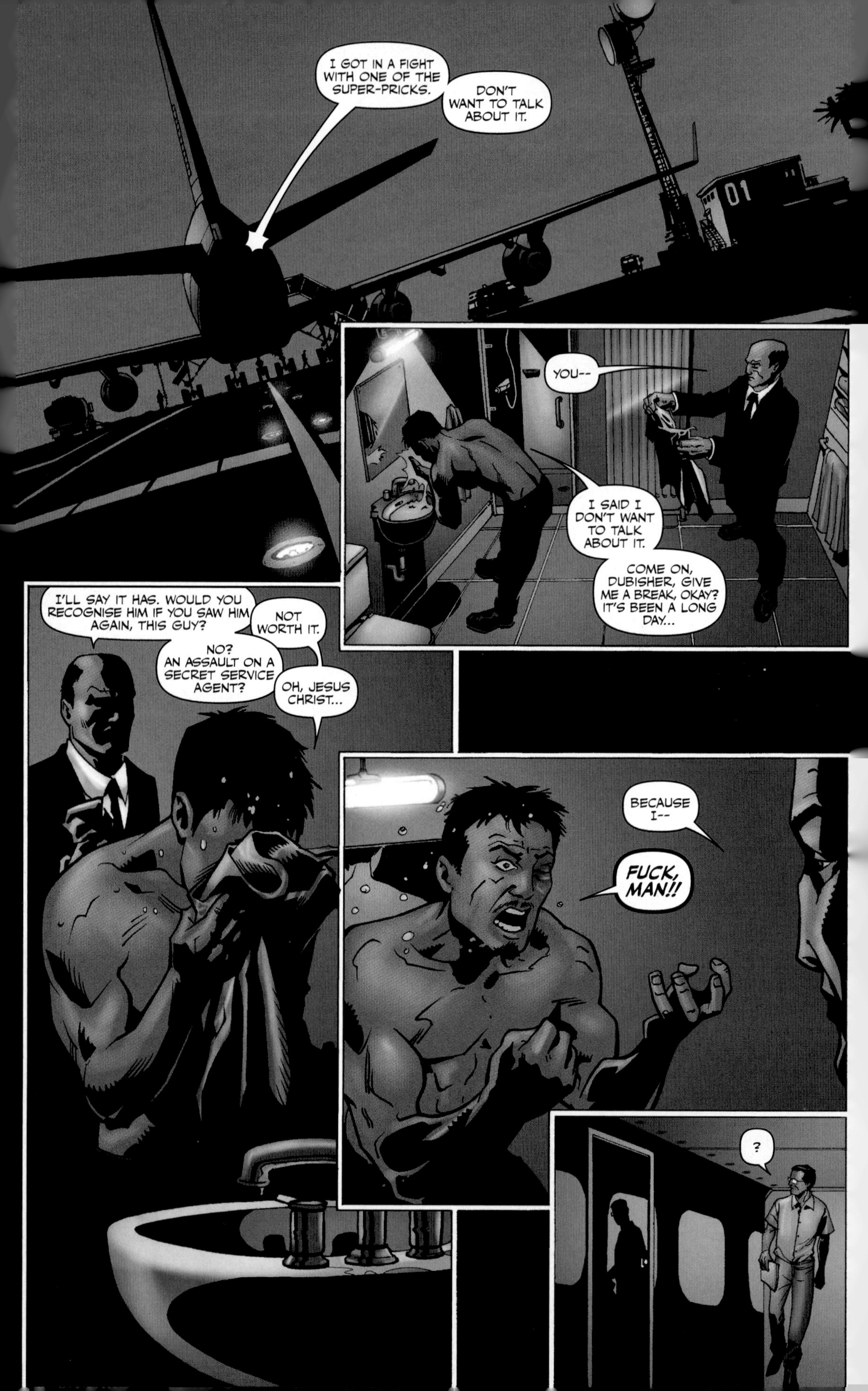
I GOT IN A FIGHT WITH ONE OF THE SUPER-PRICKS.
DON'T WANT TO TALK ABOUT IT.
YOU--
I SAID I DON'T WANT TO TALK ABOUT IT.
COME ON, DUBISHER, GIVE ME A BREAK, OKAY? IT'S BEEN A LONG DAY...
I'LL SAY IT HAS. WOULD YOU RECOGNISE HIM IF YOU SAW HIM AGAIN, THIS GUY?
NOT WORTH IT.
NO? AN ASSAULT ON A SECRET SERVICE AGENT?
OH, JESUS CHRIST...
BECAUSE I--
FUCK, MAN!!
?

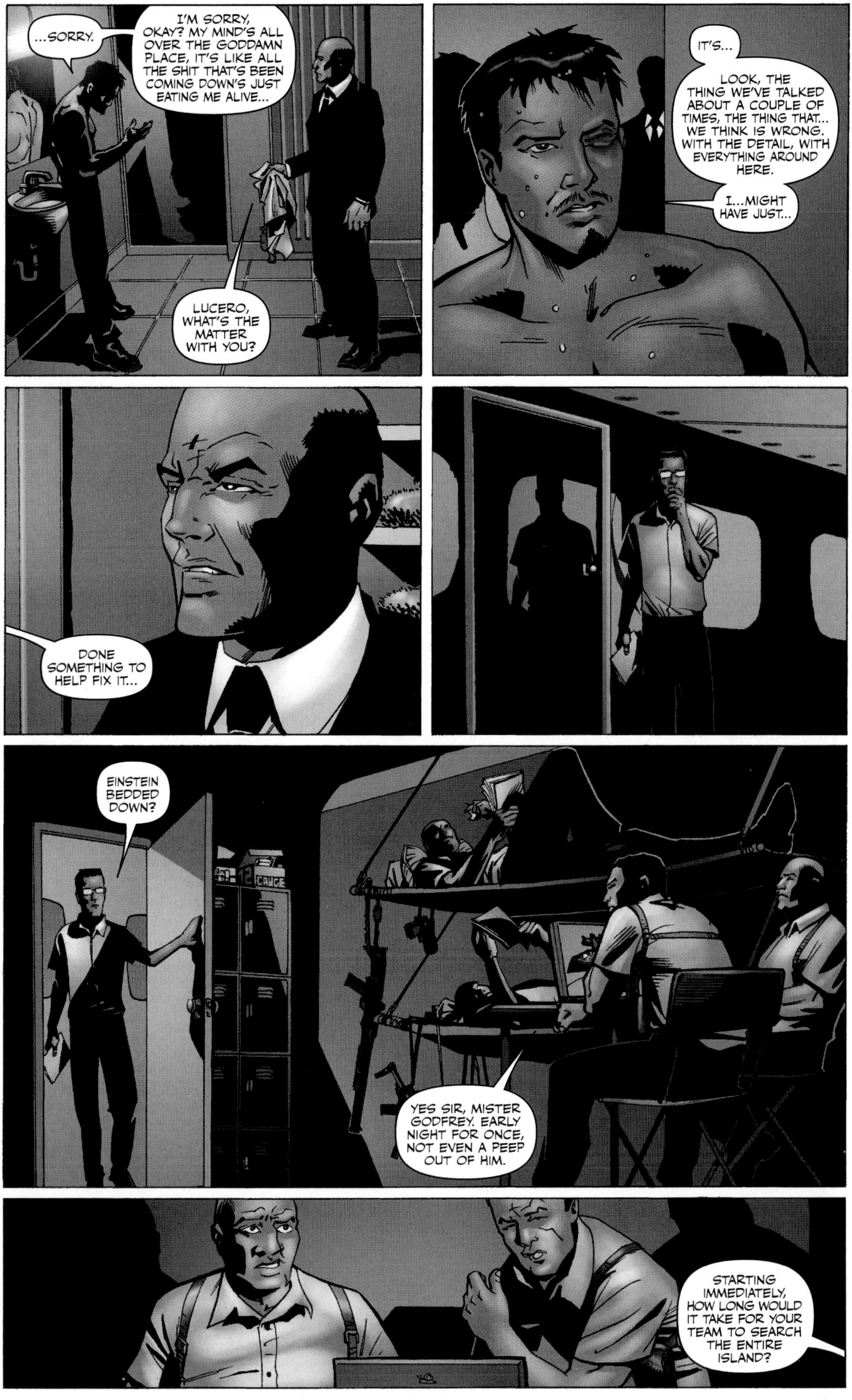
...SORRY.
I'M SORRY, OKAY? MY MIND'S ALL OVER THE GODDAMN PLACE, IT'S LIKE ALL THE SHIT THAT'S BEEN COMING DOWN'S JUST EATING ME ALIVE...
LUCERO, WHAT'S THE MATTER WITH YOU?
IT'S...
LOOK, THE THING WE'VE TALKED ABOUT A COUPLE OF TIMES, THE THING THAT... WE THINK IS WRONG. WITH THE DETAIL, WITH EVERYTHING AROUND HERE.
I...MIGHT HAVE JUST...
DONE SOMETHING TO HELP FIX IT...
EINSTEIN BEDDED DOWN?
YES SIR, MISTER GODFREY. EARLY NIGHT FOR ONCE, NOT EVEN A PEEP OUT OF HIM.
STARTING IMMEDIATELY, HOW LONG WOULD IT TAKE FOR YOUR TEAM TO SEARCH THE ENTIRE ISLAND?

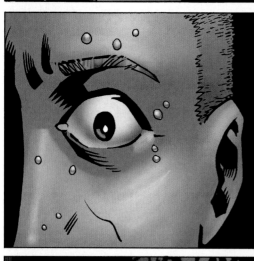

WHY'S HE NO' TOLD THEM ABOUT US?

AN' WHY--

WHY...

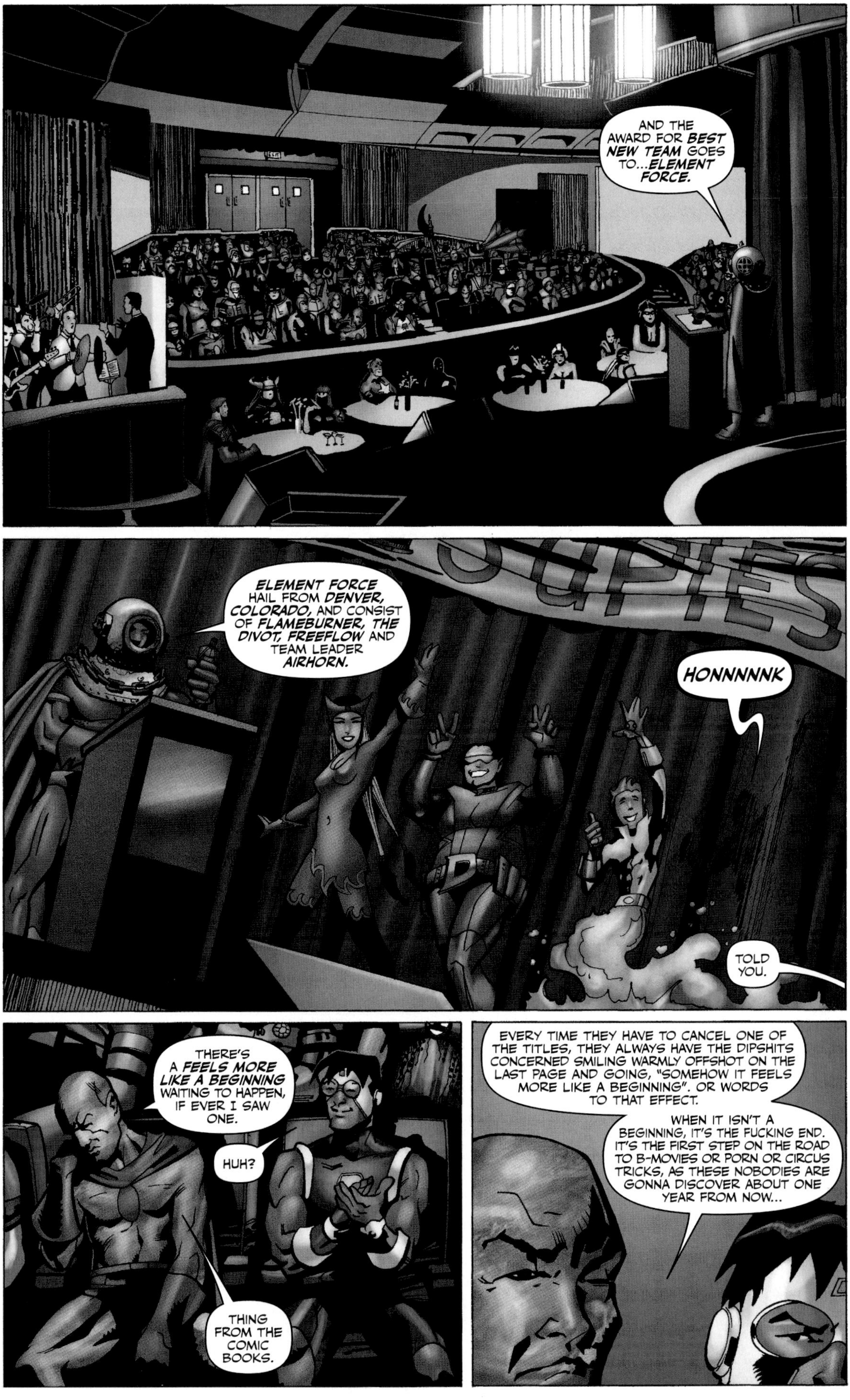
AND THE AWARD FOR **BEST NEW TEAM** GOES TO...**ELEMENT FORCE.**
ELEMENT FORCE HAIL FROM **DENVER, COLORADO,** AND CONSIST OF **FLAMEBURNER, THE DIVOT, FREEFLOW** AND TEAM LEADER **AIRHORN.**
HONNNNNK
TOLD YOU.
THERE'S A **FEELS MORE LIKE A BEGINNING** WAITING TO HAPPEN, IF EVER I SAW ONE.
HUH?
THING FROM THE COMIC BOOKS.
EVERY TIME THEY HAVE TO CANCEL ONE OF THE TITLES, THEY ALWAYS HAVE THE DIPSHITS CONCERNED SMILING WARMLY OFFSHOT ON THE LAST PAGE AND GOING, "SOMEHOW IT FEELS MORE LIKE A BEGINNING". OR WORDS TO THAT EFFECT.
WHEN IT ISN'T A BEGINNING, IT'S THE FUCKING END. IT'S THE FIRST STEP ON THE ROAD TO B-MOVIES OR PORN OR CIRCUS TRICKS, AS THESE NOBODIES ARE GONNA DISCOVER ABOUT ONE YEAR FROM NOW...

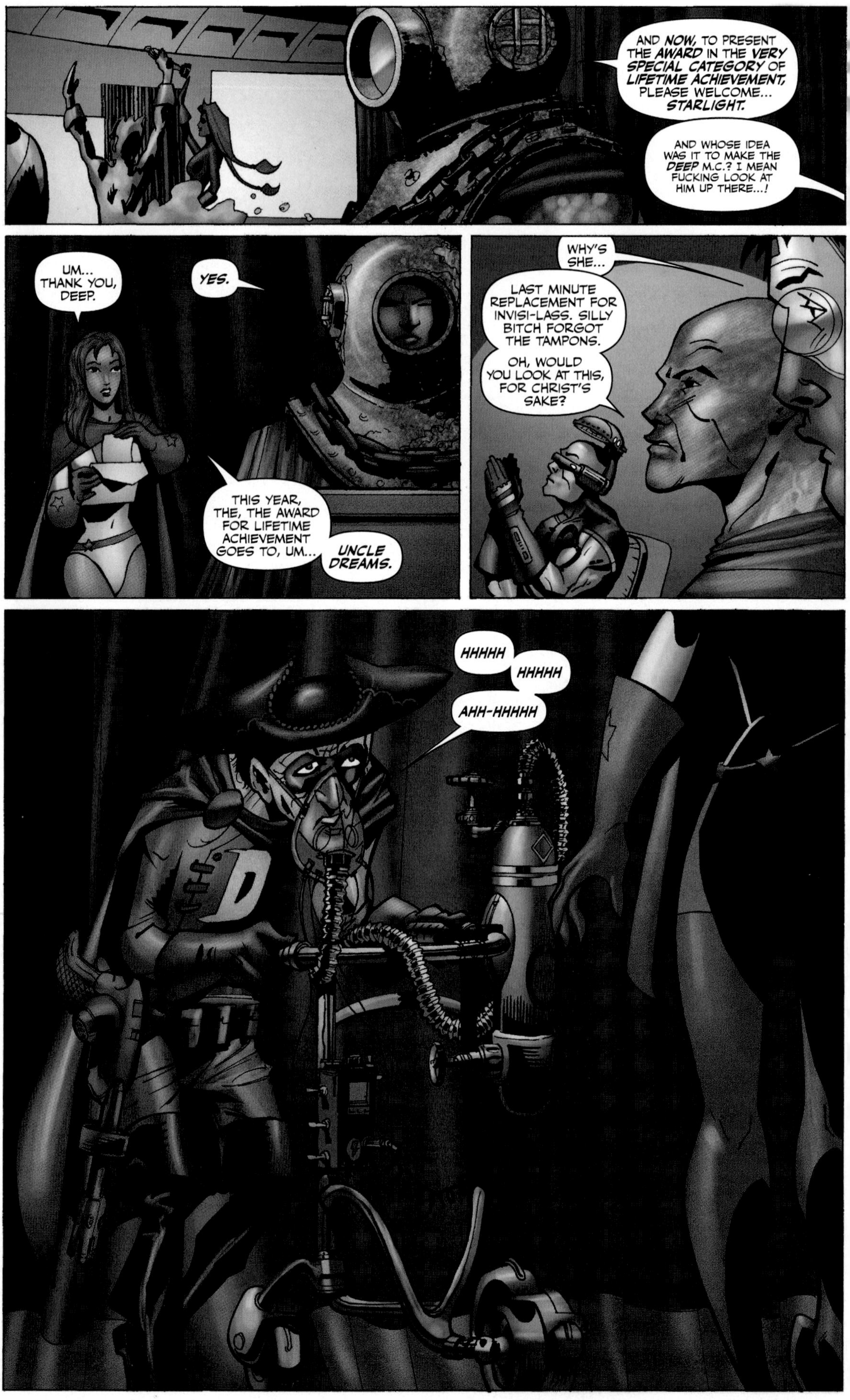

AND NOW, TO PRESENT THE AWARD IN THE VERY SPECIAL CATEGORY OF LIFETIME ACHIEVEMENT, PLEASE WELCOME... STARLIGHT.
AND WHOSE IDEA WAS IT TO MAKE THE DEEP M.C.? I MEAN FUCKING LOOK AT HIM UP THERE...!
UM... THANK YOU, DEEP.
YES.
THIS YEAR, THE, THE AWARD FOR LIFETIME ACHIEVEMENT GOES TO, UM...
UNCLE DREAMS.
WHY'S SHE...
LAST MINUTE REPLACEMENT FOR INVISI-LASS. SILLY BITCH FORGOT THE TAMPONS.
OH, WOULD YOU LOOK AT THIS, FOR CHRIST'S SAKE?
HHHHH
HHHHH
AHH-HHHHH

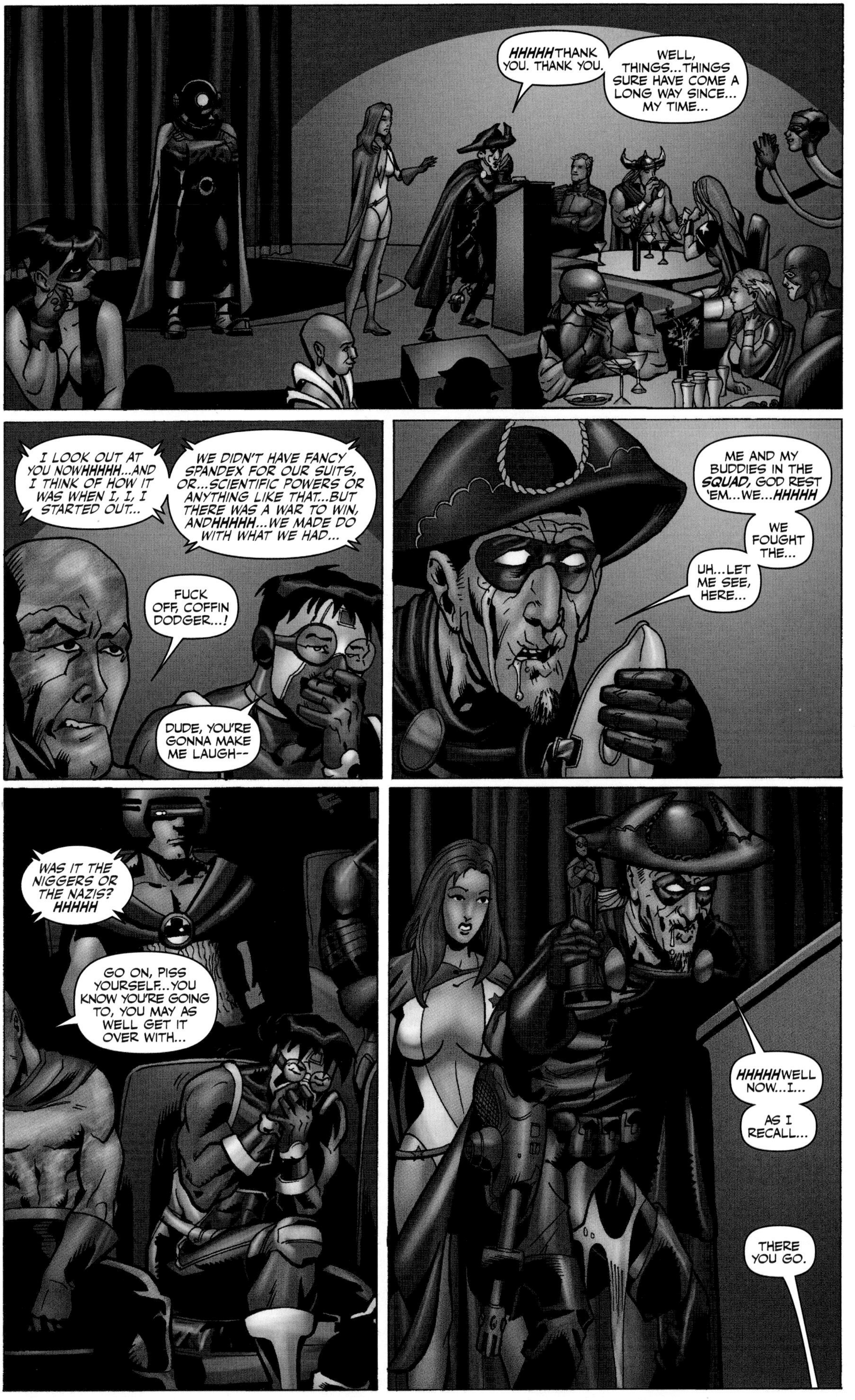

HHHHH THANK YOU. THANK YOU.
WELL, THINGS...THINGS SURE HAVE COME A LONG WAY SINCE... MY TIME...
I LOOK OUT AT YOU NOWHHHHH...AND I THINK OF HOW IT WAS WHEN I, I, I STARTED OUT...
WE DIDN'T HAVE FANCY SPANDEX FOR OUR SUITS, OR...SCIENTIFIC POWERS OR ANYTHING LIKE THAT...BUT THERE WAS A WAR TO WIN, ANDHHHHH...WE MADE DO WITH WHAT WE HAD...
FUCK OFF, COFFIN DODGER...!
DUDE, YOU'RE GONNA MAKE ME LAUGH--
ME AND MY BUDDIES IN THE SQUAD, GOD REST 'EM...WE...HHHHH
WE FOUGHT THE...
UH...LET ME SEE, HERE...
WAS IT THE NIGGERS OR THE NAZIS? HHHHH
GO ON, PISS YOURSELF...YOU KNOW YOU'RE GOING TO, YOU MAY AS WELL GET IT OVER WITH...
HHHHH WELL NOW...I...
AS I RECALL...
THERE YOU GO.

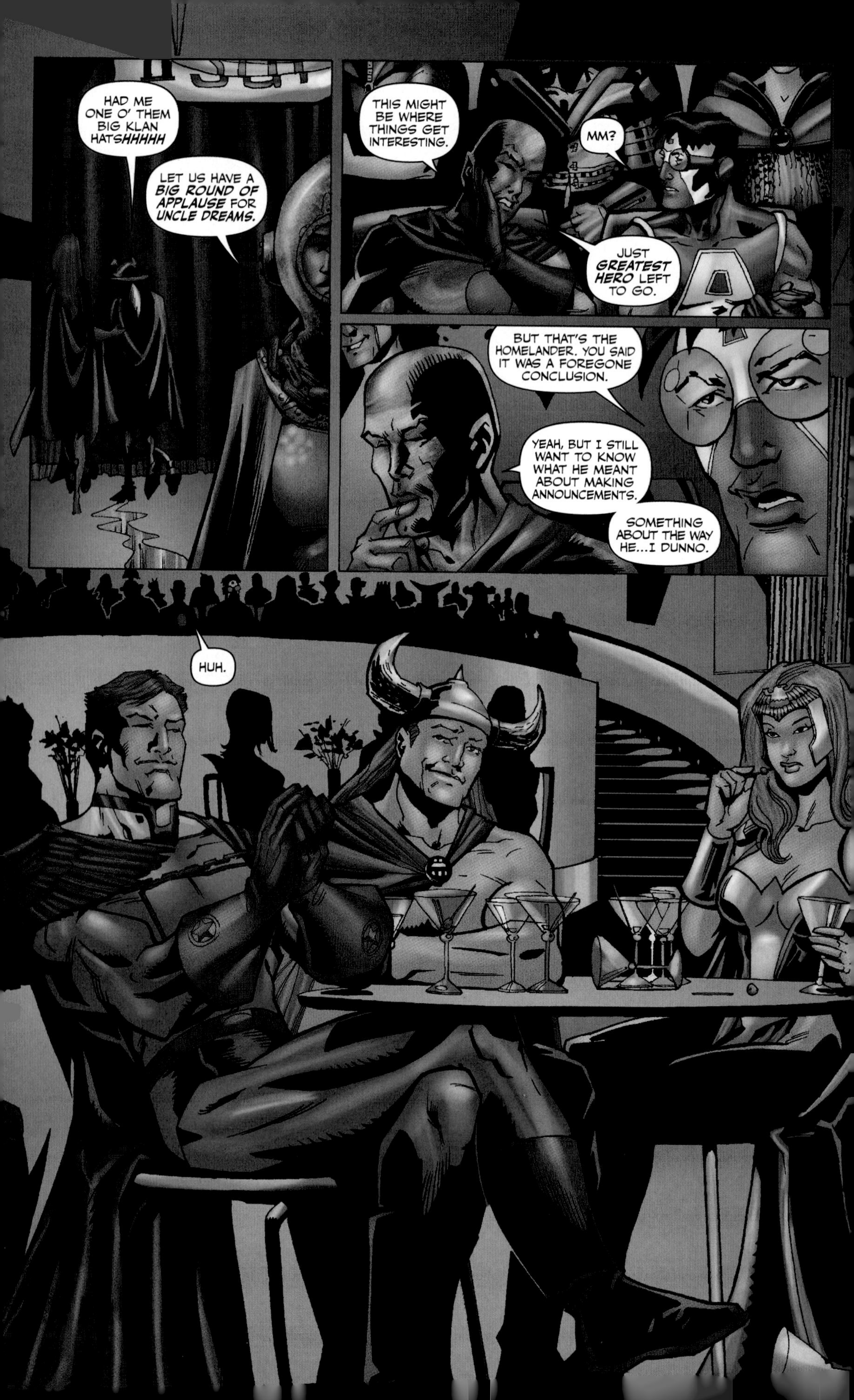
HAD ME ONE O' THEM BIG KLAN HATSHHHHH
LET US HAVE A BIG ROUND OF APPLAUSE FOR UNCLE DREAMS.
THIS MIGHT BE WHERE THINGS GET INTERESTING.
MM?
JUST GREATEST HERO LEFT TO GO.
BUT THAT'S THE HOMELANDER. YOU SAID IT WAS A FOREGONE CONCLUSION.
YEAH, BUT I STILL WANT TO KNOW WHAT HE MEANT ABOUT MAKING ANNOUNCEMENTS.
SOMETHING ABOUT THE WAY HE...I DUNNO.
HUH.

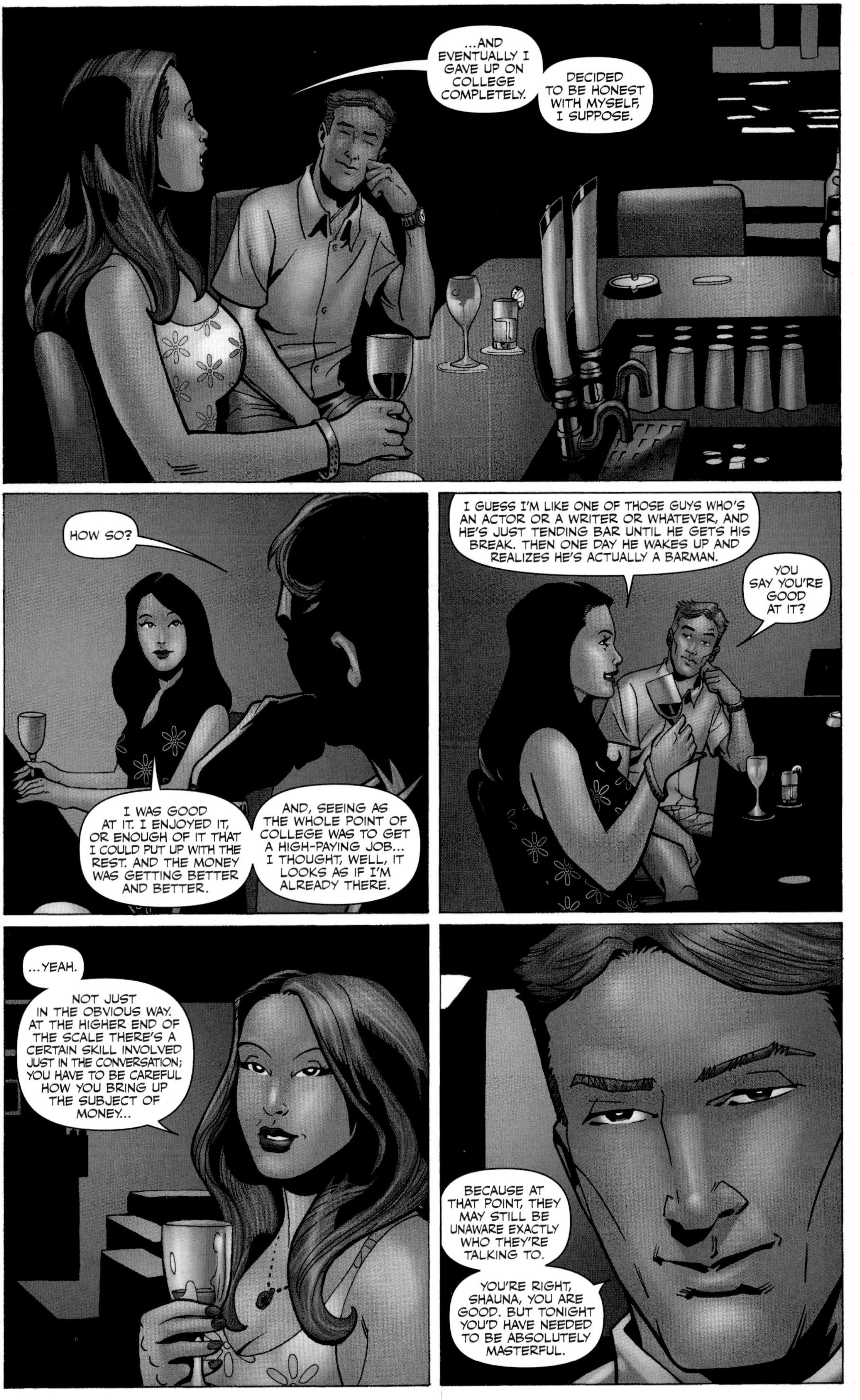
...AND EVENTUALLY I GAVE UP ON COLLEGE COMPLETELY.
DECIDED TO BE HONEST WITH MYSELF, I SUPPOSE.
HOW SO?
I WAS GOOD AT IT. I ENJOYED IT, OR ENOUGH OF IT THAT I COULD PUT UP WITH THE REST. AND THE MONEY WAS GETTING BETTER AND BETTER.
AND, SEEING AS THE WHOLE POINT OF COLLEGE WAS TO GET A HIGH-PAYING JOB... I THOUGHT, WELL, IT LOOKS AS IF I'M ALREADY THERE.
I GUESS I'M LIKE ONE OF THOSE GUYS WHO'S AN ACTOR OR A WRITER OR WHATEVER, AND HE'S JUST TENDING BAR UNTIL HE GETS HIS BREAK. THEN ONE DAY HE WAKES UP AND REALIZES HE'S ACTUALLY A BARMAN.
YOU SAY YOU'RE GOOD AT IT?
...YEAH.
NOT JUST IN THE OBVIOUS WAY. AT THE HIGHER END OF THE SCALE THERE'S A CERTAIN SKILL INVOLVED JUST IN THE CONVERSATION; YOU HAVE TO BE CAREFUL HOW YOU BRING UP THE SUBJECT OF MONEY...
BECAUSE AT THAT POINT, THEY MAY STILL BE UNAWARE EXACTLY WHO THEY'RE TALKING TO.
YOU'RE RIGHT, SHAUNA, YOU ARE GOOD. BUT TONIGHT YOU'D HAVE NEEDED TO BE ABSOLUTELY MASTERFUL.

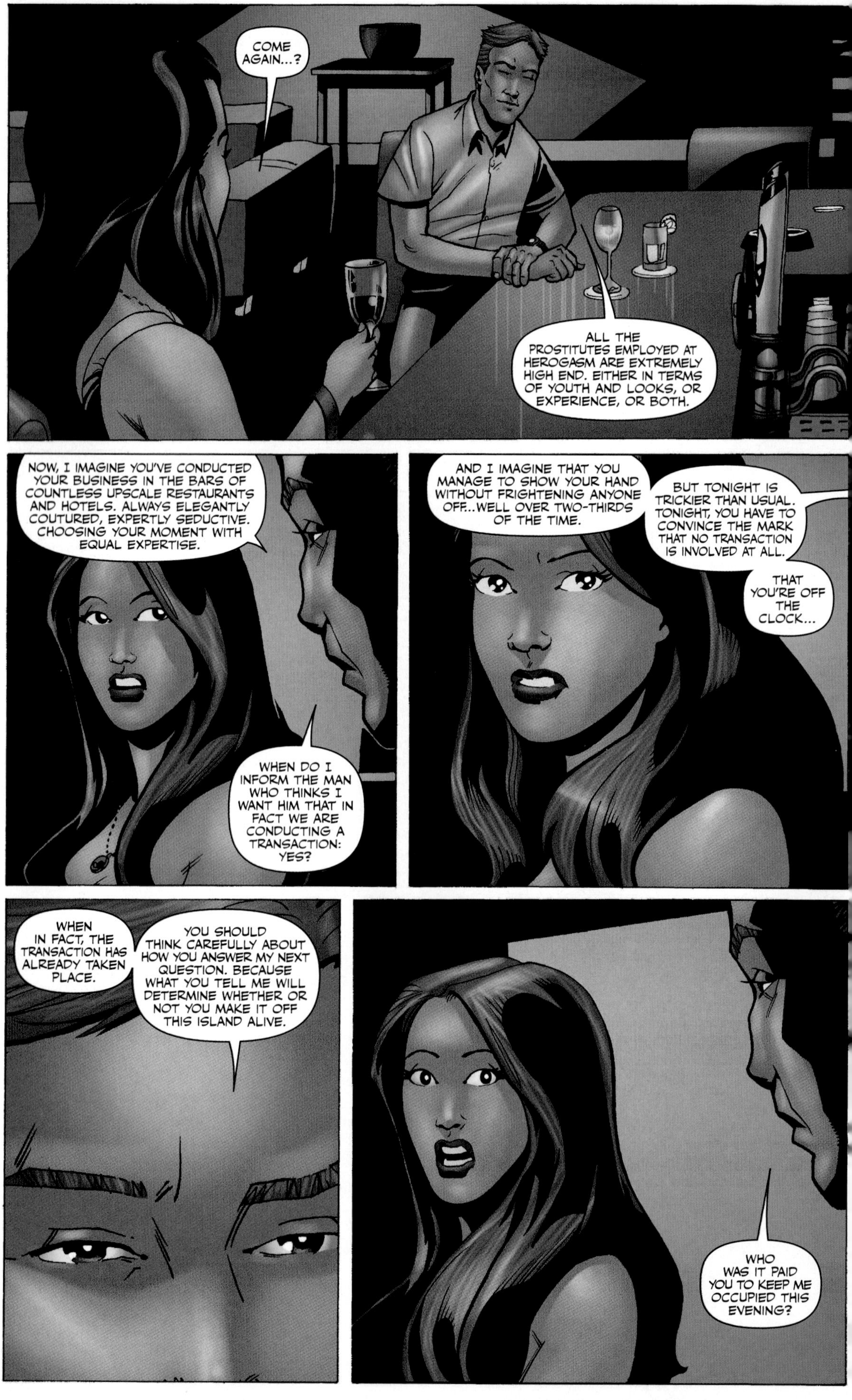

COME AGAIN...?
ALL THE PROSTITUTES EMPLOYED AT HEROGASM ARE EXTREMELY HIGH END. EITHER IN TERMS OF YOUTH AND LOOKS, OR EXPERIENCE, OR BOTH.
NOW, I IMAGINE YOU'VE CONDUCTED YOUR BUSINESS IN THE BARS OF COUNTLESS UPSCALE RESTAURANTS AND HOTELS. ALWAYS ELEGANTLY COUTURED, EXPERTLY SEDUCTIVE. CHOOSING YOUR MOMENT WITH EQUAL EXPERTISE.
WHEN DO I INFORM THE MAN WHO THINKS I WANT HIM THAT IN FACT WE ARE CONDUCTING A TRANSACTION: YES?
AND I IMAGINE THAT YOU MANAGE TO SHOW YOUR HAND WITHOUT FRIGHTENING ANYONE OFF...WELL OVER TWO-THIRDS OF THE TIME.
BUT TONIGHT IS TRICKIER THAN USUAL. TONIGHT, YOU HAVE TO CONVINCE THE MARK THAT NO TRANSACTION IS INVOLVED AT ALL.
THAT YOU'RE OFF THE CLOCK...
WHEN IN FACT, THE TRANSACTION HAS ALREADY TAKEN PLACE.
YOU SHOULD THINK CAREFULLY ABOUT HOW YOU ANSWER MY NEXT QUESTION. BECAUSE WHAT YOU TELL ME WILL DETERMINE WHETHER OR NOT YOU MAKE IT OFF THIS ISLAND ALIVE.
WHO WAS IT PAID YOU TO KEEP ME OCCUPIED THIS EVENING?

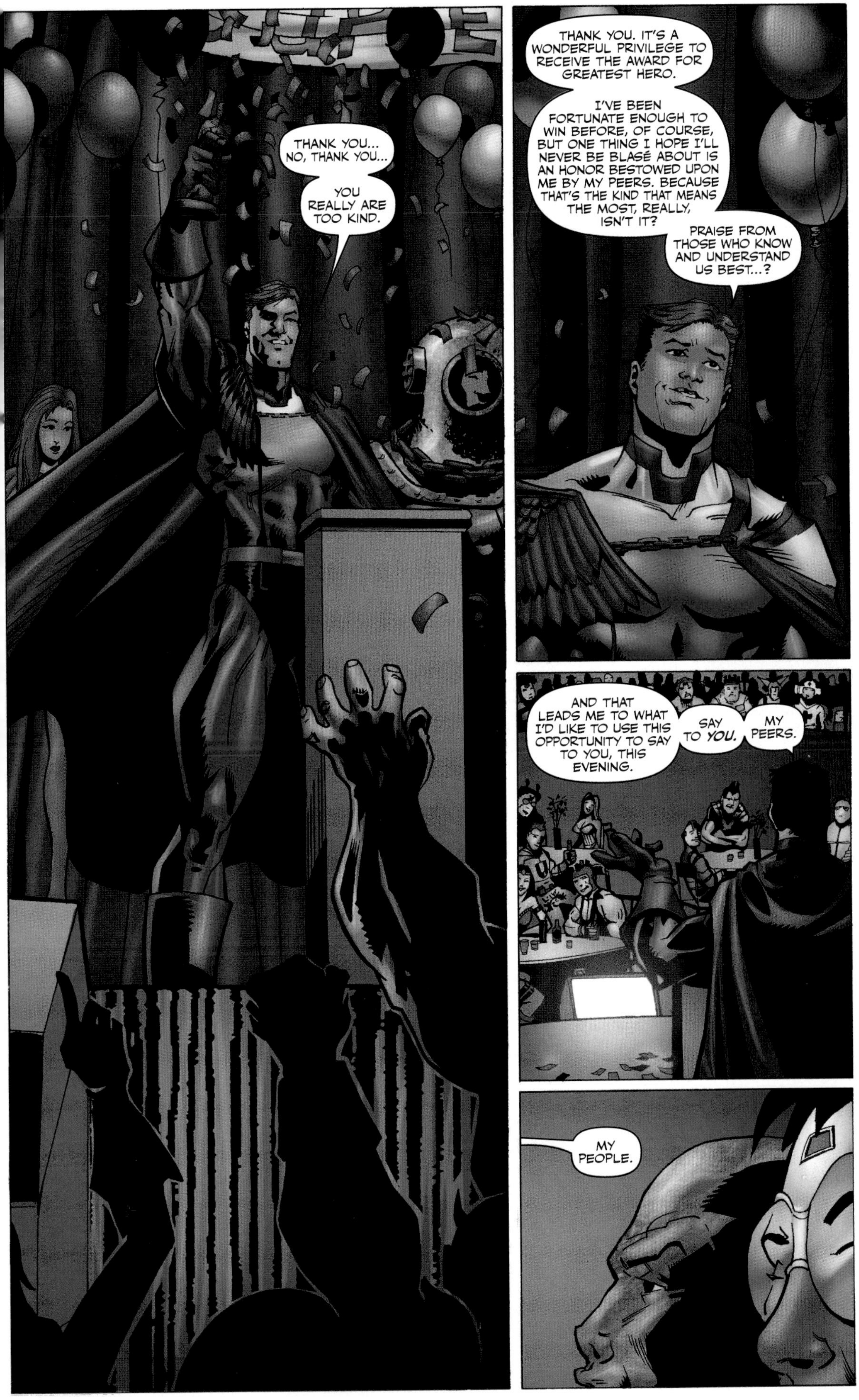
THANK YOU... NO, THANK YOU...
YOU REALLY ARE TOO KIND.
THANK YOU. IT'S A WONDERFUL PRIVILEGE TO RECEIVE THE AWARD FOR GREATEST HERO.
I'VE BEEN FORTUNATE ENOUGH TO WIN BEFORE, OF COURSE, BUT ONE THING I HOPE I'LL NEVER BE BLASÉ ABOUT IS AN HONOR BESTOWED UPON ME BY MY PEERS. BECAUSE THAT'S THE KIND THAT MEANS THE MOST, REALLY, ISN'T IT?
PRAISE FROM THOSE WHO KNOW AND UNDERSTAND US BEST...?
AND THAT LEADS ME TO WHAT I'D LIKE TO USE THIS OPPORTUNITY TO SAY TO YOU, THIS EVENING.
SAY TO *YOU*.
MY PEERS.
MY PEOPLE.

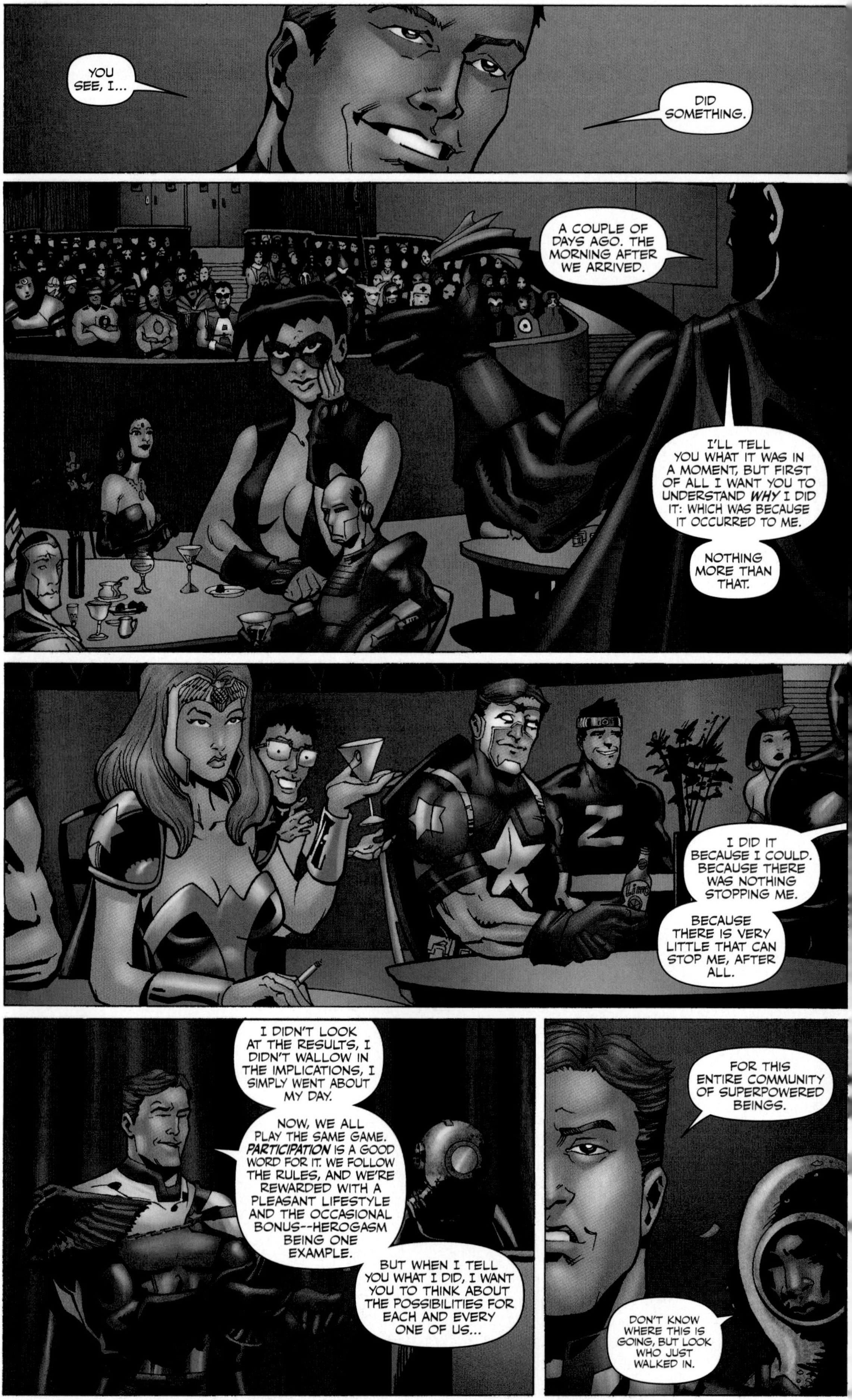
YOU SEE, I...
DID SOMETHING.
A COUPLE OF DAYS AGO. THE MORNING AFTER WE ARRIVED.
I'LL TELL YOU WHAT IT WAS IN A MOMENT, BUT FIRST OF ALL I WANT YOU TO UNDERSTAND *WHY* I DID IT: WHICH WAS BECAUSE IT OCCURRED TO ME.
NOTHING MORE THAN THAT.
I DID IT BECAUSE I COULD. BECAUSE THERE WAS NOTHING STOPPING ME.
BECAUSE THERE IS VERY LITTLE THAT CAN STOP ME, AFTER ALL.
I DIDN'T LOOK AT THE RESULTS, I DIDN'T WALLOW IN THE IMPLICATIONS, I SIMPLY WENT ABOUT MY DAY.
NOW, WE ALL PLAY THE SAME GAME. *PARTICIPATION* IS A GOOD WORD FOR IT. WE FOLLOW THE RULES, AND WE'RE REWARDED WITH A PLEASANT LIFESTYLE AND THE OCCASIONAL BONUS--HEROGASM BEING ONE EXAMPLE.
BUT WHEN I TELL YOU WHAT I DID, I WANT YOU TO THINK ABOUT THE POSSIBILITIES FOR EACH AND EVERY ONE OF US...
FOR THIS ENTIRE COMMUNITY OF SUPERPOWERED BEINGS.
DON'T KNOW WHERE THIS IS GOING, BUT LOOK WHO JUST WALKED IN.

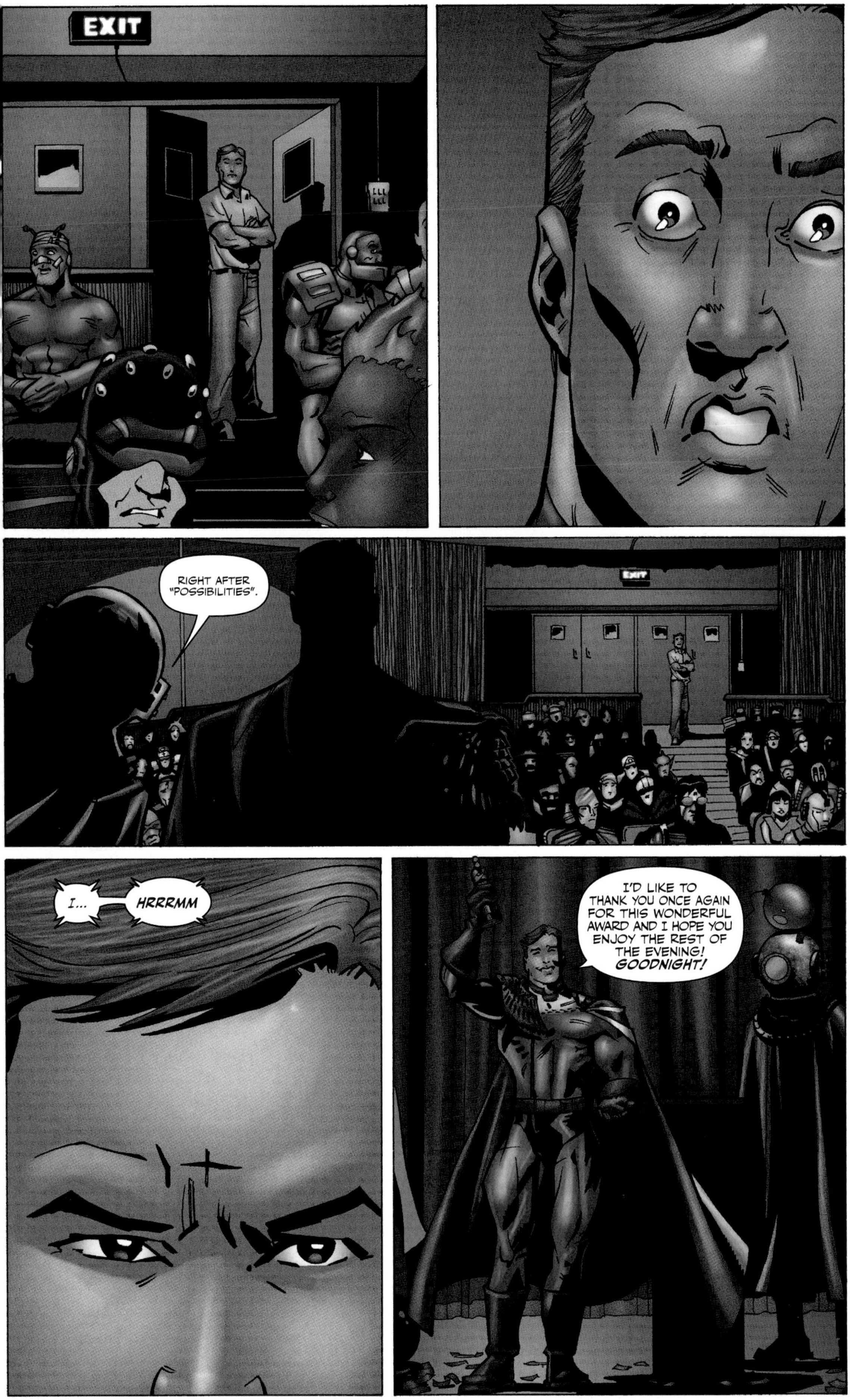
EXIT
RIGHT AFTER "POSSIBILITIES".
EXIT
I...
HRRRMM
I'D LIKE TO THANK YOU ONCE AGAIN FOR THIS WONDERFUL AWARD AND I HOPE YOU ENJOY THE REST OF THE EVENING! *GOODNIGHT!*

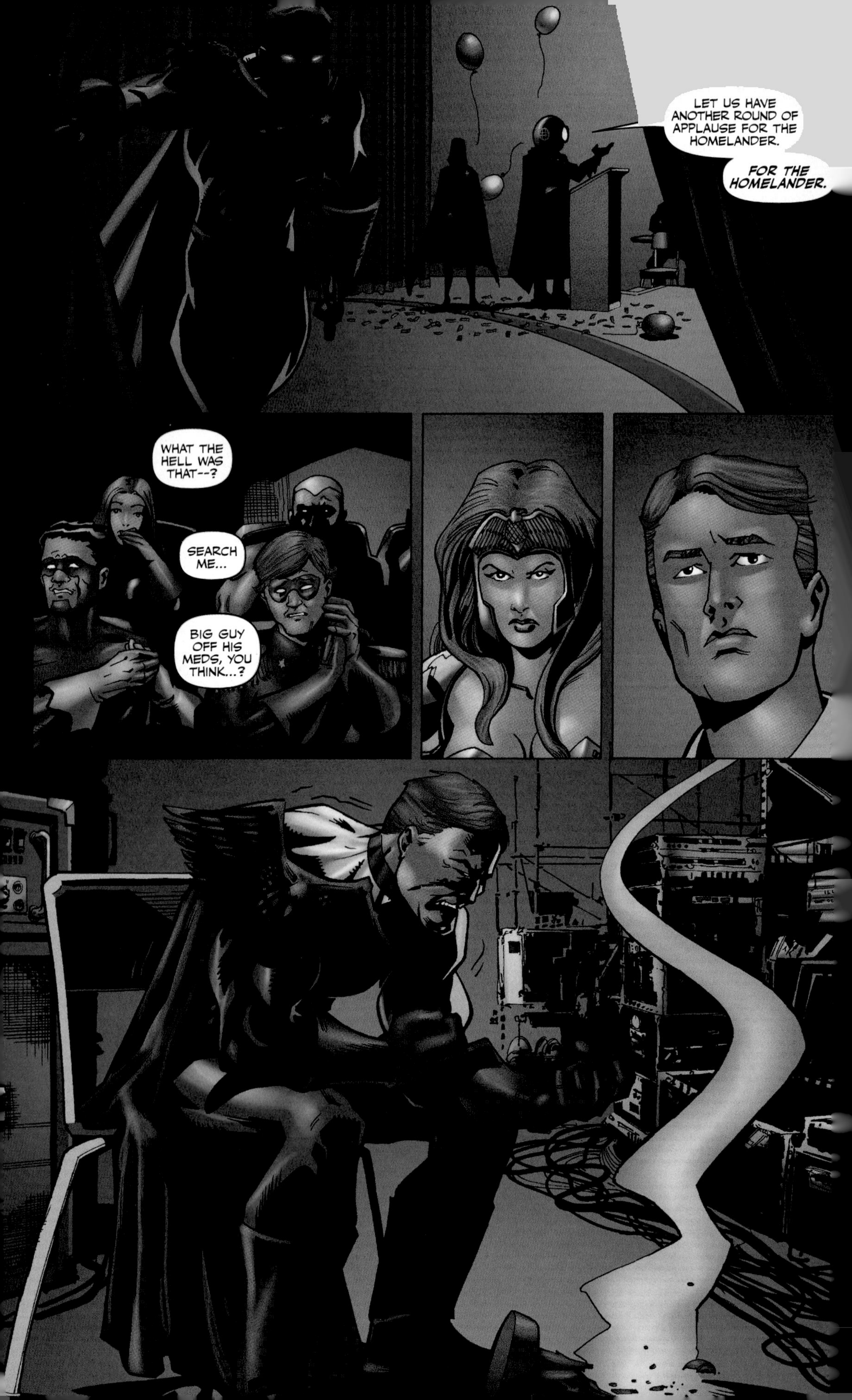
LET US HAVE ANOTHER ROUND OF APPLAUSE FOR THE HOMELANDER.
FOR THE HOMELANDER.
WHAT THE HELL WAS THAT--?
SEARCH ME...
BIG GUY OFF HIS MEDS, YOU THINK...?

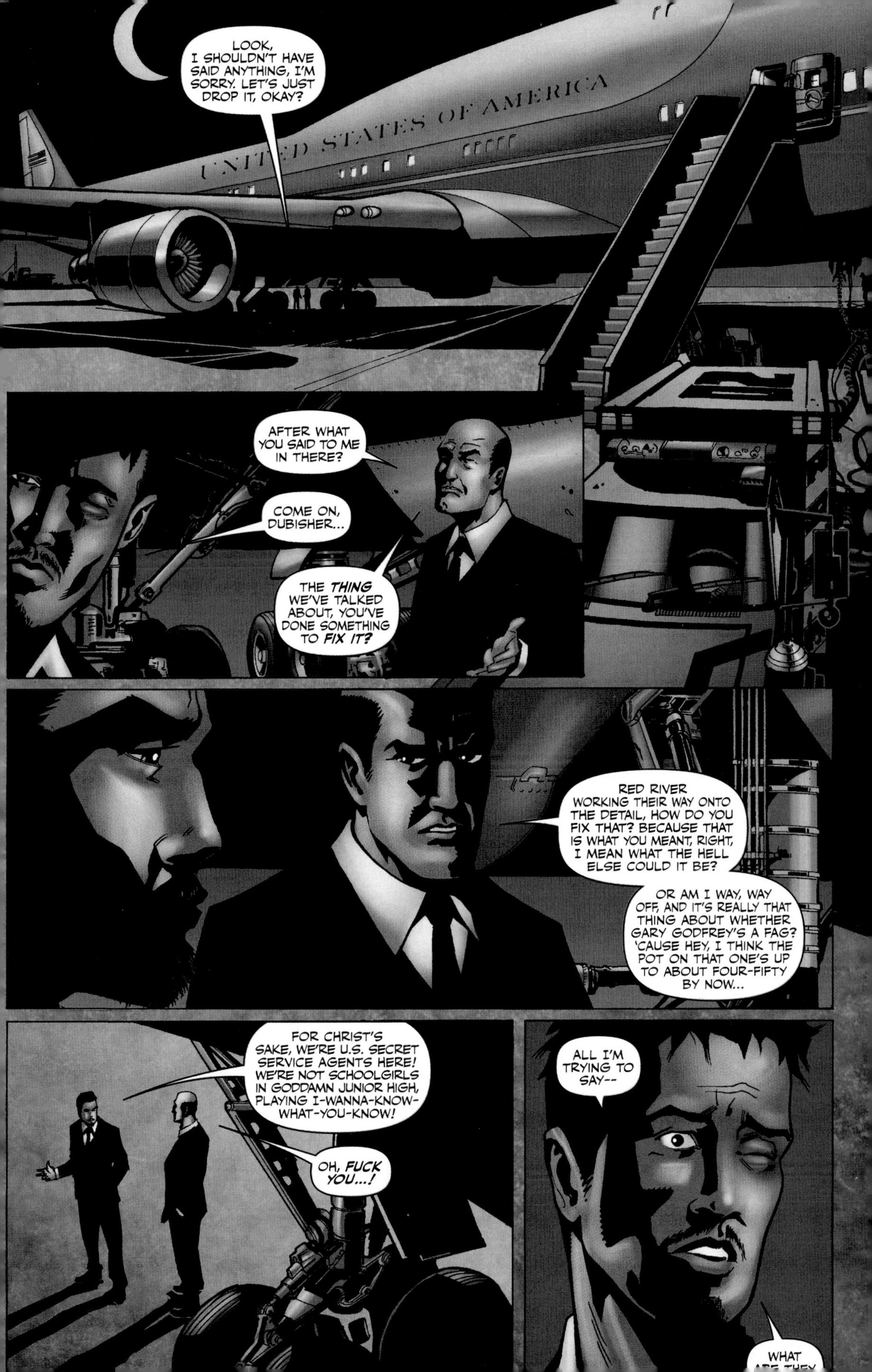

LOOK, I SHOULDN'T HAVE SAID ANYTHING, I'M SORRY. LET'S JUST DROP IT, OKAY?
UNITED STATES OF AMERICA
AFTER WHAT YOU SAID TO ME IN THERE?
COME ON, DUBISHER...
THE *THING* WE'VE TALKED ABOUT, YOU'VE DONE SOMETHING TO *FIX IT?*
RED RIVER WORKING THEIR WAY ONTO THE DETAIL, HOW DO YOU FIX THAT? BECAUSE THAT IS WHAT YOU MEANT, RIGHT, I MEAN WHAT THE HELL ELSE COULD IT BE?
OR AM I WAY, WAY OFF, AND IT'S REALLY THAT THING ABOUT WHETHER GARY GODFREY'S A FAG? 'CAUSE HEY, I THINK THE POT ON THAT ONE'S UP TO ABOUT FOUR-FIFTY BY NOW...
FOR CHRIST'S SAKE, WE'RE U.S. SECRET SERVICE AGENTS HERE! WE'RE NOT SCHOOLGIRLS IN GODDAMN JUNIOR HIGH, PLAYING I-WANNA-KNOW-WHAT-YOU-KNOW!
OH, *FUCK YOU...!*
ALL I'M TRYING TO SAY--
WHAT

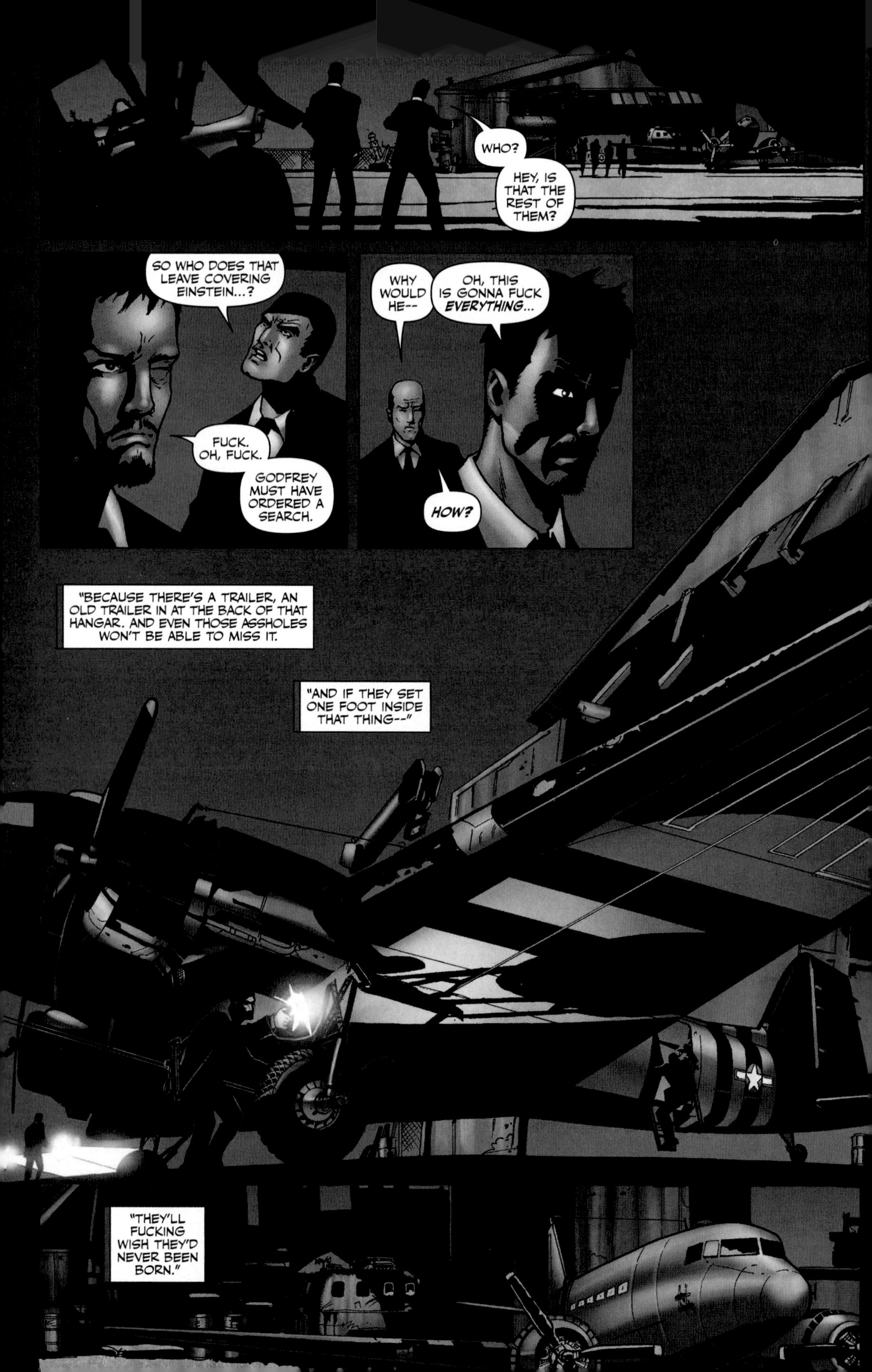
WHO?
HEY, IS THAT THE REST OF THEM?
SO WHO DOES THAT LEAVE COVERING EINSTEIN...?
FUCK. OH, FUCK.
GODFREY MUST HAVE ORDERED A SEARCH.
WHY WOULD HE--
OH, THIS IS GONNA FUCK *EVERYTHING*...
HOW?
"BECAUSE THERE'S A TRAILER, AN OLD TRAILER IN AT THE BACK OF THAT HANGAR. AND EVEN THOSE ASSHOLES WON'T BE ABLE TO MISS IT.
"AND IF THEY SET ONE FOOT INSIDE THAT THING--"
"THEY'LL FUCKING WISH THEY'D NEVER BEEN BORN."

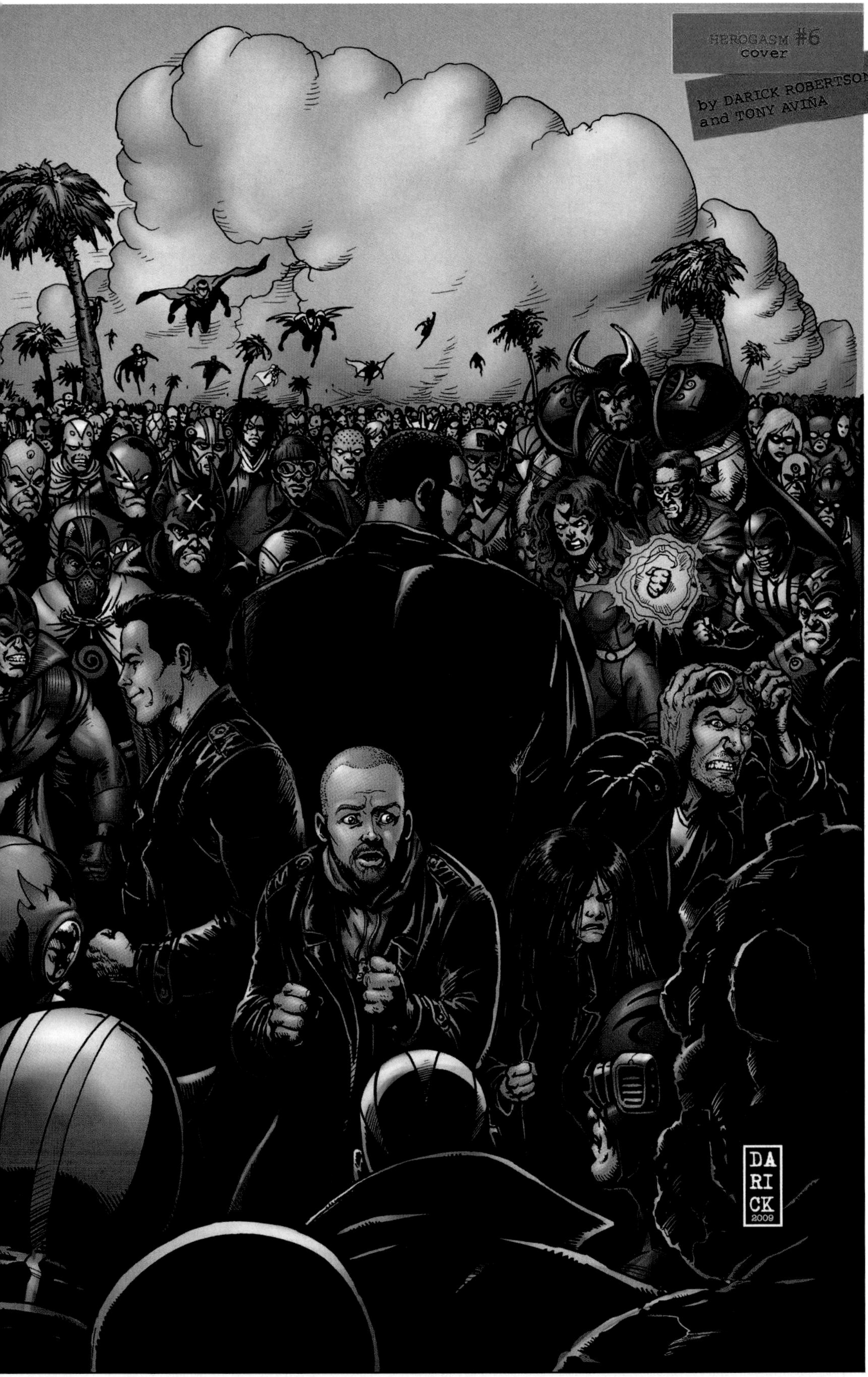
DA
RI
CK
2009

HEROGASM #6
cover

by DARICK ROBERTSON
and TONY AVIÑA

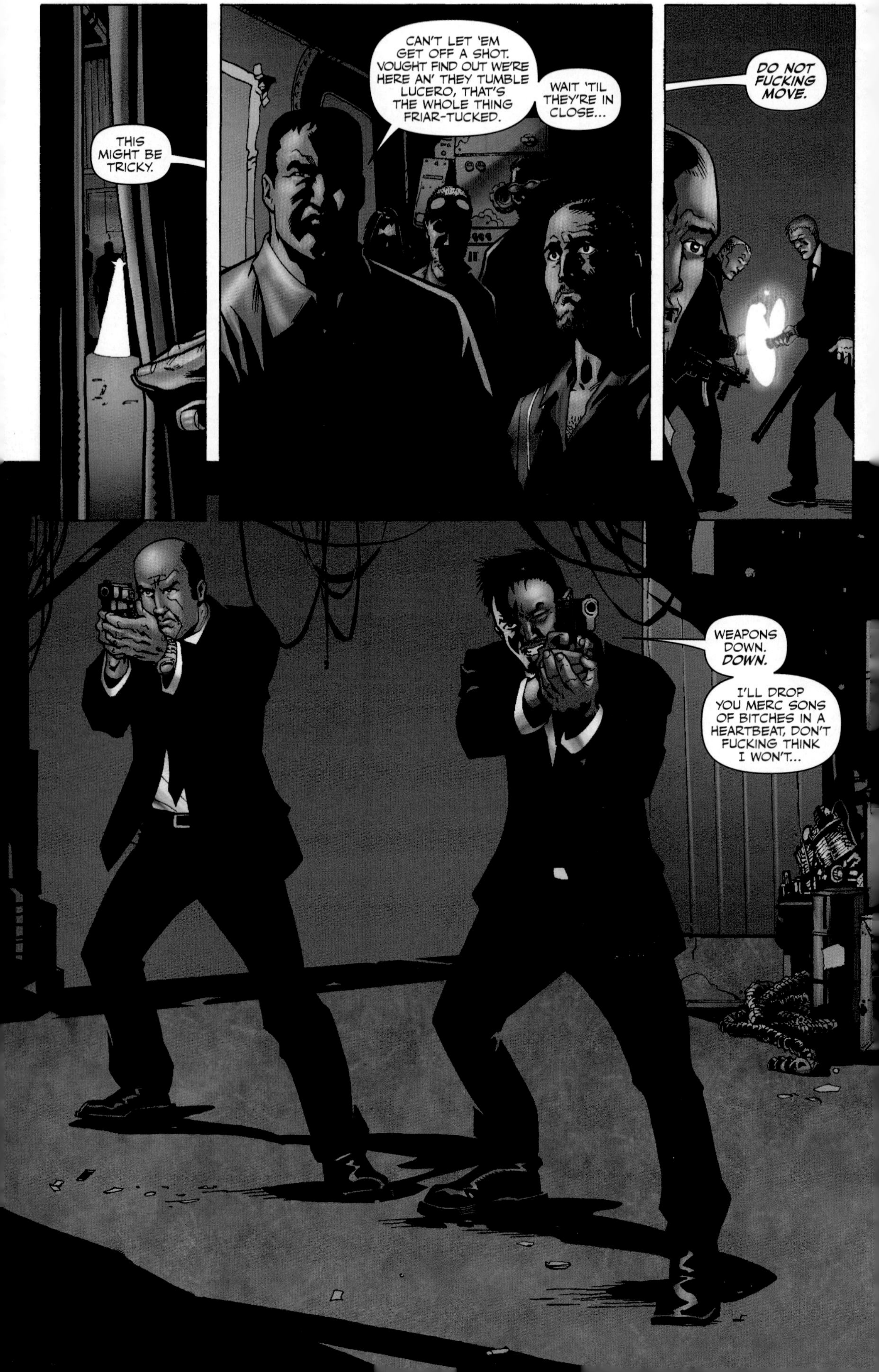
THIS MIGHT BE TRICKY.
CAN'T LET 'EM GET OFF A SHOT. VOUGHT FIND OUT WE'RE HERE AN' THEY TUMBLE LUCERO, THAT'S THE WHOLE THING FRIAR-TUCKED.
WAIT 'TIL THEY'RE IN CLOSE...
DO NOT FUCKING MOVE.
WEAPONS DOWN. DOWN.
I'LL DROP YOU MERC SONS OF BITCHES IN A HEARTBEAT, DON'T FUCKING THINK I WON'T...

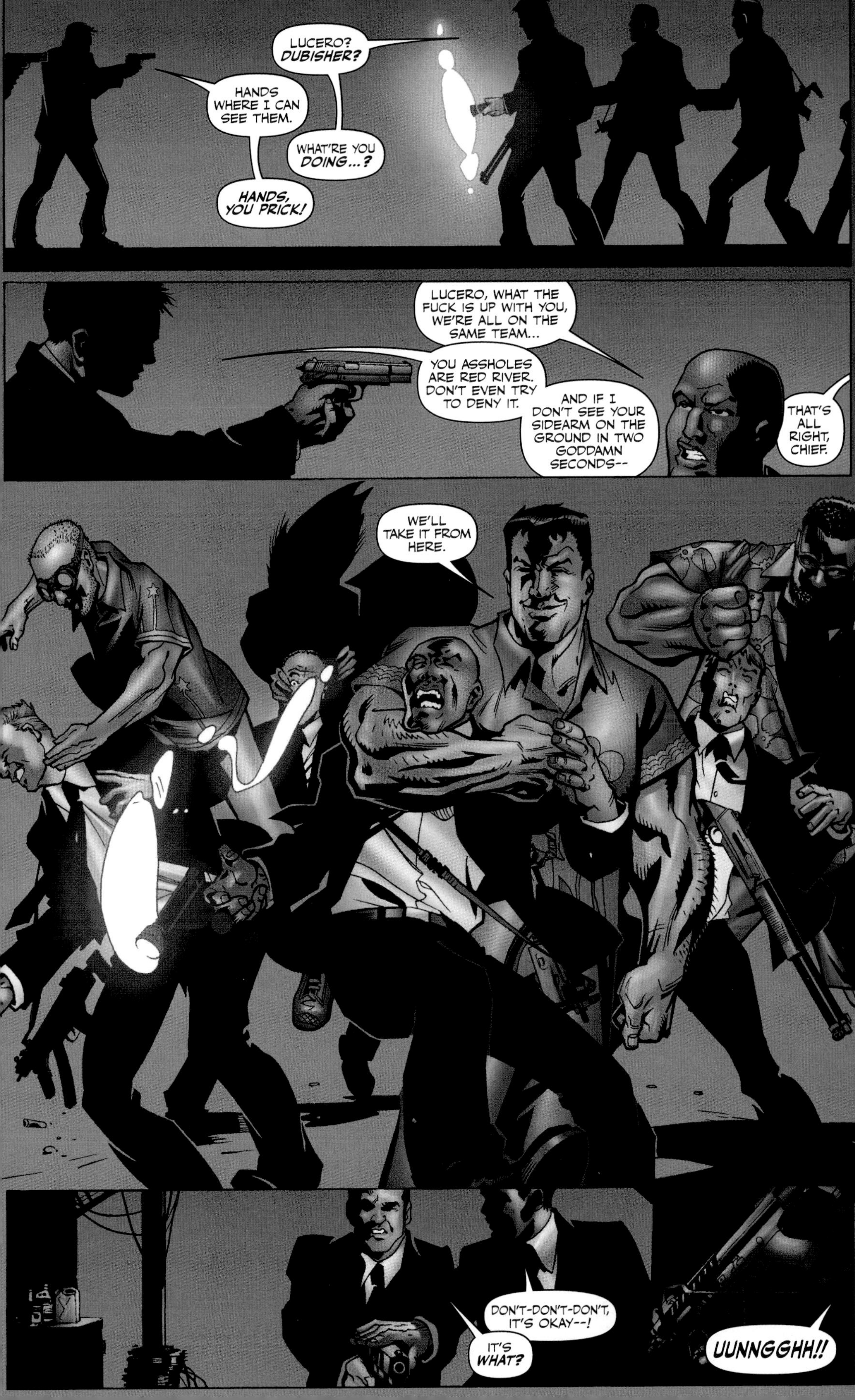

LUCERO? DUBISHER?
HANDS WHERE I CAN SEE THEM.
WHAT'RE YOU DOING...?
HANDS, YOU PRICK!
LUCERO, WHAT THE FUCK IS UP WITH YOU, WE'RE ALL ON THE SAME TEAM...
YOU ASSHOLES ARE RED RIVER. DON'T EVEN TRY TO DENY IT.
AND IF I DON'T SEE YOUR SIDEARM ON THE GROUND IN TWO GODDAMN SECONDS--
THAT'S ALL RIGHT, CHIEF.
WE'LL TAKE IT FROM HERE.
DON'T-DON'T-DON'T, IT'S OKAY--!
IT'S WHAT?
UUNNGGHH!!

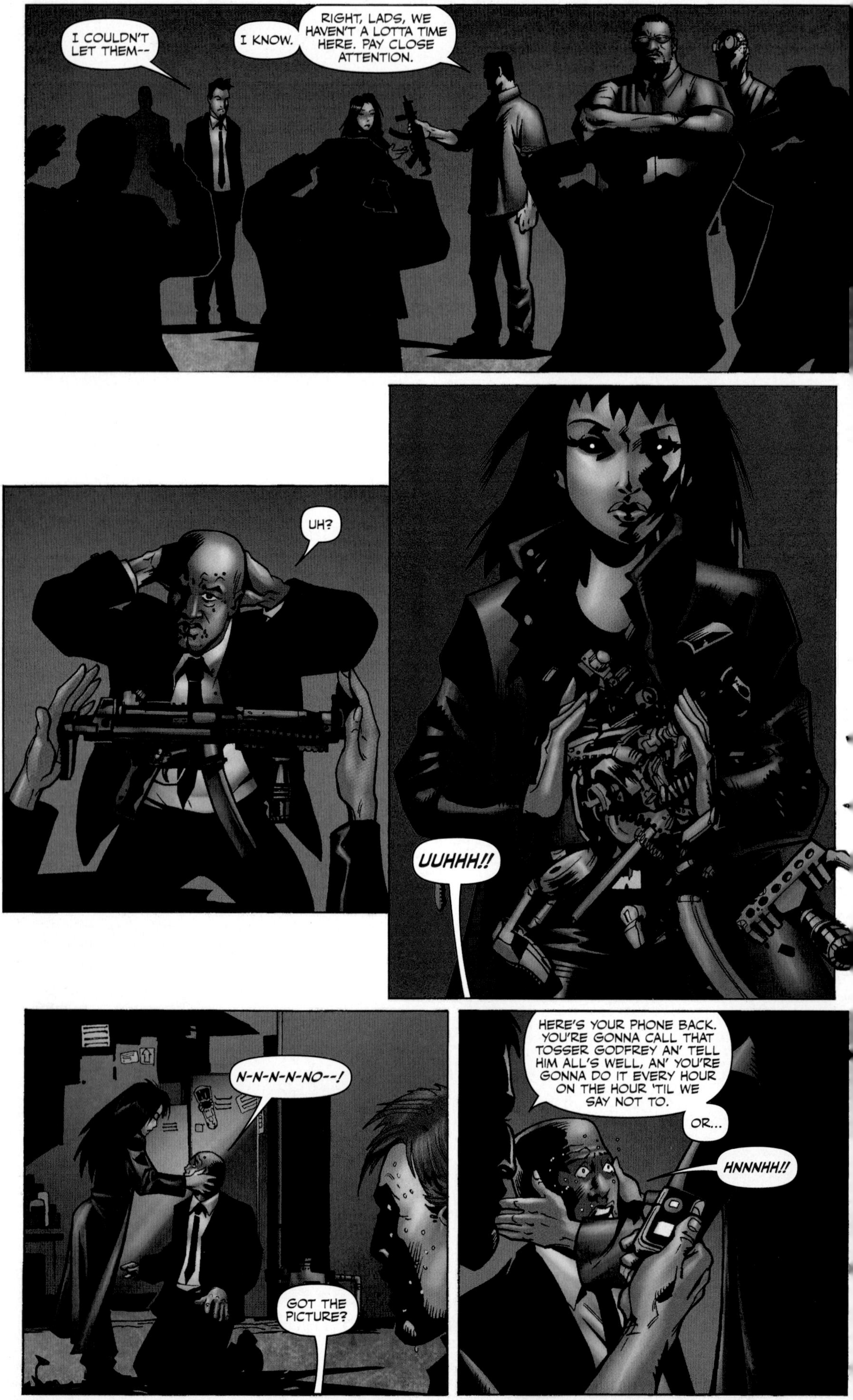
I COULDN'T LET THEM--
I KNOW.
RIGHT, LADS, WE HAVEN'T A LOTTA TIME HERE. PAY CLOSE ATTENTION.
UH?
UUHHH!!
N-N-N-N-NO--!
GOT THE PICTURE?
HERE'S YOUR PHONE BACK. YOU'RE GONNA CALL THAT TOSSER GODFREY AN' TELL HIM ALL'S WELL, AN' YOU'RE GONNA DO IT EVERY HOUR ON THE HOUR 'TIL WE SAY NOT TO.
OR...
HNNNHH!!

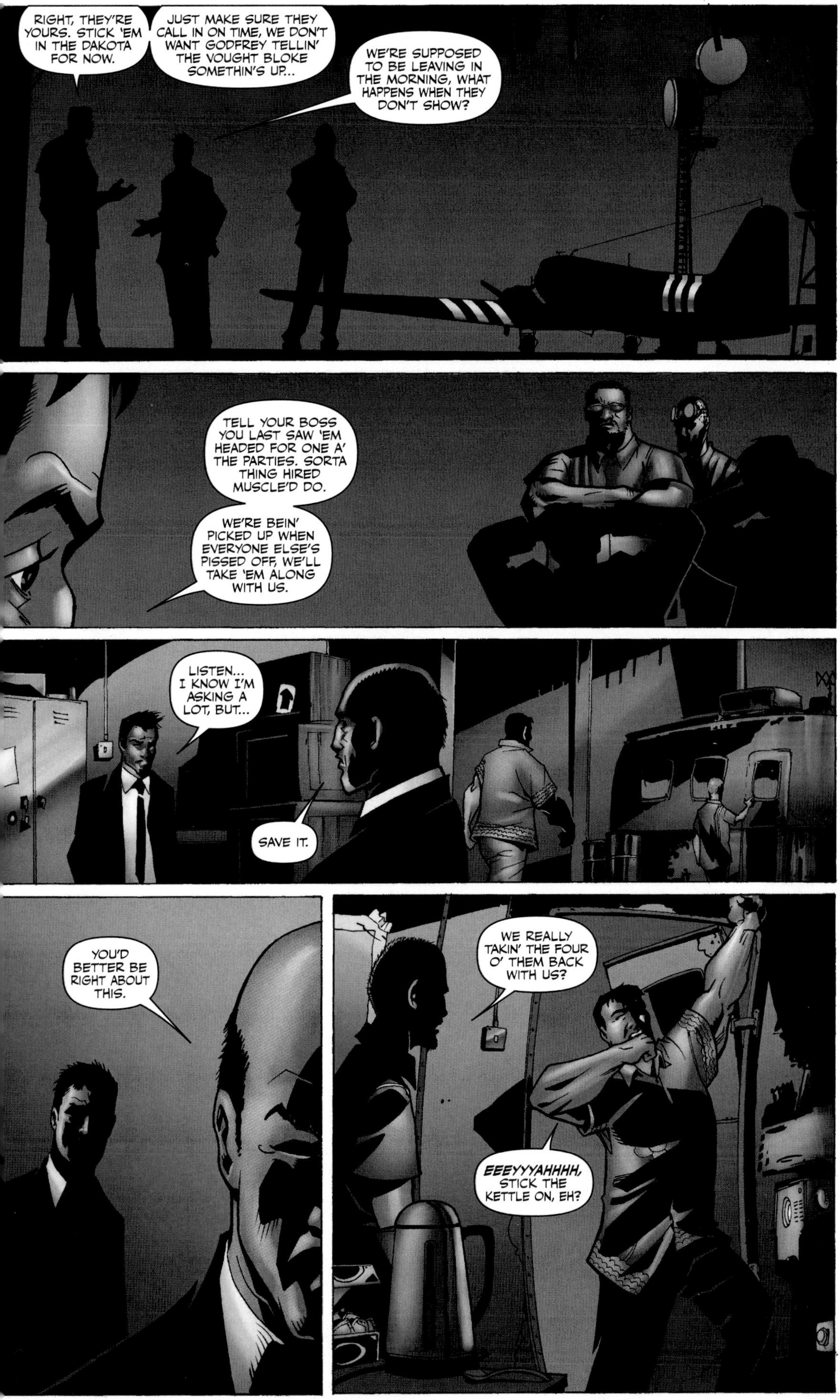
RIGHT, THEY'RE YOURS. STICK 'EM IN THE DAKOTA FOR NOW.
JUST MAKE SURE THEY CALL IN ON TIME, WE DON'T WANT GODFREY TELLIN' THE VOUGHT BLOKE SOMETHIN'S UP...
WE'RE SUPPOSED TO BE LEAVING IN THE MORNING, WHAT HAPPENS WHEN THEY DON'T SHOW?
TELL YOUR BOSS YOU LAST SAW 'EM HEADED FOR ONE A' THE PARTIES. SORTA THING HIRED MUSCLE'D DO.
WE'RE BEIN' PICKED UP WHEN EVERYONE ELSE'S PISSED OFF, WE'LL TAKE 'EM ALONG WITH US.
LISTEN... I KNOW I'M ASKING A LOT, BUT...
SAVE IT.
YOU'D BETTER BE RIGHT ABOUT THIS.
WE REALLY TAKIN' THE FOUR O' THEM BACK WITH US?
EEEYYYAHHHH, STICK THE KETTLE ON, EH?

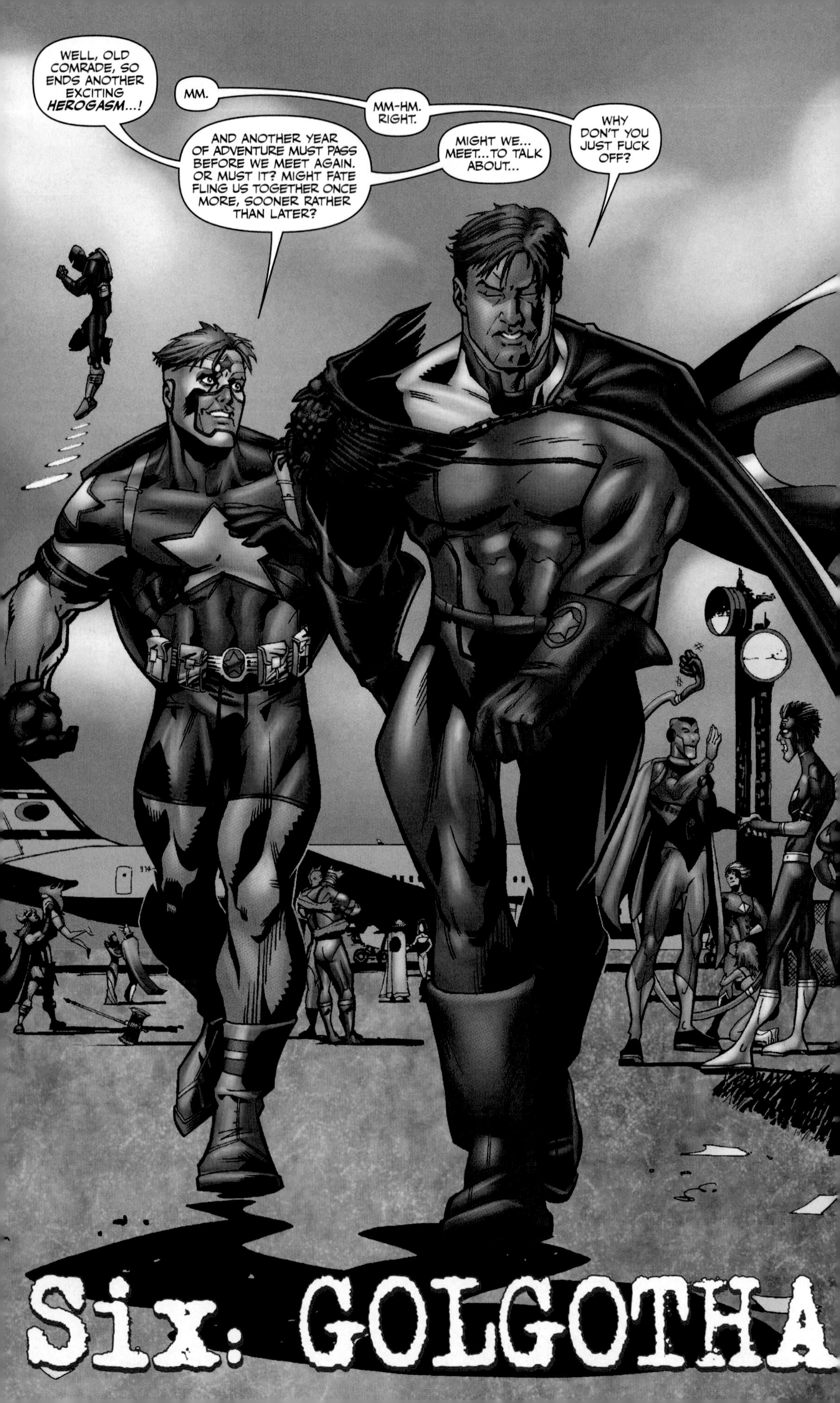
WELL, OLD COMRADE, SO ENDS ANOTHER EXCITING HEROGASM...!
MM.
AND ANOTHER YEAR OF ADVENTURE MUST PASS BEFORE WE MEET AGAIN. OR MUST IT? MIGHT FATE FLING US TOGETHER ONCE MORE, SOONER RATHER THAN LATER?
MM-HM. RIGHT.
MIGHT WE... MEET...TO TALK ABOUT...
WHY DON'T YOU JUST FUCK OFF?
Six: GOLGOTHA

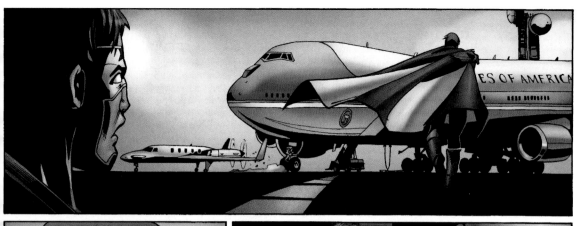

...I BEG YOUR PARDON, COULD YOU REPEAT THAT?

YES, CORRECT. SHAUNA MATTHESON. SHE'S ON THE HEROGASM MANIFEST.

NO, NOT ON THE FLIGHT. HAVE HER MET AT L.A.X.

GOOD.

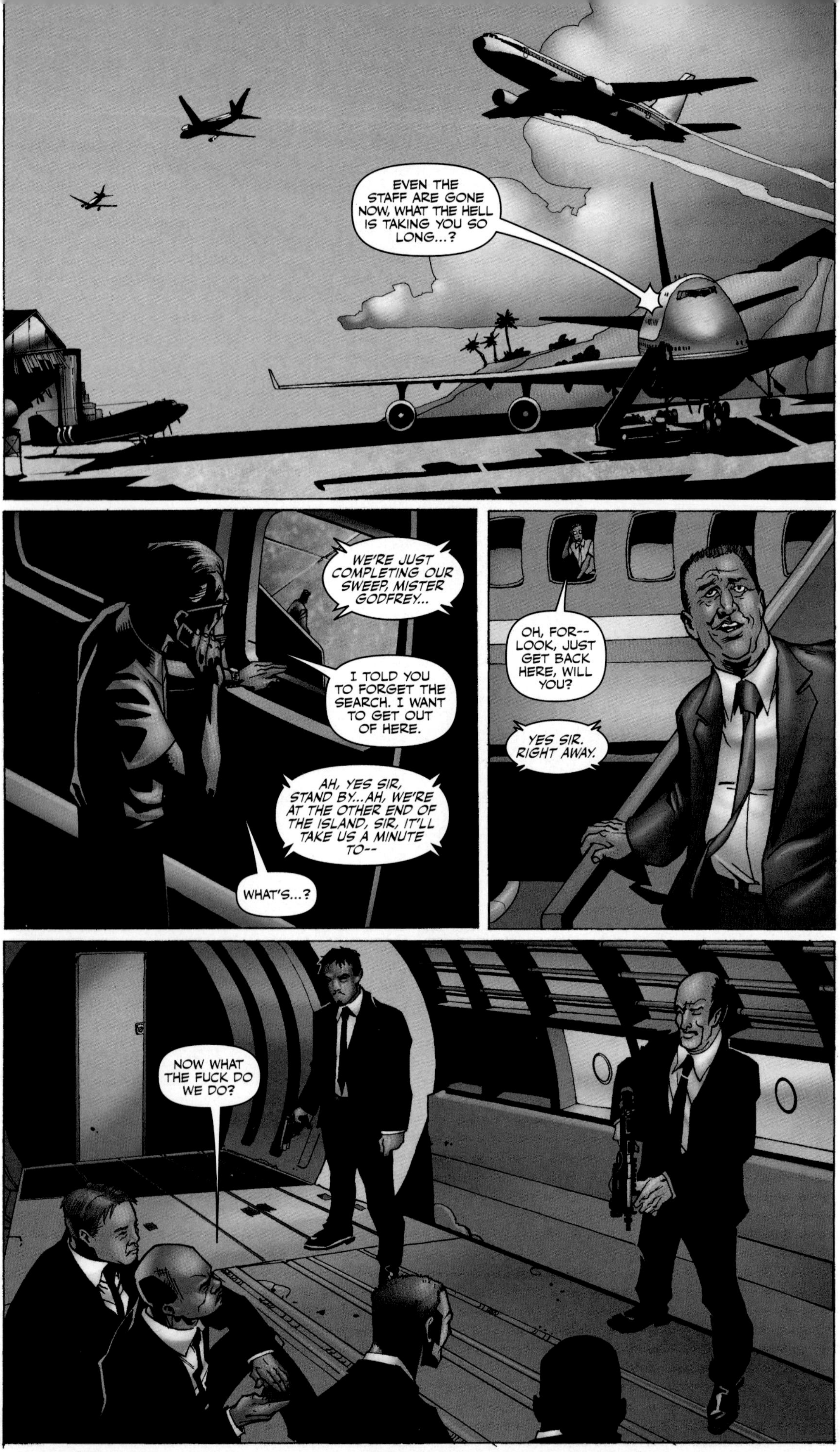
EVEN THE STAFF ARE GONE NOW, WHAT THE HELL IS TAKING YOU SO LONG...?
WE'RE JUST COMPLETING OUR SWEEP, MISTER GODFREY...
I TOLD YOU TO FORGET THE SEARCH. I WANT TO GET OUT OF HERE.
AH, YES SIR, STAND BY...AH, WE'RE AT THE OTHER END OF THE ISLAND, SIR, IT'LL TAKE US A MINUTE TO--
WHAT'S...?
OH, FOR-- LOOK, JUST GET BACK HERE, WILL YOU?
YES SIR. RIGHT AWAY.
NOW WHAT THE FUCK DO WE DO?

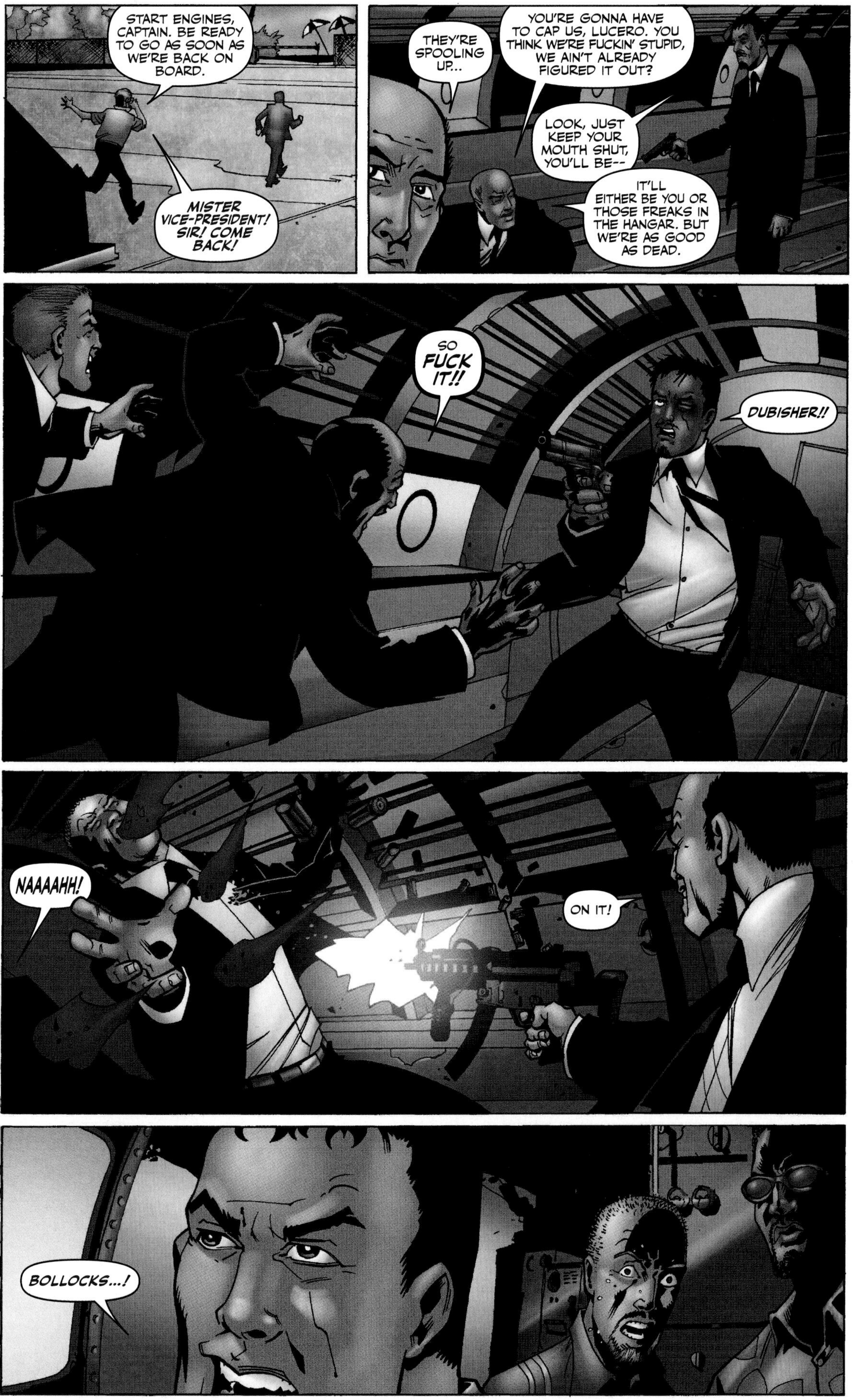
START ENGINES, CAPTAIN. BE READY TO GO AS SOON AS WE'RE BACK ON BOARD.
MISTER VICE-PRESIDENT! SIR! COME BACK!
THEY'RE SPOOLING UP...
YOU'RE GONNA HAVE TO CAP US, LUCERO. YOU THINK WE'RE FUCKIN' STUPID, WE AIN'T ALREADY FIGURED IT OUT?
LOOK, JUST KEEP YOUR MOUTH SHUT, YOU'LL BE--
IT'LL EITHER BE YOU OR THOSE FREAKS IN THE HANGAR. BUT WE'RE AS GOOD AS DEAD.
SO FUCK IT!!
DUBISHER!!
NAAAAHH!
ON IT!
BOLLOCKS...!

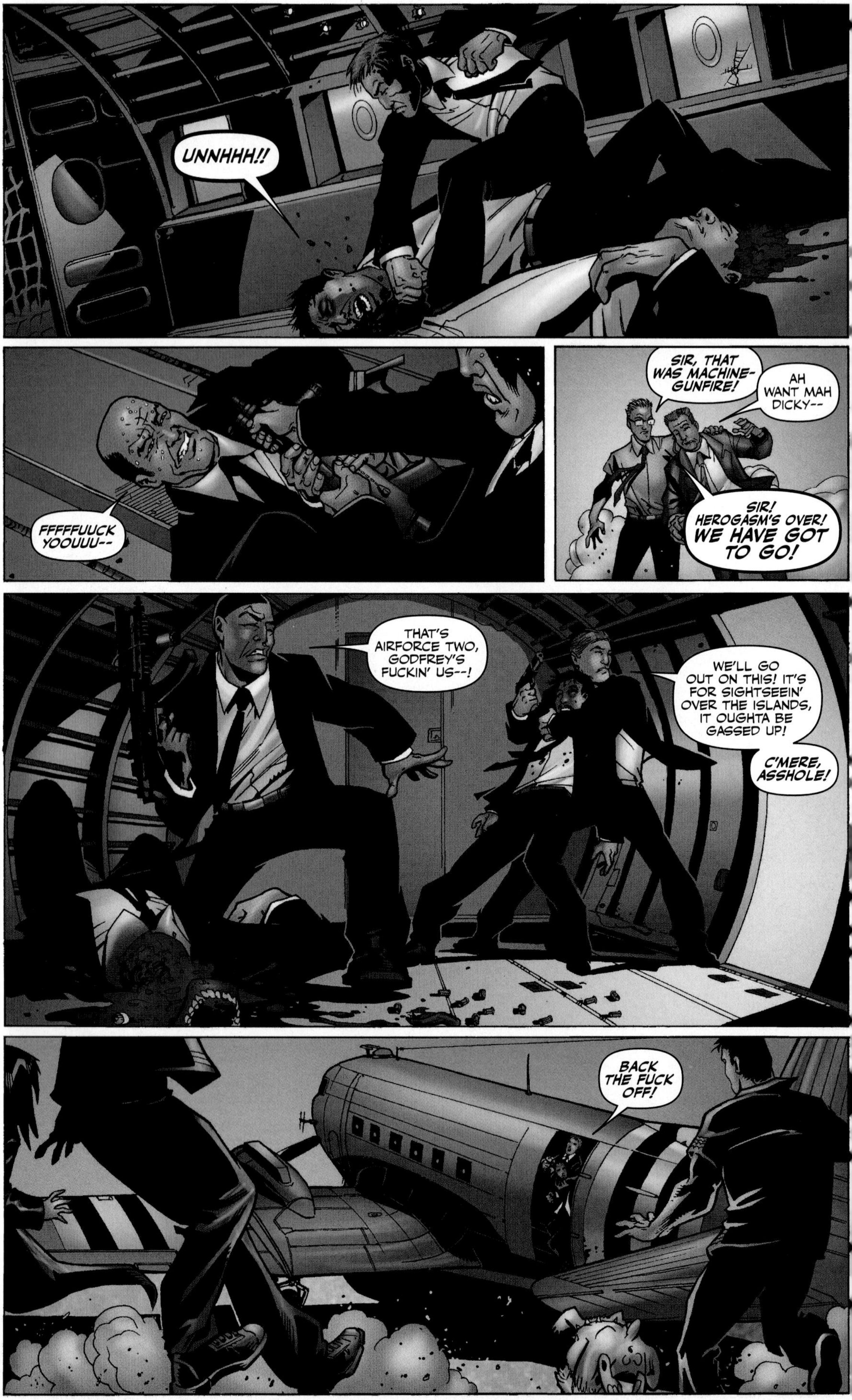
UNNHHH!!
FFFFFUUCK YOOUUU--
SIR, THAT WAS MACHINE-GUNFIRE!
AH WANT MAH DICKY--
SIR! HEROGASM'S OVER! WE HAVE GOT TO GO!
THAT'S AIRFORCE TWO, GODFREY'S FUCKIN' US--!
WE'LL GO OUT ON THIS! IT'S FOR SIGHTSEEIN' OVER THE ISLANDS, IT OUGHTA BE GASSED UP!
C'MERE, ASSHOLE!
BACK THE FUCK OFF!

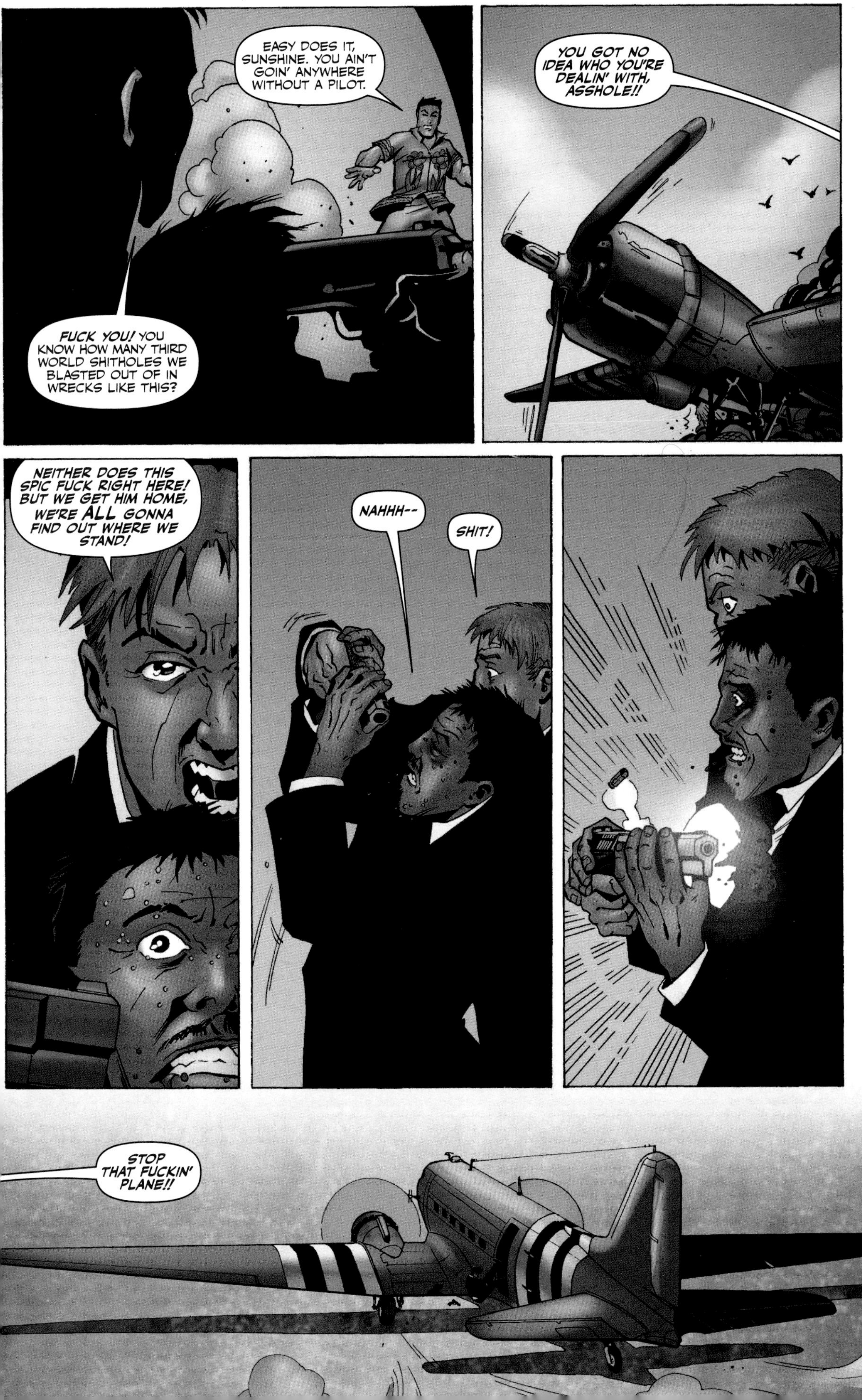
EASY DOES IT, SUNSHINE. YOU AIN'T GOIN' ANYWHERE WITHOUT A PILOT.
FUCK YOU! YOU KNOW HOW MANY THIRD WORLD SHITHOLES WE BLASTED OUT OF IN WRECKS LIKE THIS?
YOU GOT NO IDEA WHO YOU'RE DEALIN' WITH, ASSHOLE!!
NEITHER DOES THIS SPIC FUCK RIGHT HERE! BUT WE GET HIM HOME, WE'RE ALL GONNA FIND OUT WHERE WE STAND!
NAHHH--
SHIT!
STOP THAT FUCKIN' PLANE!!

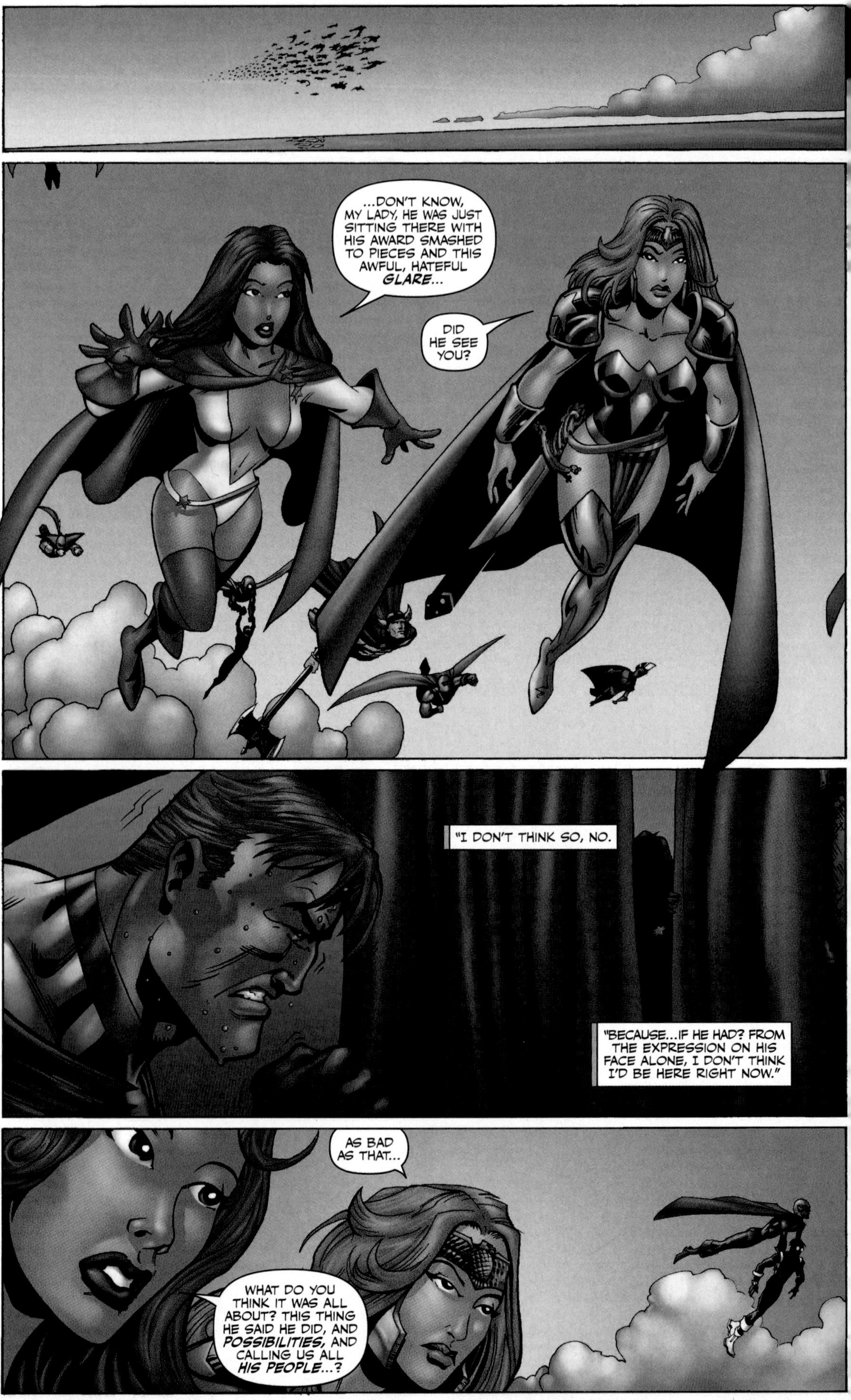
...DON'T KNOW, MY LADY, HE WAS JUST SITTING THERE WITH HIS AWARD SMASHED TO PIECES AND THIS AWFUL, HATEFUL GLARE...
DID HE SEE YOU?
"I DON'T THINK SO, NO.
"BECAUSE...IF HE HAD? FROM THE EXPRESSION ON HIS FACE ALONE, I DON'T THINK I'D BE HERE RIGHT NOW."
AS BAD AS THAT...
WHAT DO YOU THINK IT WAS ALL ABOUT? THIS THING HE SAID HE DID, AND POSSIBILITIES, AND CALLING US ALL HIS PEOPLE...?

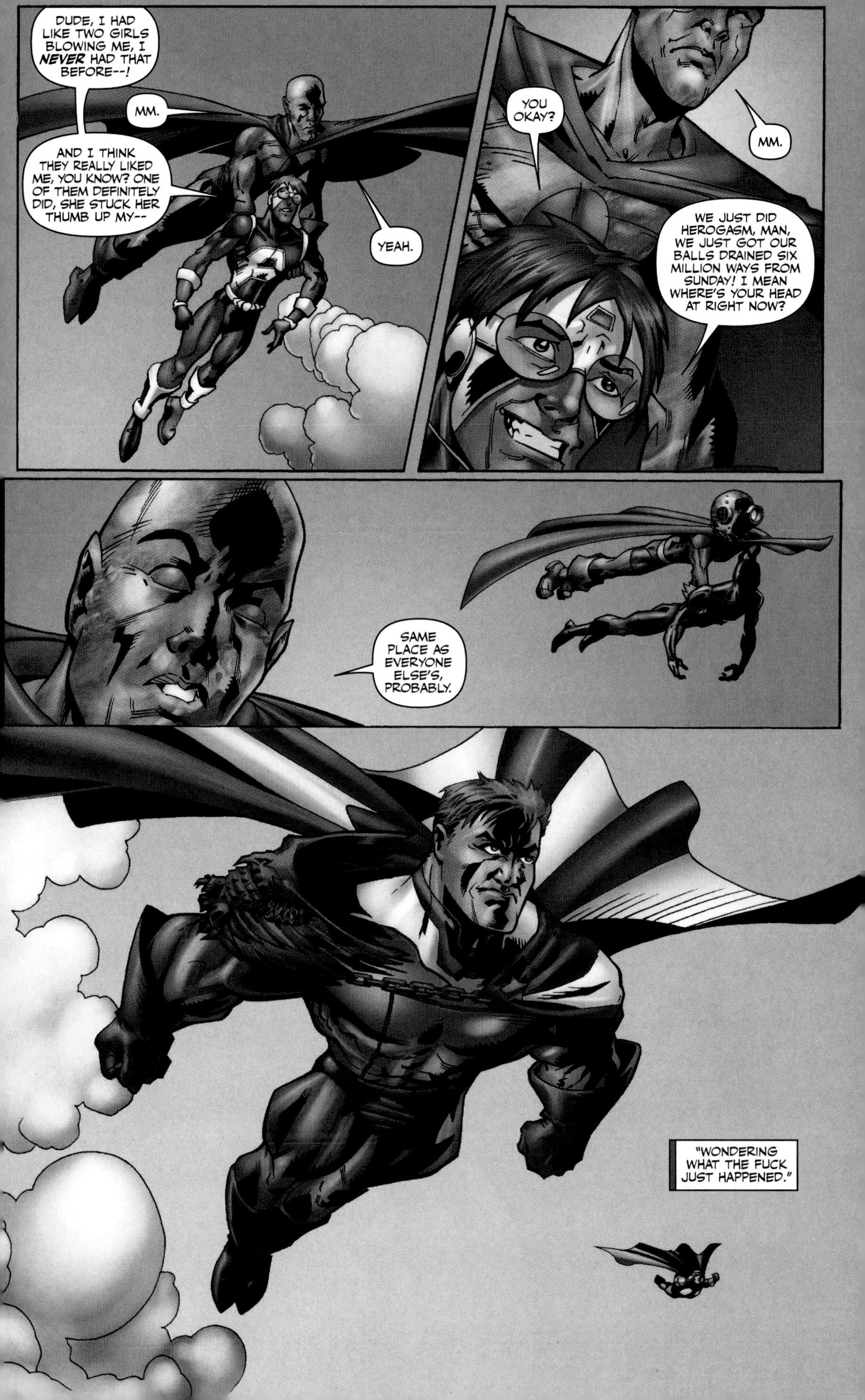

DUDE, I HAD LIKE TWO GIRLS BLOWING ME, I NEVER HAD THAT BEFORE--!
MM.
AND I THINK THEY REALLY LIKED ME, YOU KNOW? ONE OF THEM DEFINITELY DID, SHE STUCK HER THUMB UP MY--
YEAH.
YOU OKAY?
MM.
WE JUST DID HEROGASM, MAN, WE JUST GOT OUR BALLS DRAINED SIX MILLION WAYS FROM SUNDAY! I MEAN WHERE'S YOUR HEAD AT RIGHT NOW?
SAME PLACE AS EVERYONE ELSE'S, PROBABLY.
"WONDERING WHAT THE FUCK JUST HAPPENED."

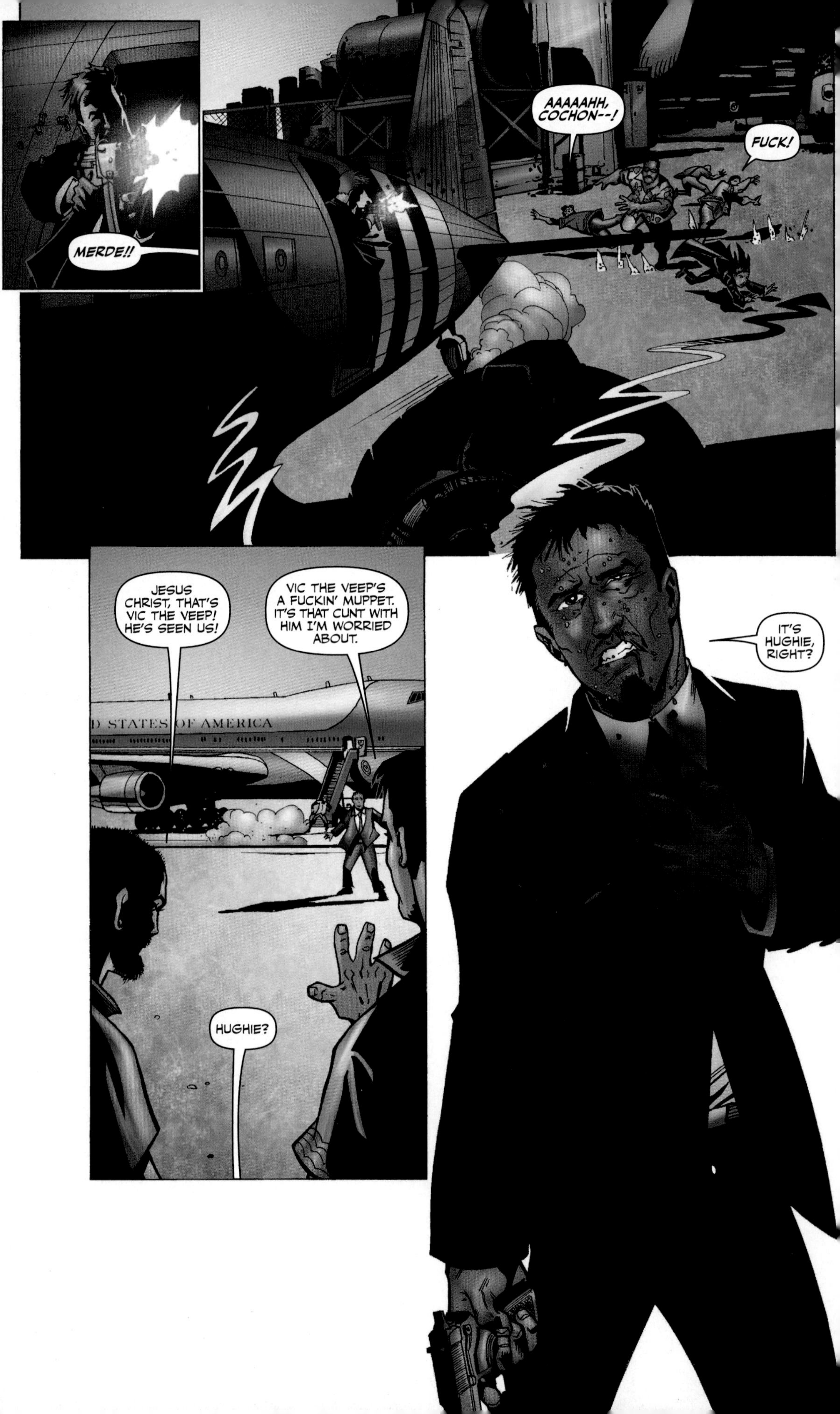
MERDE!!
AAAAAAHH, COCHON--!
FUCK!
JESUS CHRIST, THAT'S VIC THE VEEP! HE'S SEEN US!
VIC THE VEEP'S A FUCKIN' MUPPET. IT'S THAT CUNT WITH HIM I'M WORRIED ABOUT.
D STATES OF AMERICA
HUGHIE?
IT'S HUGHIE, RIGHT?

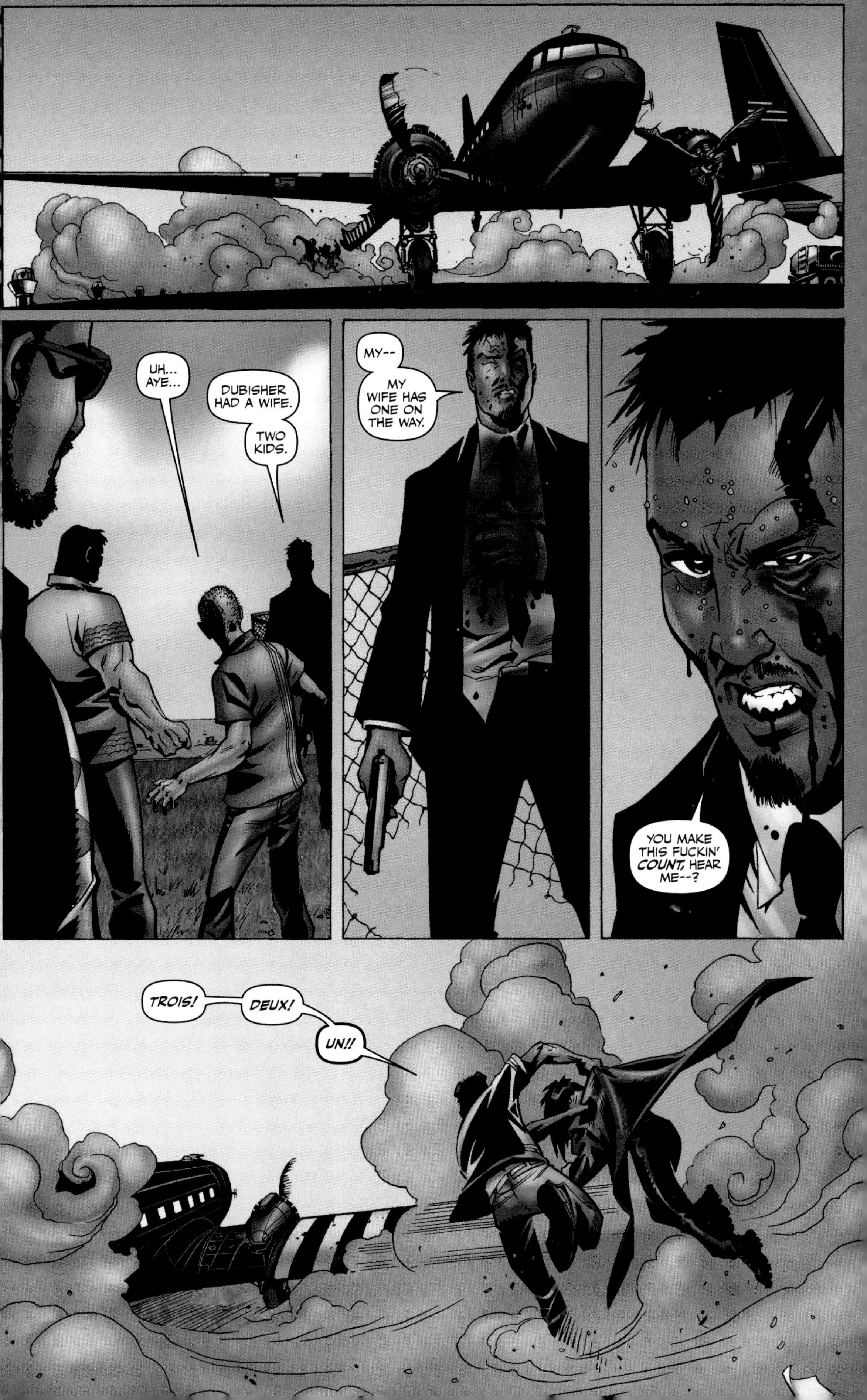
UH... AYE...
DUBISHER HAD A WIFE.
TWO KIDS.
MY--
MY WIFE HAS ONE ON THE WAY.
YOU MAKE THIS FUCKIN' COUNT, HEAR ME--?
TROIS!
DEUX!
UN!!

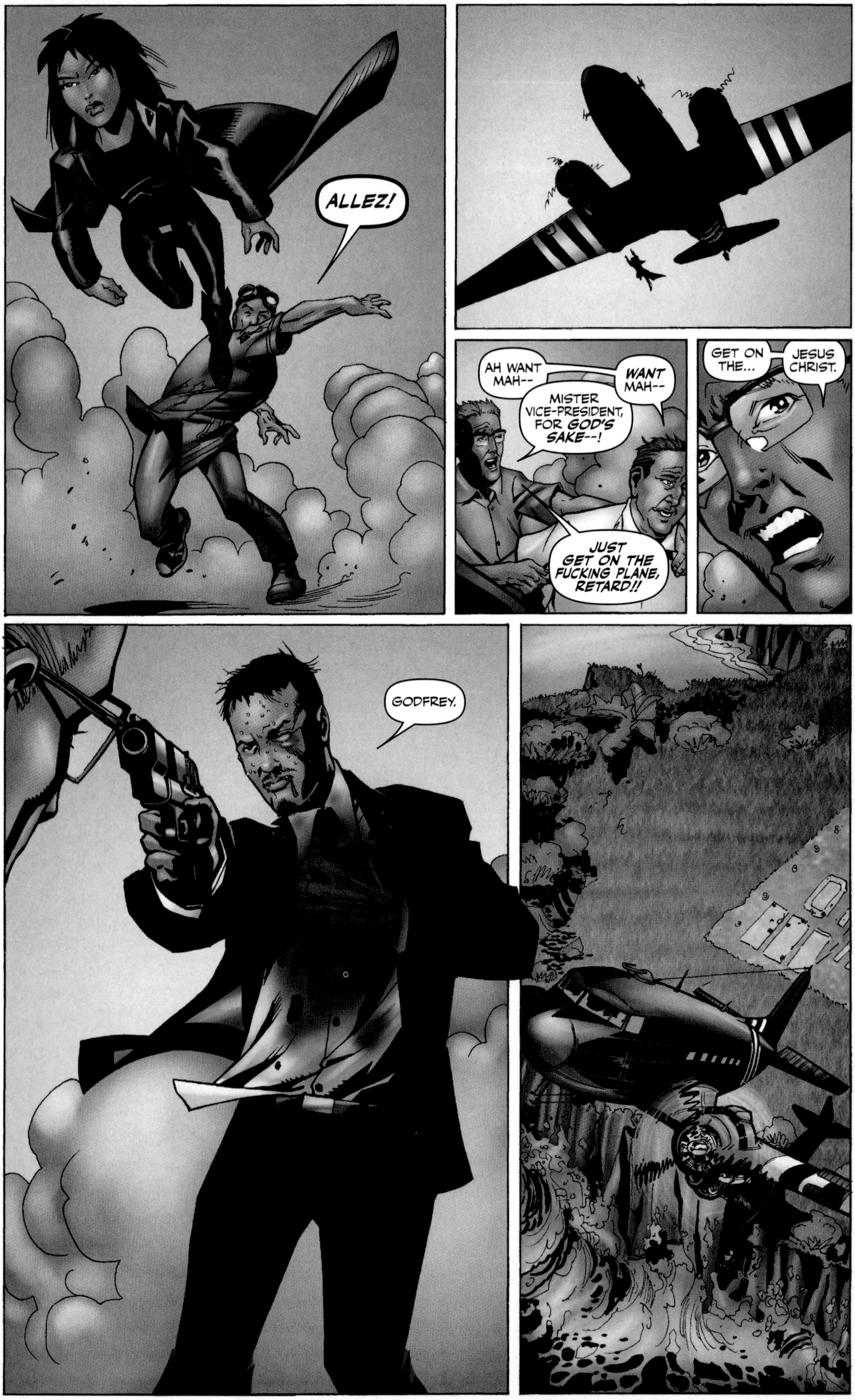
ALLEZ!
AH WANT MAH--
WANT MAH--
MISTER VICE-PRESIDENT, FOR GOD'S SAKE--!
JUST GET ON THE FUCKING PLANE, RETARD!!
GET ON THE...
JESUS CHRIST.
GODFREY.

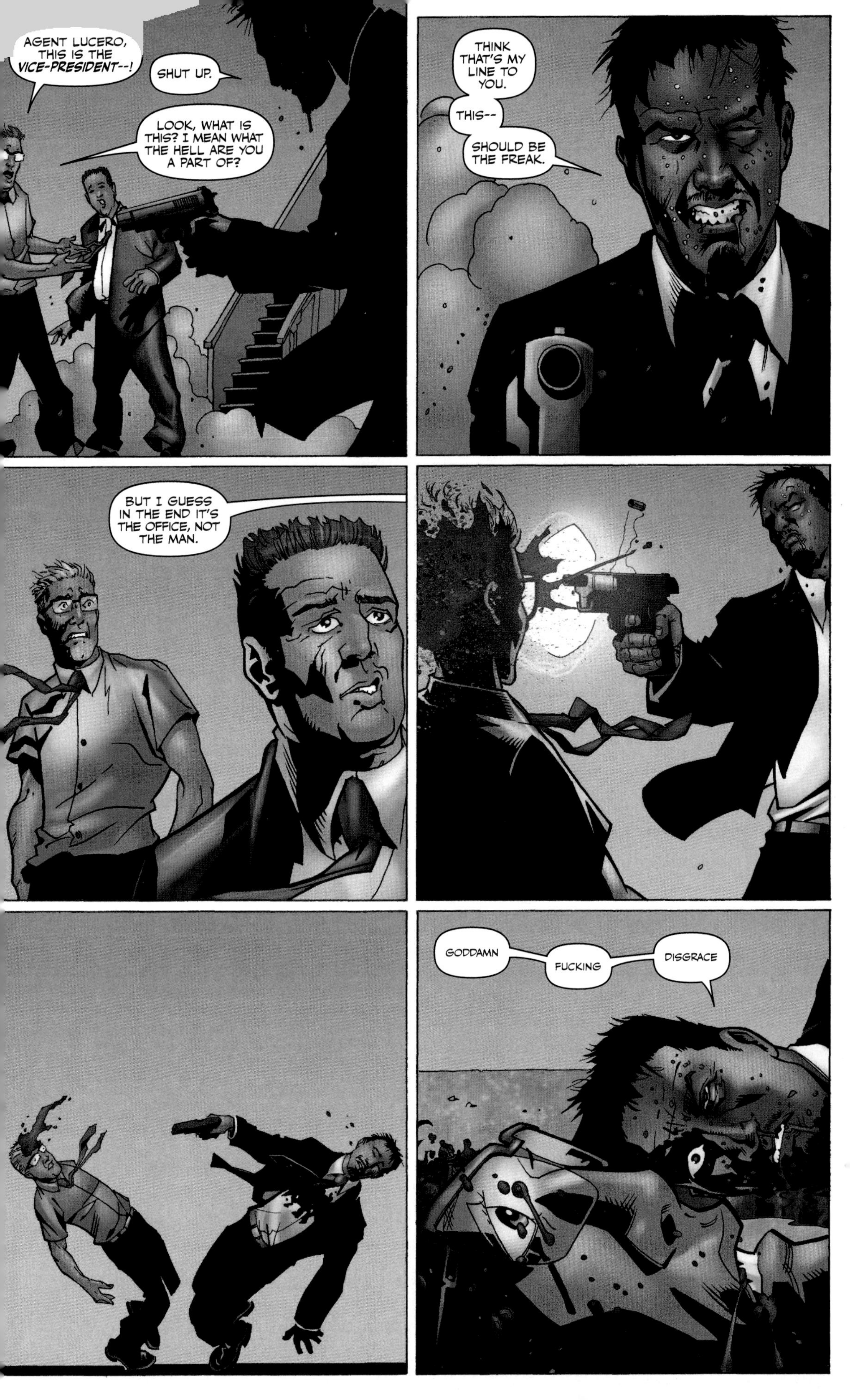
AGENT LUCERO, THIS IS THE VICE-PRESIDENT--!
SHUT UP.
LOOK, WHAT IS THIS? I MEAN WHAT THE HELL ARE YOU A PART OF?
THINK THAT'S MY LINE TO YOU.
THIS--
SHOULD BE THE FREAK.
BUT I GUESS IN THE END IT'S THE OFFICE, NOT THE MAN.
GODDAMN
FUCKING
DISGRACE

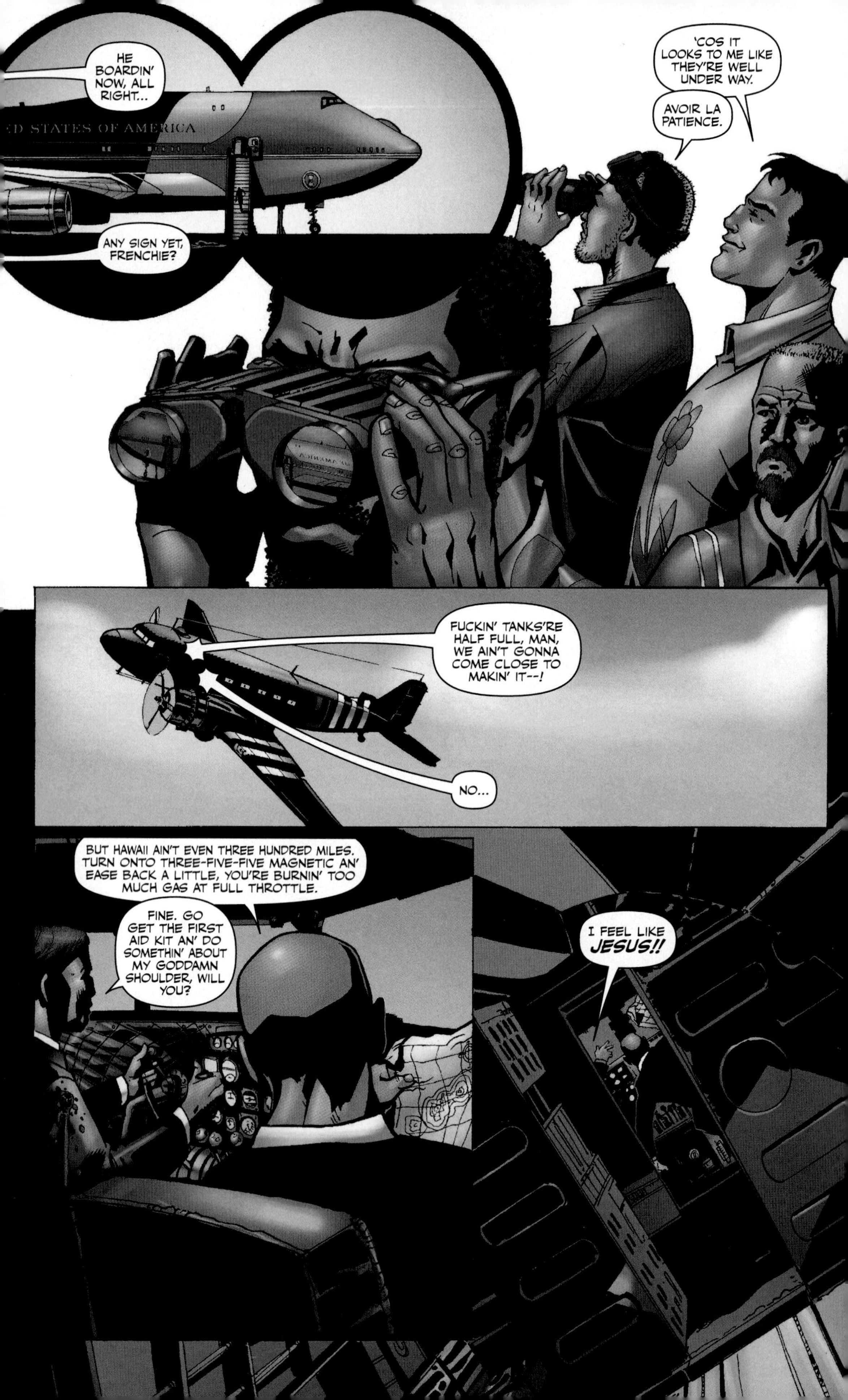
HE BOARDIN' NOW, ALL RIGHT...
ED STATES OF AMERICA
ANY SIGN YET, FRENCHIE?
'COS IT LOOKS TO ME LIKE THEY'RE WELL UNDER WAY.
AVOIR LA PATIENCE.
FUCKIN' TANKS'RE HALF FULL, MAN, WE AIN'T GONNA COME CLOSE TO MAKIN' IT--!
NO...
BUT HAWAII AIN'T EVEN THREE HUNDRED MILES. TURN ONTO THREE-FIVE-FIVE MAGNETIC AN' EASE BACK A LITTLE, YOU'RE BURNIN' TOO MUCH GAS AT FULL THROTTLE.
FINE. GO GET THE FIRST AID KIT AN' DO SOMETHIN' ABOUT MY GODDAMN SHOULDER, WILL YOU?
I FEEL LIKE *JESUS!!*

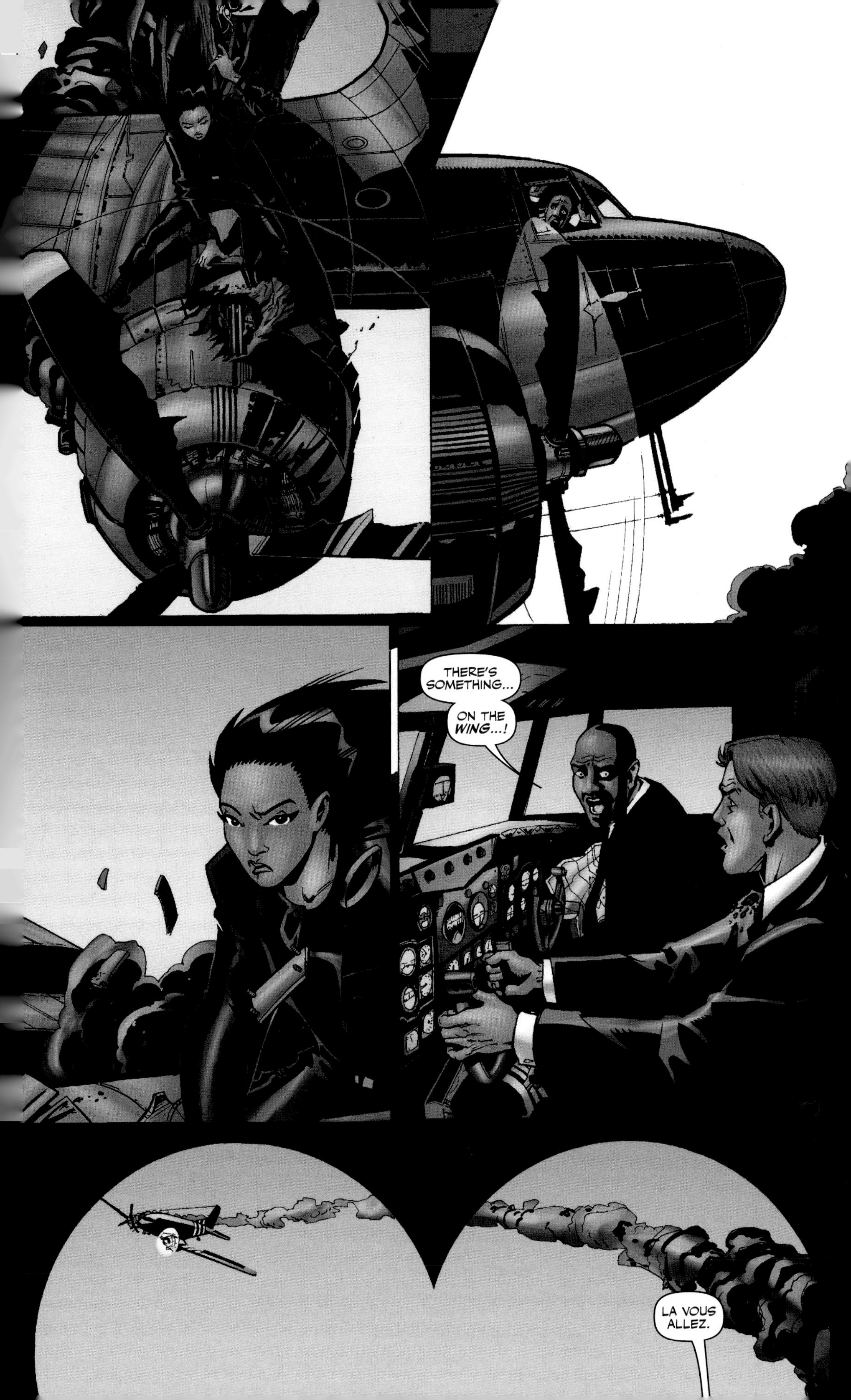
THERE'S SOMETHING...
ON THE *WING*...!
LA VOUS ALLEZ.

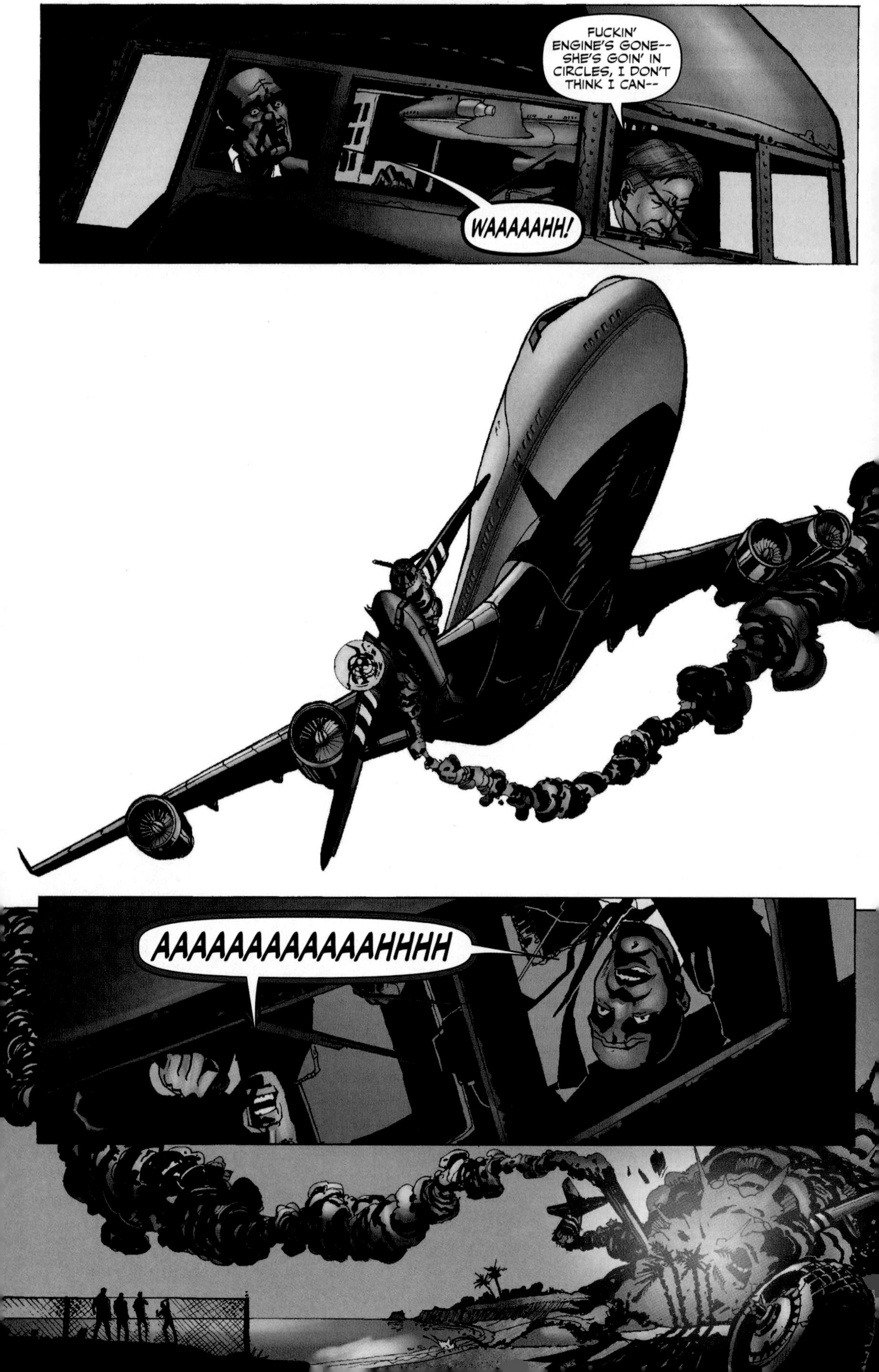
FUCKIN' ENGINE'S GONE-- SHE'S GOIN' IN CIRCLES, I DON'T THINK I CAN--
WAAAAAHH!
AAAAAAAAAAAAHHHH

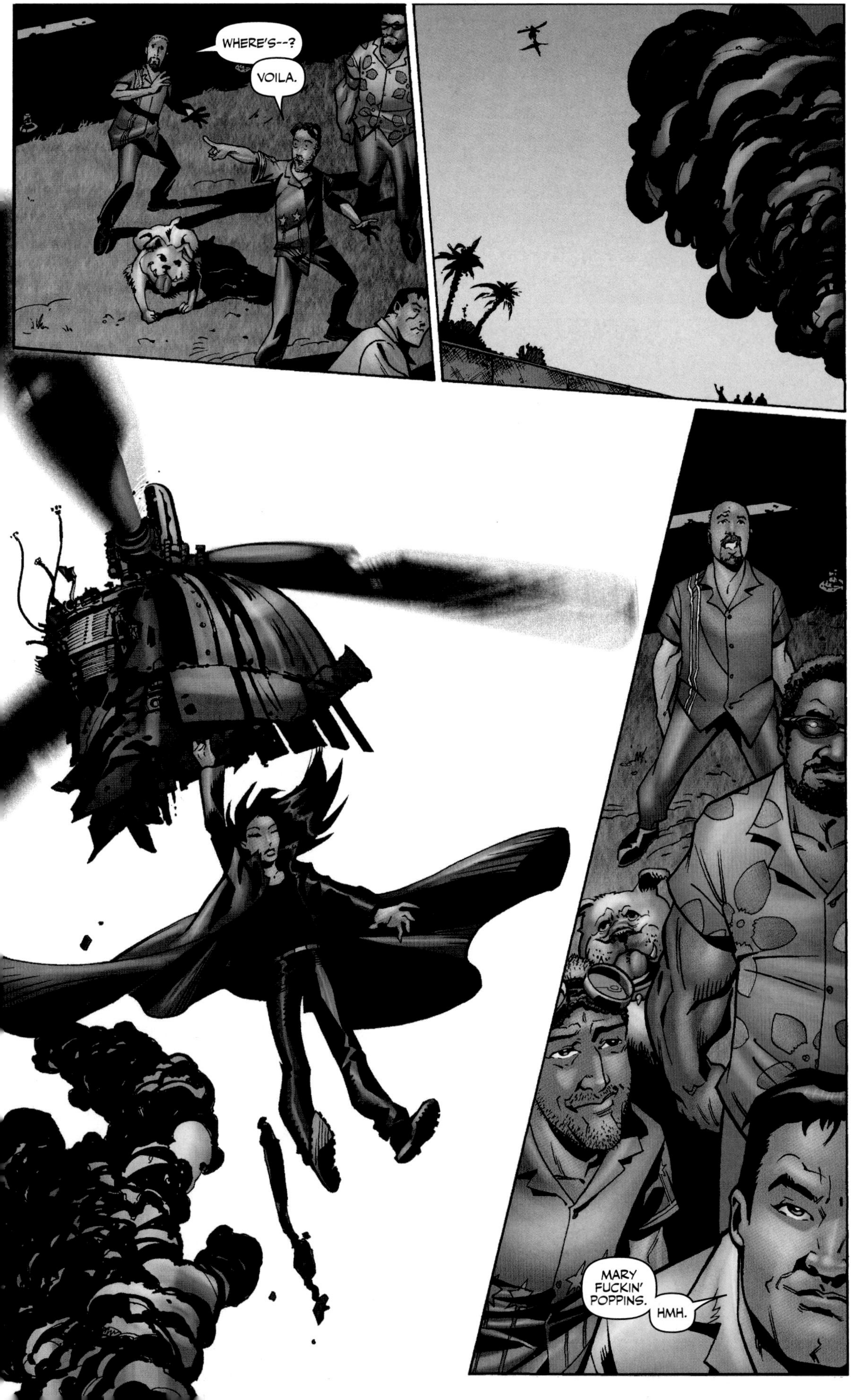
WHERE'S--?
VOILA.
MARY FUCKIN' POPPINS.
HMH.

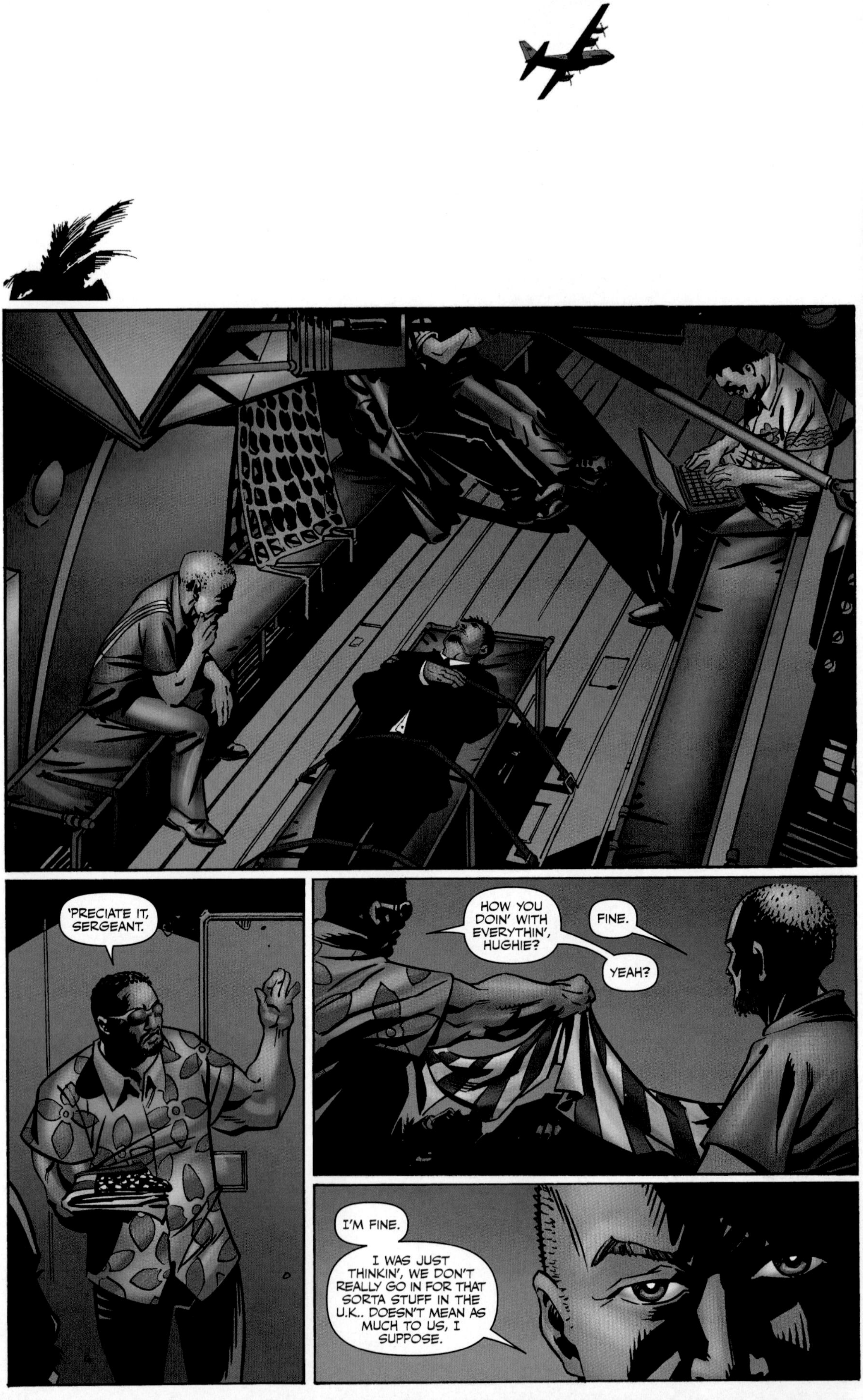
'PRECIATE IT, SERGEANT.
HOW YOU DOIN' WITH EVERYTHIN', HUGHIE?
FINE.
YEAH?
I'M FINE.
I WAS JUST THINKIN', WE DON'T REALLY GO IN FOR THAT SORTA STUFF IN THE U.K.. DOESN'T MEAN AS MUCH TO US, I SUPPOSE.

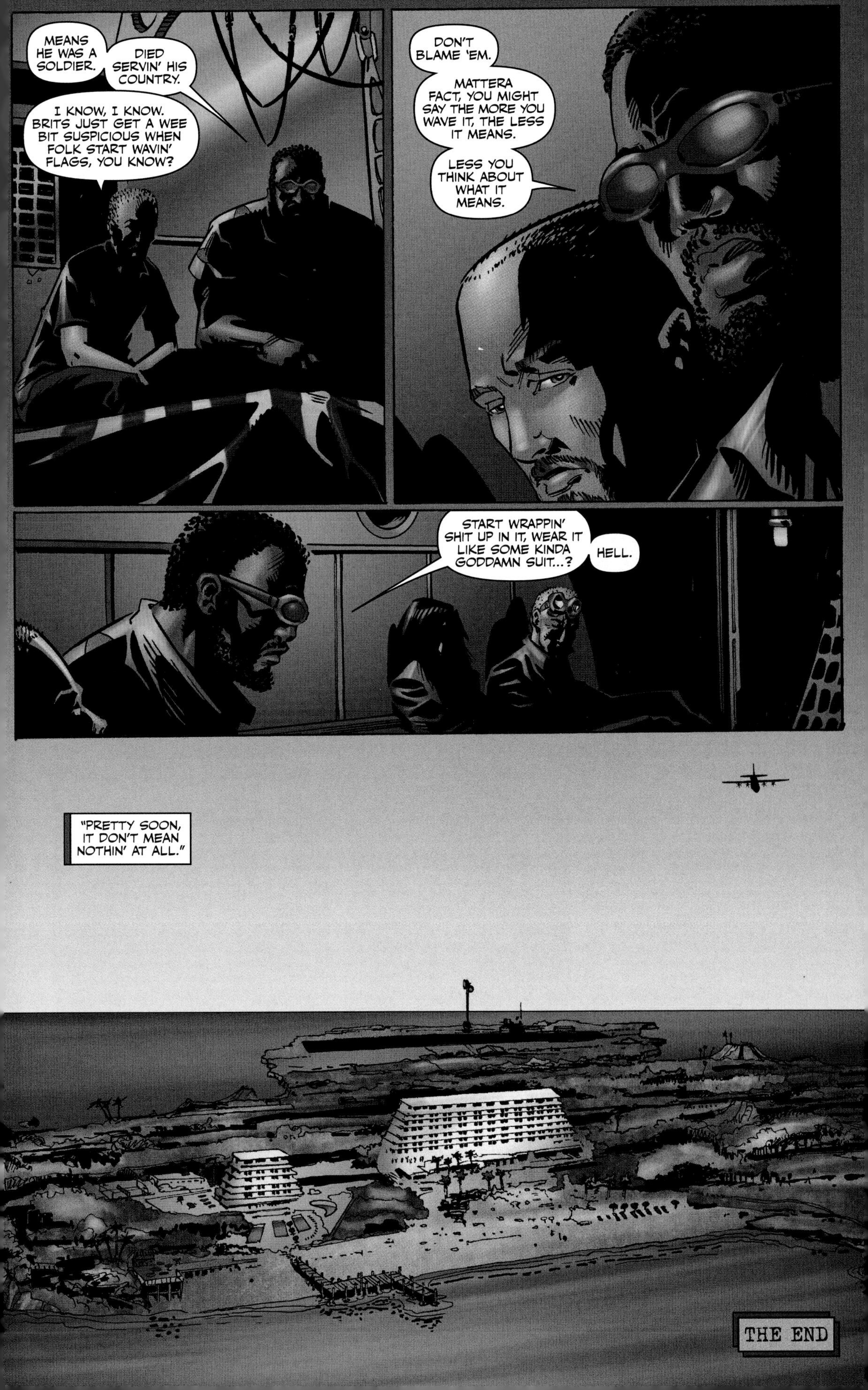
MEANS HE WAS A SOLDIER.
DIED SERVIN' HIS COUNTRY.
I KNOW, I KNOW. BRITS JUST GET A WEE BIT SUSPICIOUS WHEN FOLK START WAVIN' FLAGS, YOU KNOW?
DON'T BLAME 'EM.
MATTERA FACT, YOU MIGHT SAY THE MORE YOU WAVE IT, THE LESS IT MEANS.
LESS YOU THINK ABOUT WHAT IT MEANS.
START WRAPPIN' SHIT UP IN IT, WEAR IT LIKE SOME KINDA GODDAMN SUIT...?
HELL.
"PRETTY SOON, IT DON'T MEAN NOTHIN' AT ALL."
THE END

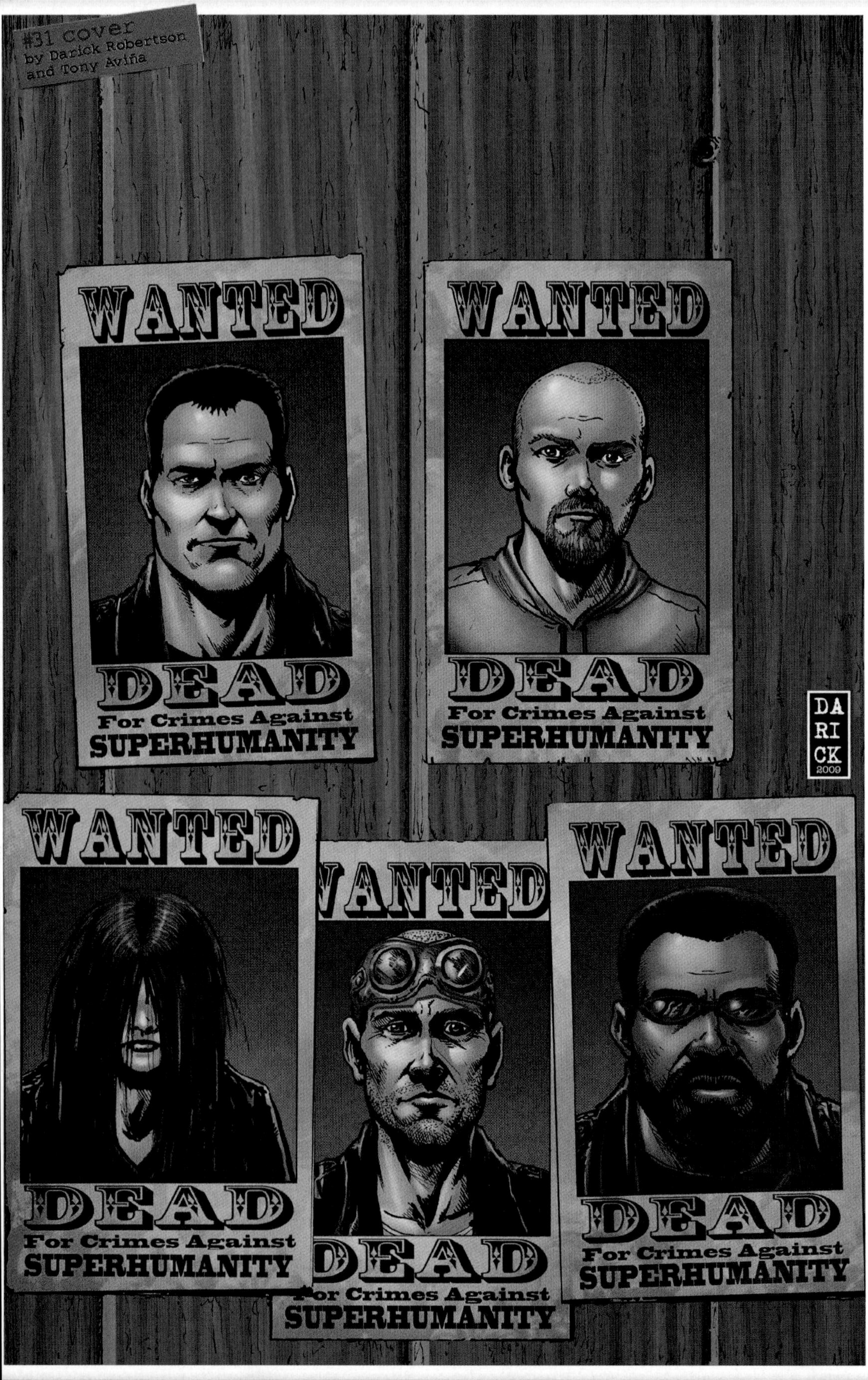
WANTED
DEAD
For Crimes Against
SUPERHUMANITY
WANTED
DEAD
For Crimes Against
SUPERHUMANITY
DARICK 2009
WANTED
DEAD
For Crimes Against
SUPERHUMANITY
WANTED
DEAD
For Crimes Against
SUPERHUMANITY
WANTED
DEAD
For Crimes Against
SUPERHUMANITY

#31 cover
by Darick Robertson
and Tony Aviña

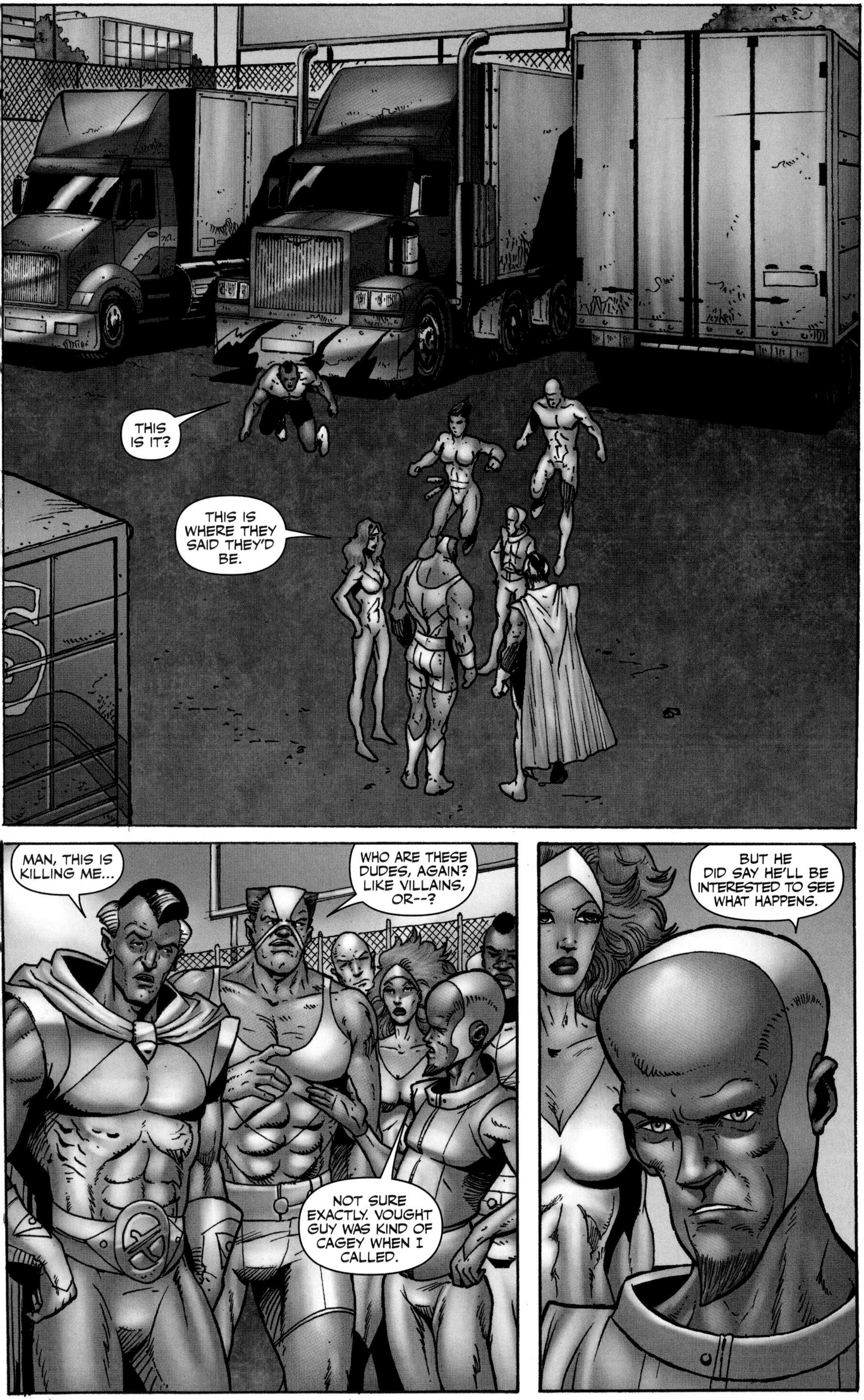
THIS IS IT?
THIS IS WHERE THEY SAID THEY'D BE.
MAN, THIS IS KILLING ME...
WHO ARE THESE DUDES, AGAIN? LIKE VILLAINS, OR--?
NOT SURE EXACTLY. VOUGHT GUY WAS KIND OF CAGEY WHEN I CALLED.
BUT HE DID SAY HE'LL BE INTERESTED TO SEE WHAT HAPPENS.

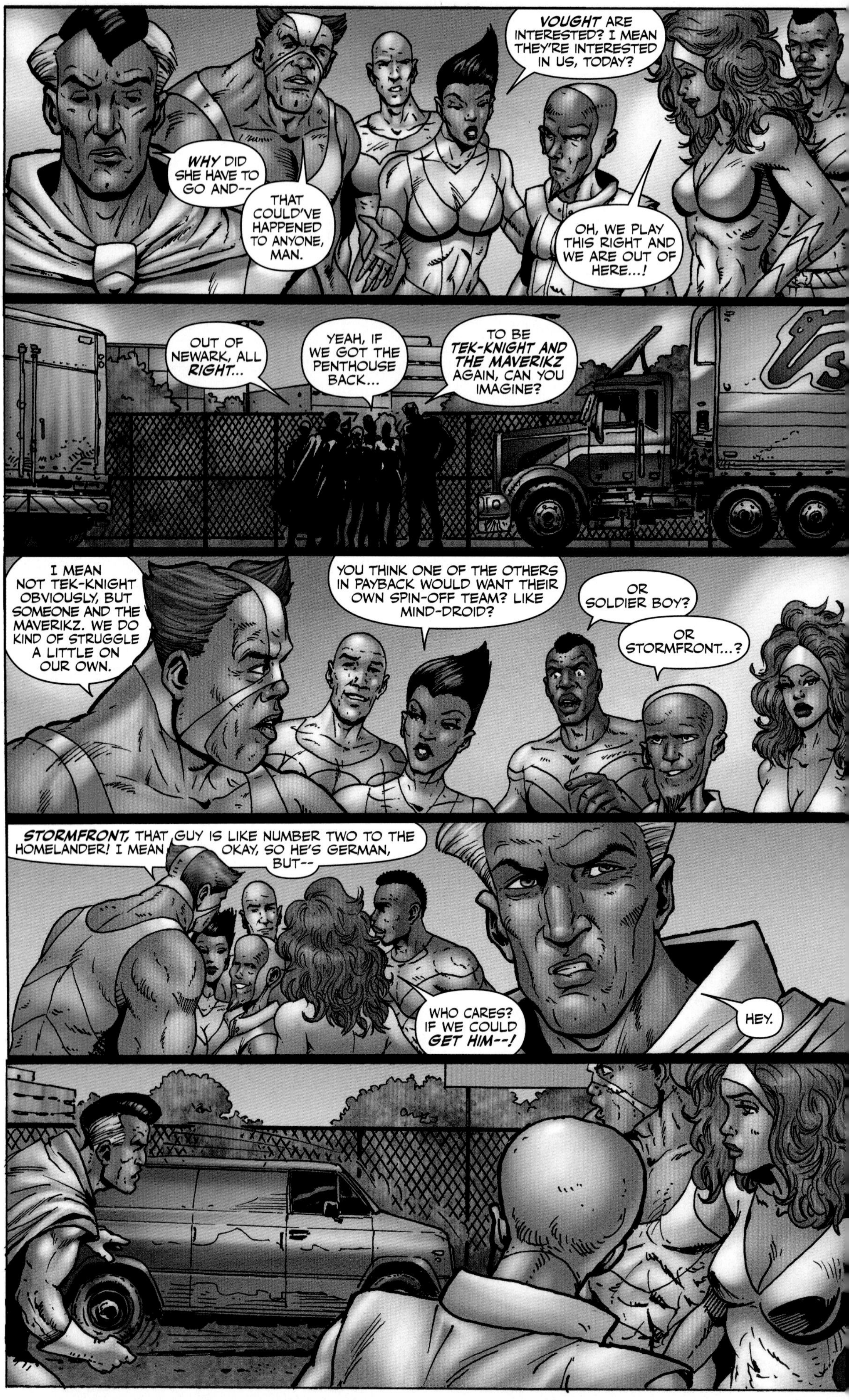
VOUGHT ARE INTERESTED? I MEAN THEY'RE INTERESTED IN US, TODAY?
WHY DID SHE HAVE TO GO AND--
THAT COULD'VE HAPPENED TO ANYONE, MAN.
OH, WE PLAY THIS RIGHT AND WE ARE OUT OF HERE...!
OUT OF NEWARK, ALL RIGHT...
YEAH, IF WE GOT THE PENTHOUSE BACK...
TO BE TEK-KNIGHT AND THE MAVERIKZ AGAIN, CAN YOU IMAGINE?
I MEAN NOT TEK-KNIGHT OBVIOUSLY, BUT SOMEONE AND THE MAVERIKZ. WE DO KIND OF STRUGGLE A LITTLE ON OUR OWN.
YOU THINK ONE OF THE OTHERS IN PAYBACK WOULD WANT THEIR OWN SPIN-OFF TEAM? LIKE MIND-DROID?
OR SOLDIER BOY?
OR STORMFRONT...?
STORMFRONT, THAT GUY IS LIKE NUMBER TWO TO THE HOMELANDER! I MEAN OKAY, SO HE'S GERMAN, BUT--
WHO CARES? IF WE COULD GET HIM--!
HEY.

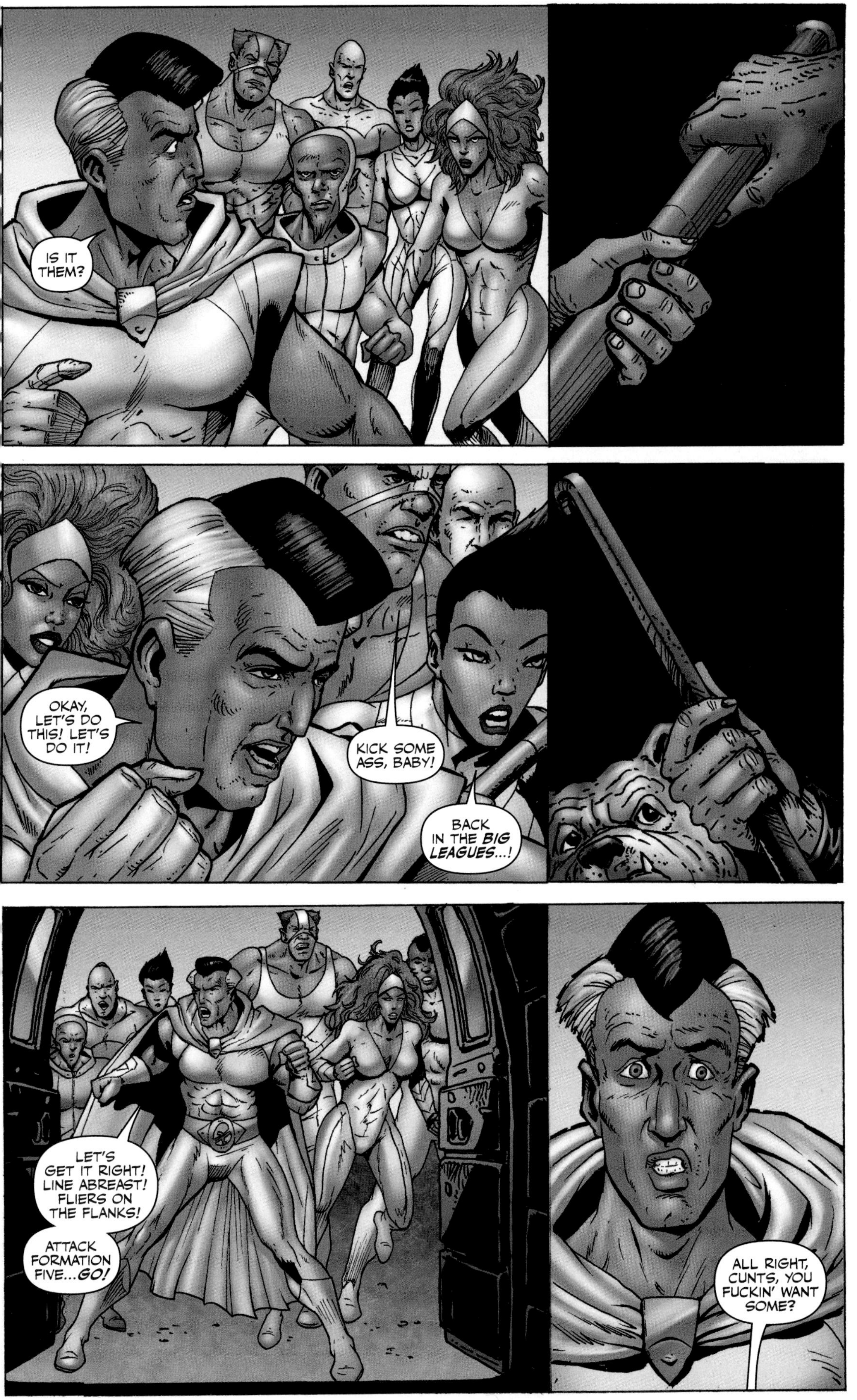
IS IT THEM?
OKAY, LET'S DO THIS! LET'S DO IT!
KICK SOME ASS, BABY!
BACK IN THE *BIG LEAGUES*...!
LET'S GET IT RIGHT! LINE ABREAST! FLIERS ON THE FLANKS!
ATTACK FORMATION FIVE...*GO!*
ALL RIGHT, CUNTS, YOU FUCKIN' WANT SOME?

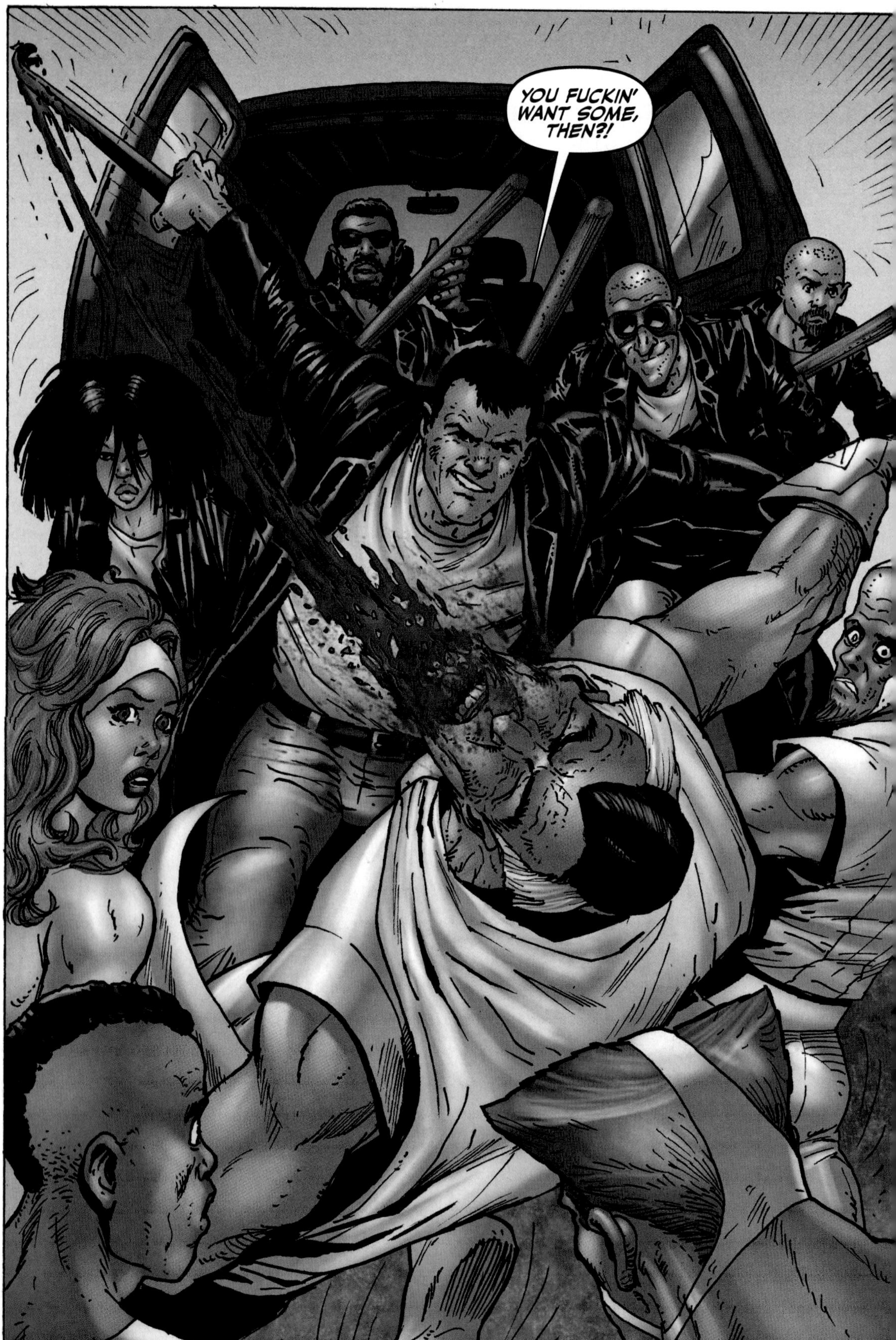
YOU FUCKIN' WANT SOME, THEN?!

THE SELF-PRESERVATION SOCIETY
part one

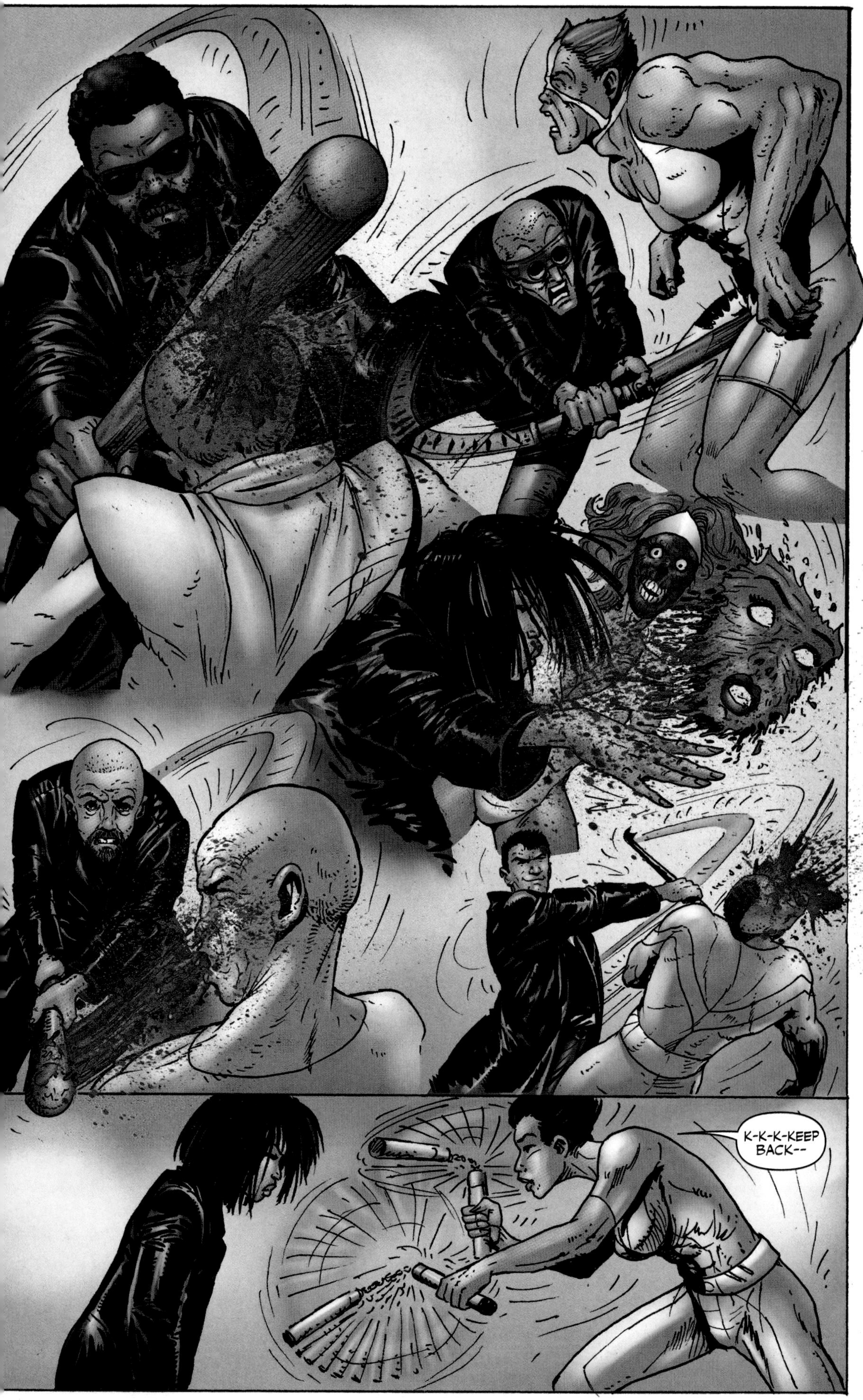
K-K-K-KEEP BACK--

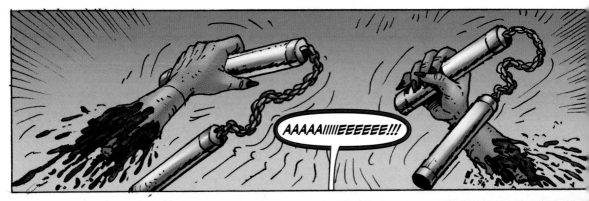

AAAAAIIIIIEEEEEEE!!!

STUPID BASTARD--

FUCKIN' STUPID BASTARD-- AAARRRRHHH--!

EASY, HUGHIE.

UH?!

IDEA IS THE SUPES STAY SCARED.

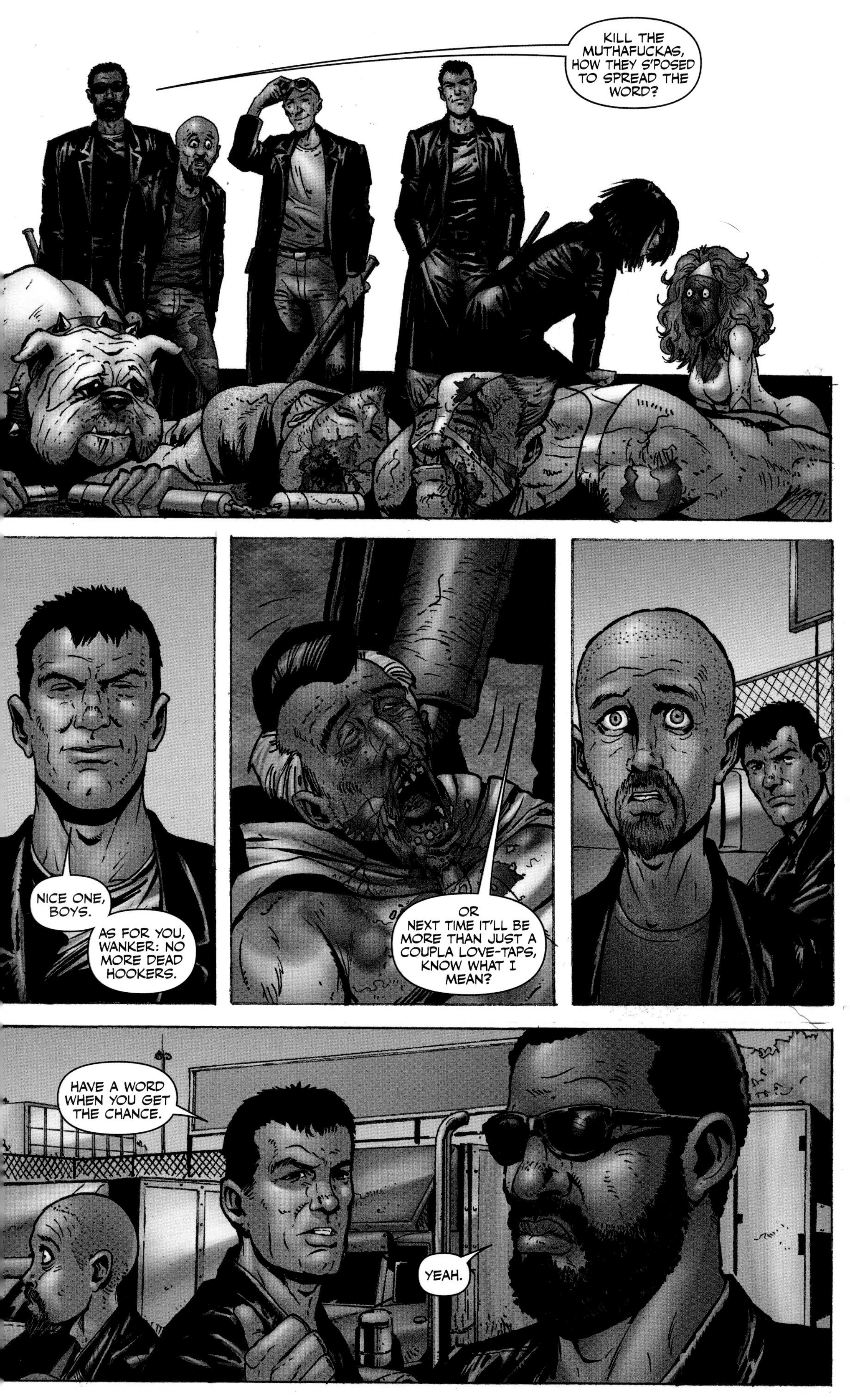
KILL THE MUTHAFUCKAS, HOW THEY S'POSED TO SPREAD THE WORD?
NICE ONE, BOYS.
AS FOR YOU, WANKER: NO MORE DEAD HOOKERS.
OR NEXT TIME IT'LL BE MORE THAN JUST A COUPLA LOVE-TAPS, KNOW WHAT I MEAN?
HAVE A WORD WHEN YOU GET THE CHANCE.
YEAH.

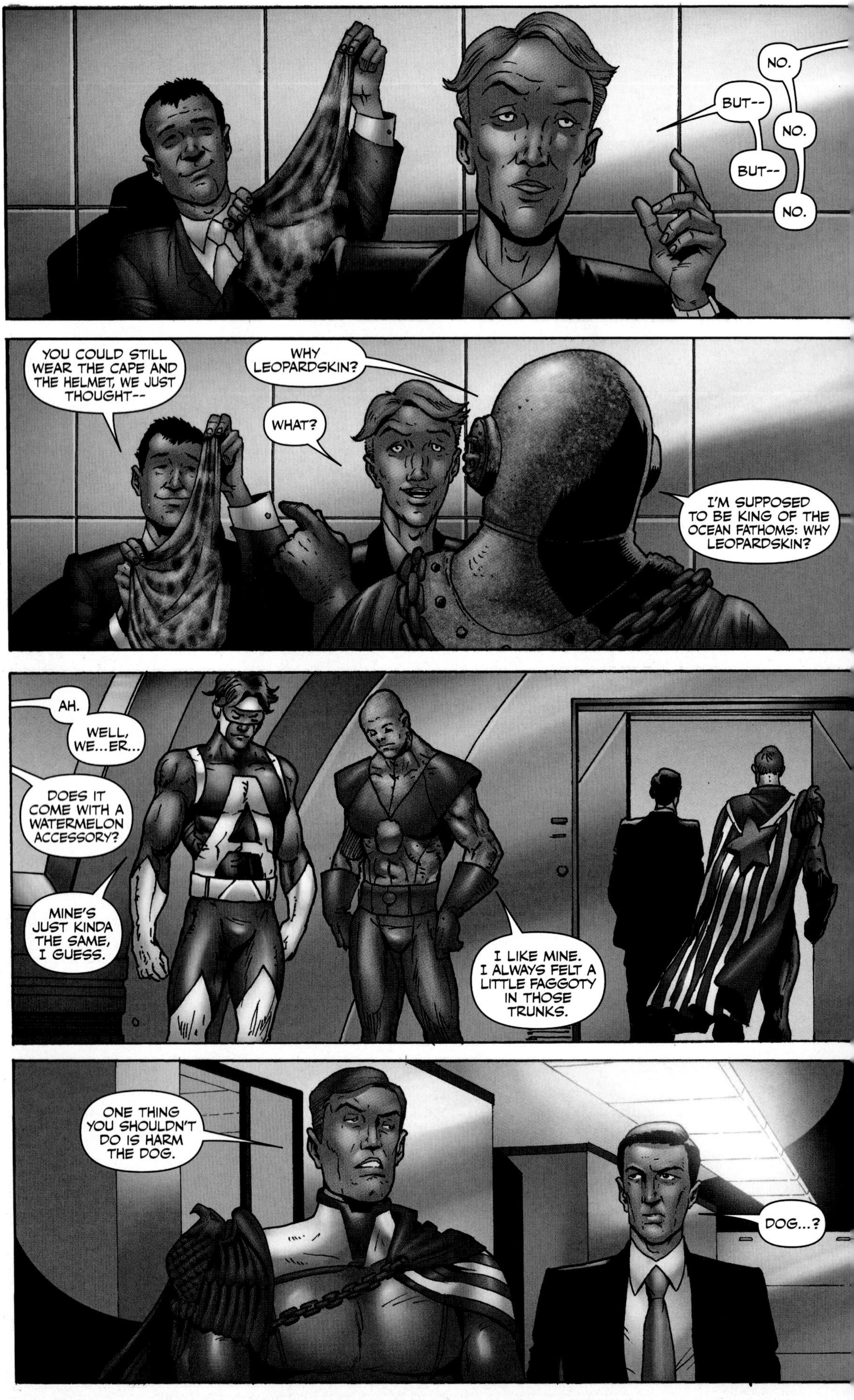
NO.
BUT--
NO.
BUT--
NO.
YOU COULD STILL WEAR THE CAPE AND THE HELMET, WE JUST THOUGHT--
WHY LEOPARDSKIN?
WHAT?
I'M SUPPOSED TO BE KING OF THE OCEAN FATHOMS: WHY LEOPARDSKIN?
AH.
WELL, WE...ER...
DOES IT COME WITH A WATERMELON ACCESSORY?
MINE'S JUST KINDA THE SAME, I GUESS.
I LIKE MINE. I ALWAYS FELT A LITTLE FAGGOTY IN THOSE TRUNKS.
ONE THING YOU SHOULDN'T DO IS HARM THE DOG.
DOG...?

HEY, ARE WE ALL GETTING--

NOT NOW.

THE DOG, THE ONE HE TAKES EVERYWHERE WITH HIM. IF YOU WANT TO AVOID PUSHING HIM TOO FAR, YOU SHOULD KEEP IT OUT OF THE FIRING LINE.

I'M SORRY, WHO ARE WE TALKING ABOUT?

BUTCHER...

YOU DON'T HAVE TO CONCERN YOURSELF ABOUT THAT.

BUT IS IT UNDER WAY? HAVE YOU OKAYED THE OPERATION?

I DO APPRECIATE THE INFORMATION, THOUGH.

REALLY.

WE'LL LEAVE THE CONSULTANTS WITH YOU FOR A COUPLE OF DAYS, JUST TO KEEP THE COSTUME TRANSITION AS SMOOTH AS POSSIBLE.

WHERE'S STARLIGHT, INCIDENTALLY? THEY'RE GOING TO WANT TO SPEAK TO HER.

NO IDEA.

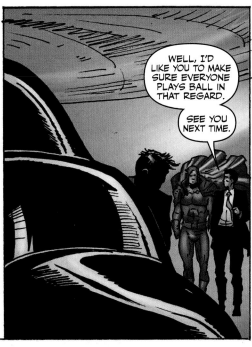

WELL, I'D LIKE YOU TO MAKE SURE EVERYONE PLAYS BALL IN THAT REGARD.

SEE YOU NEXT TIME.

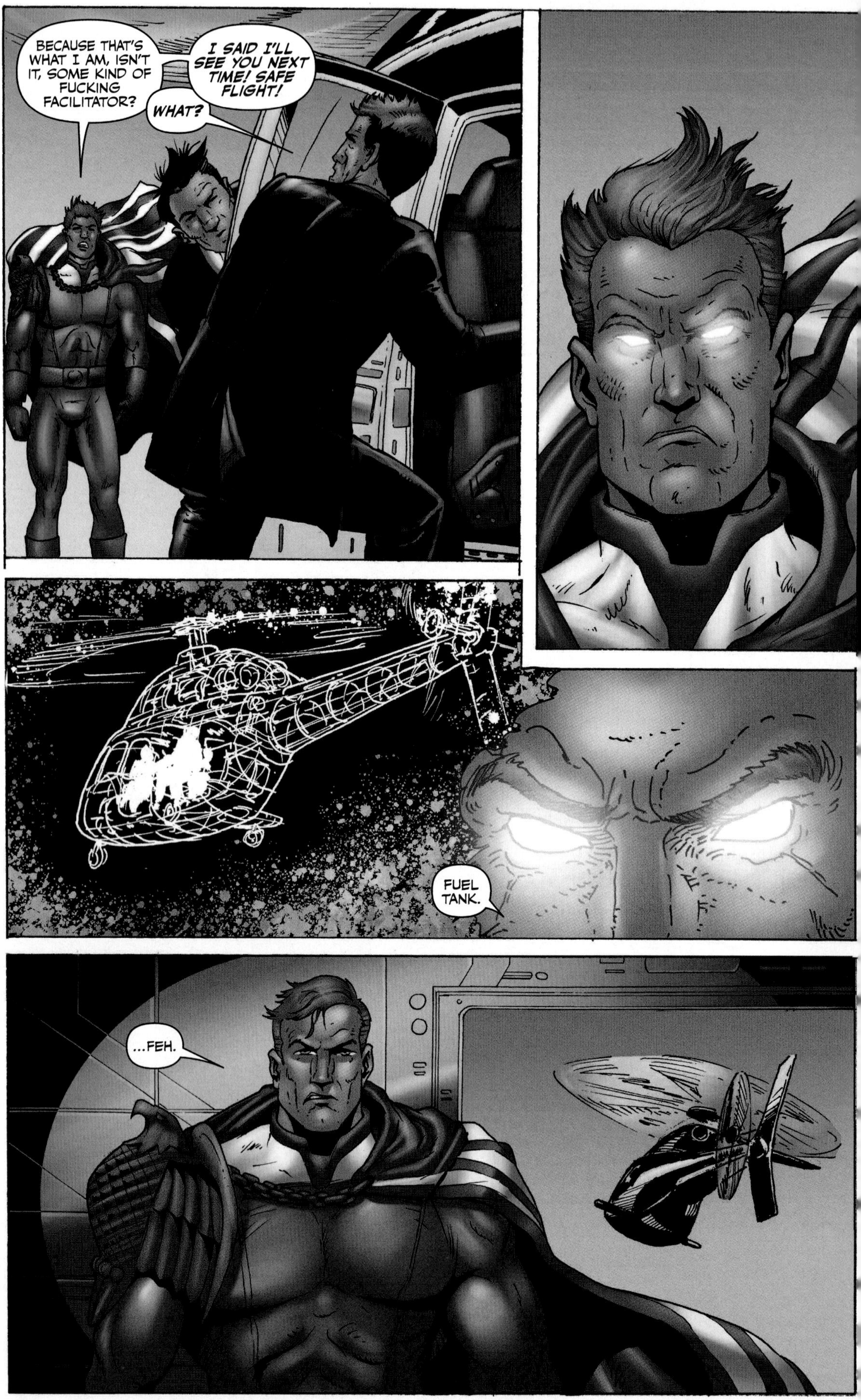
BECAUSE THAT'S WHAT I AM, ISN'T IT, SOME KIND OF FUCKING FACILITATOR?
I SAID I'LL SEE YOU NEXT TIME! SAFE FLIGHT!
WHAT?
FUEL TANK.
...FEH.

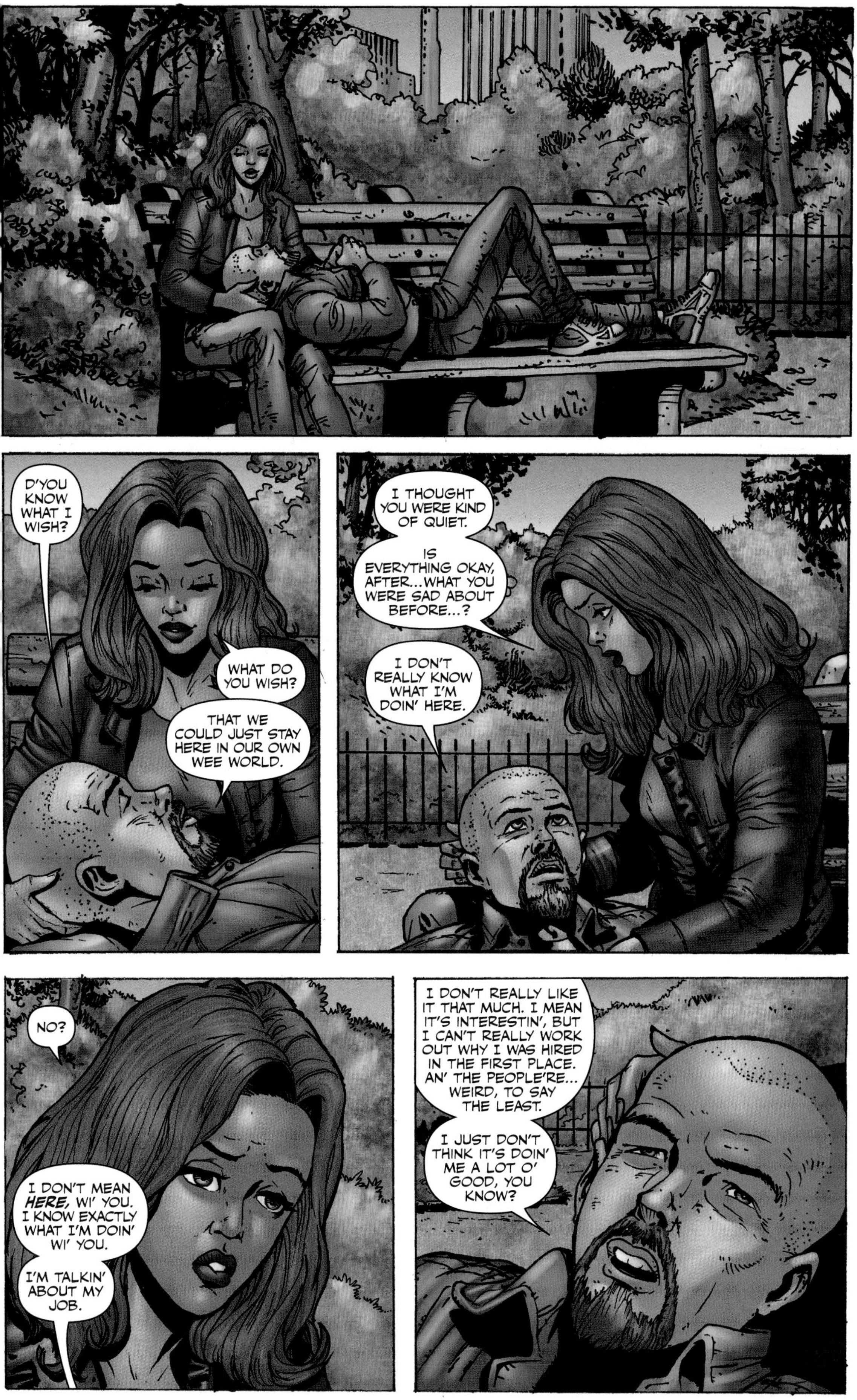
D'YOU KNOW WHAT I WISH?
WHAT DO YOU WISH?
THAT WE COULD JUST STAY HERE IN OUR OWN WEE WORLD.
I THOUGHT YOU WERE KIND OF QUIET.
IS EVERYTHING OKAY, AFTER...WHAT YOU WERE SAD ABOUT BEFORE...?
I DON'T REALLY KNOW WHAT I'M DOIN' HERE.
NO?
I DON'T MEAN HERE, WI' YOU. I KNOW EXACTLY WHAT I'M DOIN' WI' YOU.
I'M TALKIN' ABOUT MY JOB.
I DON'T REALLY LIKE IT THAT MUCH. I MEAN IT'S INTERESTIN', BUT I CAN'T REALLY WORK OUT WHY I WAS HIRED IN THE FIRST PLACE. AN' THE PEOPLE'RE... WEIRD, TO SAY THE LEAST.
I JUST DON'T THINK IT'S DOIN' ME A LOT O' GOOD, YOU KNOW?

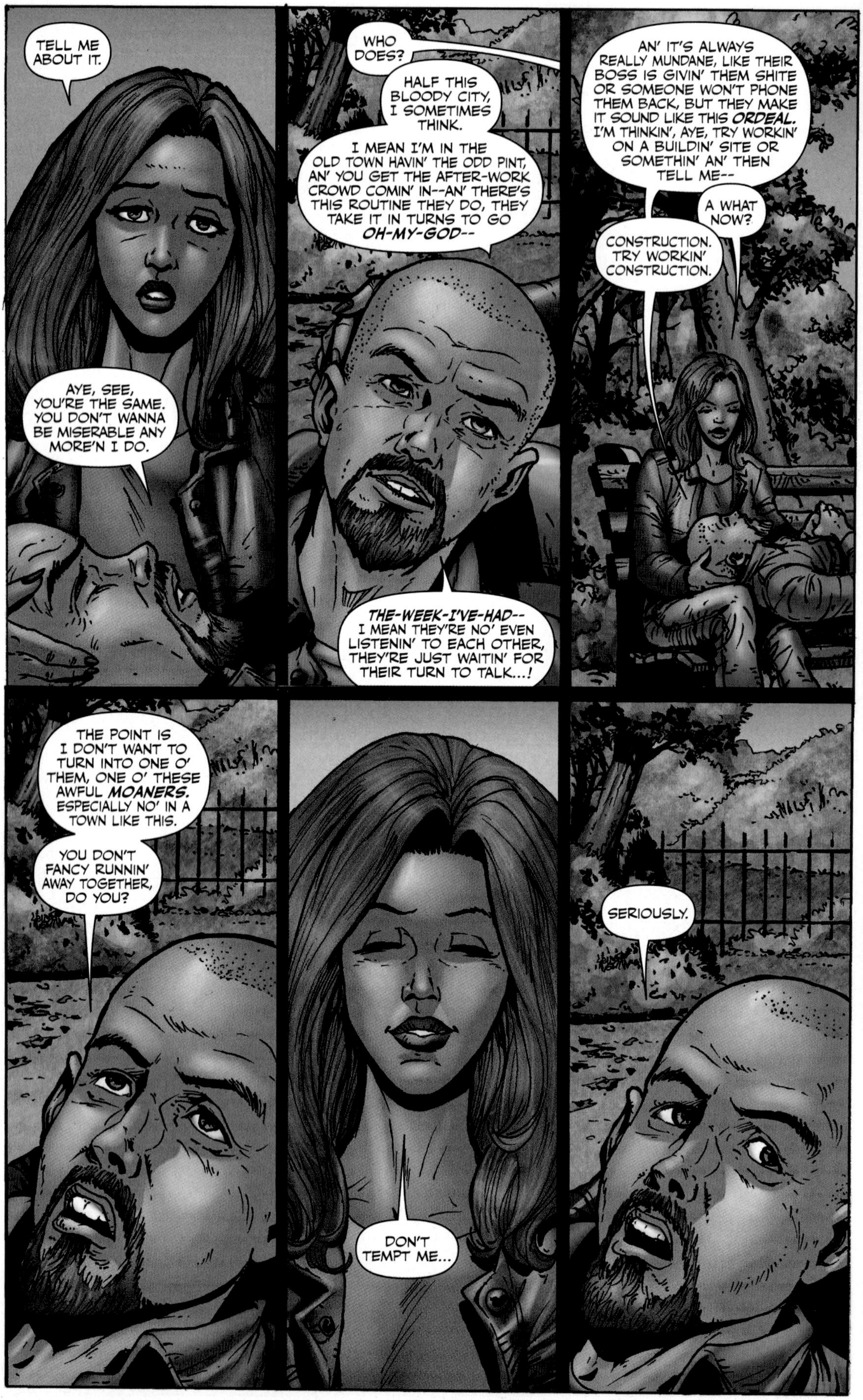
TELL ME ABOUT IT.
AYE, SEE, YOU'RE THE SAME. YOU DON'T WANNA BE MISERABLE ANY MORE'N I DO.
WHO DOES?
HALF THIS BLOODY CITY, I SOMETIMES THINK.
I MEAN I'M IN THE OLD TOWN HAVIN' THE ODD PINT, AN' YOU GET THE AFTER-WORK CROWD COMIN' IN--AN' THERE'S THIS ROUTINE THEY DO, THEY TAKE IT IN TURNS TO GO OH-MY-GOD--
THE-WEEK-I'VE-HAD-- I MEAN THEY'RE NO' EVEN LISTENIN' TO EACH OTHER, THEY'RE JUST WAITIN' FOR THEIR TURN TO TALK...!
AN' IT'S ALWAYS REALLY MUNDANE, LIKE THEIR BOSS IS GIVIN' THEM SHITE OR SOMEONE WON'T PHONE THEM BACK, BUT THEY MAKE IT SOUND LIKE THIS ORDEAL. I'M THINKIN', AYE, TRY WORKIN' ON A BUILDIN' SITE OR SOMETHIN' AN' THEN TELL ME--
A WHAT NOW?
CONSTRUCTION. TRY WORKIN' CONSTRUCTION.
THE POINT IS I DON'T WANT TO TURN INTO ONE O' THEM, ONE O' THESE AWFUL MOANERS. ESPECIALLY NO' IN A TOWN LIKE THIS.
YOU DON'T FANCY RUNNIN' AWAY TOGETHER, DO YOU?
DON'T TEMPT ME...
SERIOUSLY.

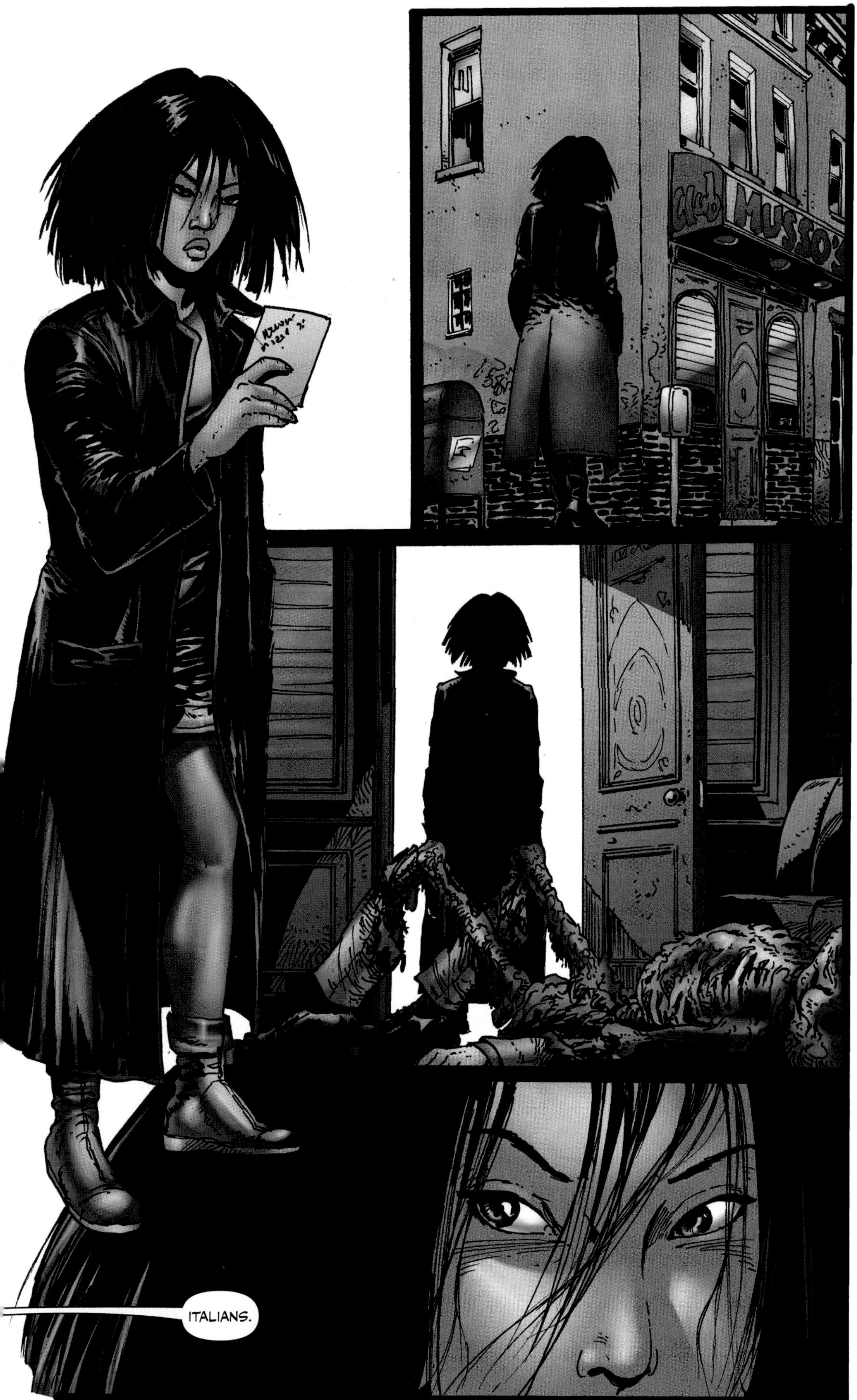
club MUSSO'S
ITALIANS.

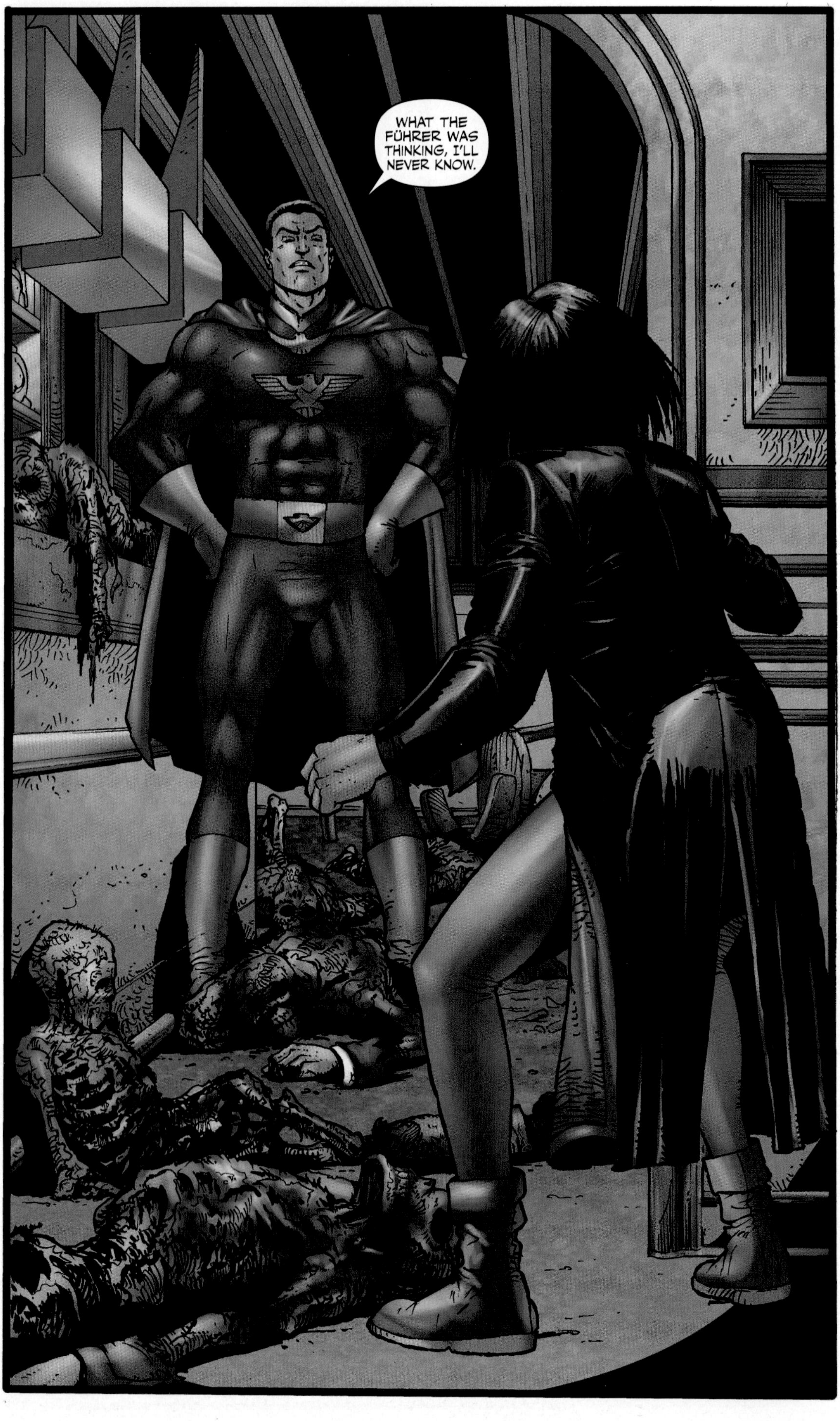
WHAT THE FÜHRER WAS THINKING, I'LL NEVER KNOW.

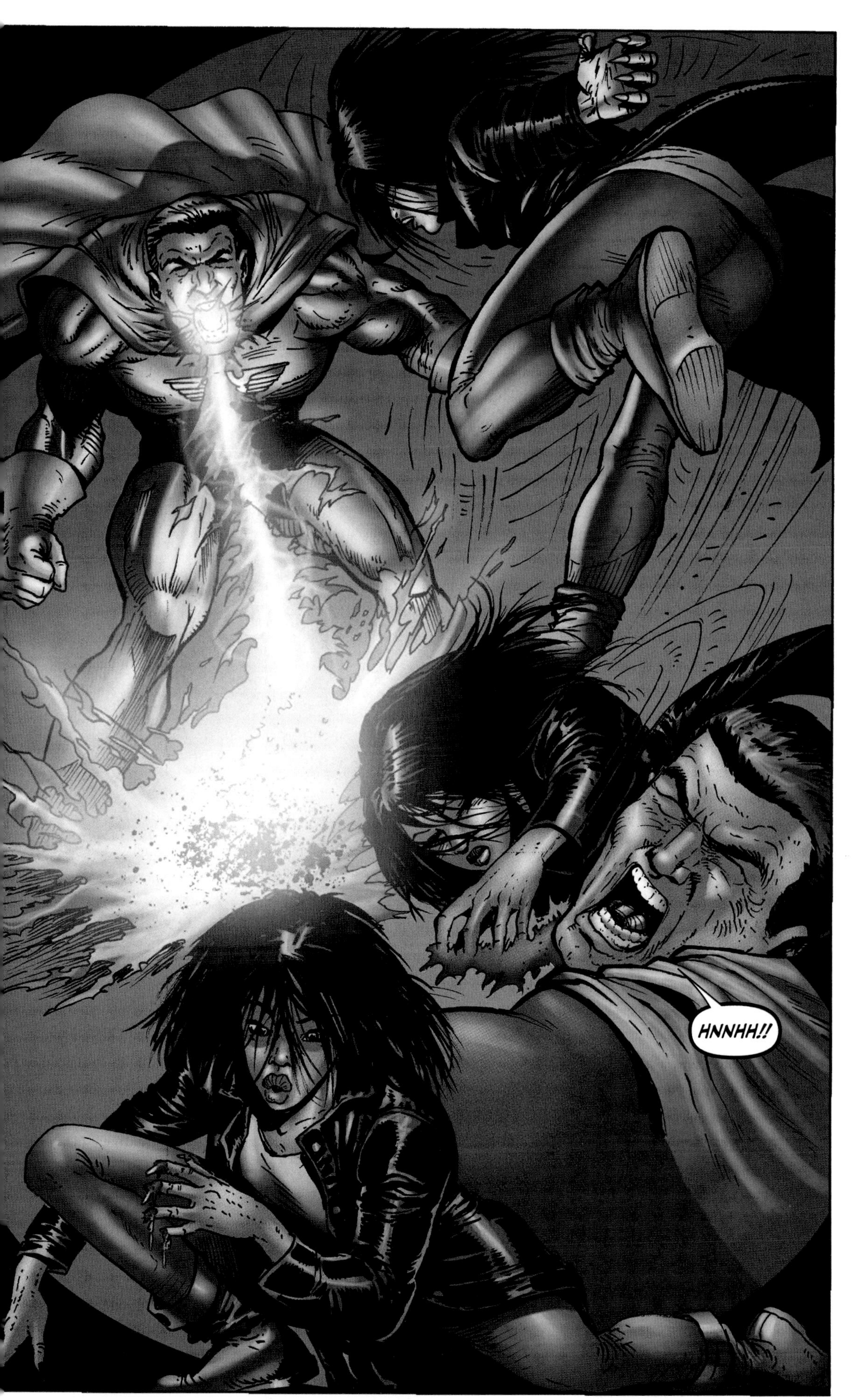
HNNHH!!

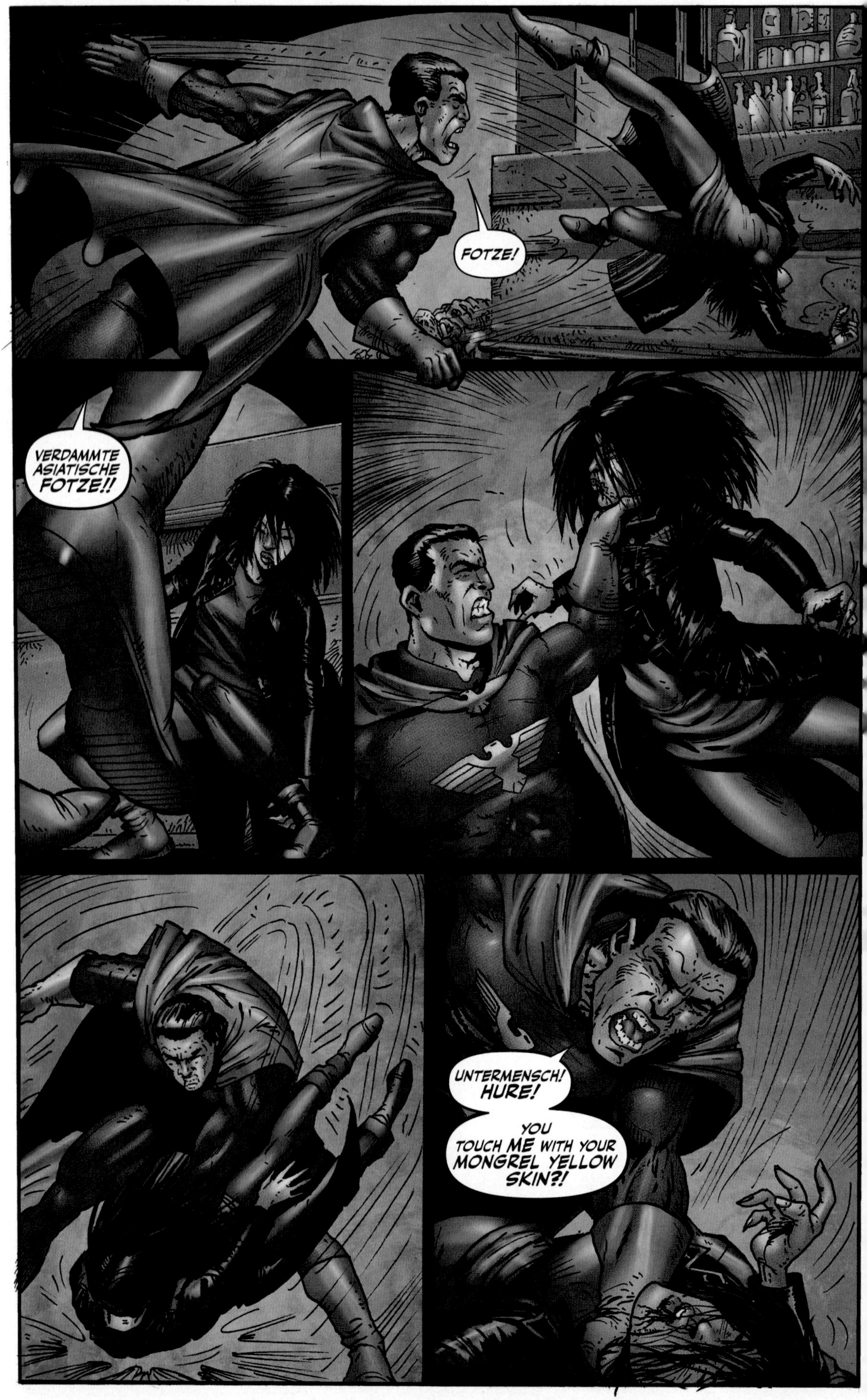
FOTZE!
VERDAMMTE ASIATISCHE FOTZE!!
UNTERMENSCH! HURE!
YOU TOUCH ME WITH YOUR MONGREL YELLOW SKIN?!

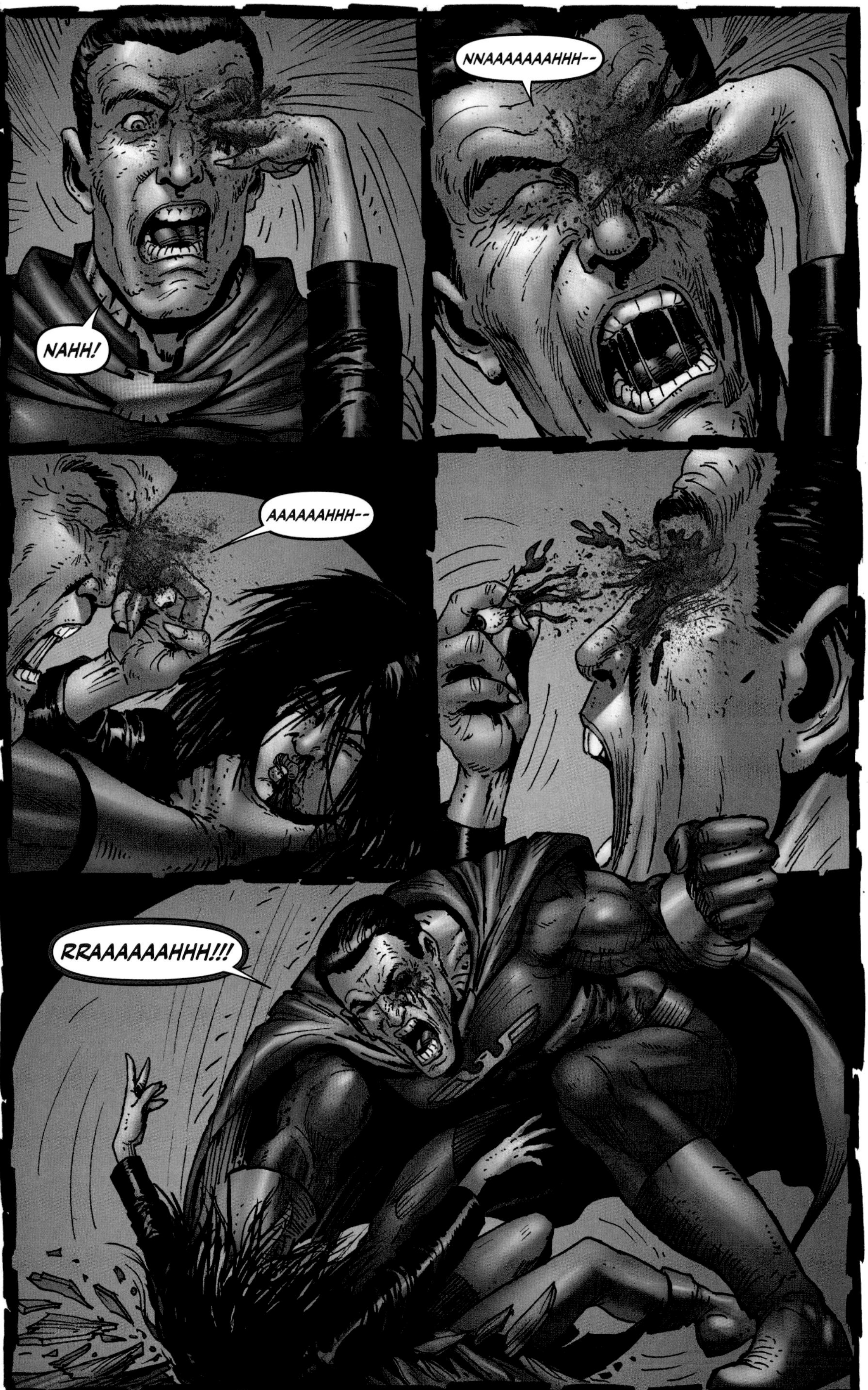
NAHH!
NNAAAAAAAAHHH--
AAAAAAHHH--
RRAAAAAAAHHH!!!

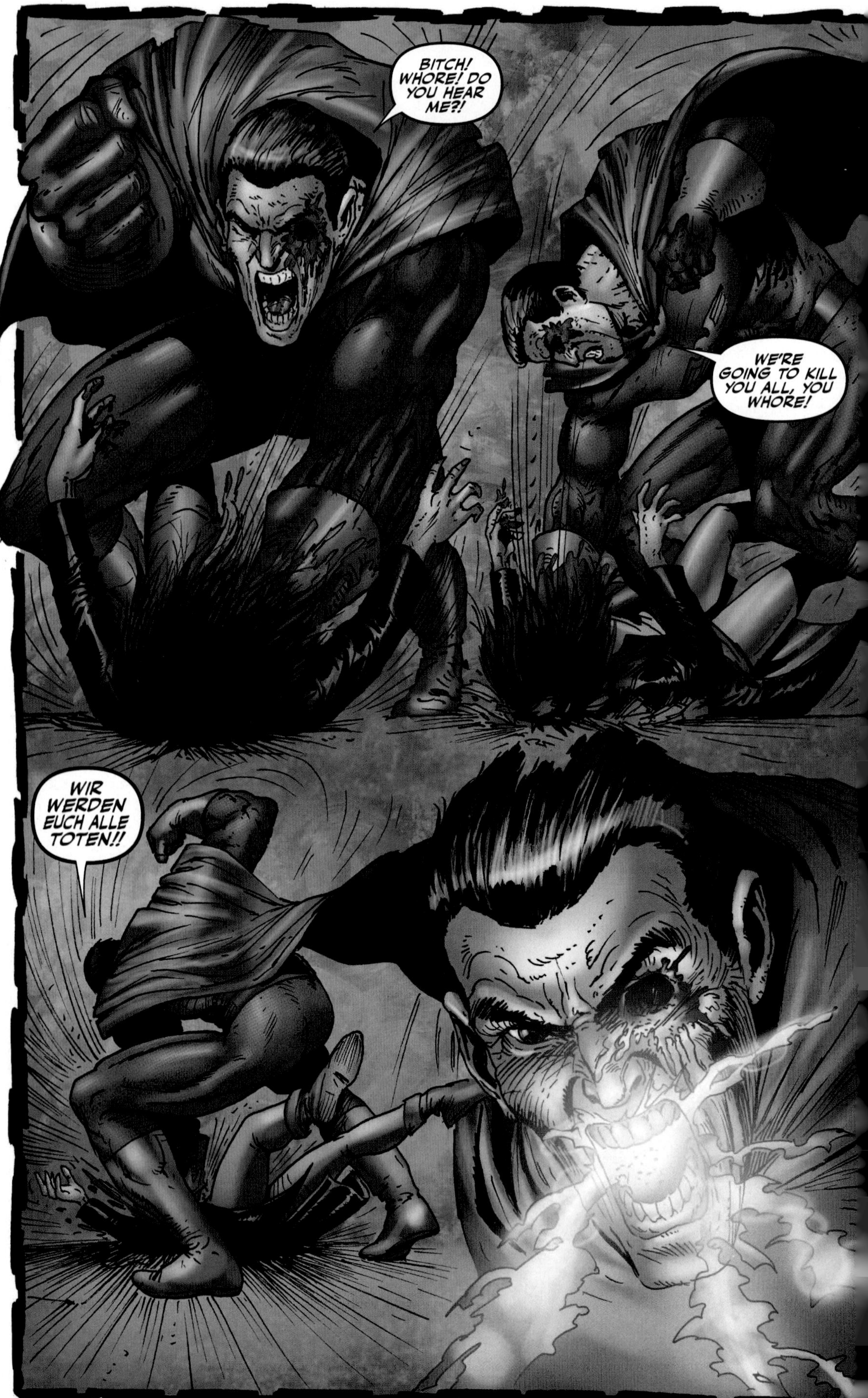
BITCH! WHORE! DO YOU HEAR ME?!
WE'RE GOING TO KILL YOU ALL, YOU WHORE!
WIR WERDEN EUCH ALLE TOTEN!!

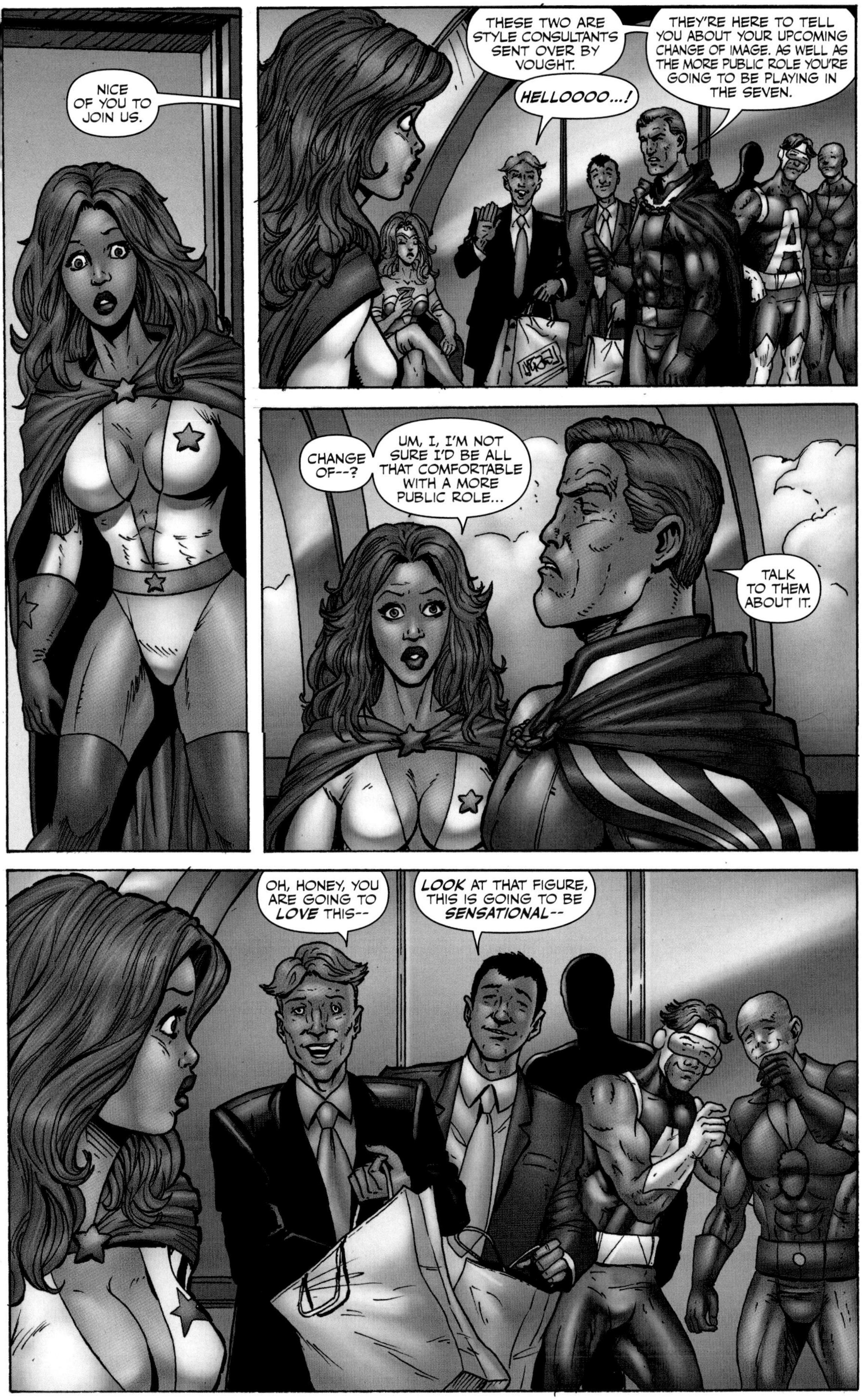
NICE OF YOU TO JOIN US.
THESE TWO ARE STYLE CONSULTANTS SENT OVER BY VOUGHT.
HELLOOOO...!
THEY'RE HERE TO TELL YOU ABOUT YOUR UPCOMING CHANGE OF IMAGE. AS WELL AS THE MORE PUBLIC ROLE YOU'RE GOING TO BE PLAYING IN THE SEVEN.
CHANGE OF--?
UM, I, I'M NOT SURE I'D BE ALL THAT COMFORTABLE WITH A MORE PUBLIC ROLE...
TALK TO THEM ABOUT IT.
OH, HONEY, YOU ARE GOING TO LOVE THIS--
LOOK AT THAT FIGURE, THIS IS GOING TO BE SENSATIONAL--

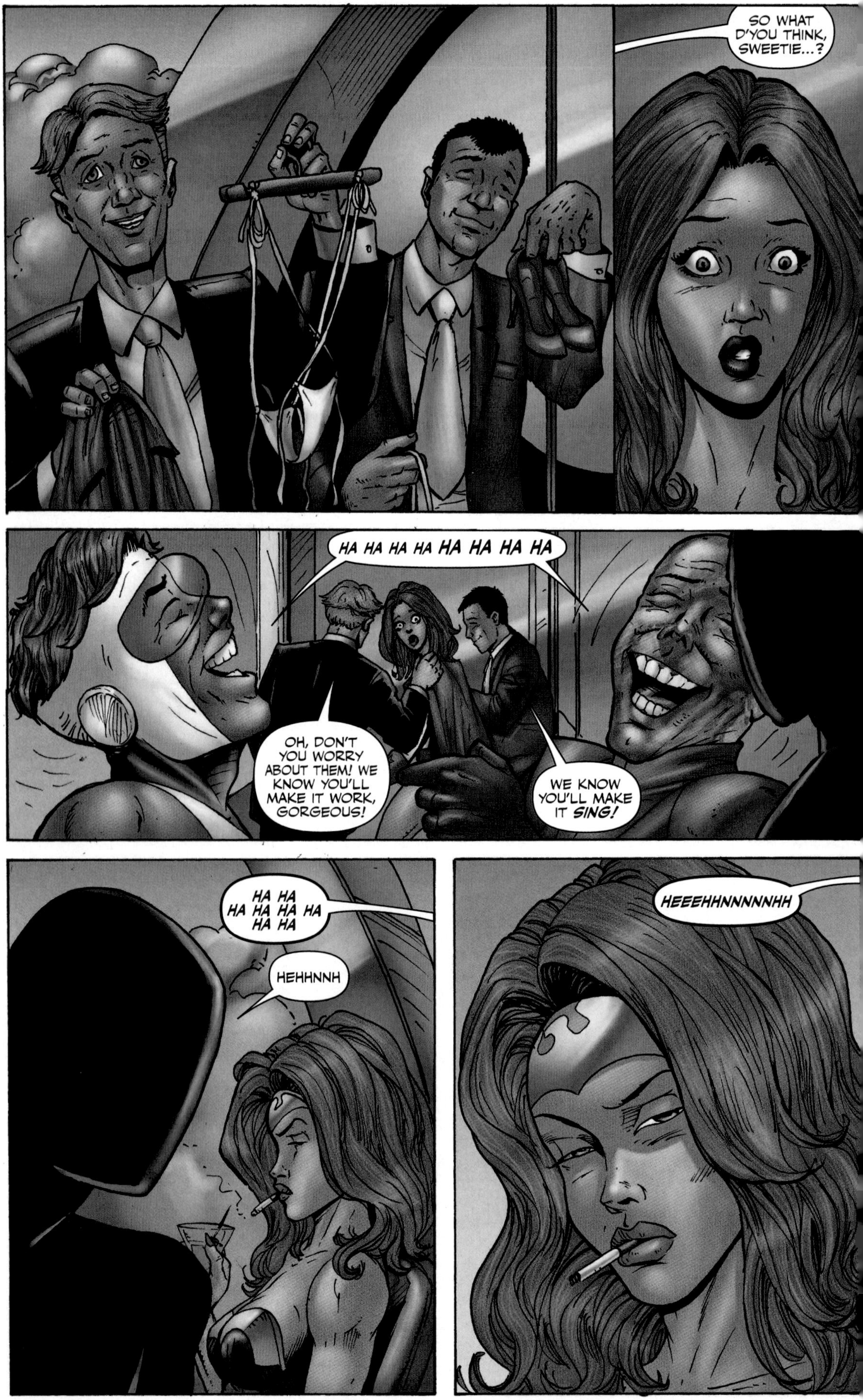
SO WHAT D'YOU THINK, SWEETIE...?
HA HA HA HA HA HA HA HA
OH, DON'T YOU WORRY ABOUT THEM! WE KNOW YOU'LL MAKE IT WORK, GORGEOUS!
WE KNOW YOU'LL MAKE IT SING!
HA HA HA HA HA HA HA HA
HEHHNNH
HEEEHHNNNNNHH

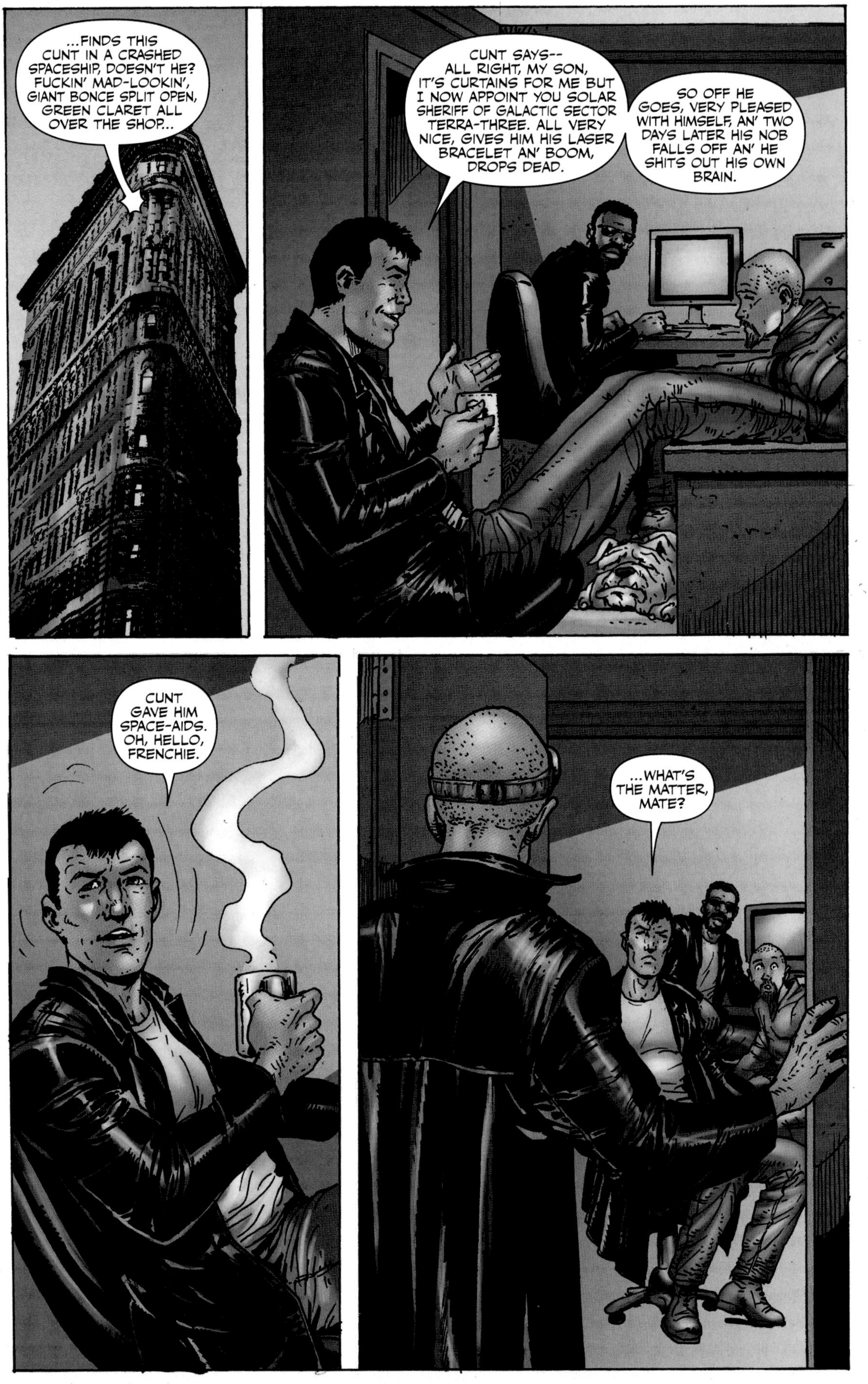
...FINDS THIS CUNT IN A CRASHED SPACESHIP, DOESN'T HE? FUCKIN' MAD-LOOKIN', GIANT BONCE SPLIT OPEN, GREEN CLARET ALL OVER THE SHOP...
CUNT SAYS-- ALL RIGHT, MY SON, IT'S CURTAINS FOR ME BUT I NOW APPOINT YOU SOLAR SHERIFF OF GALACTIC SECTOR TERRA-THREE. ALL VERY NICE, GIVES HIM HIS LASER BRACELET AN' BOOM, DROPS DEAD.
SO OFF HE GOES, VERY PLEASED WITH HIMSELF, AN' TWO DAYS LATER HIS NOB FALLS OFF AN' HE SHITS OUT HIS OWN BRAIN.
CUNT GAVE HIM SPACE-AIDS. OH, HELLO, FRENCHIE.
...WHAT'S THE MATTER, MATE?

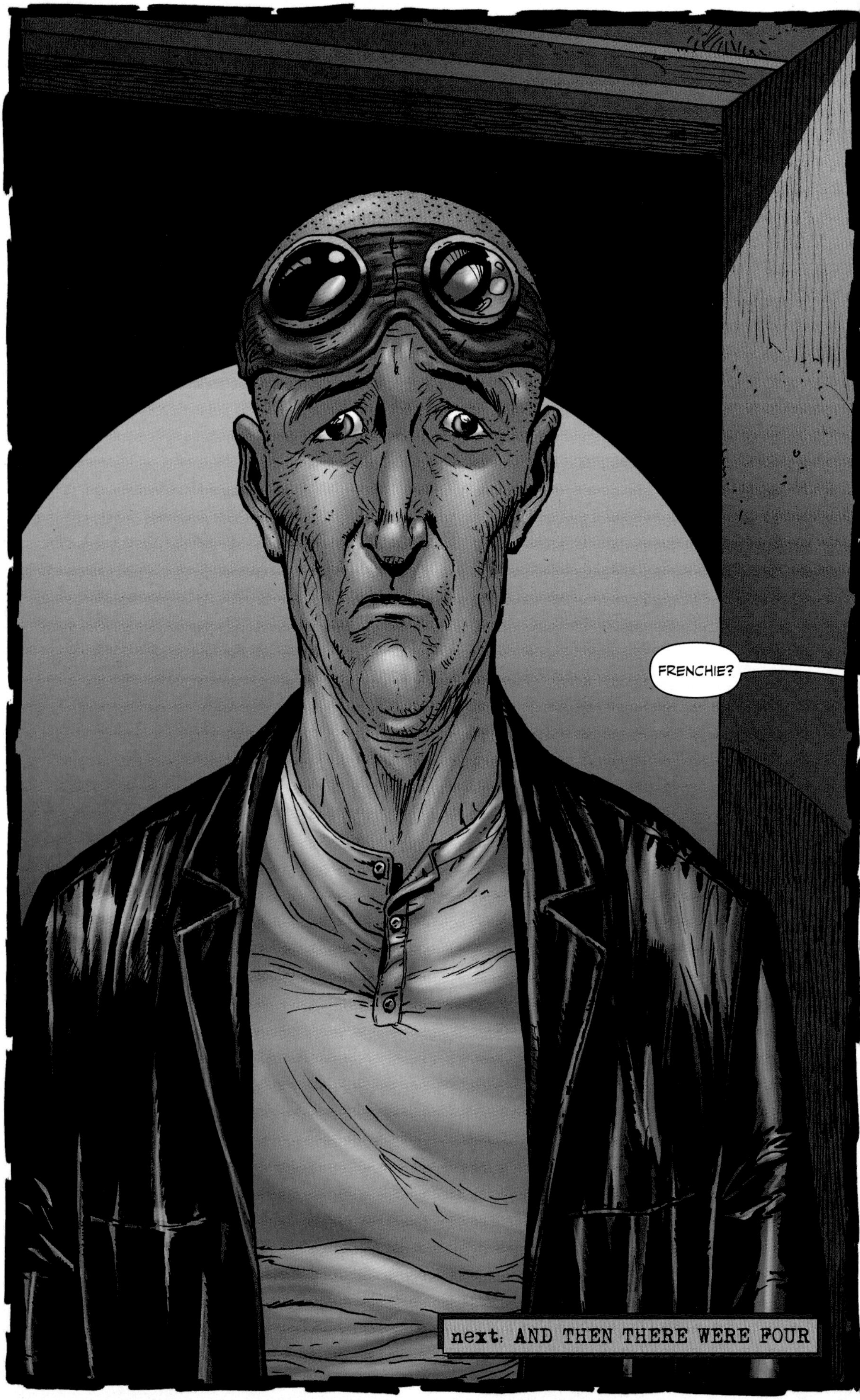
FRENCHIE?
next: AND THEN THERE WERE FOUR

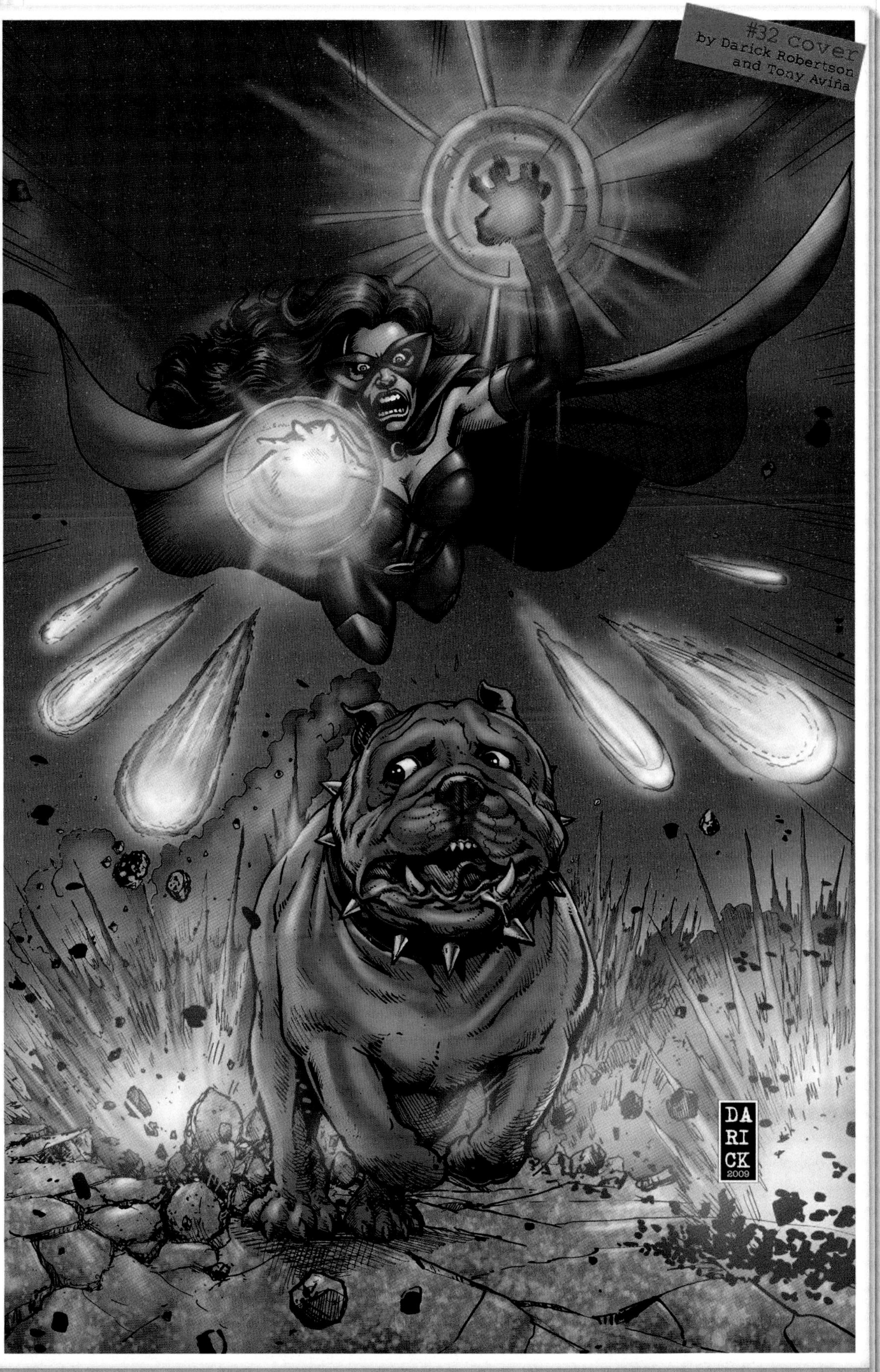
#32 cover
by Darick Robertson
and Tony Aviña
DA
RI
CK
2009

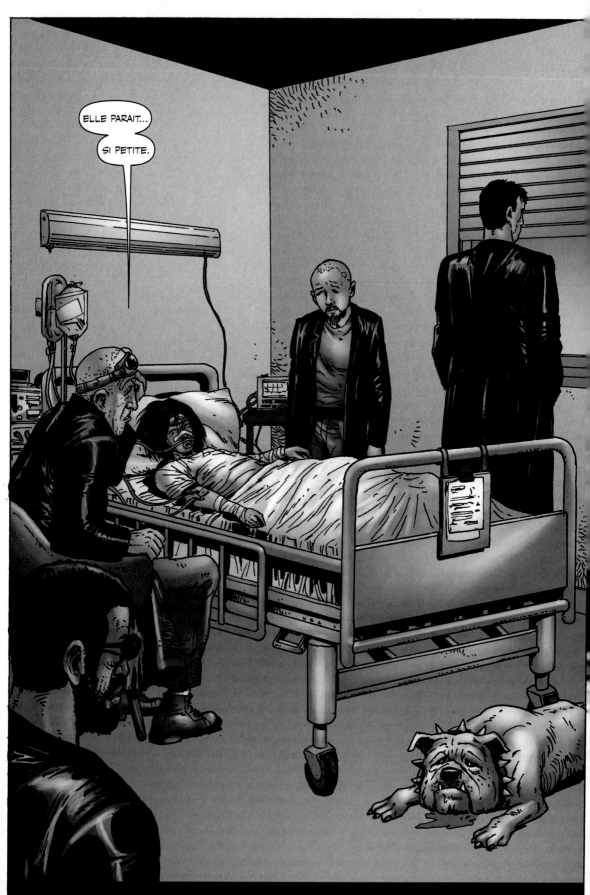

THE SELF-PRESERVATION SOCIETY
part two

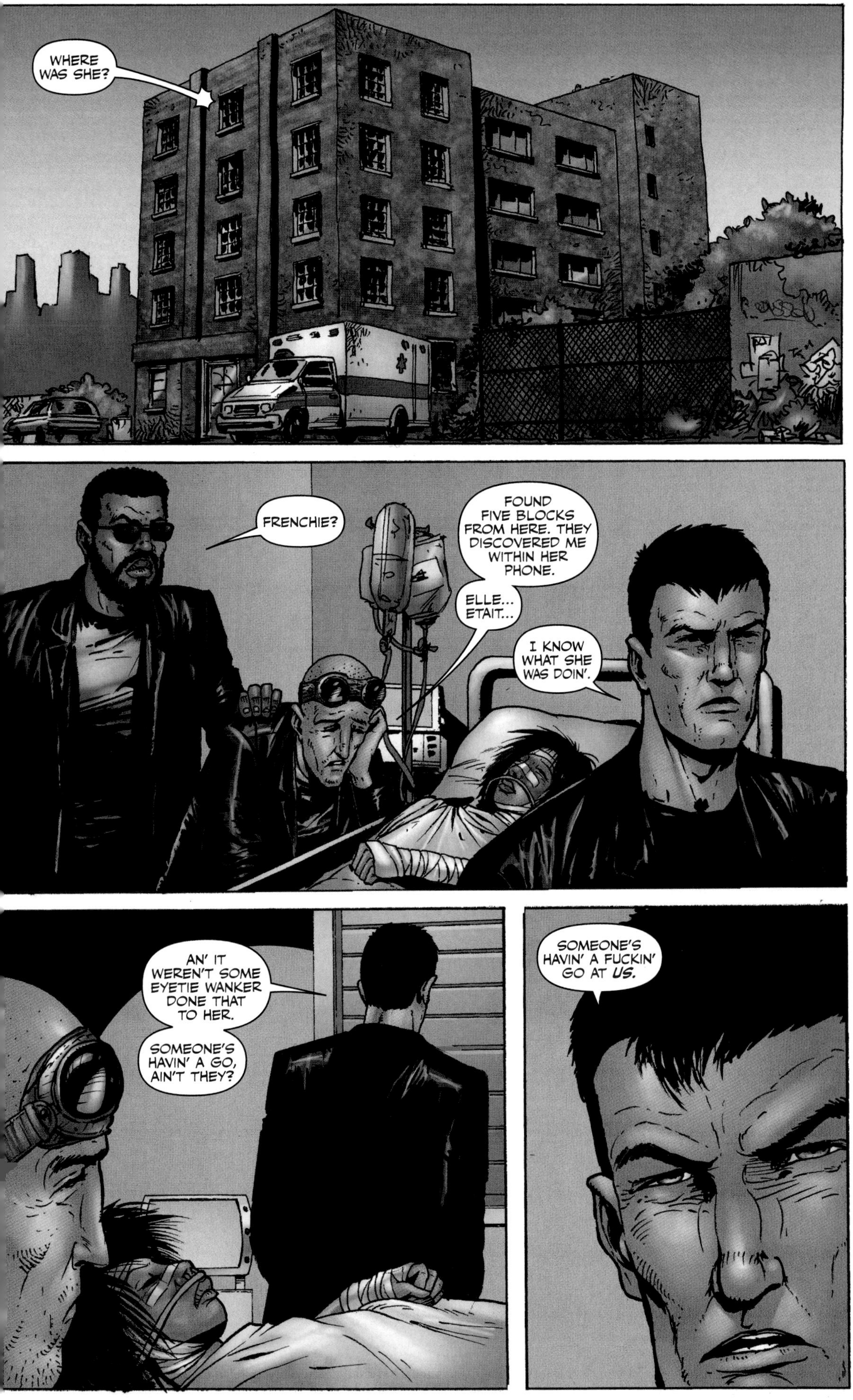
WHERE WAS SHE?
FRENCHIE?
FOUND FIVE BLOCKS FROM HERE. THEY DISCOVERED ME WITHIN HER PHONE.
ELLE... ETAIT...
I KNOW WHAT SHE WAS DOIN'.
AN' IT WEREN'T SOME EYETIE WANKER DONE THAT TO HER.
SOMEONE'S HAVIN' A GO, AIN'T THEY?
SOMEONE'S HAVIN' A FUCKIN' GO AT *US*.

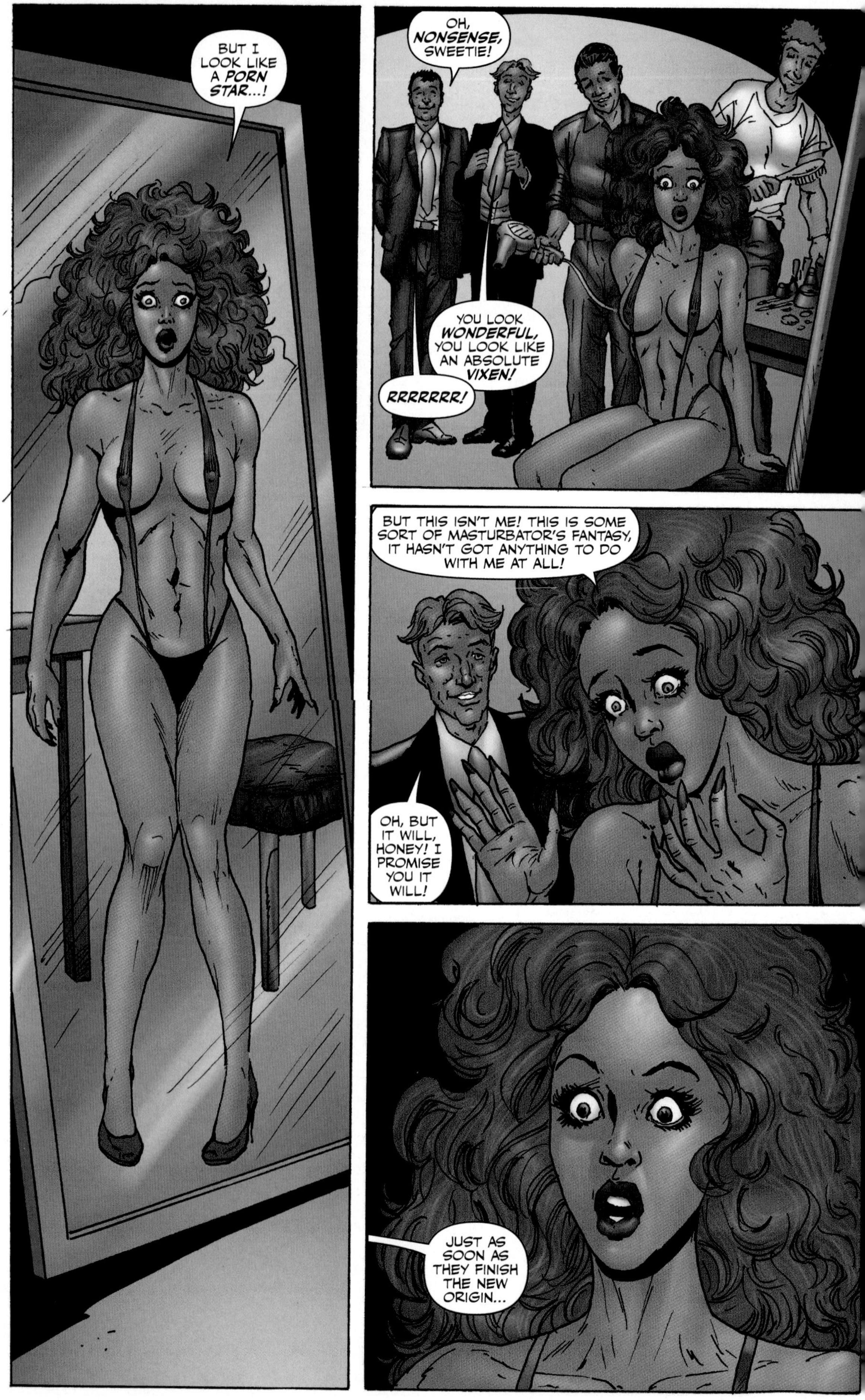
BUT I LOOK LIKE A PORN STAR...!
OH, NONSENSE, SWEETIE!
YOU LOOK WONDERFUL, YOU LOOK LIKE AN ABSOLUTE VIXEN!
RRRRRRR!
BUT THIS ISN'T ME! THIS IS SOME SORT OF MASTURBATOR'S FANTASY, IT HASN'T GOT ANYTHING TO DO WITH ME AT ALL!
OH, BUT IT WILL, HONEY! I PROMISE YOU IT WILL!
JUST AS SOON AS THEY FINISH THE NEW ORIGIN...

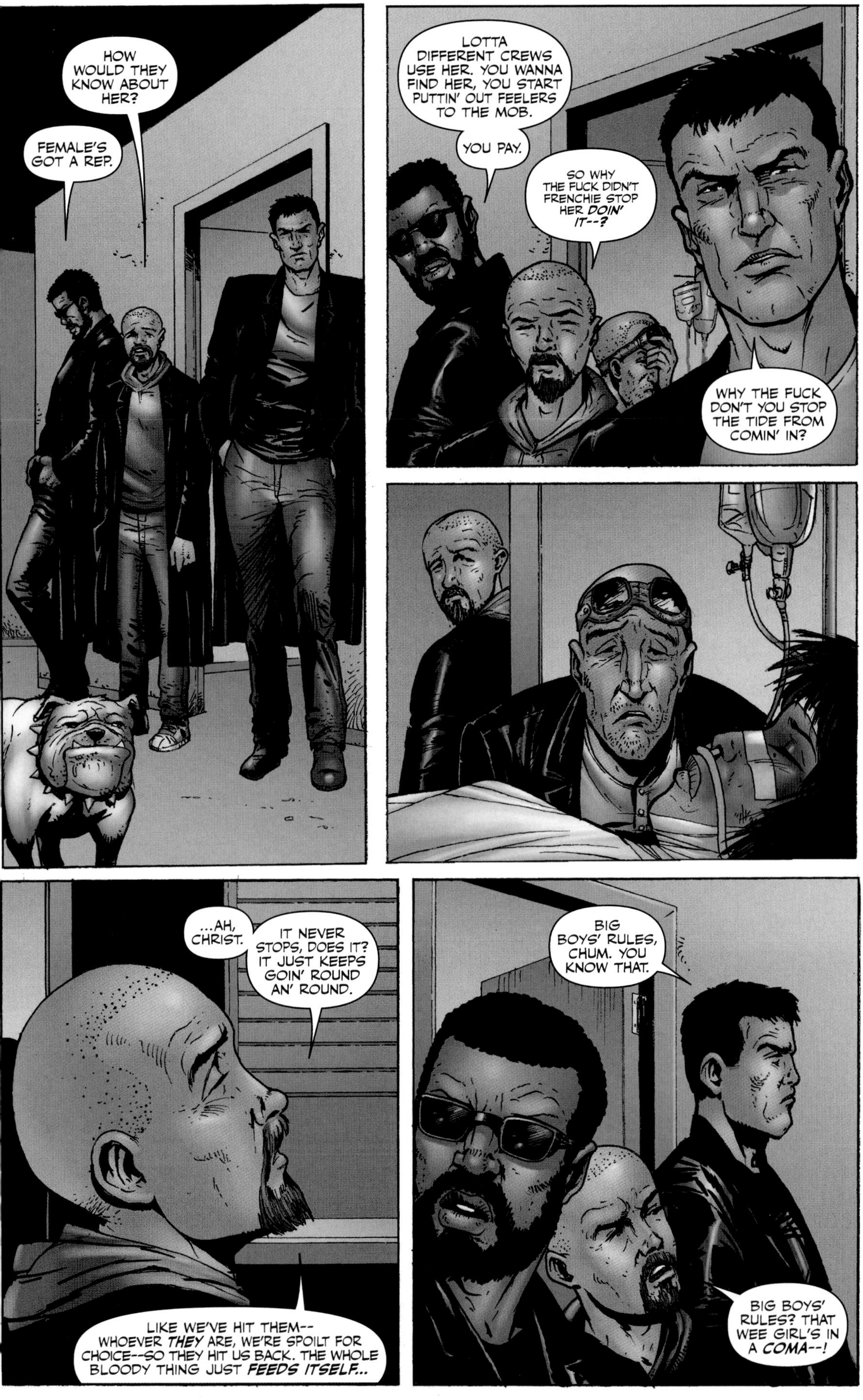
HOW WOULD THEY KNOW ABOUT HER?
FEMALE'S GOT A REP.
LOTTA DIFFERENT CREWS USE HER. YOU WANNA FIND HER, YOU START PUTTIN' OUT FEELERS TO THE MOB.
YOU PAY.
SO WHY THE FUCK DIDN'T FRENCHIE STOP HER *DOIN' IT--?*
WHY THE FUCK DON'T YOU STOP THE TIDE FROM COMIN' IN?
...AH, CHRIST.
IT NEVER STOPS, DOES IT? IT JUST KEEPS GOIN' ROUND AN' ROUND.
LIKE WE'VE HIT THEM-- WHOEVER *THEY* ARE, WE'RE SPOILT FOR CHOICE--SO THEY HIT US BACK. THE WHOLE BLOODY THING JUST *FEEDS ITSELF...*
BIG BOYS' RULES, CHUM. YOU KNOW THAT.
BIG BOYS' RULES? THAT WEE GIRL'S IN A *COMA--!*

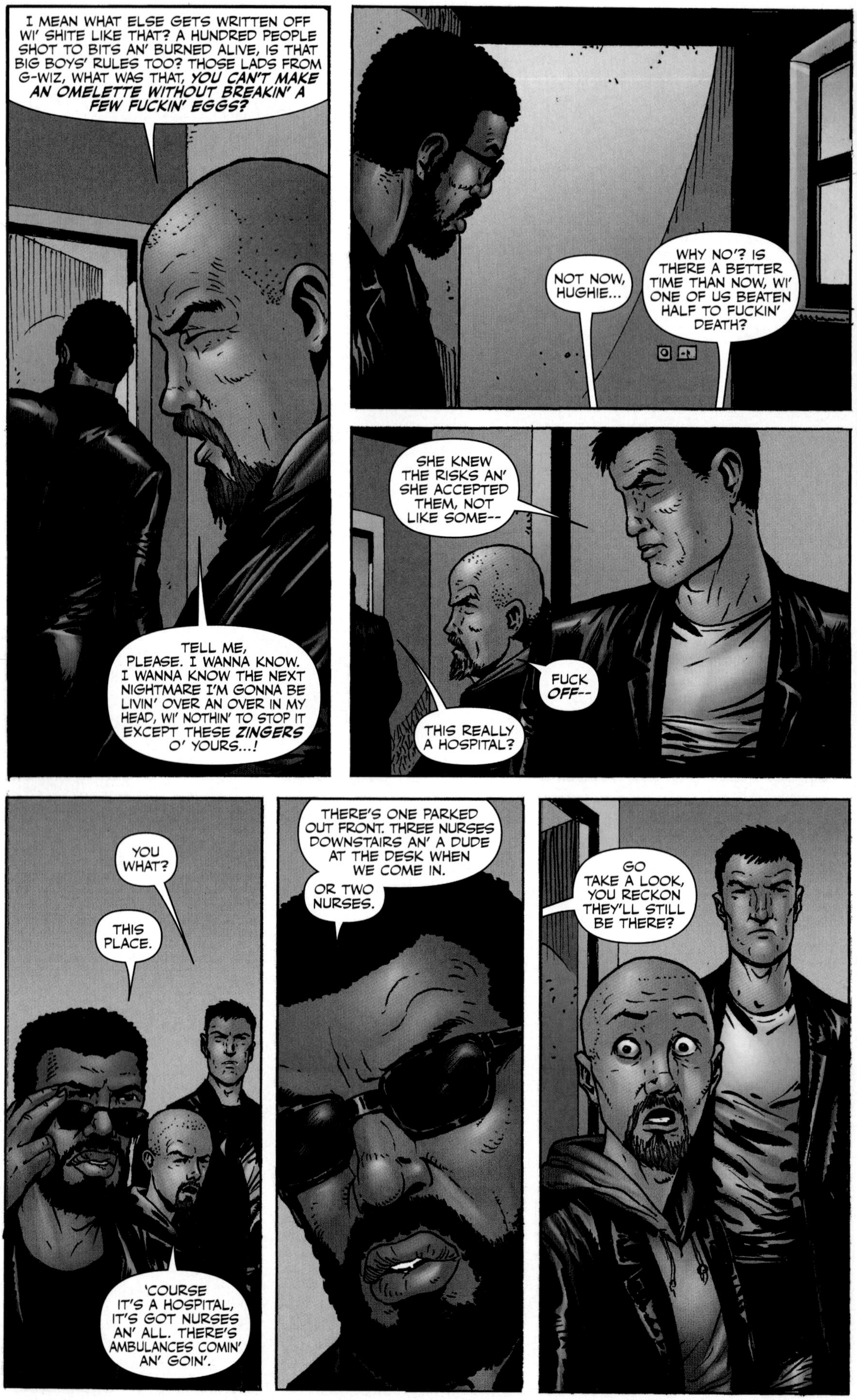
I MEAN WHAT ELSE GETS WRITTEN OFF WI' SHITE LIKE THAT? A HUNDRED PEOPLE SHOT TO BITS AN' BURNED ALIVE, IS THAT BIG BOYS' RULES TOO? THOSE LADS FROM G-WIZ, WHAT WAS THAT, *YOU CAN'T MAKE AN OMELETTE WITHOUT BREAKIN' A FEW FUCKIN' EGGS?*
TELL ME, PLEASE. I WANNA KNOW. I WANNA KNOW THE NEXT NIGHTMARE I'M GONNA BE LIVIN' OVER AN OVER IN MY HEAD, WI' NOTHIN' TO STOP IT EXCEPT THESE *ZINGERS* O' YOURS...!
NOT NOW, HUGHIE...
WHY NO'? IS THERE A BETTER TIME THAN NOW, WI' ONE OF US BEATEN HALF TO FUCKIN' DEATH?
SHE KNEW THE RISKS AN' SHE ACCEPTED THEM, NOT LIKE SOME--
FUCK *OFF*--
THIS REALLY A HOSPITAL?
YOU WHAT?
THIS PLACE.
'COURSE IT'S A HOSPITAL, IT'S GOT NURSES AN' ALL. THERE'S AMBULANCES COMIN' AN' GOIN'.
THERE'S ONE PARKED OUT FRONT. THREE NURSES DOWNSTAIRS AN' A DUDE AT THE DESK WHEN WE COME IN.
OR TWO NURSES.
GO TAKE A LOOK, YOU RECKON THEY'LL STILL BE THERE?

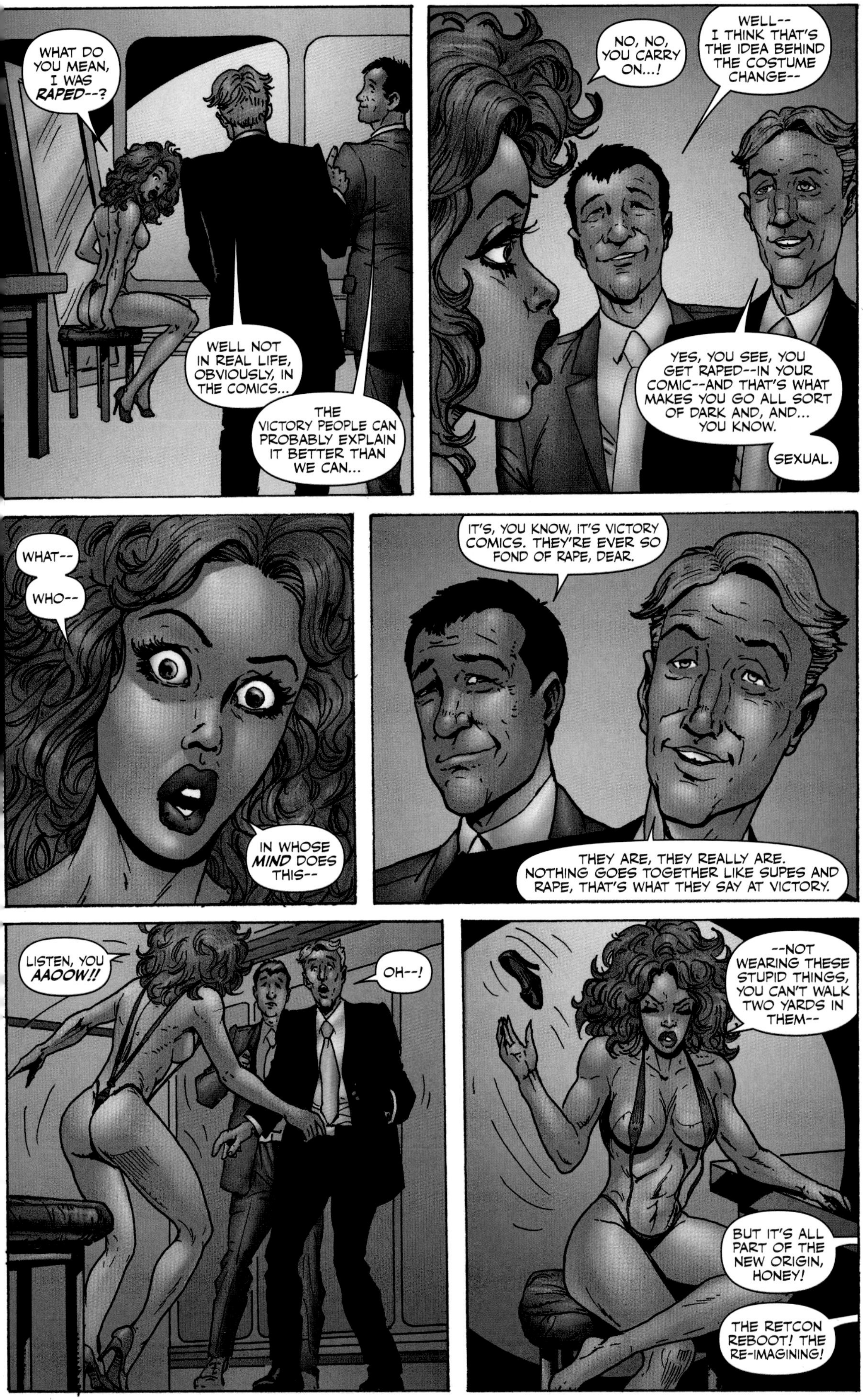
WHAT DO YOU MEAN, I WAS *RAPED*--?
WELL NOT IN REAL LIFE, OBVIOUSLY, IN THE COMICS...
THE VICTORY PEOPLE CAN PROBABLY EXPLAIN IT BETTER THAN WE CAN...
NO, NO, YOU CARRY ON...!
WELL-- I THINK THAT'S THE IDEA BEHIND THE COSTUME CHANGE--
YES, YOU SEE, YOU GET RAPED--IN YOUR COMIC--AND THAT'S WHAT MAKES YOU GO ALL SORT OF DARK AND, AND... YOU KNOW.
SEXUAL.
WHAT--
WHO--
IN WHOSE *MIND* DOES THIS--
IT'S, YOU KNOW, IT'S VICTORY COMICS. THEY'RE EVER SO FOND OF RAPE, DEAR.
THEY ARE, THEY REALLY ARE. NOTHING GOES TOGETHER LIKE SUPES AND RAPE, THAT'S WHAT THEY SAY AT VICTORY.
LISTEN, YOU *AAOOW!!*
OH--!
--NOT WEARING THESE STUPID THINGS, YOU CAN'T WALK TWO YARDS IN THEM--
BUT IT'S ALL PART OF THE NEW ORIGIN, HONEY!
THE RETCON REBOOT! THE RE-IMAGINING!

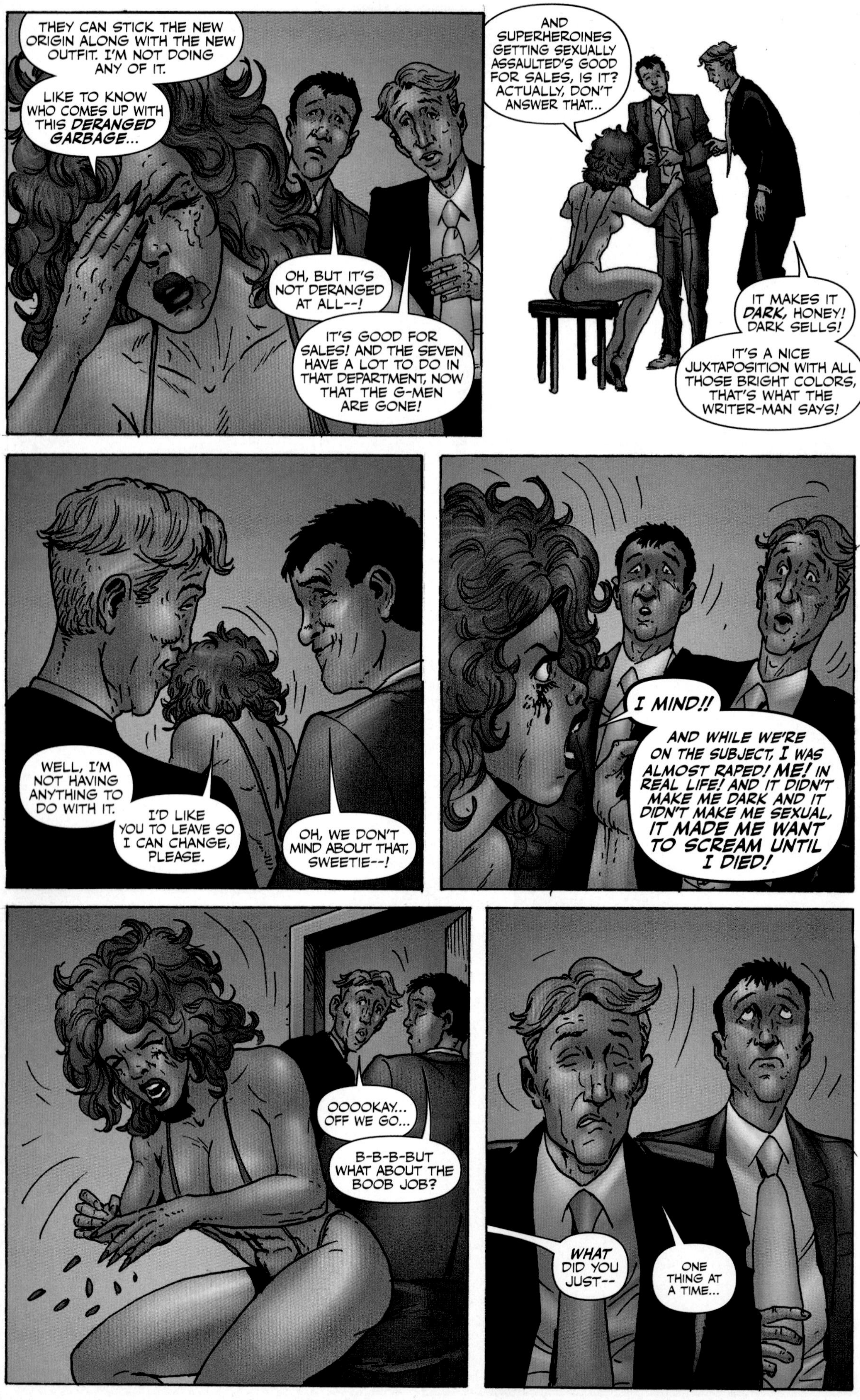
THEY CAN STICK THE NEW ORIGIN ALONG WITH THE NEW OUTFIT. I'M NOT DOING ANY OF IT.
LIKE TO KNOW WHO COMES UP WITH THIS *DERANGED GARBAGE*...
OH, BUT IT'S NOT DERANGED AT ALL--!
IT'S GOOD FOR SALES! AND THE SEVEN HAVE A LOT TO DO IN THAT DEPARTMENT, NOW THAT THE G-MEN ARE GONE!
AND SUPERHEROINES GETTING SEXUALLY ASSAULTED'S GOOD FOR SALES, IS IT? ACTUALLY, DON'T ANSWER THAT...
IT MAKES IT *DARK*, HONEY! DARK SELLS!
IT'S A NICE JUXTAPOSITION WITH ALL THOSE BRIGHT COLORS, THAT'S WHAT THE WRITER-MAN SAYS!
WELL, I'M NOT HAVING ANYTHING TO DO WITH IT.
I'D LIKE YOU TO LEAVE SO I CAN CHANGE, PLEASE.
OH, WE DON'T MIND ABOUT THAT, SWEETIE--!
I MIND!!
AND WHILE WE'RE ON THE SUBJECT, I WAS ALMOST RAPED! ME! IN REAL LIFE! AND IT DIDN'T MAKE ME DARK AND IT DIDN'T MAKE ME SEXUAL, IT MADE ME WANT TO SCREAM UNTIL I DIED!
OOOOKAY... OFF WE GO...
B-B-B-BUT WHAT ABOUT THE BOOB JOB?
WHAT DID YOU JUST--
ONE THING AT A TIME...

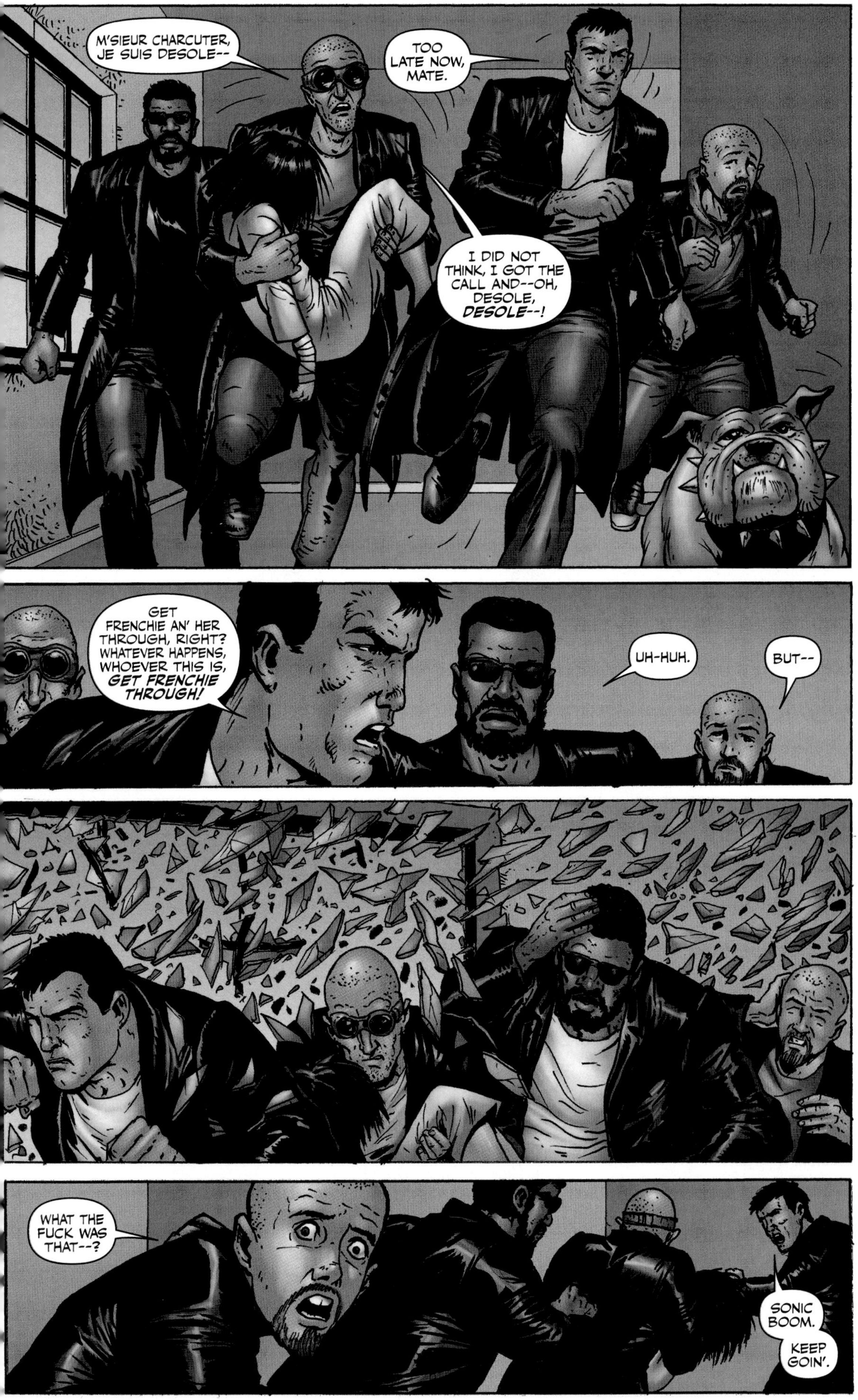
M'SIEUR CHARCUTER, JE SUIS DESOLE--
TOO LATE NOW, MATE.
I DID NOT THINK, I GOT THE CALL AND--OH, DESOLE, DESOLE--!
GET FRENCHIE AN' HER THROUGH, RIGHT? WHATEVER HAPPENS, WHOEVER THIS IS, GET FRENCHIE THROUGH!
UH-HUH.
BUT--
WHAT THE FUCK WAS THAT--?
SONIC BOOM.
KEEP GOIN'.

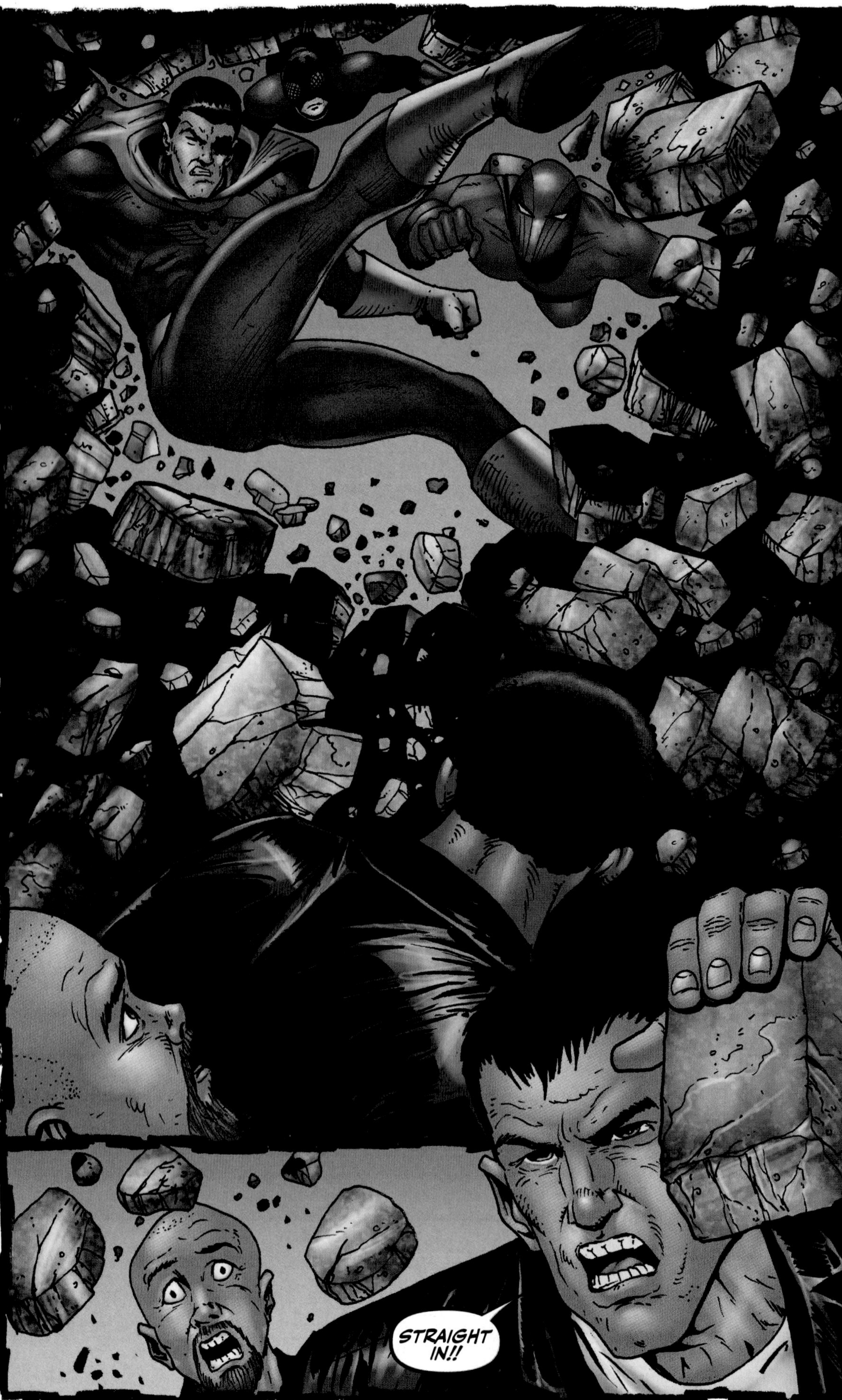
STRAIGHT IN!!

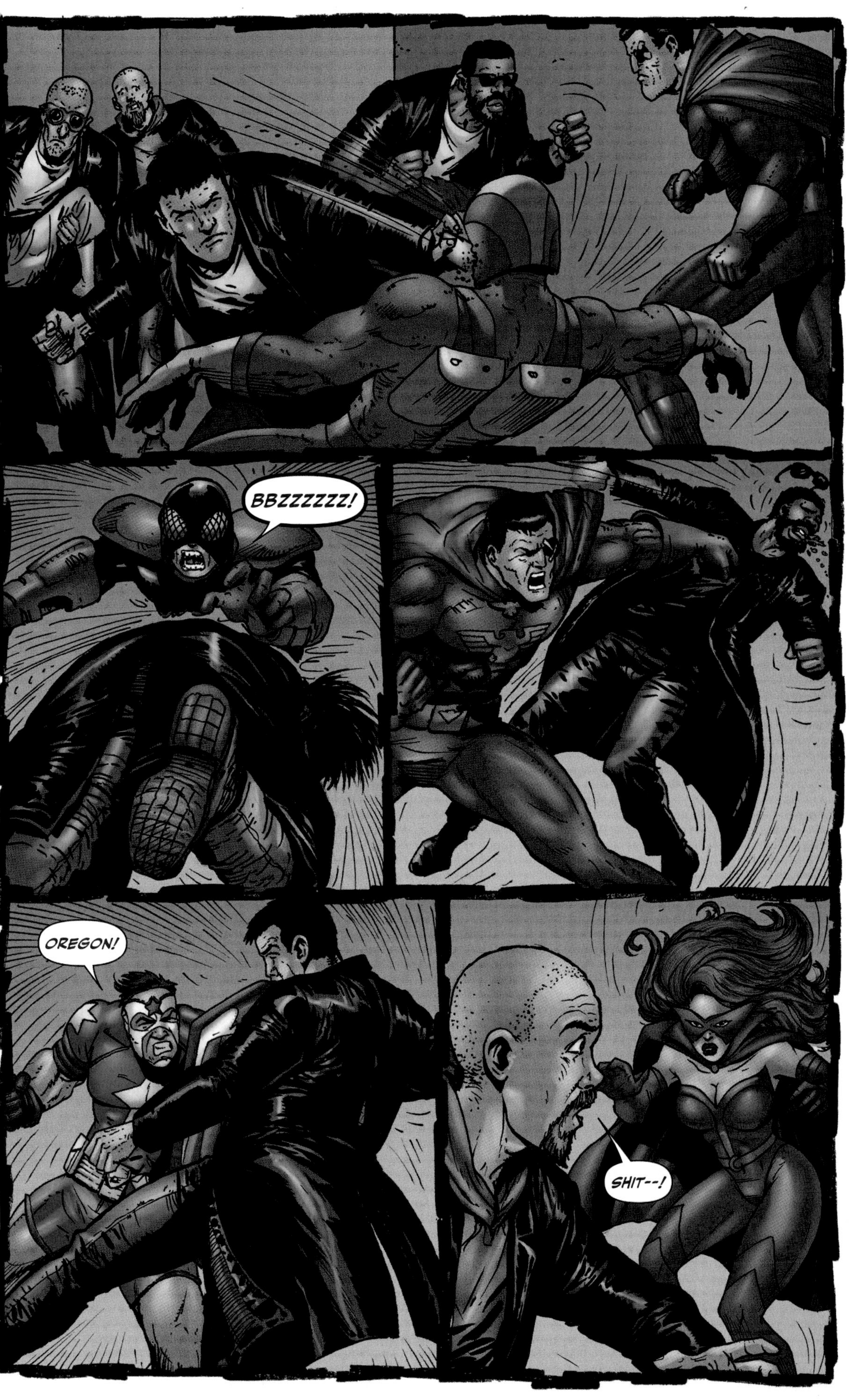
BBZZZZZZ!
OREGON!
SHIT--!

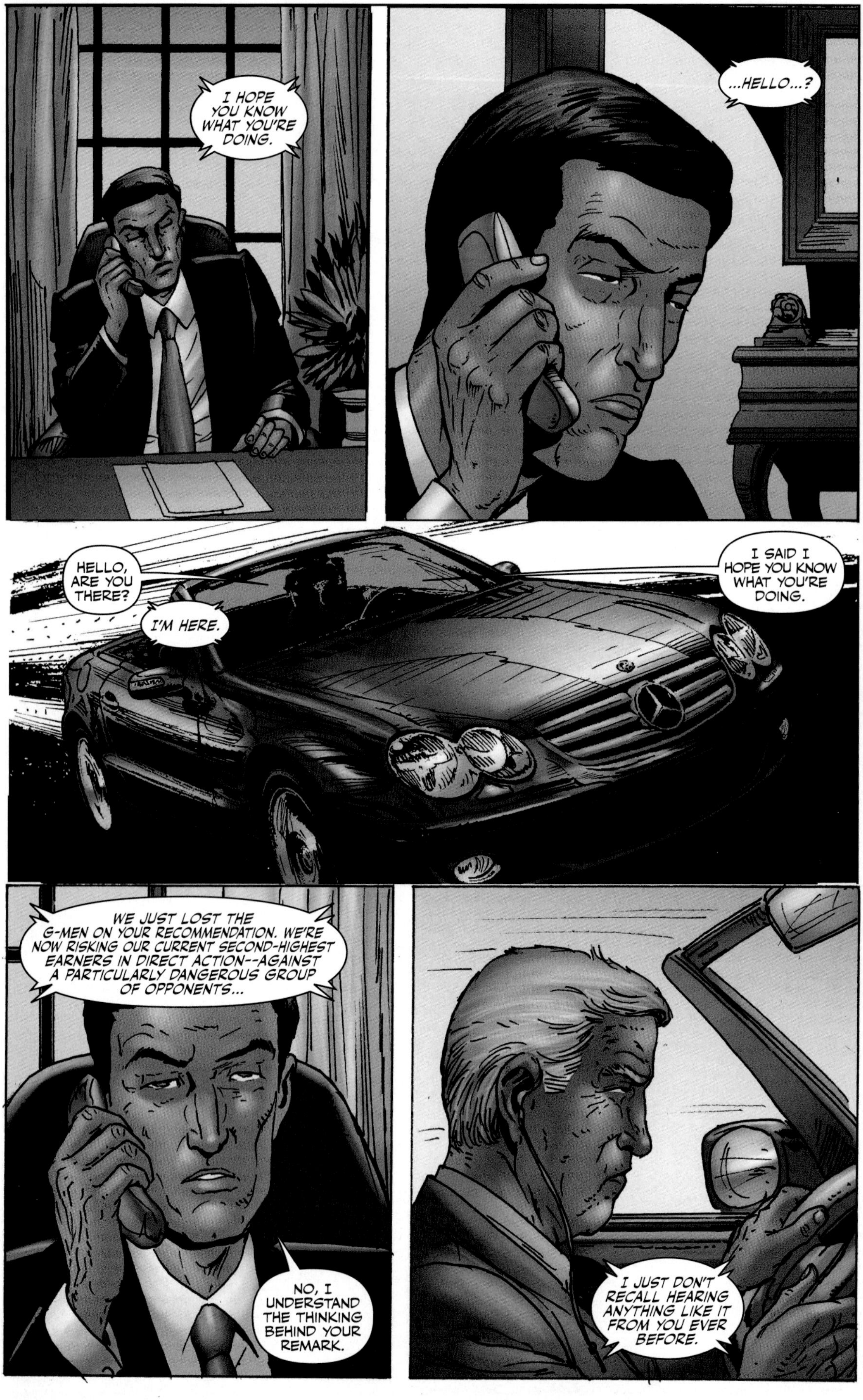
I HOPE YOU KNOW WHAT YOU'RE DOING.
...HELLO...?
HELLO, ARE YOU THERE?
I'M HERE.
I SAID I HOPE YOU KNOW WHAT YOU'RE DOING.
WE JUST LOST THE G-MEN ON YOUR RECOMMENDATION. WE'RE NOW RISKING OUR CURRENT SECOND-HIGHEST EARNERS IN DIRECT ACTION--AGAINST A PARTICULARLY DANGEROUS GROUP OF OPPONENTS...
NO, I UNDERSTAND THE THINKING BEHIND YOUR REMARK.
I JUST DON'T RECALL HEARING ANYTHING LIKE IT FROM YOU EVER BEFORE.

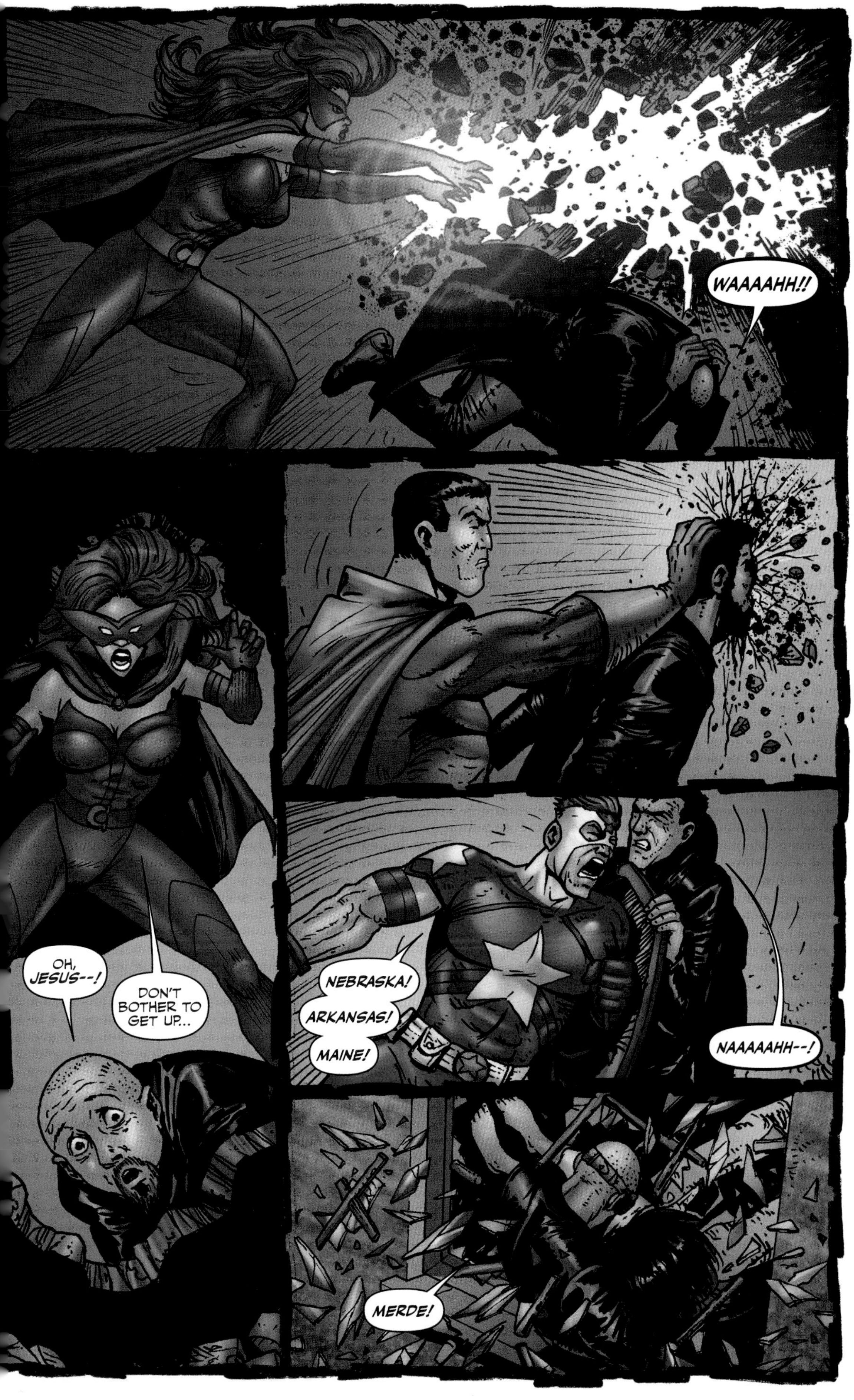
WAAAAHH!!
OH, JESUS--!
DON'T BOTHER TO GET UP...
NEBRASKA!
ARKANSAS!
MAINE!
NAAAAAHH--!
MERDE!

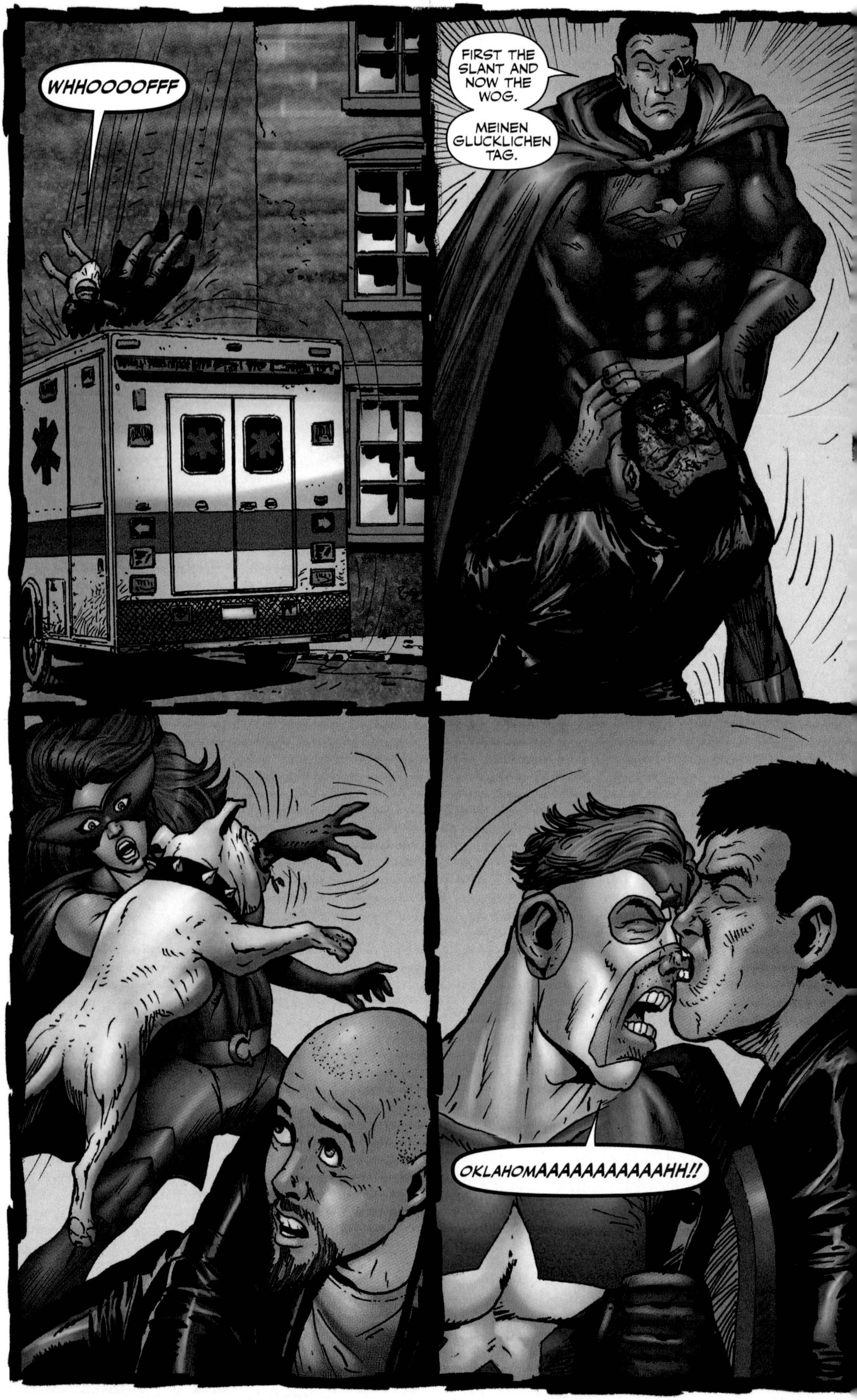
WHHOOOOFFF
FIRST THE SLANT AND NOW THE WOG.
MEINEN GLUCKLICHEN TAG.
OKLAHOMAAAAAAAAAAAAH!!

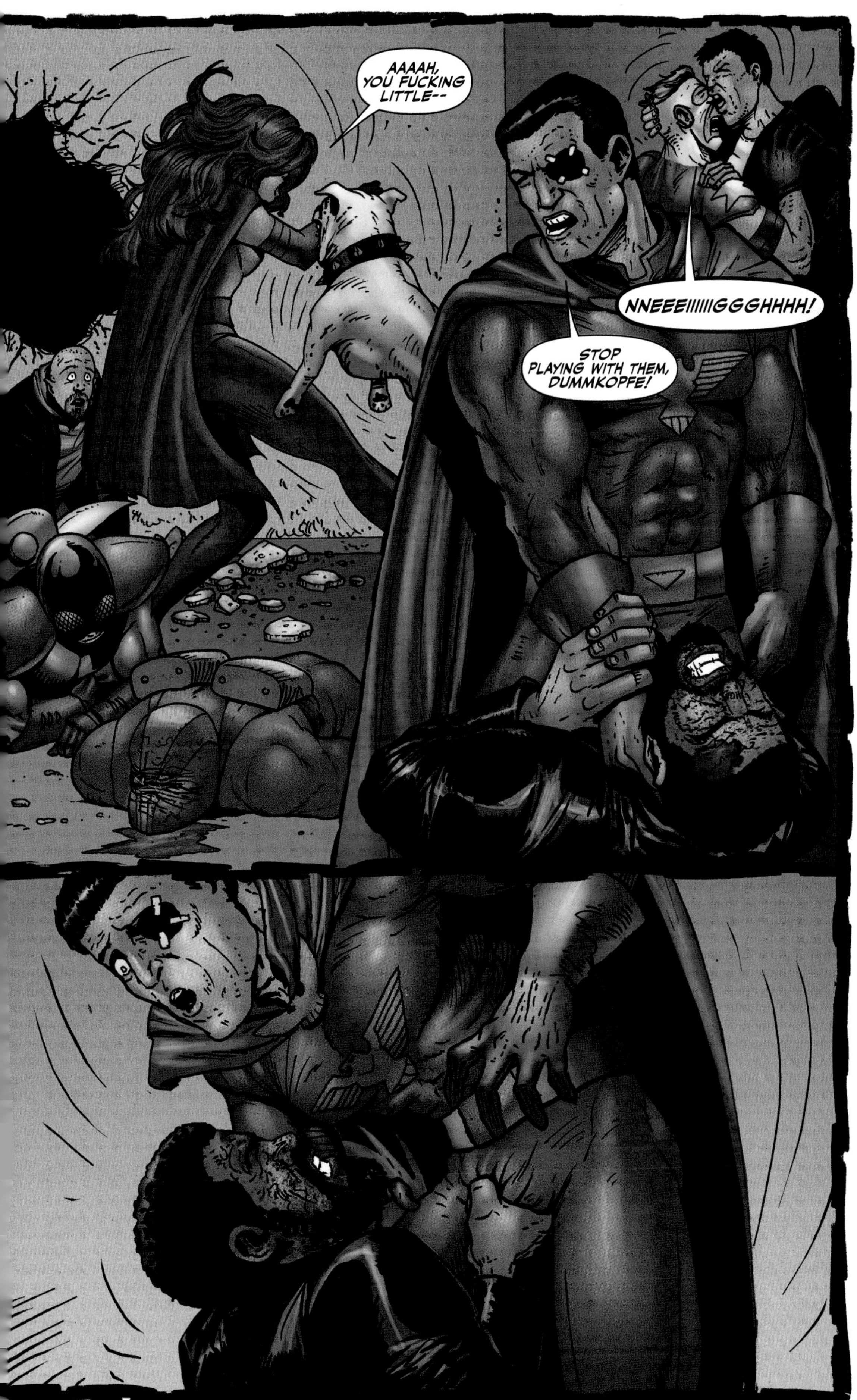
AAAAH, YOU FUCKING LITTLE--
NNEEEIIIIIIGGGHHHH!
STOP PLAYING WITH THEM, DUMMKOPFE!

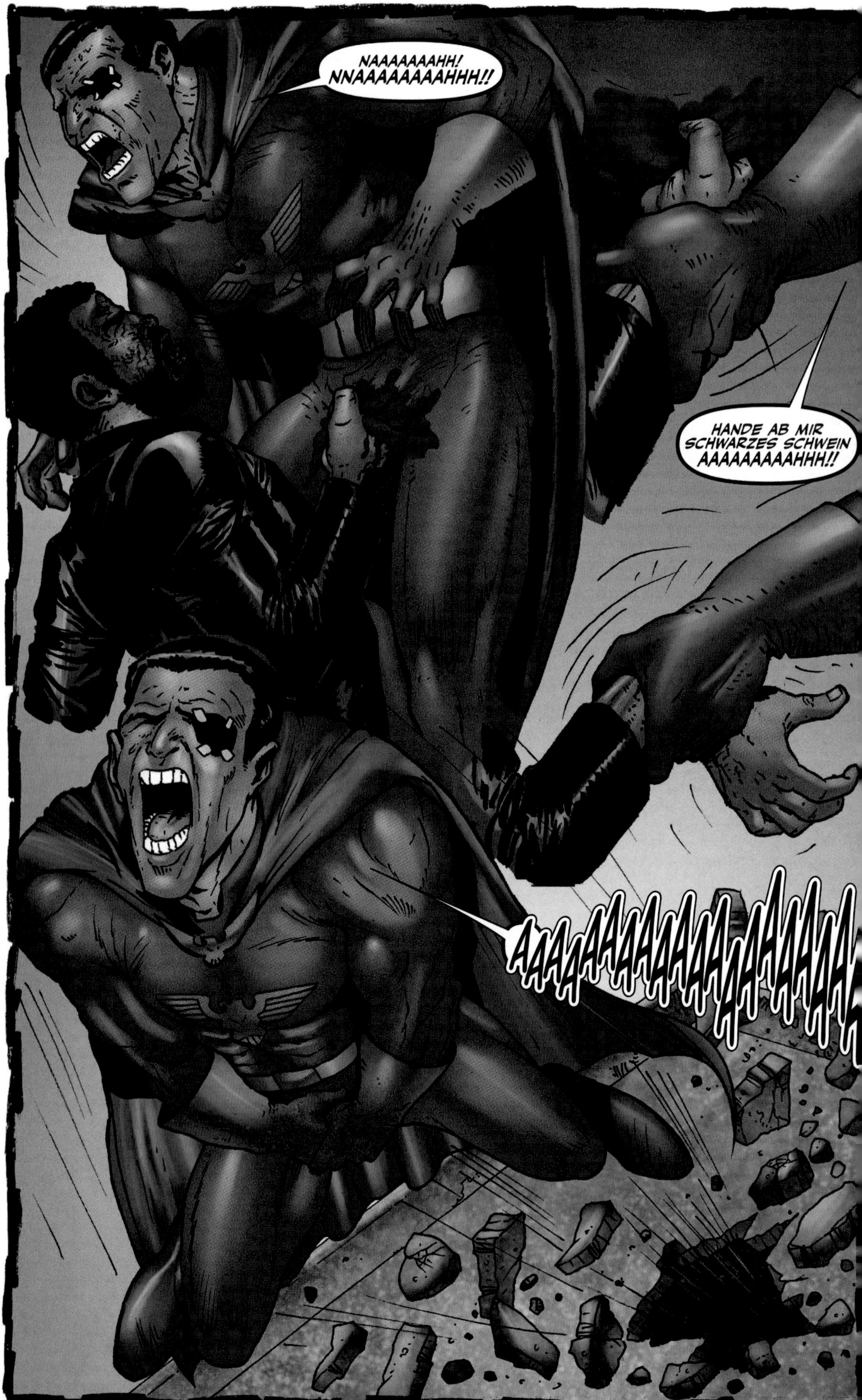
NAAAAAAAAHH!
NNAAAAAAAAAHHH!!
HANDE AB MIR
SCHWARZES SCHWEIN
AAAAAAAAAHHH!!
AAAAAAAAAAAAAAAAAAA

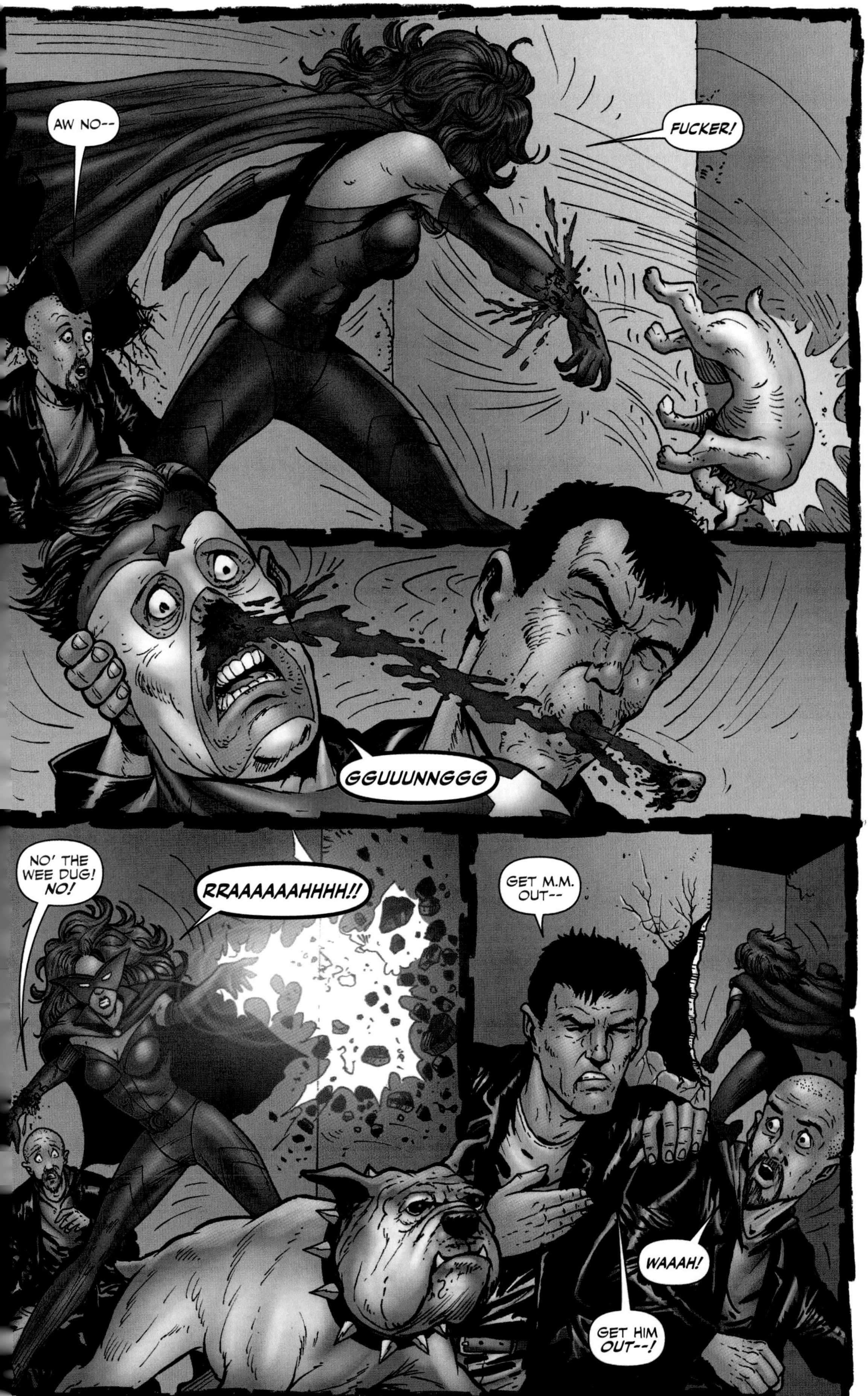
AW NO--
FUCKER!
GGUUUNNGGG
NO' THE WEE DUG! NO!
RRAAAAAAHHHH!!
GET M.M. OUT--
WAAAH!
GET HIM OUT--!

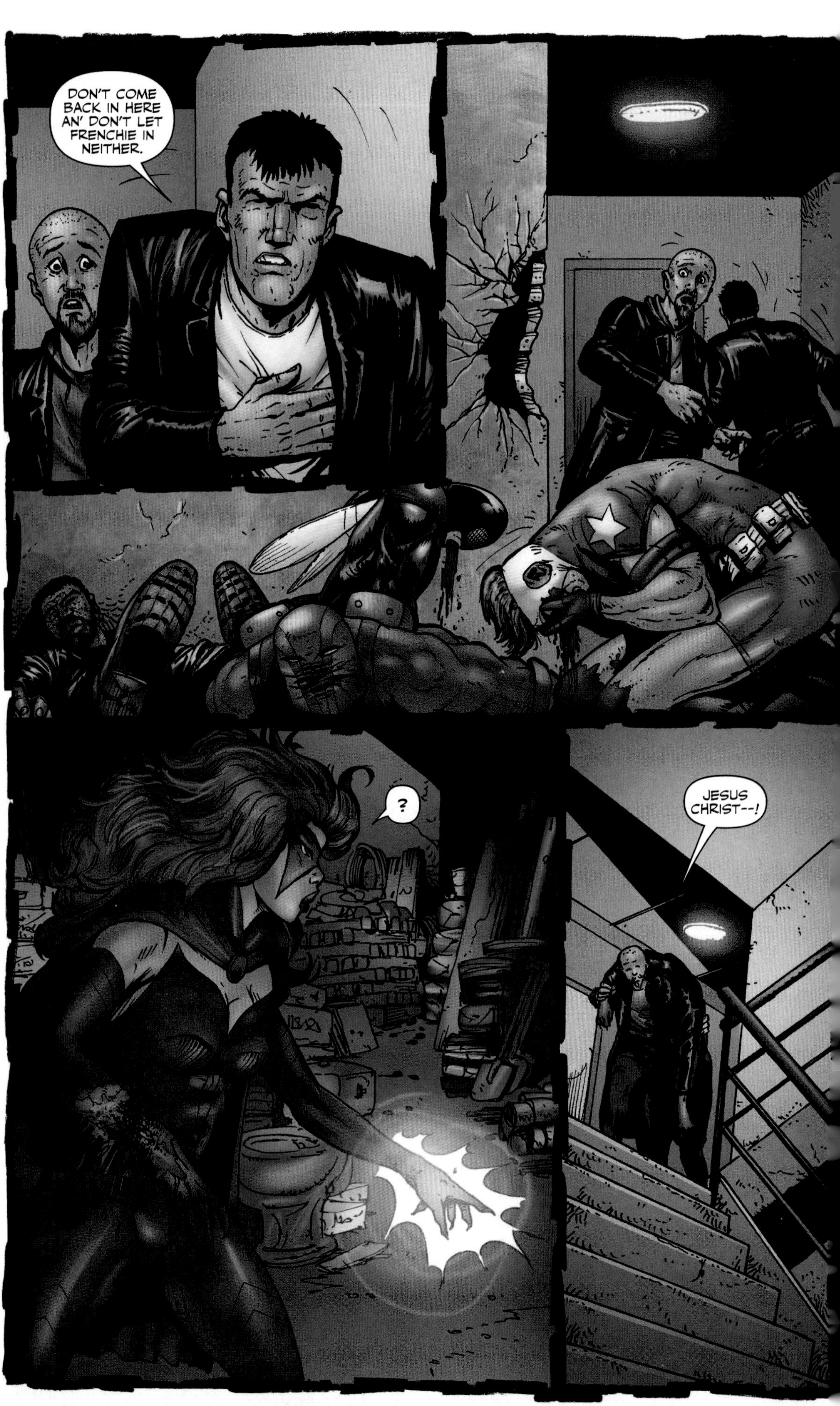
DON'T COME BACK IN HERE AN' DON'T LET FRENCHIE IN NEITHER.
?
JESUS CHRIST--!

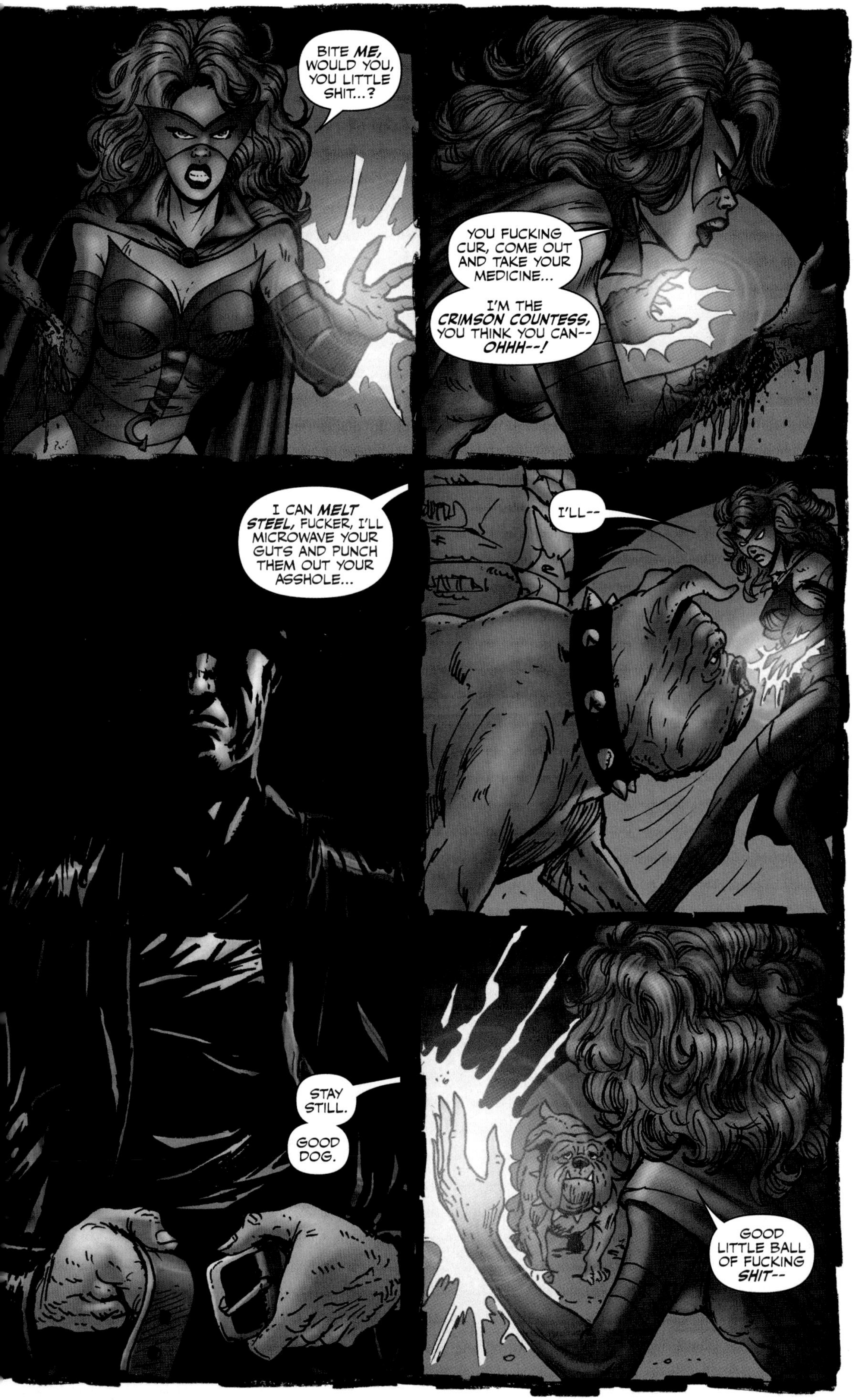
BITE ME, WOULD YOU, YOU LITTLE SHIT...?
YOU FUCKING CUR, COME OUT AND TAKE YOUR MEDICINE...
I'M THE CRIMSON COUNTESS, YOU THINK YOU CAN-- OHHH--!
I CAN MELT STEEL, FUCKER, I'LL MICROWAVE YOUR GUTS AND PUNCH THEM OUT YOUR ASSHOLE...
I'LL--
STAY STILL.
GOOD DOG.
GOOD LITTLE BALL OF FUCKING SHIT--

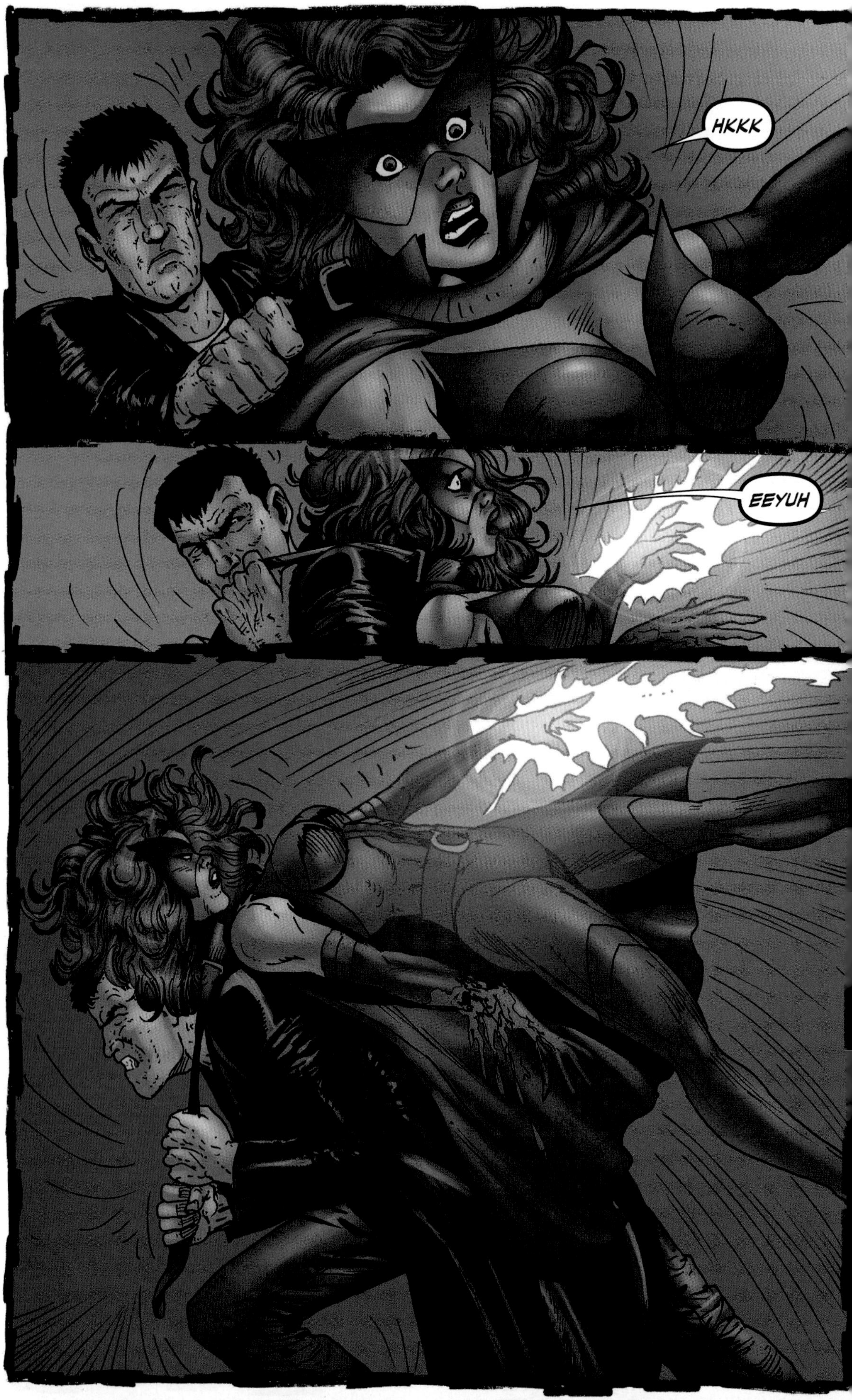
HKKK
EEYUH

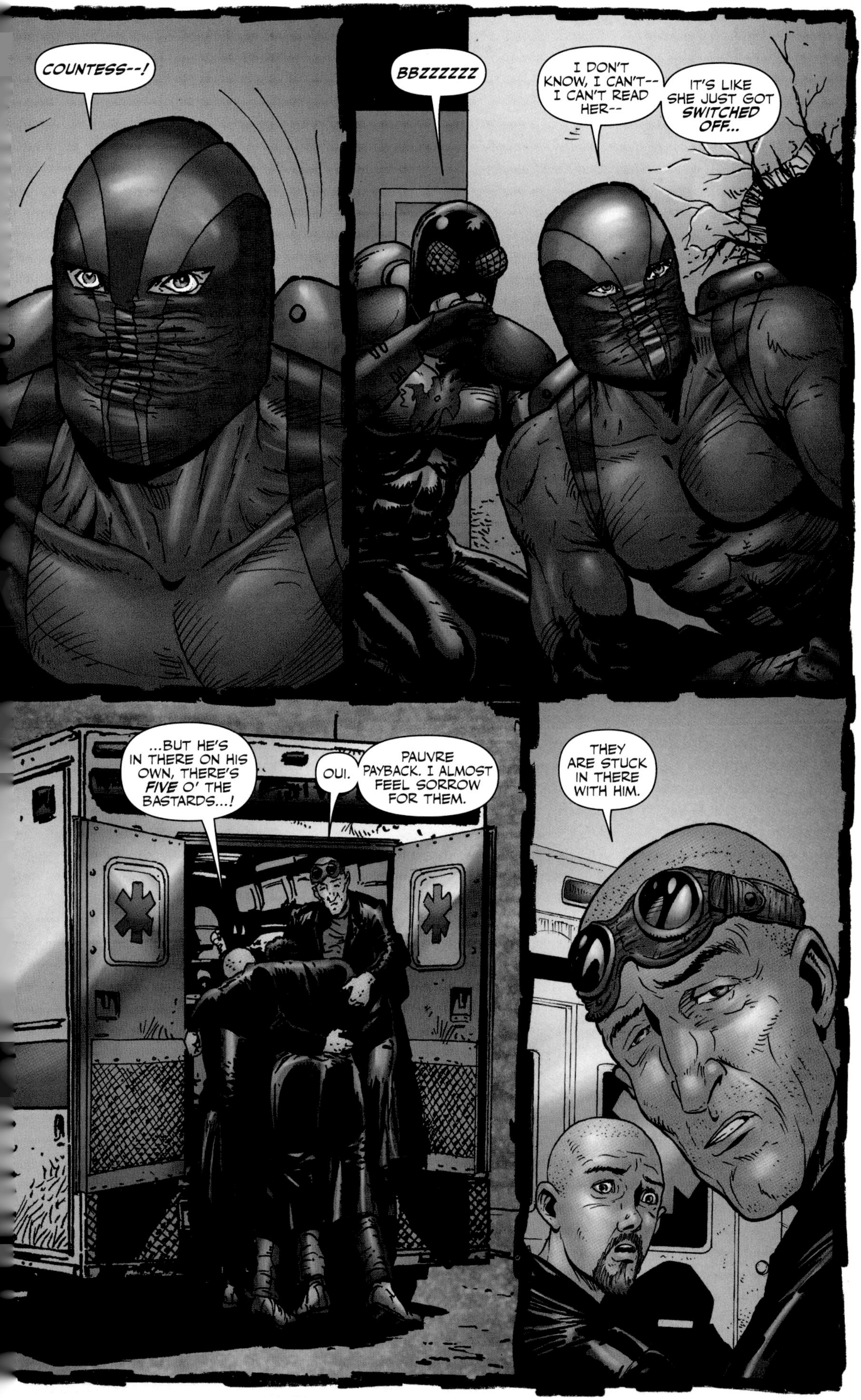
COUNTESS--!
BBZZZZZZ
I DON'T KNOW, I CAN'T-- I CAN'T READ HER--
IT'S LIKE SHE JUST GOT SWITCHED OFF...
...BUT HE'S IN THERE ON HIS OWN, THERE'S FIVE O' THE BASTARDS...!
OUI.
PAUVRE PAYBACK. I ALMOST FEEL SORROW FOR THEM.
THEY ARE STUCK IN THERE WITH HIM.

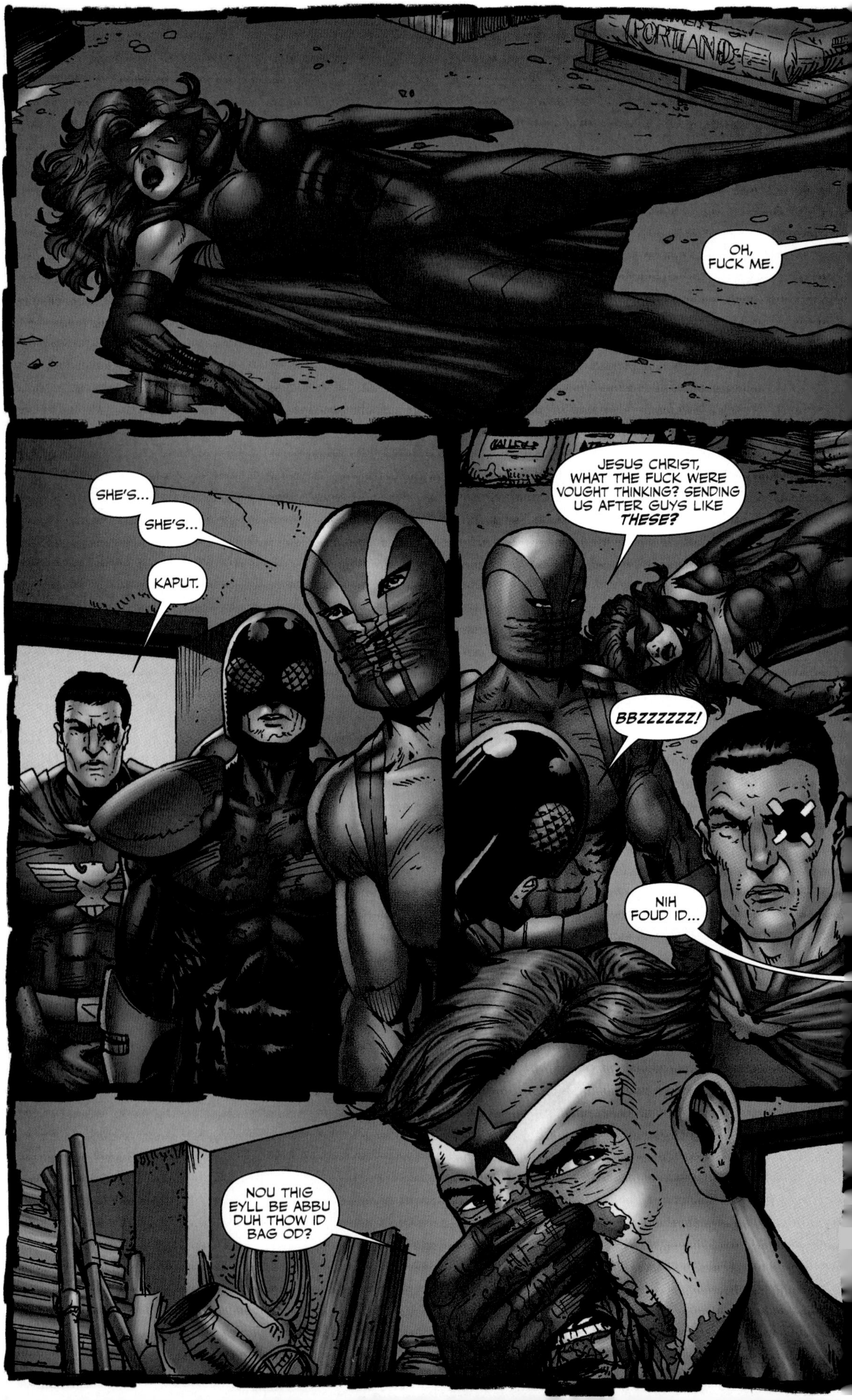
OH, FUCK ME.
SHE'S...
SHE'S...
KAPUT.
JESUS CHRIST, WHAT THE FUCK WERE VOUGHT THINKING? SENDING US AFTER GUYS LIKE THESE?
BBZZZZZZ!
NIH FOUD ID...
NOU THIG EYLL BE ABBU DUH THOW ID BAG OD?
PORTLAND

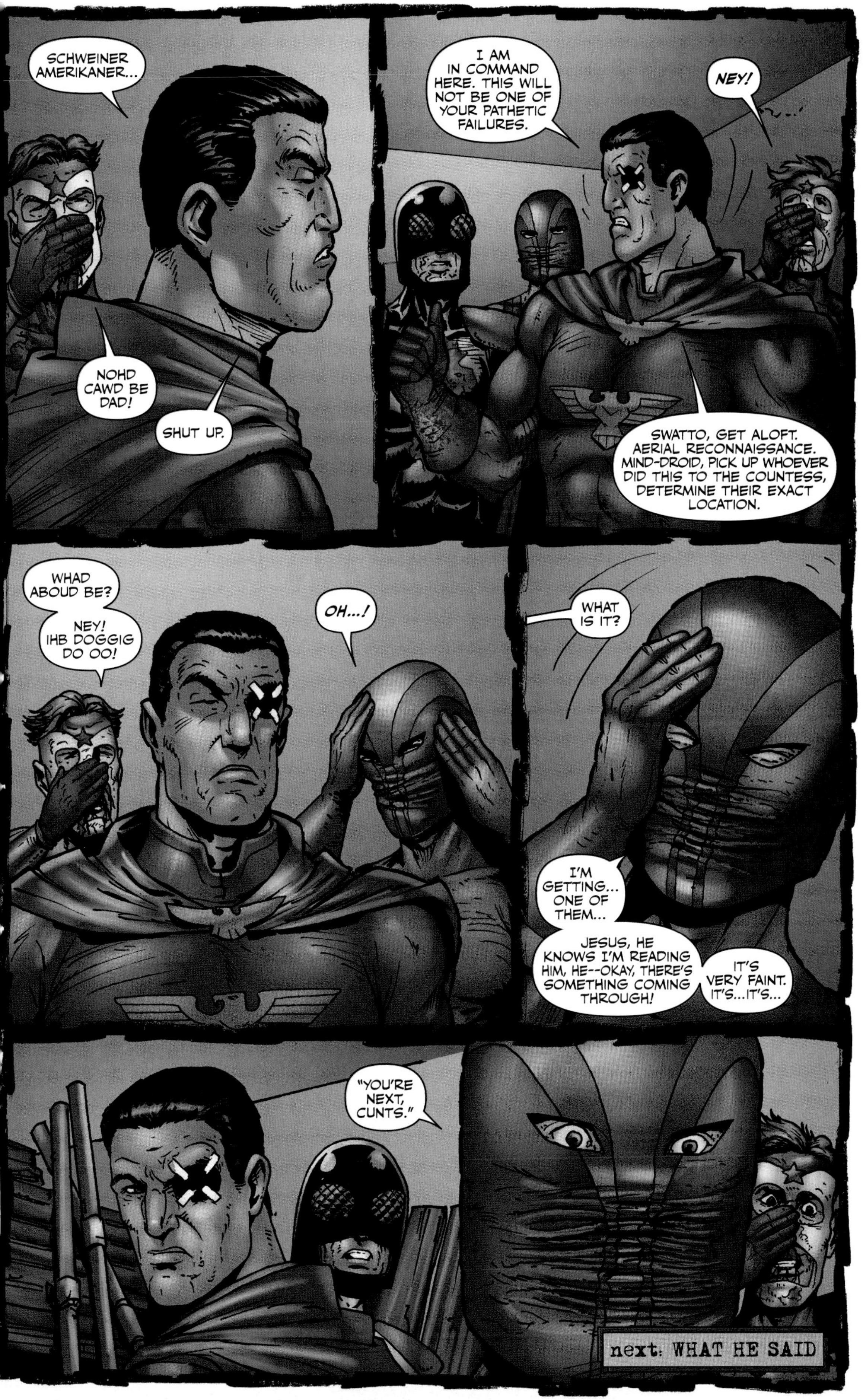
SCHWEINER AMERIKANER...
NOHD CAWD BE DAD!
SHUT UP.
I AM IN COMMAND HERE. THIS WILL NOT BE ONE OF YOUR PATHETIC FAILURES.
NEY!
SWATTO, GET ALOFT. AERIAL RECONNAISSANCE. MIND-DROID, PICK UP WHOEVER DID THIS TO THE COUNTESS, DETERMINE THEIR EXACT LOCATION.
WHAD ABOUD BE?
NEY! IHB DOGGIG DO OO!
OH...!
WHAT IS IT?
I'M GETTING... ONE OF THEM...
JESUS, HE KNOWS I'M READING HIM, HE--OKAY, THERE'S SOMETHING COMING THROUGH!
IT'S VERY FAINT. IT'S...IT'S...
"YOU'RE NEXT, CUNTS."
next: WHAT HE SAID

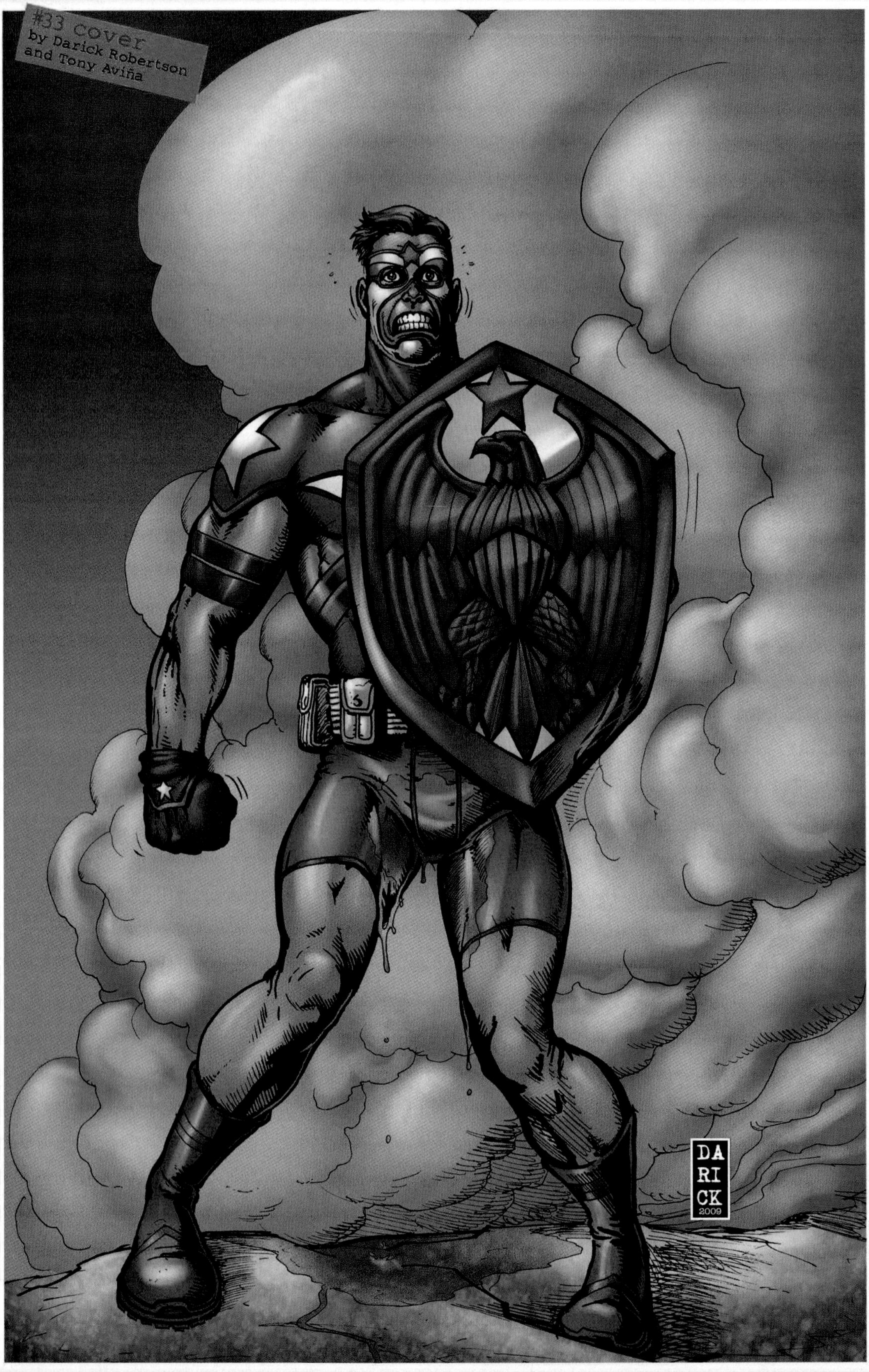
#33 cover
by Darick Robertson
and Tony Aviña
DA
RI
CK
2009

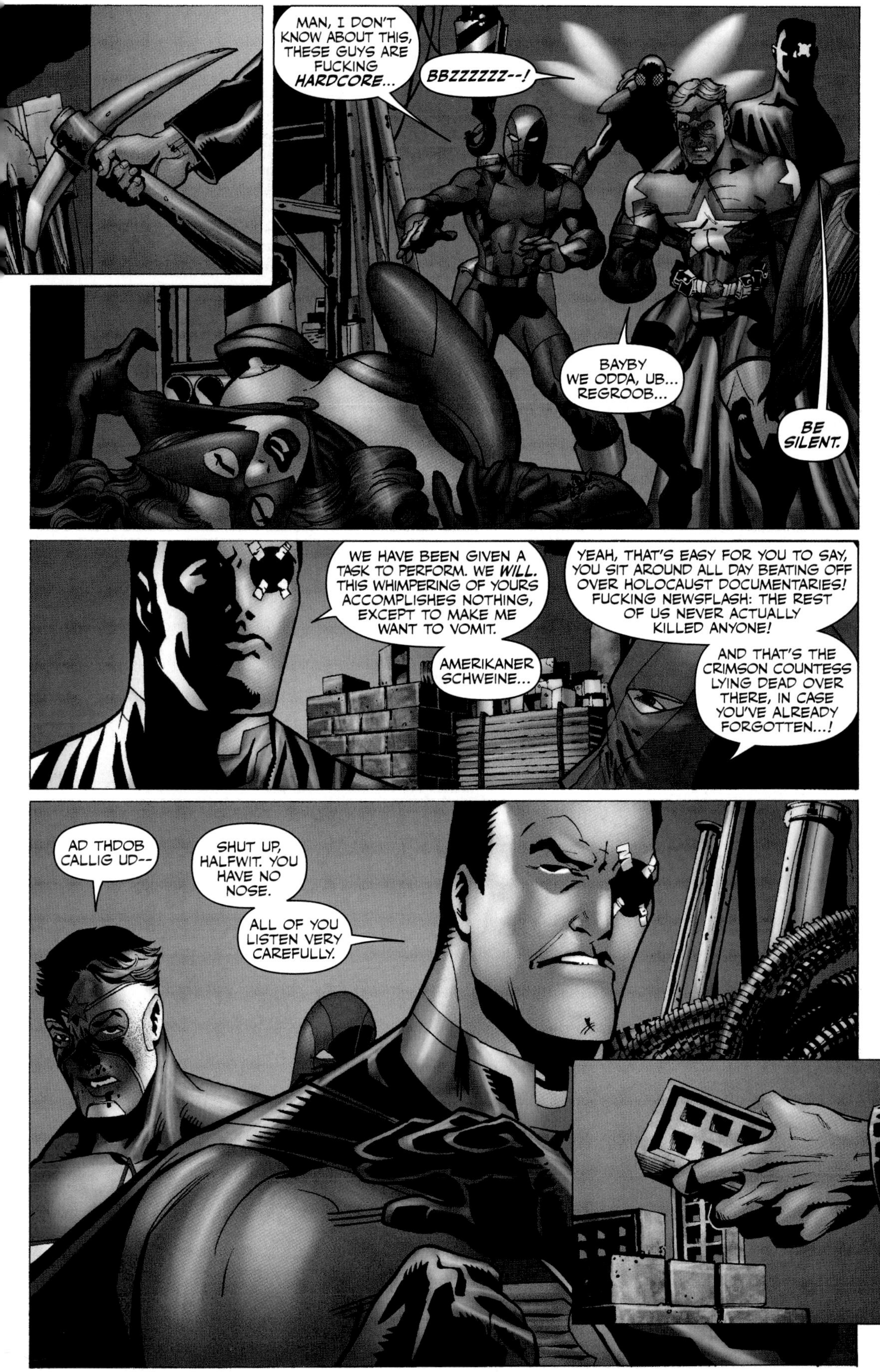
MAN, I DON'T KNOW ABOUT THIS, THESE GUYS ARE FUCKING *HARDCORE*...
BBZZZZZZ--!
BAYBY WE ODDA, UB... REGROOB...
BE SILENT.
WE HAVE BEEN GIVEN A TASK TO PERFORM. WE *WILL.* THIS WHIMPERING OF YOURS ACCOMPLISHES NOTHING, EXCEPT TO MAKE ME WANT TO VOMIT.
AMERIKANER SCHWEINE...
YEAH, THAT'S EASY FOR YOU TO SAY, YOU SIT AROUND ALL DAY BEATING OFF OVER HOLOCAUST DOCUMENTARIES! FUCKING NEWSFLASH: THE REST OF US NEVER ACTUALLY KILLED ANYONE!
AND THAT'S THE CRIMSON COUNTESS LYING DEAD OVER THERE, IN CASE YOU'VE ALREADY FORGOTTEN...!
AD THDOB CALLIG UD--
SHUT UP, HALFWIT. YOU HAVE NO NOSE.
ALL OF YOU LISTEN VERY CAREFULLY.

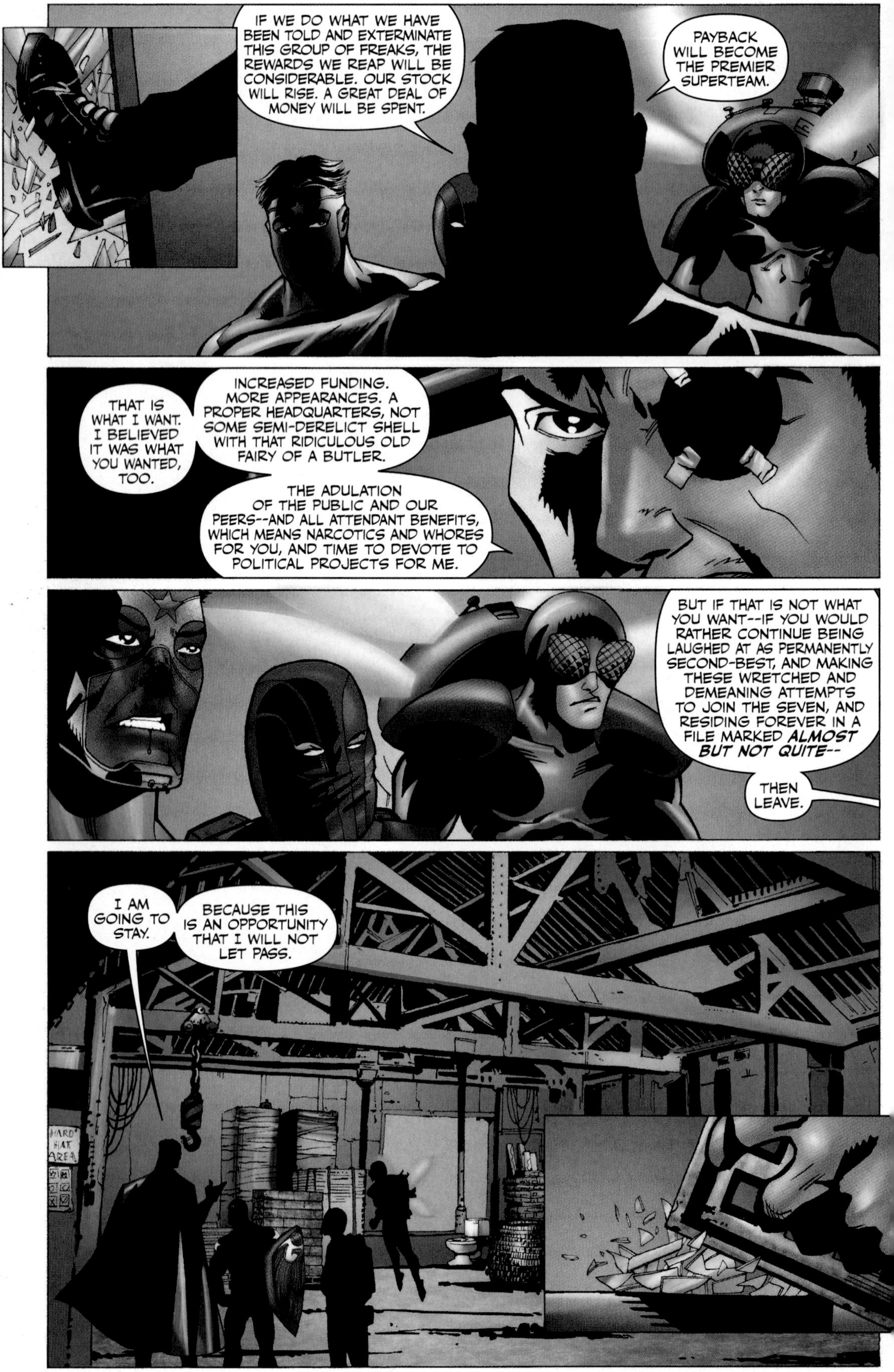
IF WE DO WHAT WE HAVE BEEN TOLD AND EXTERMINATE THIS GROUP OF FREAKS, THE REWARDS WE REAP WILL BE CONSIDERABLE. OUR STOCK WILL RISE. A GREAT DEAL OF MONEY WILL BE SPENT.
PAYBACK WILL BECOME THE PREMIER SUPERTEAM.
INCREASED FUNDING. MORE APPEARANCES. A PROPER HEADQUARTERS, NOT SOME SEMI-DERELICT SHELL WITH THAT RIDICULOUS OLD FAIRY OF A BUTLER.
THE ADULATION OF THE PUBLIC AND OUR PEERS--AND ALL ATTENDANT BENEFITS, WHICH MEANS NARCOTICS AND WHORES FOR YOU, AND TIME TO DEVOTE TO POLITICAL PROJECTS FOR ME.
THAT IS WHAT I WANT. I BELIEVED IT WAS WHAT YOU WANTED, TOO.
BUT IF THAT IS NOT WHAT YOU WANT--IF YOU WOULD RATHER CONTINUE BEING LAUGHED AT AS PERMANENTLY SECOND-BEST, AND MAKING THESE WRETCHED AND DEMEANING ATTEMPTS TO JOIN THE SEVEN, AND RESIDING FOREVER IN A FILE MARKED *ALMOST BUT NOT QUITE*--
THEN LEAVE.
I AM GOING TO STAY.
BECAUSE THIS IS AN OPPORTUNITY THAT I WILL NOT LET PASS.
HARD HAT AREA

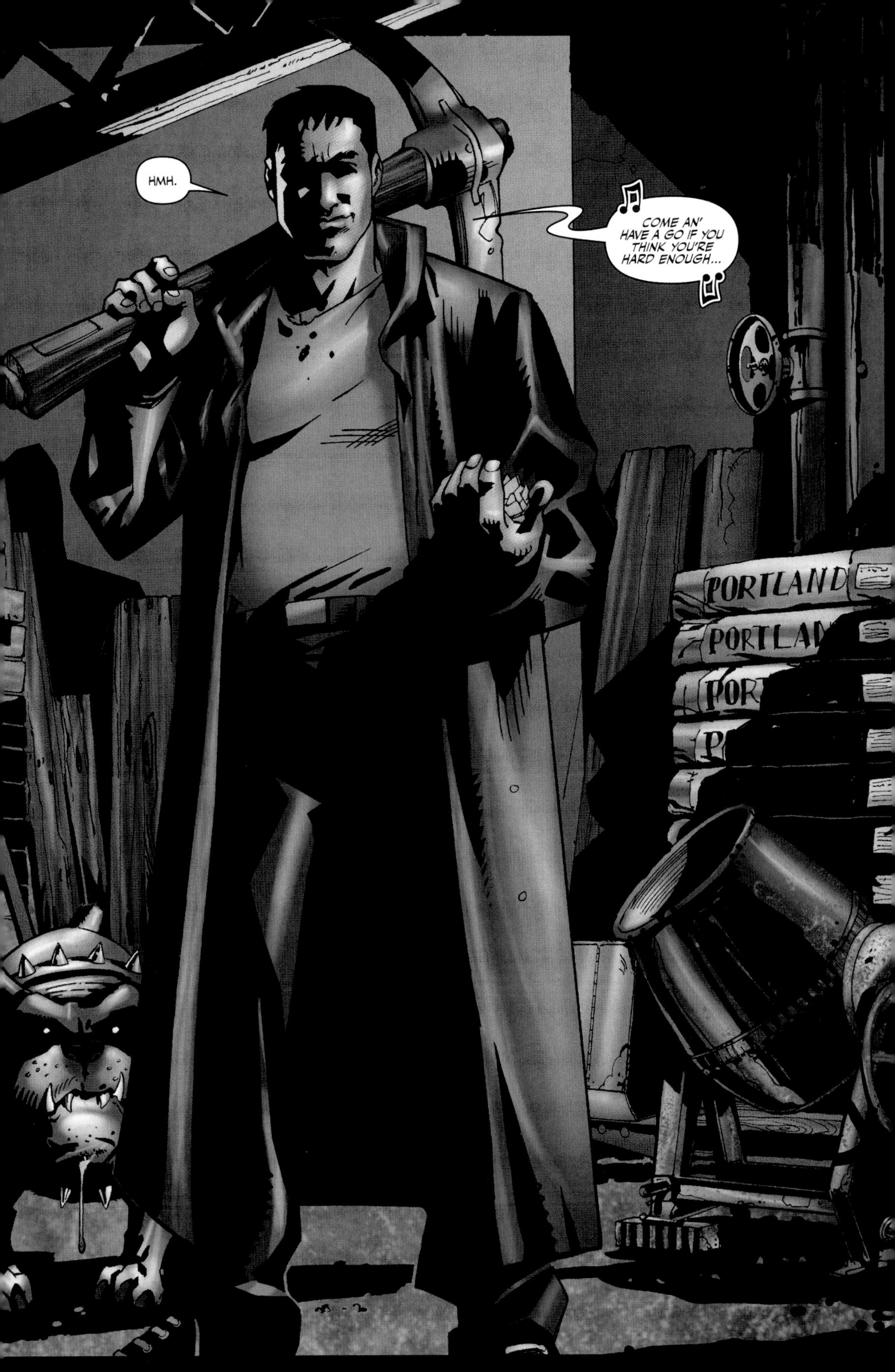
HMH.
COME AN' HAVE A GO IF YOU THINK YOU'RE HARD ENOUGH...
PORTLAND

THE SELF-PRESERVATION SOCIETY
part three

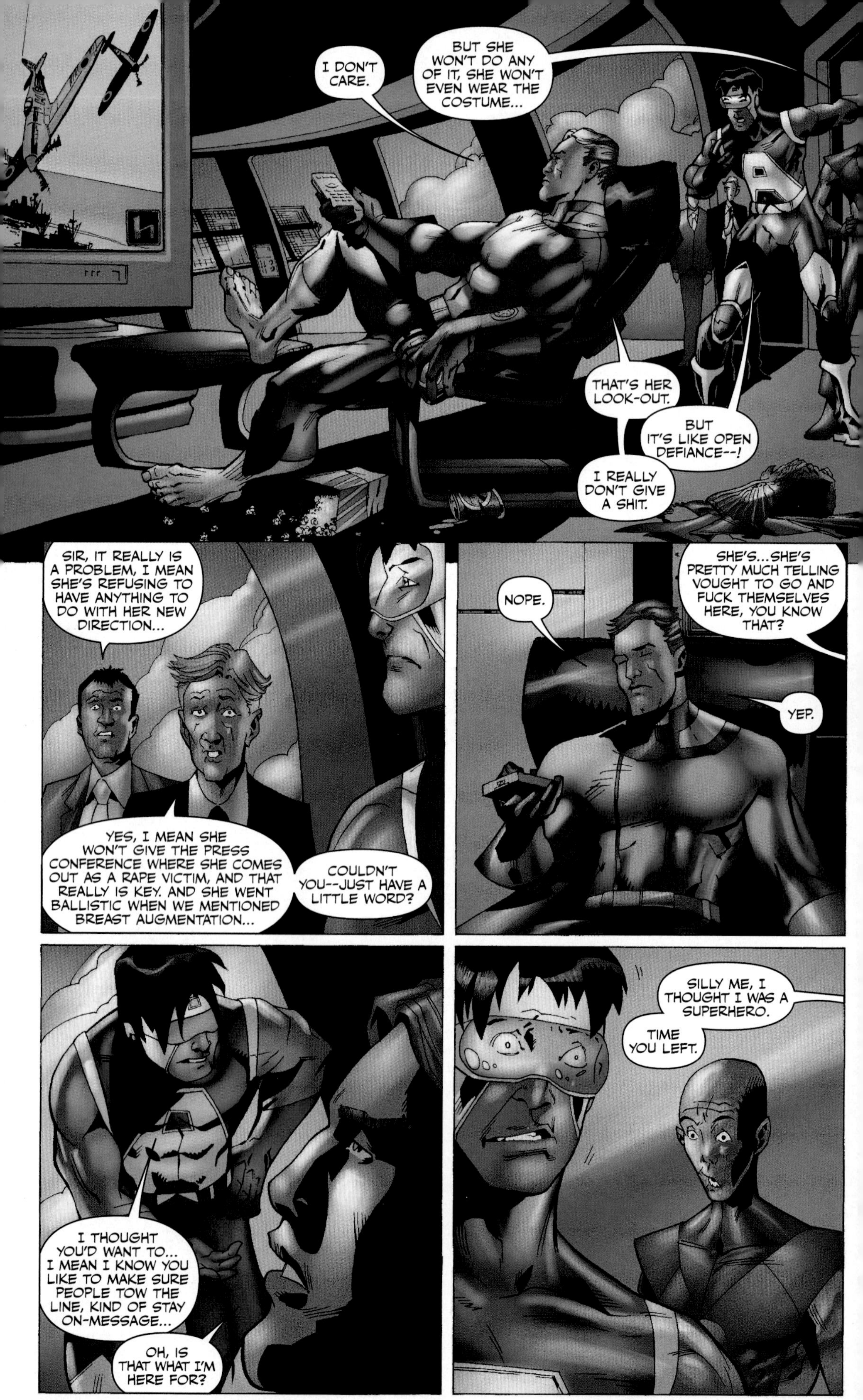

BUT SHE WON'T DO ANY OF IT, SHE WON'T EVEN WEAR THE COSTUME...
I DON'T CARE.
THAT'S HER LOOK-OUT.
BUT IT'S LIKE OPEN DEFIANCE--!
I REALLY DON'T GIVE A SHIT.
SIR, IT REALLY IS A PROBLEM, I MEAN SHE'S REFUSING TO HAVE ANYTHING TO DO WITH HER NEW DIRECTION...
YES, I MEAN SHE WON'T GIVE THE PRESS CONFERENCE WHERE SHE COMES OUT AS A RAPE VICTIM, AND THAT REALLY IS KEY. AND SHE WENT BALLISTIC WHEN WE MENTIONED BREAST AUGMENTATION...
COULDN'T YOU--JUST HAVE A LITTLE WORD?
NOPE.
SHE'S...SHE'S PRETTY MUCH TELLING VOUGHT TO GO AND FUCK THEMSELVES HERE, YOU KNOW THAT?
YEP.
I THOUGHT YOU'D WANT TO... I MEAN I KNOW YOU LIKE TO MAKE SURE PEOPLE TOW THE LINE, KIND OF STAY ON-MESSAGE...
OH, IS THAT WHAT I'M HERE FOR?
SILLY ME, I THOUGHT I WAS A SUPERHERO.
TIME YOU LEFT.

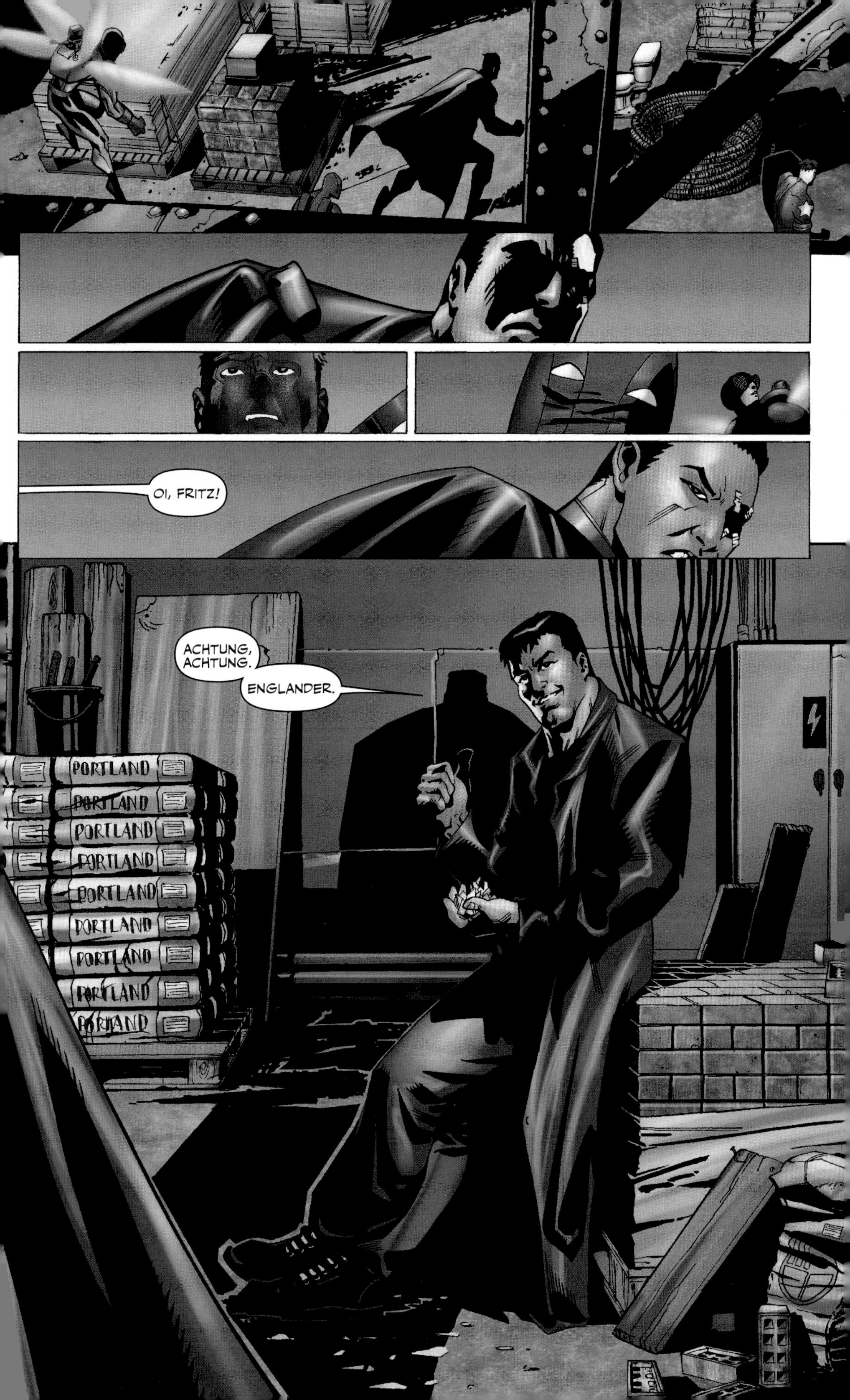
OI, FRITZ!
ACHTUNG, ACHTUNG.
ENGLANDER.
PORTLAND

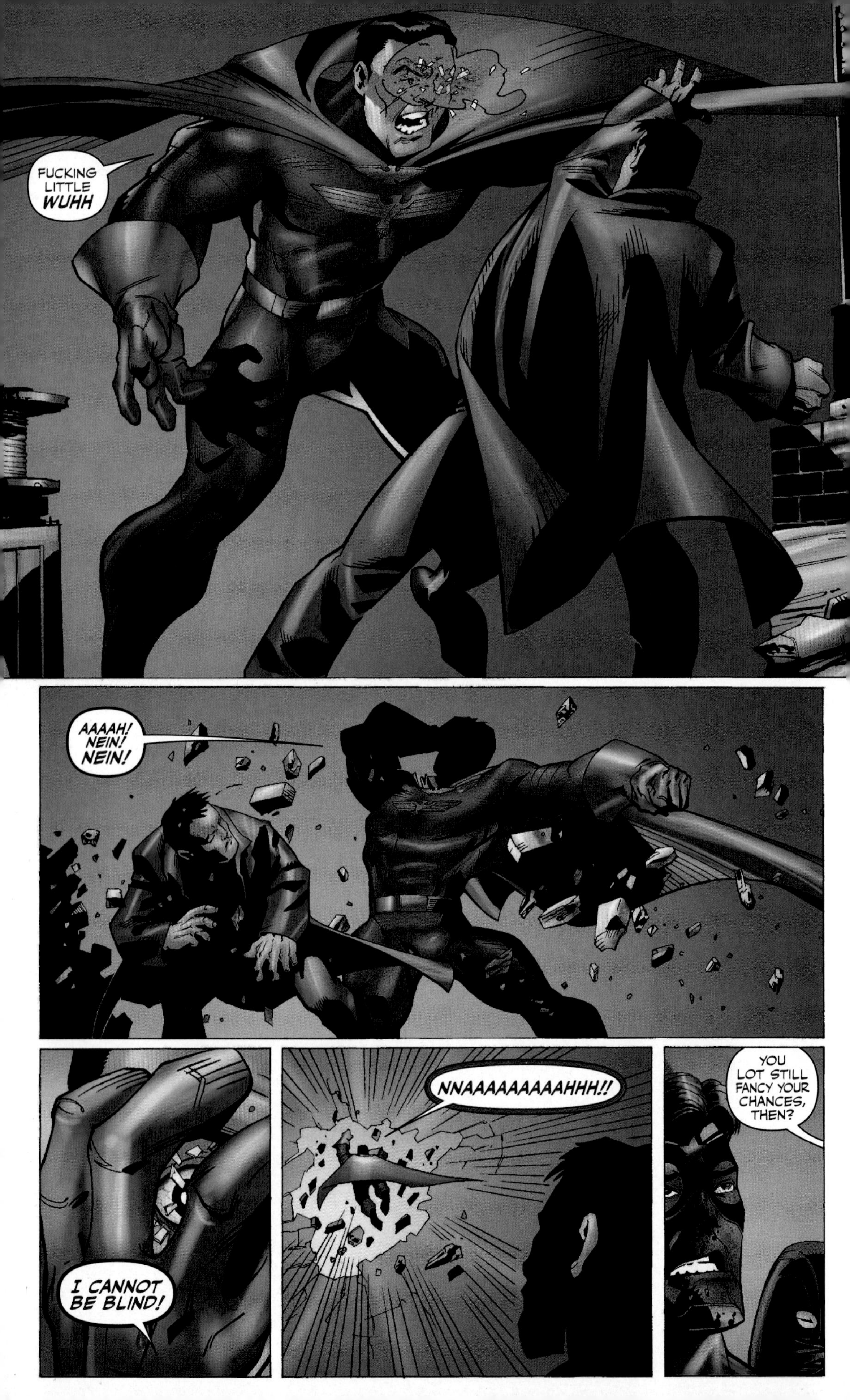
FUCKING LITTLE *WUHH*
AAAAH! NEIN! NEIN!
I CANNOT BE BLIND!
NNAAAAAAAAAAHHH!!
YOU LOT STILL FANCY YOUR CHANCES, THEN?

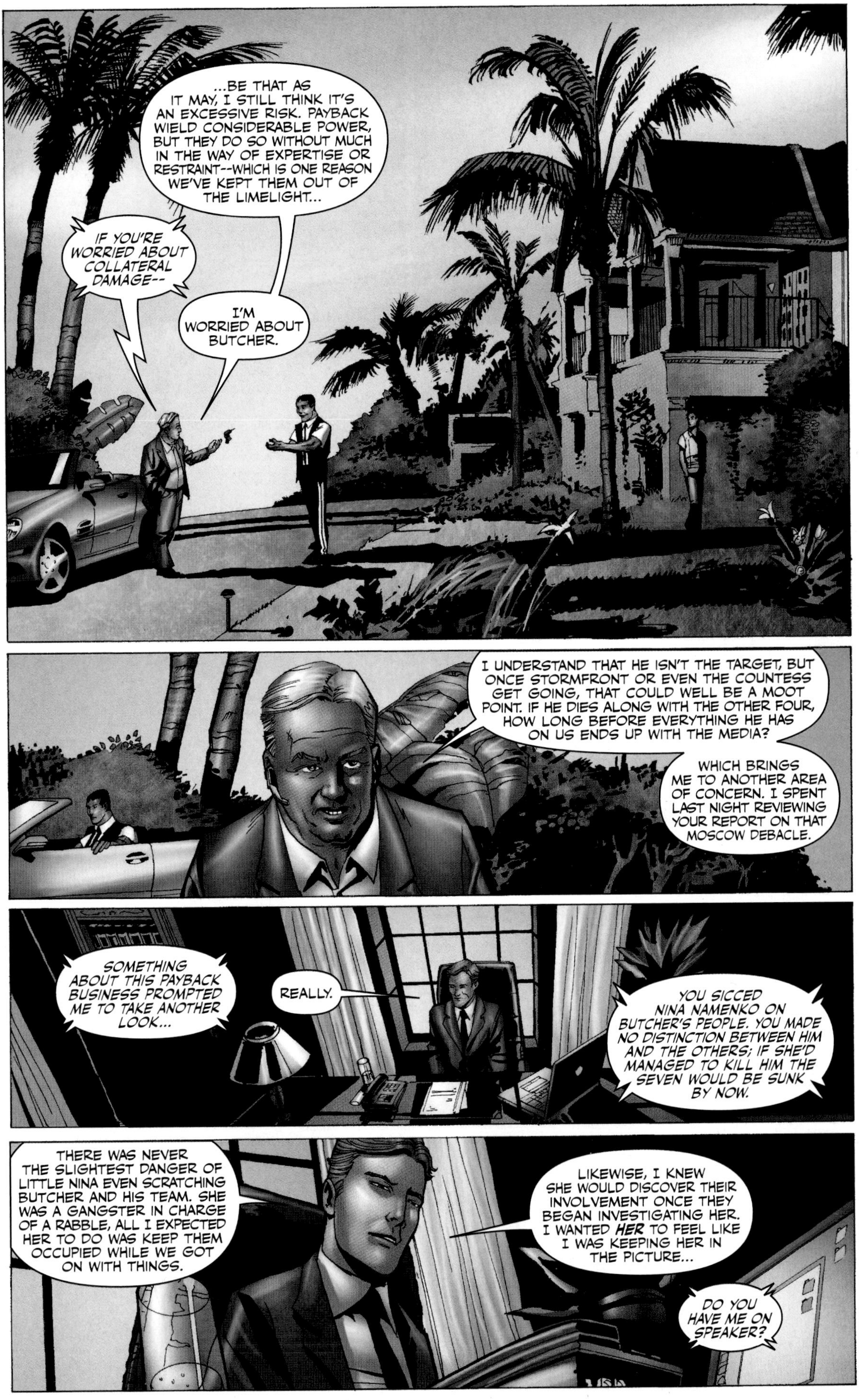
...BE THAT AS IT MAY, I STILL THINK IT'S AN EXCESSIVE RISK. PAYBACK WIELD CONSIDERABLE POWER, BUT THEY DO SO WITHOUT MUCH IN THE WAY OF EXPERTISE OR RESTRAINT--WHICH IS ONE REASON WE'VE KEPT THEM OUT OF THE LIMELIGHT...
IF YOU'RE WORRIED ABOUT COLLATERAL DAMAGE--
I'M WORRIED ABOUT BUTCHER.
I UNDERSTAND THAT HE ISN'T THE TARGET, BUT ONCE STORMFRONT OR EVEN THE COUNTESS GET GOING, THAT COULD WELL BE A MOOT POINT. IF HE DIES ALONG WITH THE OTHER FOUR, HOW LONG BEFORE EVERYTHING HE HAS ON US ENDS UP WITH THE MEDIA?
WHICH BRINGS ME TO ANOTHER AREA OF CONCERN. I SPENT LAST NIGHT REVIEWING YOUR REPORT ON THAT MOSCOW DEBACLE.
SOMETHING ABOUT THIS PAYBACK BUSINESS PROMPTED ME TO TAKE ANOTHER LOOK...
REALLY.
YOU SICCED NINA NAMENKO ON BUTCHER'S PEOPLE. YOU MADE NO DISTINCTION BETWEEN HIM AND THE OTHERS; IF SHE'D MANAGED TO KILL HIM THE SEVEN WOULD BE SUNK BY NOW.
THERE WAS NEVER THE SLIGHTEST DANGER OF LITTLE NINA EVEN SCRATCHING BUTCHER AND HIS TEAM. SHE WAS A GANGSTER IN CHARGE OF A RABBLE, ALL I EXPECTED HER TO DO WAS KEEP THEM OCCUPIED WHILE WE GOT ON WITH THINGS.
LIKEWISE, I KNEW SHE WOULD DISCOVER THEIR INVOLVEMENT ONCE THEY BEGAN INVESTIGATING HER. I WANTED HER TO FEEL LIKE I WAS KEEPING HER IN THE PICTURE...
DO YOU HAVE ME ON SPEAKER?

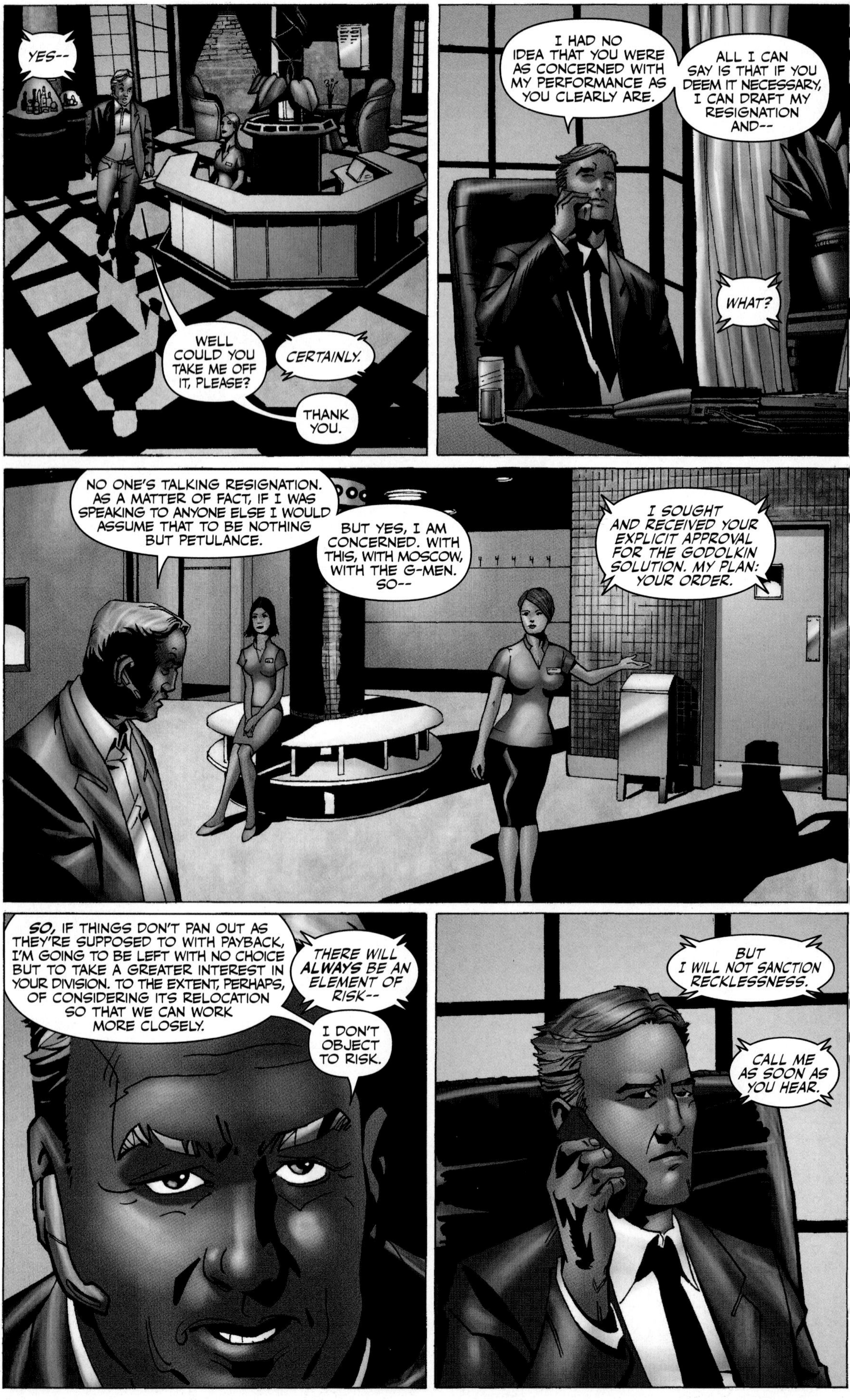
YES--
WELL COULD YOU TAKE ME OFF IT, PLEASE?
CERTAINLY.
THANK YOU.
I HAD NO IDEA THAT YOU WERE AS CONCERNED WITH MY PERFORMANCE AS YOU CLEARLY ARE.
ALL I CAN SAY IS THAT IF YOU DEEM IT NECESSARY, I CAN DRAFT MY RESIGNATION AND--
WHAT?
NO ONE'S TALKING RESIGNATION. AS A MATTER OF FACT, IF I WAS SPEAKING TO ANYONE ELSE I WOULD ASSUME THAT TO BE NOTHING BUT PETULANCE.
BUT YES, I AM CONCERNED. WITH THIS, WITH MOSCOW, WITH THE G-MEN. SO--
I SOUGHT AND RECEIVED YOUR EXPLICIT APPROVAL FOR THE GODOLKIN SOLUTION. MY PLAN: YOUR ORDER.
SO, IF THINGS DON'T PAN OUT AS THEY'RE SUPPOSED TO WITH PAYBACK, I'M GOING TO BE LEFT WITH NO CHOICE BUT TO TAKE A GREATER INTEREST IN YOUR DIVISION. TO THE EXTENT, PERHAPS, OF CONSIDERING ITS RELOCATION SO THAT WE CAN WORK MORE CLOSELY.
THERE WILL ALWAYS BE AN ELEMENT OF RISK--
I DON'T OBJECT TO RISK.
BUT I WILL NOT SANCTION RECKLESSNESS.
CALL ME AS SOON AS YOU HEAR.

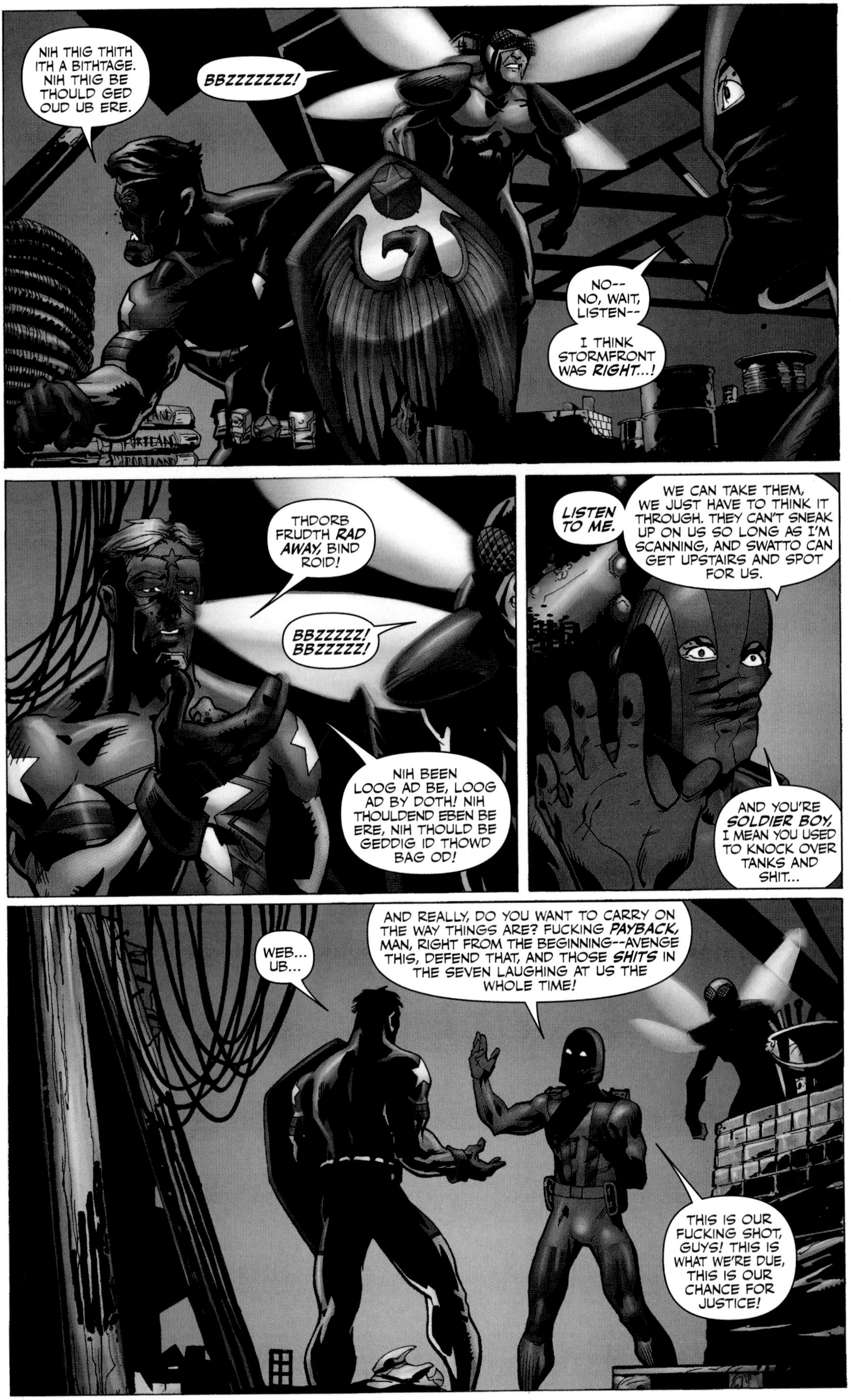
NIH THIG THITH ITH A BITHTAGE. NIH THIG BE THOULD GED OUD UB ERE.
BBZZZZZZZ!
NO-- NO, WAIT, LISTEN--
I THINK STORMFRONT WAS RIGHT...!
THDORB FRUDTH RAD AWAY, BIND ROID!
BBZZZZZ! BBZZZZZ!
NIH BEEN LOOG AD BE, LOOG AD BY DOTH! NIH THOULDEND EBEN BE ERE, NIH THOULD BE GEDDIG ID THOWD BAG OD!
LISTEN TO ME.
WE CAN TAKE THEM, WE JUST HAVE TO THINK IT THROUGH. THEY CAN'T SNEAK UP ON US SO LONG AS I'M SCANNING, AND SWATTO CAN GET UPSTAIRS AND SPOT FOR US.
AND YOU'RE SOLDIER BOY, I MEAN YOU USED TO KNOCK OVER TANKS AND SHIT...
WEB... UB...
AND REALLY, DO YOU WANT TO CARRY ON THE WAY THINGS ARE? FUCKING PAYBACK, MAN, RIGHT FROM THE BEGINNING--AVENGE THIS, DEFEND THAT, AND THOSE SHITS IN THE SEVEN LAUGHING AT US THE WHOLE TIME!
THIS IS OUR FUCKING SHOT, GUYS! THIS IS WHAT WE'RE DUE, THIS IS OUR CHANCE FOR JUSTICE!

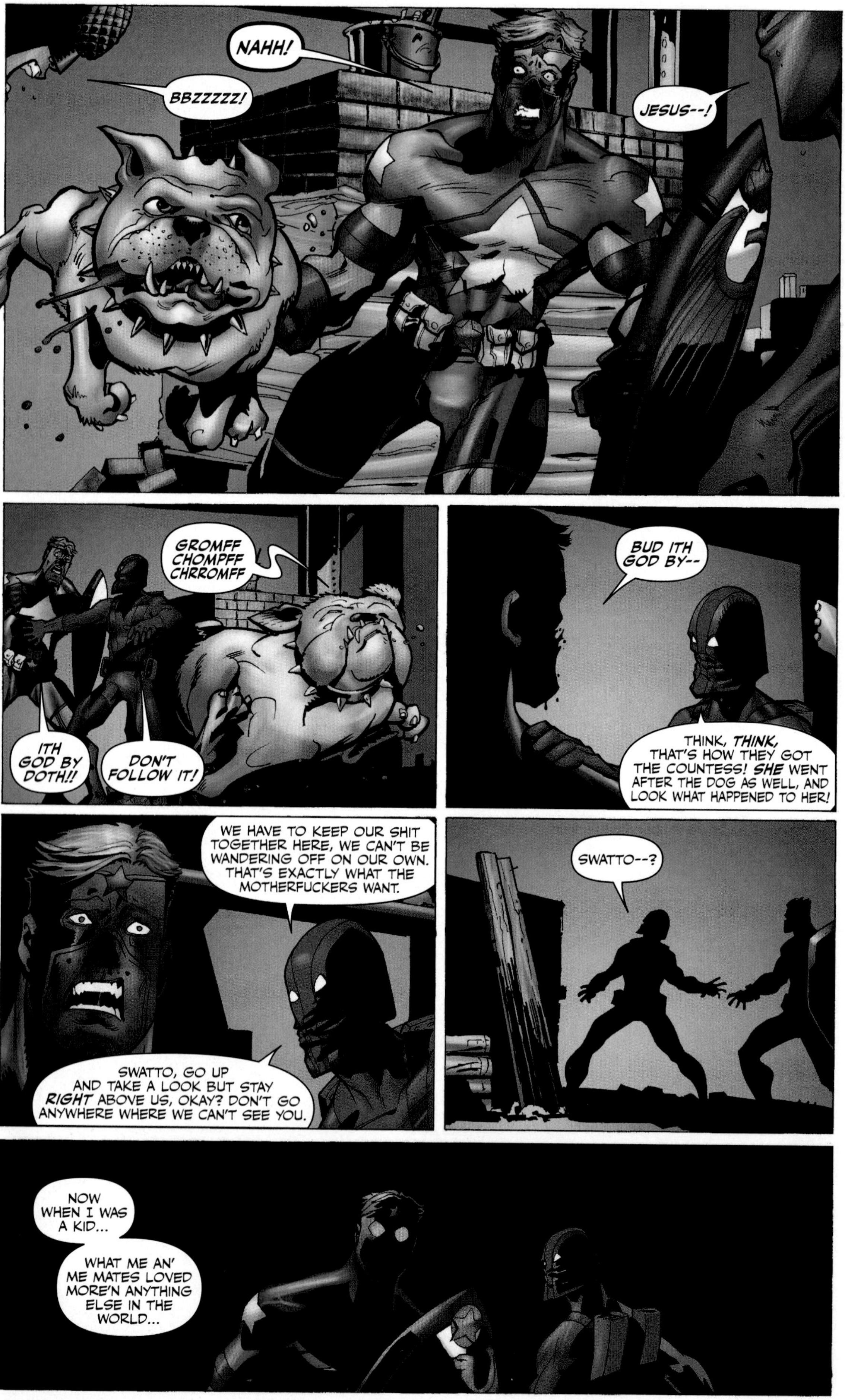
NAHH!
BBZZZZZ!
JESUS--!
GROMFF CHOMPFF CHRROMFF
ITH GOD BY DOTH!!
DON'T FOLLOW IT!
BUD ITH GOD BY--
THINK, THINK, THAT'S HOW THEY GOT THE COUNTESS! SHE WENT AFTER THE DOG AS WELL, AND LOOK WHAT HAPPENED TO HER!
WE HAVE TO KEEP OUR SHIT TOGETHER HERE, WE CAN'T BE WANDERING OFF ON OUR OWN. THAT'S EXACTLY WHAT THE MOTHERFUCKERS WANT.
SWATTO, GO UP AND TAKE A LOOK BUT STAY RIGHT ABOVE US, OKAY? DON'T GO ANYWHERE WHERE WE CAN'T SEE YOU.
SWATTO--?
NOW WHEN I WAS A KID...
WHAT ME AN' ME MATES LOVED MORE'N ANYTHING ELSE IN THE WORLD...

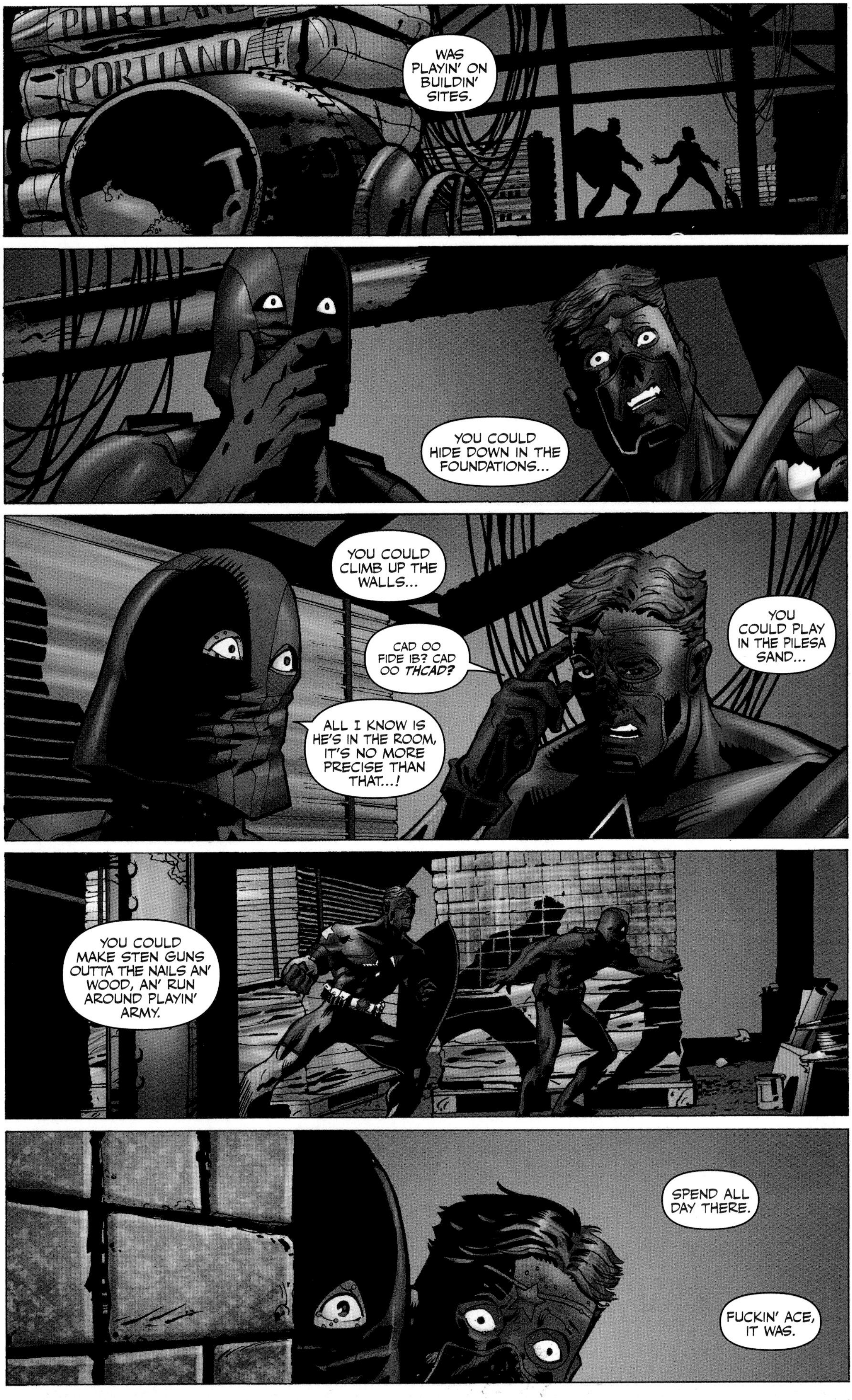
PORTLAND
WAS PLAYIN' ON BUILDIN' SITES.
YOU COULD HIDE DOWN IN THE FOUNDATIONS...
YOU COULD CLIMB UP THE WALLS...
YOU COULD PLAY IN THE PILESA SAND...
CAD OO FIDE IB? CAD OO *THCAD?*
ALL I KNOW IS HE'S IN THE ROOM, IT'S NO MORE PRECISE THAN THAT...!
YOU COULD MAKE STEN GUNS OUTTA THE NAILS AN' WOOD, AN' RUN AROUND PLAYIN' ARMY.
SPEND ALL DAY THERE.
FUCKIN' ACE, IT WAS.

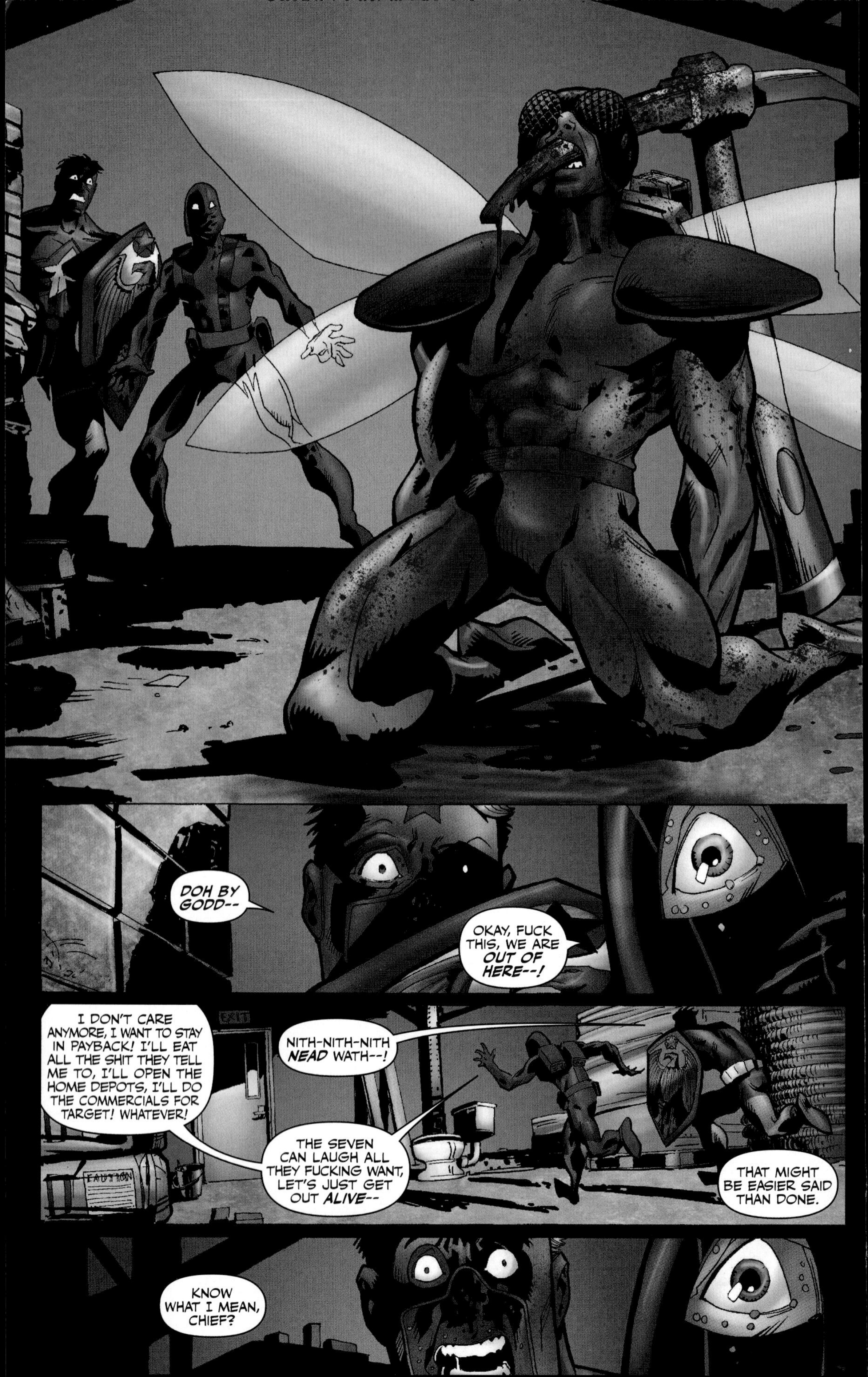
DOH BY GODD--
OKAY, FUCK THIS, WE ARE *OUT OF HERE--!*
I DON'T CARE ANYMORE, I WANT TO STAY IN PAYBACK! I'LL EAT ALL THE SHIT THEY TELL ME TO, I'LL OPEN THE HOME DEPOTS, I'LL DO THE COMMERCIALS FOR TARGET! WHATEVER!
NITH-NITH-NITH *NEAD* WATH--!
THE SEVEN CAN LAUGH ALL THEY FUCKING WANT, LET'S JUST GET OUT *ALIVE--*
EXIT
CAUTION
THAT MIGHT BE EASIER SAID THAN DONE.
KNOW WHAT I MEAN, CHIEF?

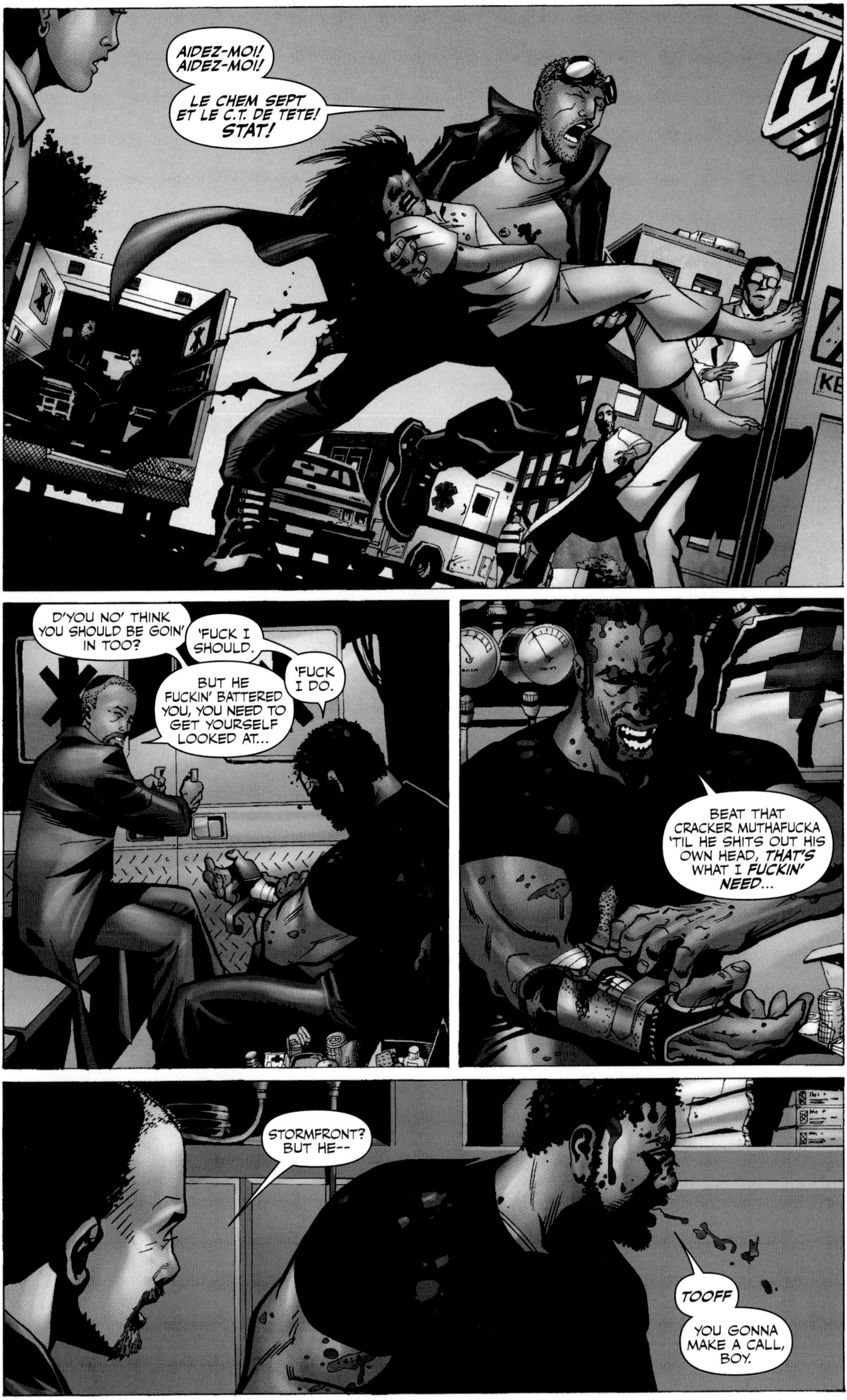
AIDEZ-MOI! AIDEZ-MOI!
LE CHEM SEPT ET LE C.T. DE TETE! STAT!
D'YOU NO' THINK YOU SHOULD BE GOIN' IN TOO?
'FUCK I SHOULD.
BUT HE FUCKIN' BATTERED YOU, YOU NEED TO GET YOURSELF LOOKED AT...
'FUCK I DO.
BEAT THAT CRACKER MUTHAFUCKA 'TIL HE SHITS OUT HIS OWN HEAD, THAT'S WHAT I FUCKIN' NEED...
STORMFRONT? BUT HE--
TOOFF
YOU GONNA MAKE A CALL, BOY.

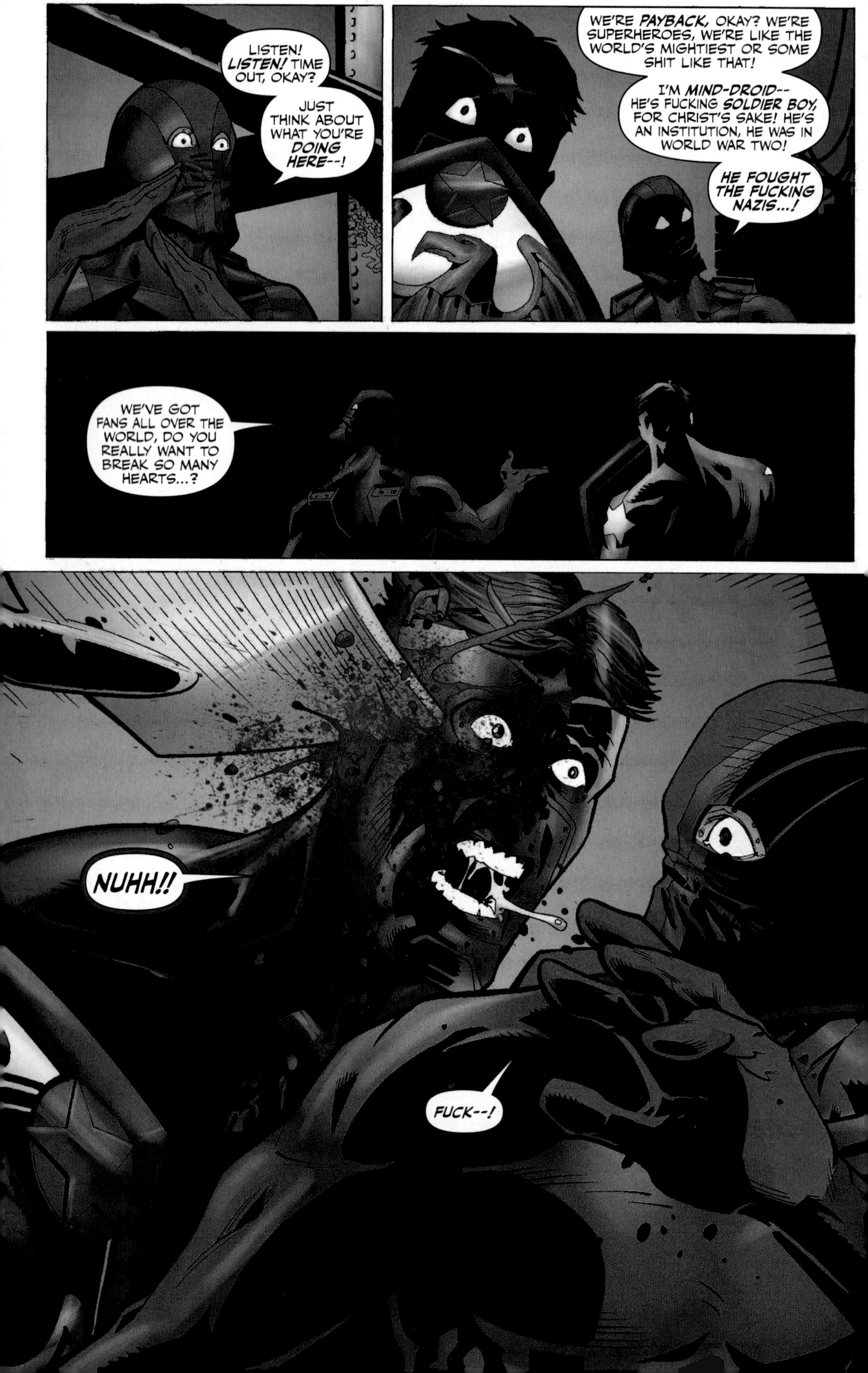
LISTEN! LISTEN! TIME OUT, OKAY?
JUST THINK ABOUT WHAT YOU'RE DOING HERE--!
WE'RE PAYBACK, OKAY? WE'RE SUPERHEROES, WE'RE LIKE THE WORLD'S MIGHTIEST OR SOME SHIT LIKE THAT!
I'M MIND-DROID-- HE'S FUCKING SOLDIER BOY, FOR CHRIST'S SAKE! HE'S AN INSTITUTION, HE WAS IN WORLD WAR TWO!
HE FOUGHT THE FUCKING NAZIS...!
WE'VE GOT FANS ALL OVER THE WORLD, DO YOU REALLY WANT TO BREAK SO MANY HEARTS...?
NUHH!!
FUCK--!

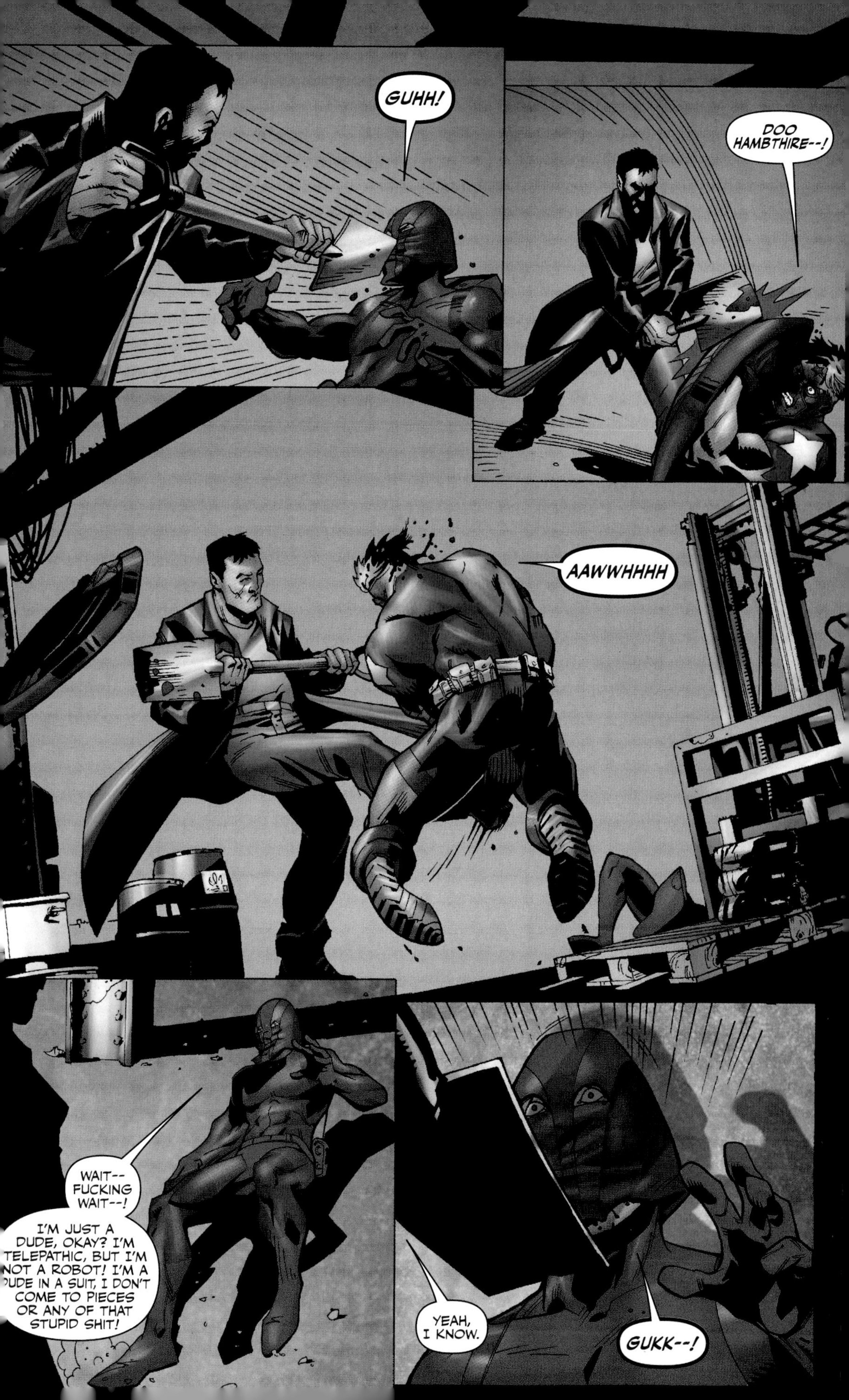
GUHH!
DOO HAMBTHIRE--!
AAWWHHHH
WAIT-- FUCKING WAIT--!
I'M JUST A DUDE, OKAY? I'M TELEPATHIC, BUT I'M NOT A ROBOT! I'M A DUDE IN A SUIT, I DON'T COME TO PIECES OR ANY OF THAT STUPID SHIT!
YEAH, I KNOW.
GUKK--!

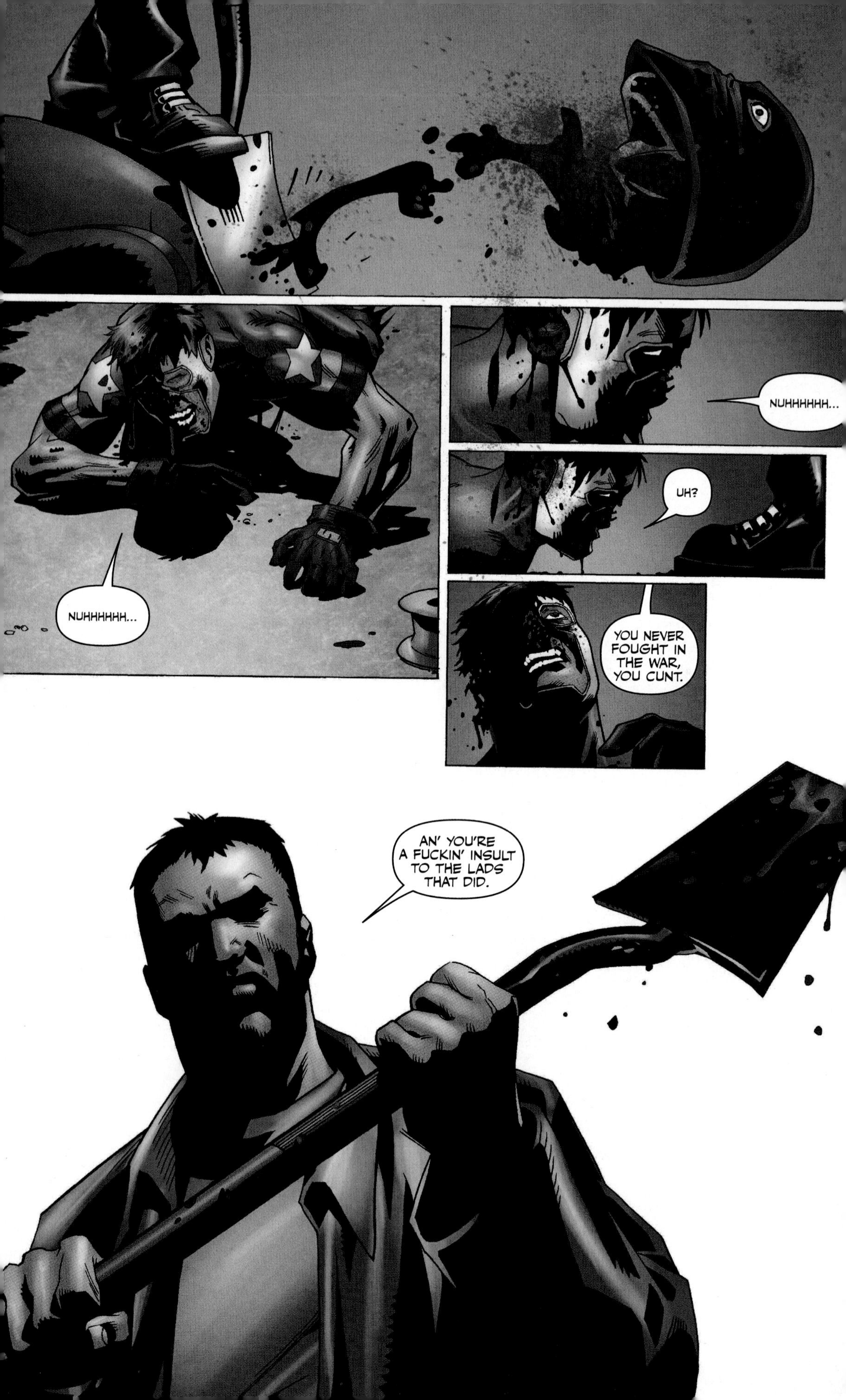
NUHHHHHH...
NUHHHHHH...
UH?
YOU NEVER FOUGHT IN THE WAR, YOU CUNT.
AN' YOU'RE A FUCKIN' INSULT TO THE LADS THAT DID.

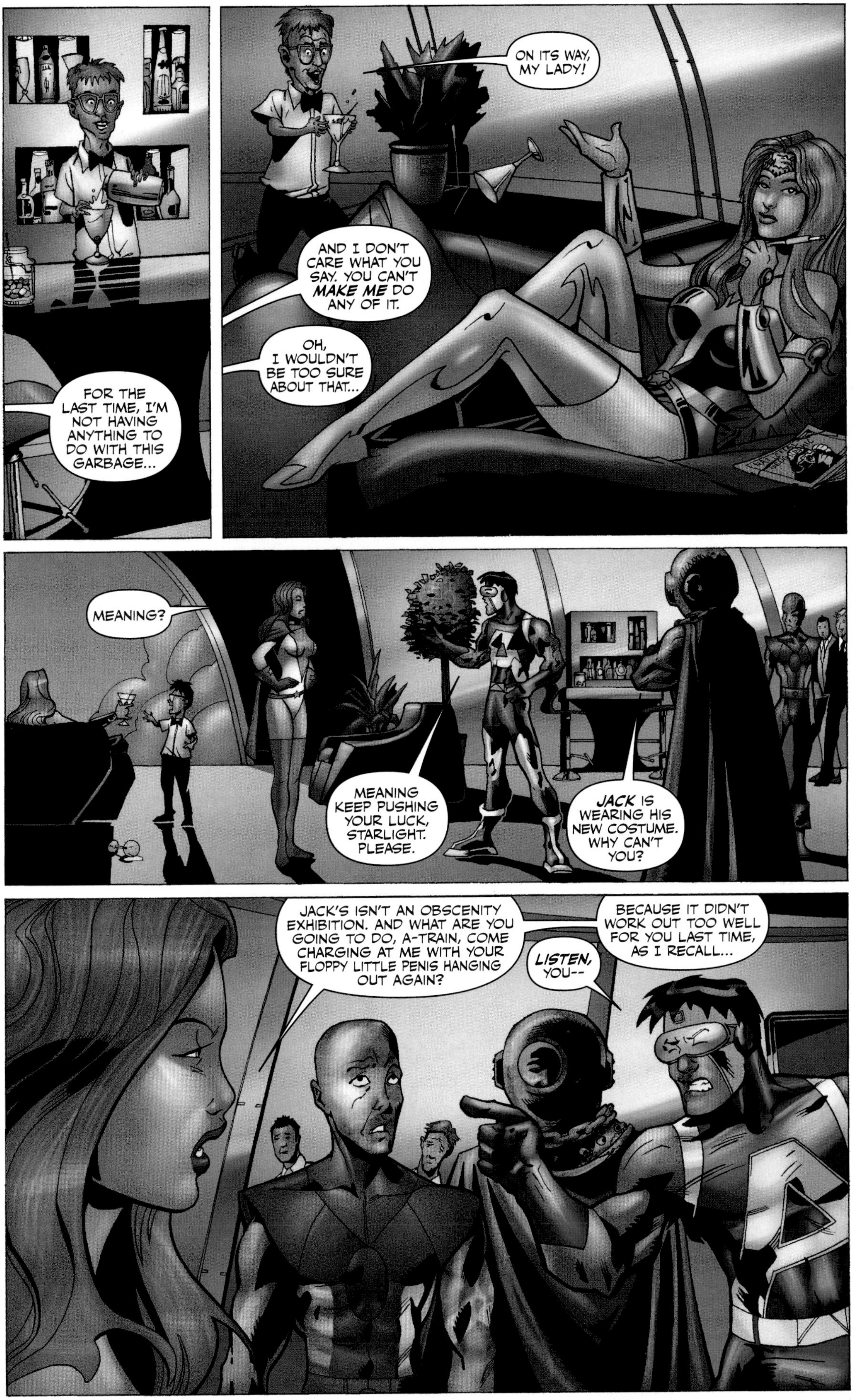
FOR THE LAST TIME, I'M NOT HAVING ANYTHING TO DO WITH THIS GARBAGE...
ON ITS WAY, MY LADY!
AND I DON'T CARE WHAT YOU SAY. YOU CAN'T *MAKE ME* DO ANY OF IT.
OH, I WOULDN'T BE TOO SURE ABOUT THAT...
MEANING?
MEANING KEEP PUSHING YOUR LUCK, STARLIGHT. PLEASE.
JACK IS WEARING HIS NEW COSTUME. WHY CAN'T YOU?
JACK'S ISN'T AN OBSCENITY EXHIBITION. AND WHAT ARE YOU GOING TO DO, A-TRAIN, COME CHARGING AT ME WITH YOUR FLOPPY LITTLE PENIS HANGING OUT AGAIN?
BECAUSE IT DIDN'T WORK OUT TOO WELL FOR YOU LAST TIME, AS I RECALL...
LISTEN, YOU--

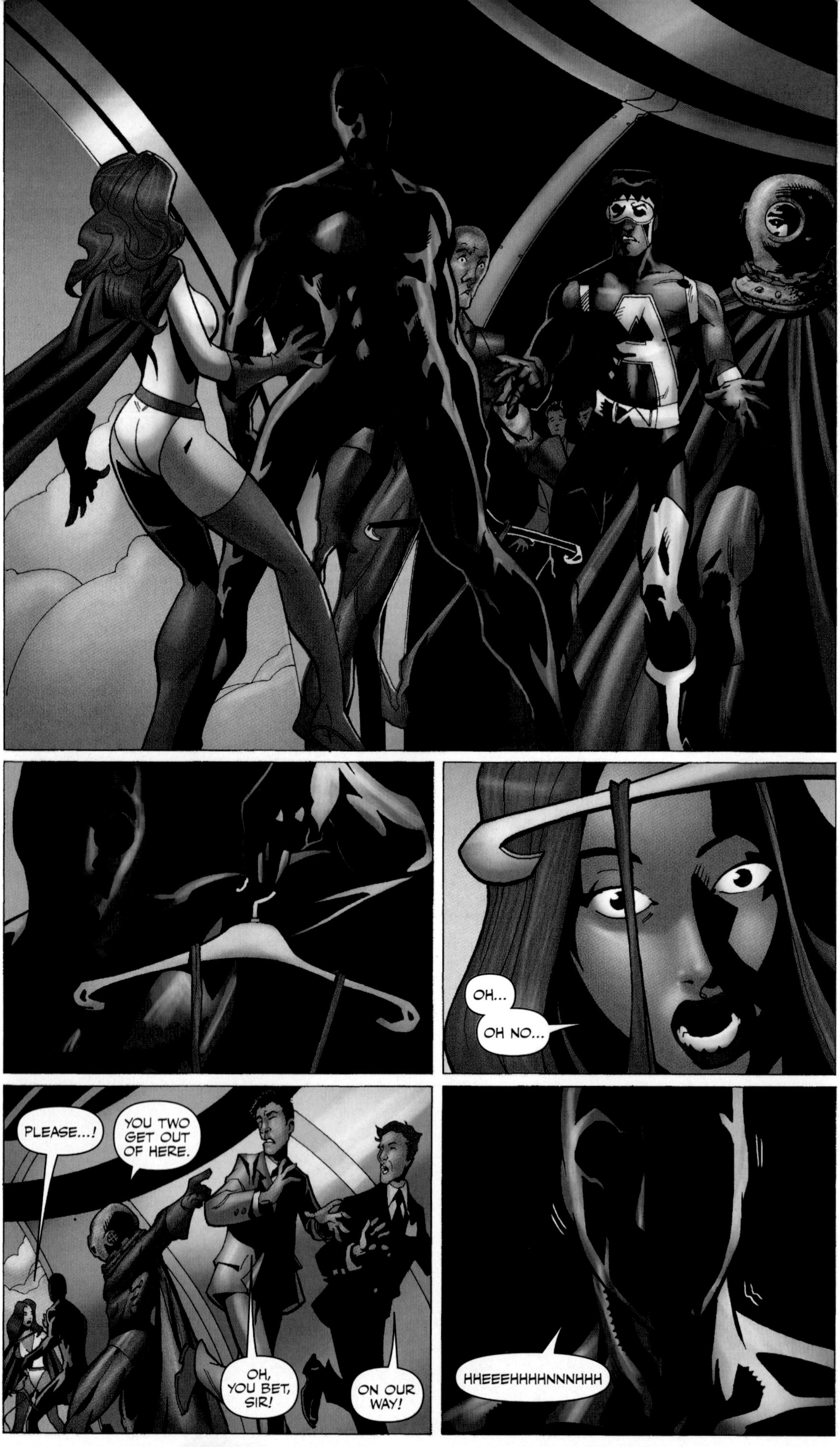
OH...
OH NO...
PLEASE...!
YOU TWO GET OUT OF HERE.
OH, YOU BET, SIR!
ON OUR WAY!
HHEEEHHHHNNNHHH

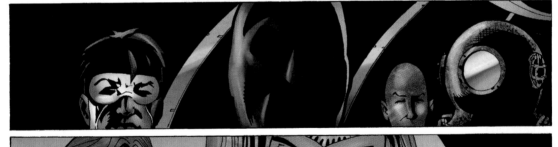

MY-- MY LADY--!

WHAT?

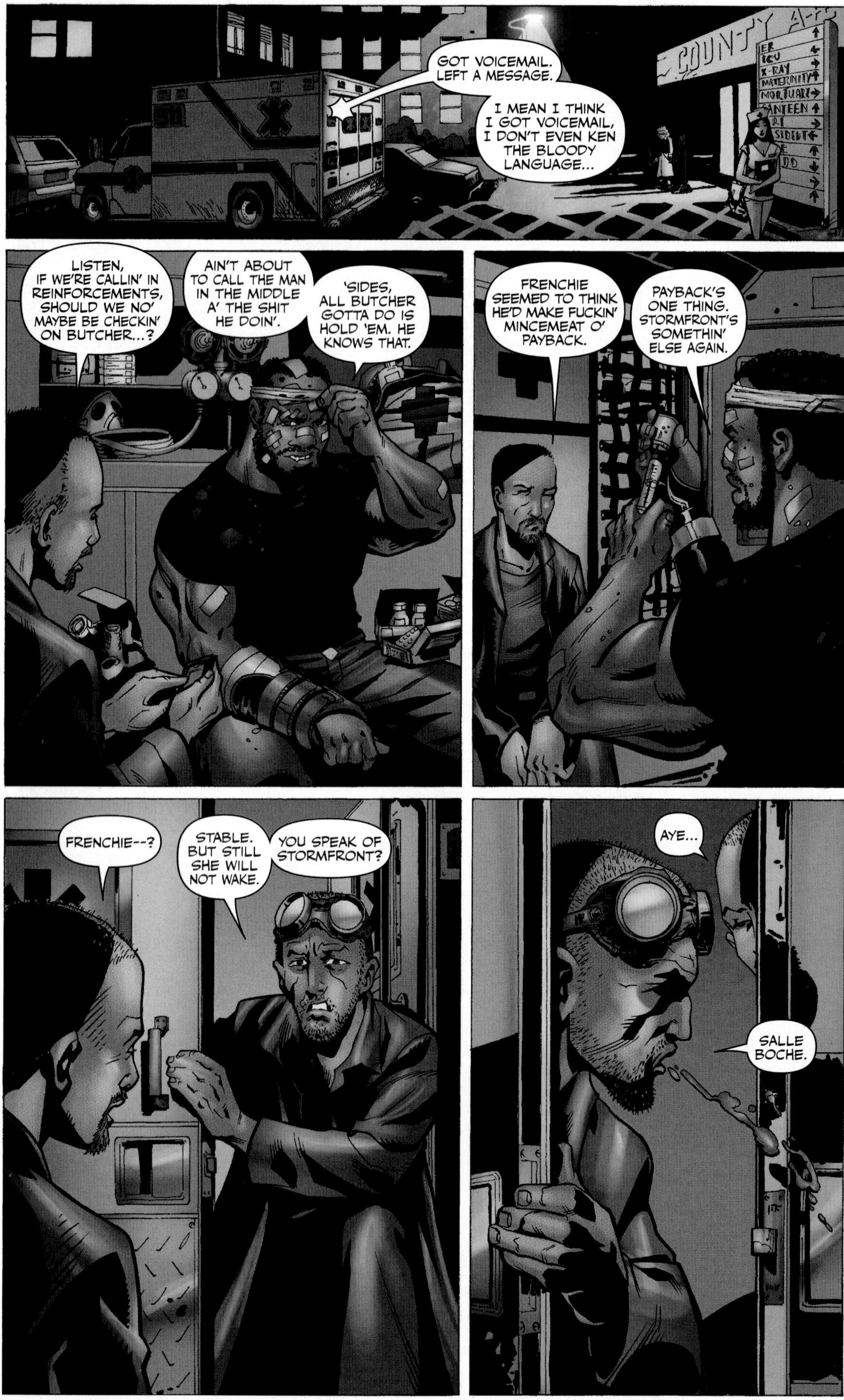
COUNTY
ER
ICU
X-RAY
MATERNITY
MORTUARY
CANTEEN
GOT VOICEMAIL. LEFT A MESSAGE.
I MEAN I THINK I GOT VOICEMAIL, I DON'T EVEN KEN THE BLOODY LANGUAGE...
LISTEN, IF WE'RE CALLIN' IN REINFORCEMENTS, SHOULD WE NO' MAYBE BE CHECKIN' ON BUTCHER...?
AIN'T ABOUT TO CALL THE MAN IN THE MIDDLE A' THE SHIT HE DOIN'.
'SIDES, ALL BUTCHER GOTTA DO IS HOLD 'EM. HE KNOWS THAT.
FRENCHIE SEEMED TO THINK HE'D MAKE FUCKIN' MINCEMEAT O' PAYBACK.
PAYBACK'S ONE THING. STORMFRONT'S SOMETHIN' ELSE AGAIN.
FRENCHIE--?
STABLE. BUT STILL SHE WILL NOT WAKE.
YOU SPEAK OF STORMFRONT?
AYE...
SALLE BOCHE.

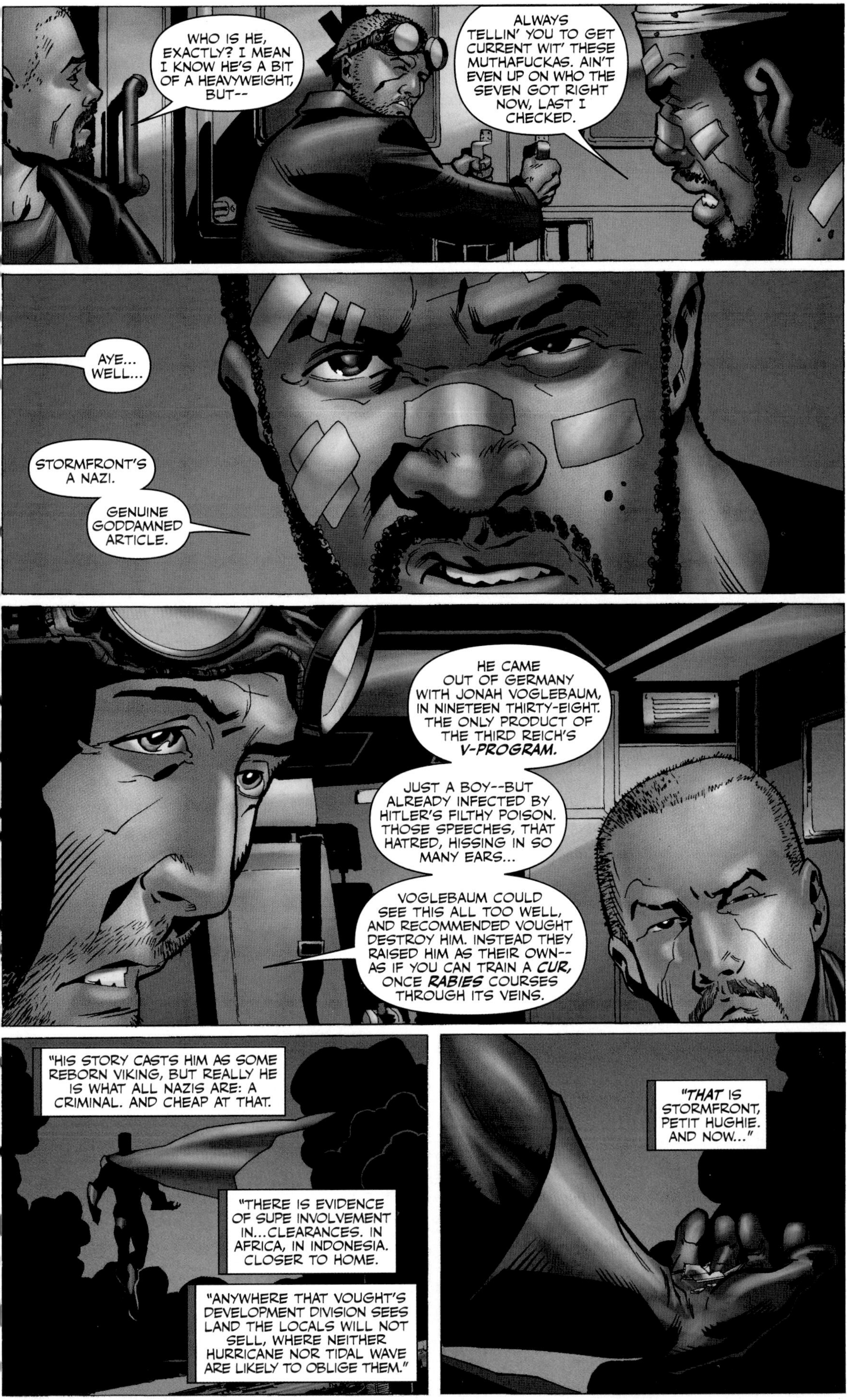
WHO IS HE, EXACTLY? I MEAN I KNOW HE'S A BIT OF A HEAVYWEIGHT, BUT--
ALWAYS TELLIN' YOU TO GET CURRENT WIT' THESE MUTHAFUCKAS. AIN'T EVEN UP ON WHO THE SEVEN GOT RIGHT NOW, LAST I CHECKED.
AYE... WELL...
STORMFRONT'S A NAZI.
GENUINE GODDAMNED ARTICLE.
HE CAME OUT OF GERMANY WITH JONAH VOGLEBAUM, IN NINETEEN THIRTY-EIGHT. THE ONLY PRODUCT OF THE THIRD REICH'S ***V-PROGRAM.***
JUST A BOY--BUT ALREADY INFECTED BY HITLER'S FILTHY POISON. THOSE SPEECHES, THAT HATRED, HISSING IN SO MANY EARS...
VOGLEBAUM COULD SEE THIS ALL TOO WELL, AND RECOMMENDED VOUGHT DESTROY HIM. INSTEAD THEY RAISED HIM AS THEIR OWN--AS IF YOU CAN TRAIN A ***CUR,*** ONCE ***RABIES*** COURSES THROUGH ITS VEINS.
"HIS STORY CASTS HIM AS SOME REBORN VIKING, BUT REALLY HE IS WHAT ALL NAZIS ARE: A CRIMINAL. AND CHEAP AT THAT.
"THERE IS EVIDENCE OF SUPE INVOLVEMENT IN...CLEARANCES. IN AFRICA, IN INDONESIA. CLOSER TO HOME.
"ANYWHERE THAT VOUGHT'S DEVELOPMENT DIVISION SEES LAND THE LOCALS WILL NOT SELL, WHERE NEITHER HURRICANE NOR TIDAL WAVE ARE LIKELY TO OBLIGE THEM."
"***THAT*** IS STORMFRONT, PETIT HUGHIE. AND NOW..."

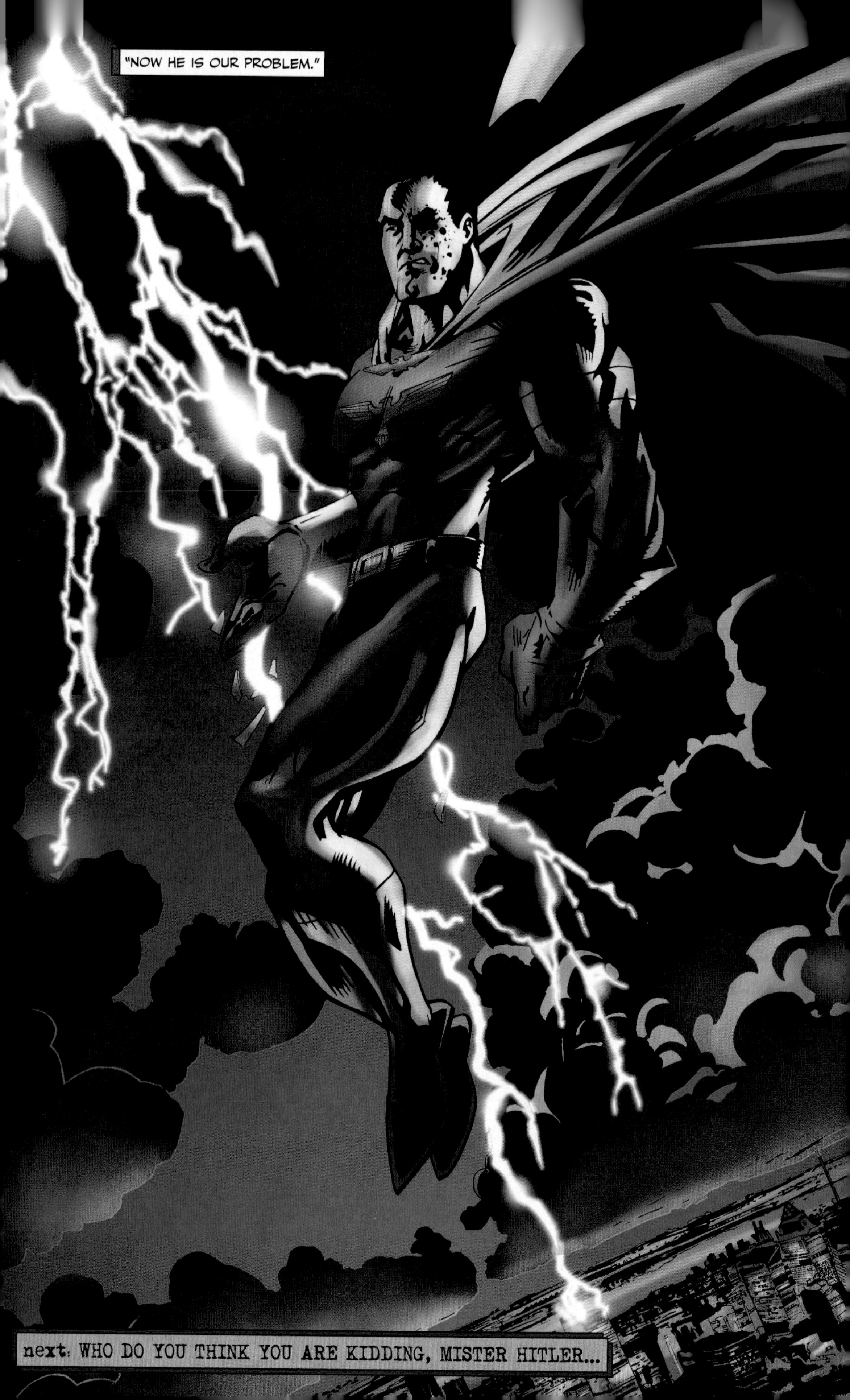
"NOW HE IS OUR PROBLEM."
next: WHO DO YOU THINK YOU ARE KIDDING, MISTER HITLER...

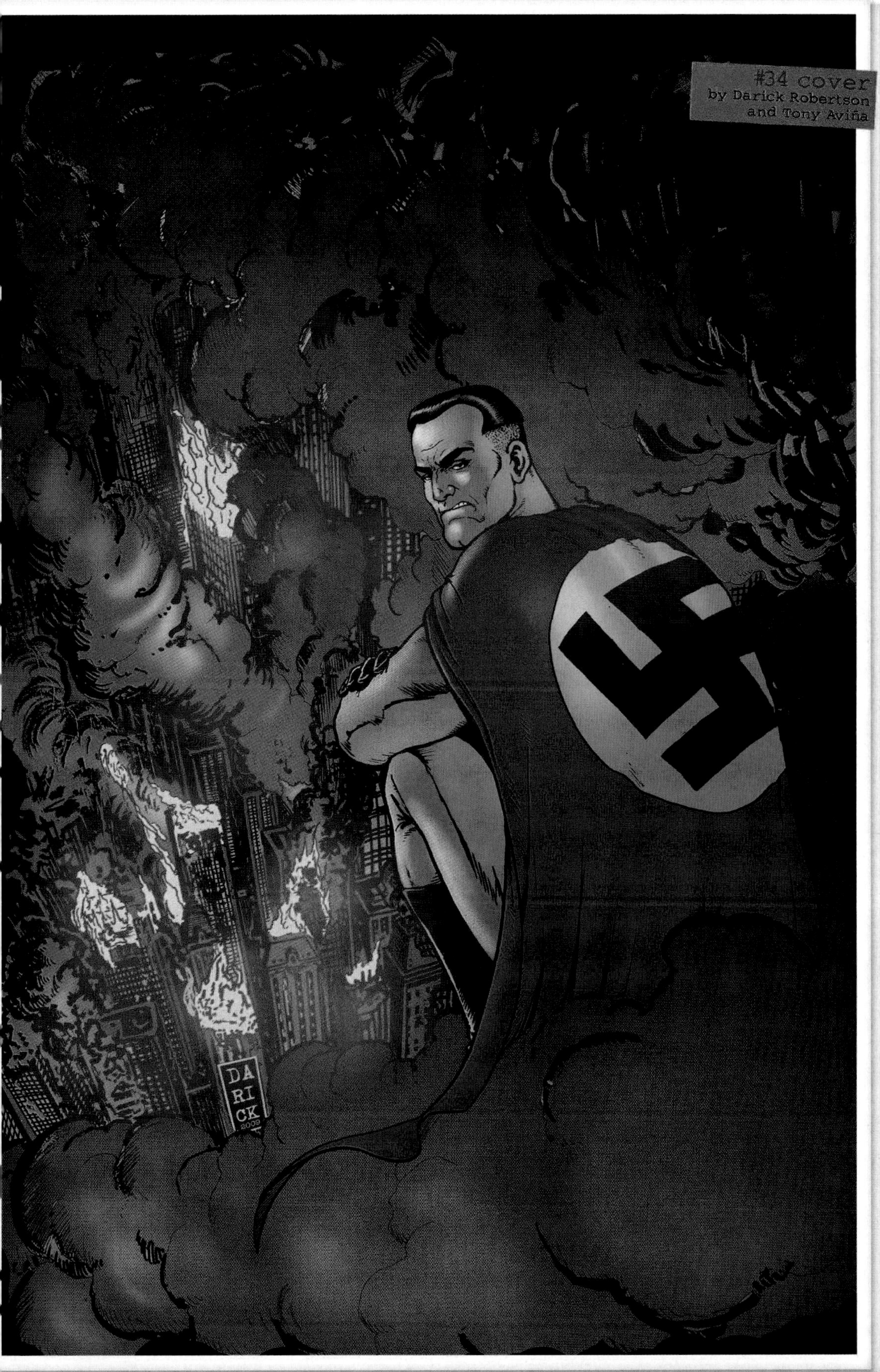
DARICK 2009

#34 cover
by Darick Robertson
and Tony Aviña

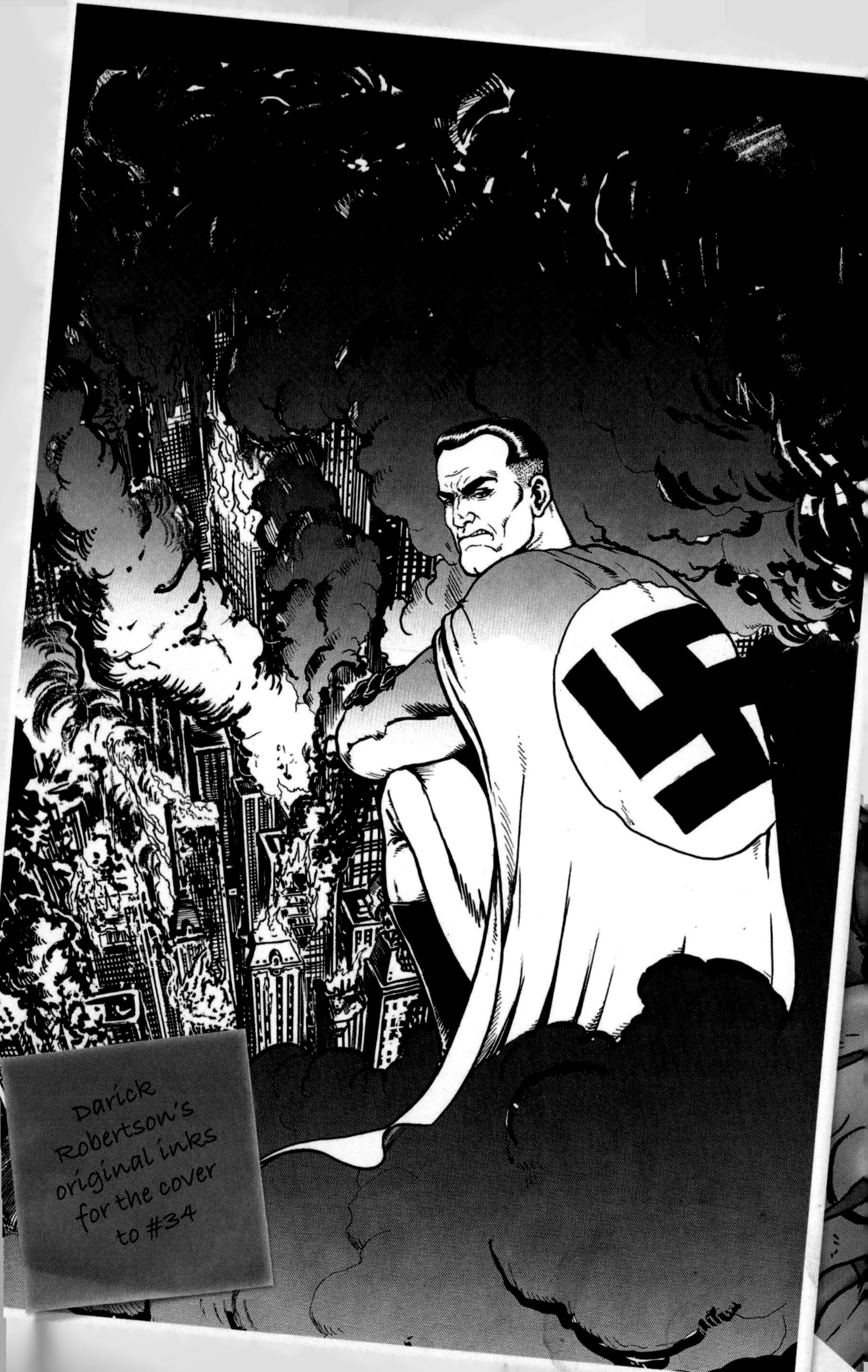

Darick Robertson's original inks for the cover to #34

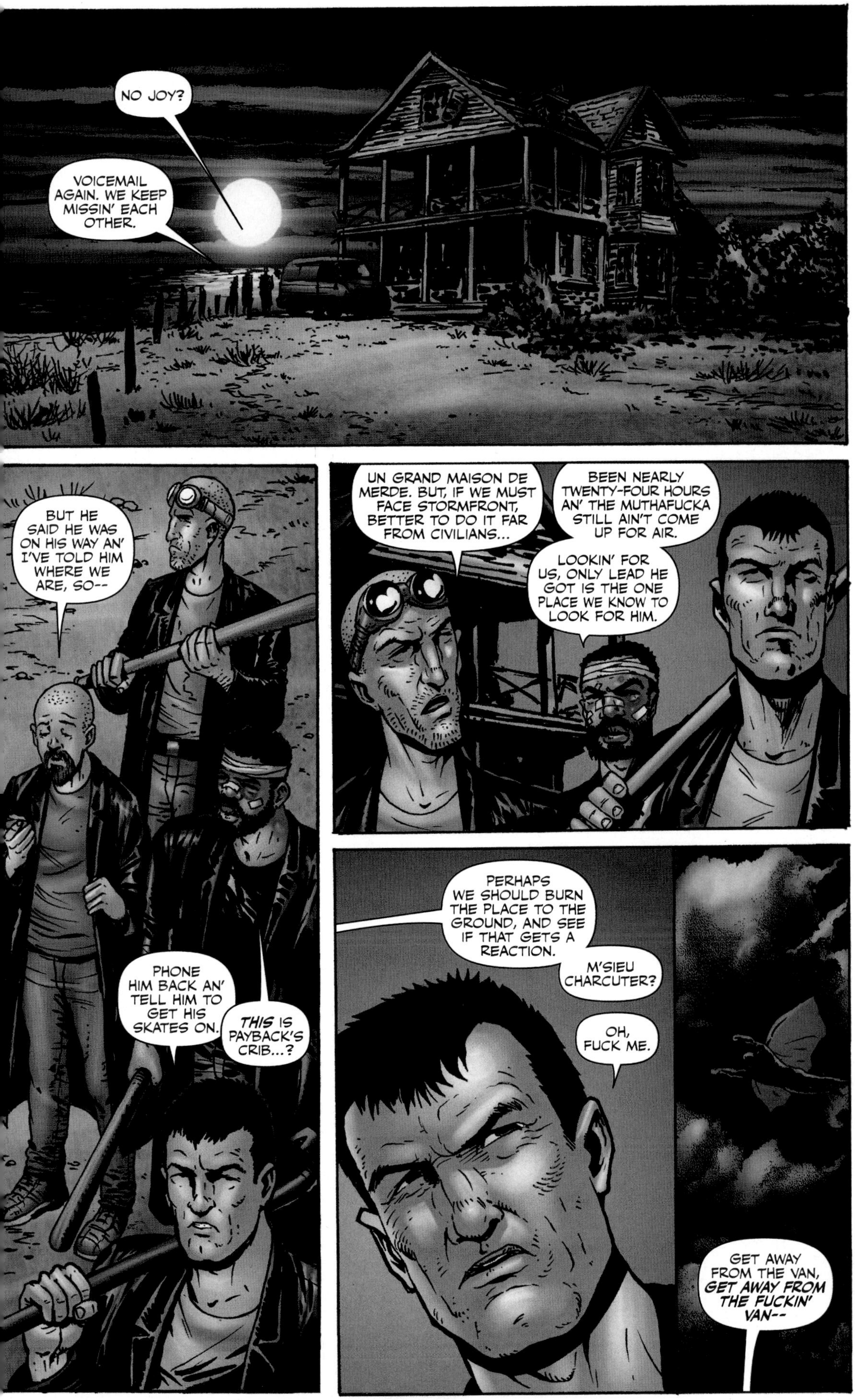

NO JOY?
VOICEMAIL AGAIN. WE KEEP MISSIN' EACH OTHER.
BUT HE SAID HE WAS ON HIS WAY AN' I'VE TOLD HIM WHERE WE ARE, SO--
PHONE HIM BACK AN' TELL HIM TO GET HIS SKATES ON.
THIS IS PAYBACK'S CRIB...?
UN GRAND MAISON DE MERDE. BUT, IF WE MUST FACE STORMFRONT, BETTER TO DO IT FAR FROM CIVILIANS...
BEEN NEARLY TWENTY-FOUR HOURS AN' THE MUTHAFUCKA STILL AIN'T COME UP FOR AIR.
LOOKIN' FOR US, ONLY LEAD HE GOT IS THE ONE PLACE WE KNOW TO LOOK FOR HIM.
PERHAPS WE SHOULD BURN THE PLACE TO THE GROUND, AND SEE IF THAT GETS A REACTION.
M'SIEU CHARCUTER?
OH, FUCK ME.
GET AWAY FROM THE VAN, ***GET AWAY FROM THE FUCKIN' VAN--***

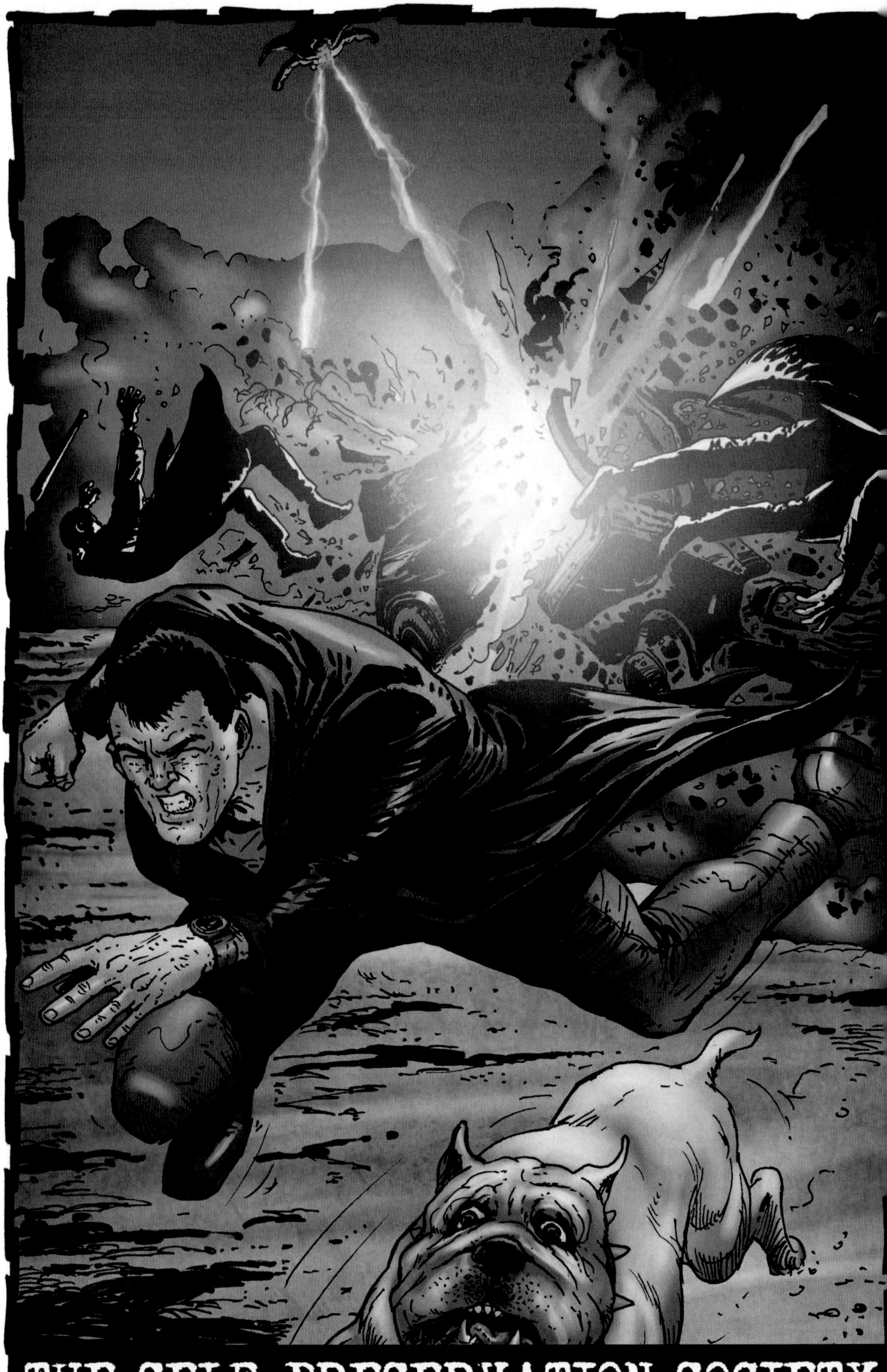

THE SELF-PRESERVATION SOCIETY
conclusion

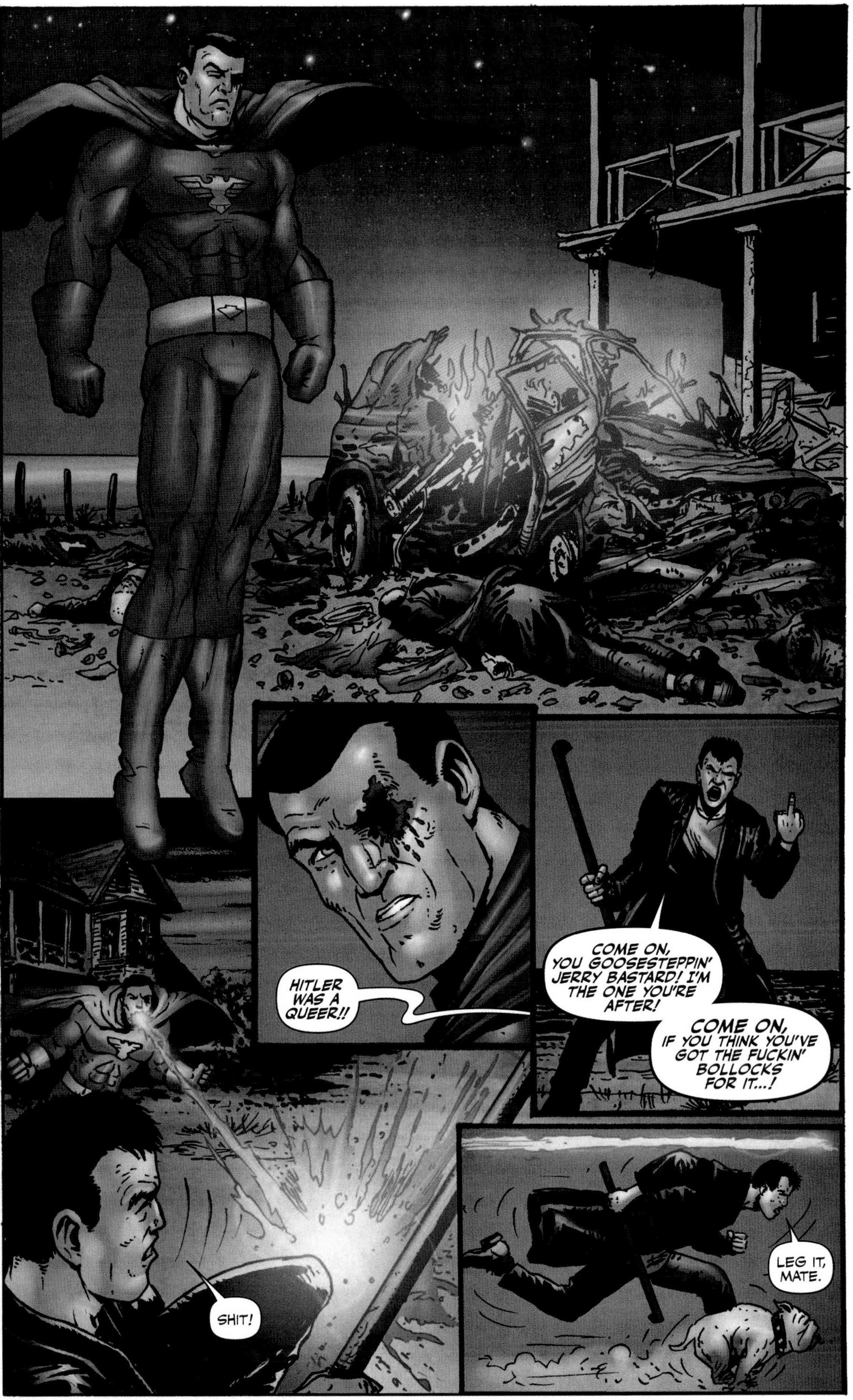
HITLER WAS A QUEER!!
COME ON, YOU GOOSESTEPPIN' JERRY BASTARD! I'M THE ONE YOU'RE AFTER!
COME ON, IF YOU THINK YOU'VE GOT THE FUCKIN' BOLLOCKS FOR IT...!
SHIT!
LEG IT, MATE.

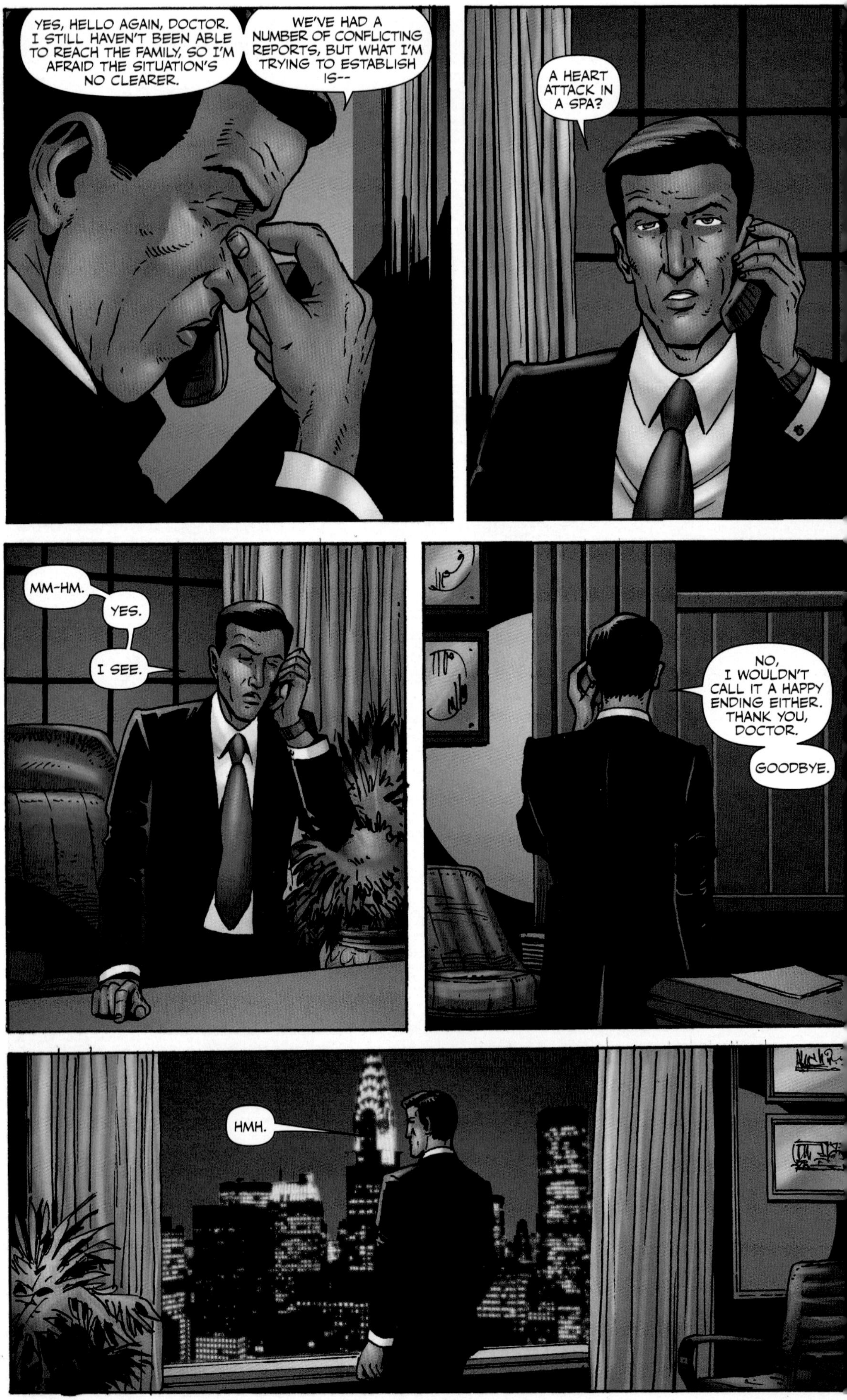

YES, HELLO AGAIN, DOCTOR. I STILL HAVEN'T BEEN ABLE TO REACH THE FAMILY, SO I'M AFRAID THE SITUATION'S NO CLEARER.
WE'VE HAD A NUMBER OF CONFLICTING REPORTS, BUT WHAT I'M TRYING TO ESTABLISH IS--
A HEART ATTACK IN A SPA?
MM-HM.
YES.
I SEE.
NO, I WOULDN'T CALL IT A HAPPY ENDING EITHER. THANK YOU, DOCTOR.
GOODBYE.
HMH.

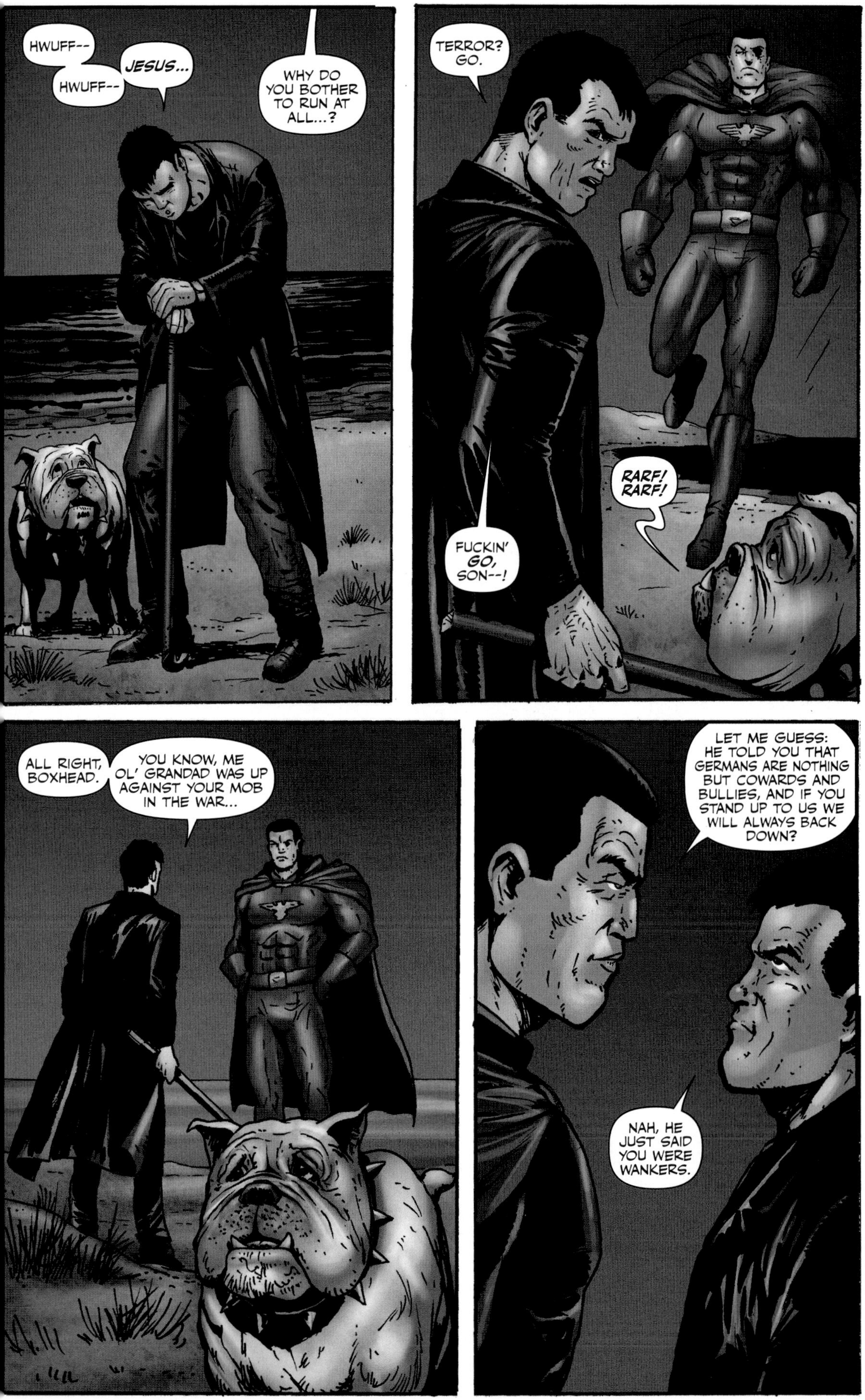

HWUFF--
HWUFF--
JESUS...
WHY DO YOU BOTHER TO RUN AT ALL...?
TERROR? GO.
FUCKIN' GO, SON--!
RARF! RARF!
ALL RIGHT, BOXHEAD.
YOU KNOW, ME OL' GRANDAD WAS UP AGAINST YOUR MOB IN THE WAR...
LET ME GUESS: HE TOLD YOU THAT GERMANS ARE NOTHING BUT COWARDS AND BULLIES, AND IF YOU STAND UP TO US WE WILL ALWAYS BACK DOWN?
NAH, HE JUST SAID YOU WERE WANKERS.

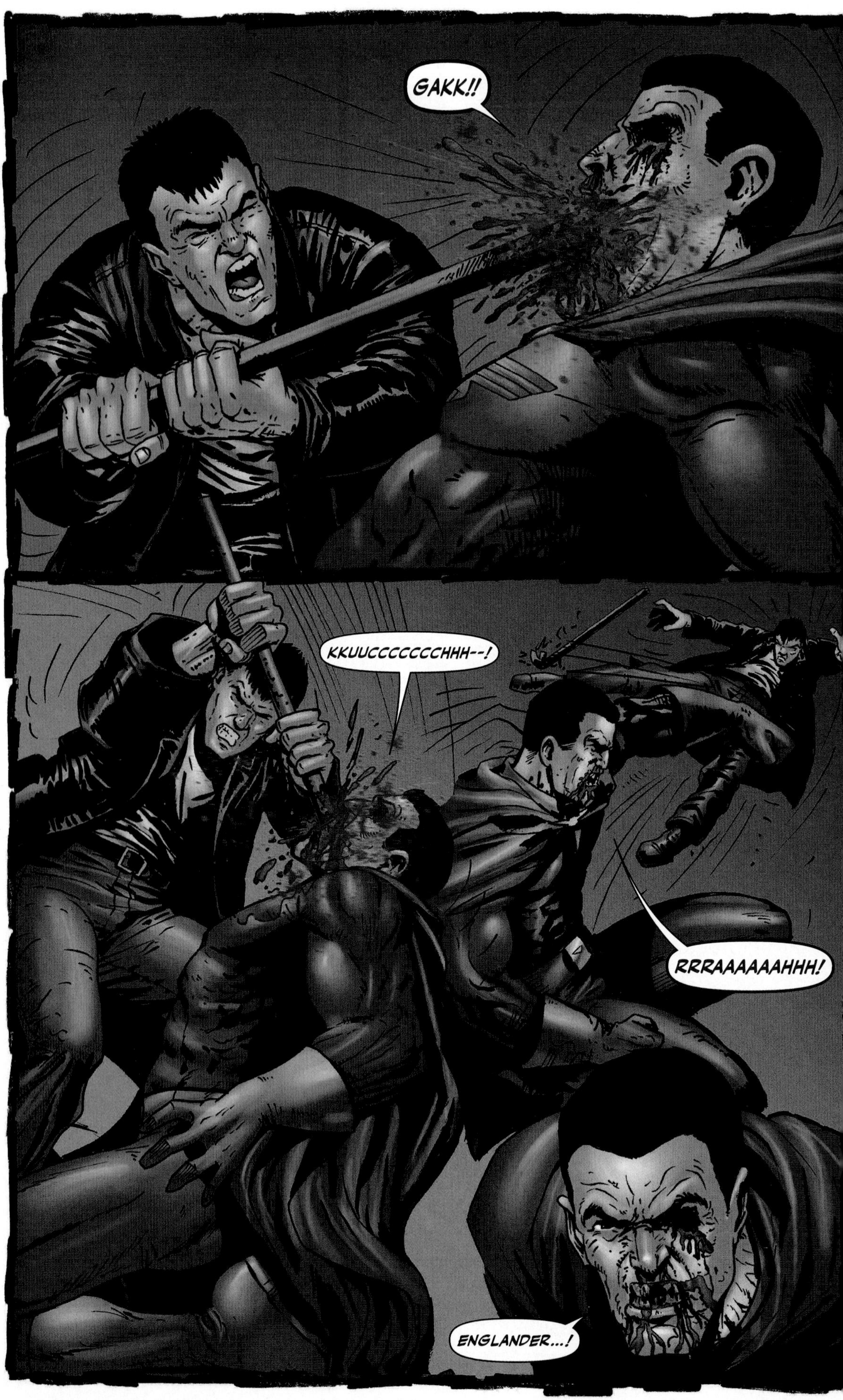
GAKK!!
KKUUCCCCCCCHHH--!
RRRAAAAAAHHH!
ENGLANDER...!

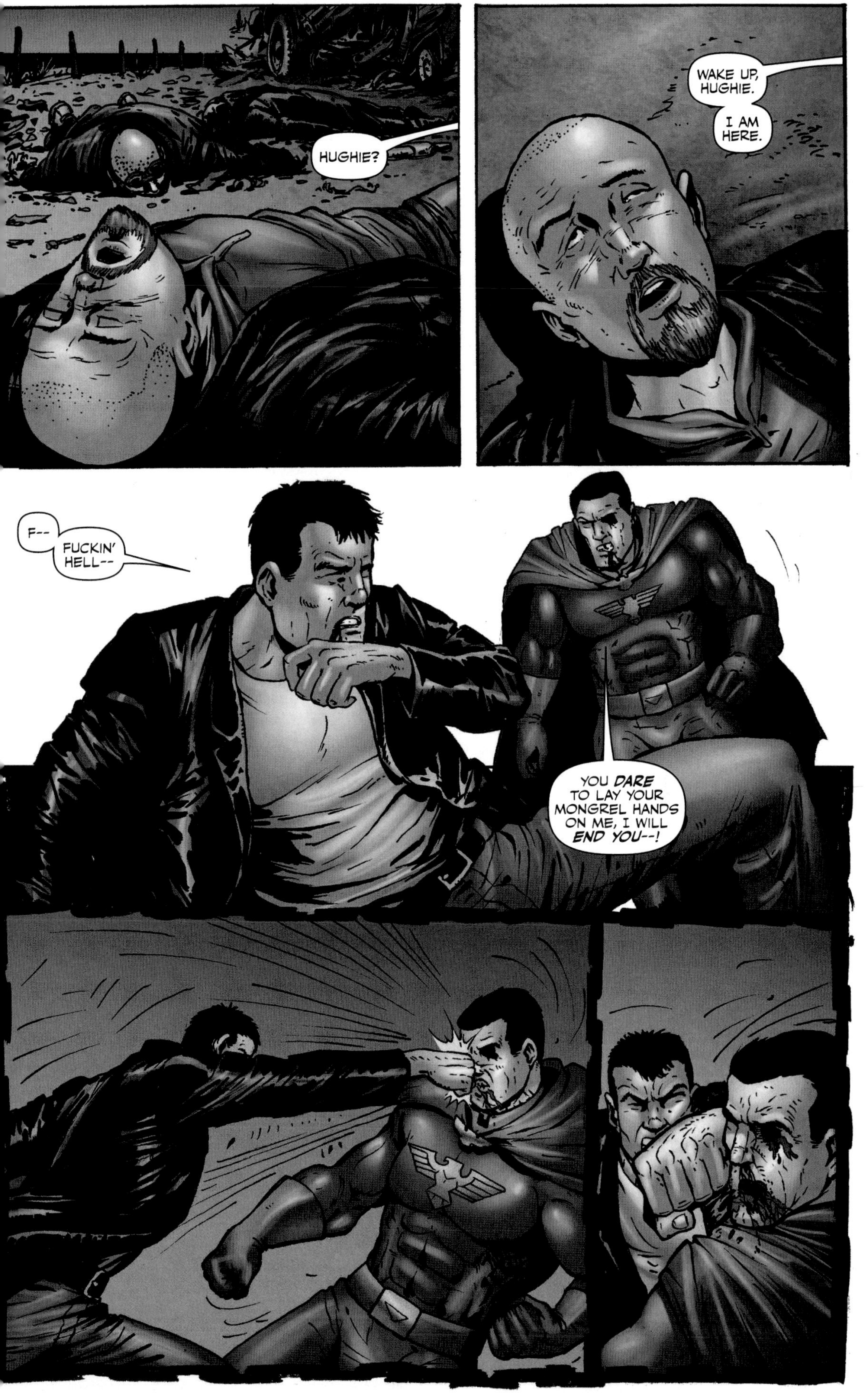
HUGHIE?
WAKE UP, HUGHIE.
I AM HERE.
F--
FUCKIN' HELL--
YOU DARE TO LAY YOUR MONGREL HANDS ON ME, I WILL END YOU--!

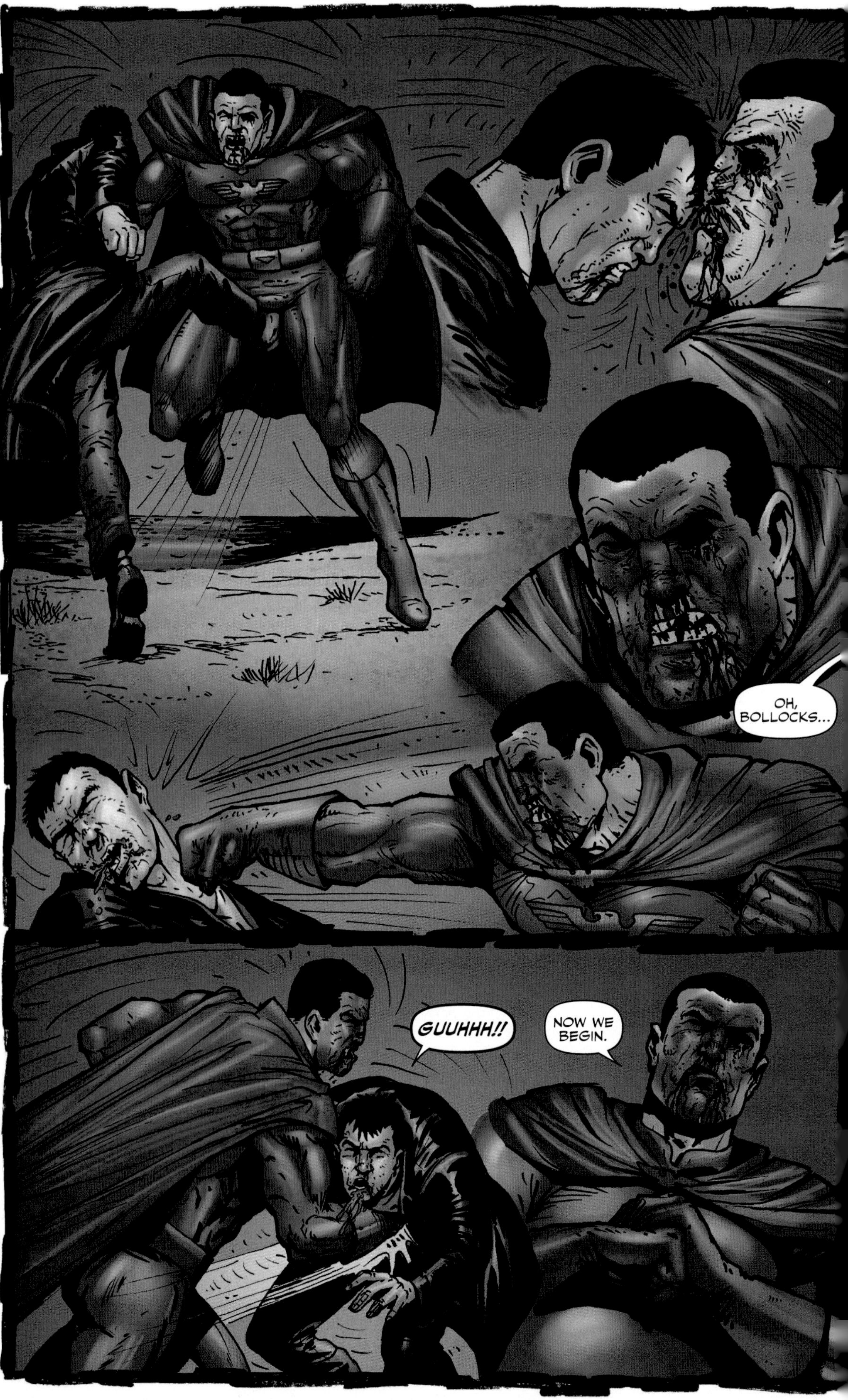
OH, BOLLOCKS...
GUUHHH!!
NOW WE BEGIN.

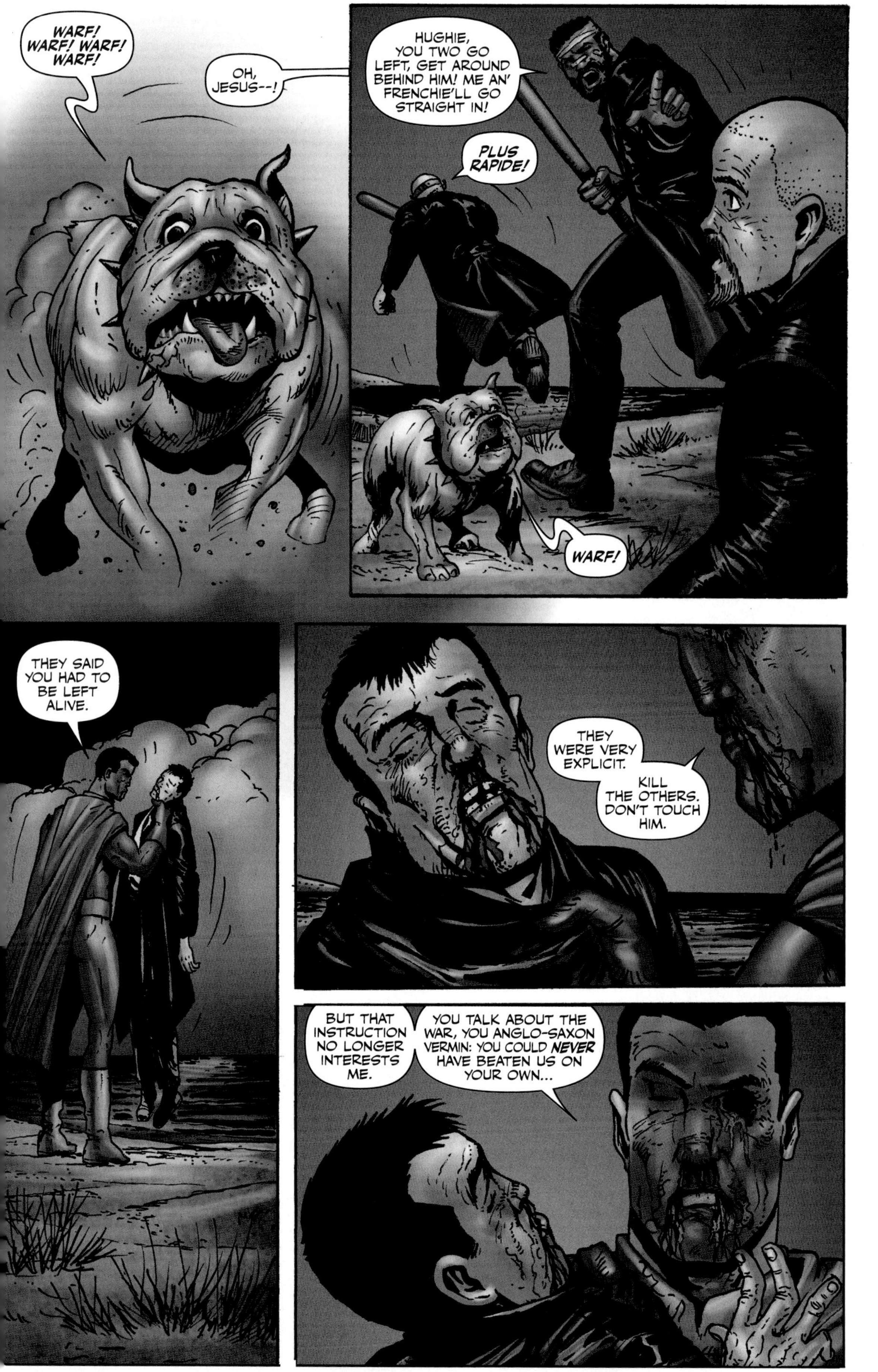
WARF! WARF! WARF! WARF! WARF!
OH, JESUS--!
HUGHIE, YOU TWO GO LEFT, GET AROUND BEHIND HIM! ME AN' FRENCHIE'LL GO STRAIGHT IN!
PLUS RAPIDE!
WARF!
THEY SAID YOU HAD TO BE LEFT ALIVE.
THEY WERE VERY EXPLICIT.
KILL THE OTHERS. DON'T TOUCH HIM.
BUT THAT INSTRUCTION NO LONGER INTERESTS ME.
YOU TALK ABOUT THE WAR, YOU ANGLO-SAXON VERMIN: YOU COULD NEVER HAVE BEATEN US ON YOUR OWN...

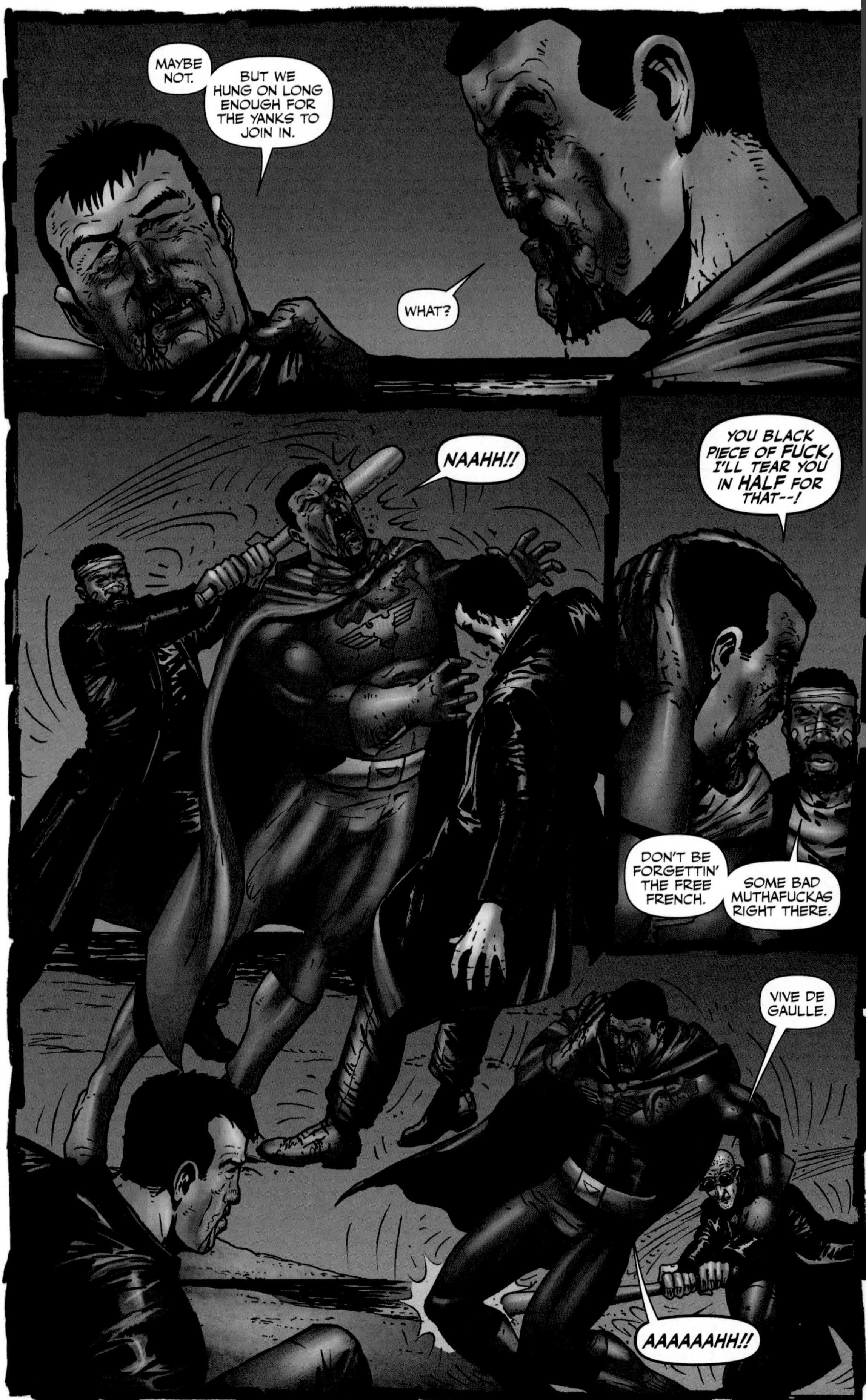
MAYBE NOT.
BUT WE HUNG ON LONG ENOUGH FOR THE YANKS TO JOIN IN.
WHAT?
NAAHH!!
YOU BLACK PIECE OF FUCK, I'LL TEAR YOU IN HALF FOR THAT--!
DON'T BE FORGETTIN' THE FREE FRENCH.
SOME BAD MUTHAFUCKAS RIGHT THERE.
VIVE DE GAULLE.
AAAAAAHH!!

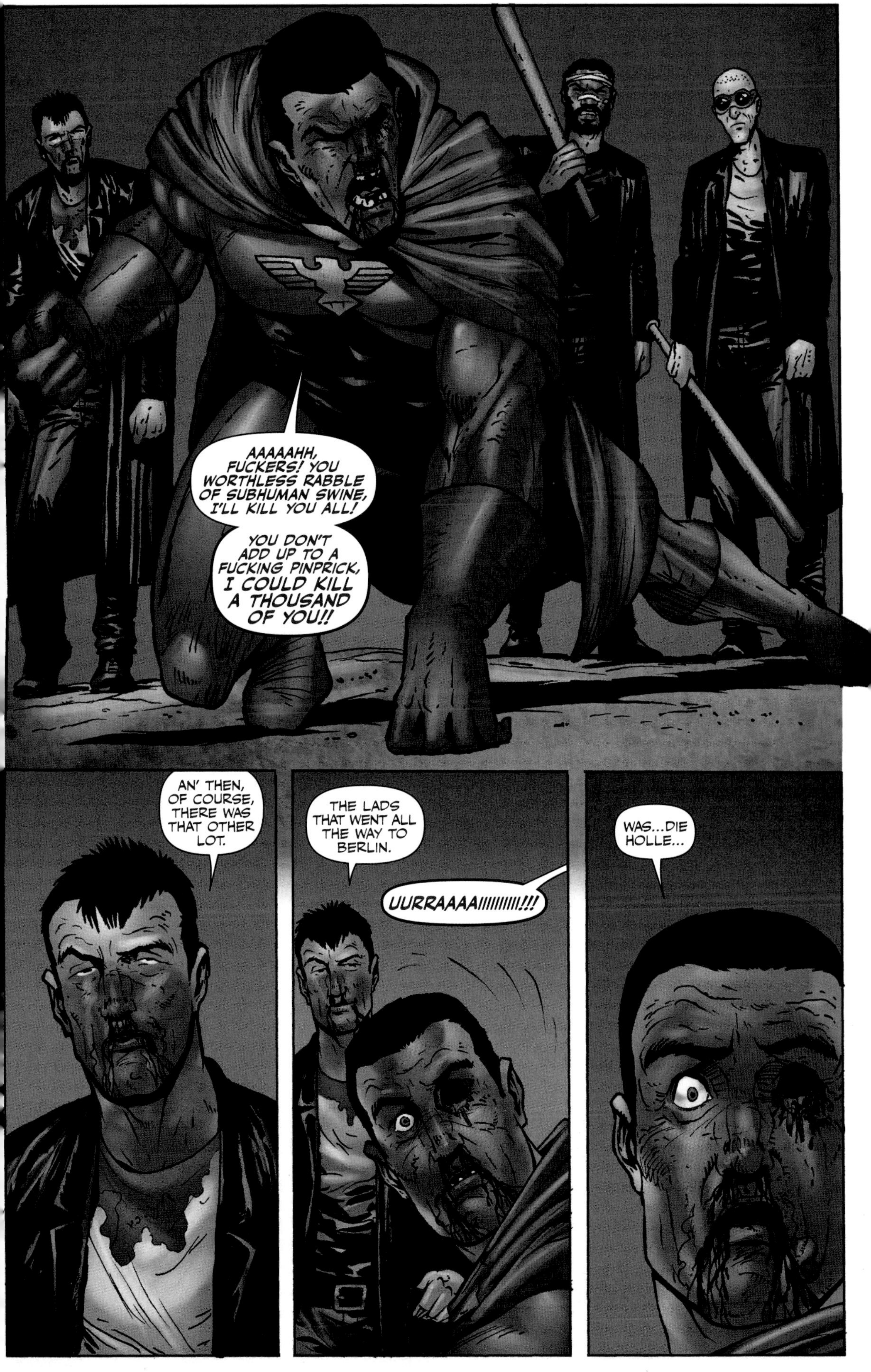
AAAAAHH, FUCKERS! YOU WORTHLESS RABBLE OF SUBHUMAN SWINE, I'LL KILL YOU ALL!
YOU DON'T ADD UP TO A FUCKING PINPRICK, I COULD KILL A THOUSAND OF YOU!!
AN' THEN, OF COURSE, THERE WAS THAT OTHER LOT.
THE LADS THAT WENT ALL THE WAY TO BERLIN.
UURRAAAAIIIIIIIIIII!!!
WAS...DIE HOLLE...

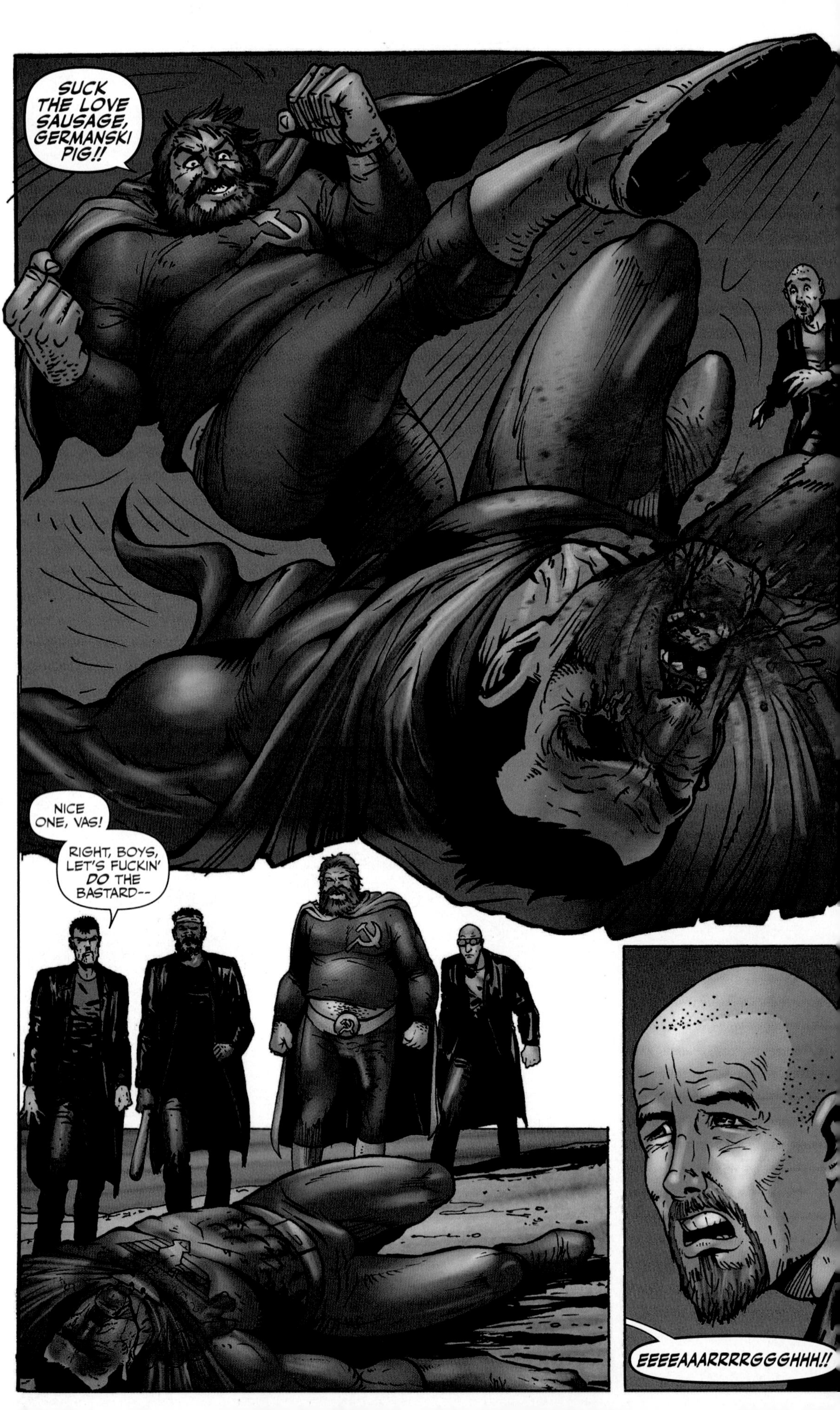
SUCK THE LOVE SAUSAGE, GERMANSKI PIG!!
NICE ONE, VAS!
RIGHT, BOYS, LET'S FUCKIN' *DO* THE BASTARD--
EEEEAAARRRRGGGHHH!!

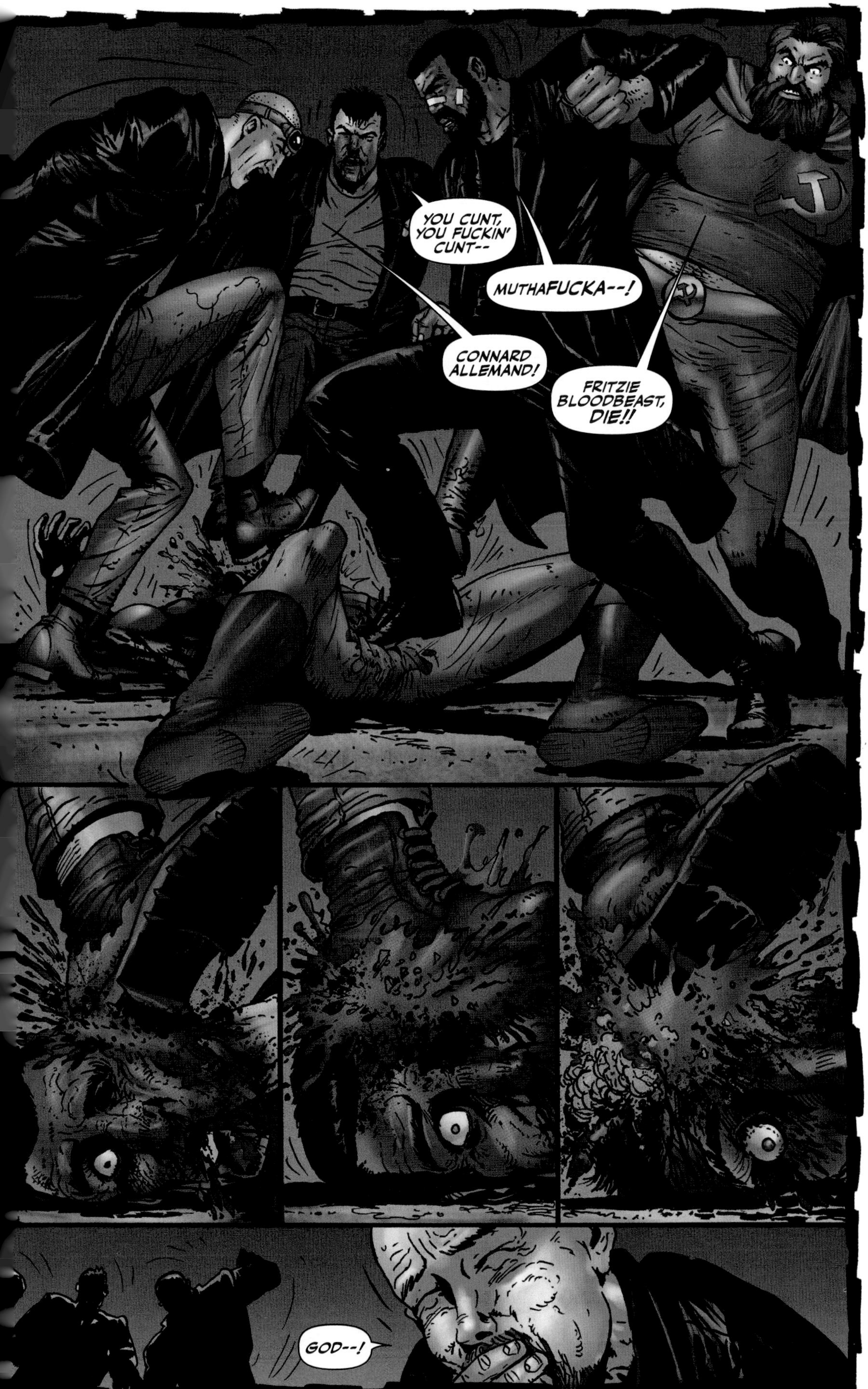
YOU CUNT, YOU FUCKIN' CUNT--
MUTHAFUCKA--!
CONNARD ALLEMAND!
FRITZIE BLOODBEAST, DIE!!
GOD--!

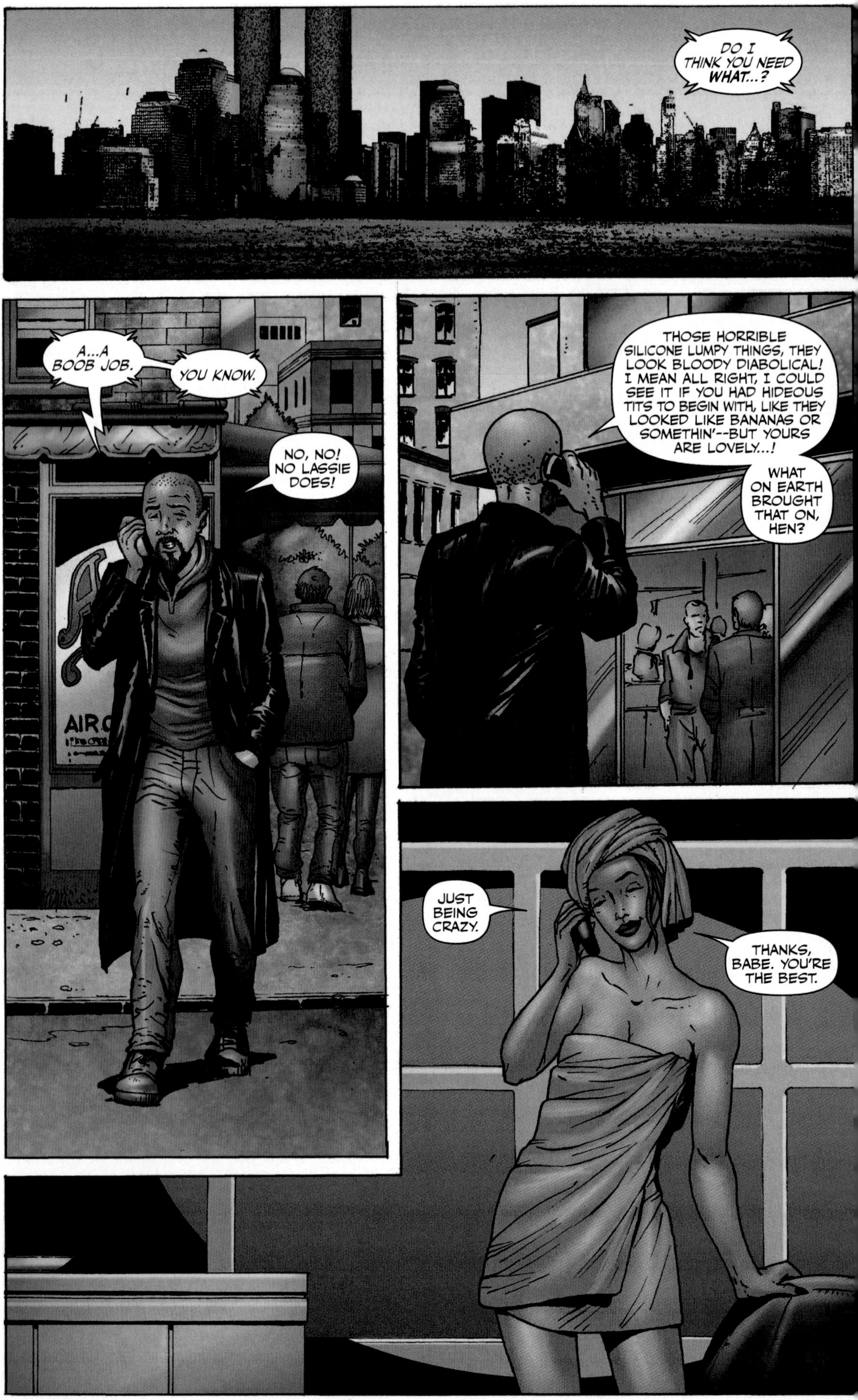
DO I THINK YOU NEED WHAT...?
A...A BOOB JOB.
YOU KNOW.
NO, NO! NO LASSIE DOES!
THOSE HORRIBLE SILICONE LUMPY THINGS, THEY LOOK BLOODY DIABOLICAL! I MEAN ALL RIGHT, I COULD SEE IT IF YOU HAD HIDEOUS TITS TO BEGIN WITH, LIKE THEY LOOKED LIKE BANANAS OR SOMETHIN'--BUT YOURS ARE LOVELY...!
WHAT ON EARTH BROUGHT THAT ON, HEN?
JUST BEING CRAZY.
THANKS, BABE. YOU'RE THE BEST.

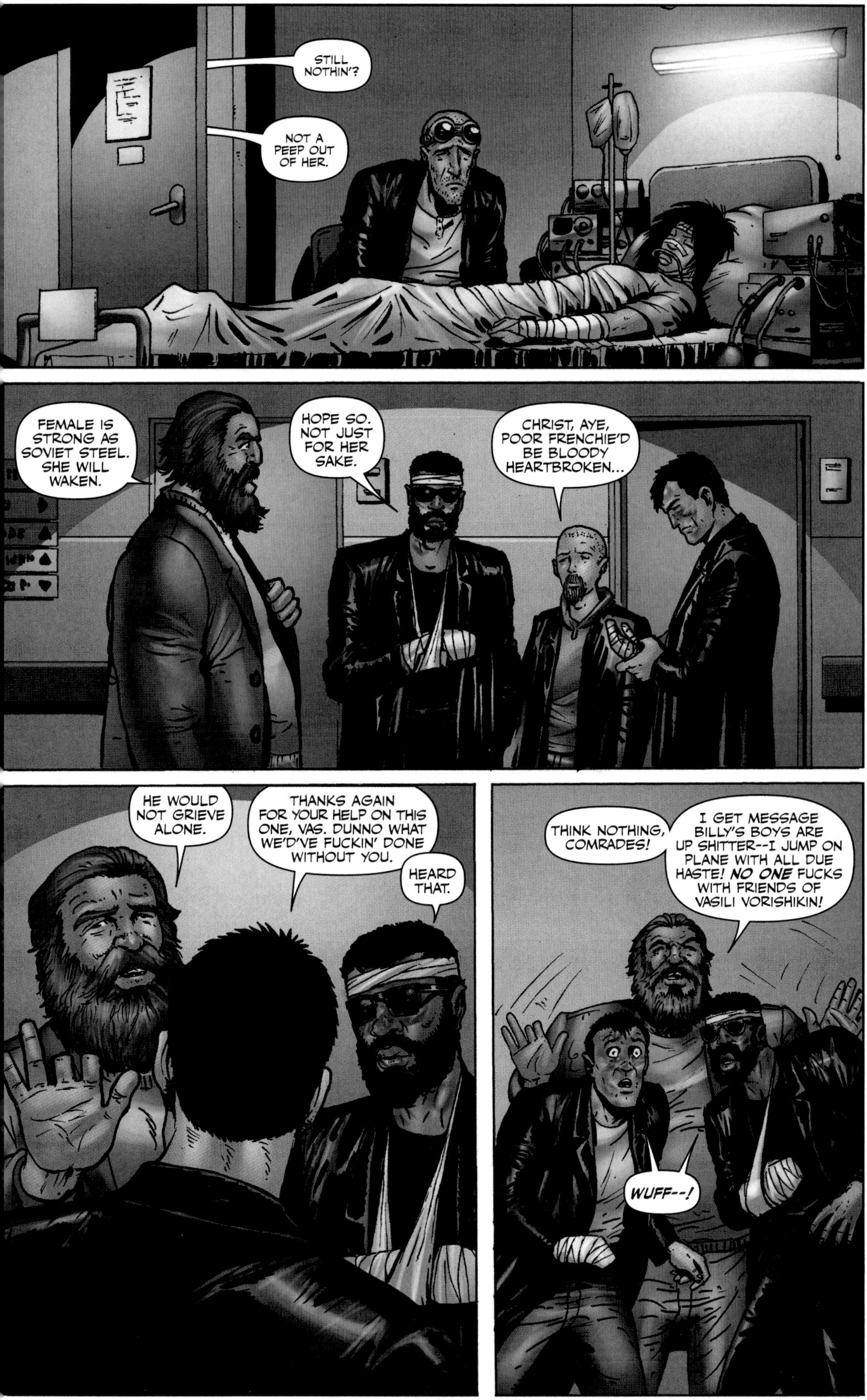
STILL NOTHIN'?
NOT A PEEP OUT OF HER.
FEMALE IS STRONG AS SOVIET STEEL. SHE WILL WAKEN.
HOPE SO. NOT JUST FOR HER SAKE.
CHRIST, AYE, POOR FRENCHIE'D BE BLOODY HEARTBROKEN...
HE WOULD NOT GRIEVE ALONE.
THANKS AGAIN FOR YOUR HELP ON THIS ONE, VAS. DUNNO WHAT WE'D'VE FUCKIN' DONE WITHOUT YOU.
HEARD THAT.
THINK NOTHING, COMRADES!
I GET MESSAGE BILLY'S BOYS ARE UP SHITTER--I JUMP ON PLANE WITH ALL DUE HASTE! NO ONE FUCKS WITH FRIENDS OF VASILI VORISHIKIN!
WUFF--!

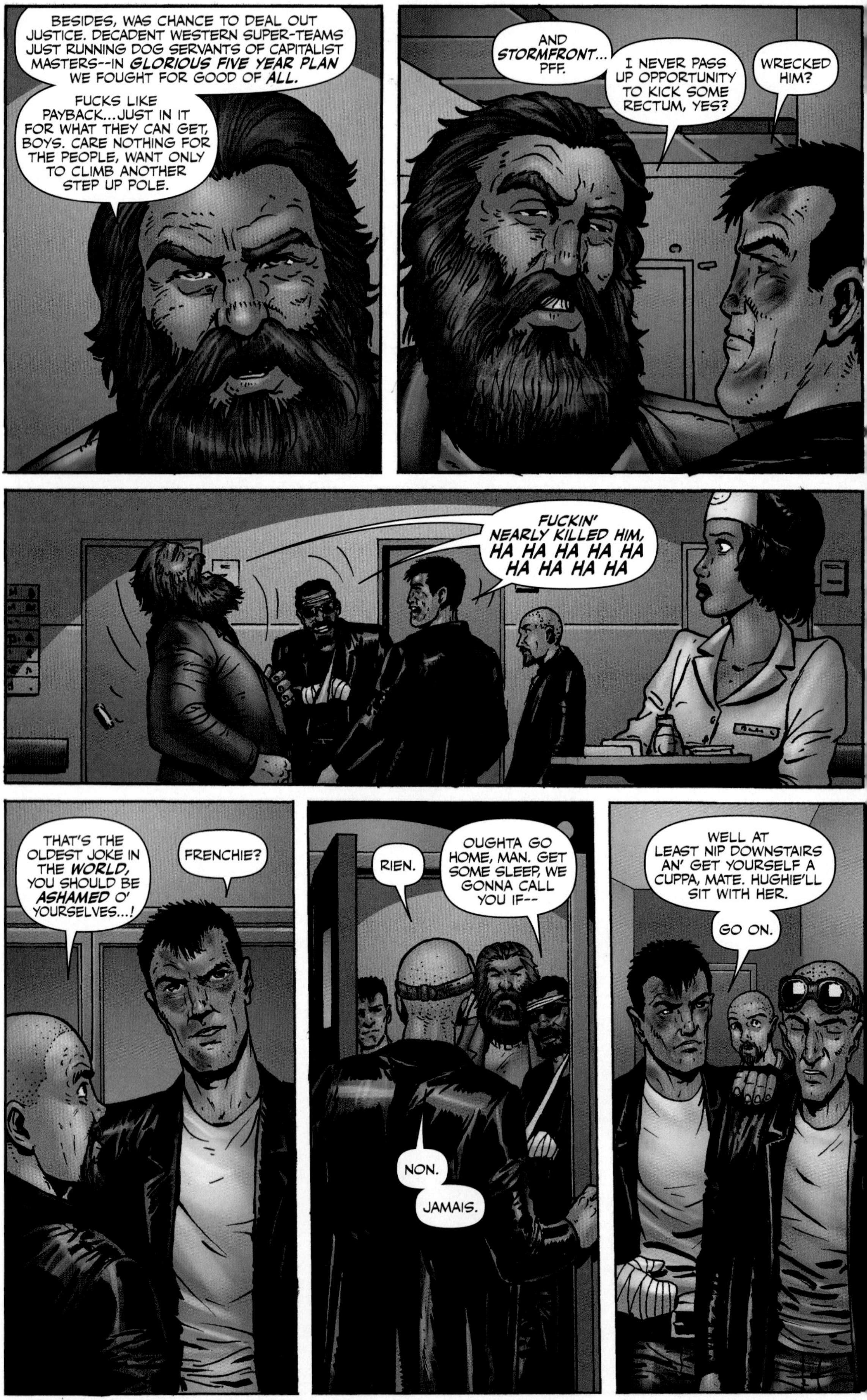
BESIDES, WAS CHANCE TO DEAL OUT JUSTICE. DECADENT WESTERN SUPER-TEAMS JUST RUNNING DOG SERVANTS OF CAPITALIST MASTERS--IN *GLORIOUS FIVE YEAR PLAN* WE FOUGHT FOR GOOD OF *ALL.*
FUCKS LIKE PAYBACK...JUST IN IT FOR WHAT THEY CAN GET, BOYS. CARE NOTHING FOR THE PEOPLE, WANT ONLY TO CLIMB ANOTHER STEP UP POLE.
AND *STORMFRONT*... PFF.
I NEVER PASS UP OPPORTUNITY TO KICK SOME RECTUM, YES?
WRECKED HIM?
FUCKIN' NEARLY KILLED HIM, *HA HA HA HA HA HA HA HA HA*
THAT'S THE OLDEST JOKE IN THE *WORLD,* YOU SHOULD BE *ASHAMED* O' YOURSELVES...!
FRENCHIE?
RIEN.
OUGHTA GO HOME, MAN. GET SOME SLEEP, WE GONNA CALL YOU IF--
NON.
JAMAIS.
WELL AT LEAST NIP DOWNSTAIRS AN' GET YOURSELF A CUPPA, MATE. HUGHIE'LL SIT WITH HER.
GO ON.

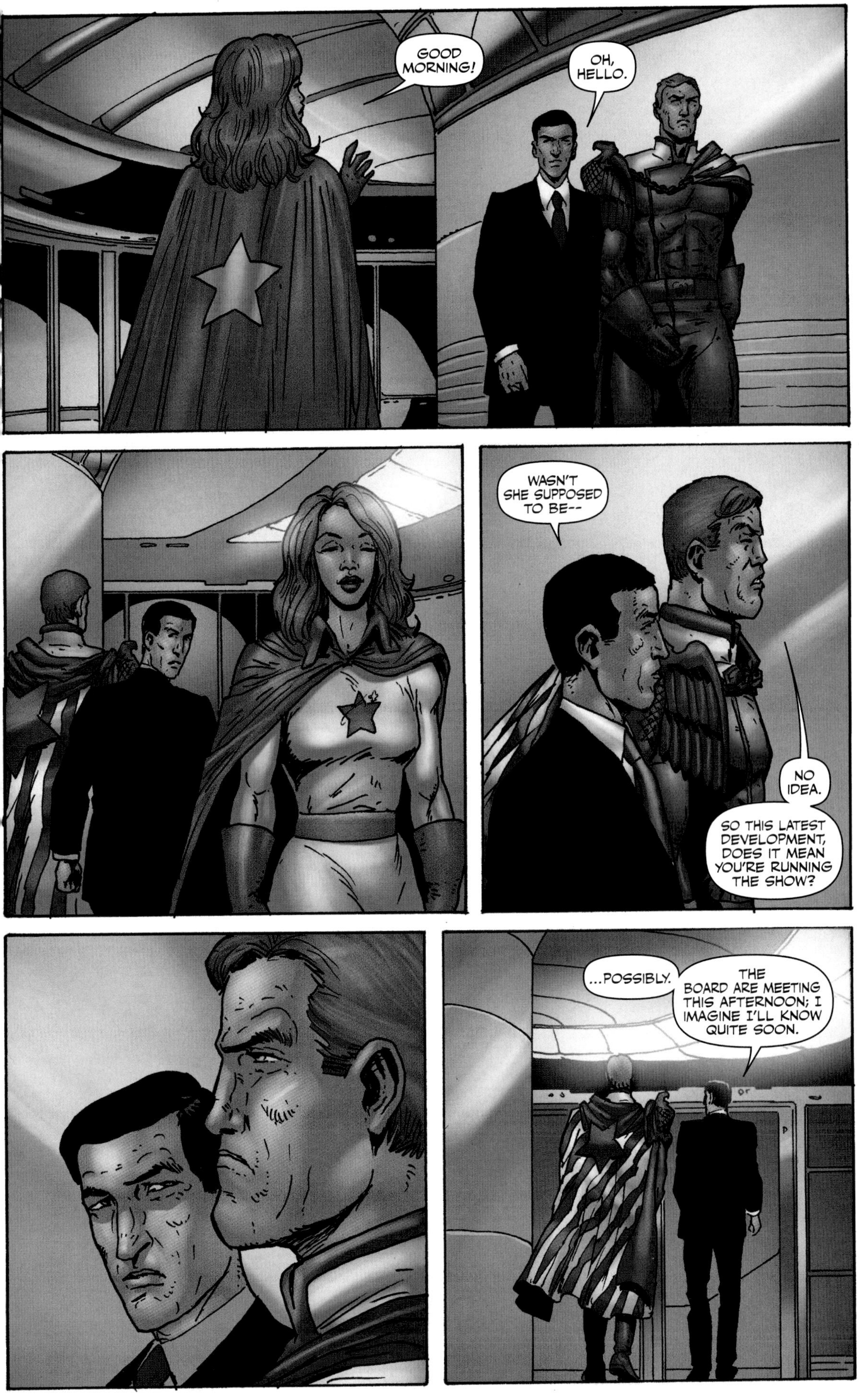
GOOD MORNING!
OH, HELLO.
WASN'T SHE SUPPOSED TO BE--
NO IDEA.
SO THIS LATEST DEVELOPMENT, DOES IT MEAN YOU'RE RUNNING THE SHOW?
...POSSIBLY.
THE BOARD ARE MEETING THIS AFTERNOON; I IMAGINE I'LL KNOW QUITE SOON.

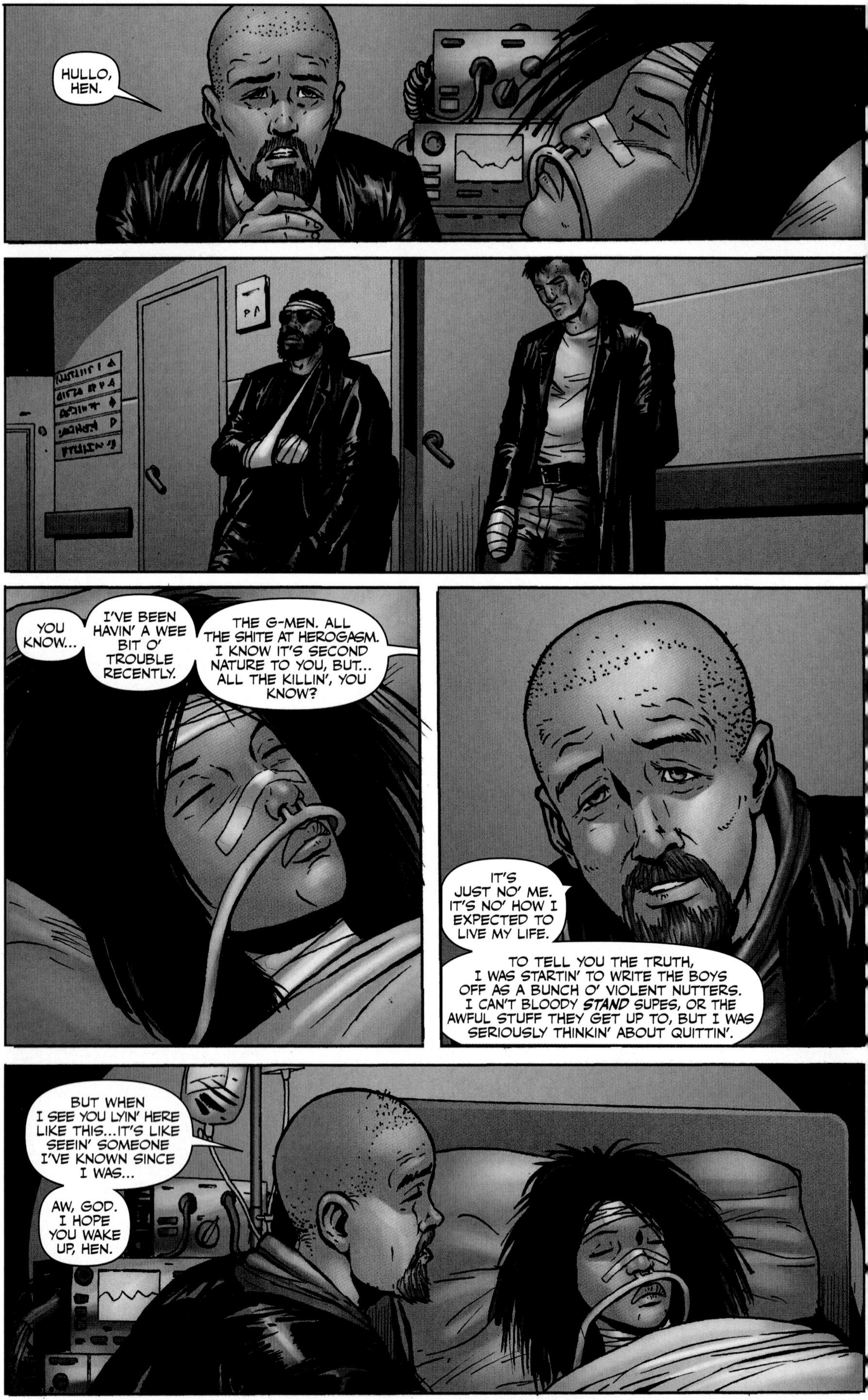
HULLO, HEN.
YOU KNOW...
I'VE BEEN HAVIN' A WEE BIT O' TROUBLE RECENTLY.
THE G-MEN. ALL THE SHITE AT HEROGASM. I KNOW IT'S SECOND NATURE TO YOU, BUT... ALL THE KILLIN', YOU KNOW?
IT'S JUST NO' ME. IT'S NO' HOW I EXPECTED TO LIVE MY LIFE.
TO TELL YOU THE TRUTH, I WAS STARTIN' TO WRITE THE BOYS OFF AS A BUNCH O' VIOLENT NUTTERS. I CAN'T BLOODY STAND SUPES, OR THE AWFUL STUFF THEY GET UP TO, BUT I WAS SERIOUSLY THINKIN' ABOUT QUITTIN'.
BUT WHEN I SEE YOU LYIN' HERE LIKE THIS...IT'S LIKE SEEIN' SOMEONE I'VE KNOWN SINCE I WAS...
AW, GOD. I HOPE YOU WAKE UP, HEN.

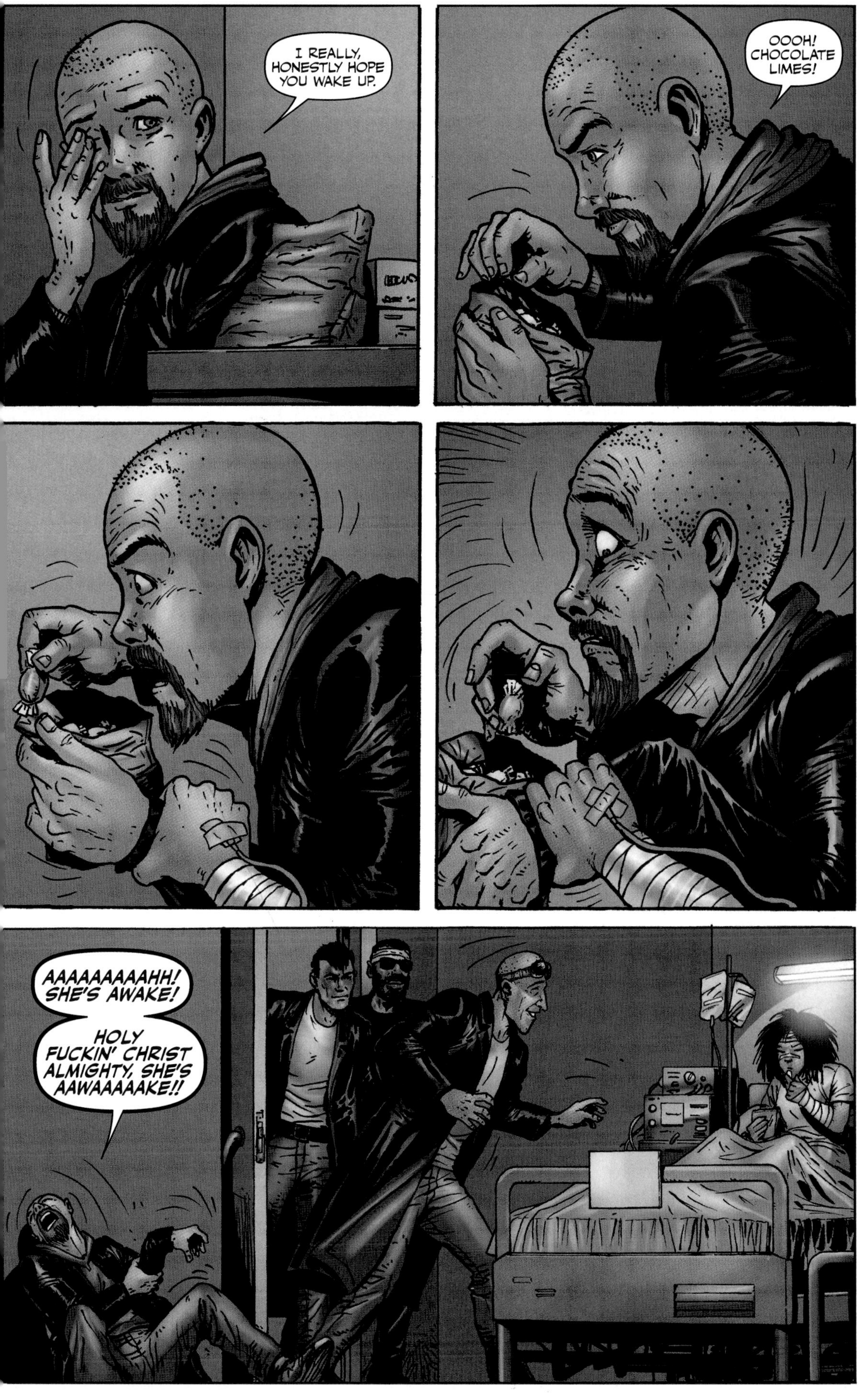
I REALLY, HONESTLY HOPE YOU WAKE UP.
OOOH! CHOCOLATE LIMES!
AAAAAAAAAHH! SHE'S AWAKE!
HOLY FUCKIN' CHRIST ALMIGHTY, SHE'S AAWAAAAAKE!!

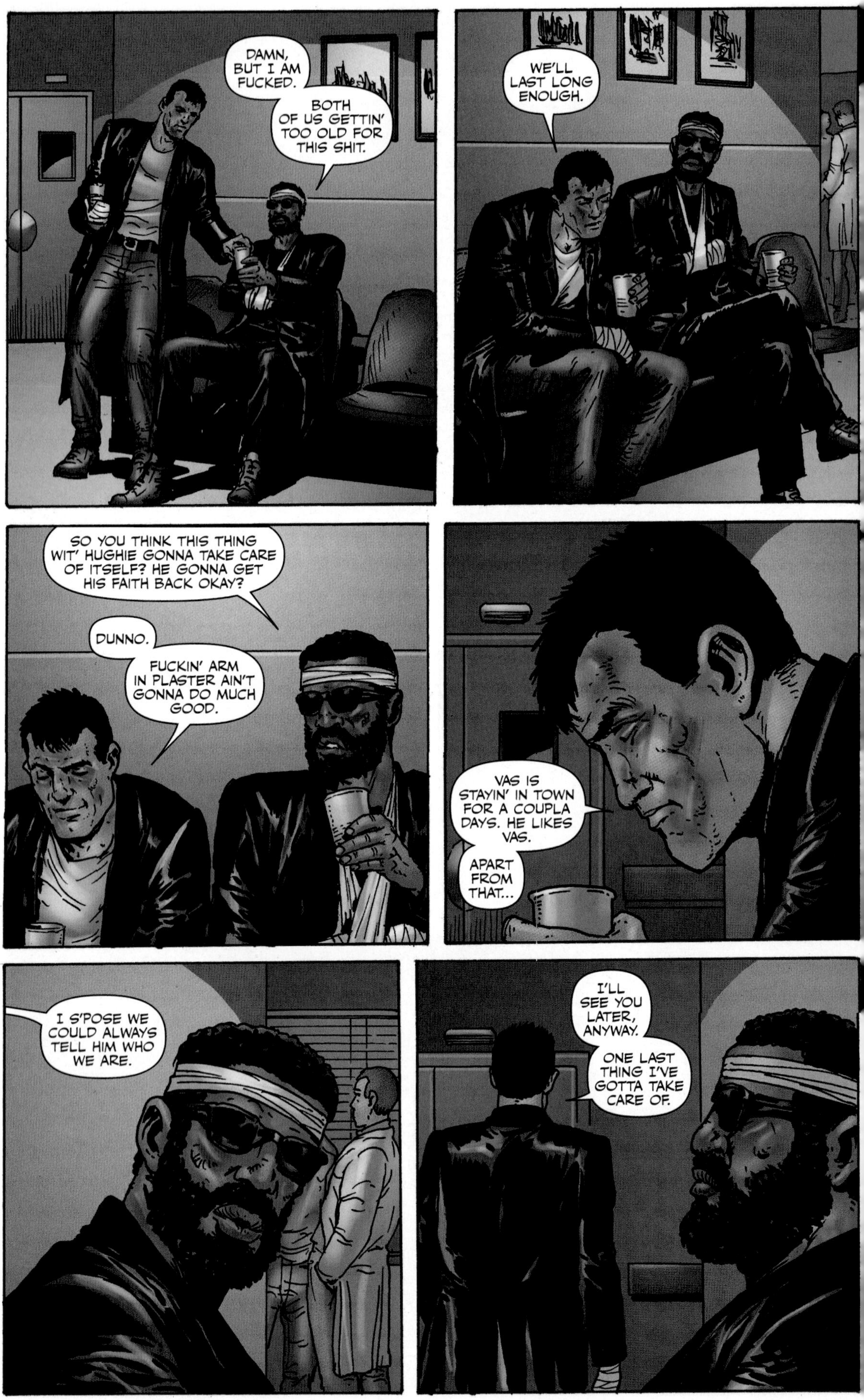
DAMN, BUT I AM FUCKED.
BOTH OF US GETTIN' TOO OLD FOR THIS SHIT.
WE'LL LAST LONG ENOUGH.
SO YOU THINK THIS THING WIT' HUGHIE GONNA TAKE CARE OF ITSELF? HE GONNA GET HIS FAITH BACK OKAY?
DUNNO.
FUCKIN' ARM IN PLASTER AIN'T GONNA DO MUCH GOOD.
VAS IS STAYIN' IN TOWN FOR A COUPLA DAYS. HE LIKES VAS.
APART FROM THAT...
I S'POSE WE COULD ALWAYS TELL HIM WHO WE ARE.
I'LL SEE YOU LATER, ANYWAY.
ONE LAST THING I'VE GOTTA TAKE CARE OF.

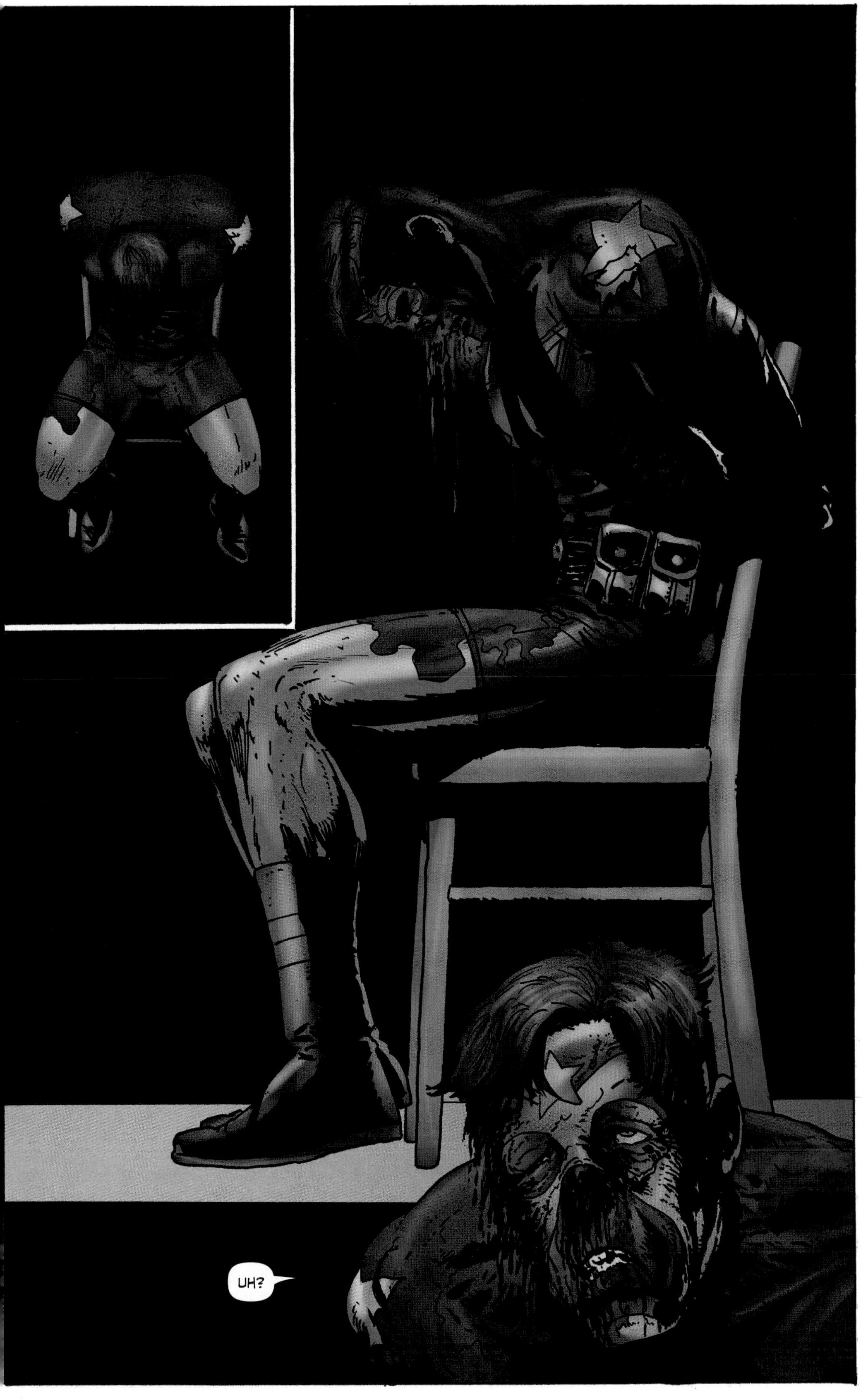
UH?

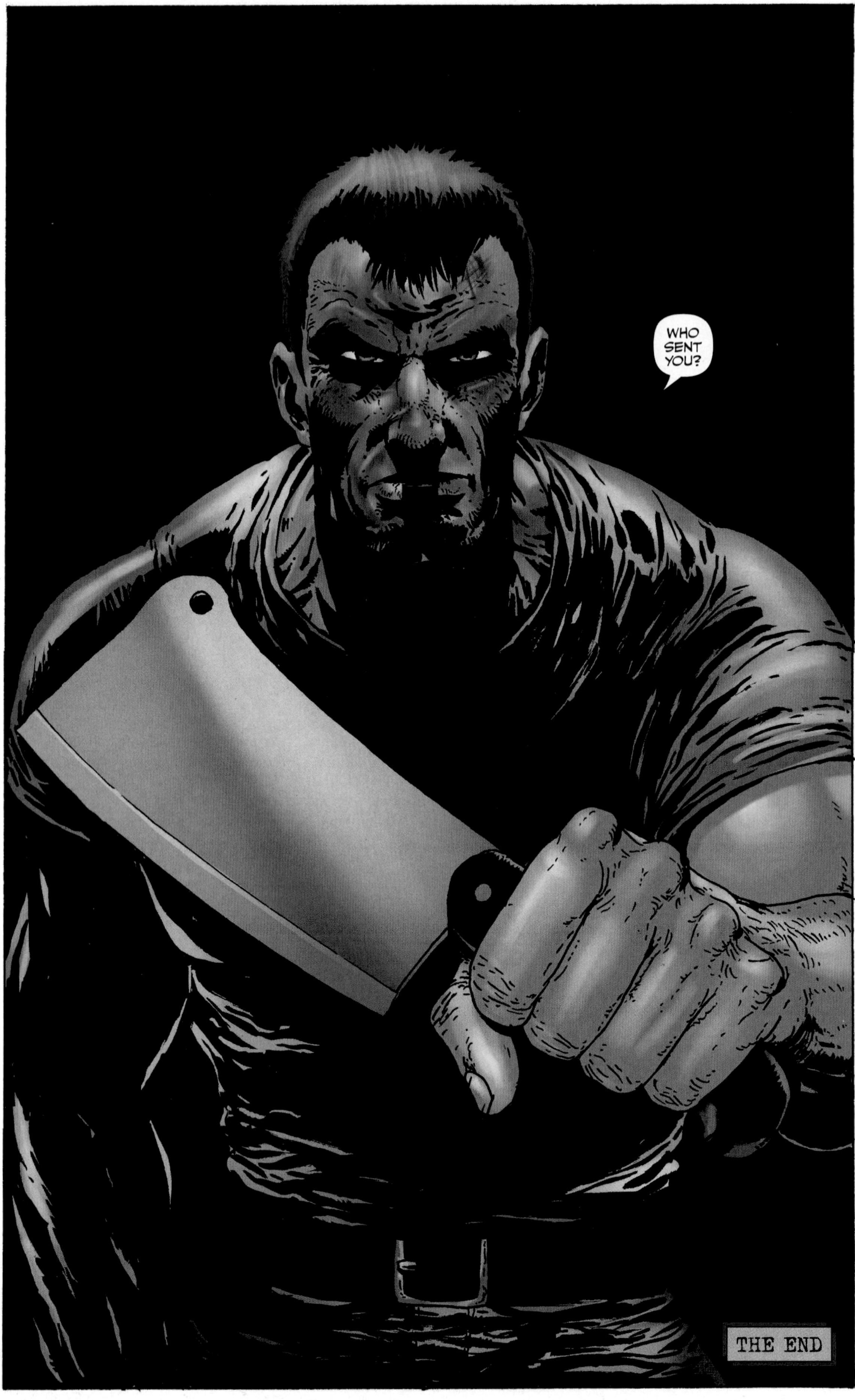
WHO SENT YOU?
THE END

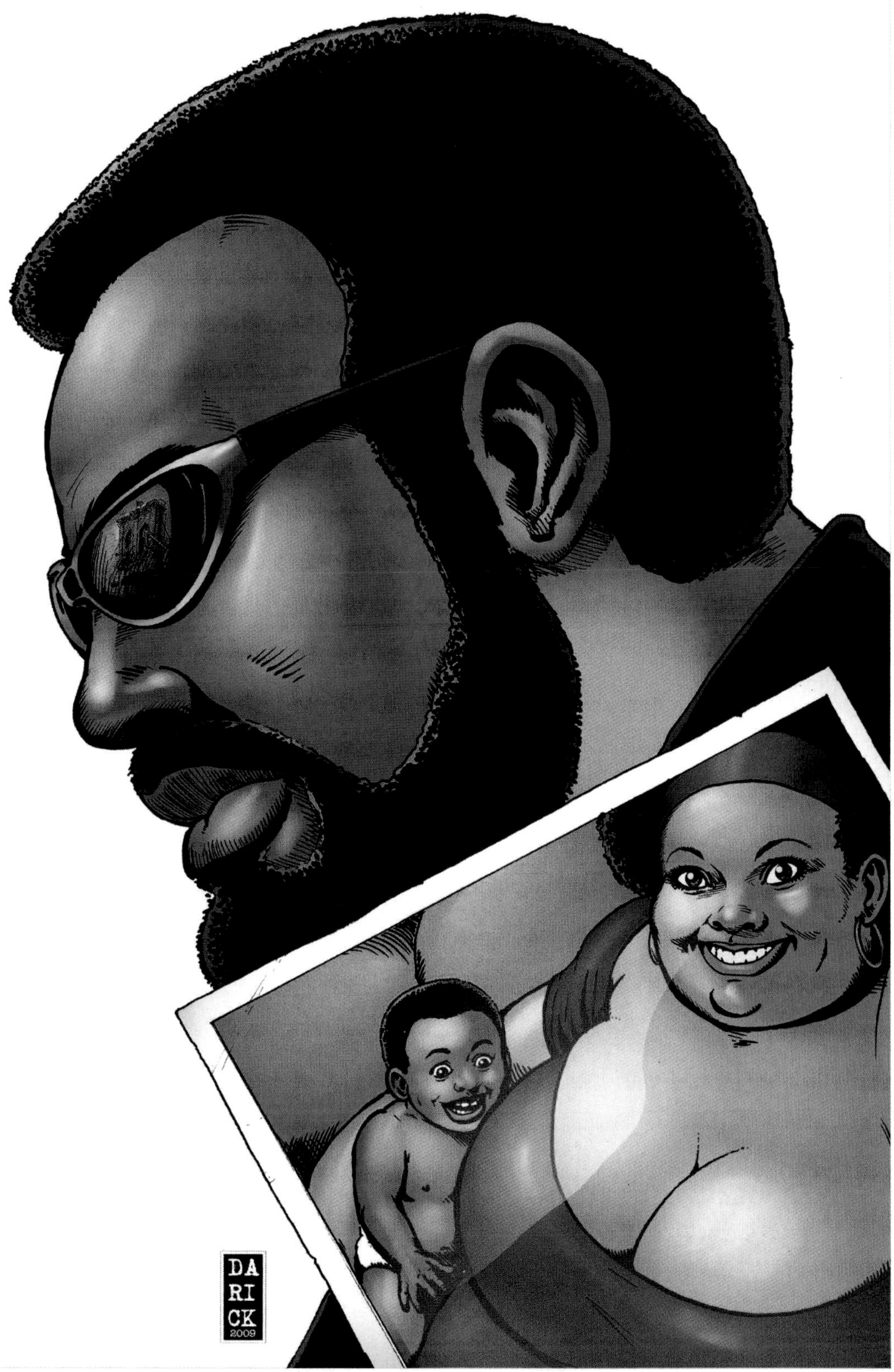
DA
RI
CK
2009

#35 cover
by Darick Robertson
and Tony Aviña

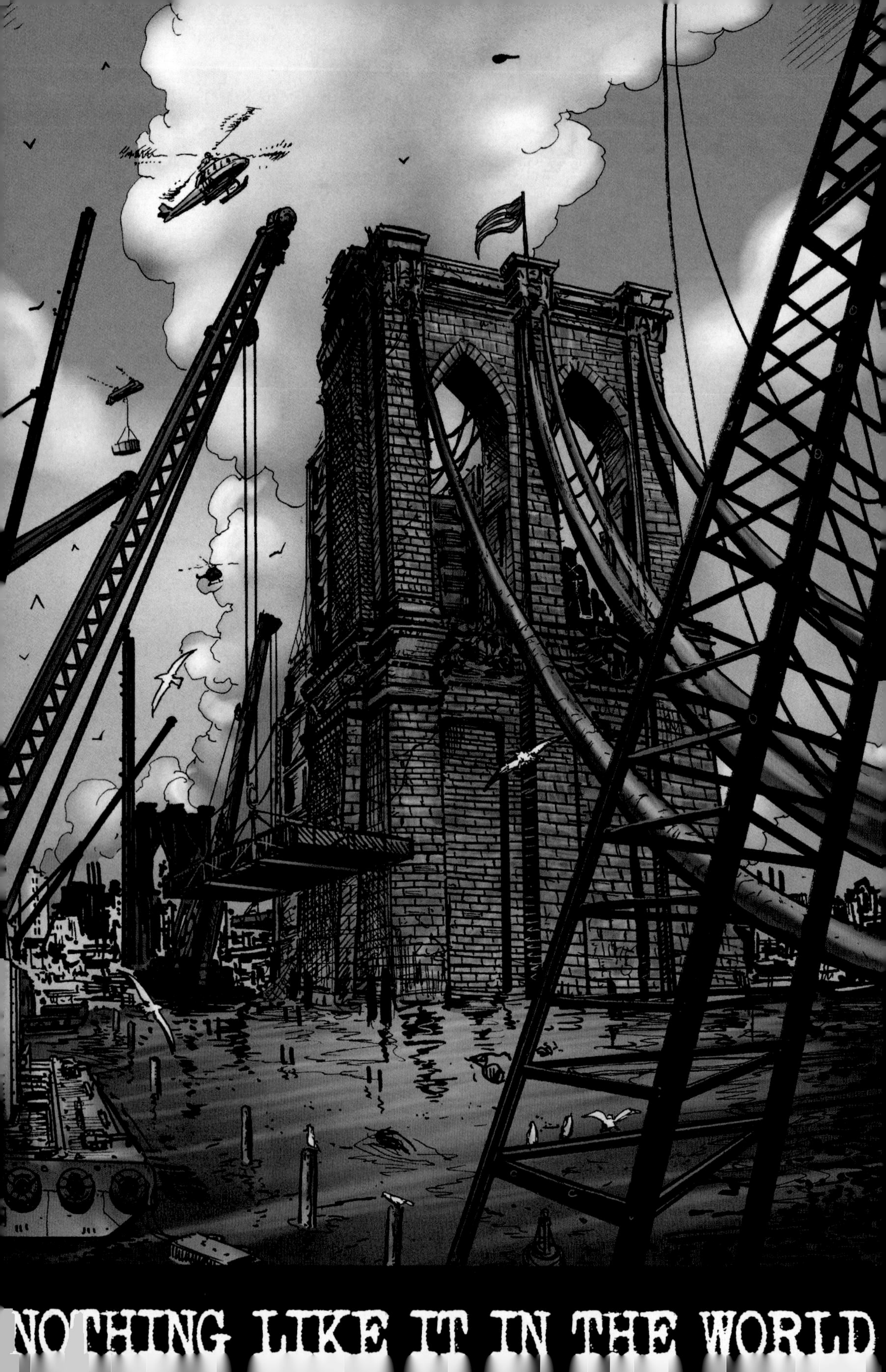

NOTHING LIKE IT IN THE WORLD

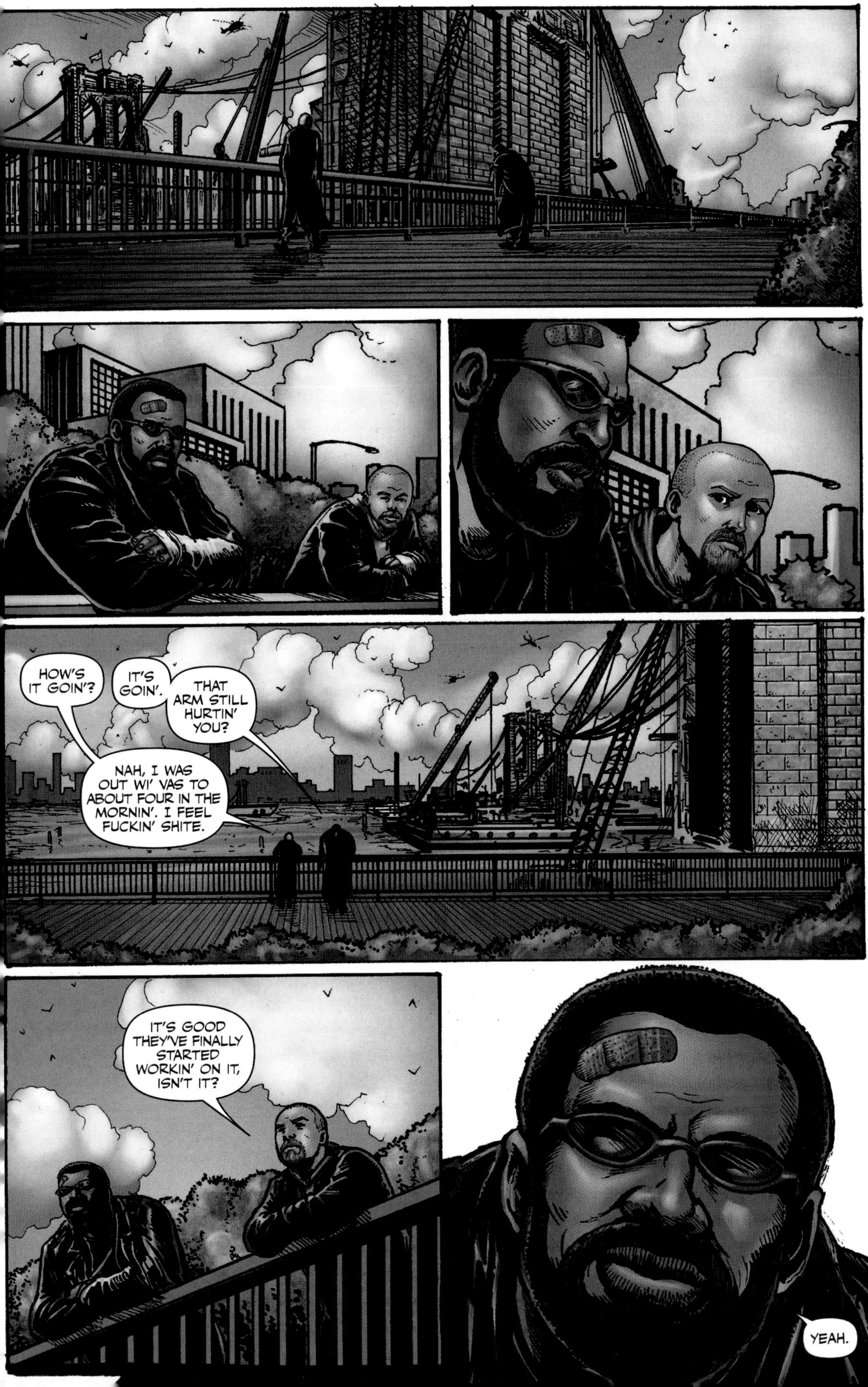
HOW'S IT GOIN'?
IT'S GOIN'.
THAT ARM STILL HURTIN' YOU?
NAH, I WAS OUT WI' VAS TO ABOUT FOUR IN THE MORNIN'. I FEEL FUCKIN' SHITE.
IT'S GOOD THEY'VE FINALLY STARTED WORKIN' ON IT, ISN'T IT?
YEAH.

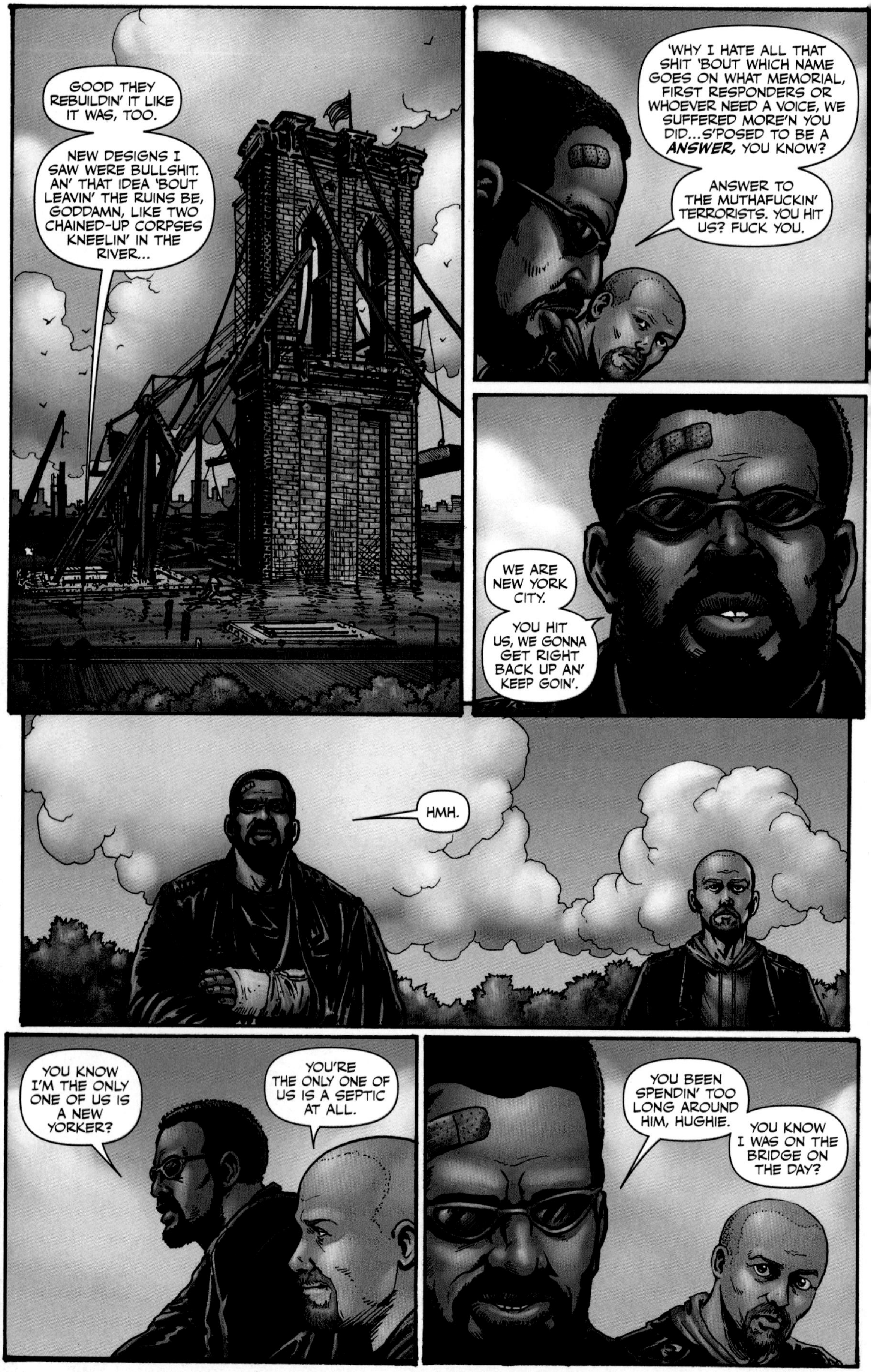
GOOD THEY REBUILDIN' IT LIKE IT WAS, TOO.
NEW DESIGNS I SAW WERE BULLSHIT. AN' THAT IDEA 'BOUT LEAVIN' THE RUINS BE, GODDAMN, LIKE TWO CHAINED-UP CORPSES KNEELIN' IN THE RIVER...
'WHY I HATE ALL THAT SHIT 'BOUT WHICH NAME GOES ON WHAT MEMORIAL, FIRST RESPONDERS OR WHOEVER NEED A VOICE, WE SUFFERED MORE'N YOU DID...S'POSED TO BE A ANSWER, YOU KNOW?
ANSWER TO THE MUTHAFUCKIN' TERRORISTS. YOU HIT US? FUCK YOU.
WE ARE NEW YORK CITY.
YOU HIT US, WE GONNA GET RIGHT BACK UP AN' KEEP GOIN'.
HMH.
YOU KNOW I'M THE ONLY ONE OF US IS A NEW YORKER?
YOU'RE THE ONLY ONE OF US IS A SEPTIC AT ALL.
YOU BEEN SPENDIN' TOO LONG AROUND HIM, HUGHIE.
YOU KNOW I WAS ON THE BRIDGE ON THE DAY?

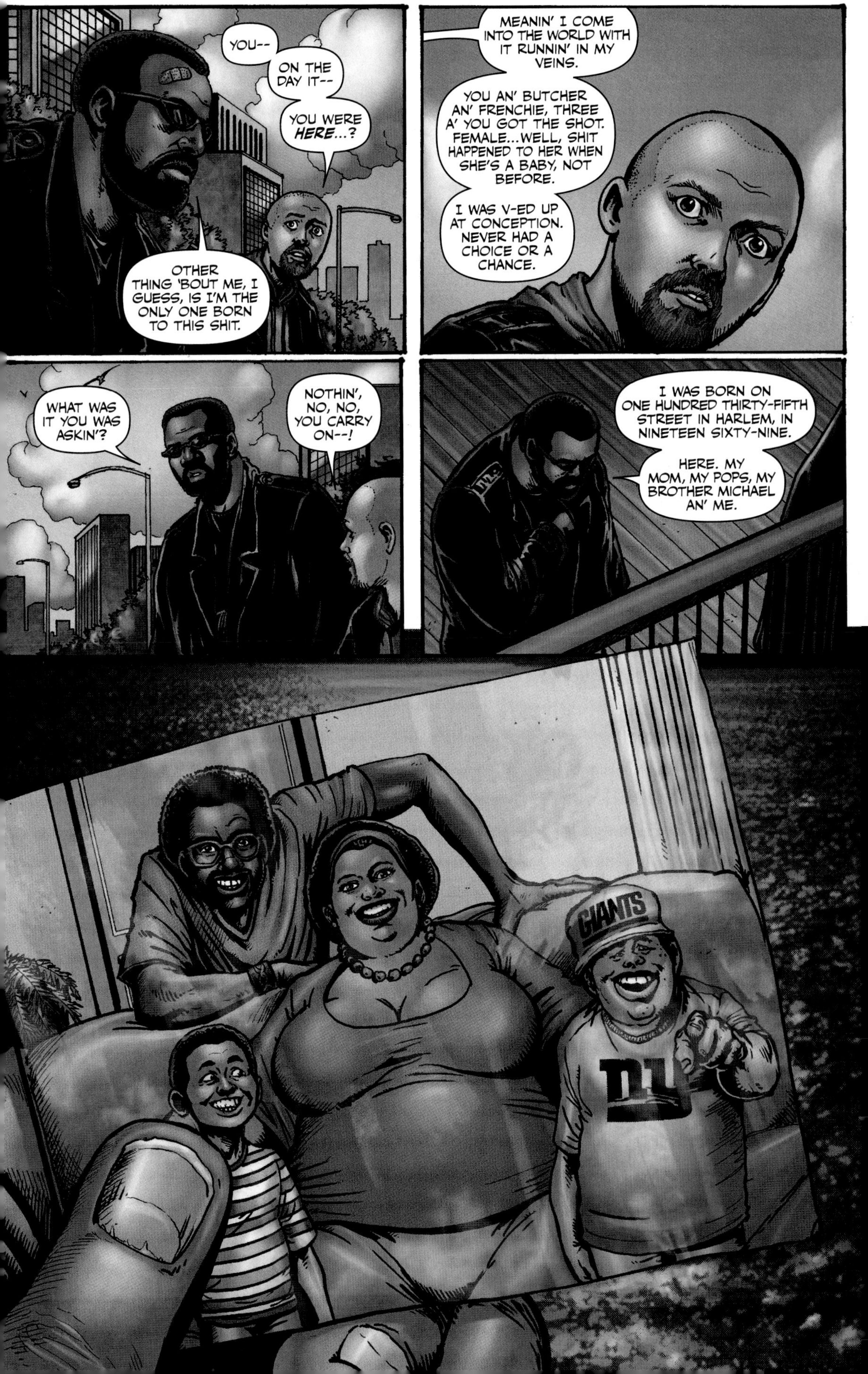
YOU--
ON THE DAY IT--
YOU WERE *HERE*...?
OTHER THING 'BOUT ME, I GUESS, IS I'M THE ONLY ONE BORN TO THIS SHIT.
MEANIN' I COME INTO THE WORLD WITH IT RUNNIN' IN MY VEINS.
YOU AN' BUTCHER AN' FRENCHIE, THREE A' YOU GOT THE SHOT. FEMALE...WELL, SHIT HAPPENED TO HER WHEN SHE'S A BABY, NOT BEFORE.
I WAS V-ED UP AT CONCEPTION. NEVER HAD A CHOICE OR A CHANCE.
WHAT WAS IT YOU WAS ASKIN'?
NOTHIN', NO, NO, YOU CARRY ON--!
I WAS BORN ON ONE HUNDRED THIRTY-FIFTH STREET IN HARLEM, IN NINETEEN SIXTY-NINE.
HERE. MY MOM, MY POPS, MY BROTHER MICHAEL AN' ME.
GIANTS

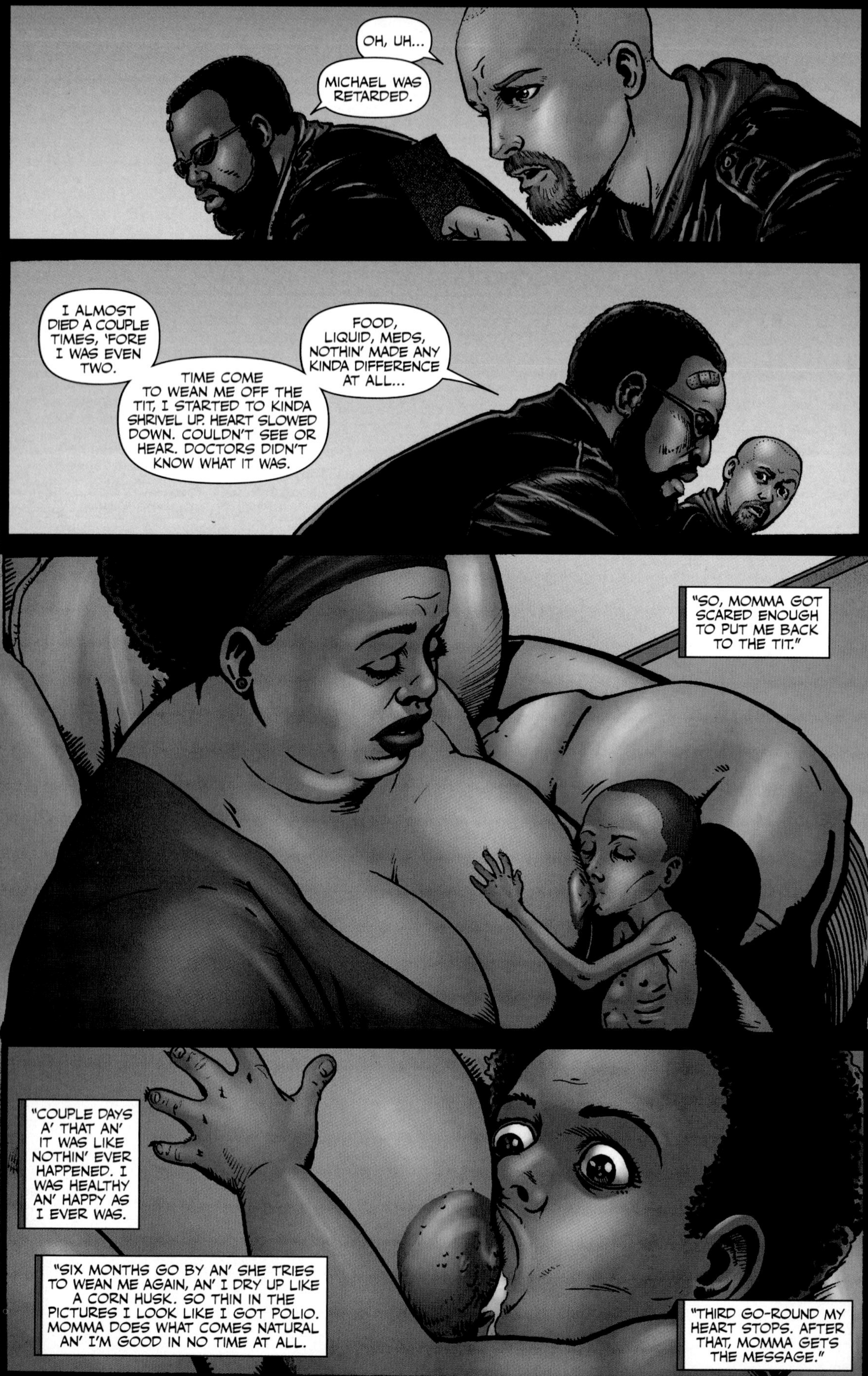
OH, UH...
MICHAEL WAS RETARDED.
I ALMOST DIED A COUPLE TIMES, 'FORE I WAS EVEN TWO.
TIME COME TO WEAN ME OFF THE TIT, I STARTED TO KINDA SHRIVEL UP. HEART SLOWED DOWN. COULDN'T SEE OR HEAR. DOCTORS DIDN'T KNOW WHAT IT WAS.
FOOD, LIQUID, MEDS, NOTHIN' MADE ANY KINDA DIFFERENCE AT ALL...
"SO, MOMMA GOT SCARED ENOUGH TO PUT ME BACK TO THE TIT."
"COUPLE DAYS A' THAT AN' IT WAS LIKE NOTHIN' EVER HAPPENED. I WAS HEALTHY AN' HAPPY AS I EVER WAS.
"SIX MONTHS GO BY AN' SHE TRIES TO WEAN ME AGAIN, AN' I DRY UP LIKE A CORN HUSK. SO THIN IN THE PICTURES I LOOK LIKE I GOT POLIO. MOMMA DOES WHAT COMES NATURAL AN' I'M GOOD IN NO TIME AT ALL.
"THIRD GO-ROUND MY HEART STOPS. AFTER THAT, MOMMA GETS THE MESSAGE."

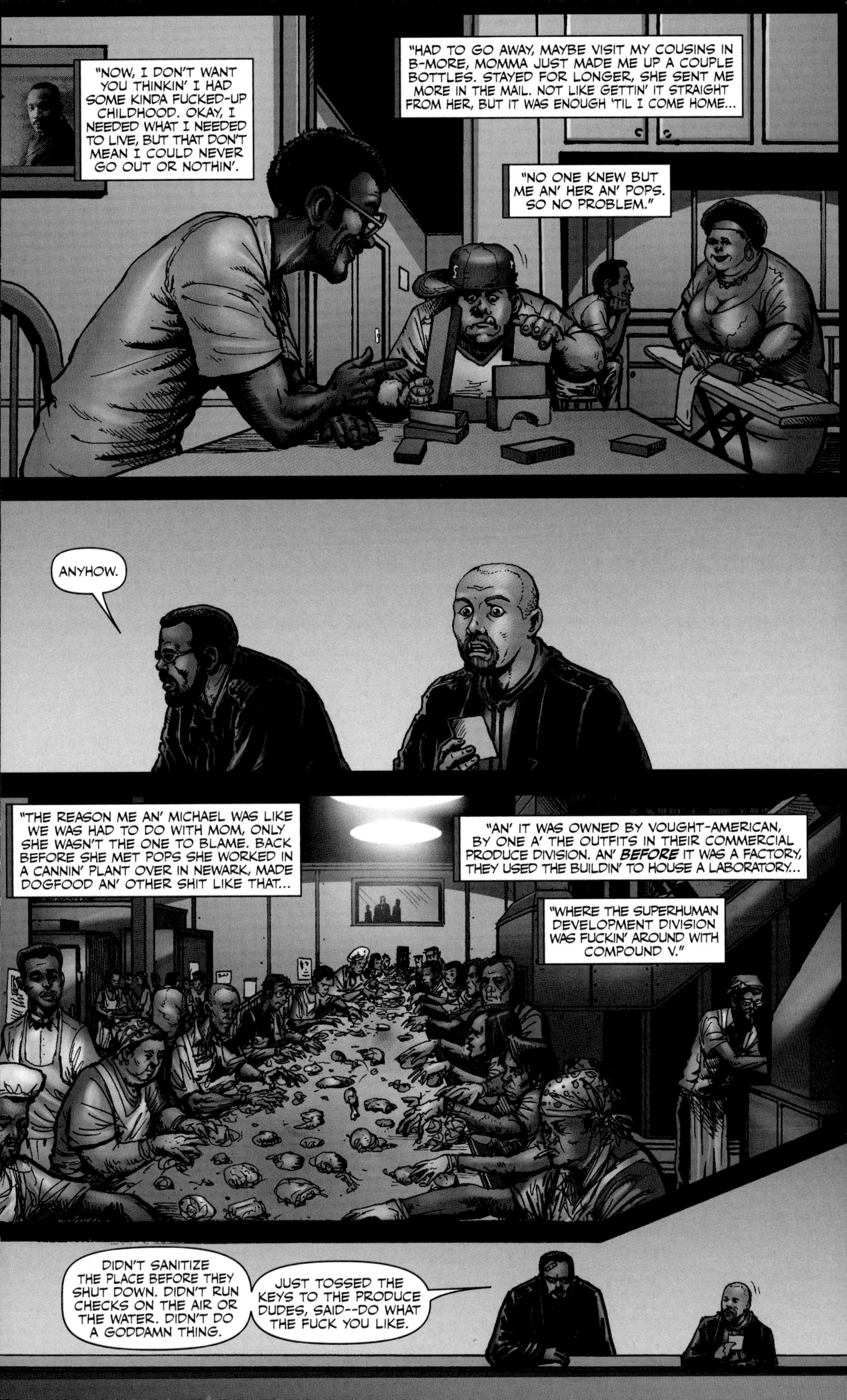
"NOW, I DON'T WANT YOU THINKIN' I HAD SOME KINDA FUCKED-UP CHILDHOOD. OKAY, I NEEDED WHAT I NEEDED TO LIVE, BUT THAT DON'T MEAN I COULD NEVER GO OUT OR NOTHIN'.
"HAD TO GO AWAY, MAYBE VISIT MY COUSINS IN B-MORE, MOMMA JUST MADE ME UP A COUPLE BOTTLES. STAYED FOR LONGER, SHE SENT ME MORE IN THE MAIL. NOT LIKE GETTIN' IT STRAIGHT FROM HER, BUT IT WAS ENOUGH 'TIL I COME HOME...
"NO ONE KNEW BUT ME AN' HER AN' POPS. SO NO PROBLEM."
ANYHOW.
"THE REASON ME AN' MICHAEL WAS LIKE WE WAS HAD TO DO WITH MOM, ONLY SHE WASN'T THE ONE TO BLAME. BACK BEFORE SHE MET POPS SHE WORKED IN A CANNIN' PLANT OVER IN NEWARK, MADE DOGFOOD AN' OTHER SHIT LIKE THAT...
"AN' IT WAS OWNED BY VOUGHT-AMERICAN, BY ONE A' THE OUTFITS IN THEIR COMMERCIAL PRODUCE DIVISION. AN' BEFORE IT WAS A FACTORY, THEY USED THE BUILDIN' TO HOUSE A LABORATORY...
"WHERE THE SUPERHUMAN DEVELOPMENT DIVISION WAS FUCKIN' AROUND WITH COMPOUND V."
DIDN'T SANITIZE THE PLACE BEFORE THEY SHUT DOWN. DIDN'T RUN CHECKS ON THE AIR OR THE WATER. DIDN'T DO A GODDAMN THING.
JUST TOSSED THE KEYS TO THE PRODUCE DUDES, SAID--DO WHAT THE FUCK YOU LIKE.

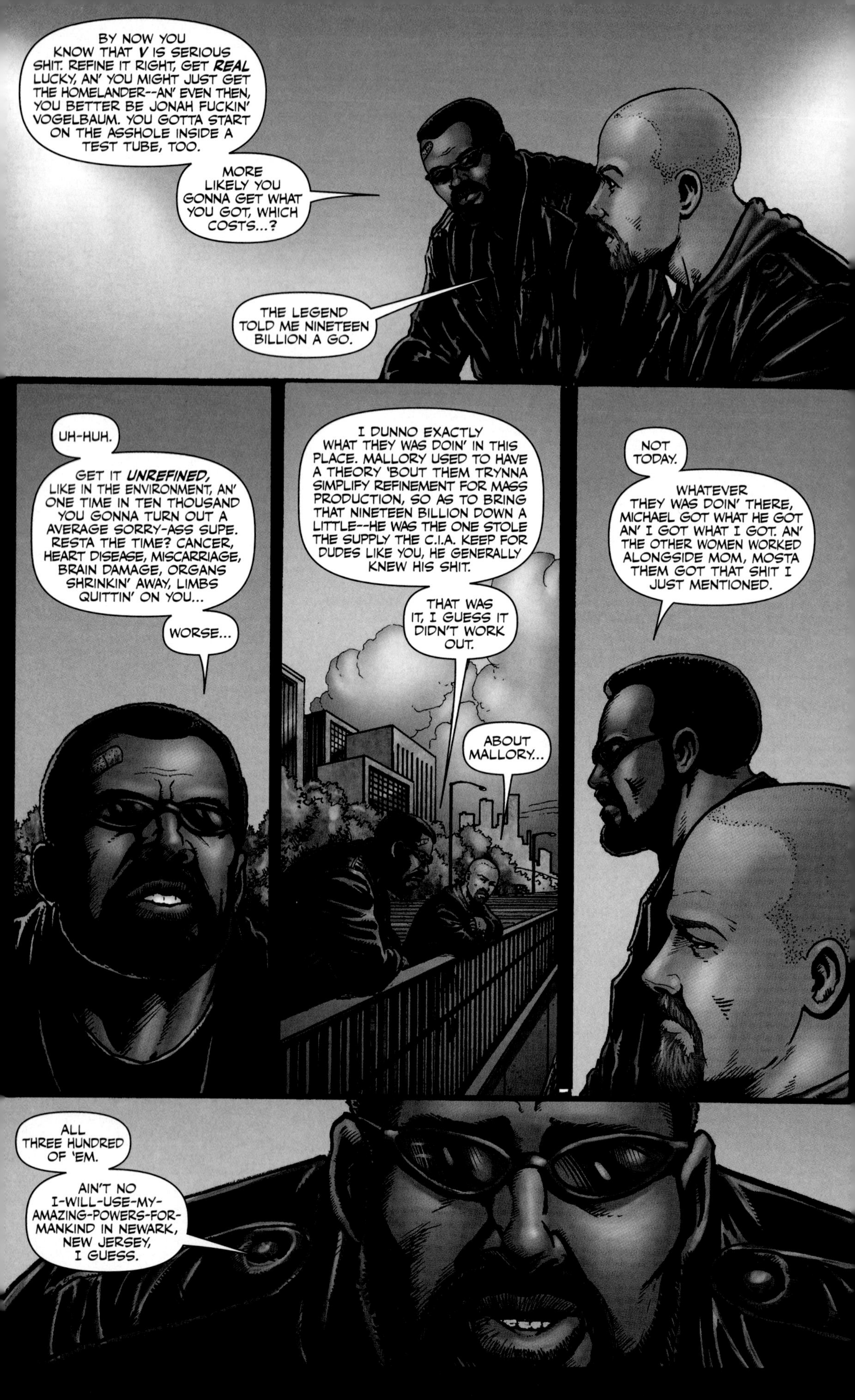
BY NOW YOU KNOW THAT V IS SERIOUS SHIT. REFINE IT RIGHT, GET REAL LUCKY, AN' YOU MIGHT JUST GET THE HOMELANDER--AN' EVEN THEN, YOU BETTER BE JONAH FUCKIN' VOGELBAUM. YOU GOTTA START ON THE ASSHOLE INSIDE A TEST TUBE, TOO.
MORE LIKELY YOU GONNA GET WHAT YOU GOT, WHICH COSTS...?
THE LEGEND TOLD ME NINETEEN BILLION A GO.
UH-HUH.
GET IT UNREFINED, LIKE IN THE ENVIRONMENT, AN' ONE TIME IN TEN THOUSAND YOU GONNA TURN OUT A AVERAGE SORRY-ASS SUPE. RESTA THE TIME? CANCER, HEART DISEASE, MISCARRIAGE, BRAIN DAMAGE, ORGANS SHRINKIN' AWAY, LIMBS QUITTIN' ON YOU...
WORSE...
I DUNNO EXACTLY WHAT THEY WAS DOIN' IN THIS PLACE. MALLORY USED TO HAVE A THEORY 'BOUT THEM TRYNNA SIMPLIFY REFINEMENT FOR MASS PRODUCTION, SO AS TO BRING THAT NINETEEN BILLION DOWN A LITTLE--HE WAS THE ONE STOLE THE SUPPLY THE C.I.A. KEEP FOR DUDES LIKE YOU, HE GENERALLY KNEW HIS SHIT.
THAT WAS IT, I GUESS IT DIDN'T WORK OUT.
ABOUT MALLORY...
NOT TODAY.
WHATEVER THEY WAS DOIN' THERE, MICHAEL GOT WHAT HE GOT AN' I GOT WHAT I GOT. AN' THE OTHER WOMEN WORKED ALONGSIDE MOM, MOSTA THEM GOT THAT SHIT I JUST MENTIONED.
ALL THREE HUNDRED OF 'EM.
AIN'T NO I-WILL-USE-MY-AMAZING-POWERS-FOR-MANKIND IN NEWARK, NEW JERSEY, I GUESS.

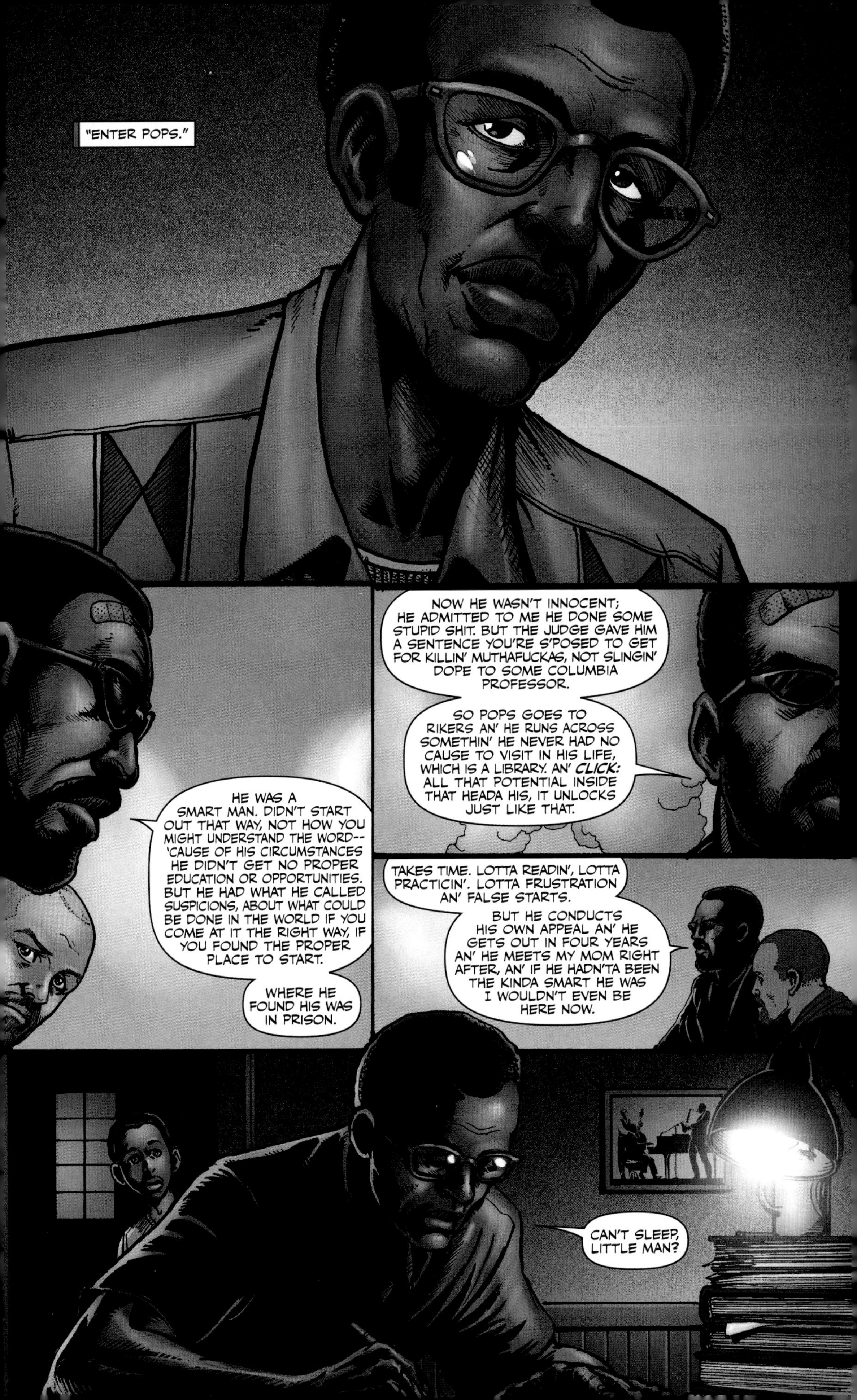
"ENTER POPS."
HE WAS A SMART MAN. DIDN'T START OUT THAT WAY, NOT HOW YOU MIGHT UNDERSTAND THE WORD-- 'CAUSE OF HIS CIRCUMSTANCES HE DIDN'T GET NO PROPER EDUCATION OR OPPORTUNITIES. BUT HE HAD WHAT HE CALLED SUSPICIONS, ABOUT WHAT COULD BE DONE IN THE WORLD IF YOU COME AT IT THE RIGHT WAY, IF YOU FOUND THE PROPER PLACE TO START.
WHERE HE FOUND HIS WAS IN PRISON.
NOW HE WASN'T INNOCENT; HE ADMITTED TO ME HE DONE SOME STUPID SHIT. BUT THE JUDGE GAVE HIM A SENTENCE YOU'RE S'POSED TO GET FOR KILLIN' MUTHAFUCKAS, NOT SLINGIN' DOPE TO SOME COLUMBIA PROFESSOR.
SO POPS GOES TO RIKERS AN' HE RUNS ACROSS SOMETHIN' HE NEVER HAD NO CAUSE TO VISIT IN HIS LIFE, WHICH IS A LIBRARY. AN' *CLICK:* ALL THAT POTENTIAL INSIDE THAT HEADA HIS, IT UNLOCKS JUST LIKE THAT.
TAKES TIME. LOTTA READIN', LOTTA PRACTICIN'. LOTTA FRUSTRATION AN' FALSE STARTS.
BUT HE CONDUCTS HIS OWN APPEAL AN' HE GETS OUT IN FOUR YEARS AN' HE MEETS MY MOM RIGHT AFTER, AN' IF HE HADN'TA BEEN THE KINDA SMART HE WAS I WOULDN'T EVEN BE HERE NOW.
CAN'T SLEEP, LITTLE MAN?

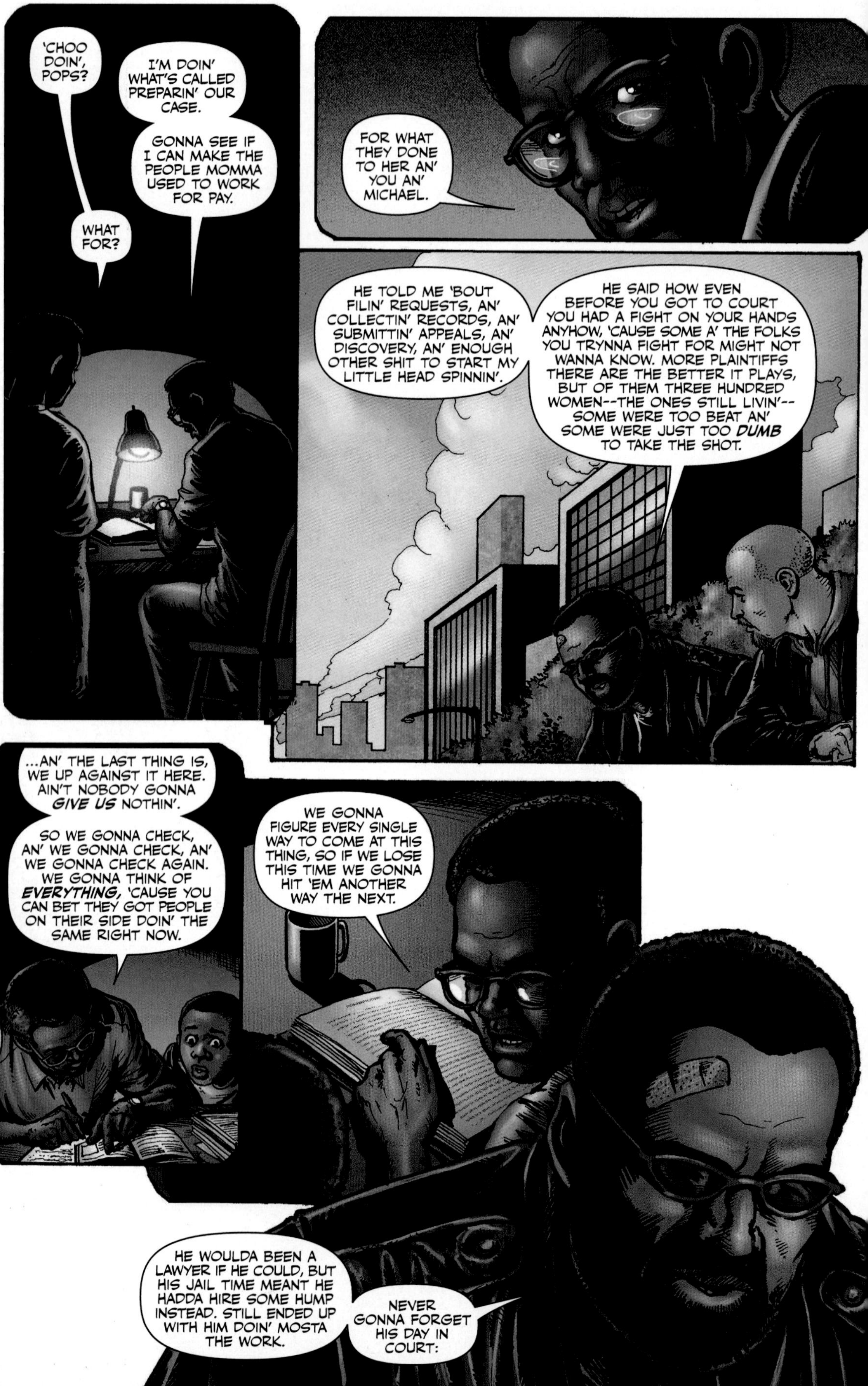
'CHOO DOIN', POPS?
I'M DOIN' WHAT'S CALLED PREPARIN' OUR CASE.
GONNA SEE IF I CAN MAKE THE PEOPLE MOMMA USED TO WORK FOR PAY.
WHAT FOR?
FOR WHAT THEY DONE TO HER AN' YOU AN' MICHAEL.
HE TOLD ME 'BOUT FILIN' REQUESTS, AN' COLLECTIN' RECORDS, AN' SUBMITTIN' APPEALS, AN' DISCOVERY, AN' ENOUGH OTHER SHIT TO START MY LITTLE HEAD SPINNIN'.
HE SAID HOW EVEN BEFORE YOU GOT TO COURT YOU HAD A FIGHT ON YOUR HANDS ANYHOW, 'CAUSE SOME A' THE FOLKS YOU TRYNNA FIGHT FOR MIGHT NOT WANNA KNOW. MORE PLAINTIFFS THERE ARE THE BETTER IT PLAYS, BUT OF THEM THREE HUNDRED WOMEN--THE ONES STILL LIVIN'--SOME WERE TOO BEAT AN' SOME WERE JUST TOO *DUMB* TO TAKE THE SHOT.
...AN' THE LAST THING IS, WE UP AGAINST IT HERE. AIN'T NOBODY GONNA ***GIVE US*** NOTHIN'.
SO WE GONNA CHECK, AN' WE GONNA CHECK, AN' WE GONNA CHECK AGAIN. WE GONNA THINK OF ***EVERYTHING,*** 'CAUSE YOU CAN BET THEY GOT PEOPLE ON THEIR SIDE DOIN' THE SAME RIGHT NOW.
WE GONNA FIGURE EVERY SINGLE WAY TO COME AT THIS THING, SO IF WE LOSE THIS TIME WE GONNA HIT 'EM ANOTHER WAY THE NEXT.
HE WOULDA BEEN A LAWYER IF HE COULD, BUT HIS JAIL TIME MEANT HE HADDA HIRE SOME HUMP INSTEAD. STILL ENDED UP WITH HIM DOIN' MOSTA THE WORK.
NEVER GONNA FORGET HIS DAY IN COURT:

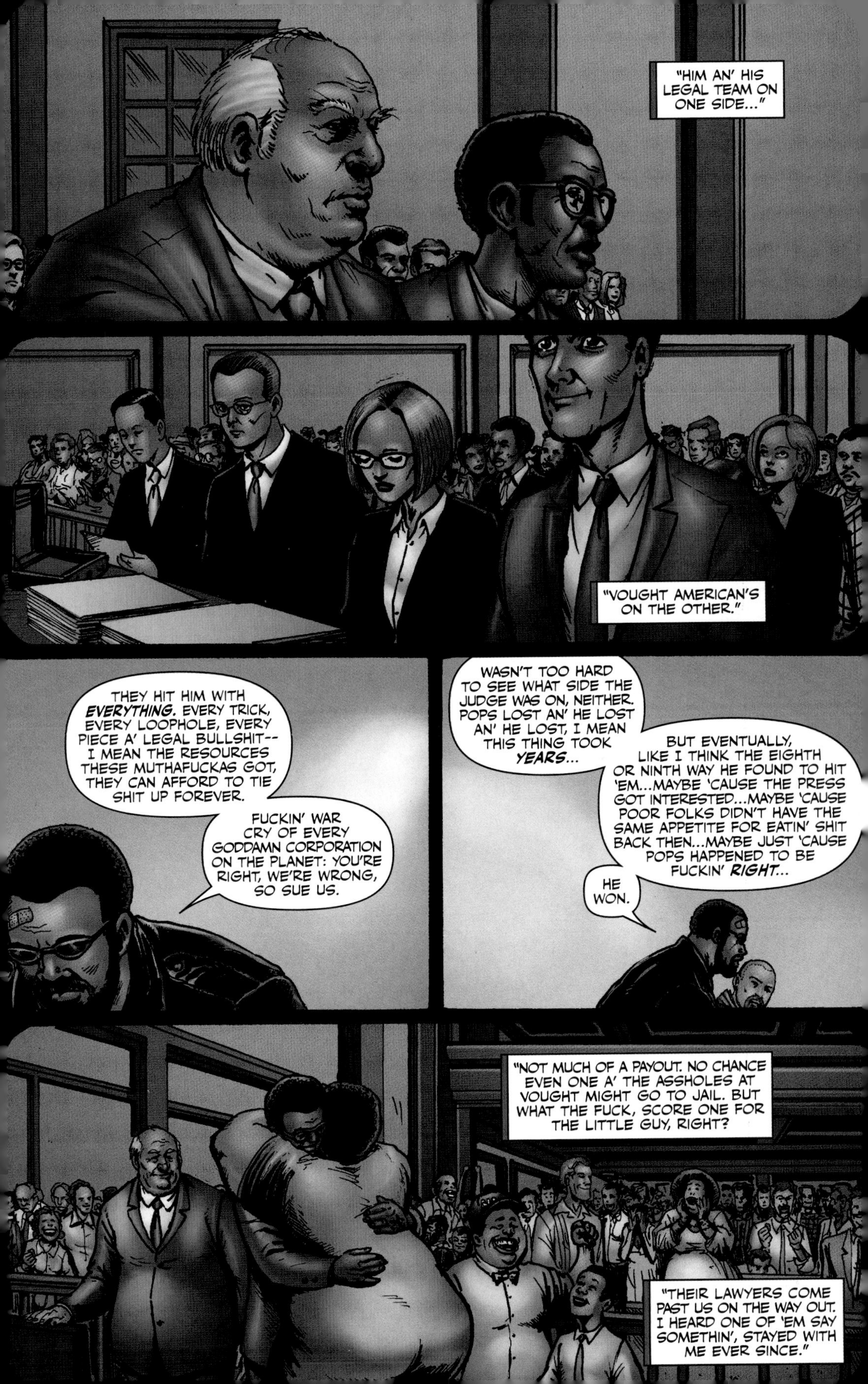
"HIM AN' HIS LEGAL TEAM ON ONE SIDE..."
"VOUGHT AMERICAN'S ON THE OTHER."
THEY HIT HIM WITH *EVERYTHING.* EVERY TRICK, EVERY LOOPHOLE, EVERY PIECE A' LEGAL BULLSHIT-- I MEAN THE RESOURCES THESE MUTHAFUCKAS GOT, THEY CAN AFFORD TO TIE SHIT UP FOREVER.
FUCKIN' WAR CRY OF EVERY GODDAMN CORPORATION ON THE PLANET: YOU'RE RIGHT, WE'RE WRONG, SO SUE US.
WASN'T TOO HARD TO SEE WHAT SIDE THE JUDGE WAS ON, NEITHER. POPS LOST AN' HE LOST AN' HE LOST, I MEAN THIS THING TOOK *YEARS*...
BUT EVENTUALLY, LIKE I THINK THE EIGHTH OR NINTH WAY HE FOUND TO HIT 'EM...MAYBE 'CAUSE THE PRESS GOT INTERESTED...MAYBE 'CAUSE POOR FOLKS DIDN'T HAVE THE SAME APPETITE FOR EATIN' SHIT BACK THEN...MAYBE JUST 'CAUSE POPS HAPPENED TO BE FUCKIN' *RIGHT*...
HE WON.
"NOT MUCH OF A PAYOUT. NO CHANCE EVEN ONE A' THE ASSHOLES AT VOUGHT MIGHT GO TO JAIL. BUT WHAT THE FUCK, SCORE ONE FOR THE LITTLE GUY, RIGHT?
"THEIR LAWYERS COME PAST US ON THE WAY OUT. I HEARD ONE OF 'EM SAY SOMETHIN', STAYED WITH ME EVER SINCE."

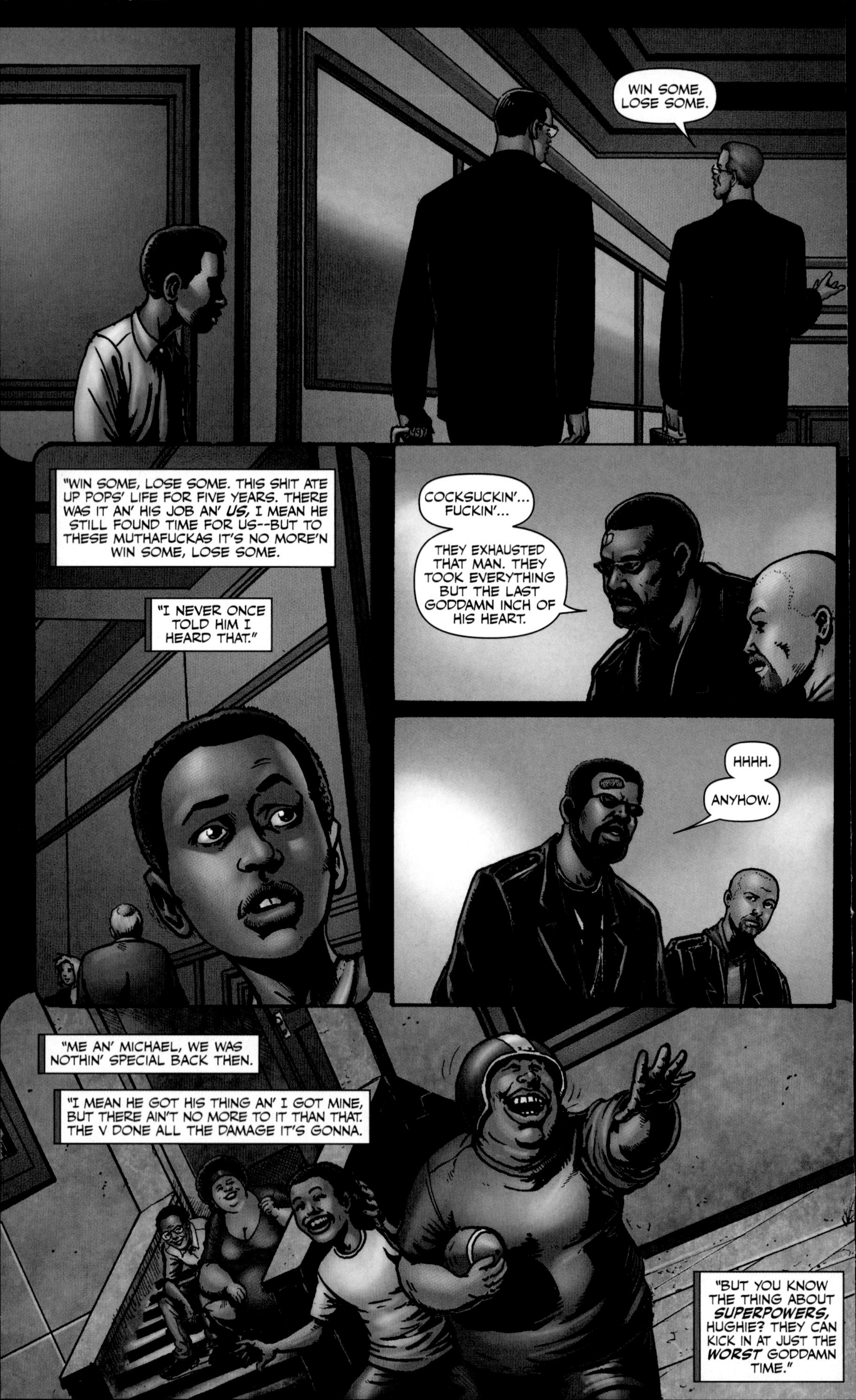
WIN SOME, LOSE SOME.
"WIN SOME, LOSE SOME. THIS SHIT ATE UP POPS' LIFE FOR FIVE YEARS. THERE WAS IT AN' HIS JOB AN' US, I MEAN HE STILL FOUND TIME FOR US--BUT TO THESE MUTHAFUCKAS IT'S NO MORE'N WIN SOME, LOSE SOME.
"I NEVER ONCE TOLD HIM I HEARD THAT."
COCKSUCKIN'... FUCKIN'...
THEY EXHAUSTED THAT MAN. THEY TOOK EVERYTHING BUT THE LAST GODDAMN INCH OF HIS HEART.
HHHH.
ANYHOW.
"ME AN' MICHAEL, WE WAS NOTHIN' SPECIAL BACK THEN.
"I MEAN HE GOT HIS THING AN' I GOT MINE, BUT THERE AIN'T NO MORE TO IT THAN THAT. THE V DONE ALL THE DAMAGE IT'S GONNA.
"BUT YOU KNOW THE THING ABOUT SUPERPOWERS, HUGHIE? THEY CAN KICK IN AT JUST THE WORST GODDAMN TIME."

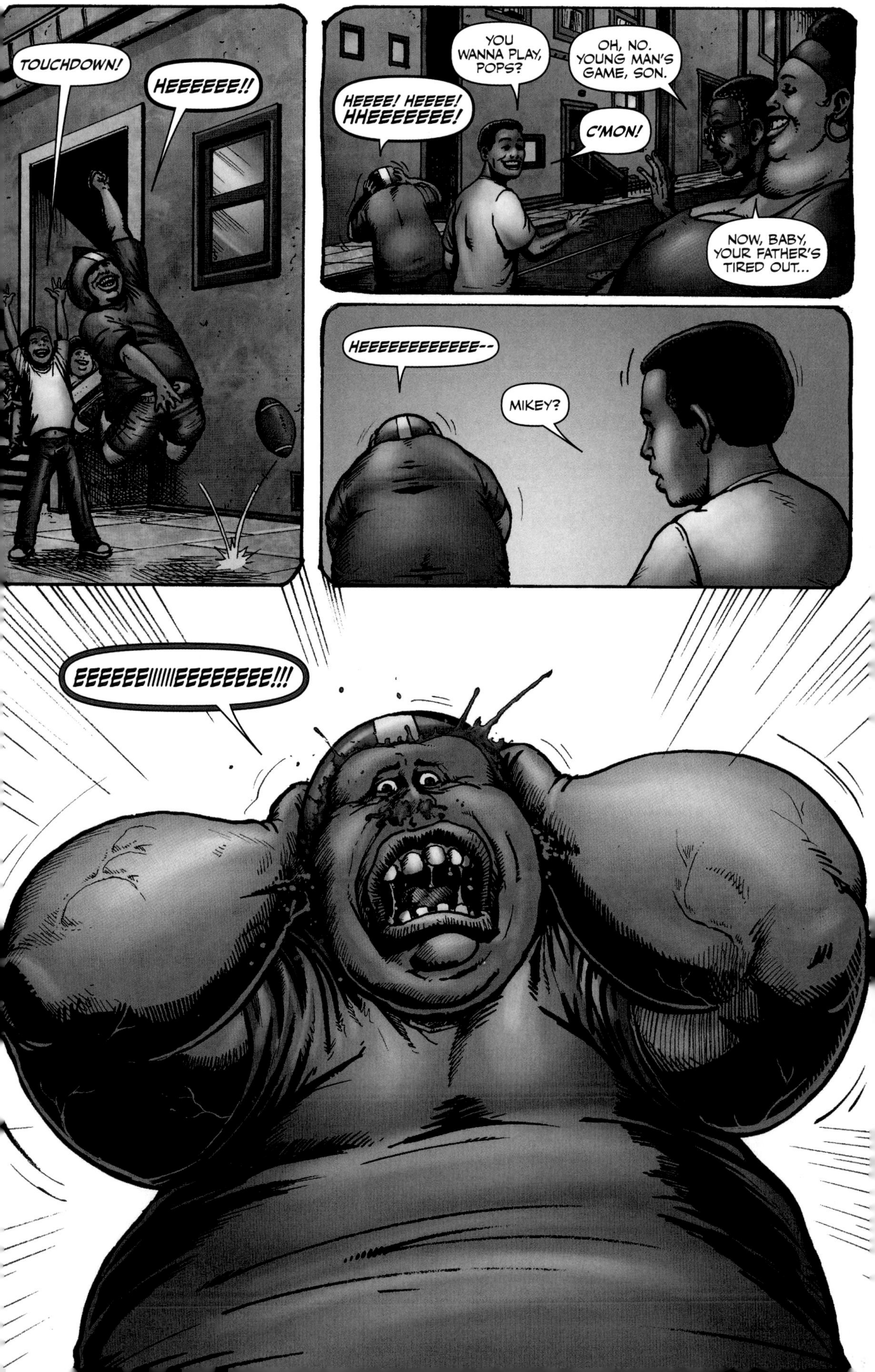
TOUCHDOWN!
HEEEEEE!!
YOU WANNA PLAY, POPS?
OH, NO. YOUNG MAN'S GAME, SON.
HEEEE! HEEEE! HHEEEEEEE!
C'MON!
NOW, BABY, YOUR FATHER'S TIRED OUT...
HEEEEEEEEEEEE--
MIKEY?
EEEEEEIIIIIIIEEEEEEEE!!!

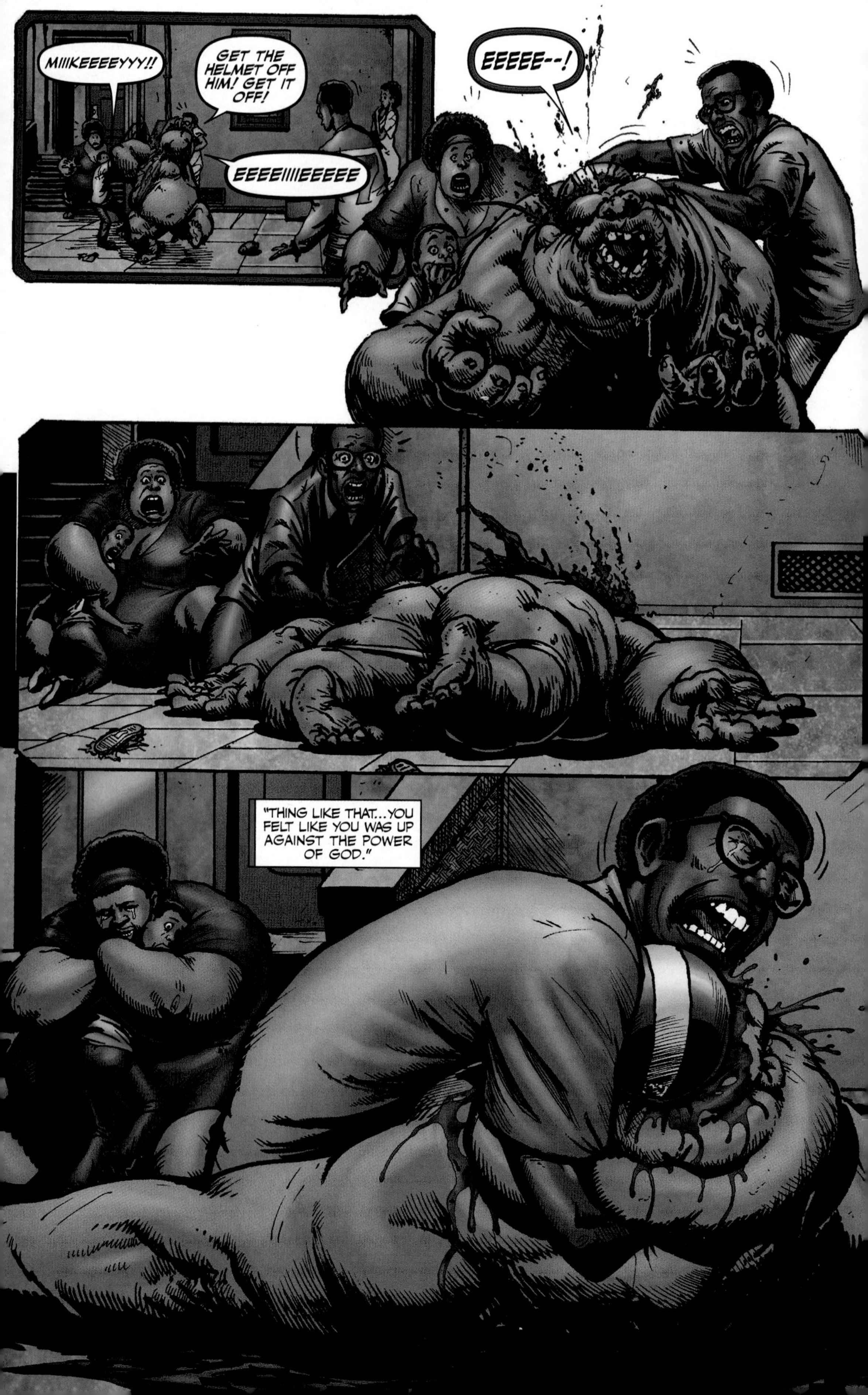
MIIIKEEEEYYY!!
GET THE HELMET OFF HIM! GET IT OFF!
EEEEIIIIEEEEE
EEEEE--!
"THING LIKE THAT...YOU FELT LIKE YOU WAS UP AGAINST THE POWER OF GOD."

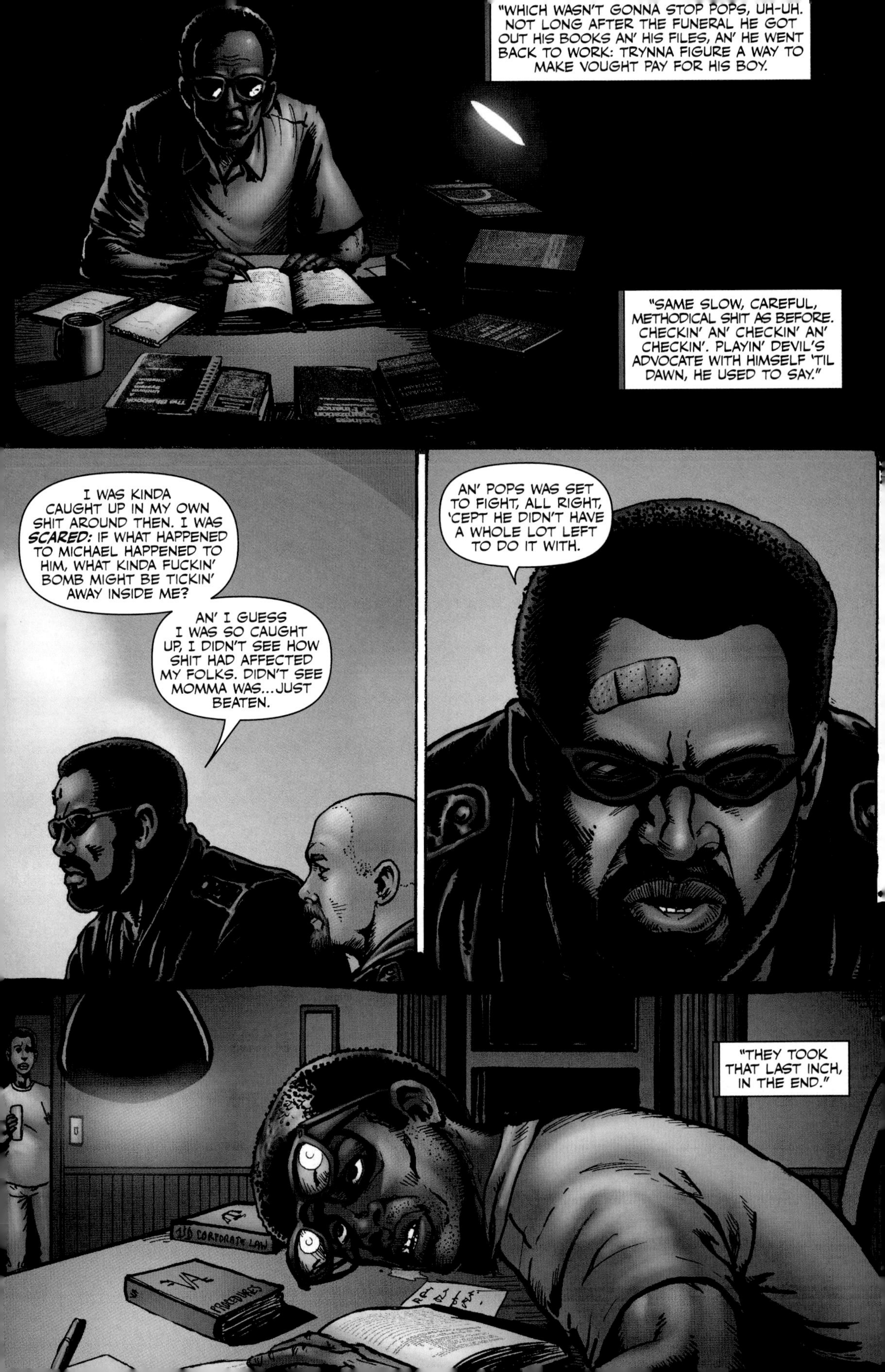
"WHICH WASN'T GONNA STOP POPS, UH-UH. NOT LONG AFTER THE FUNERAL HE GOT OUT HIS BOOKS AN' HIS FILES, AN' HE WENT BACK TO WORK: TRYNNA FIGURE A WAY TO MAKE VOUGHT PAY FOR HIS BOY.
"SAME SLOW, CAREFUL, METHODICAL SHIT AS BEFORE. CHECKIN' AN' CHECKIN' AN' CHECKIN'. PLAYIN' DEVIL'S ADVOCATE WITH HIMSELF 'TIL DAWN, HE USED TO SAY."
I WAS KINDA CAUGHT UP IN MY OWN SHIT AROUND THEN. I WAS *SCARED:* IF WHAT HAPPENED TO MICHAEL HAPPENED TO HIM, WHAT KINDA FUCKIN' BOMB MIGHT BE TICKIN' AWAY INSIDE ME?
AN' I GUESS I WAS SO CAUGHT UP, I DIDN'T SEE HOW SHIT HAD AFFECTED MY FOLKS. DIDN'T SEE MOMMA WAS...JUST BEATEN.
AN' POPS WAS SET TO FIGHT, ALL RIGHT, 'CEPT HE DIDN'T HAVE A WHOLE LOT LEFT TO DO IT WITH.
"THEY TOOK THAT LAST INCH, IN THE END."
CORPORATE LAW
PROCEDURES

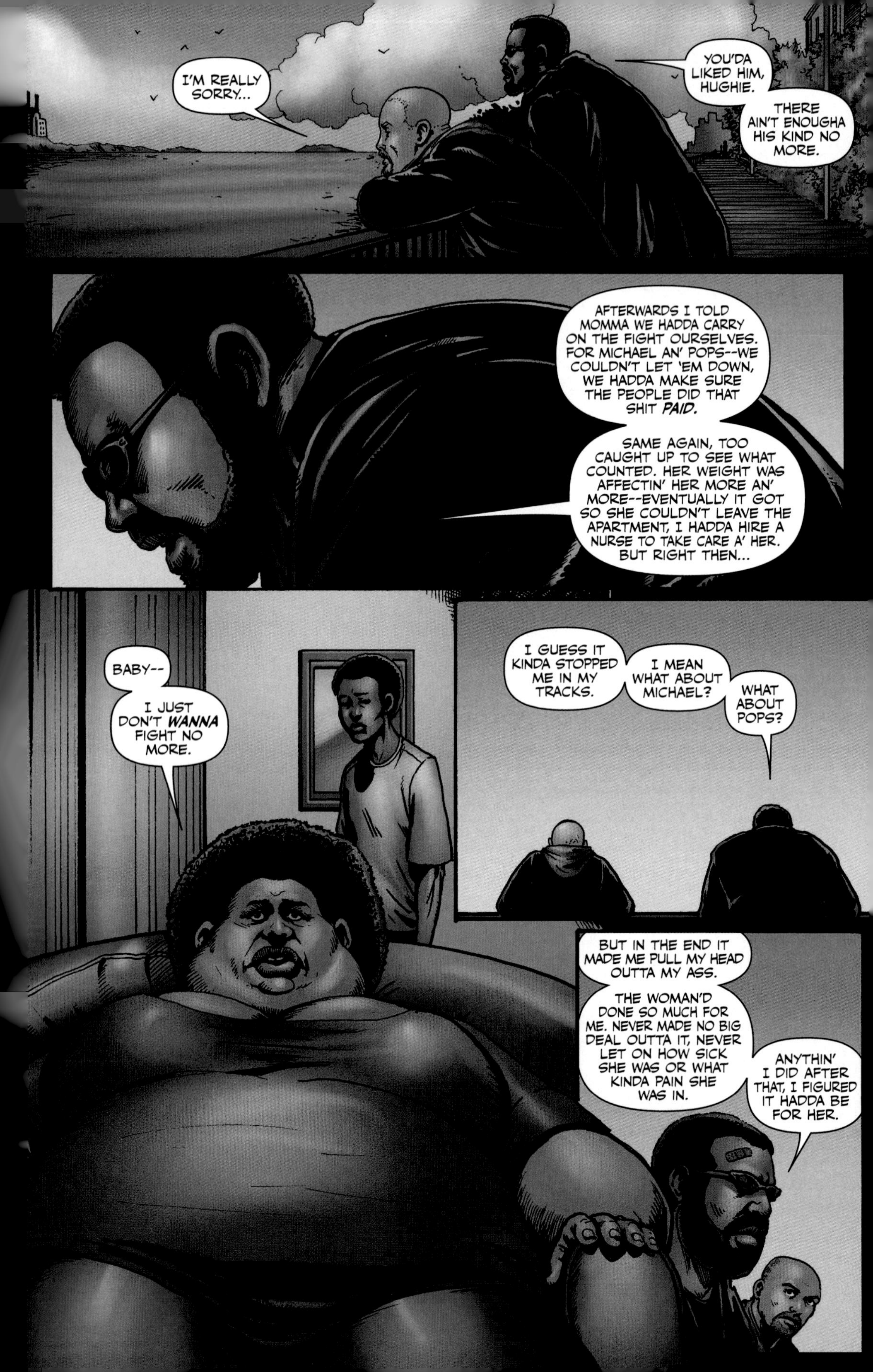
I'M REALLY SORRY...
YOU'DA LIKED HIM, HUGHIE.
THERE AIN'T ENOUGHA HIS KIND NO MORE.
AFTERWARDS I TOLD MOMMA WE HADDA CARRY ON THE FIGHT OURSELVES. FOR MICHAEL AN' POPS--WE COULDN'T LET 'EM DOWN, WE HADDA MAKE SURE THE PEOPLE DID THAT SHIT *PAID.*
SAME AGAIN, TOO CAUGHT UP TO SEE WHAT COUNTED. HER WEIGHT WAS AFFECTIN' HER MORE AN' MORE--EVENTUALLY IT GOT SO SHE COULDN'T LEAVE THE APARTMENT, I HADDA HIRE A NURSE TO TAKE CARE A' HER. BUT RIGHT THEN...
BABY--
I JUST DON'T *WANNA* FIGHT NO MORE.
I GUESS IT KINDA STOPPED ME IN MY TRACKS.
I MEAN WHAT ABOUT MICHAEL?
WHAT ABOUT POPS?
BUT IN THE END IT MADE ME PULL MY HEAD OUTTA MY ASS.
THE WOMAN'D DONE SO MUCH FOR ME. NEVER MADE NO BIG DEAL OUTTA IT, NEVER LET ON HOW SICK SHE WAS OR WHAT KINDA PAIN SHE WAS IN.
ANYTHIN' I DID AFTER THAT, I FIGURED IT HADDA BE FOR HER.

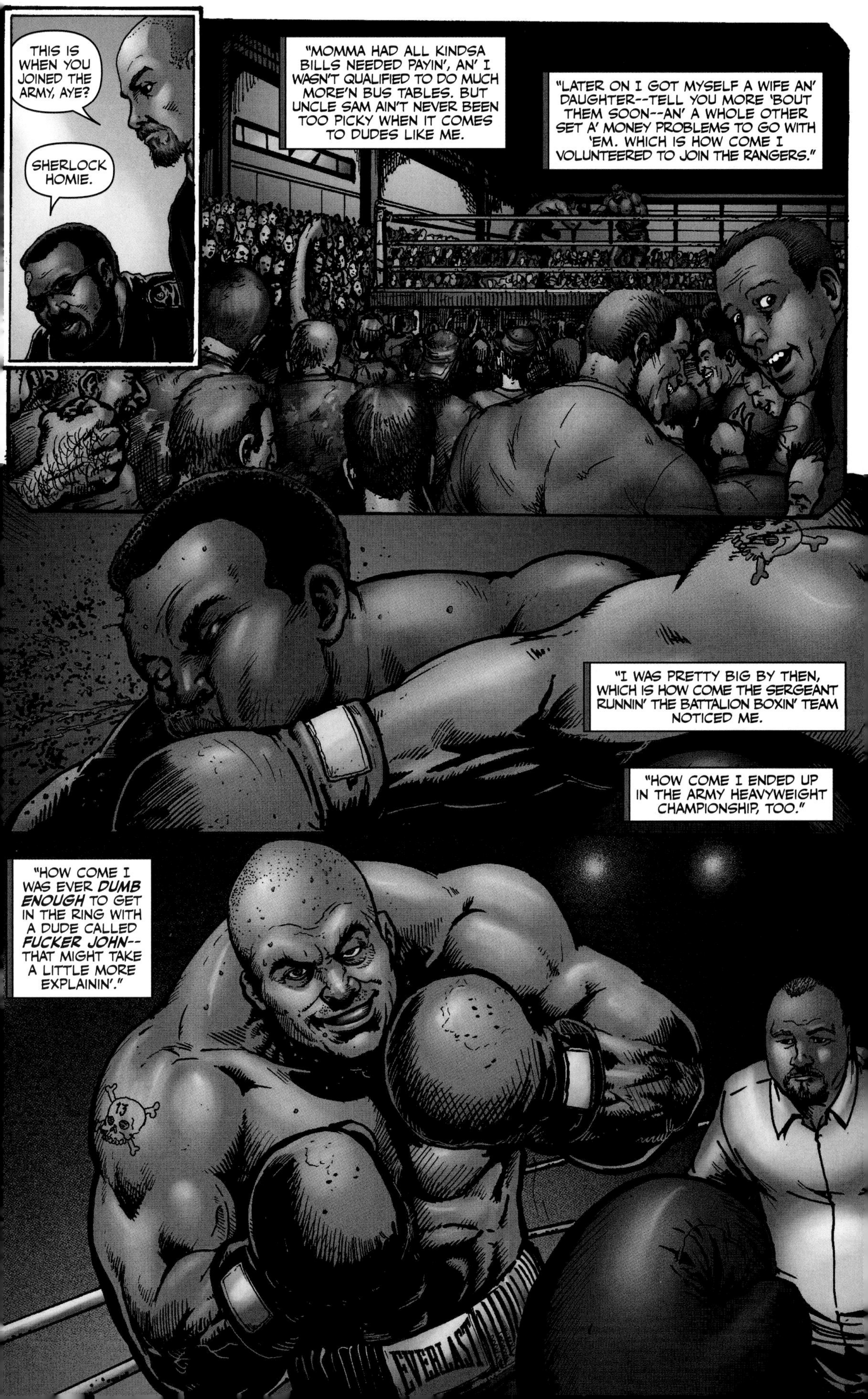
THIS IS WHEN YOU JOINED THE ARMY, AYE?
SHERLOCK HOMIE.
"MOMMA HAD ALL KINDSA BILLS NEEDED PAYIN', AN' I WASN'T QUALIFIED TO DO MUCH MORE'N BUS TABLES. BUT UNCLE SAM AIN'T NEVER BEEN TOO PICKY WHEN IT COMES TO DUDES LIKE ME.
"LATER ON I GOT MYSELF A WIFE AN' DAUGHTER--TELL YOU MORE 'BOUT THEM SOON--AN' A WHOLE OTHER SET A' MONEY PROBLEMS TO GO WITH 'EM. WHICH IS HOW COME I VOLUNTEERED TO JOIN THE RANGERS."
"I WAS PRETTY BIG BY THEN, WHICH IS HOW COME THE SERGEANT RUNNIN' THE BATTALION BOXIN' TEAM NOTICED ME.
"HOW COME I ENDED UP IN THE ARMY HEAVYWEIGHT CHAMPIONSHIP, TOO."
"HOW COME I WAS EVER *DUMB ENOUGH* TO GET IN THE RING WITH A DUDE CALLED *FUCKER JOHN*--THAT MIGHT TAKE A LITTLE MORE EXPLAININ'."
EVERLAST

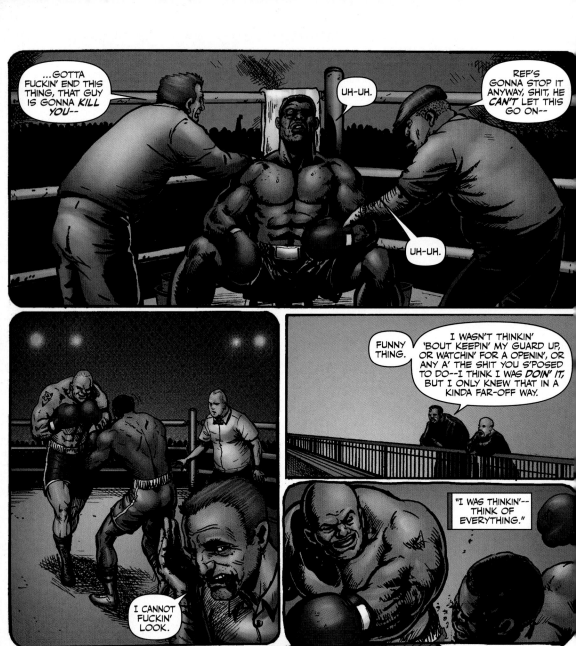

...GOTTA FUCKIN' END THIS THING, THAT GUY IS GONNA *KILL YOU*--

UH-UH.

REF'S GONNA STOP IT ANYWAY, SHIT, HE *CAN'T* LET THIS GO ON--

UH-UH.

I CANNOT FUCKIN' LOOK.

FUNNY THING.

I WASN'T THINKIN' 'BOUT KEEPIN' MY GUARD UP, OR WATCHIN' FOR A OPENIN', OR ANY A' THE SHIT YOU S'POSED TO DO--I THINK I WAS *DOIN' IT*, BUT I ONLY KNEW THAT IN A KINDA FAR-OFF WAY.

"I WAS THINKIN'-- THINK OF EVERYTHING."

"FIGURE EVERY SINGLE WAY."

"LOSE THIS TIME, WE GONNA HIT 'EM ANOTHER WAY THE NEXT."

YOU REMEMBER THE THING I SAID ABOUT SUPERPOWERS?

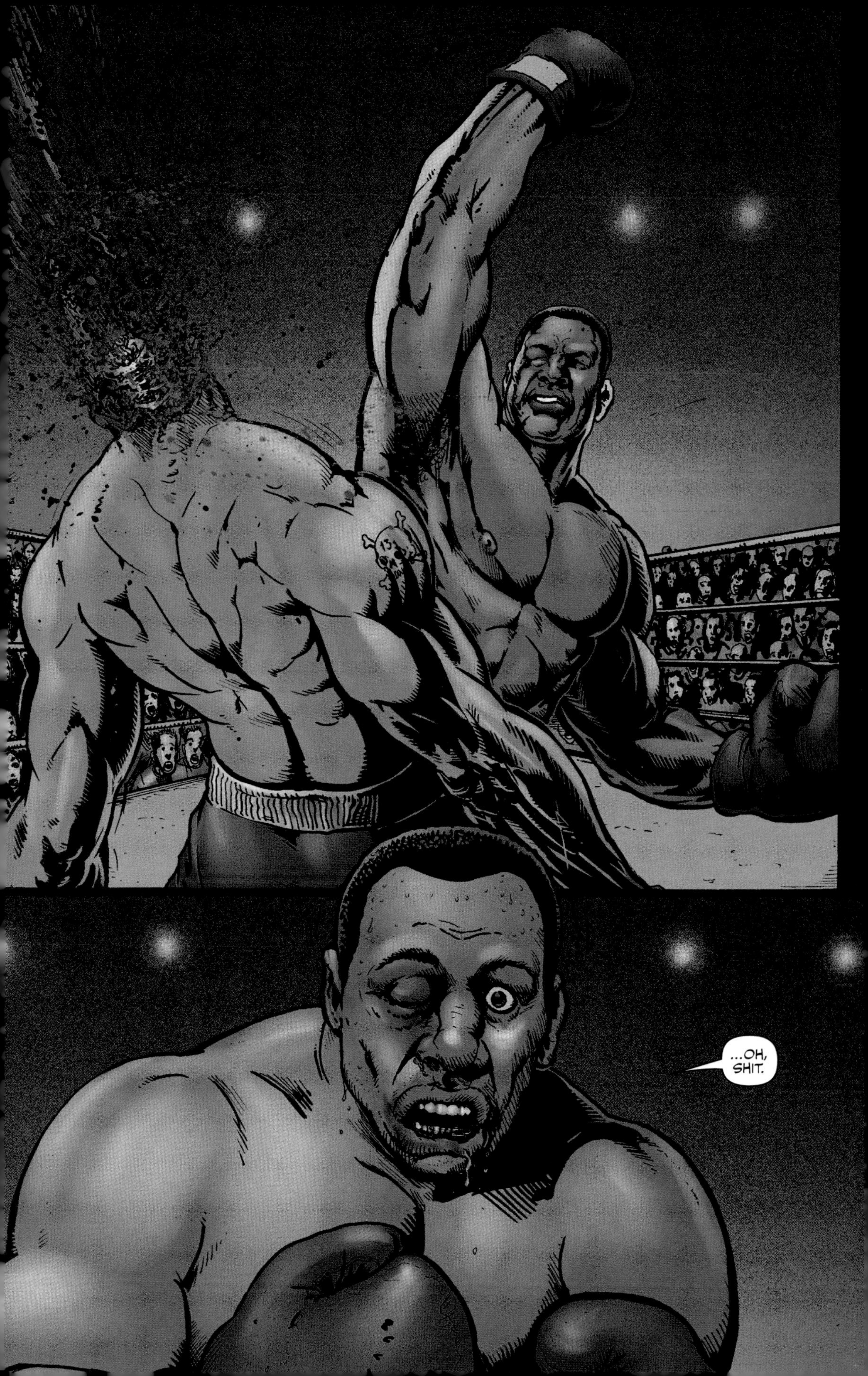
...OH, SHIT.

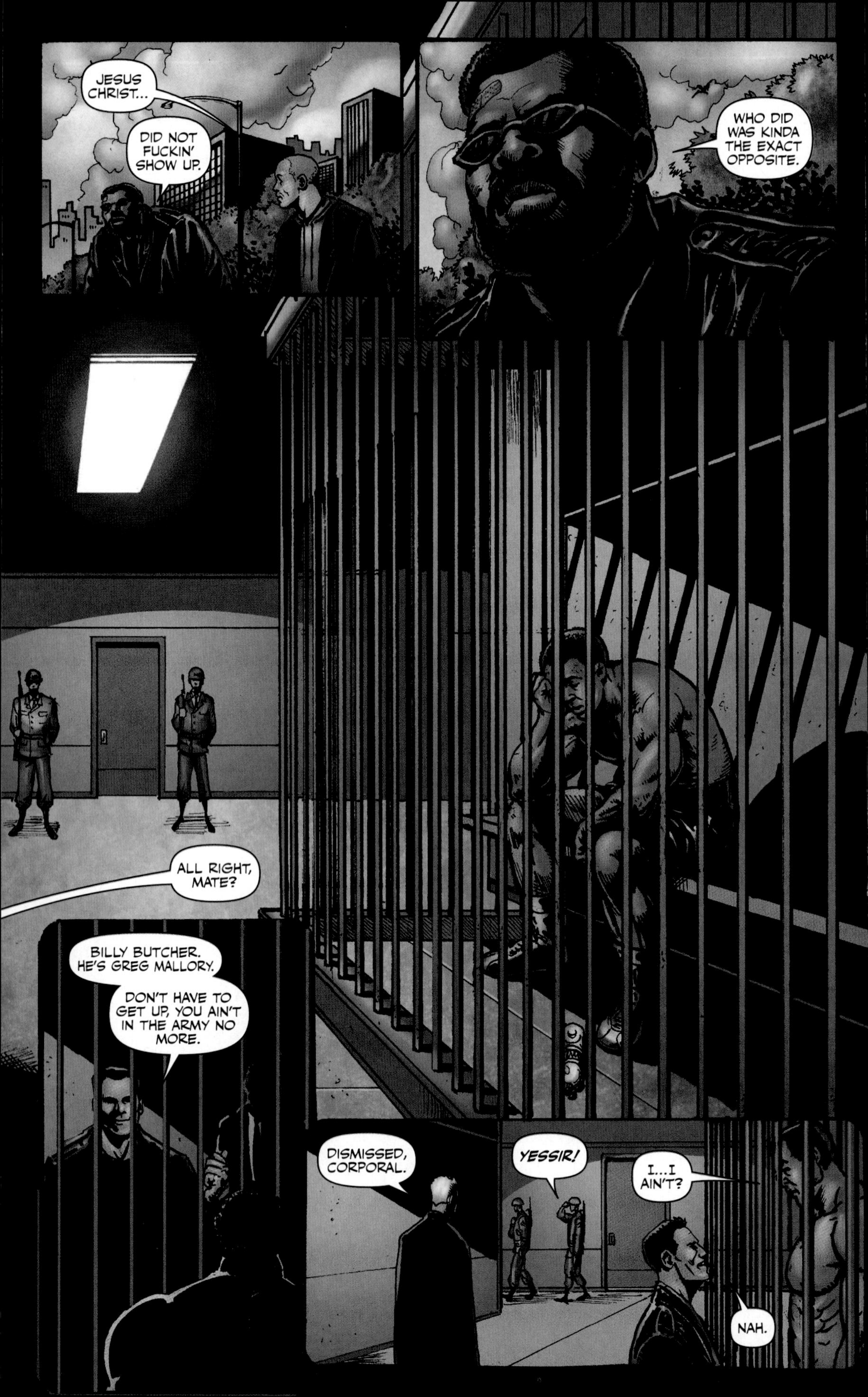
JESUS CHRIST...
DID NOT FUCKIN' SHOW UP.
WHO DID WAS KINDA THE EXACT OPPOSITE.
ALL RIGHT, MATE?
BILLY BUTCHER. HE'S GREG MALLORY.
DON'T HAVE TO GET UP, YOU AIN'T IN THE ARMY NO MORE.
DISMISSED, CORPORAL.
YESSIR!
I...I AIN'T?
NAH.

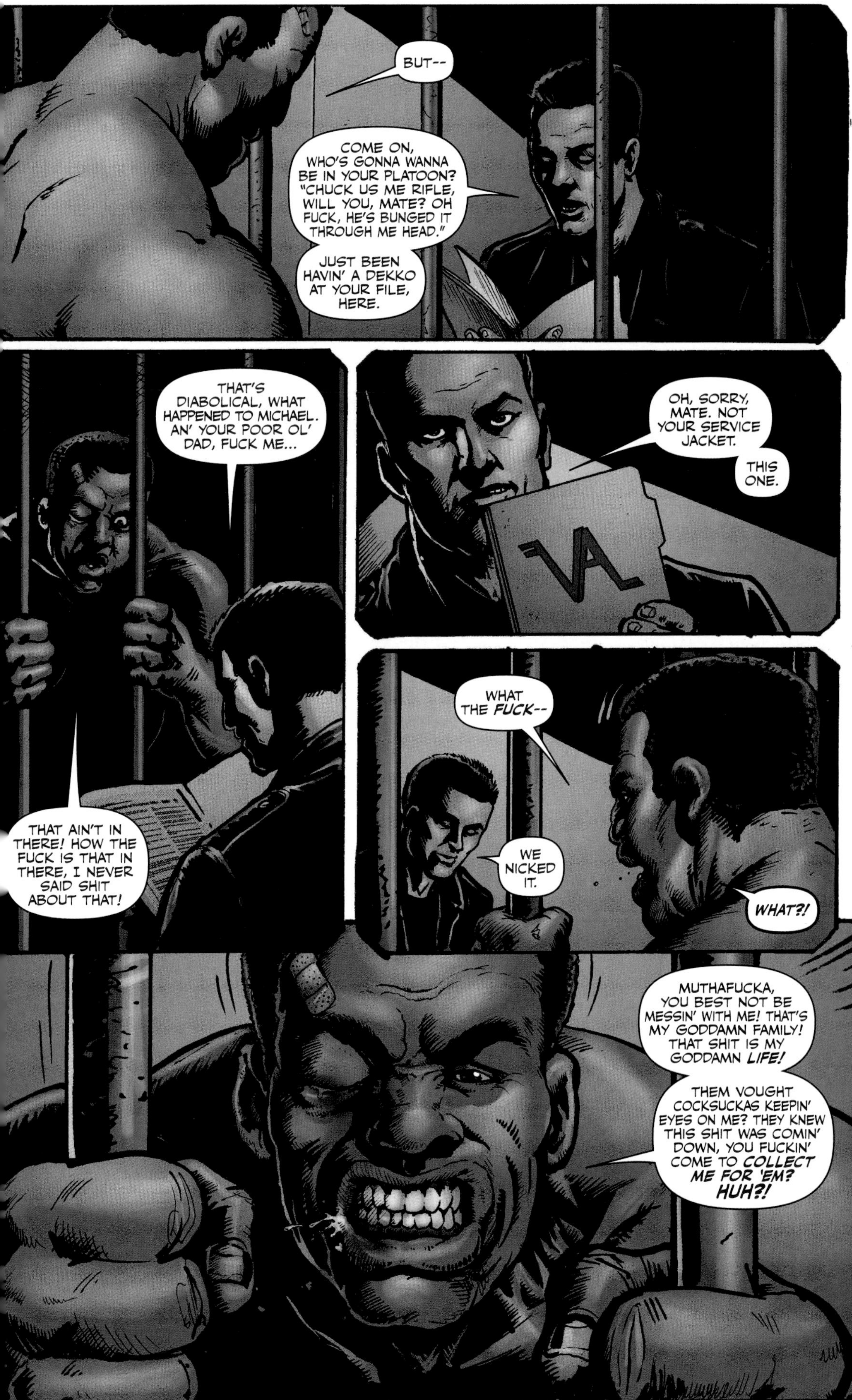
BUT--
COME ON, WHO'S GONNA WANNA BE IN YOUR PLATOON? "CHUCK US ME RIFLE, WILL YOU, MATE? OH FUCK, HE'S BUNGED IT THROUGH ME HEAD."
JUST BEEN HAVIN' A DEKKO AT YOUR FILE, HERE.
THAT'S DIABOLICAL, WHAT HAPPENED TO MICHAEL. AN' YOUR POOR OL' DAD, FUCK ME...
THAT AIN'T IN THERE! HOW THE FUCK IS THAT IN THERE, I NEVER SAID SHIT ABOUT THAT!
OH, SORRY, MATE. NOT YOUR SERVICE JACKET.
THIS ONE.
VA
WHAT THE *FUCK*--
WE NICKED IT.
WHAT?!
MUTHAFUCKA, YOU BEST NOT BE MESSIN' WITH ME! THAT'S MY GODDAMN FAMILY! THAT SHIT IS MY GODDAMN *LIFE!*
THEM VOUGHT COCKSUCKAS KEEPIN' EYES ON ME? THEY KNEW THIS SHIT WAS COMIN' DOWN, YOU FUCKIN' COME TO *COLLECT ME FOR 'EM? HUH?!*

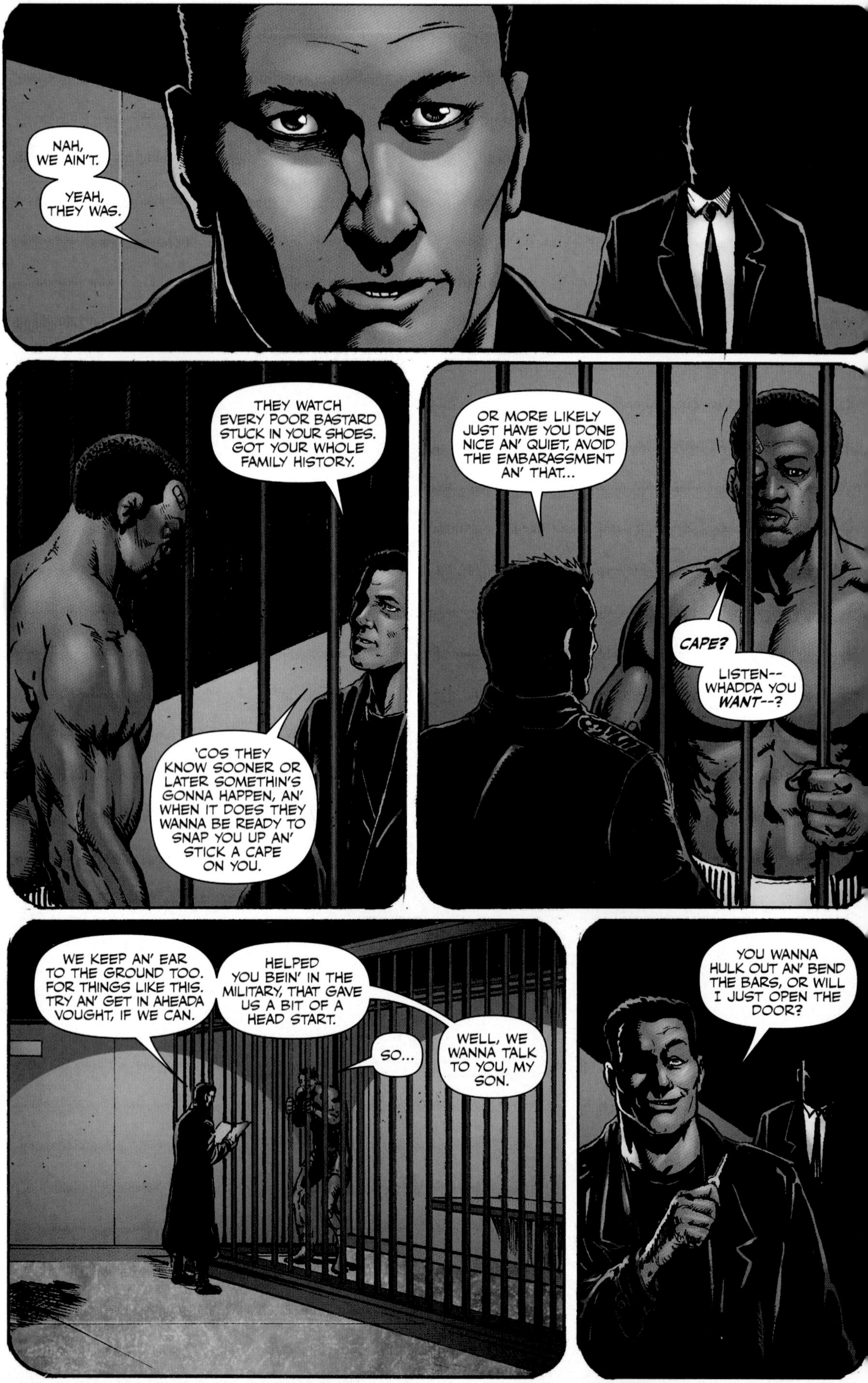
NAH, WE AIN'T.
YEAH, THEY WAS.
THEY WATCH EVERY POOR BASTARD STUCK IN YOUR SHOES. GOT YOUR WHOLE FAMILY HISTORY.
'COS THEY KNOW SOONER OR LATER SOMETHIN'S GONNA HAPPEN, AN' WHEN IT DOES THEY WANNA BE READY TO SNAP YOU UP AN' STICK A CAPE ON YOU.
OR MORE LIKELY JUST HAVE YOU DONE NICE AN' QUIET, AVOID THE EMBARASSMENT AN' THAT...
CAPE?
LISTEN-- WHADDA YOU WANT--?
WE KEEP AN' EAR TO THE GROUND TOO. FOR THINGS LIKE THIS. TRY AN' GET IN AHEADA VOUGHT, IF WE CAN.
HELPED YOU BEIN' IN THE MILITARY, THAT GAVE US A BIT OF A HEAD START.
SO...
WELL, WE WANNA TALK TO YOU, MY SON.
YOU WANNA HULK OUT AN' BEND THE BARS, OR WILL I JUST OPEN THE DOOR?

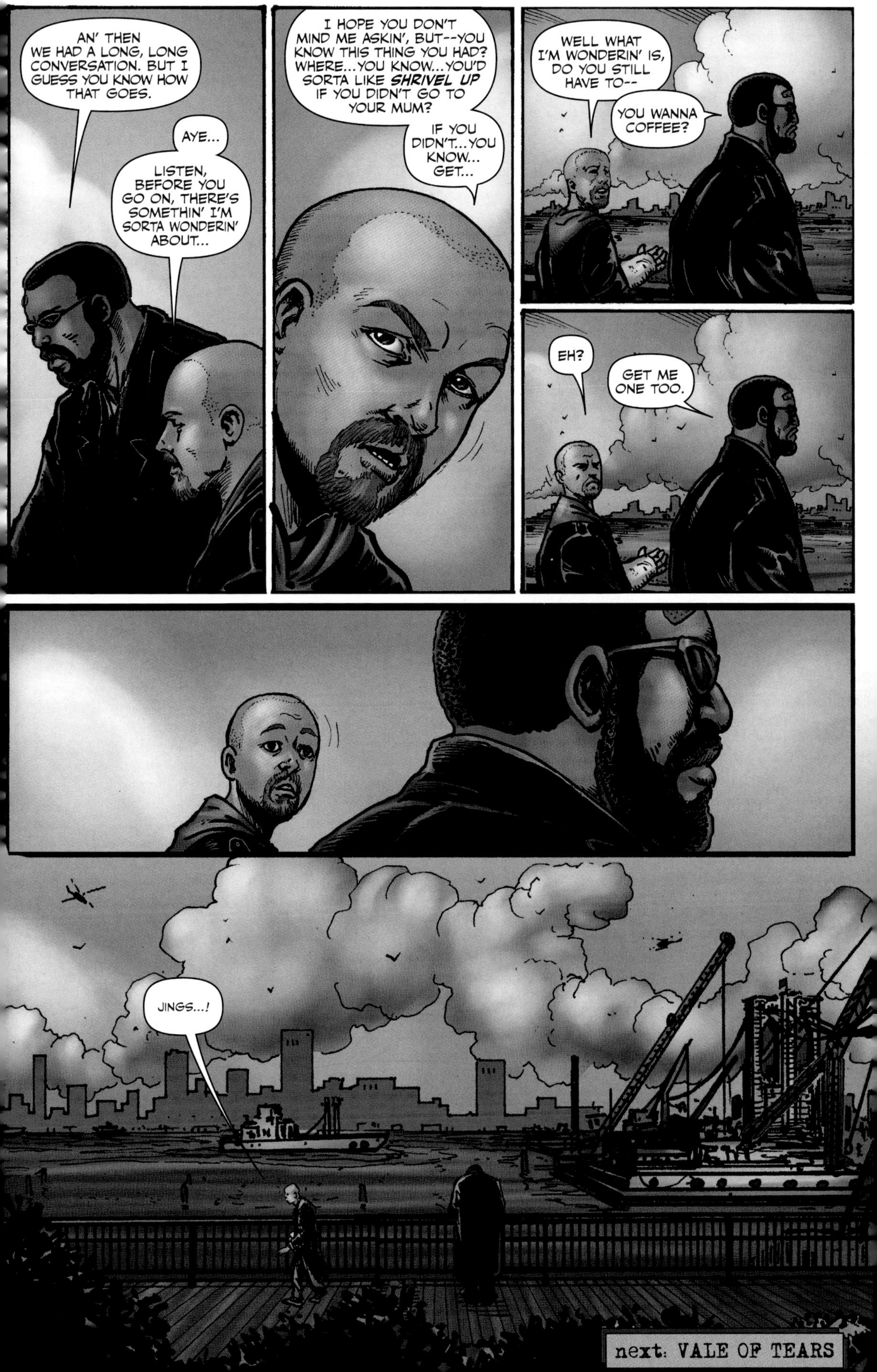
AN' THEN WE HAD A LONG, LONG CONVERSATION. BUT I GUESS YOU KNOW HOW THAT GOES.
AYE...
LISTEN, BEFORE YOU GO ON, THERE'S SOMETHIN' I'M SORTA WONDERIN' ABOUT...
I HOPE YOU DON'T MIND ME ASKIN', BUT--YOU KNOW THIS THING YOU HAD? WHERE...YOU KNOW...YOU'D SORTA LIKE SHRIVEL UP IF YOU DIDN'T GO TO YOUR MUM?
IF YOU DIDN'T...YOU KNOW... GET...
WELL WHAT I'M WONDERIN' IS, DO YOU STILL HAVE TO--
YOU WANNA COFFEE?
EH?
GET ME ONE TOO.
JINGS...!
next: VALE OF TEARS

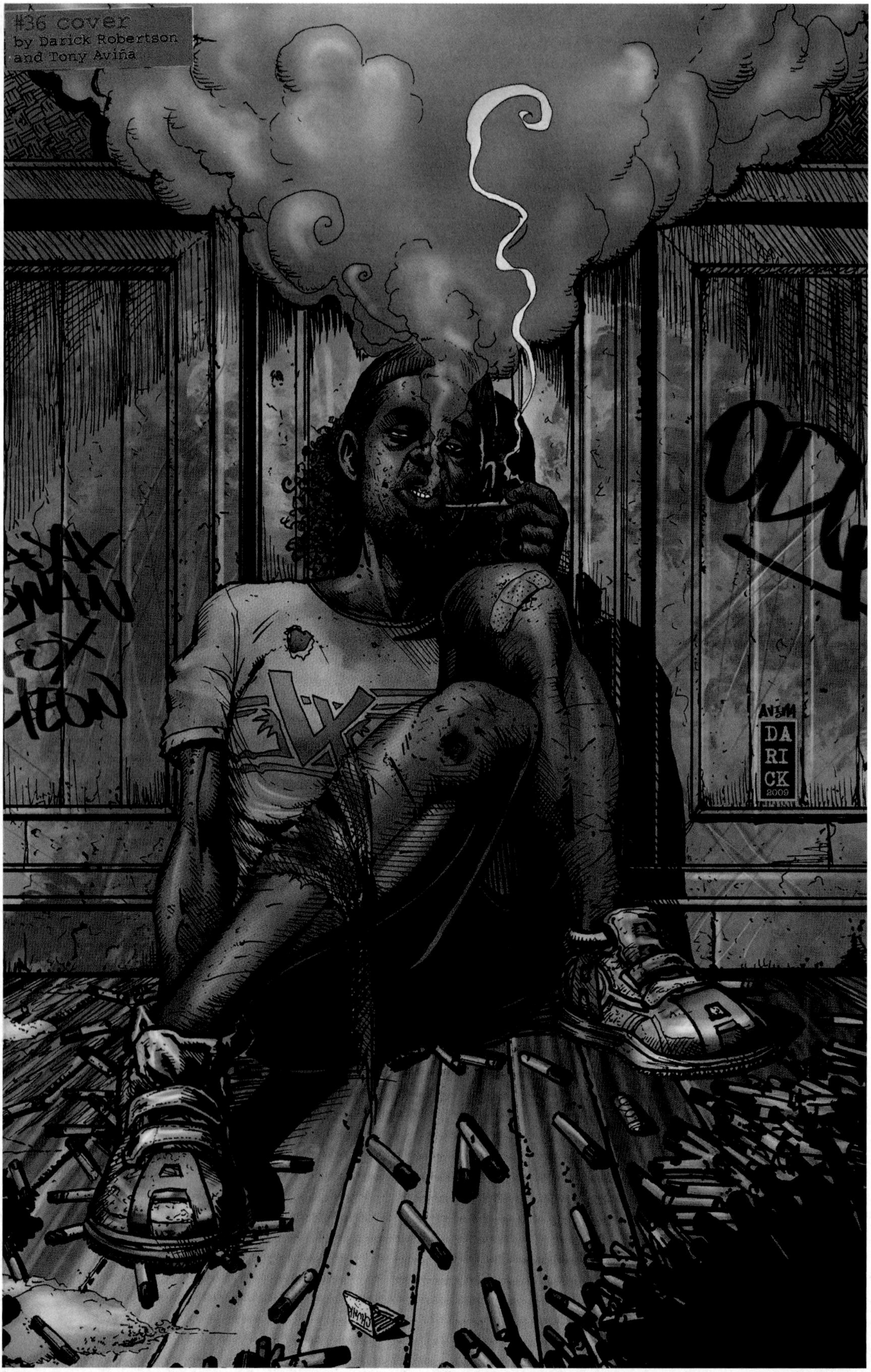
DA
RI
CK
2009

#36 cover
by Darick Robertson
and Tony Aviña

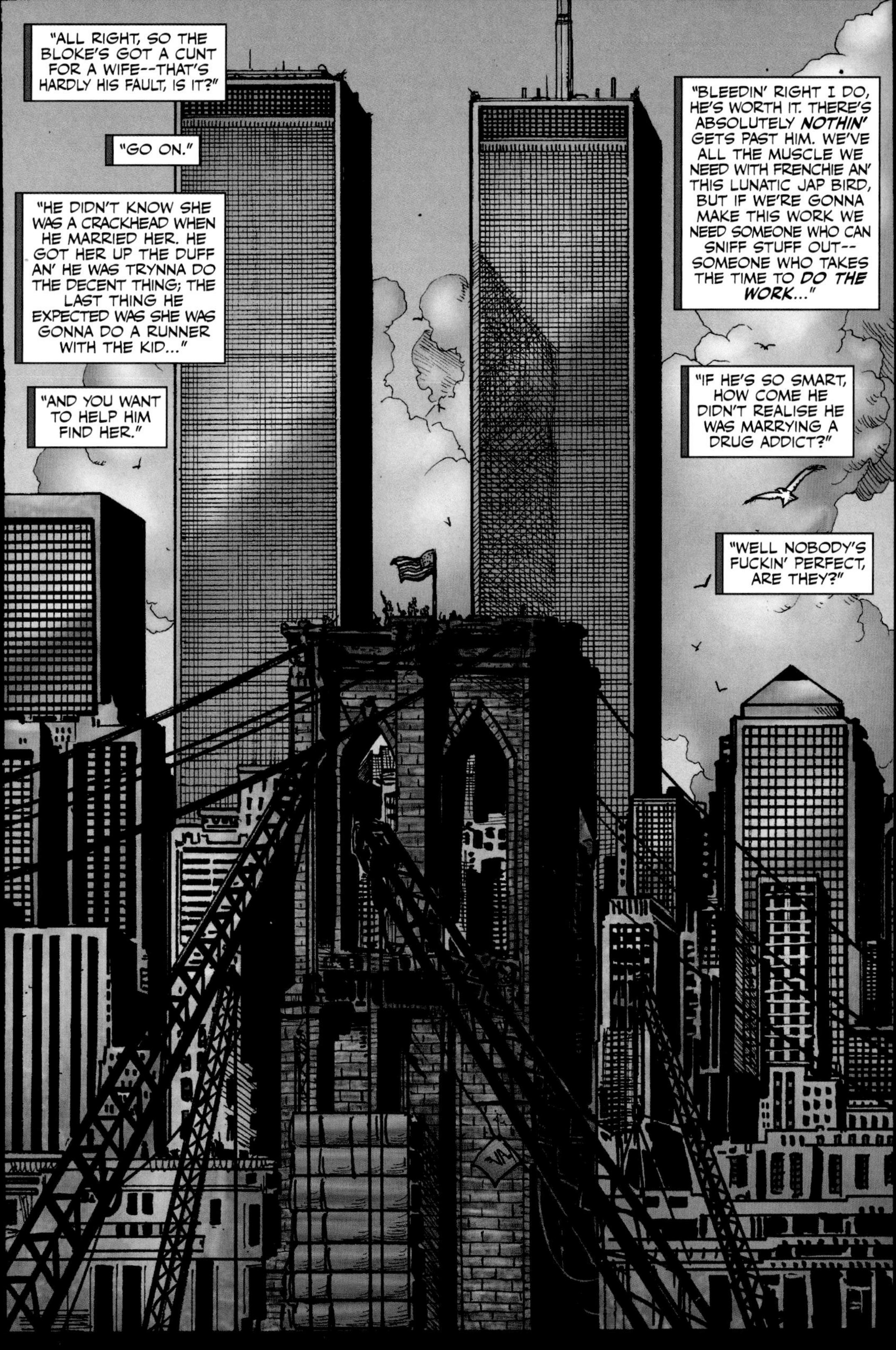
"ALL RIGHT, SO THE BLOKE'S GOT A CUNT FOR A WIFE--THAT'S HARDLY HIS FAULT, IS IT?"
"GO ON."
"HE DIDN'T KNOW SHE WAS A CRACKHEAD WHEN HE MARRIED HER. HE GOT HER UP THE DUFF AN' HE WAS TRYNNA DO THE DECENT THING; THE LAST THING HE EXPECTED WAS SHE WAS GONNA DO A RUNNER WITH THE KID..."
"AND YOU WANT TO HELP HIM FIND HER."
"BLEEDIN' RIGHT I DO, HE'S WORTH IT. THERE'S ABSOLUTELY ***NOTHIN'*** GETS PAST HIM. WE'VE ALL THE MUSCLE WE NEED WITH FRENCHIE AN' THIS LUNATIC JAP BIRD, BUT IF WE'RE GONNA MAKE THIS WORK WE NEED SOMEONE WHO CAN SNIFF STUFF OUT--SOMEONE WHO TAKES THE TIME TO ***DO THE WORK***..."
"IF HE'S SO SMART, HOW COME HE DIDN'T REALISE HE WAS MARRYING A DRUG ADDICT?"
"WELL NOBODY'S FUCKIN' PERFECT, ARE THEY?"

NOTHING LIKE IT IN THE WORLD

part two

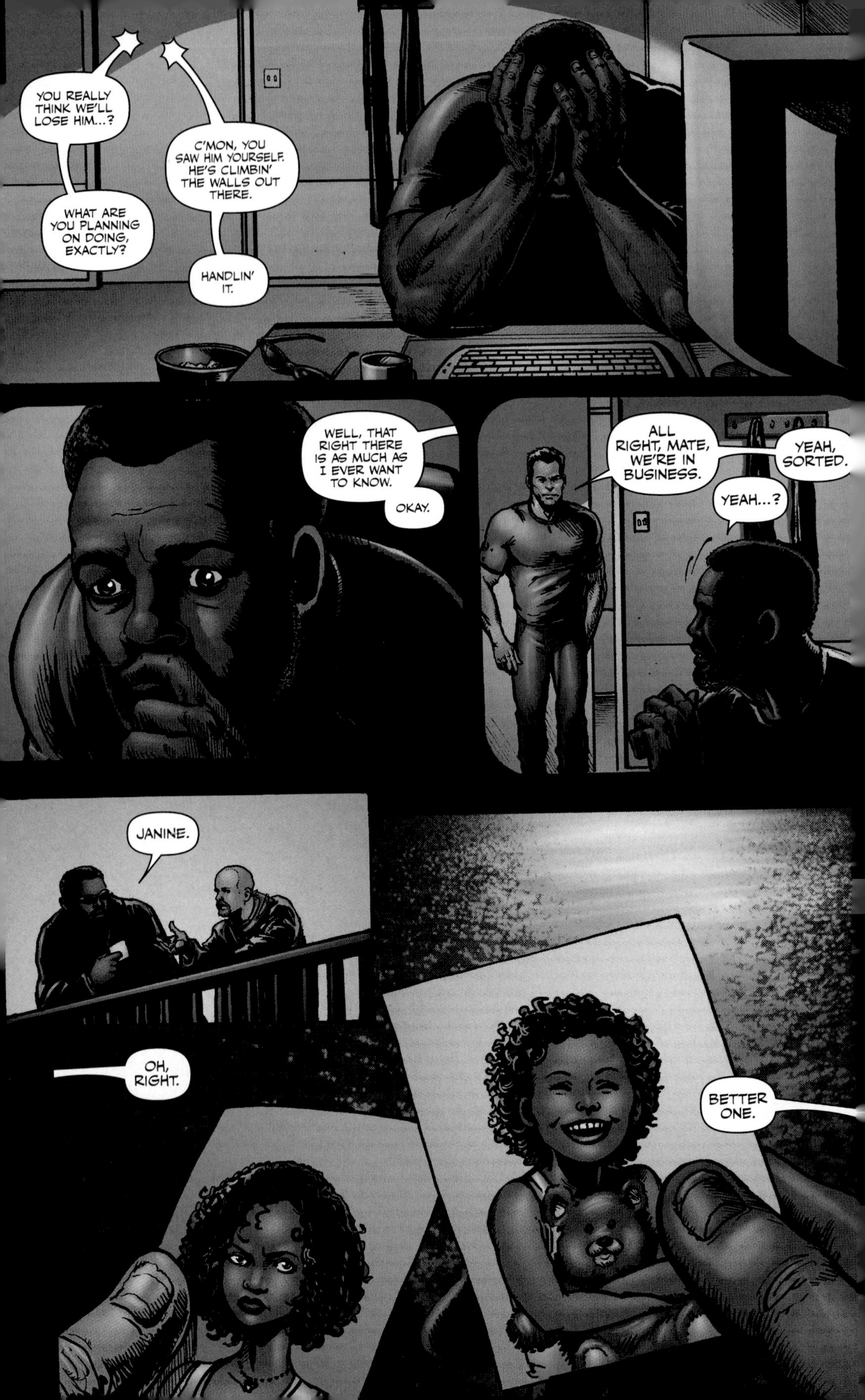
YOU REALLY THINK WE'LL LOSE HIM...?
C'MON, YOU SAW HIM YOURSELF. HE'S CLIMBIN' THE WALLS OUT THERE.
WHAT ARE YOU PLANNING ON DOING, EXACTLY?
HANDLIN' IT.
WELL, THAT RIGHT THERE IS AS MUCH AS I EVER WANT TO KNOW.
OKAY.
ALL RIGHT, MATE, WE'RE IN BUSINESS.
YEAH...?
YEAH, SORTED.
JANINE.
OH, RIGHT.
BETTER ONE.

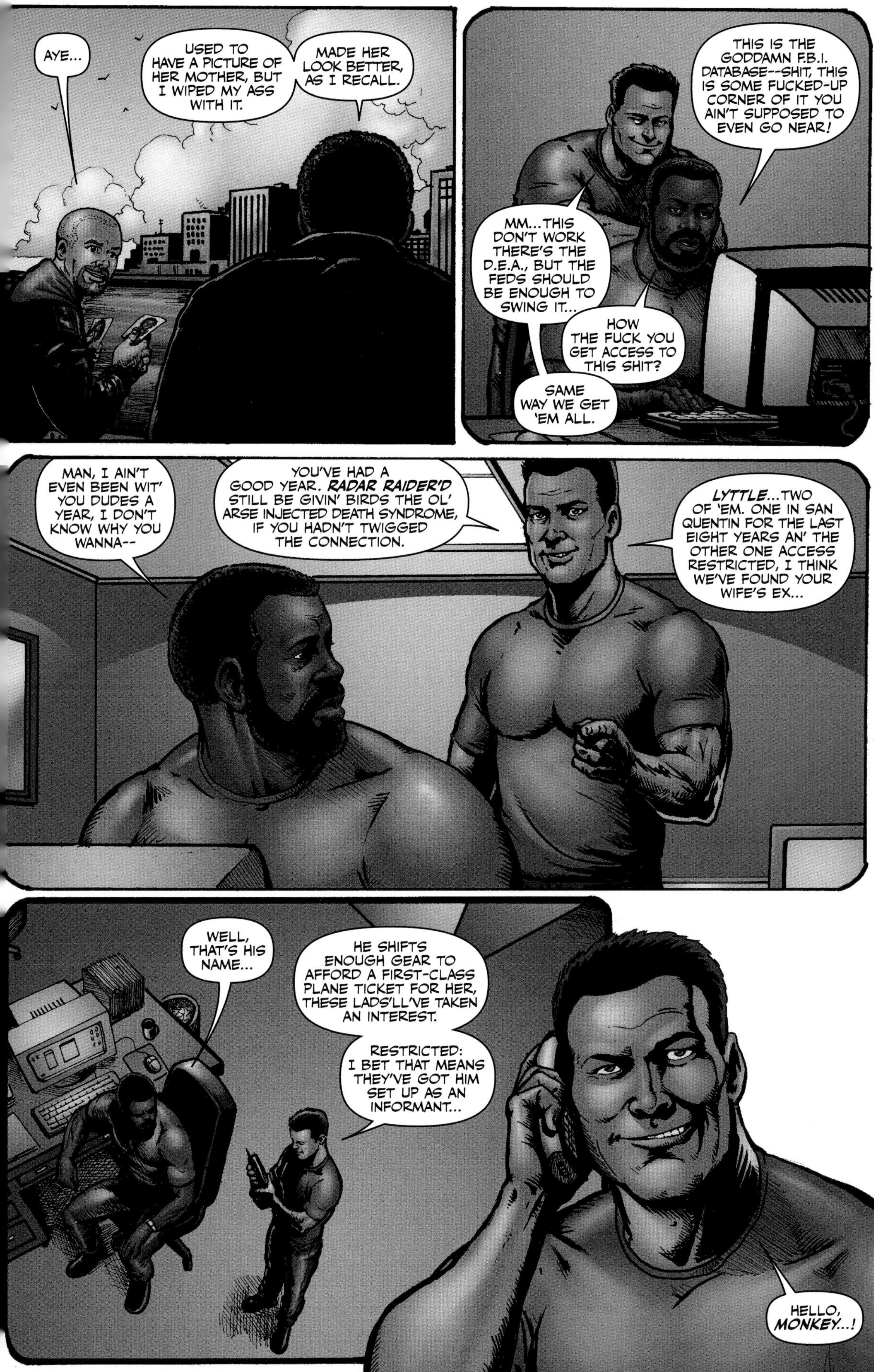
AYE...
USED TO HAVE A PICTURE OF HER MOTHER, BUT I WIPED MY ASS WITH IT.
MADE HER LOOK BETTER, AS I RECALL.
THIS IS THE GODDAMN F.B.I. DATABASE--SHIT, THIS IS SOME FUCKED-UP CORNER OF IT YOU AIN'T SUPPOSED TO EVEN GO NEAR!
MM...THIS DON'T WORK THERE'S THE D.E.A., BUT THE FEDS SHOULD BE ENOUGH TO SWING IT...
HOW THE FUCK YOU GET ACCESS TO THIS SHIT?
SAME WAY WE GET 'EM ALL.
MAN, I AIN'T EVEN BEEN WIT' YOU DUDES A YEAR, I DON'T KNOW WHY YOU WANNA--
YOU'VE HAD A GOOD YEAR. *RADAR RAIDER'D* STILL BE GIVIN' BIRDS THE OL' ARSE INJECTED DEATH SYNDROME, IF YOU HADN'T TWIGGED THE CONNECTION.
LYTTLE...TWO OF 'EM. ONE IN SAN QUENTIN FOR THE LAST EIGHT YEARS AN' THE OTHER ONE ACCESS RESTRICTED, I THINK WE'VE FOUND YOUR WIFE'S EX...
WELL, THAT'S HIS NAME...
HE SHIFTS ENOUGH GEAR TO AFFORD A FIRST-CLASS PLANE TICKET FOR HER, THESE LADS'LL'VE TAKEN AN INTEREST.
RESTRICTED: I BET THAT MEANS THEY'VE GOT HIM SET UP AS AN INFORMANT...
HELLO, *MONKEY*...!

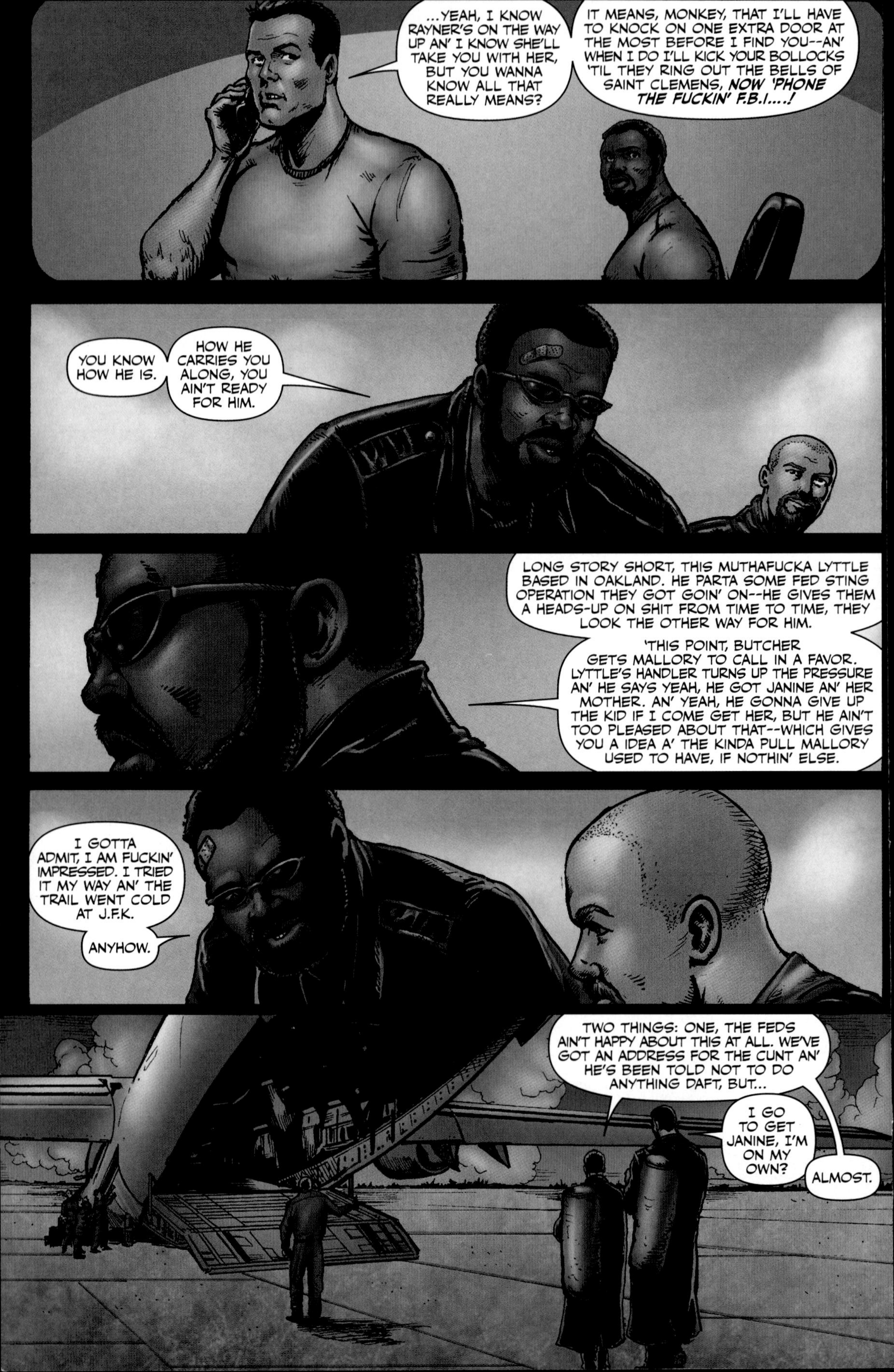
...YEAH, I KNOW RAYNER'S ON THE WAY UP AN' I KNOW SHE'LL TAKE YOU WITH HER, BUT YOU WANNA KNOW ALL THAT REALLY MEANS?
IT MEANS, MONKEY, THAT I'LL HAVE TO KNOCK ON ONE EXTRA DOOR AT THE MOST BEFORE I FIND YOU--AN' WHEN I DO I'LL KICK YOUR BOLLOCKS 'TIL THEY RING OUT THE BELLS OF SAINT CLEMENS, NOW 'PHONE THE FUCKIN' F.B.I....!
YOU KNOW HOW HE IS.
HOW HE CARRIES YOU ALONG, YOU AIN'T READY FOR HIM.
LONG STORY SHORT, THIS MUTHAFUCKA LYTTLE BASED IN OAKLAND. HE PARTA SOME FED STING OPERATION THEY GOT GOIN' ON--HE GIVES THEM A HEADS-UP ON SHIT FROM TIME TO TIME, THEY LOOK THE OTHER WAY FOR HIM.
'THIS POINT, BUTCHER GETS MALLORY TO CALL IN A FAVOR. LYTTLE'S HANDLER TURNS UP THE PRESSURE AN' HE SAYS YEAH, HE GOT JANINE AN' HER MOTHER. AN' YEAH, HE GONNA GIVE UP THE KID IF I COME GET HER, BUT HE AIN'T TOO PLEASED ABOUT THAT--WHICH GIVES YOU A IDEA A' THE KINDA PULL MALLORY USED TO HAVE, IF NOTHIN' ELSE.
I GOTTA ADMIT, I AM FUCKIN' IMPRESSED. I TRIED IT MY WAY AN' THE TRAIL WENT COLD AT J.F.K.
ANYHOW.
TWO THINGS: ONE, THE FEDS AIN'T HAPPY ABOUT THIS AT ALL. WE'VE GOT AN ADDRESS FOR THE CUNT AN' HE'S BEEN TOLD NOT TO DO ANYTHING DAFT, BUT...
I GO TO GET JANINE, I'M ON MY OWN?
ALMOST.

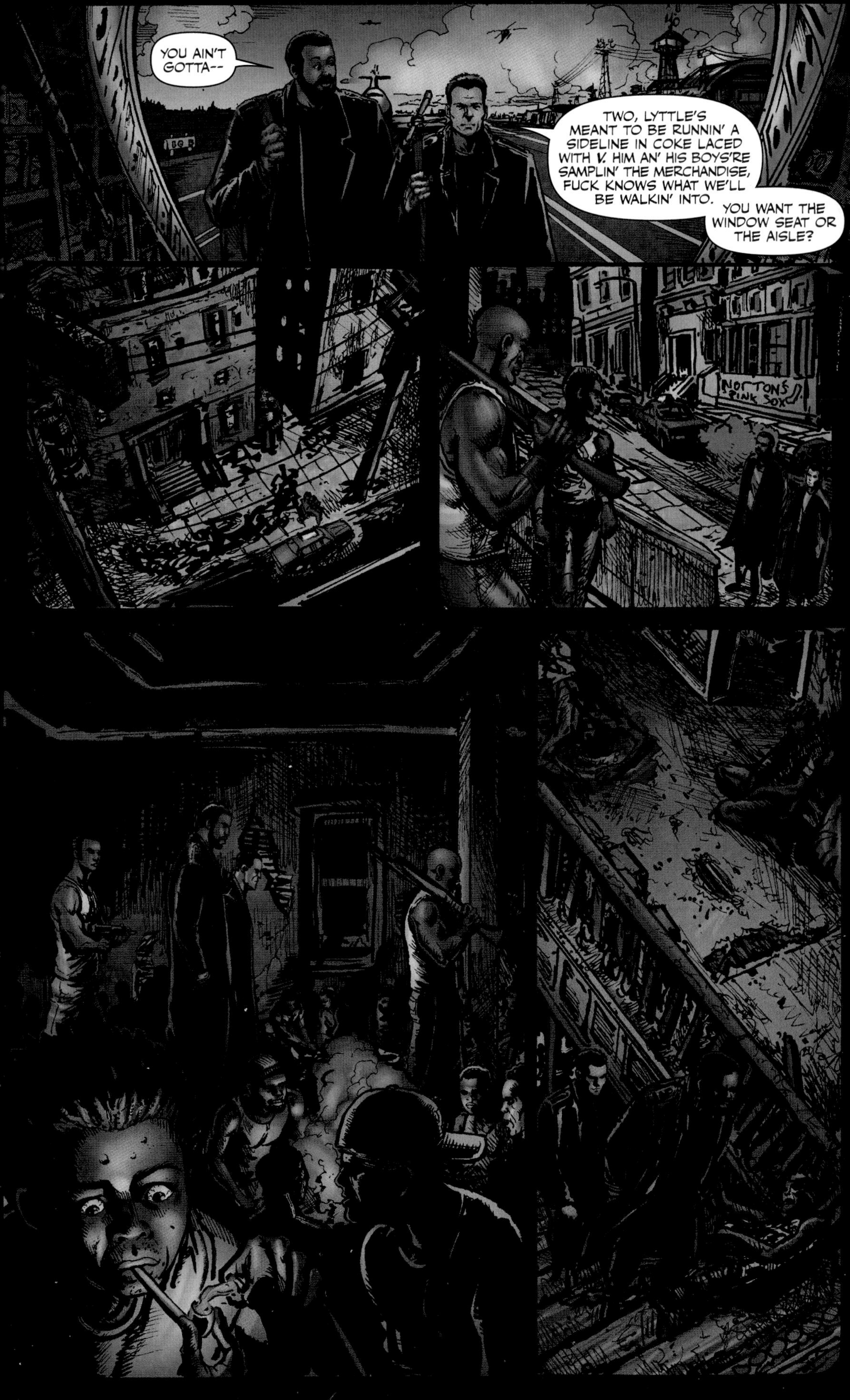
YOU AIN'T GOTTA--
TWO, LYTTLE'S MEANT TO BE RUNNIN' A SIDELINE IN COKE LACED WITH V. HIM AN' HIS BOYS'RE SAMPLIN' THE MERCHANDISE, FUCK KNOWS WHAT WE'LL BE WALKIN' INTO.
YOU WANT THE WINDOW SEAT OR THE AISLE?
NORTON'S PINK SOX

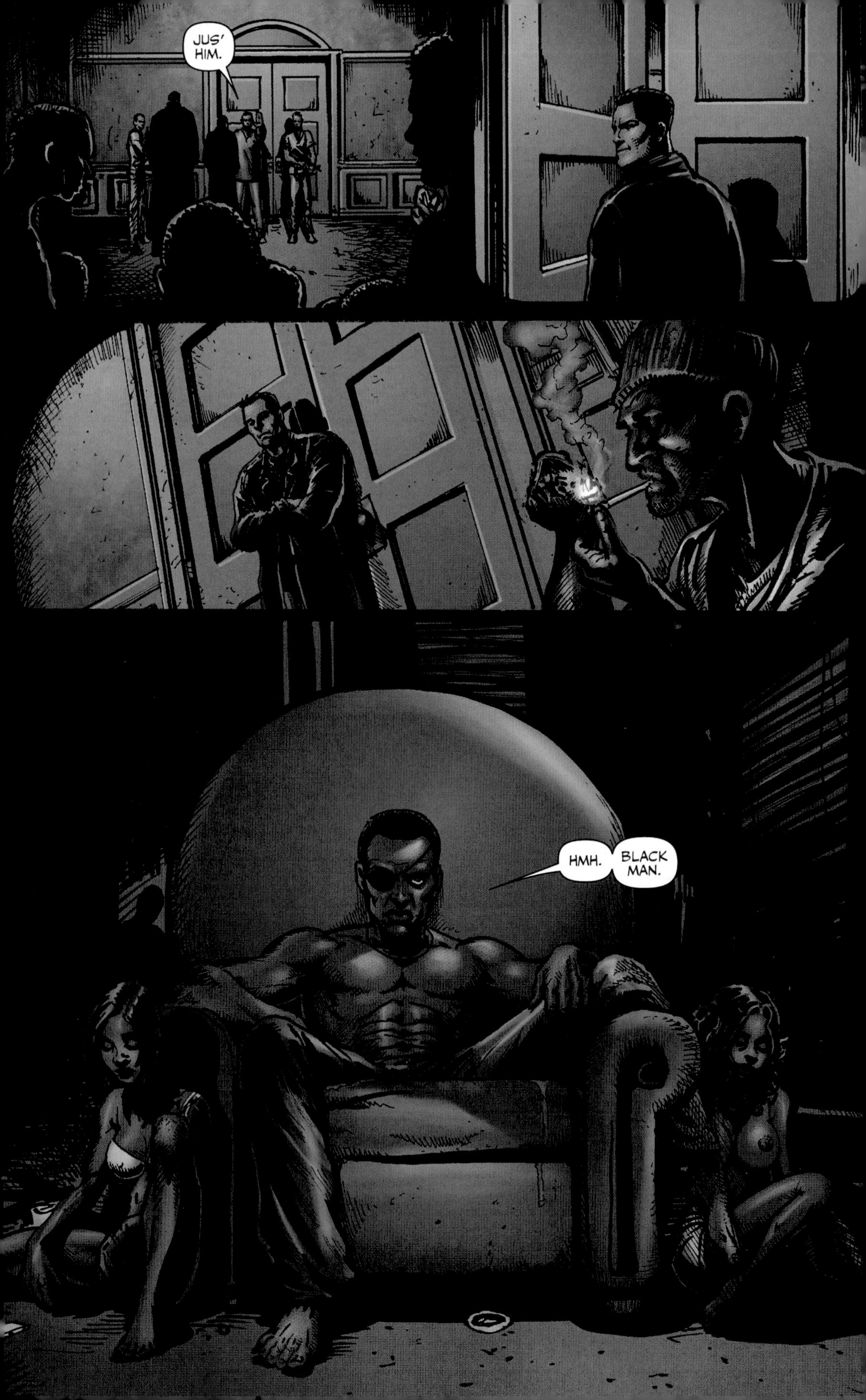
JUS' HIM.
HMH.
BLACK MAN.

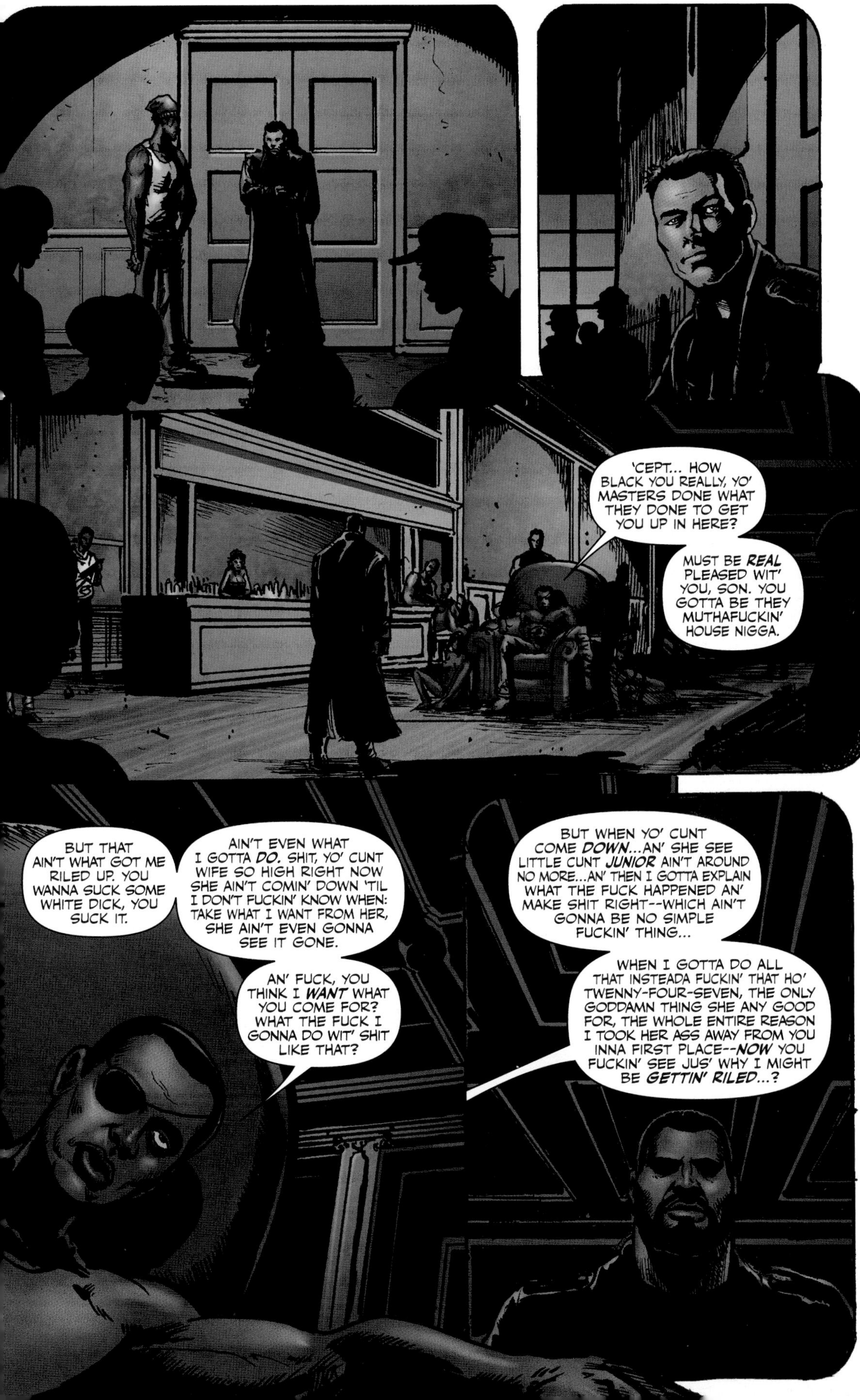
'CEPT... HOW BLACK YOU REALLY, YO' MASTERS DONE WHAT THEY DONE TO GET YOU UP IN HERE?
MUST BE REAL PLEASED WIT' YOU, SON. YOU GOTTA BE THEY MUTHAFUCKIN' HOUSE NIGGA.
BUT THAT AIN'T WHAT GOT ME RILED UP. YOU WANNA SUCK SOME WHITE DICK, YOU SUCK IT.
AIN'T EVEN WHAT I GOTTA DO. SHIT, YO' CUNT WIFE SO HIGH RIGHT NOW SHE AIN'T COMIN' DOWN 'TIL I DON'T FUCKIN' KNOW WHEN: TAKE WHAT I WANT FROM HER, SHE AIN'T EVEN GONNA SEE IT GONE.
AN' FUCK, YOU THINK I WANT WHAT YOU COME FOR? WHAT THE FUCK I GONNA DO WIT' SHIT LIKE THAT?
BUT WHEN YO' CUNT COME DOWN...AN' SHE SEE LITTLE CUNT JUNIOR AIN'T AROUND NO MORE...AN' THEN I GOTTA EXPLAIN WHAT THE FUCK HAPPENED AN' MAKE SHIT RIGHT--WHICH AIN'T GONNA BE NO SIMPLE FUCKIN' THING...
WHEN I GOTTA DO ALL THAT INSTEADA FUCKIN' THAT HO' TWENNY-FOUR-SEVEN, THE ONLY GODDAMN THING SHE ANY GOOD FOR, THE WHOLE ENTIRE REASON I TOOK HER ASS AWAY FROM YOU INNA FIRST PLACE--NOW YOU FUCKIN' SEE JUS' WHY I MIGHT BE GETTIN' RILED...?

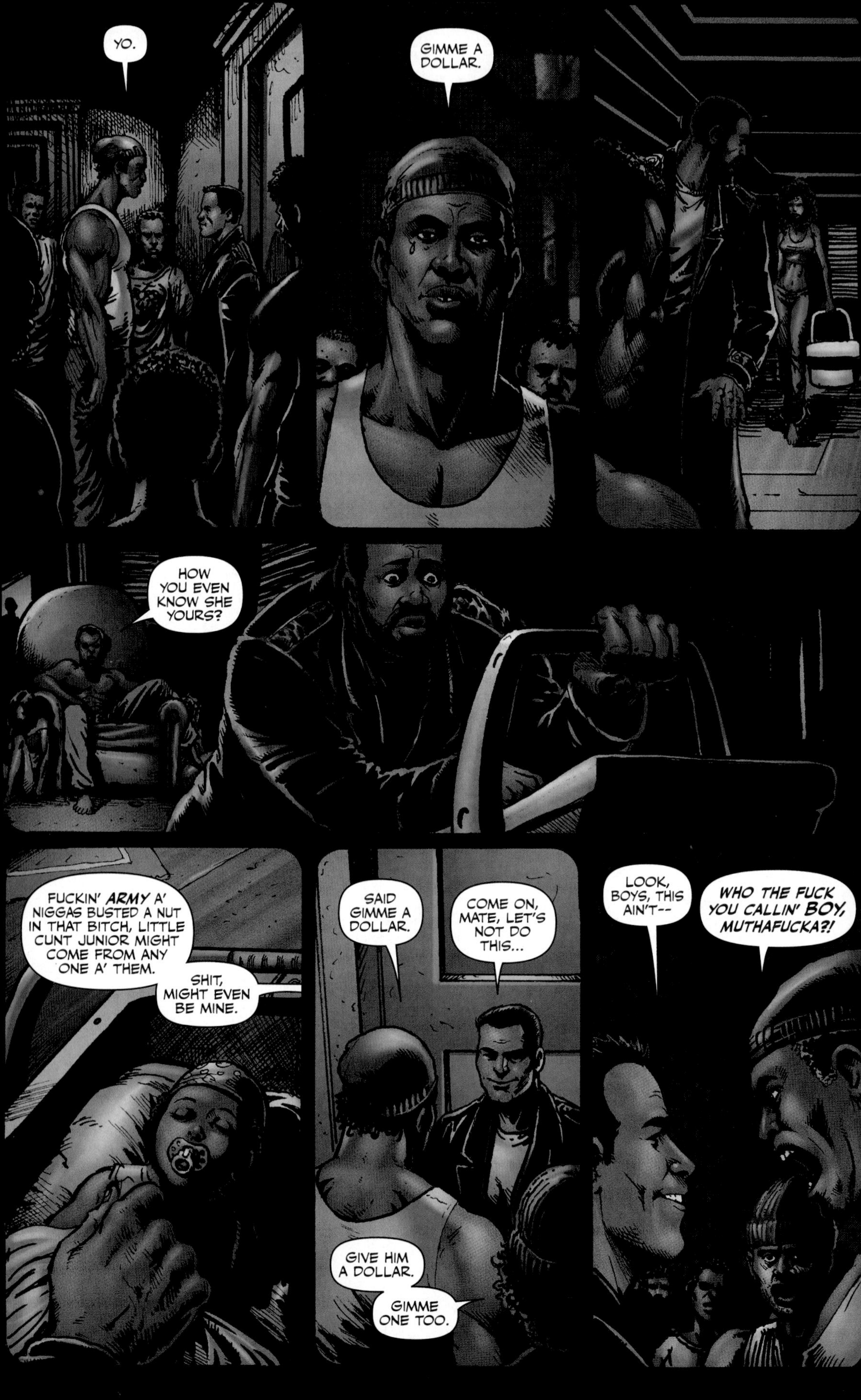
YO.
GIMME A DOLLAR.
HOW YOU EVEN KNOW SHE YOURS?
FUCKIN' ARMY A' NIGGAS BUSTED A NUT IN THAT BITCH, LITTLE CUNT JUNIOR MIGHT COME FROM ANY ONE A' THEM.
SHIT, MIGHT EVEN BE MINE.
SAID GIMME A DOLLAR.
COME ON, MATE, LET'S NOT DO THIS...
GIVE HIM A DOLLAR.
GIMME ONE TOO.
LOOK, BOYS, THIS AIN'T--
WHO THE FUCK YOU CALLIN' BOY, MUTHAFUCKA?!

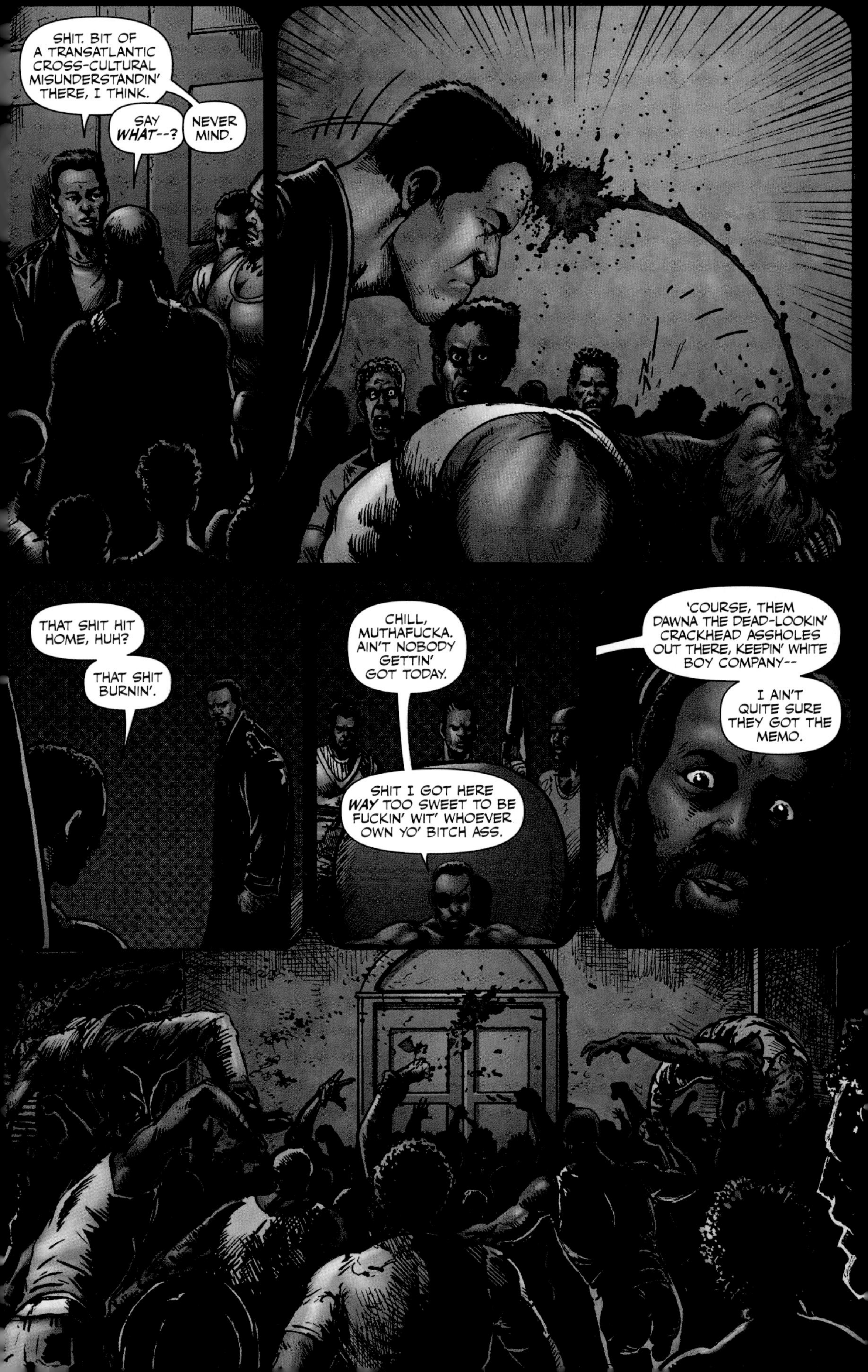
SHIT. BIT OF A TRANSATLANTIC CROSS-CULTURAL MISUNDERSTANDIN' THERE, I THINK.
SAY *WHAT*--?
NEVER MIND.
THAT SHIT HIT HOME, HUH?
THAT SHIT BURNIN'.
CHILL, MUTHAFUCKA. AIN'T NOBODY GETTIN' GOT TODAY.
SHIT I GOT HERE *WAY* TOO SWEET TO BE FUCKIN' WIT' WHOEVER OWN YO' BITCH ASS.
'COURSE, THEM DAWNA THE DEAD-LOOKIN' CRACKHEAD ASSHOLES OUT THERE, KEEPIN' WHITE BOY COMPANY--
I AIN'T QUITE SURE THEY GOT THE MEMO.

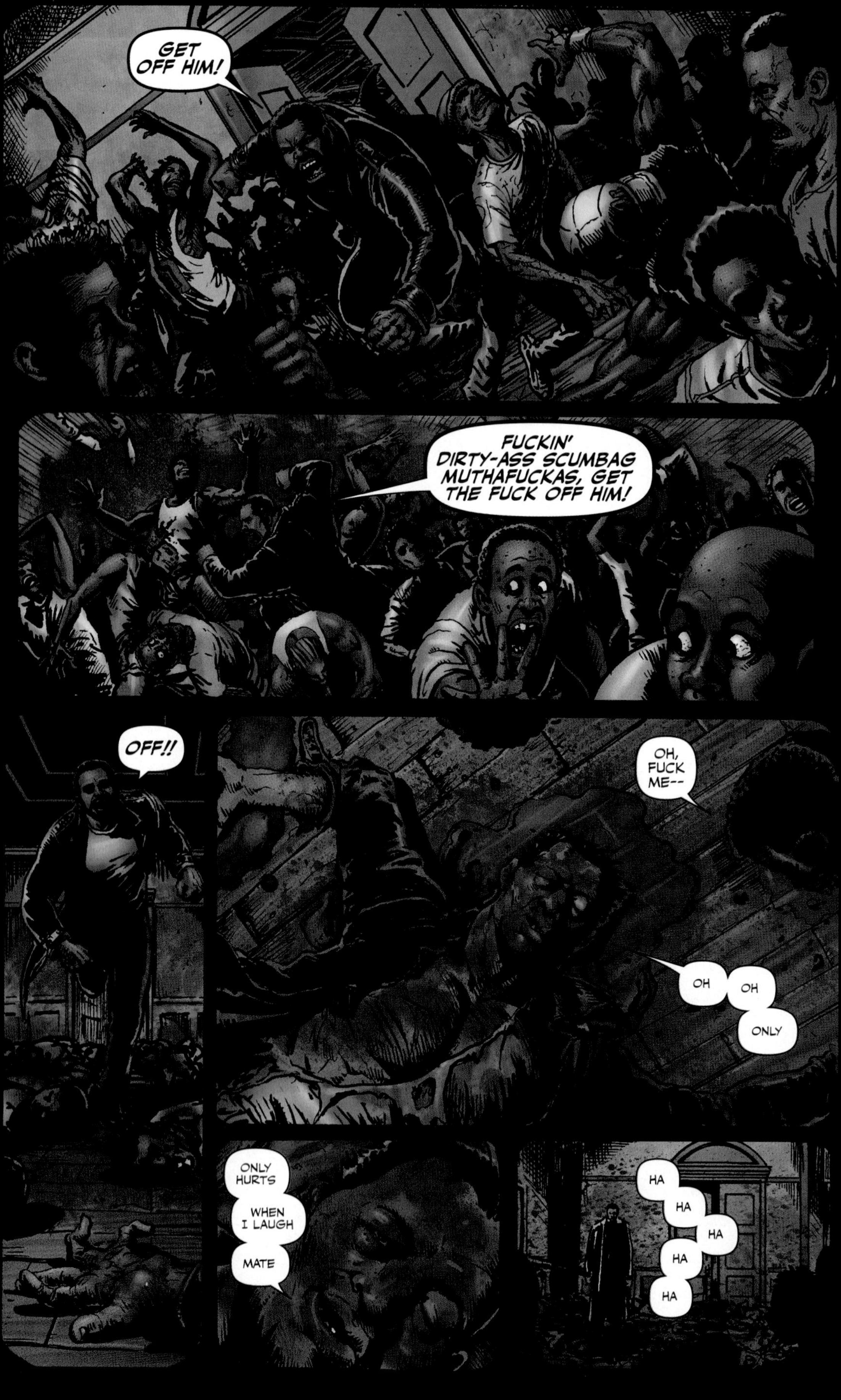
GET OFF HIM!
FUCKIN' DIRTY-ASS SCUMBAG MUTHAFUCKAS, GET THE FUCK OFF HIM!
OFF!!
OH, FUCK ME--
OH
OH
ONLY
ONLY HURTS
WHEN I LAUGH
MATE
HA
HA
HA
HA
HA

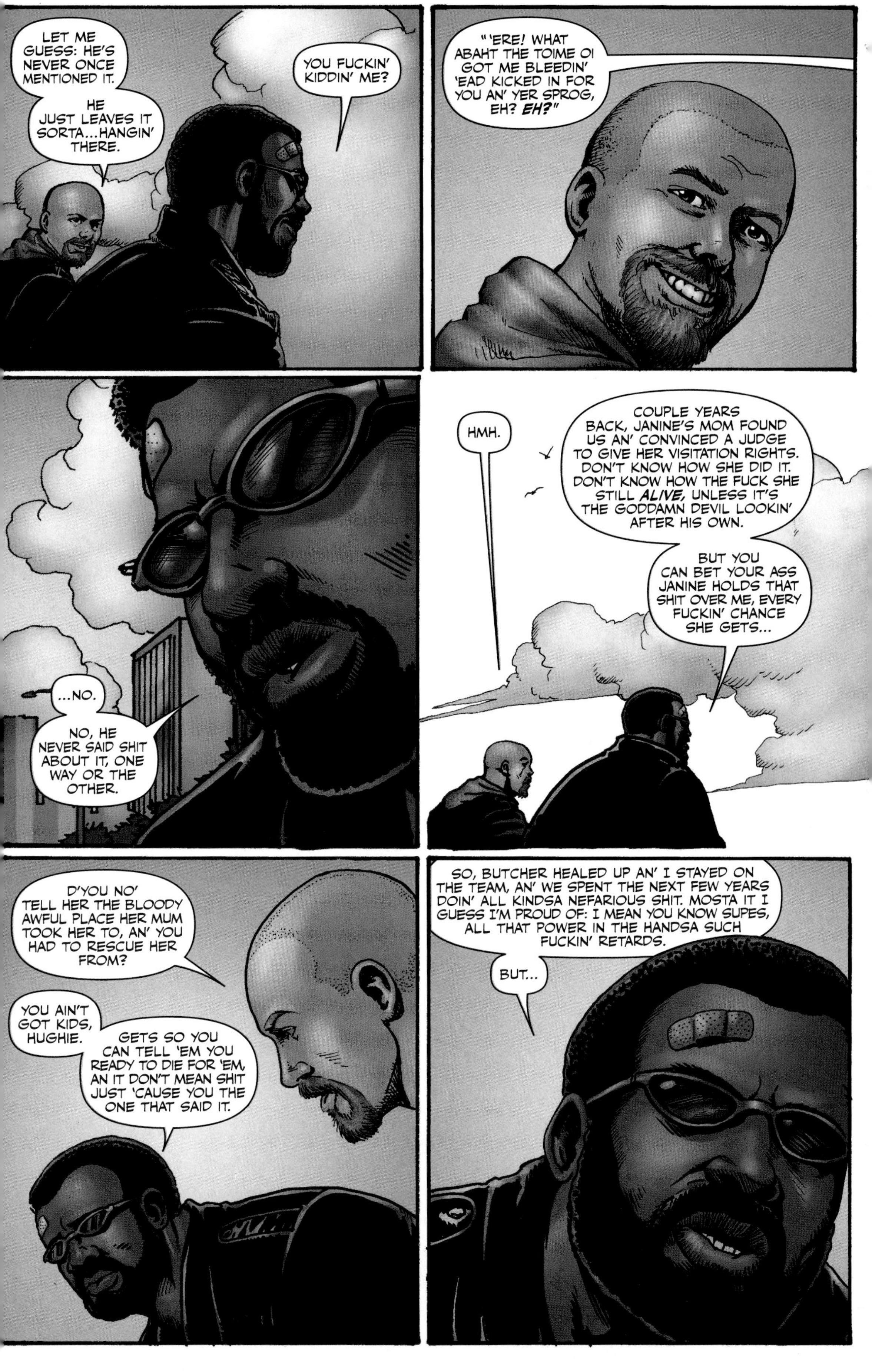
LET ME GUESS: HE'S NEVER ONCE MENTIONED IT.
HE JUST LEAVES IT SORTA...HANGIN' THERE.
YOU FUCKIN' KIDDIN' ME?
"'ERE! WHAT ABAHT THE TOIME OI GOT ME BLEEDIN' 'EAD KICKED IN FOR YOU AN' YER SPROG, EH? EH?"
...NO.
NO, HE NEVER SAID SHIT ABOUT IT, ONE WAY OR THE OTHER.
HMH.
COUPLE YEARS BACK, JANINE'S MOM FOUND US AN' CONVINCED A JUDGE TO GIVE HER VISITATION RIGHTS. DON'T KNOW HOW SHE DID IT. DON'T KNOW HOW THE FUCK SHE STILL ALIVE, UNLESS IT'S THE GODDAMN DEVIL LOOKIN' AFTER HIS OWN.
BUT YOU CAN BET YOUR ASS JANINE HOLDS THAT SHIT OVER ME, EVERY FUCKIN' CHANCE SHE GETS...
D'YOU NO' TELL HER THE BLOODY AWFUL PLACE HER MUM TOOK HER TO, AN' YOU HAD TO RESCUE HER FROM?
YOU AIN'T GOT KIDS, HUGHIE.
GETS SO YOU CAN TELL 'EM YOU READY TO DIE FOR 'EM, AN IT DON'T MEAN SHIT JUST 'CAUSE YOU THE ONE THAT SAID IT.
SO, BUTCHER HEALED UP AN' I STAYED ON THE TEAM, AN' WE SPENT THE NEXT FEW YEARS DOIN' ALL KINDSA NEFARIOUS SHIT. MOSTA IT I GUESS I'M PROUD OF: I MEAN YOU KNOW SUPES, ALL THAT POWER IN THE HANDSA SUCH FUCKIN' RETARDS.
BUT...

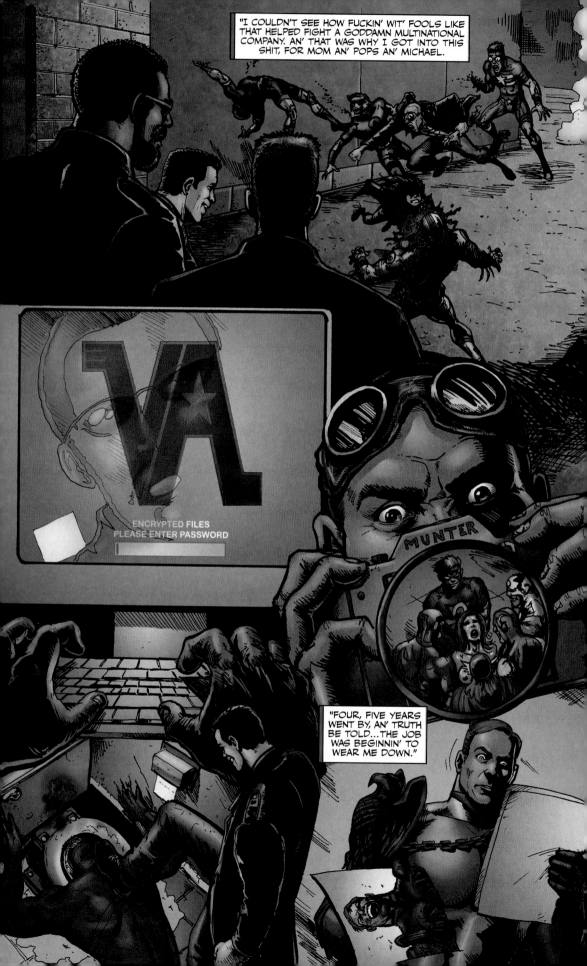

"I COULDN'T SEE HOW FUCKIN' WIT' FOOLS LIKE THAT HELPED FIGHT A GODDAMN MULTINATIONAL COMPANY. AN' THAT WAS WHY I GOT INTO THIS SHIT, FOR MOM AN' POPS AN' MICHAEL.

ENCRYPTED **FILES**
PLEASE ENTER PASSWORD

MUNTER

"FOUR, FIVE YEARS WENT BY, AN' TRUTH BE TOLD...THE JOB WAS BEGINNIN' TO WEAR ME DOWN."

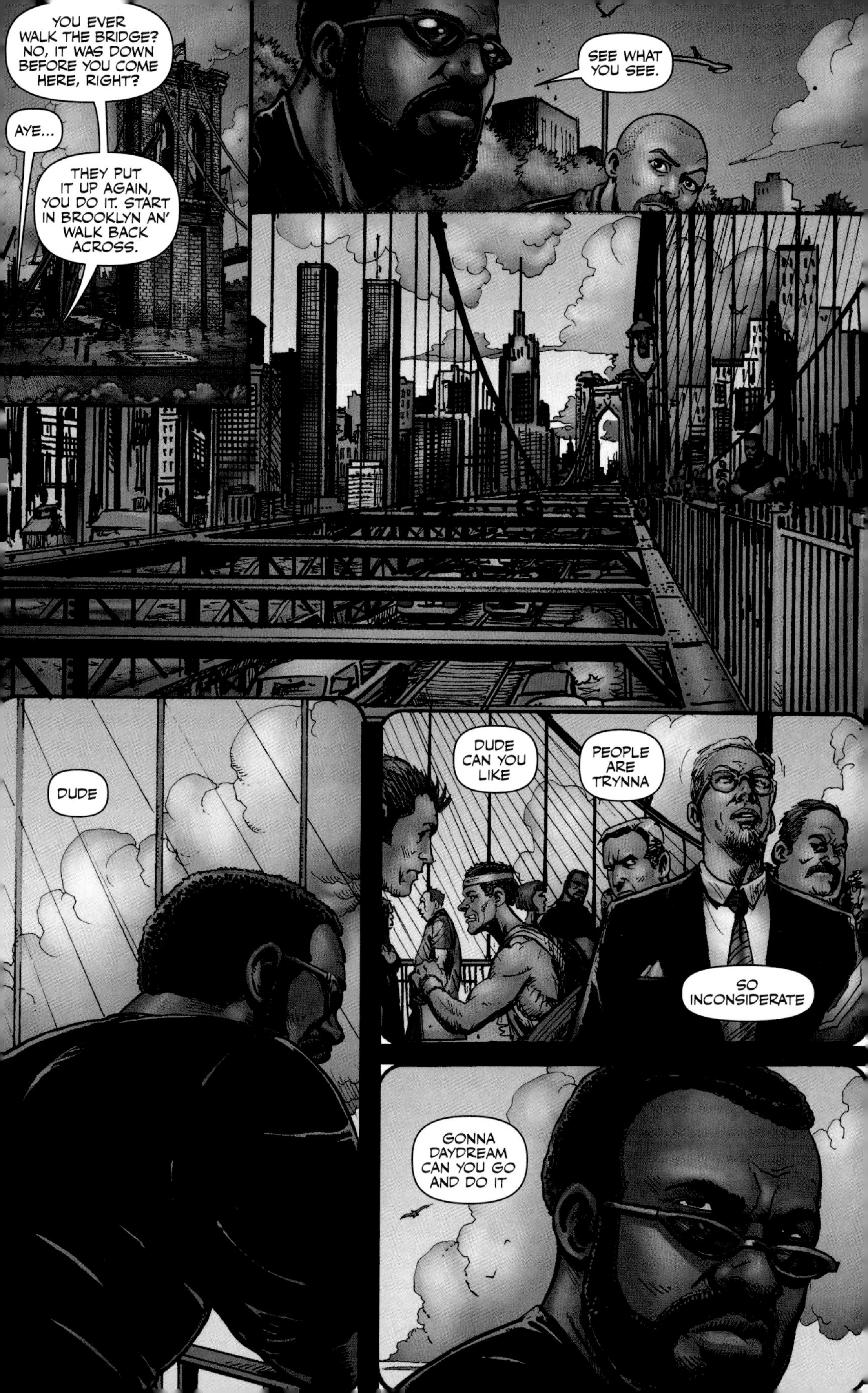
YOU EVER WALK THE BRIDGE? NO, IT WAS DOWN BEFORE YOU COME HERE, RIGHT?
AYE...
SEE WHAT YOU SEE.
THEY PUT IT UP AGAIN, YOU DO IT. START IN BROOKLYN AN' WALK BACK ACROSS.
DUDE
DUDE CAN YOU LIKE
PEOPLE ARE TRYNNA
SO INCONSIDERATE
GONNA DAYDREAM CAN YOU GO AND DO IT

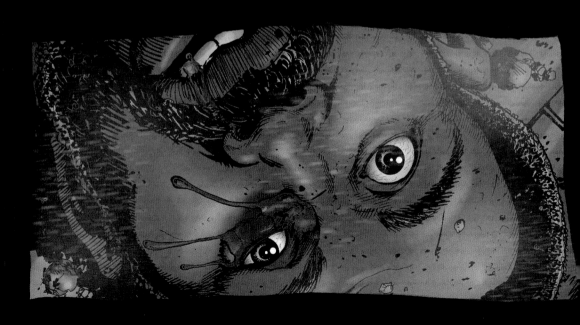

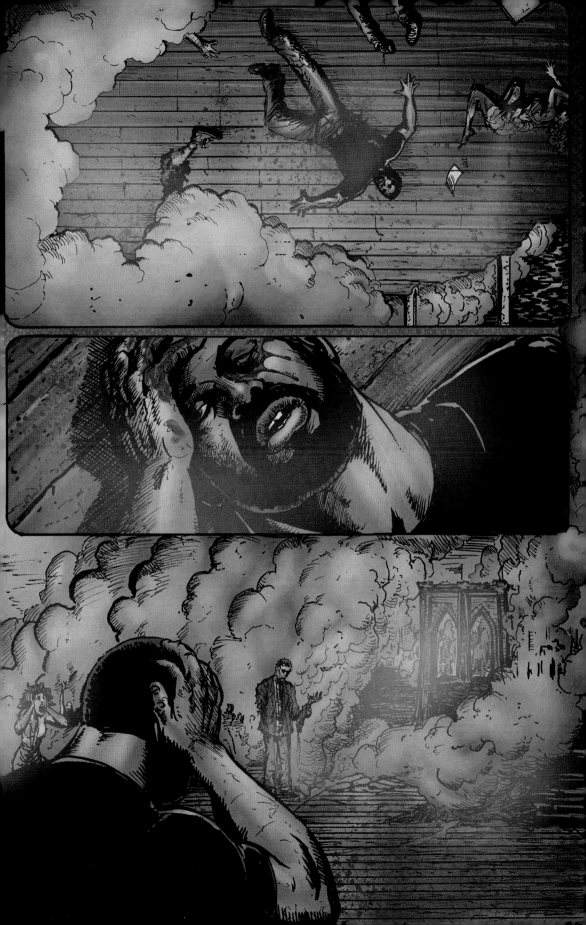

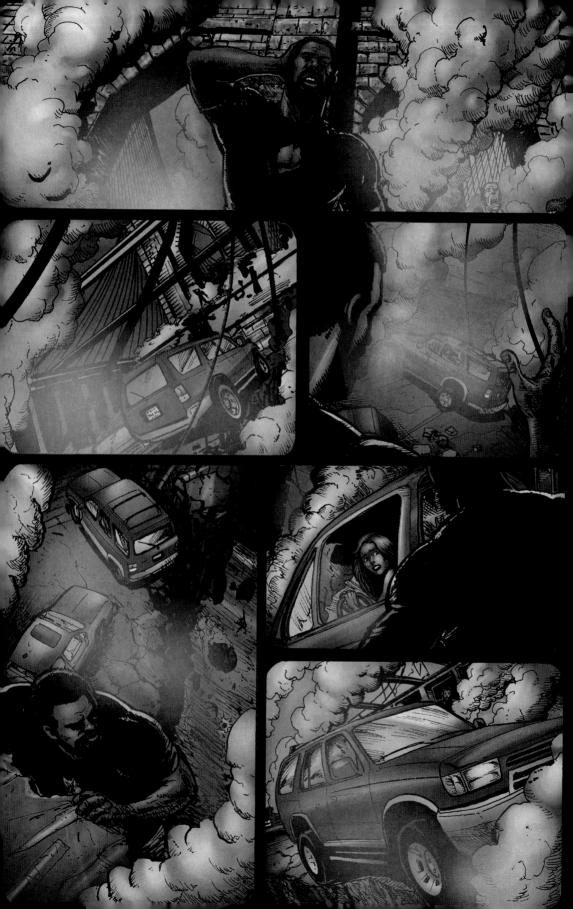

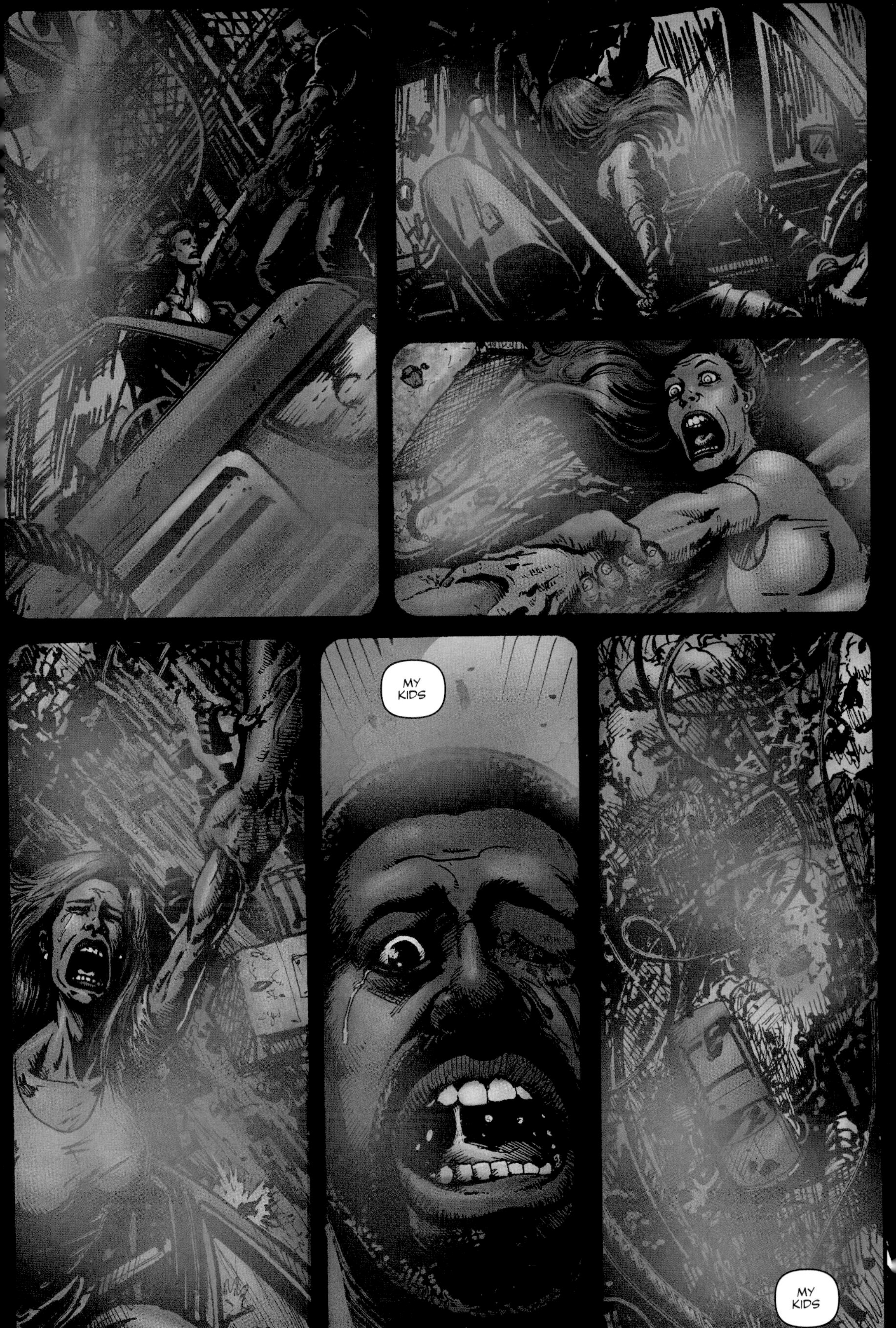
MY KIDS
MY KIDS

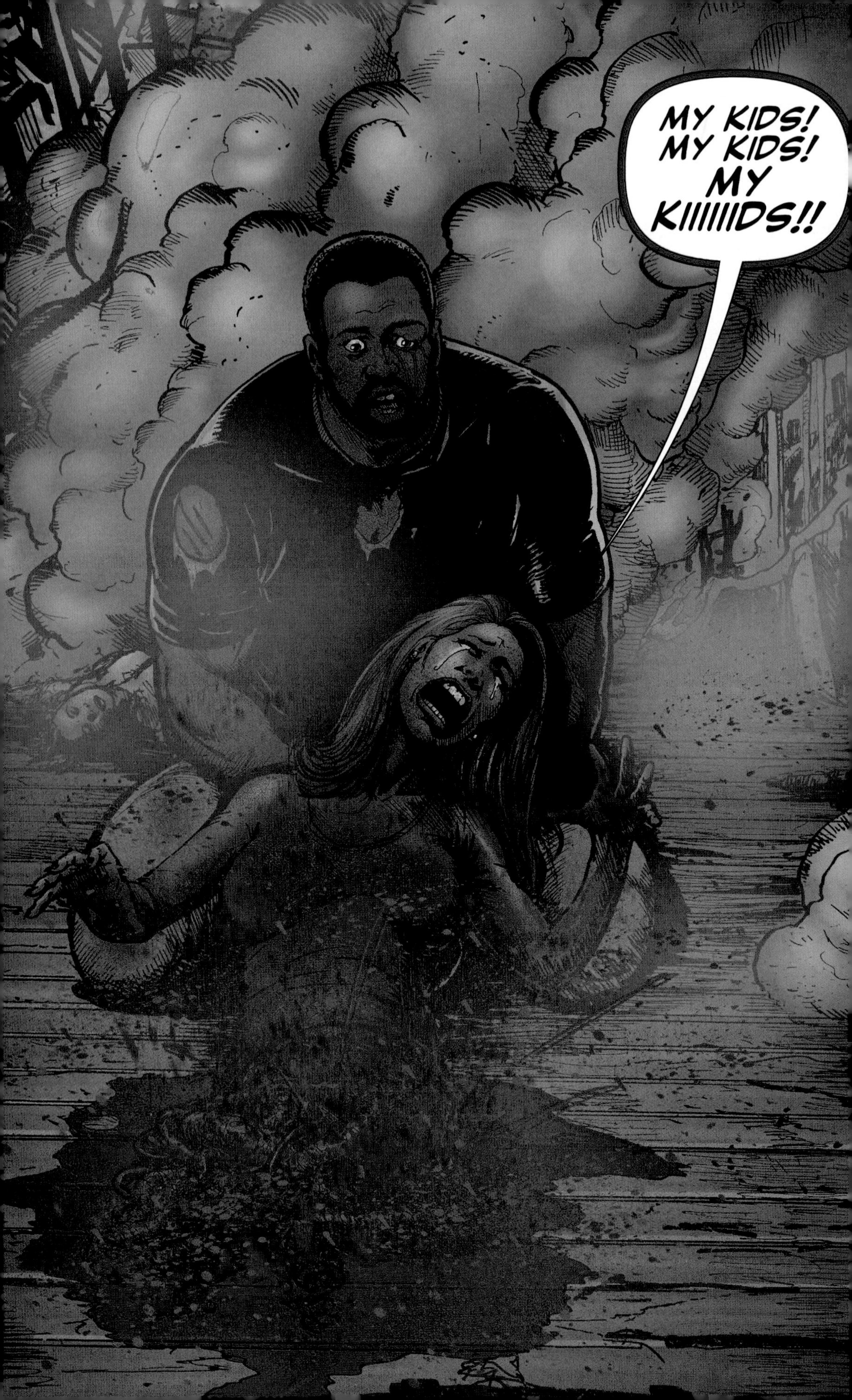
MY KIDS! MY KIDS! MY KIIIIIIDS!!

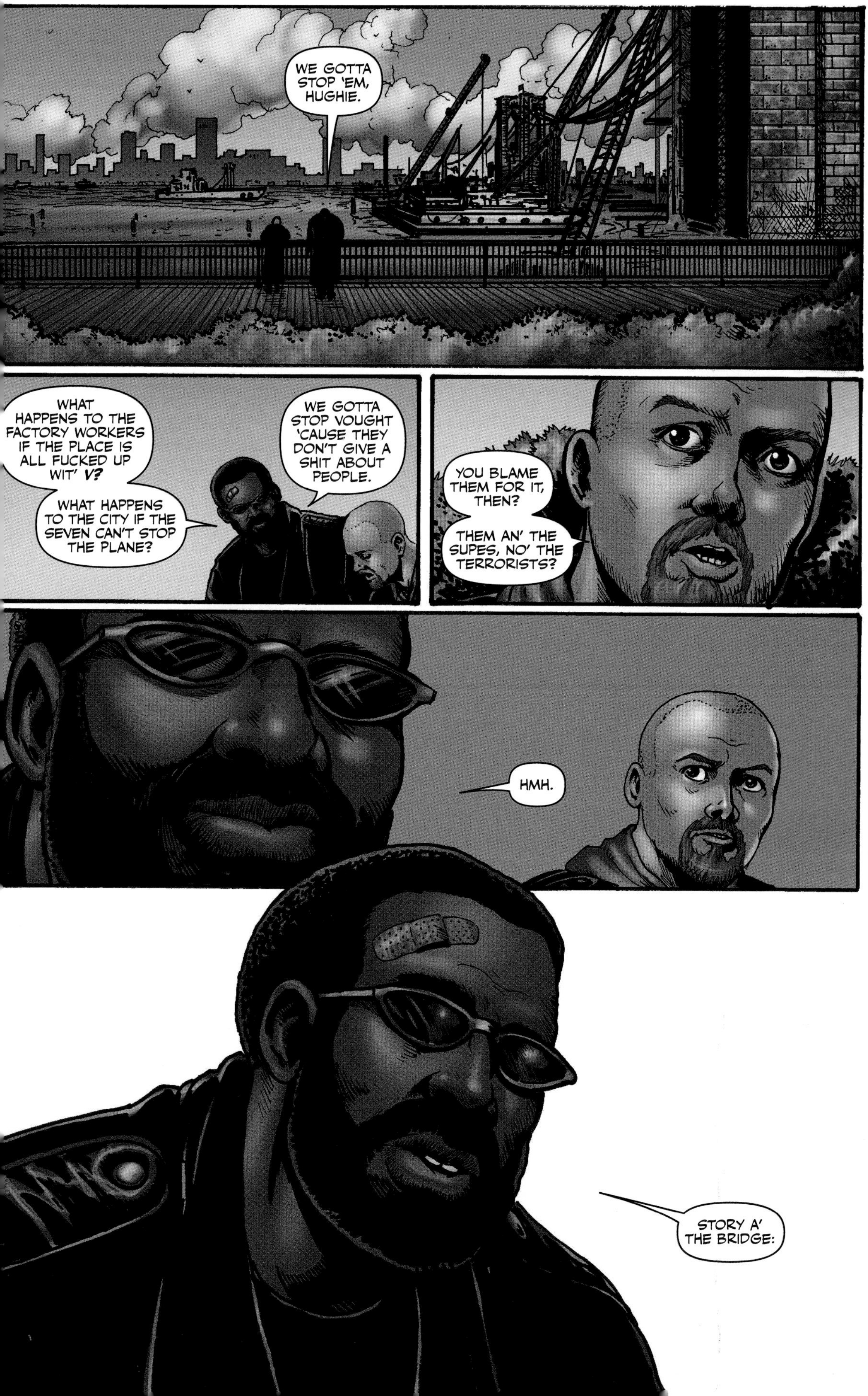
WE GOTTA STOP 'EM, HUGHIE.
WHAT HAPPENS TO THE FACTORY WORKERS IF THE PLACE IS ALL FUCKED UP WIT' *V?*
WHAT HAPPENS TO THE CITY IF THE SEVEN CAN'T STOP THE PLANE?
WE GOTTA STOP VOUGHT 'CAUSE THEY DON'T GIVE A SHIT ABOUT PEOPLE.
YOU BLAME THEM FOR IT, THEN?
THEM AN' THE SUPES, NO' THE TERRORISTS?
HMH.
STORY A' THE BRIDGE:

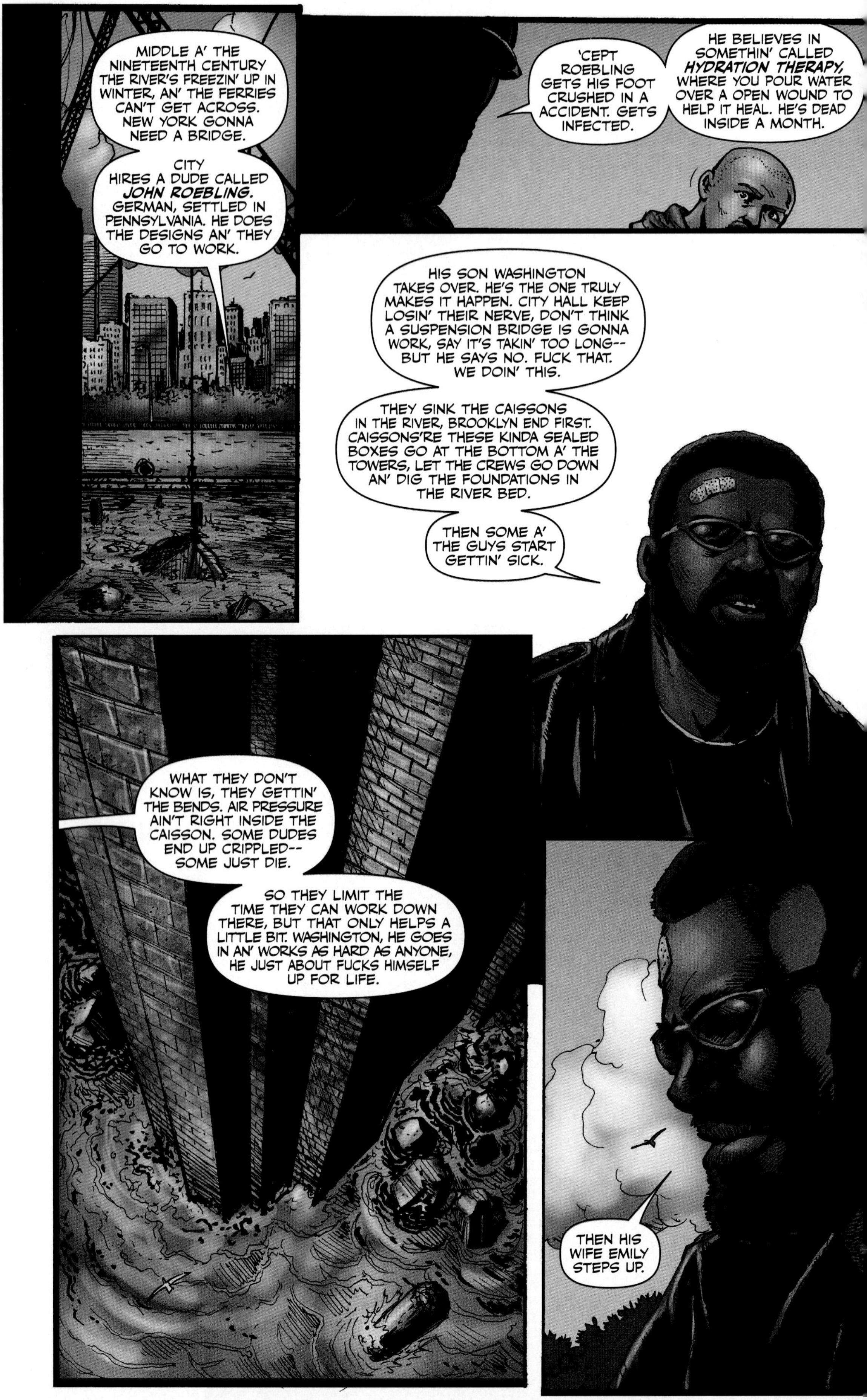
MIDDLE A' THE NINETEENTH CENTURY THE RIVER'S FREEZIN' UP IN WINTER, AN' THE FERRIES CAN'T GET ACROSS. NEW YORK GONNA NEED A BRIDGE.
CITY HIRES A DUDE CALLED *JOHN ROEBLING.* GERMAN, SETTLED IN PENNSYLVANIA. HE DOES THE DESIGNS AN' THEY GO TO WORK.
'CEPT ROEBLING GETS HIS FOOT CRUSHED IN A ACCIDENT. GETS INFECTED.
HE BELIEVES IN SOMETHIN' CALLED *HYDRATION THERAPY,* WHERE YOU POUR WATER OVER A OPEN WOUND TO HELP IT HEAL. HE'S DEAD INSIDE A MONTH.
HIS SON WASHINGTON TAKES OVER. HE'S THE ONE TRULY MAKES IT HAPPEN. CITY HALL KEEP LOSIN' THEIR NERVE, DON'T THINK A SUSPENSION BRIDGE IS GONNA WORK, SAY IT'S TAKIN' TOO LONG-- BUT HE SAYS NO. FUCK THAT. WE DOIN' THIS.
THEY SINK THE CAISSONS IN THE RIVER, BROOKLYN END FIRST. CAISSONS'RE THESE KINDA SEALED BOXES GO AT THE BOTTOM A' THE TOWERS, LET THE CREWS GO DOWN AN' DIG THE FOUNDATIONS IN THE RIVER BED.
THEN SOME A' THE GUYS START GETTIN' SICK.
WHAT THEY DON'T KNOW IS, THEY GETTIN' THE BENDS. AIR PRESSURE AIN'T RIGHT INSIDE THE CAISSON. SOME DUDES END UP CRIPPLED-- SOME JUST DIE.
SO THEY LIMIT THE TIME THEY CAN WORK DOWN THERE, BUT THAT ONLY HELPS A LITTLE BIT. WASHINGTON, HE GOES IN AN' WORKS AS HARD AS ANYONE, HE JUST ABOUT FUCKS HIMSELF UP FOR LIFE.
THEN HIS WIFE EMILY STEPS UP.

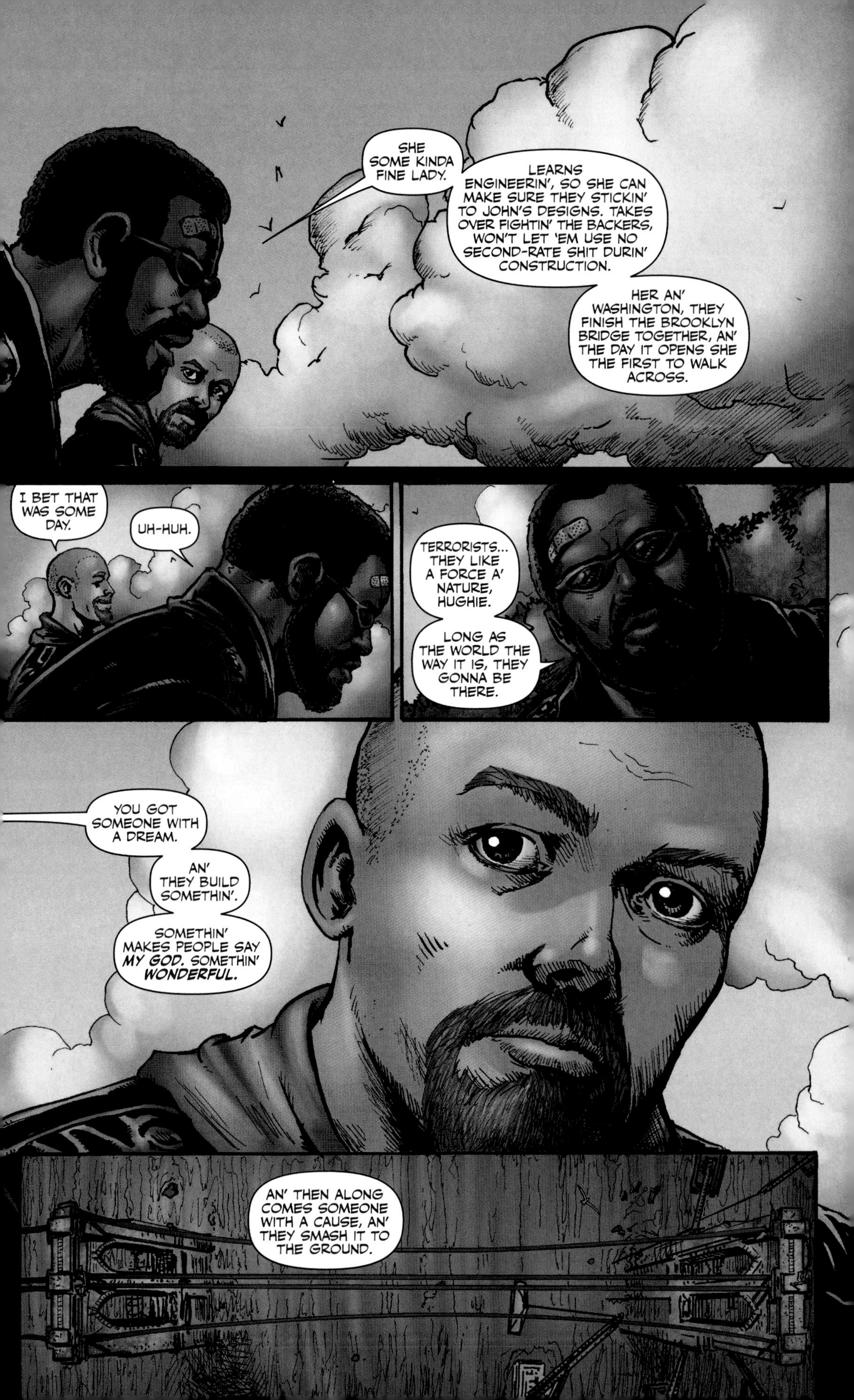
SHE SOME KINDA FINE LADY.
LEARNS ENGINEERIN', SO SHE CAN MAKE SURE THEY STICKIN' TO JOHN'S DESIGNS. TAKES OVER FIGHTIN' THE BACKERS, WON'T LET 'EM USE NO SECOND-RATE SHIT DURIN' CONSTRUCTION.
HER AN' WASHINGTON, THEY FINISH THE BROOKLYN BRIDGE TOGETHER, AN' THE DAY IT OPENS SHE THE FIRST TO WALK ACROSS.
I BET THAT WAS SOME DAY.
UH-HUH.
TERRORISTS... THEY LIKE A FORCE A' NATURE, HUGHIE.
LONG AS THE WORLD THE WAY IT IS, THEY GONNA BE THERE.
YOU GOT SOMEONE WITH A DREAM.
AN' THEY BUILD SOMETHIN'.
SOMETHIN' MAKES PEOPLE SAY *MY GOD*. SOMETHIN' ***WONDERFUL.***
AN' THEN ALONG COMES SOMEONE WITH A CAUSE, AN' THEY SMASH IT TO THE GROUND.

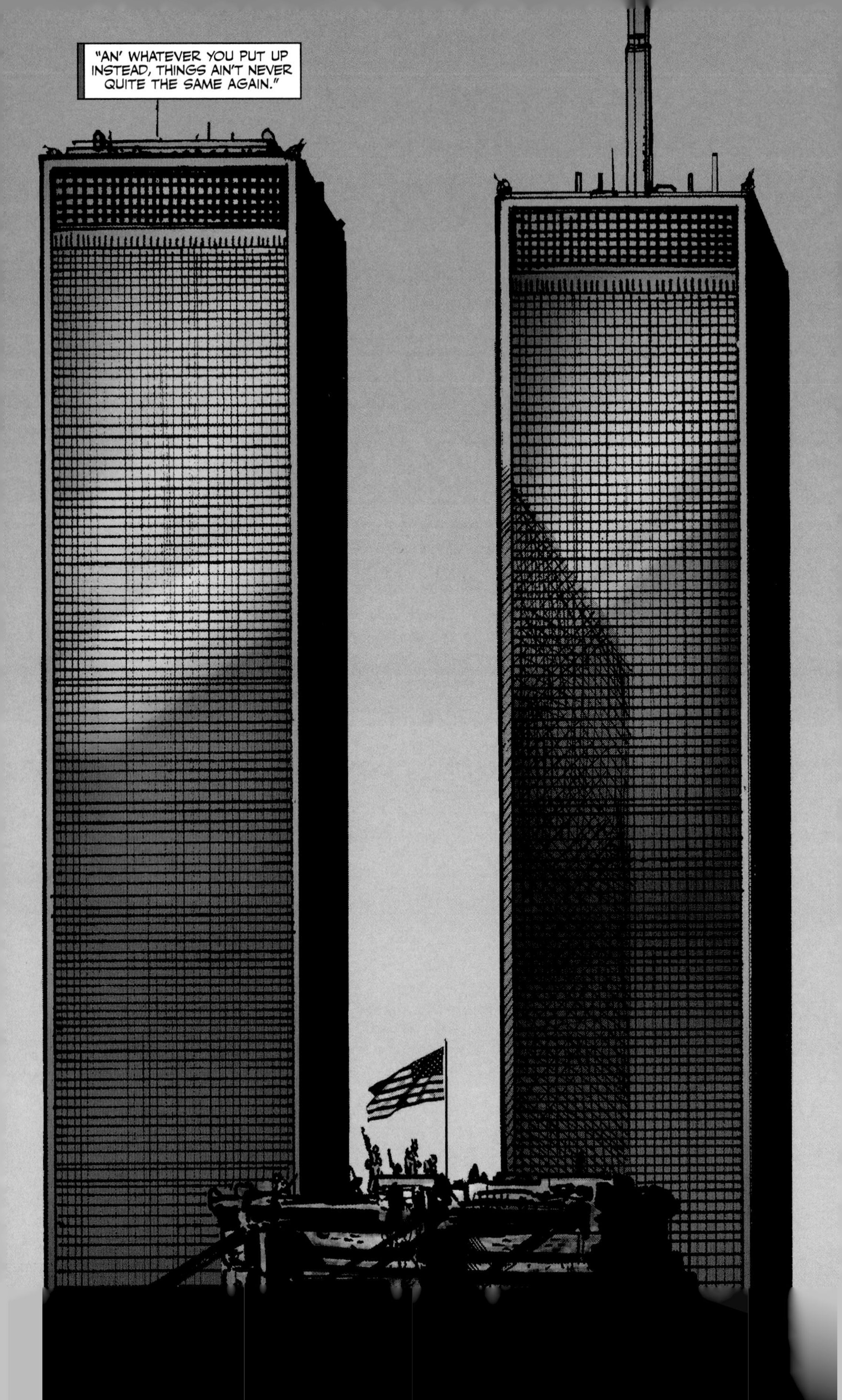
"AN' WHATEVER YOU PUT UP INSTEAD, THINGS AIN'T NEVER QUITE THE SAME AGAIN."

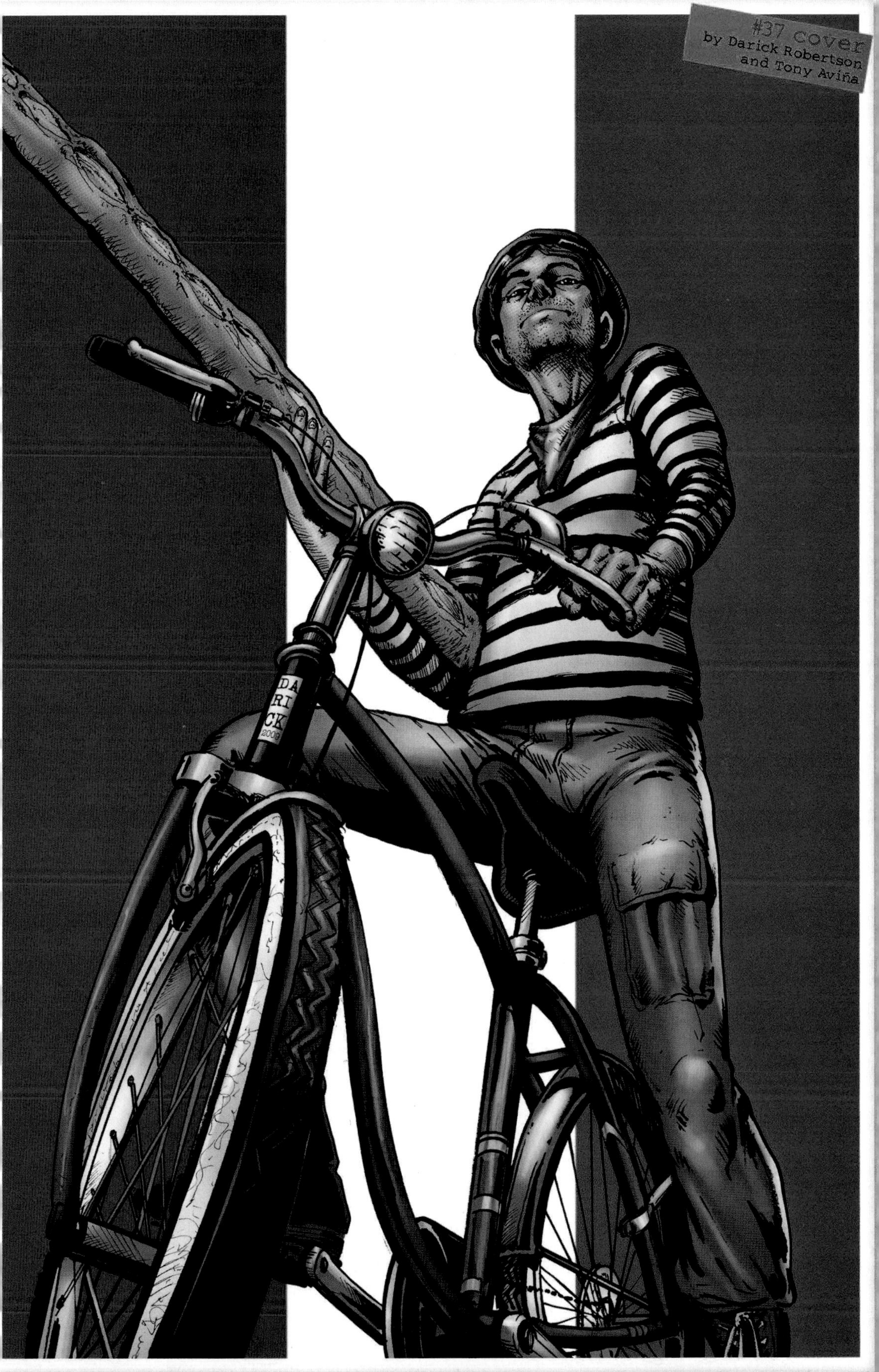
DA
RI
CK
2009

#37 cover
by Darick Robertson
and Tony Aviña

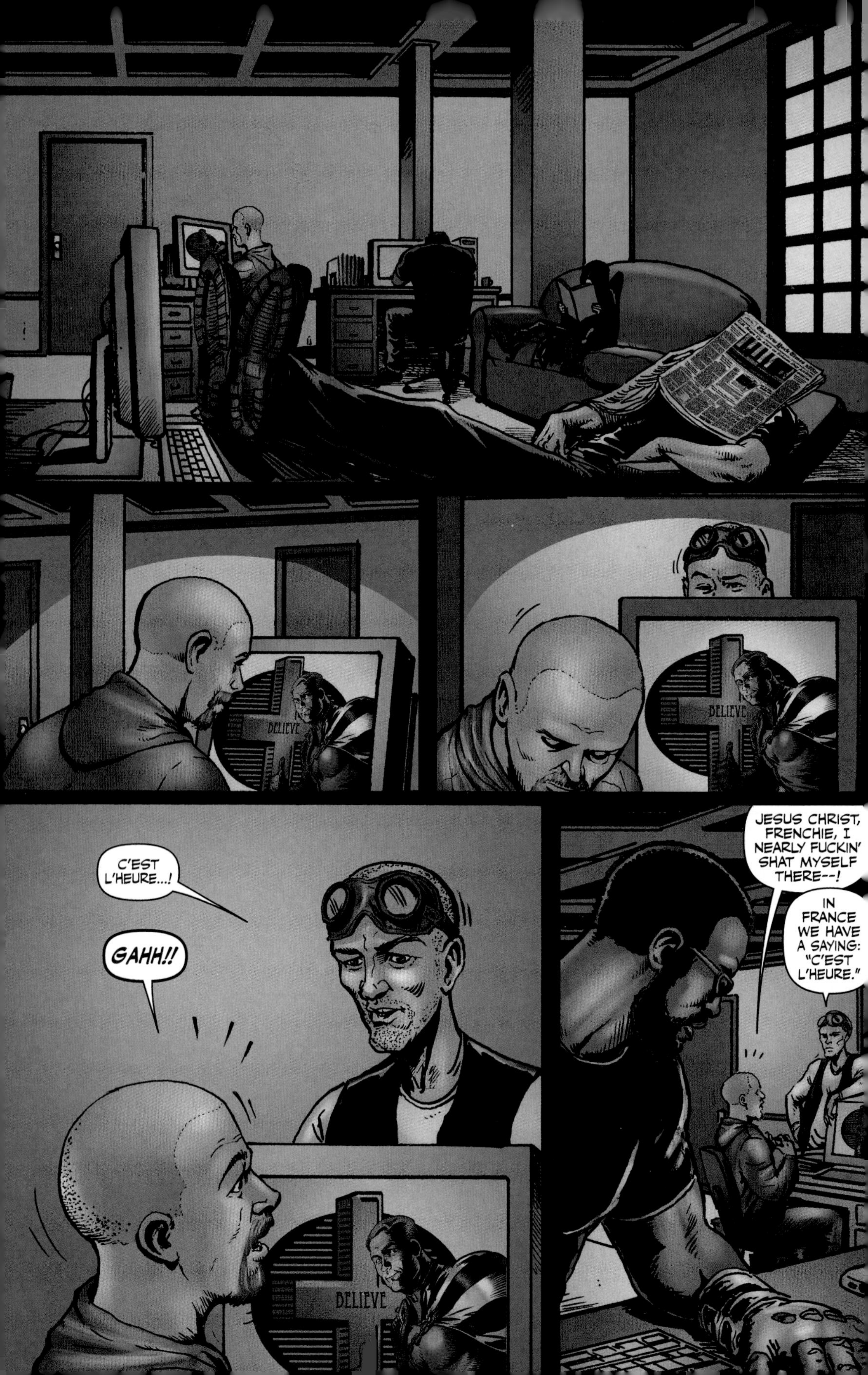
C'EST L'HEURE...!
GAHH!!
JESUS CHRIST, FRENCHIE, I NEARLY FUCKIN' SHAT MYSELF THERE--!
IN FRANCE WE HAVE A SAYING: "C'EST L'HEURE."
BELIEVE

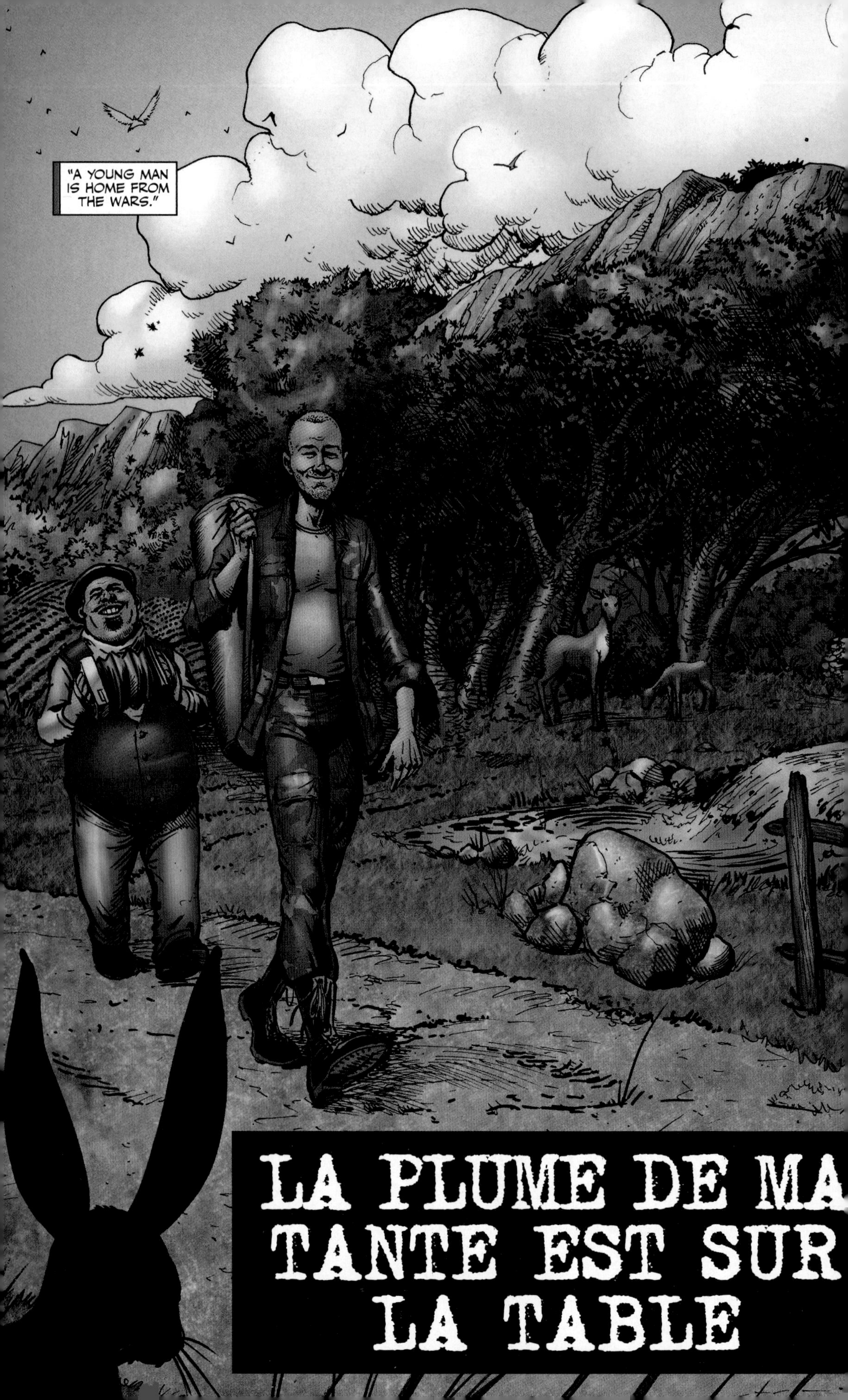
"A YOUNG MAN IS HOME FROM THE WARS."
LA PLUME DE MA TANTE EST SUR LA TABLE

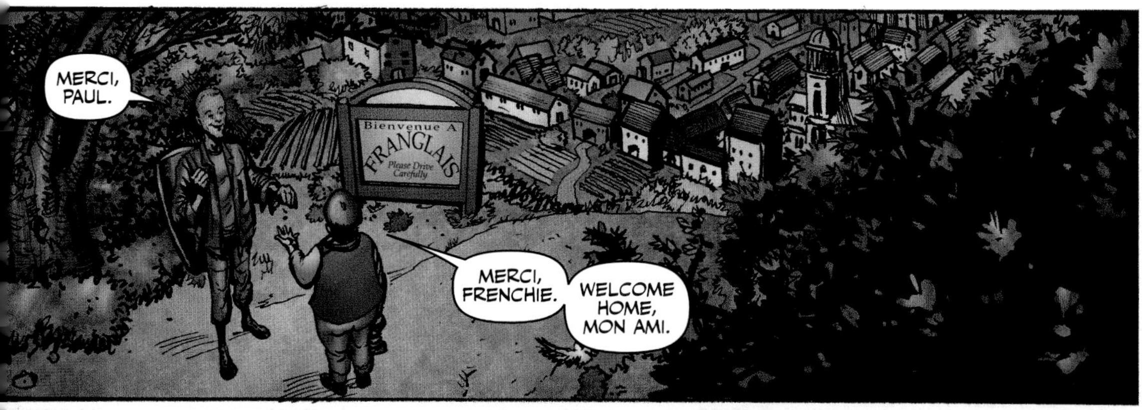
MERCI, PAUL.
Bienvenue A
FRANGLAIS
Please Drive Carefully
MERCI, FRENCHIE.
WELCOME HOME, MON AMI.

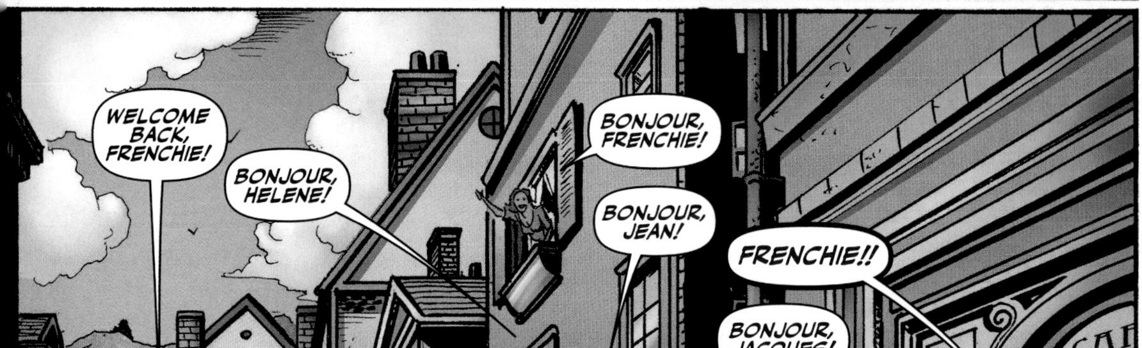
WELCOME BACK, FRENCHIE!
BONJOUR, HELENE!
BONJOUR, FRENCHIE!
BONJOUR, JEAN!
FRENCHIE!!
BONJOUR, JACQUES!
5KI2P7

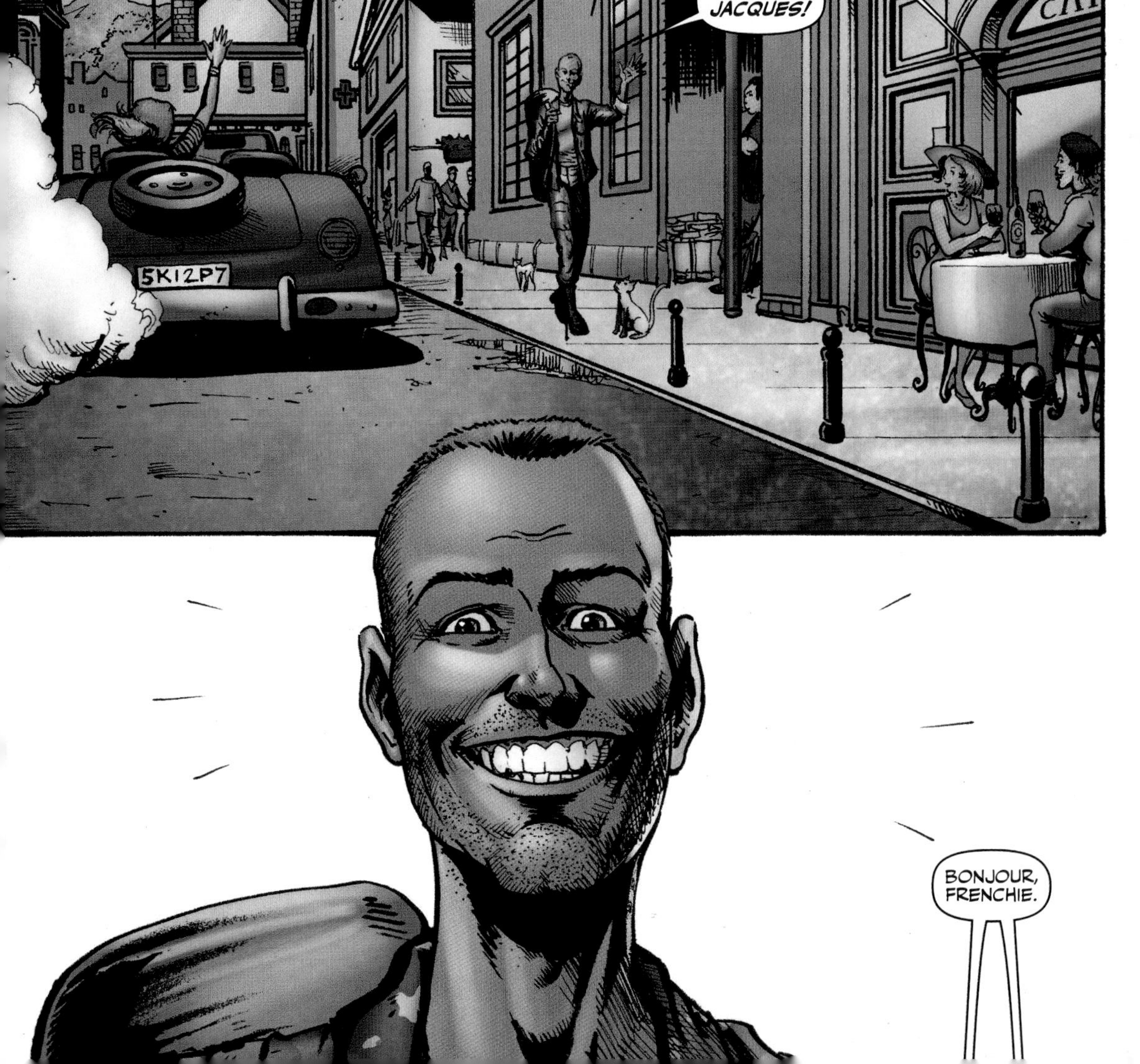
BONJOUR, FRENCHIE.

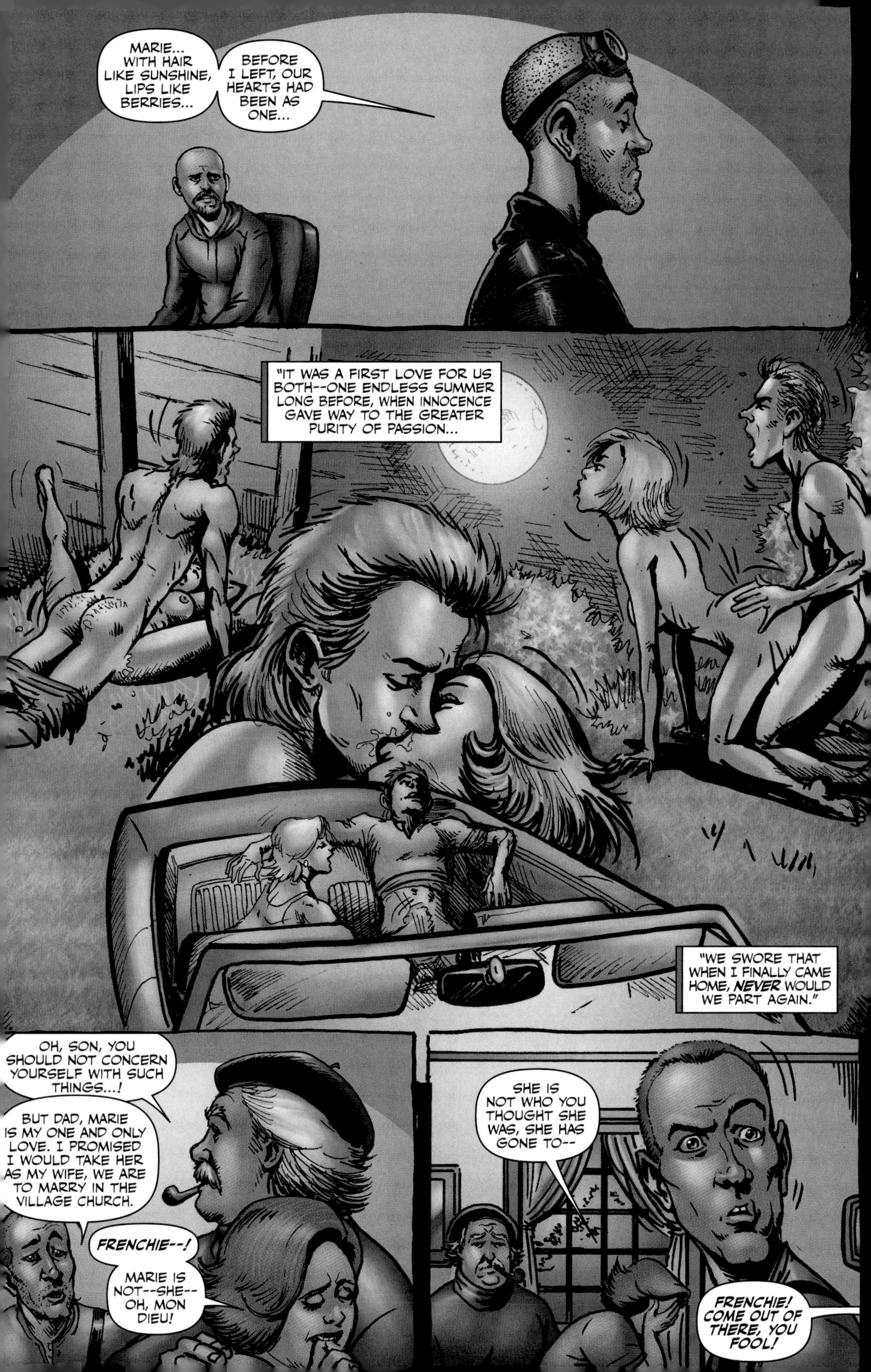
MARIE... WITH HAIR LIKE SUNSHINE, LIPS LIKE BERRIES...
BEFORE I LEFT, OUR HEARTS HAD BEEN AS ONE...
"IT WAS A FIRST LOVE FOR US BOTH--ONE ENDLESS SUMMER LONG BEFORE, WHEN INNOCENCE GAVE WAY TO THE GREATER PURITY OF PASSION...
"WE SWORE THAT WHEN I FINALLY CAME HOME, NEVER WOULD WE PART AGAIN."
OH, SON, YOU SHOULD NOT CONCERN YOURSELF WITH SUCH THINGS...!
BUT DAD, MARIE IS MY ONE AND ONLY LOVE. I PROMISED I WOULD TAKE HER AS MY WIFE, WE ARE TO MARRY IN THE VILLAGE CHURCH.
FRENCHIE--!
MARIE IS NOT--SHE--OH, MON DIEU!
SHE IS NOT WHO YOU THOUGHT SHE WAS, SHE HAS GONE TO--
FRENCHIE! COME OUT OF THERE, YOU FOOL!

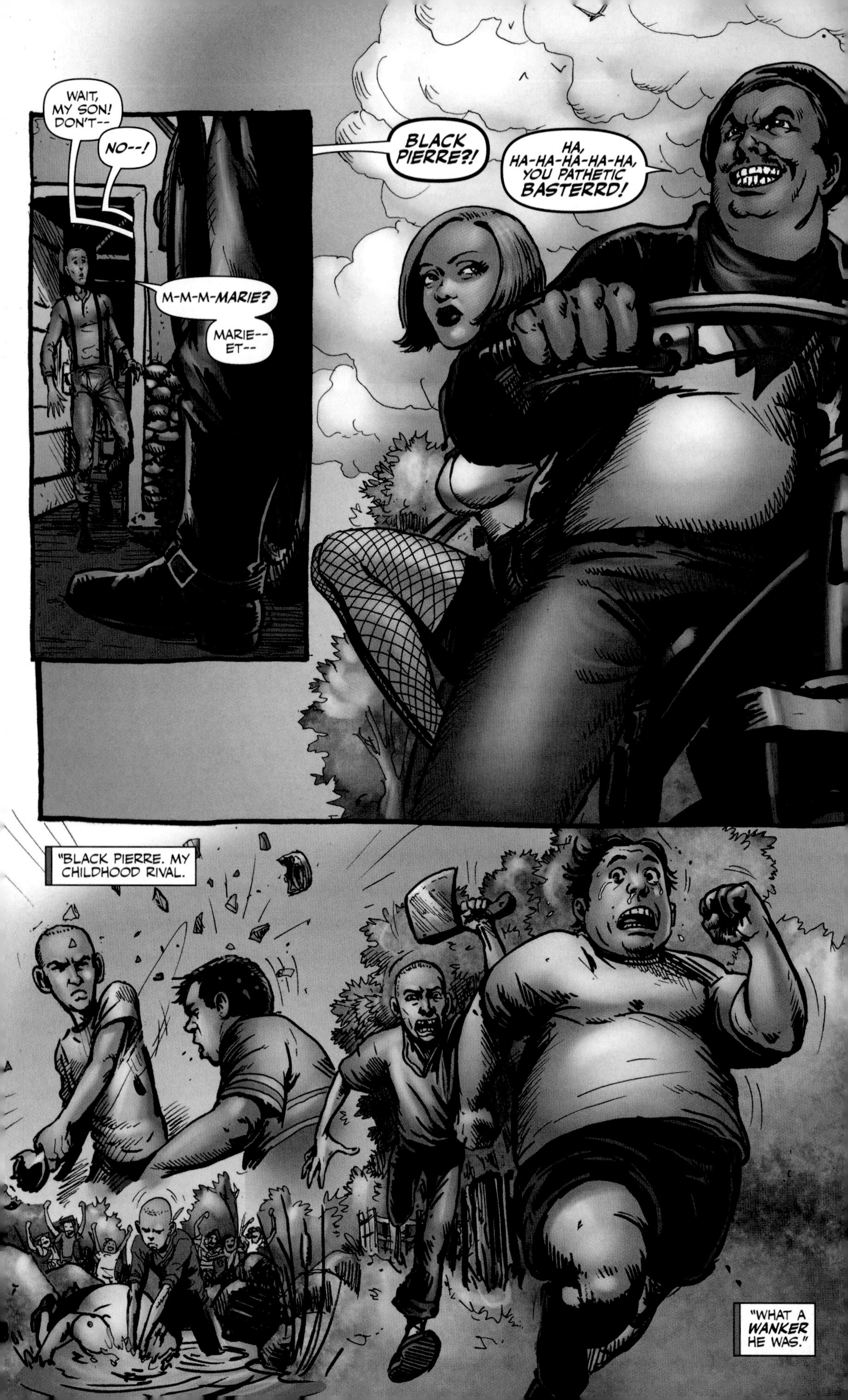
WAIT, MY SON! DON'T--
NO--!
BLACK PIERRE?!
HA, HA-HA-HA-HA-HA, YOU PATHETIC BASTERRD!
M-M-M-MARIE?
MARIE-- ET--
"BLACK PIERRE. MY CHILDHOOD RIVAL.
"WHAT A WANKER HE WAS."

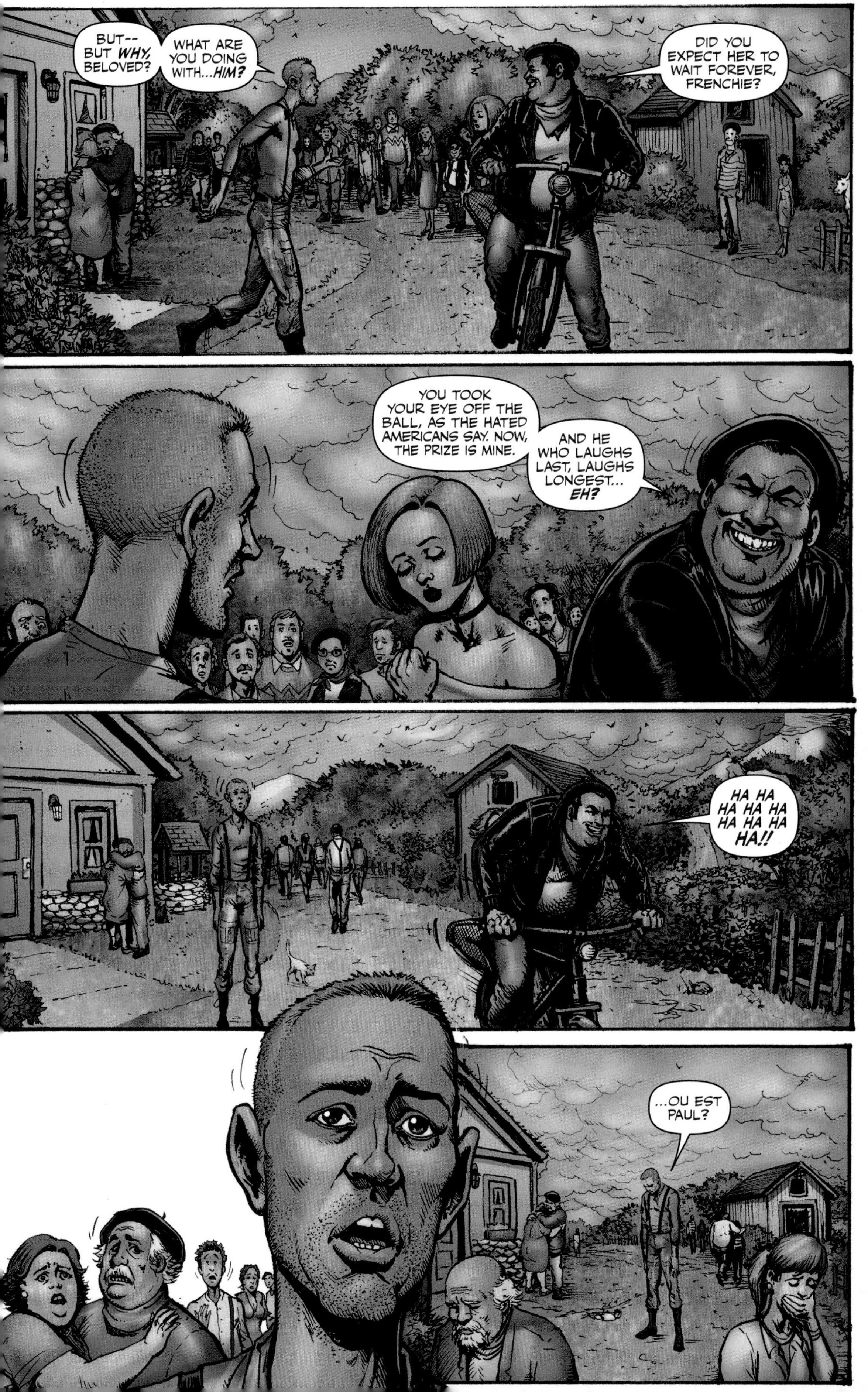
BUT-- BUT WHY, BELOVED?
WHAT ARE YOU DOING WITH...HIM?
DID YOU EXPECT HER TO WAIT FOREVER, FRENCHIE?
YOU TOOK YOUR EYE OFF THE BALL, AS THE HATED AMERICANS SAY. NOW, THE PRIZE IS MINE.
AND HE WHO LAUGHS LAST, LAUGHS LONGEST... EH?
HA HA HA HA HA HA HA HA HA!!
...OU EST PAUL?

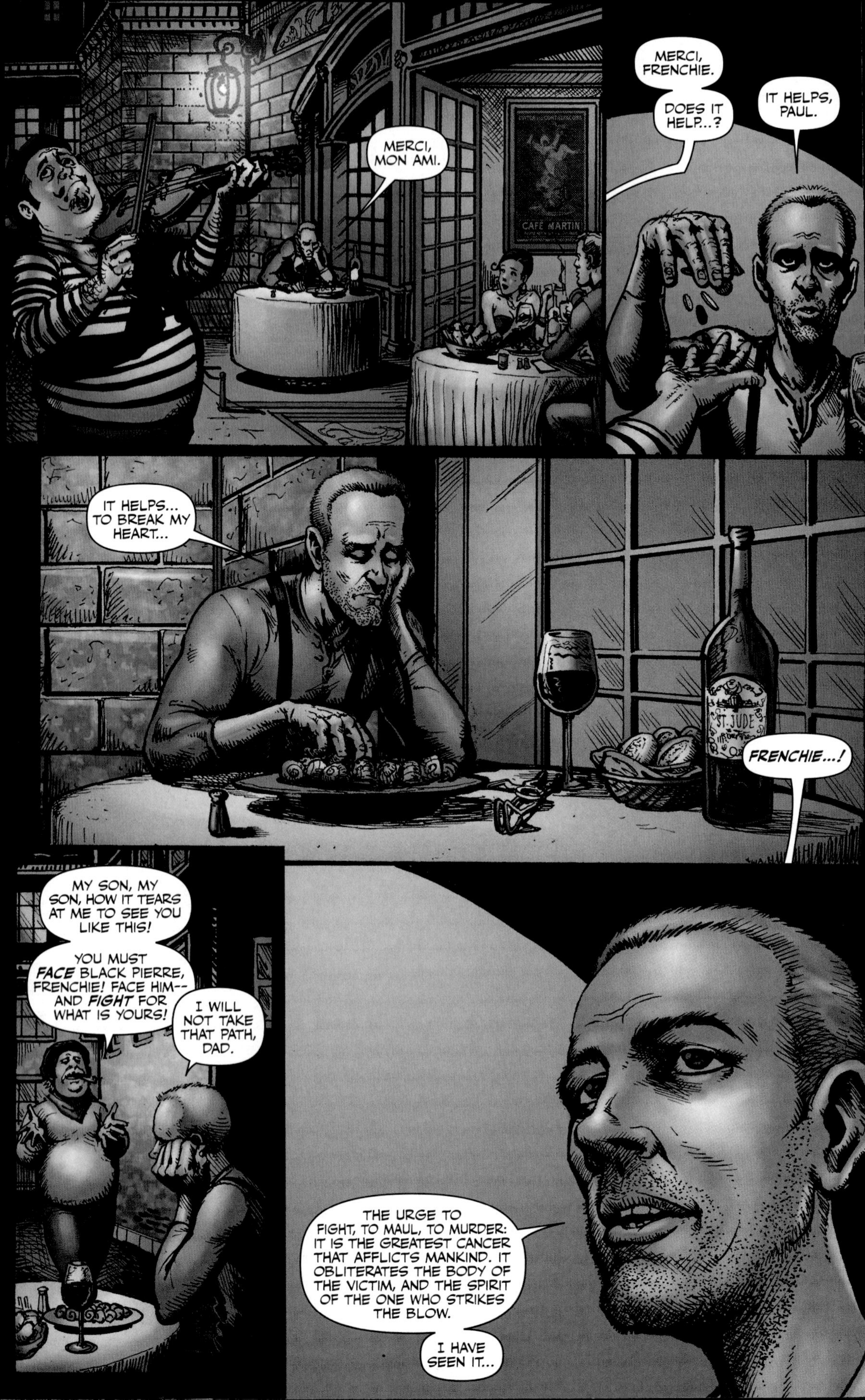
CAFÉ MARTIN
MERCI, MON AMI.
MERCI, FRENCHIE.
DOES IT HELP...?
IT HELPS, PAUL.
IT HELPS... TO BREAK MY HEART...
ST. JUDE
FRENCHIE...!
MY SON, MY SON, HOW IT TEARS AT ME TO SEE YOU LIKE THIS!
YOU MUST FACE BLACK PIERRE, FRENCHIE! FACE HIM-- AND FIGHT FOR WHAT IS YOURS!
I WILL NOT TAKE THAT PATH, DAD.
THE URGE TO FIGHT, TO MAUL, TO MURDER: IT IS THE GREATEST CANCER THAT AFFLICTS MANKIND. IT OBLITERATES THE BODY OF THE VICTIM, AND THE SPIRIT OF THE ONE WHO STRIKES THE BLOW.
I HAVE SEEN IT...

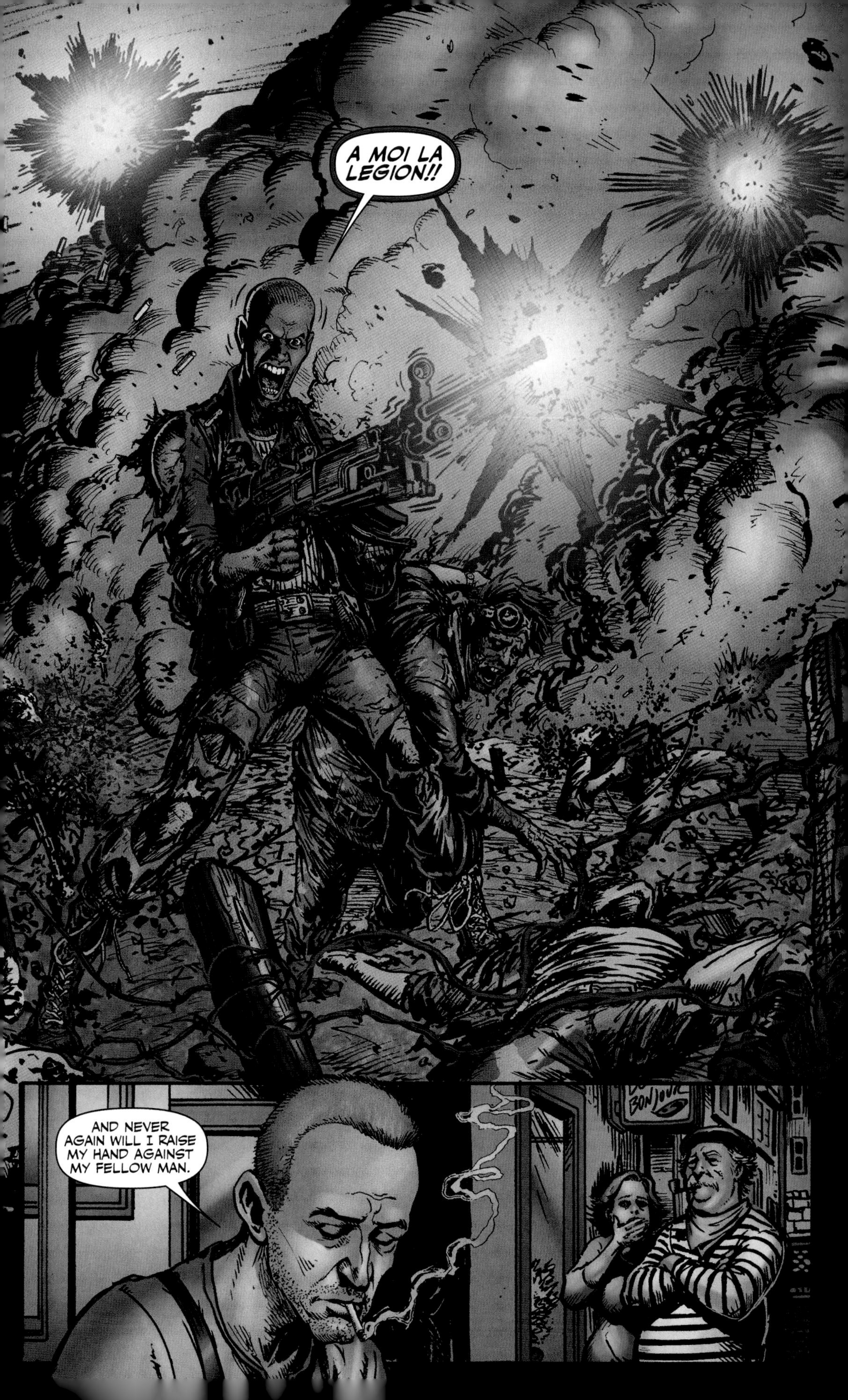
A MOI LA LEGION!!
AND NEVER AGAIN WILL I RAISE MY HAND AGAINST MY FELLOW MAN.

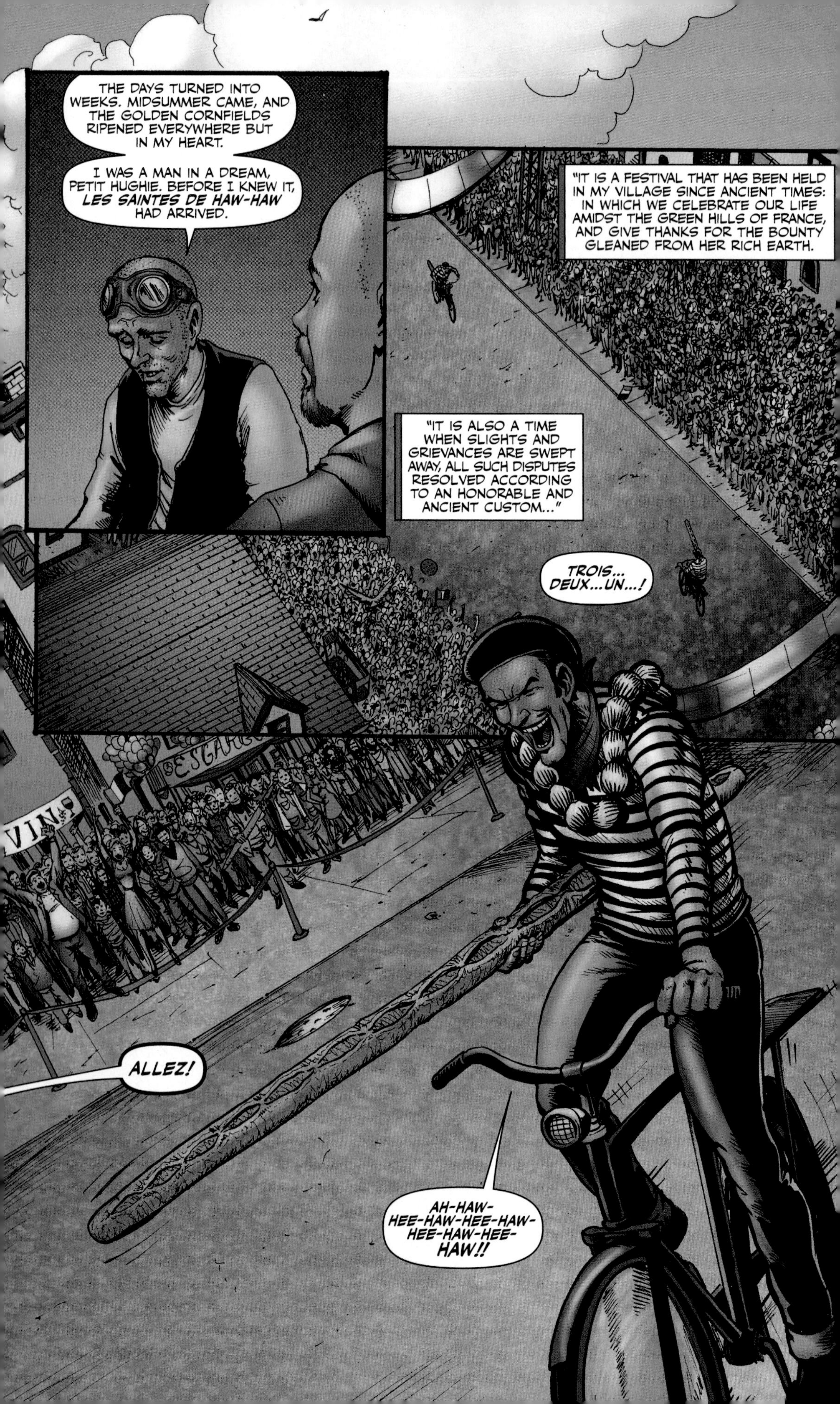
THE DAYS TURNED INTO WEEKS. MIDSUMMER CAME, AND THE GOLDEN CORNFIELDS RIPENED EVERYWHERE BUT IN MY HEART.
I WAS A MAN IN A DREAM, PETIT HUGHIE. BEFORE I KNEW IT, LES SAINTES DE HAW-HAW HAD ARRIVED.
"IT IS A FESTIVAL THAT HAS BEEN HELD IN MY VILLAGE SINCE ANCIENT TIMES: IN WHICH WE CELEBRATE OUR LIFE AMIDST THE GREEN HILLS OF FRANCE, AND GIVE THANKS FOR THE BOUNTY GLEANED FROM HER RICH EARTH.
"IT IS ALSO A TIME WHEN SLIGHTS AND GRIEVANCES ARE SWEPT AWAY, ALL SUCH DISPUTES RESOLVED ACCORDING TO AN HONORABLE AND ANCIENT CUSTOM..."
TROIS... DEUX...UN...!
ESCARGOT
VIN
ALLEZ!
AH-HAW-HEE-HAW-HEE-HAW-HEE-HAW-HEE-HAW!!

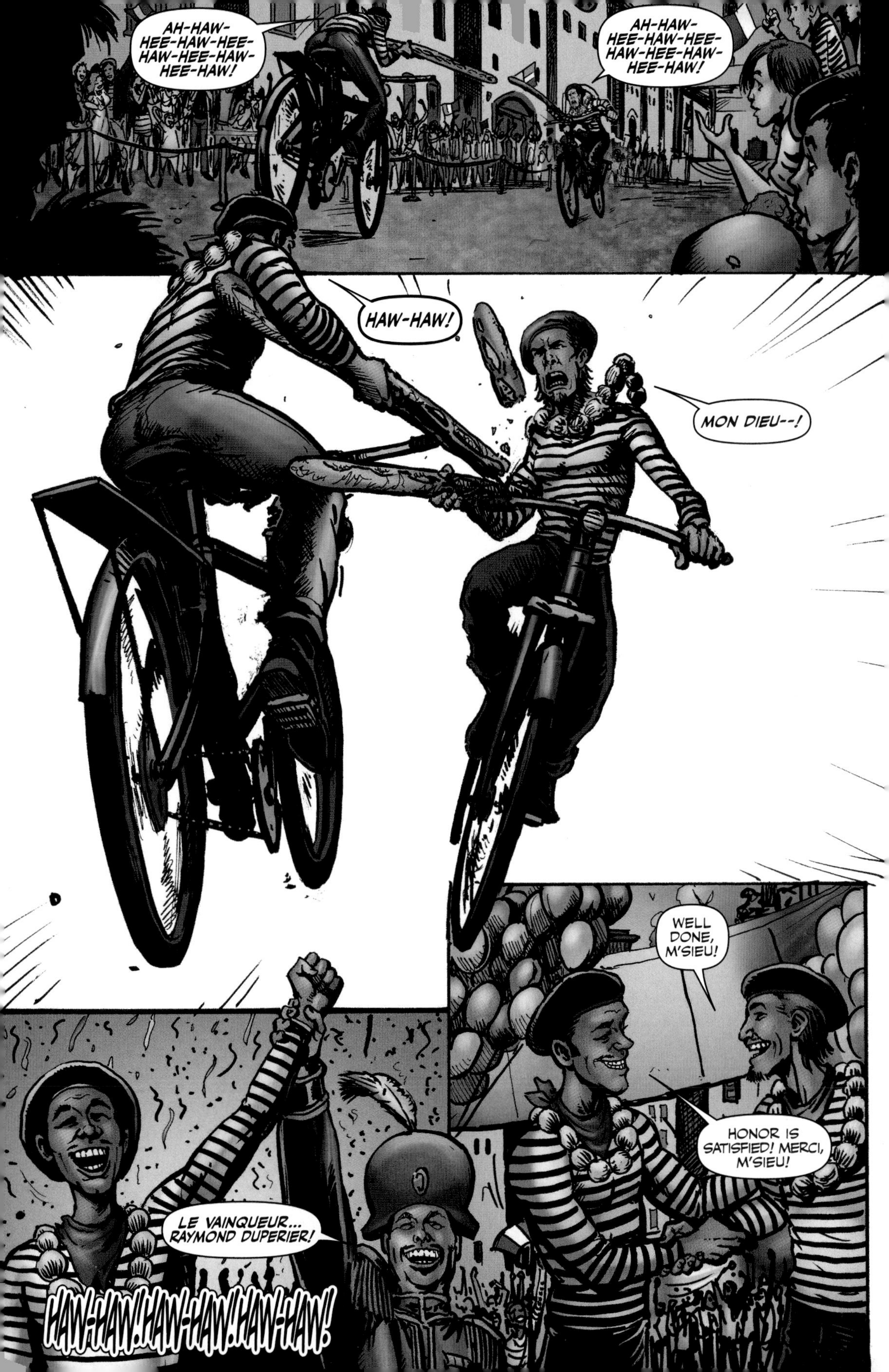
AH-HAW-HEE-HAW-HEE-HAW-HEE-HAW-HEE-HAW!
AH-HAW-HEE-HAW-HEE-HAW-HEE-HAW-HEE-HAW!
HAW-HAW!
MON DIEU--!
WELL DONE, M'SIEU!
HONOR IS SATISFIED! MERCI, M'SIEU!
LE VAINQUEUR... RAYMOND DUPERIER!
HAW-HAW! HAW-HAW! HAW-HAW!

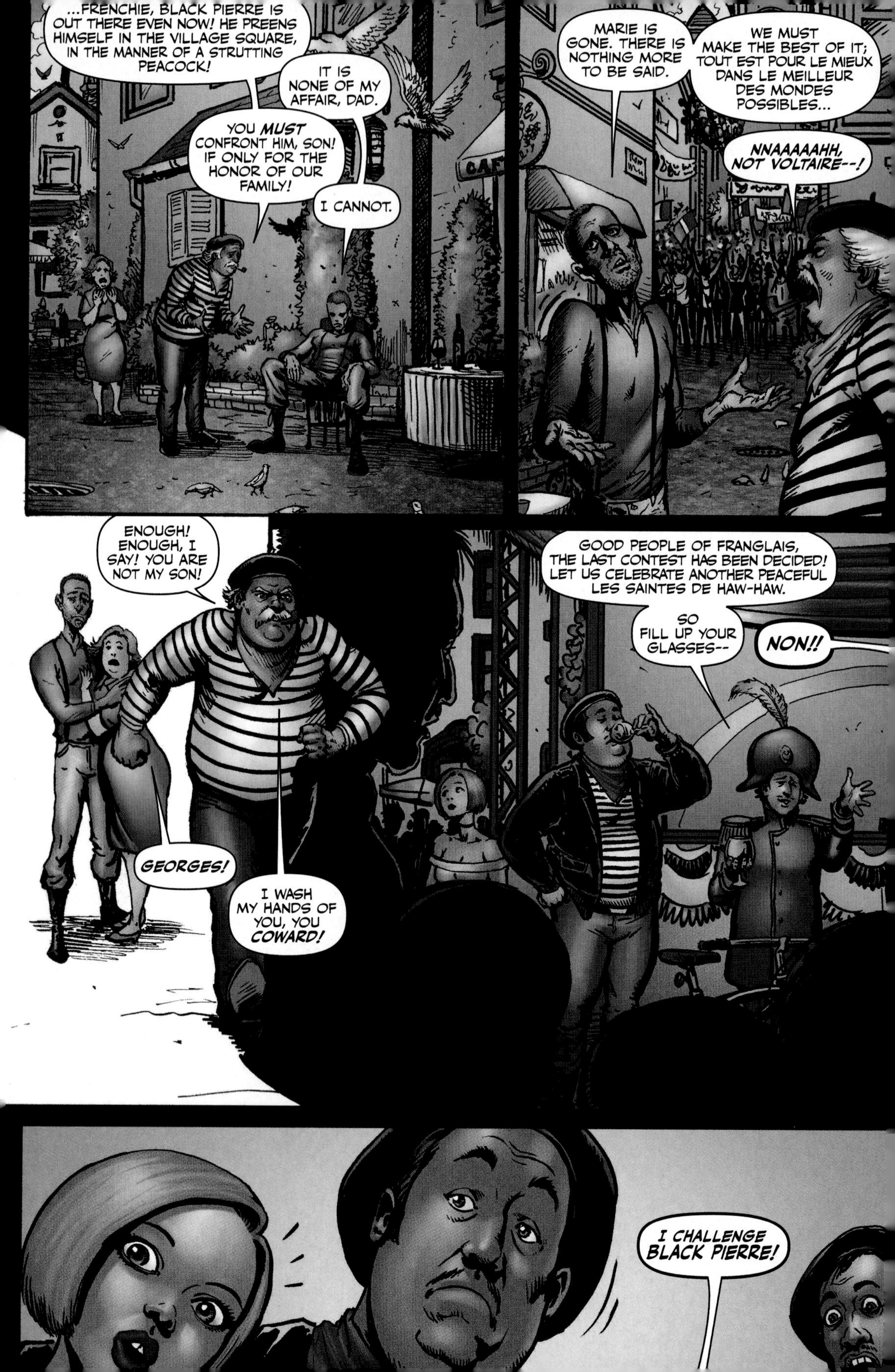
...FRENCHIE, BLACK PIERRE IS OUT THERE EVEN NOW! HE PREENS HIMSELF IN THE VILLAGE SQUARE, IN THE MANNER OF A STRUTTING PEACOCK!
IT IS NONE OF MY AFFAIR, DAD.
YOU MUST CONFRONT HIM, SON! IF ONLY FOR THE HONOR OF OUR FAMILY!
I CANNOT.
MARIE IS GONE. THERE IS NOTHING MORE TO BE SAID.
WE MUST MAKE THE BEST OF IT; TOUT EST POUR LE MIEUX DANS LE MEILLEUR DES MONDES POSSIBLES...
NNAAAAAHH, NOT VOLTAIRE--!
ENOUGH! ENOUGH, I SAY! YOU ARE NOT MY SON!
GEORGES!
I WASH MY HANDS OF YOU, YOU COWARD!
GOOD PEOPLE OF FRANGLAIS, THE LAST CONTEST HAS BEEN DECIDED! LET US CELEBRATE ANOTHER PEACEFUL LES SAINTES DE HAW-HAW.
SO FILL UP YOUR GLASSES--
NON!!
I CHALLENGE BLACK PIERRE!

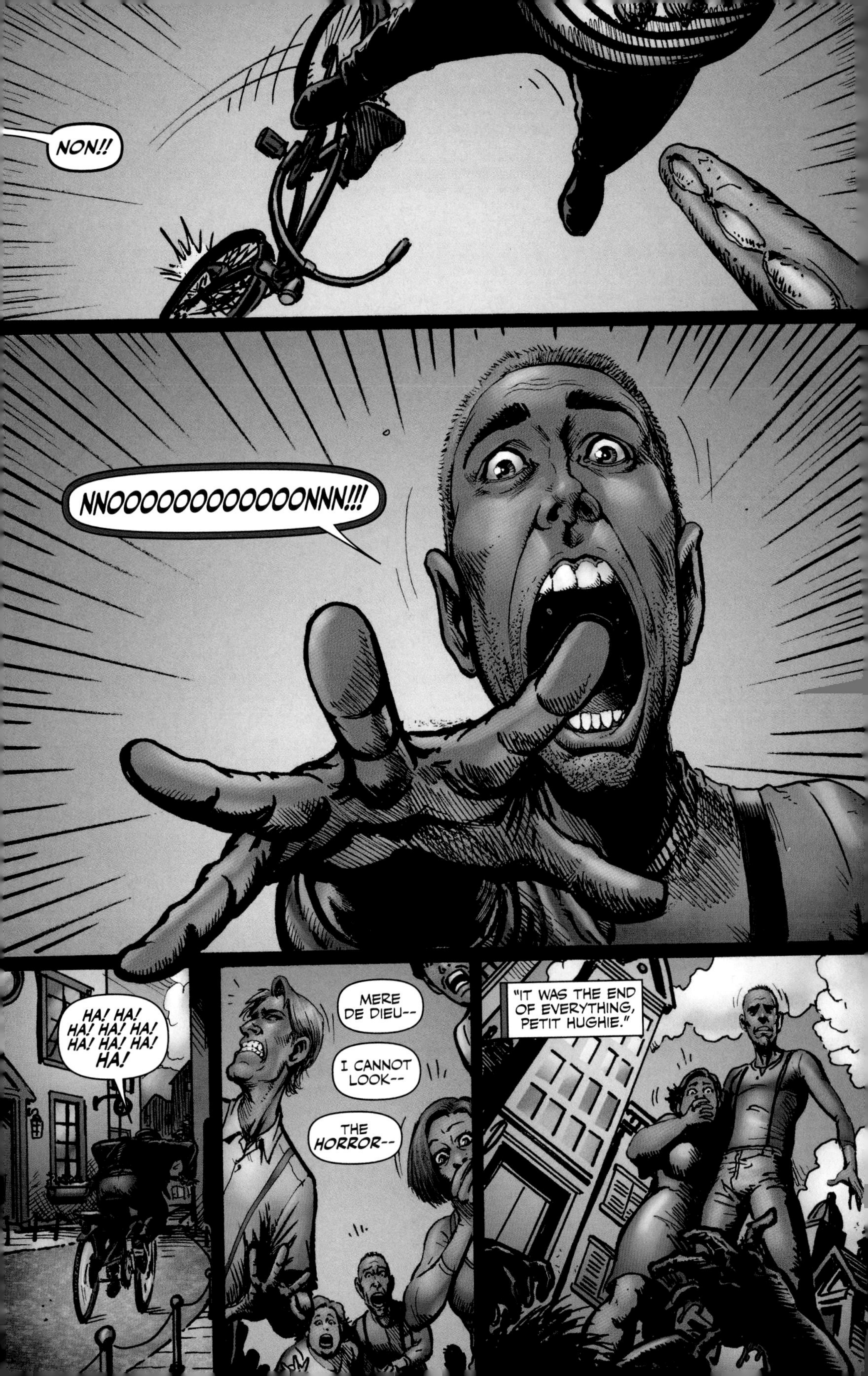

NON!!
NNOOOOOOOOOOOOONNN!!!
HA! HA! HA! HA! HA! HA! HA! HA! HA!
MERE DE DIEU--
I CANNOT LOOK--
THE HORROR--
"IT WAS THE END OF EVERYTHING, PETIT HUGHIE."

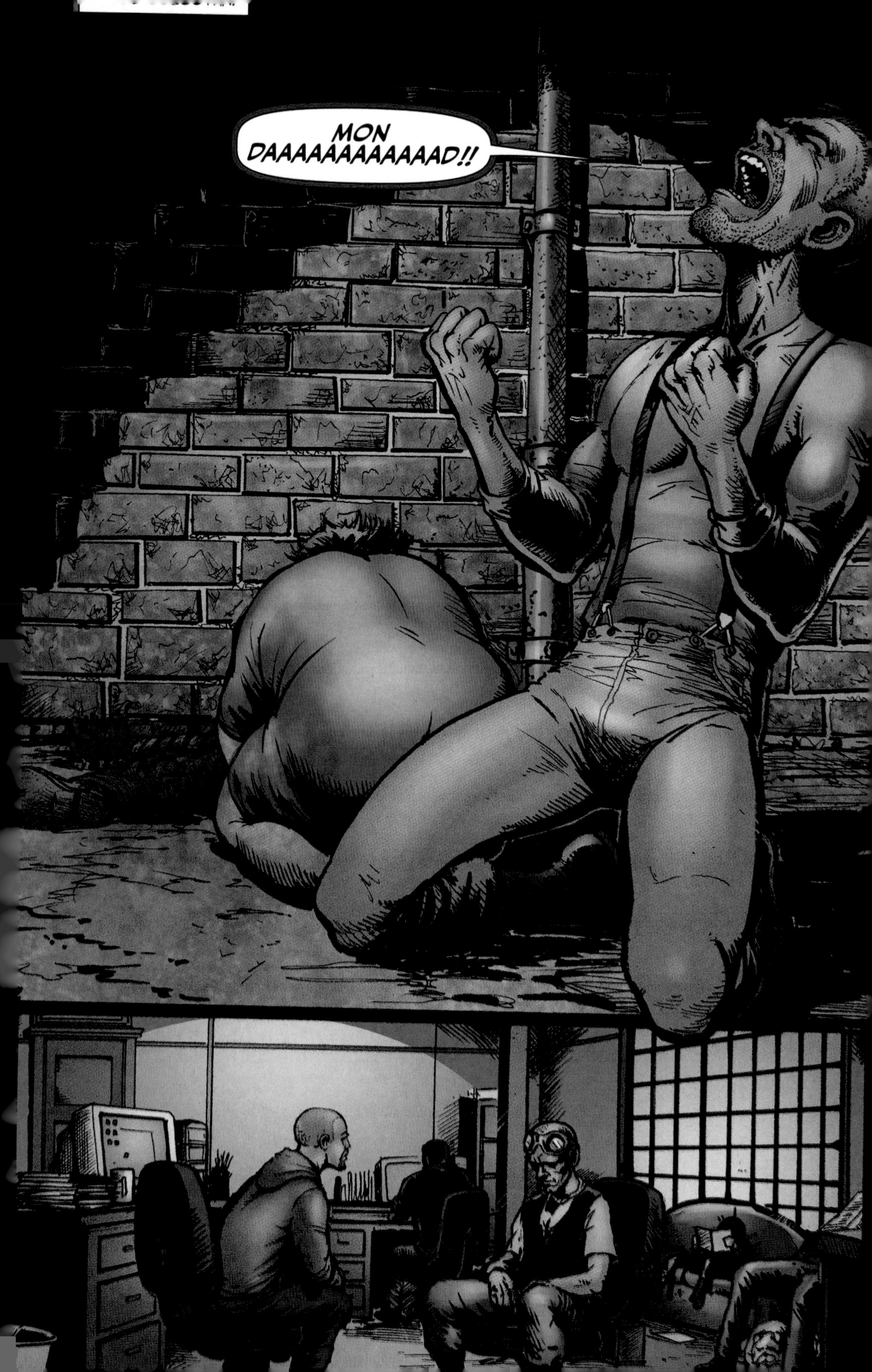
MON DAAAAAAAAAAAAD!!

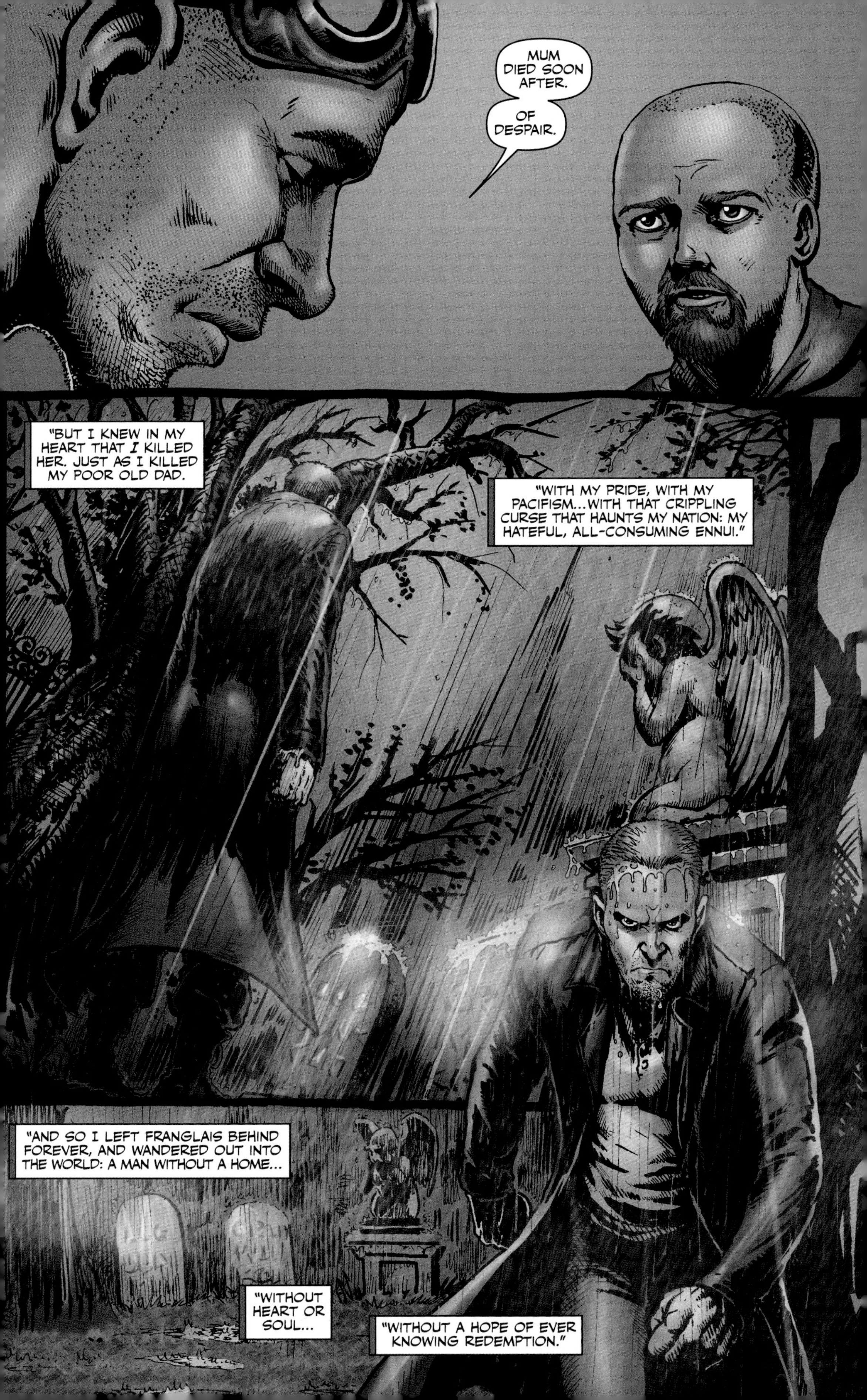
MUM DIED SOON AFTER.
OF DESPAIR.
"BUT I KNEW IN MY HEART THAT I KILLED HER. JUST AS I KILLED MY POOR OLD DAD.
"WITH MY PRIDE, WITH MY PACIFISM...WITH THAT CRIPPLING CURSE THAT HAUNTS MY NATION: MY HATEFUL, ALL-CONSUMING ENNUI."
"AND SO I LEFT FRANGLAIS BEHIND FOREVER, AND WANDERED OUT INTO THE WORLD: A MAN WITHOUT A HOME...
"WITHOUT HEART OR SOUL...
"WITHOUT A HOPE OF EVER KNOWING REDEMPTION."

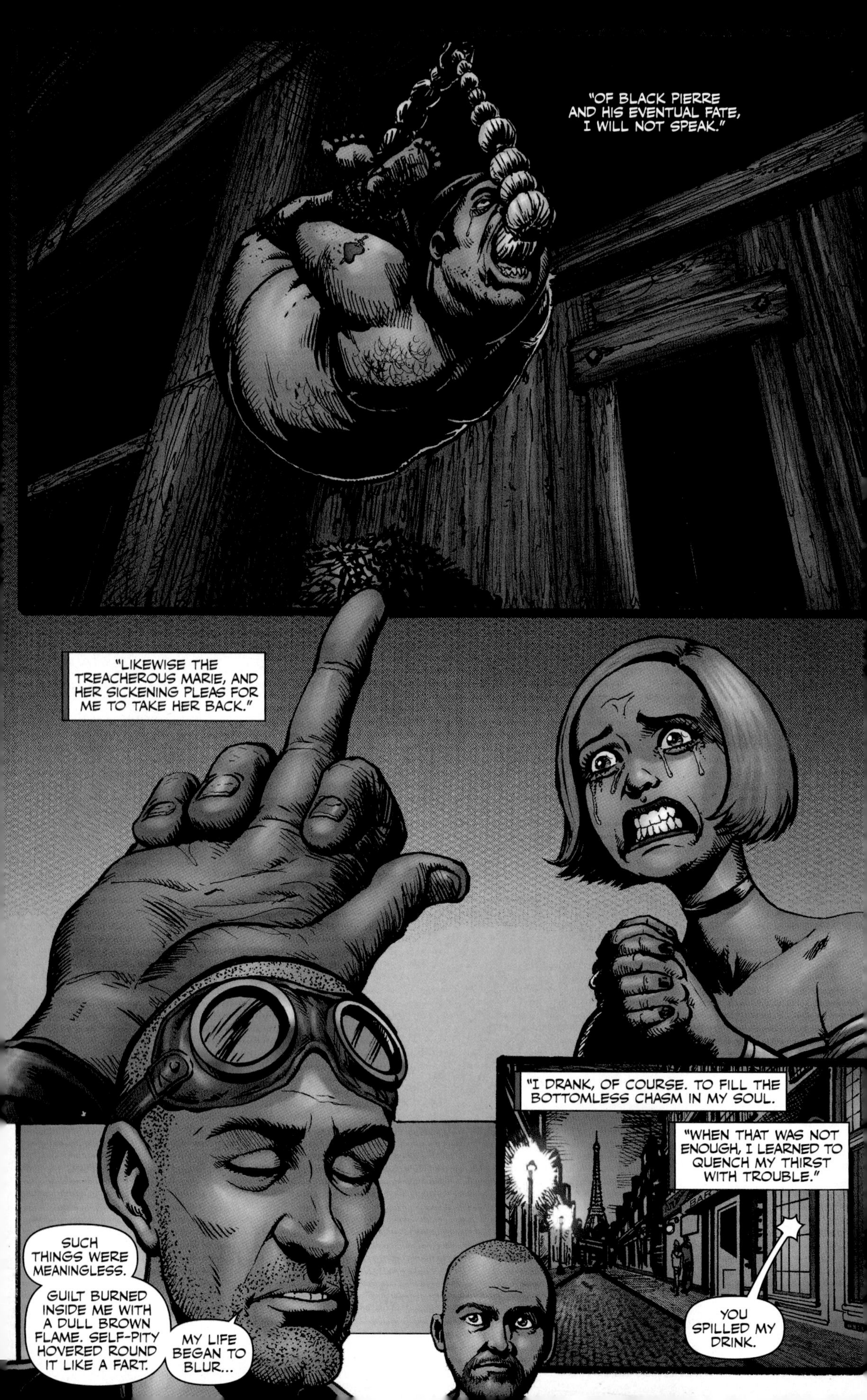
"OF BLACK PIERRE AND HIS EVENTUAL FATE, I WILL NOT SPEAK."
"LIKEWISE THE TREACHEROUS MARIE, AND HER SICKENING PLEAS FOR ME TO TAKE HER BACK."
"I DRANK, OF COURSE. TO FILL THE BOTTOMLESS CHASM IN MY SOUL.
"WHEN THAT WAS NOT ENOUGH, I LEARNED TO QUENCH MY THIRST WITH TROUBLE."
BAR
YOU SPILLED MY DRINK.
SUCH THINGS WERE MEANINGLESS.
GUILT BURNED INSIDE ME WITH A DULL BROWN FLAME. SELF-PITY HOVERED ROUND IT LIKE A FART.
MY LIFE BEGAN TO BLUR...

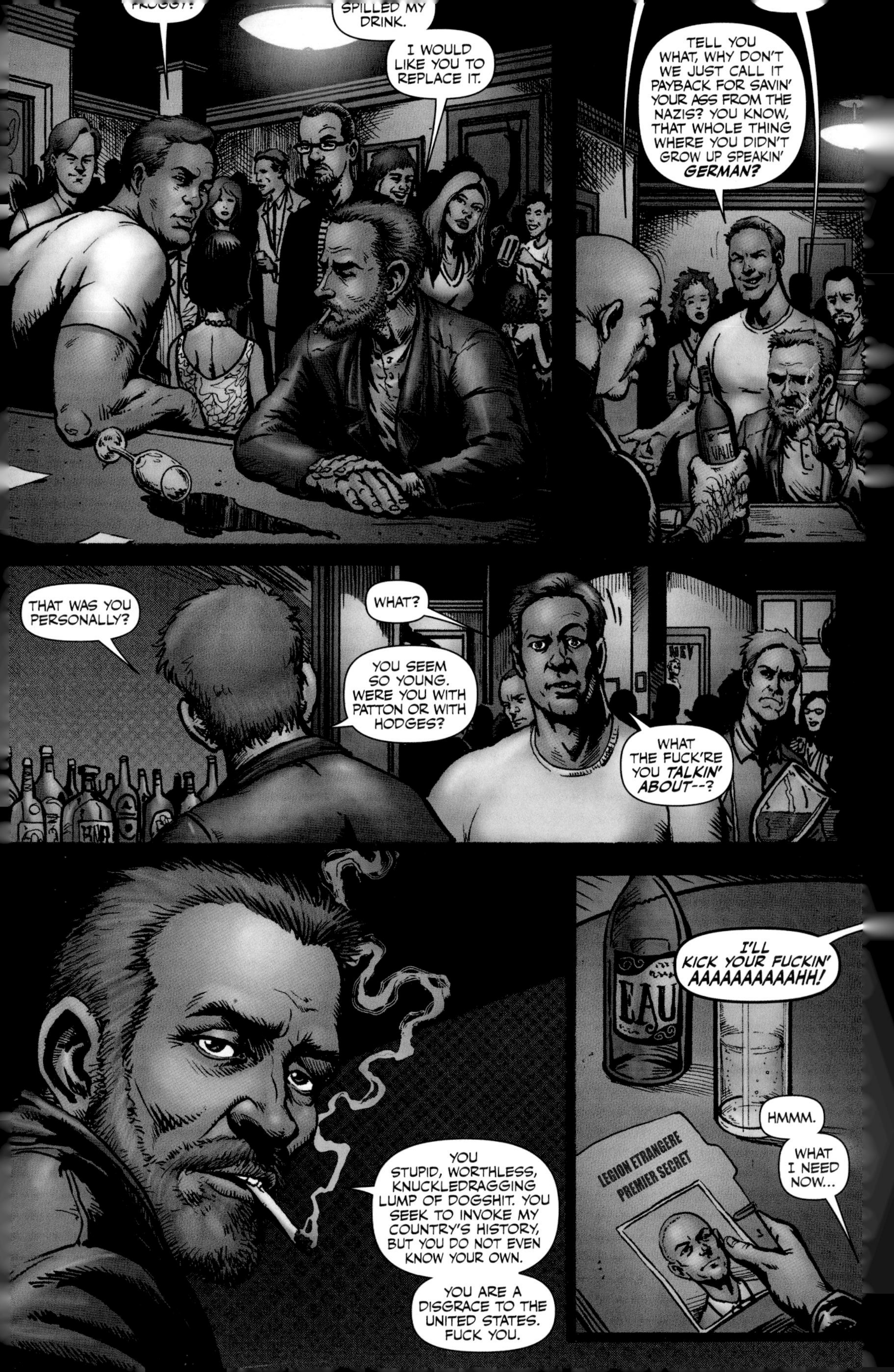
SPILLED MY DRINK.
I WOULD LIKE YOU TO REPLACE IT.
TELL YOU WHAT, WHY DON'T WE JUST CALL IT PAYBACK FOR SAVIN' YOUR ASS FROM THE NAZIS? YOU KNOW, THAT WHOLE THING WHERE YOU DIDN'T GROW UP SPEAKIN' ***GERMAN?***
THAT WAS YOU PERSONALLY?
WHAT?
YOU SEEM SO YOUNG. WERE YOU WITH PATTON OR WITH HODGES?
WHAT THE FUCK'RE YOU *TALKIN' ABOUT*--?
YOU STUPID, WORTHLESS, KNUCKLEDRAGGING LUMP OF DOGSHIT. YOU SEEK TO INVOKE MY COUNTRY'S HISTORY, BUT YOU DO NOT EVEN KNOW YOUR OWN.
YOU ARE A DISGRACE TO THE UNITED STATES. FUCK YOU.
EAU
I'LL KICK YOUR FUCKIN' AAAAAAAAAAHH!
HMMM.
WHAT I NEED NOW...
LEGION ETRANGERE
PREMIER SECRET

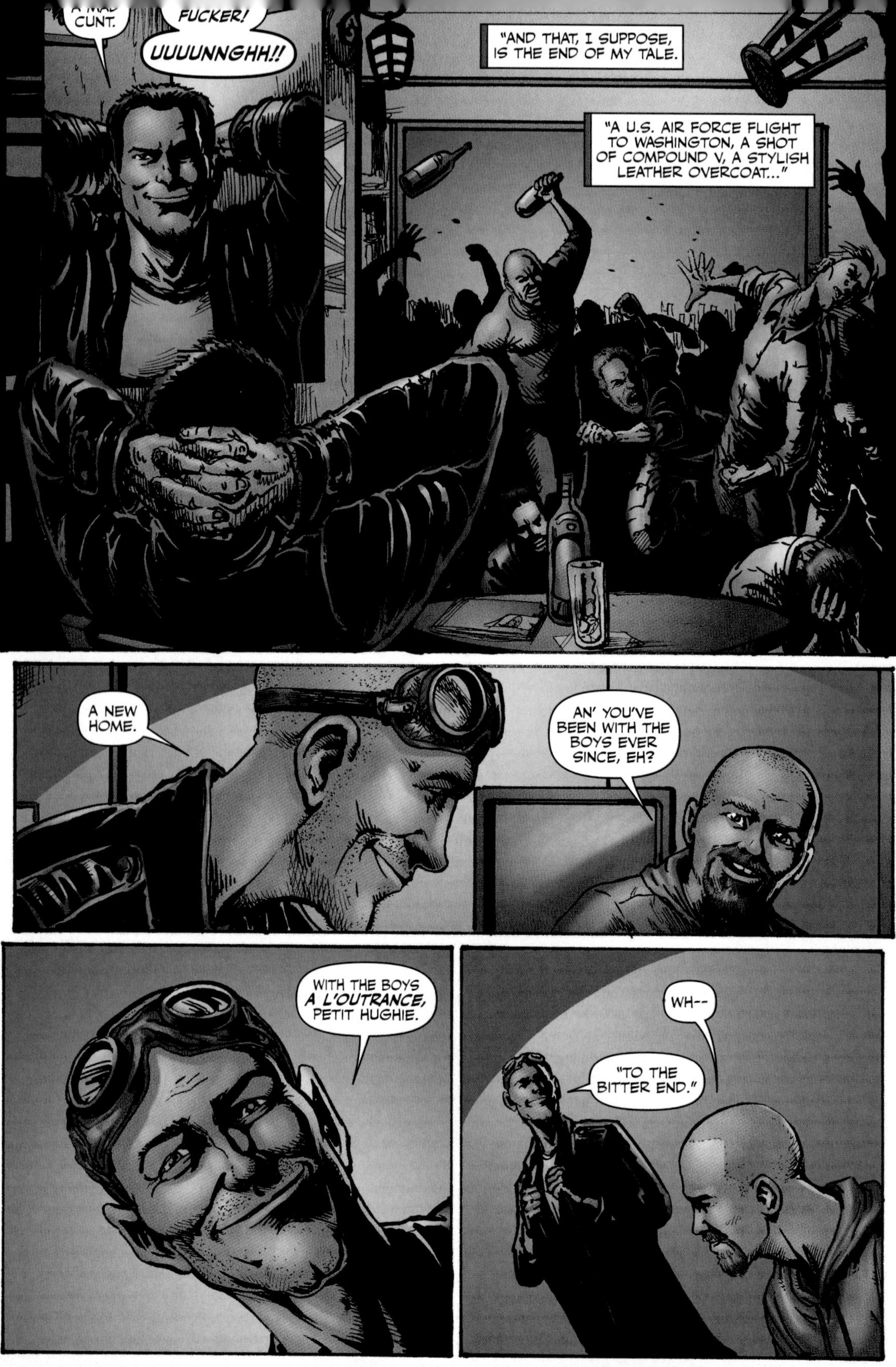

CUNT.
FUCKER!
UUUUNNGHH!!
"AND THAT, I SUPPOSE, IS THE END OF MY TALE.
"A U.S. AIR FORCE FLIGHT TO WASHINGTON, A SHOT OF COMPOUND V, A STYLISH LEATHER OVERCOAT..."
A NEW HOME.
AN' YOU'VE BEEN WITH THE BOYS EVER SINCE, EH?
WITH THE BOYS *A L'OUTRANCE,* PETIT HUGHIE.
WH--
"TO THE BITTER END."

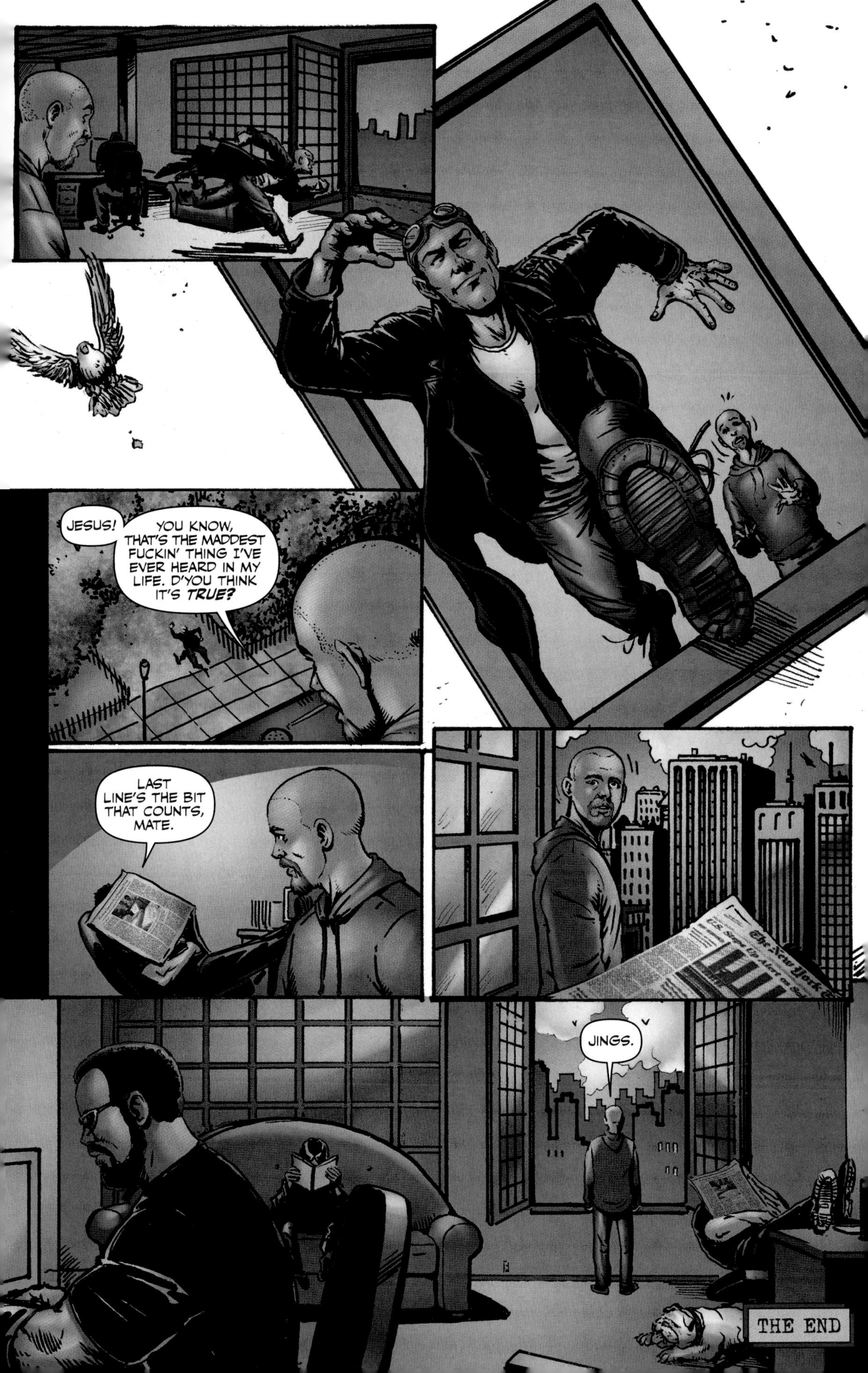
JESUS!
YOU KNOW, THAT'S THE MADDEST FUCKIN' THING I'VE EVER HEARD IN MY LIFE. D'YOU THINK IT'S TRUE?
LAST LINE'S THE BIT THAT COUNTS, MATE.
JINGS.
THE END

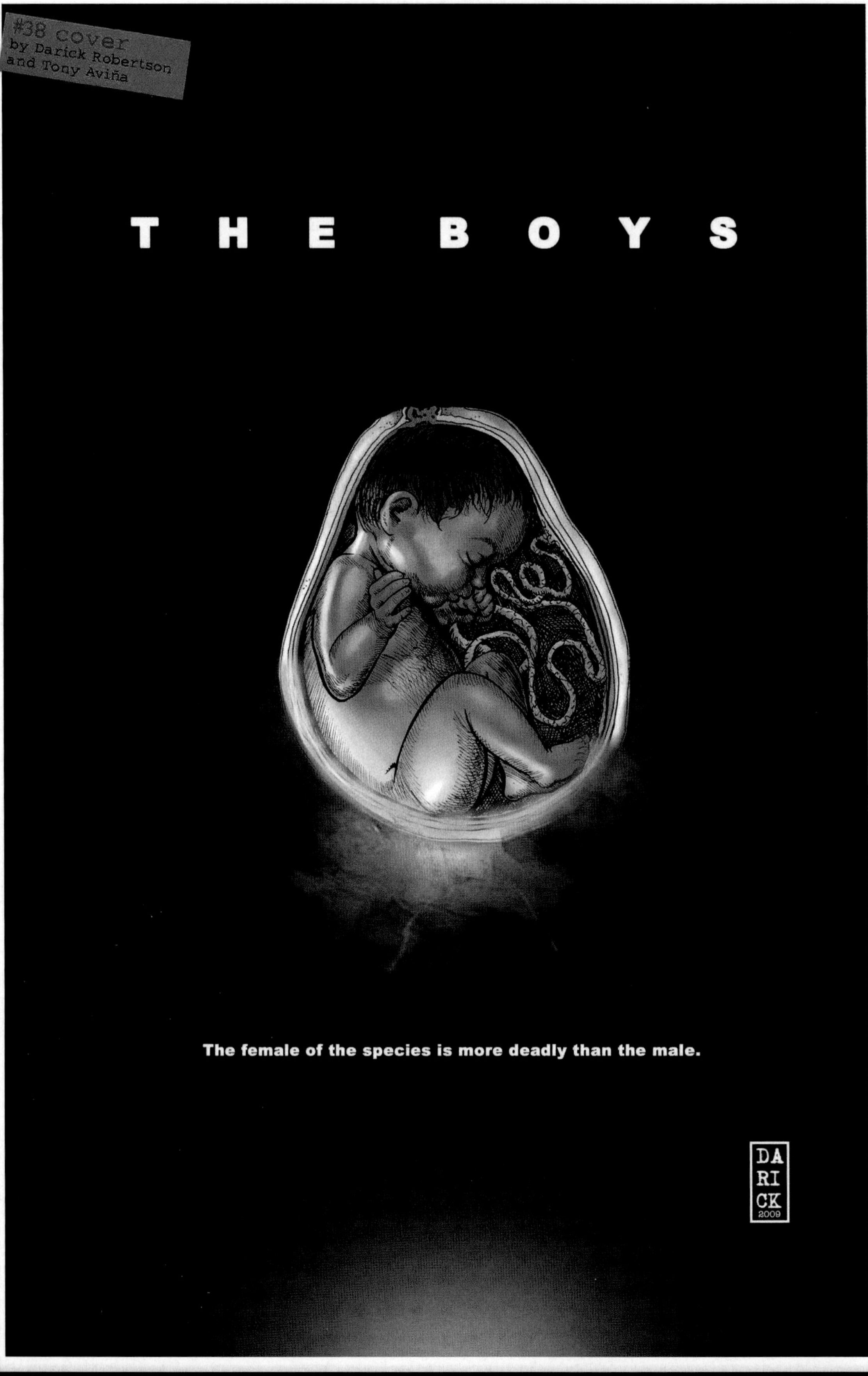
THE BOYS
The female of the species is more deadly than the male.
DARICK 2009

#38 cover
by Darick Robertson
and Tony Aviña

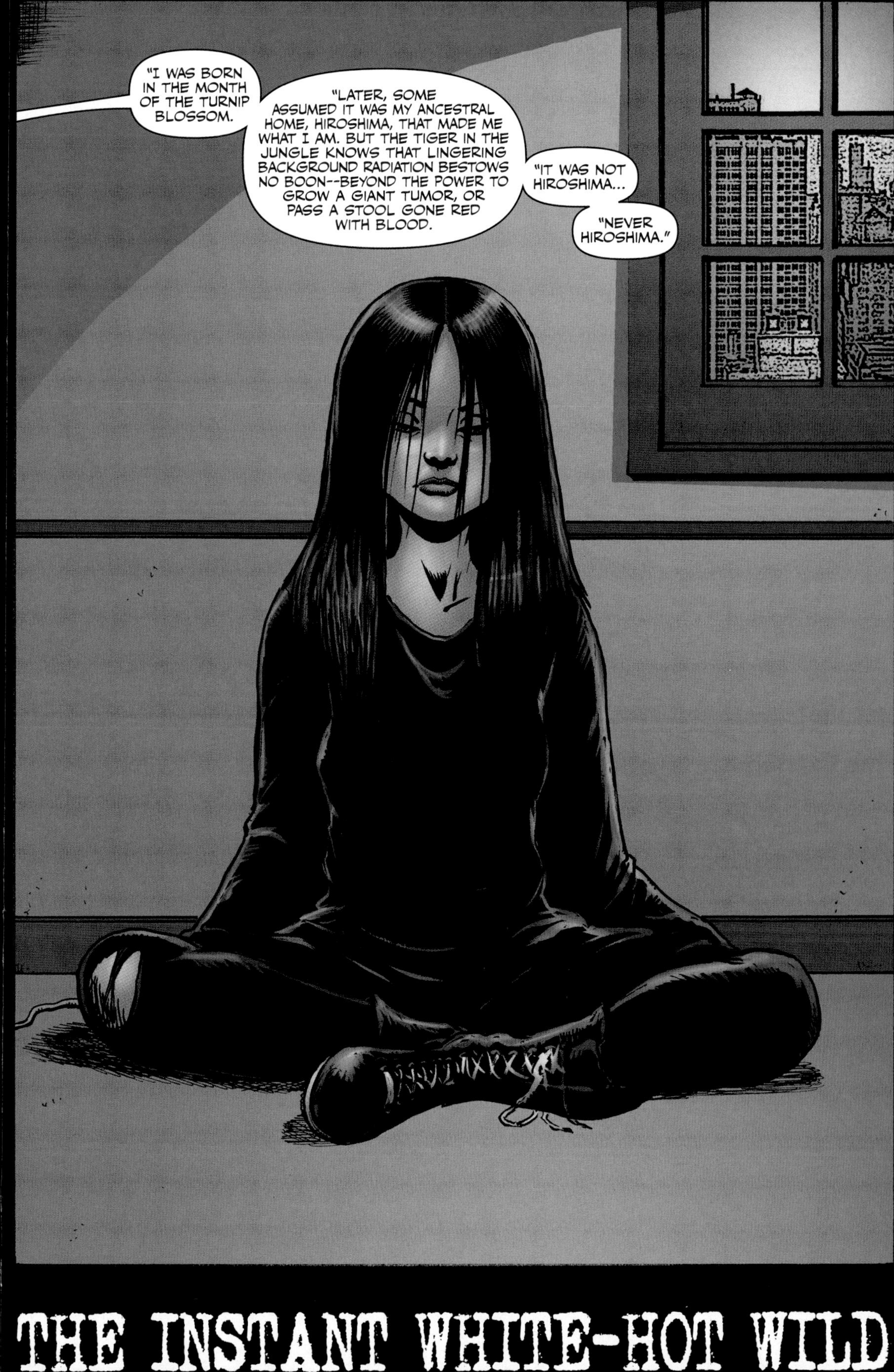
"I WAS BORN IN THE MONTH OF THE TURNIP BLOSSOM.
"LATER, SOME ASSUMED IT WAS MY ANCESTRAL HOME, HIROSHIMA, THAT MADE ME WHAT I AM. BUT THE TIGER IN THE JUNGLE KNOWS THAT LINGERING BACKGROUND RADIATION BESTOWS NO BOON--BEYOND THE POWER TO GROW A GIANT TUMOR, OR PASS A STOOL GONE RED WITH BLOOD.
"IT WAS NOT HIROSHIMA...
"NEVER HIROSHIMA."
THE INSTANT WHITE-HOT WILD

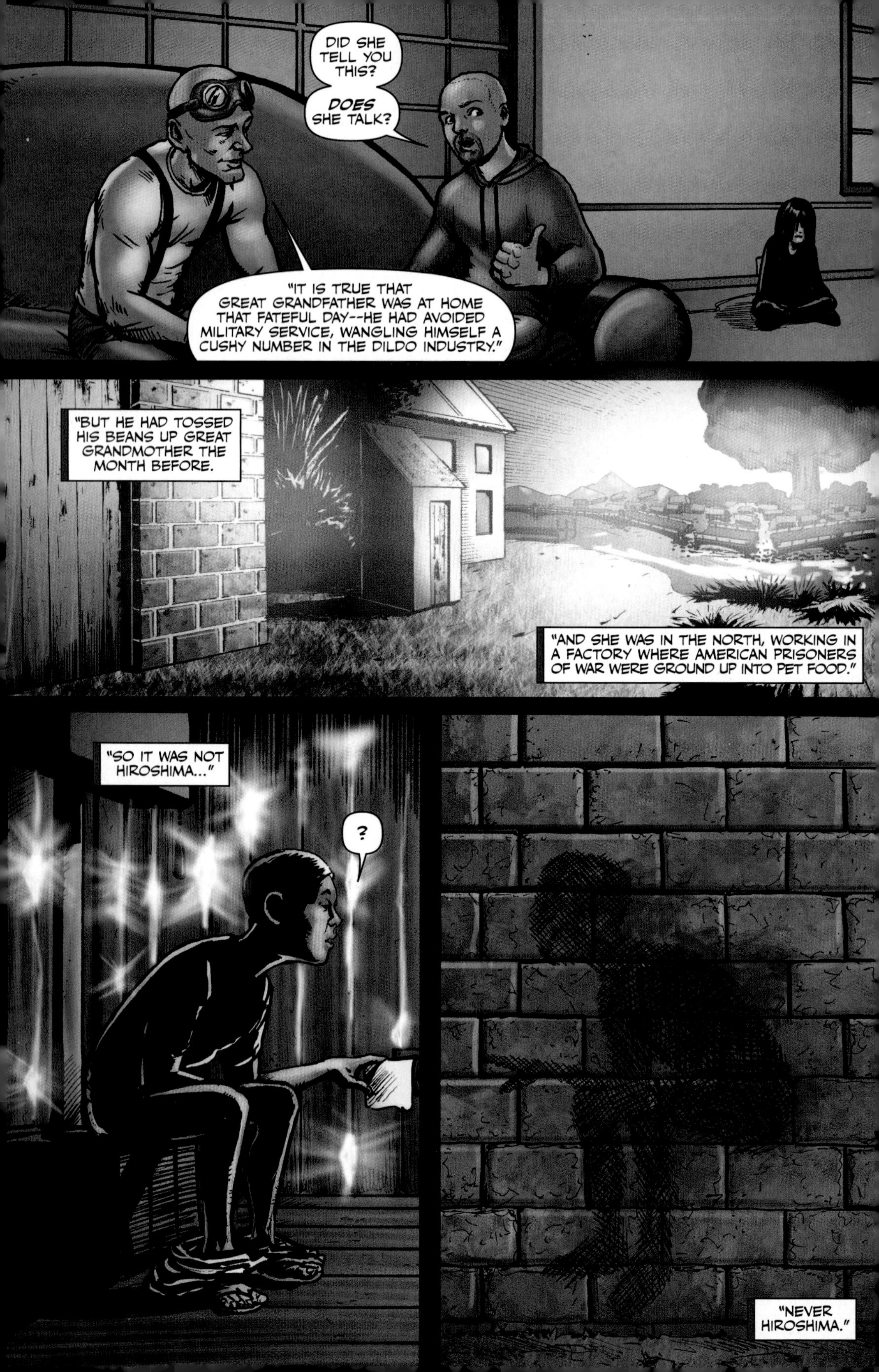
DID SHE TELL YOU THIS?
DOES SHE TALK?
"IT IS TRUE THAT GREAT GRANDFATHER WAS AT HOME THAT FATEFUL DAY--HE HAD AVOIDED MILITARY SERVICE, WANGLING HIMSELF A CUSHY NUMBER IN THE DILDO INDUSTRY."
"BUT HE HAD TOSSED HIS BEANS UP GREAT GRANDMOTHER THE MONTH BEFORE.
"AND SHE WAS IN THE NORTH, WORKING IN A FACTORY WHERE AMERICAN PRISONERS OF WAR WERE GROUND UP INTO PET FOOD."
"SO IT WAS NOT HIROSHIMA..."
?
"NEVER HIROSHIMA."

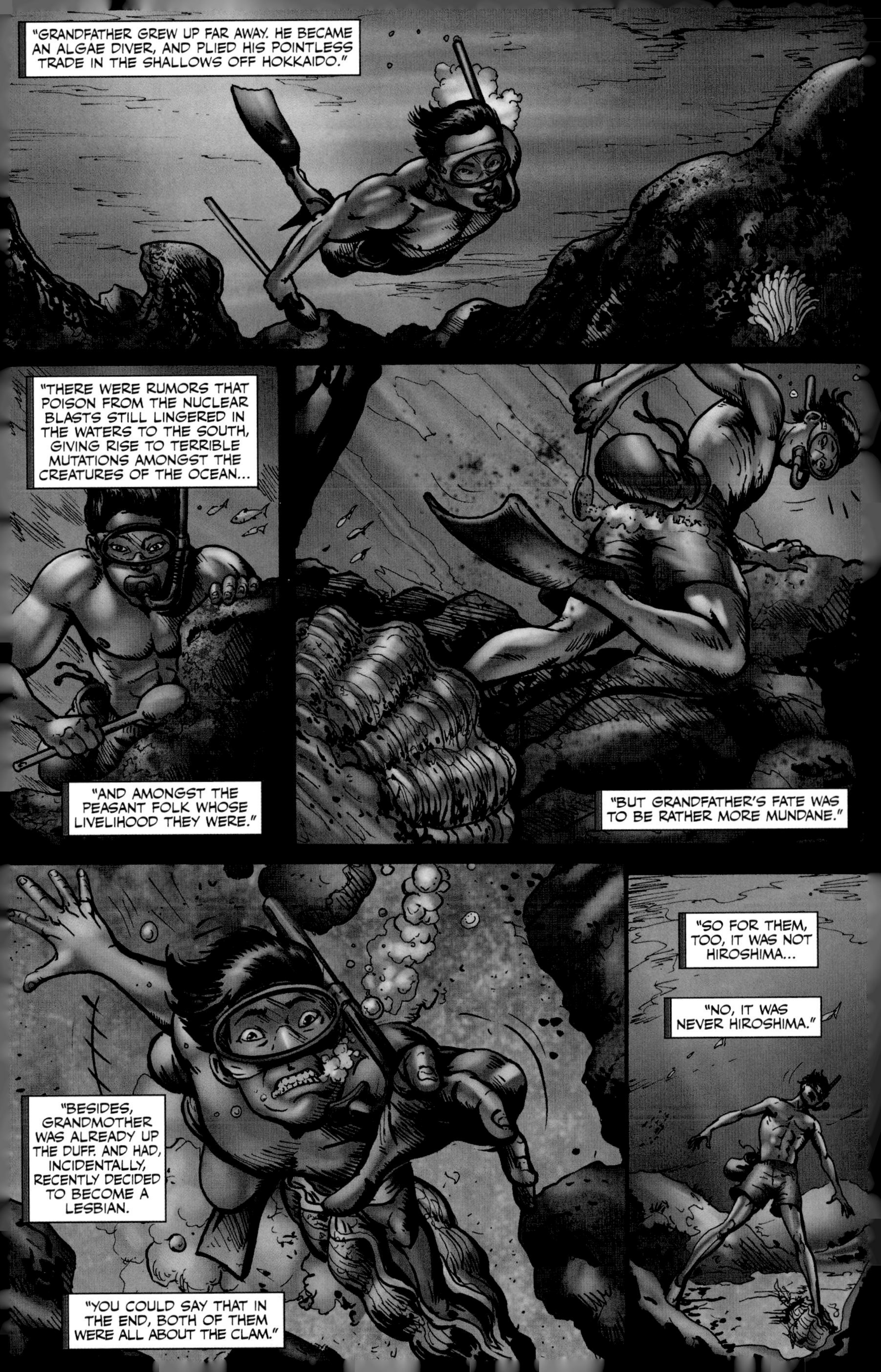
"GRANDFATHER GREW UP FAR AWAY. HE BECAME AN ALGAE DIVER, AND PLIED HIS POINTLESS TRADE IN THE SHALLOWS OFF HOKKAIDO."
"THERE WERE RUMORS THAT POISON FROM THE NUCLEAR BLASTS STILL LINGERED IN THE WATERS TO THE SOUTH, GIVING RISE TO TERRIBLE MUTATIONS AMONGST THE CREATURES OF THE OCEAN...
"AND AMONGST THE PEASANT FOLK WHOSE LIVELIHOOD THEY WERE."
"BUT GRANDFATHER'S FATE WAS TO BE RATHER MORE MUNDANE."
"BESIDES, GRANDMOTHER WAS ALREADY UP THE DUFF. AND HAD, INCIDENTALLY, RECENTLY DECIDED TO BECOME A LESBIAN.
"YOU COULD SAY THAT IN THE END, BOTH OF THEM WERE ALL ABOUT THE CLAM."
"SO FOR THEM, TOO, IT WAS NOT HIROSHIMA...
"NO, IT WAS NEVER HIROSHIMA."

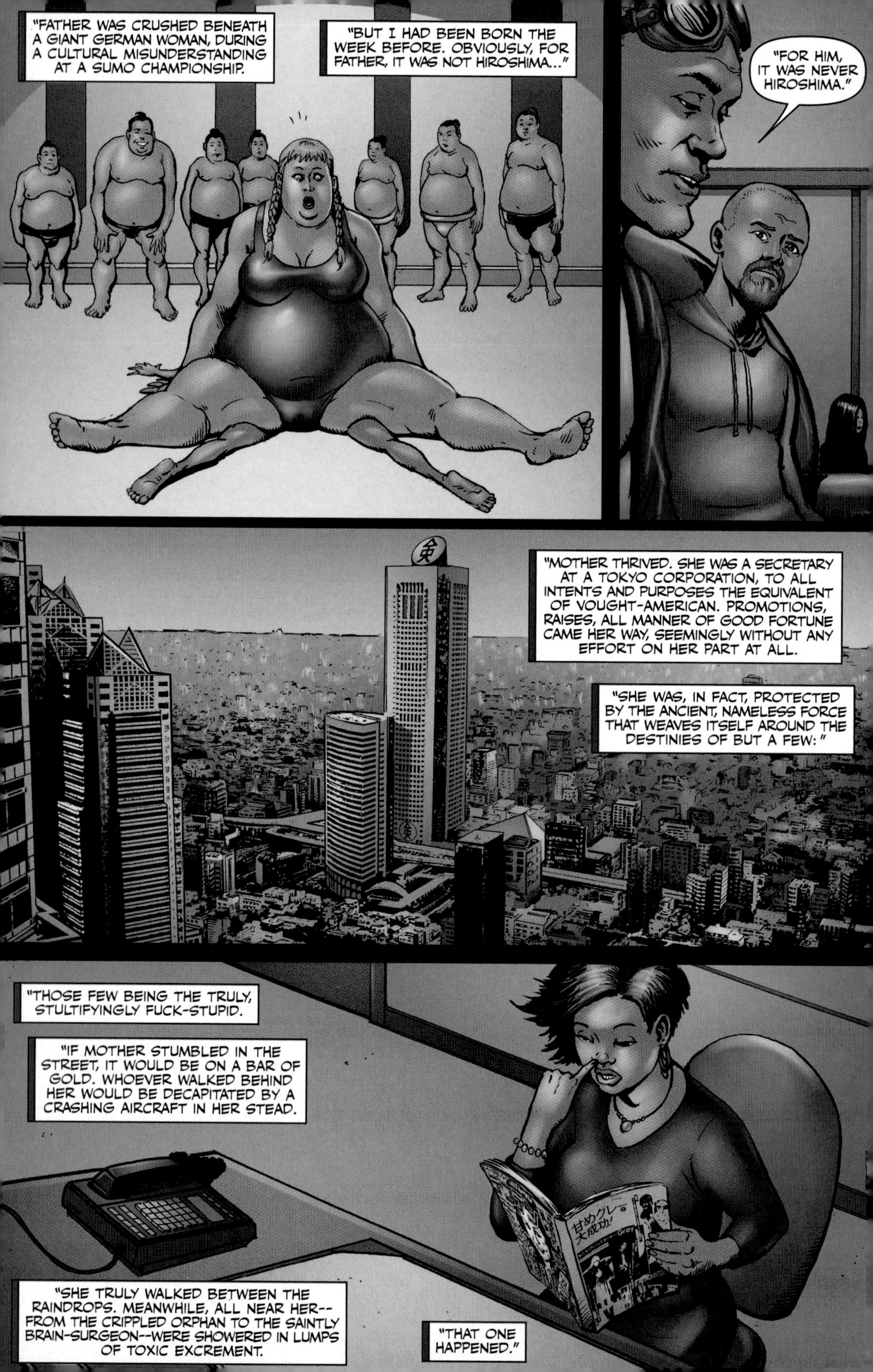
"FATHER WAS CRUSHED BENEATH A GIANT GERMAN WOMAN, DURING A CULTURAL MISUNDERSTANDING AT A SUMO CHAMPIONSHIP.
"BUT I HAD BEEN BORN THE WEEK BEFORE. OBVIOUSLY, FOR FATHER, IT WAS NOT HIROSHIMA..."
"FOR HIM, IT WAS NEVER HIROSHIMA."
"MOTHER THRIVED. SHE WAS A SECRETARY AT A TOKYO CORPORATION, TO ALL INTENTS AND PURPOSES THE EQUIVALENT OF VOUGHT-AMERICAN. PROMOTIONS, RAISES, ALL MANNER OF GOOD FORTUNE CAME HER WAY, SEEMINGLY WITHOUT ANY EFFORT ON HER PART AT ALL.
"SHE WAS, IN FACT, PROTECTED BY THE ANCIENT, NAMELESS FORCE THAT WEAVES ITSELF AROUND THE DESTINIES OF BUT A FEW:"
"THOSE FEW BEING THE TRULY, STULTIFYINGLY FUCK-STUPID.
"IF MOTHER STUMBLED IN THE STREET, IT WOULD BE ON A BAR OF GOLD. WHOEVER WALKED BEHIND HER WOULD BE DECAPITATED BY A CRASHING AIRCRAFT IN HER STEAD.
"SHE TRULY WALKED BETWEEN THE RAINDROPS. MEANWHILE, ALL NEAR HER--FROM THE CRIPPLED ORPHAN TO THE SAINTLY BRAIN-SURGEON--WERE SHOWERED IN LUMPS OF TOXIC EXCREMENT.
"THAT ONE HAPPENED."

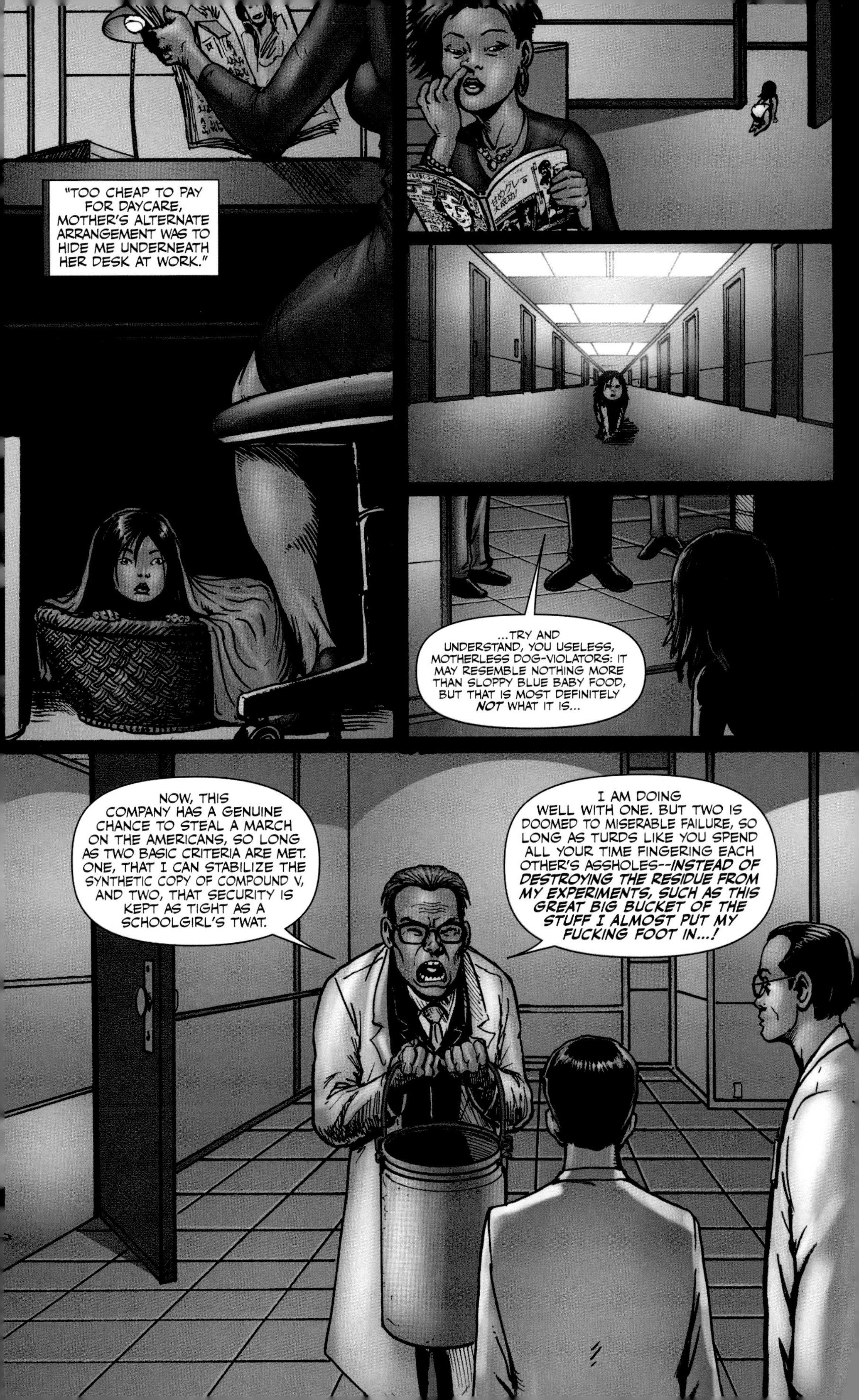
"TOO CHEAP TO PAY FOR DAYCARE, MOTHER'S ALTERNATE ARRANGEMENT WAS TO HIDE ME UNDERNEATH HER DESK AT WORK."
...TRY AND UNDERSTAND, YOU USELESS, MOTHERLESS DOG-VIOLATORS: IT MAY RESEMBLE NOTHING MORE THAN SLOPPY BLUE BABY FOOD, BUT THAT IS MOST DEFINITELY *NOT* WHAT IT IS...
NOW, THIS COMPANY HAS A GENUINE CHANCE TO STEAL A MARCH ON THE AMERICANS, SO LONG AS TWO BASIC CRITERIA ARE MET. ONE, THAT I CAN STABILIZE THE SYNTHETIC COPY OF COMPOUND V, AND TWO, THAT SECURITY IS KEPT AS TIGHT AS A SCHOOLGIRL'S TWAT.
I AM DOING WELL WITH ONE. BUT TWO IS DOOMED TO MISERABLE FAILURE, SO LONG AS TURDS LIKE YOU SPEND ALL YOUR TIME FINGERING EACH OTHER'S ASSHOLES--*INSTEAD OF DESTROYING THE RESIDUE FROM MY EXPERIMENTS, SUCH AS THIS GREAT BIG BUCKET OF THE STUFF I ALMOST PUT MY FUCKING FOOT IN...!*

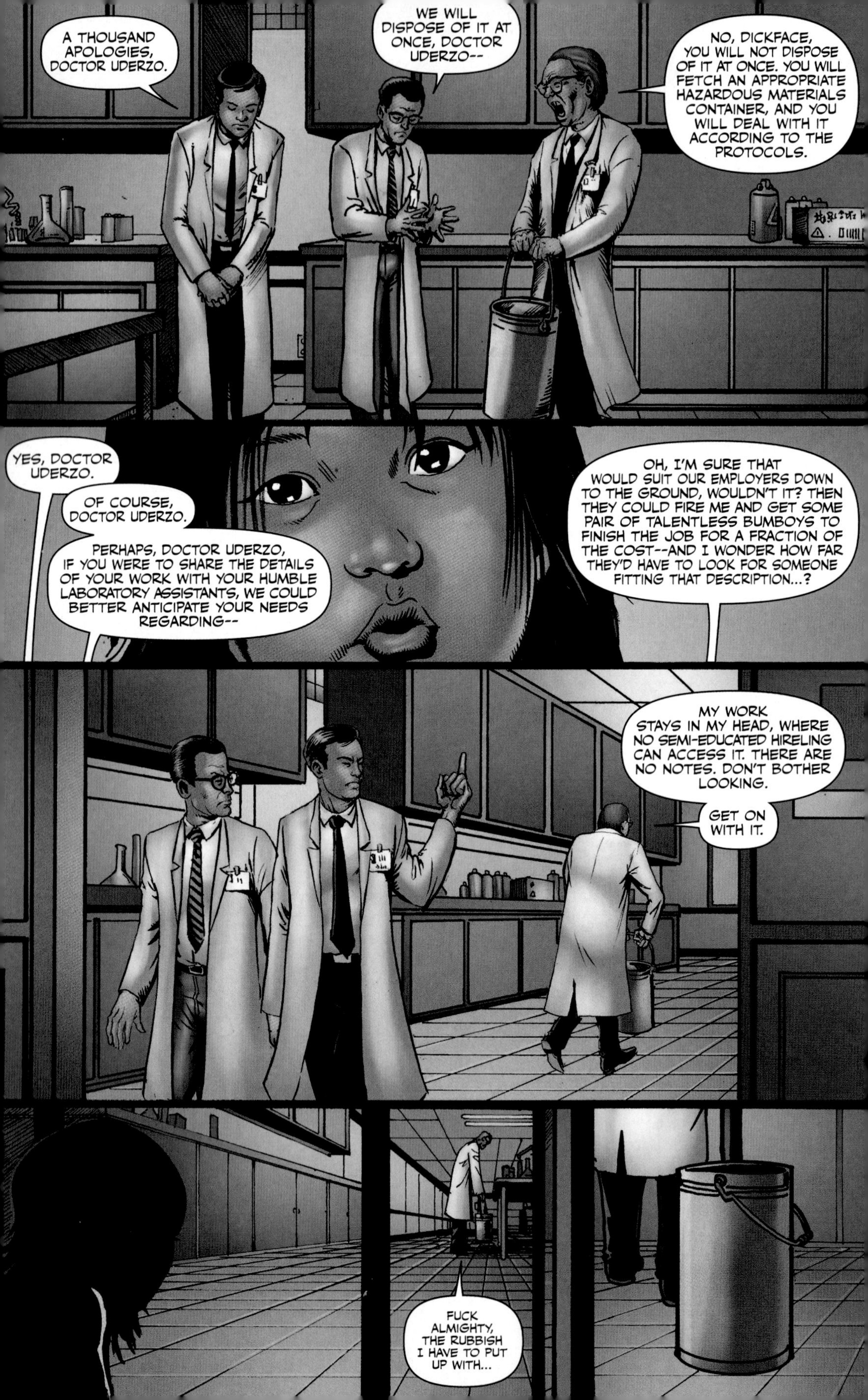
A THOUSAND APOLOGIES, DOCTOR UDERZO.
WE WILL DISPOSE OF IT AT ONCE, DOCTOR UDERZO--
NO, DICKFACE, YOU WILL NOT DISPOSE OF IT AT ONCE. YOU WILL FETCH AN APPROPRIATE HAZARDOUS MATERIALS CONTAINER, AND YOU WILL DEAL WITH IT ACCORDING TO THE PROTOCOLS.
YES, DOCTOR UDERZO.
OF COURSE, DOCTOR UDERZO.
PERHAPS, DOCTOR UDERZO, IF YOU WERE TO SHARE THE DETAILS OF YOUR WORK WITH YOUR HUMBLE LABORATORY ASSISTANTS, WE COULD BETTER ANTICIPATE YOUR NEEDS REGARDING--
OH, I'M SURE THAT WOULD SUIT OUR EMPLOYERS DOWN TO THE GROUND, WOULDN'T IT? THEN THEY COULD FIRE ME AND GET SOME PAIR OF TALENTLESS BUMBOYS TO FINISH THE JOB FOR A FRACTION OF THE COST--AND I WONDER HOW FAR THEY'D HAVE TO LOOK FOR SOMEONE FITTING THAT DESCRIPTION...?
MY WORK STAYS IN MY HEAD, WHERE NO SEMI-EDUCATED HIRELING CAN ACCESS IT. THERE ARE NO NOTES. DON'T BOTHER LOOKING.
GET ON WITH IT.
FUCK ALMIGHTY, THE RUBBISH I HAVE TO PUT UP WITH...

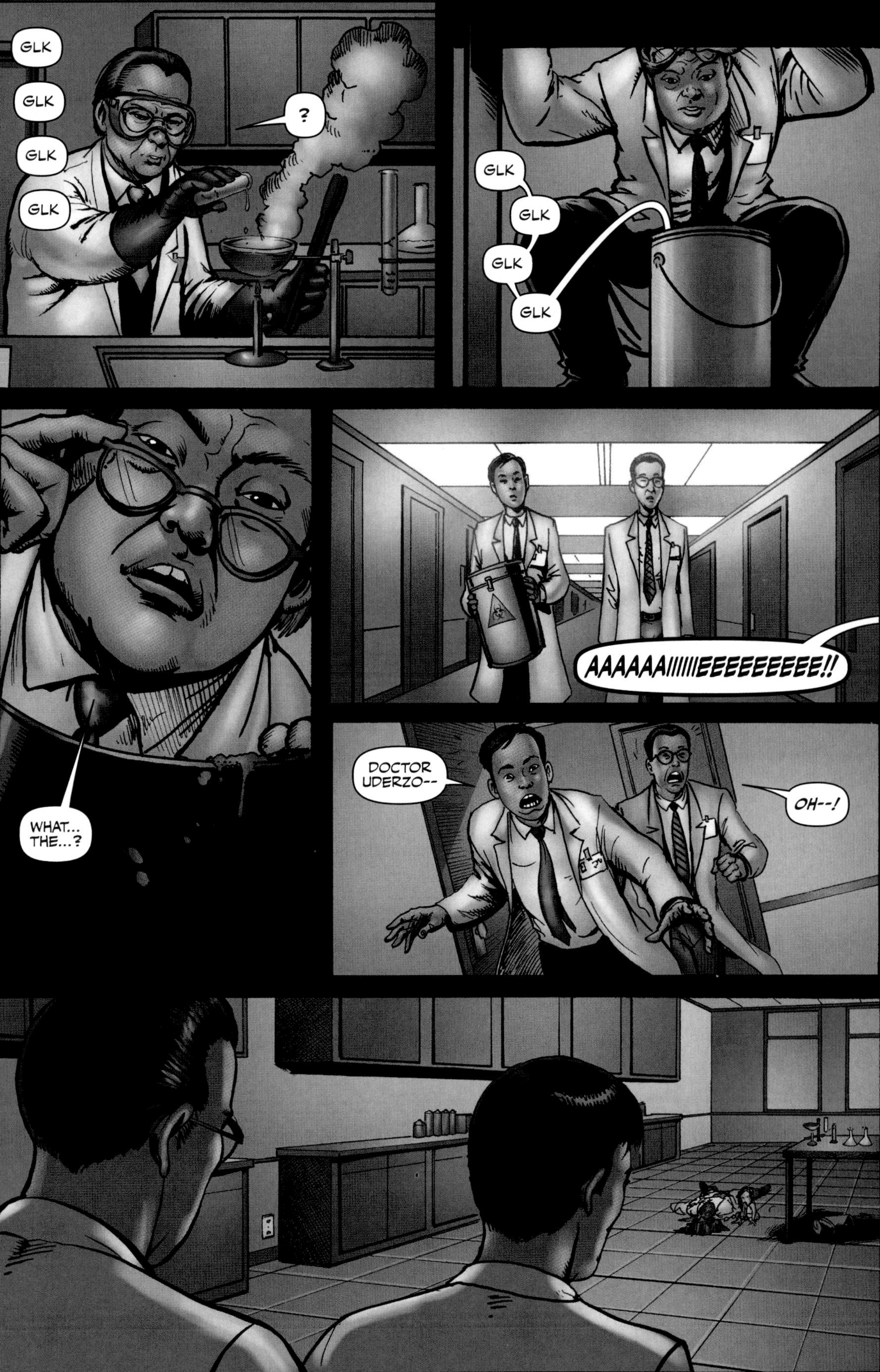
GLK
GLK
GLK
GLK
?
GLK
GLK
GLK
GLK
WHAT... THE...?
AAAAAAIIIIIIEEEEEEEEE!!
DOCTOR UDERZO--
OH--!

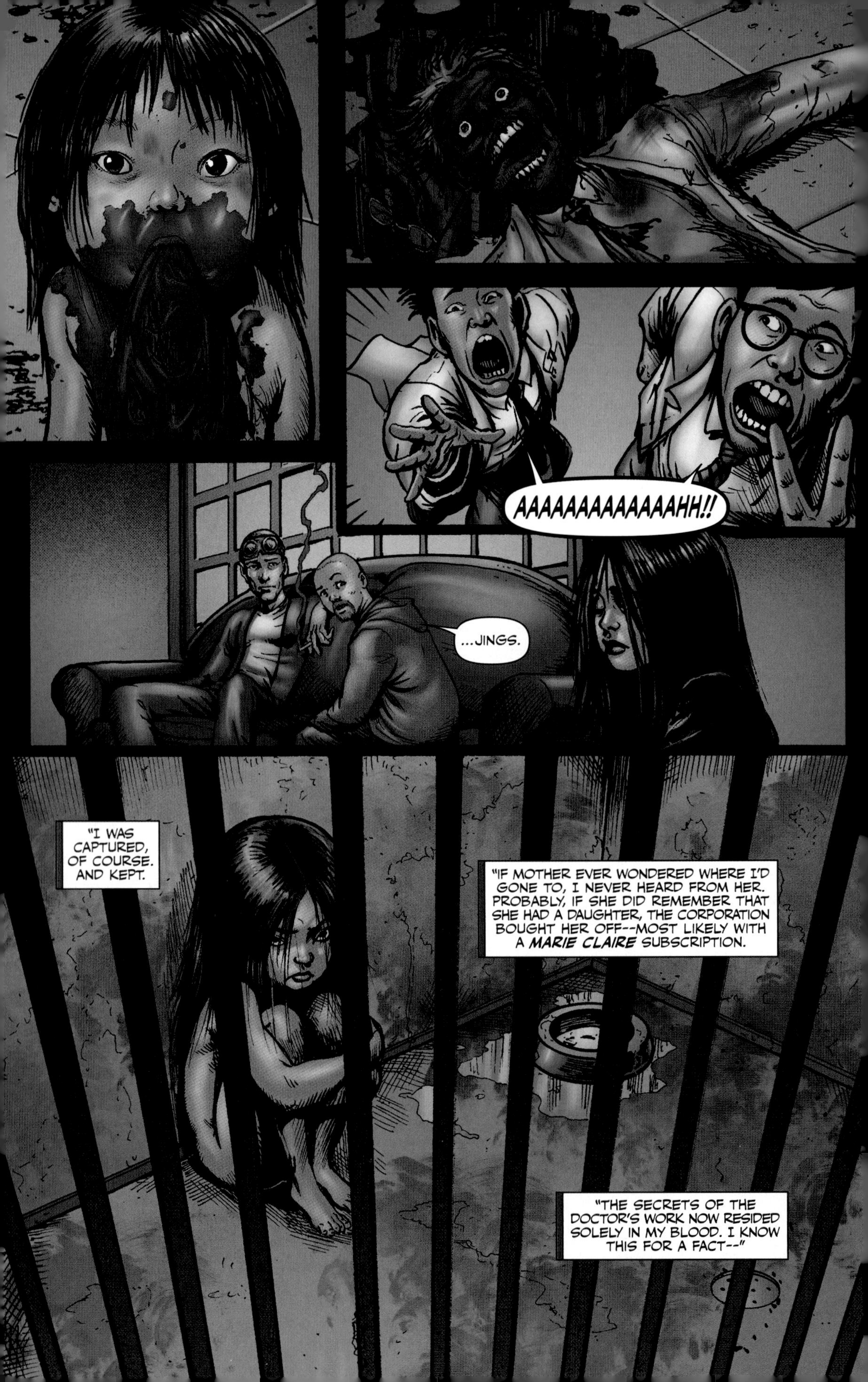
AAAAAAAAAAAAAAHH!!
...JINGS.
"I WAS CAPTURED, OF COURSE. AND KEPT.
"IF MOTHER EVER WONDERED WHERE I'D GONE TO, I NEVER HEARD FROM HER. PROBABLY, IF SHE DID REMEMBER THAT SHE HAD A DAUGHTER, THE CORPORATION BOUGHT HER OFF--MOST LIKELY WITH A MARIE CLAIRE SUBSCRIPTION.
"THE SECRETS OF THE DOCTOR'S WORK NOW RESIDED SOLELY IN MY BLOOD. I KNOW THIS FOR A FACT--"

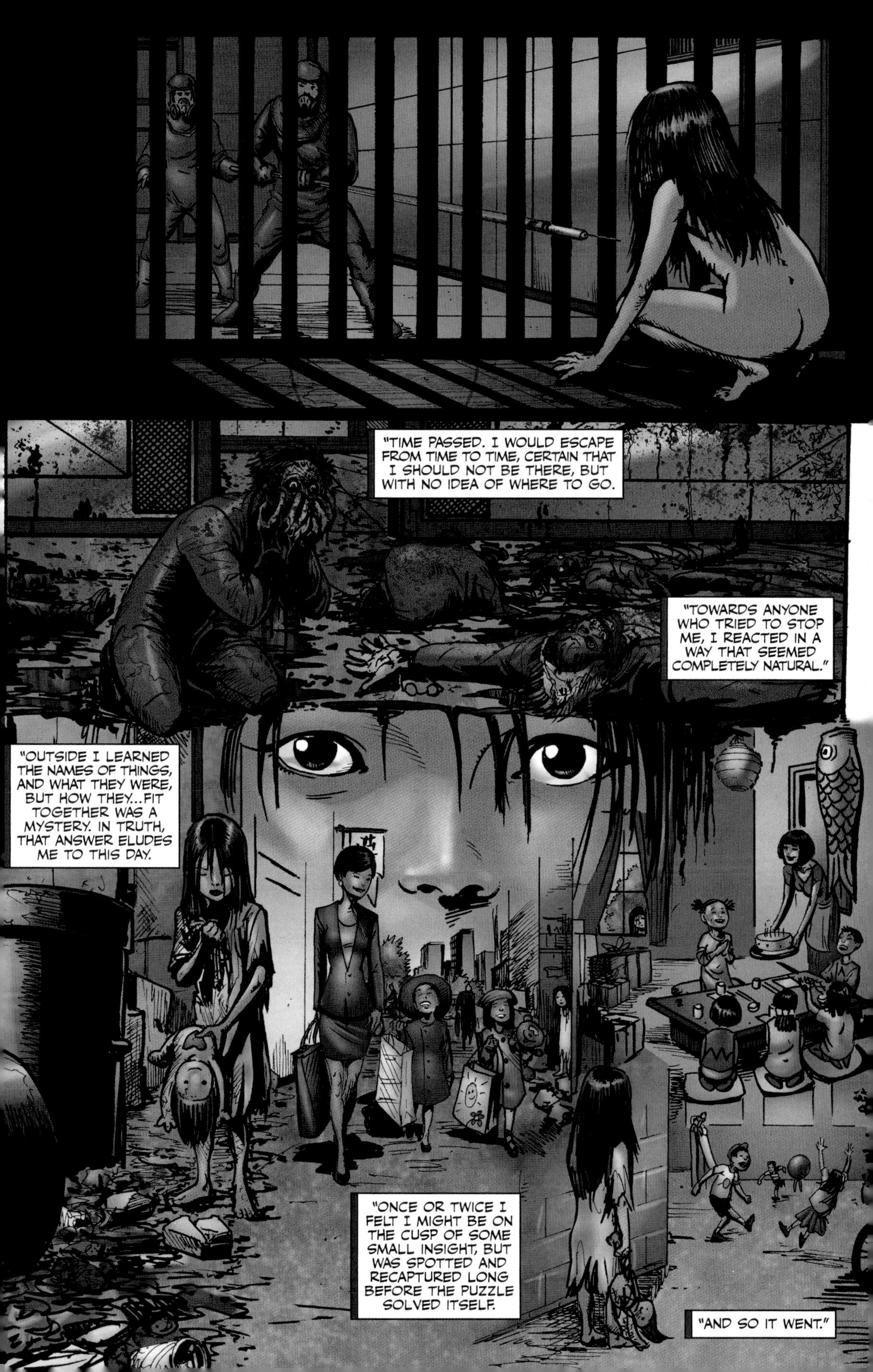
"TIME PASSED. I WOULD ESCAPE FROM TIME TO TIME, CERTAIN THAT I SHOULD NOT BE THERE, BUT WITH NO IDEA OF WHERE TO GO.
"TOWARDS ANYONE WHO TRIED TO STOP ME, I REACTED IN A WAY THAT SEEMED COMPLETELY NATURAL."
"OUTSIDE I LEARNED THE NAMES OF THINGS, AND WHAT THEY WERE, BUT HOW THEY...FIT TOGETHER WAS A MYSTERY. IN TRUTH, THAT ANSWER ELUDES ME TO THIS DAY.
"ONCE OR TWICE I FELT I MIGHT BE ON THE CUSP OF SOME SMALL INSIGHT, BUT WAS SPOTTED AND RECAPTURED LONG BEFORE THE PUZZLE SOLVED ITSELF.
"AND SO IT WENT."

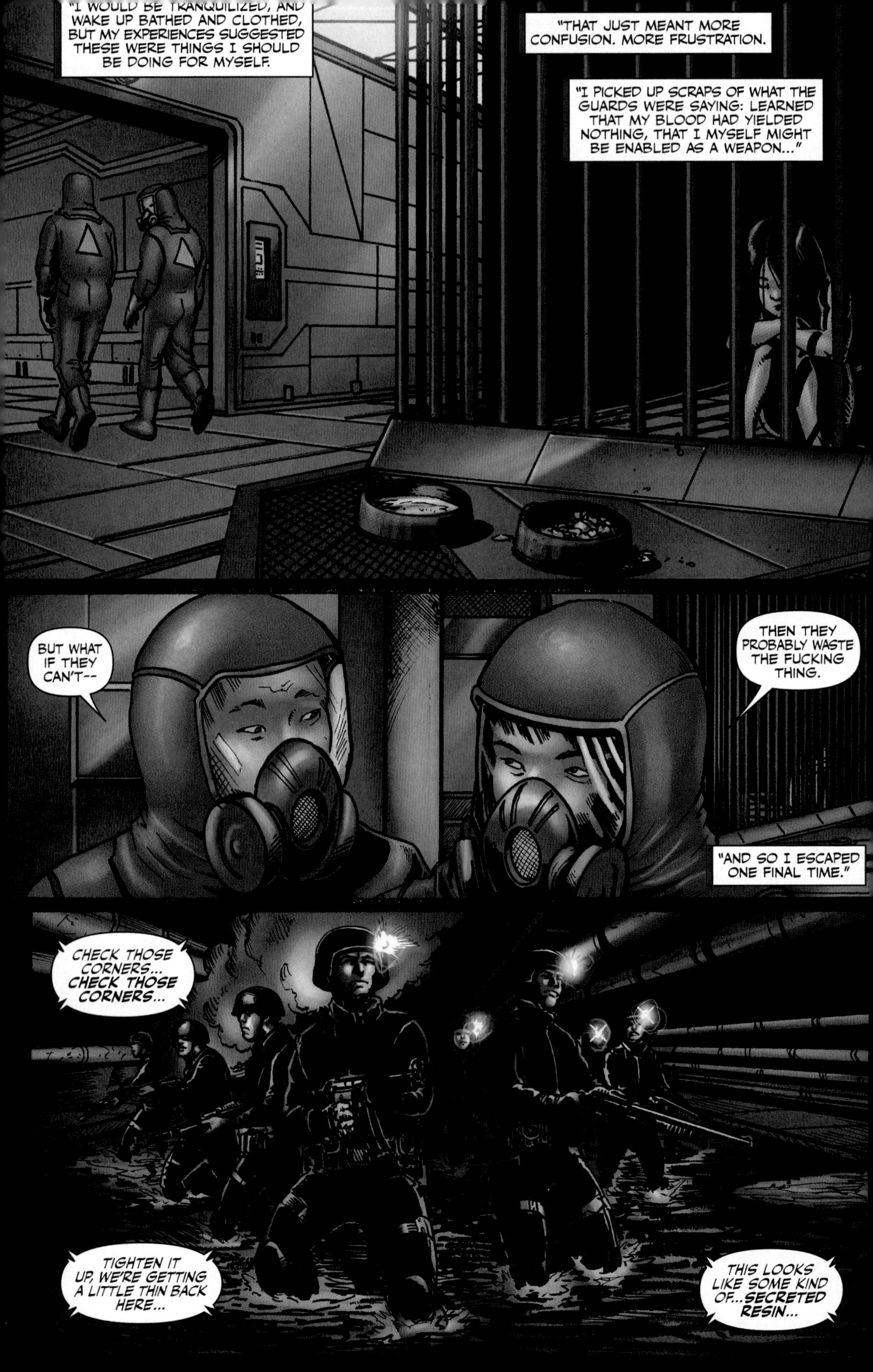
"I WOULD BE TRANQUILIZED, AND WAKE UP BATHED AND CLOTHED, BUT MY EXPERIENCES SUGGESTED THESE WERE THINGS I SHOULD BE DOING FOR MYSELF.
"THAT JUST MEANT MORE CONFUSION. MORE FRUSTRATION.
"I PICKED UP SCRAPS OF WHAT THE GUARDS WERE SAYING: LEARNED THAT MY BLOOD HAD YIELDED NOTHING, THAT I MYSELF MIGHT BE ENABLED AS A WEAPON..."
BUT WHAT IF THEY CAN'T--
THEN THEY PROBABLY WASTE THE FUCKING THING.
"AND SO I ESCAPED ONE FINAL TIME."
CHECK THOSE CORNERS... CHECK THOSE CORNERS...
TIGHTEN IT UP, WE'RE GETTING A LITTLE THIN BACK HERE...
THIS LOOKS LIKE SOME KIND OF...SECRETED RESIN...

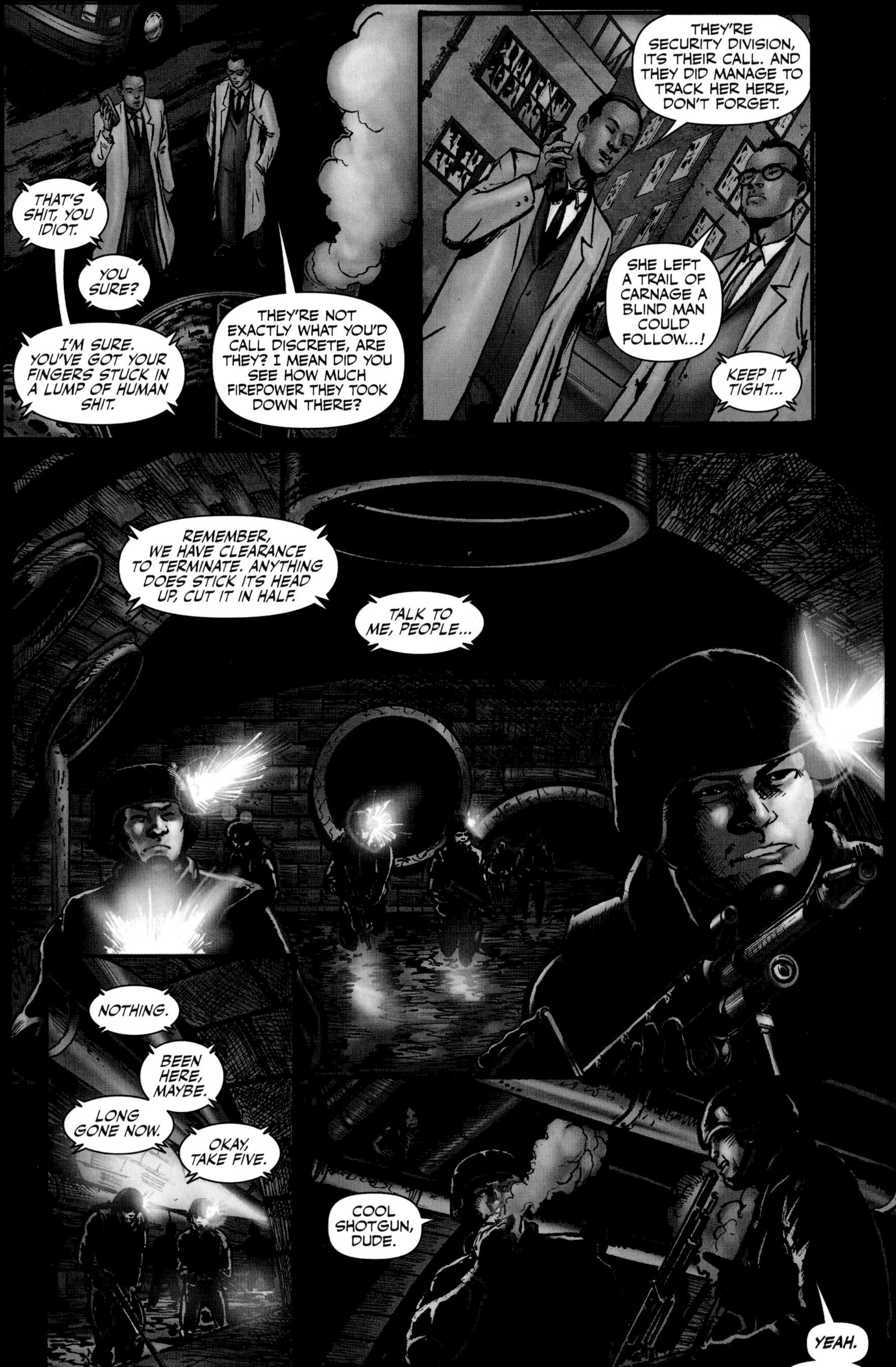
THEY'RE SECURITY DIVISION, ITS THEIR CALL. AND THEY DID MANAGE TO TRACK HER HERE, DON'T FORGET.
SHE LEFT A TRAIL OF CARNAGE A BLIND MAN COULD FOLLOW...!
KEEP IT TIGHT...
THAT'S SHIT, YOU IDIOT.
YOU SURE?
I'M SURE. YOU'VE GOT YOUR FINGERS STUCK IN A LUMP OF HUMAN SHIT.
THEY'RE NOT EXACTLY WHAT YOU'D CALL DISCRETE, ARE THEY? I MEAN DID YOU SEE HOW MUCH FIREPOWER THEY TOOK DOWN THERE?
REMEMBER, WE HAVE CLEARANCE TO TERMINATE. ANYTHING DOES STICK ITS HEAD UP, CUT IT IN HALF.
TALK TO ME, PEOPLE...
NOTHING.
BEEN HERE, MAYBE.
LONG GONE NOW.
OKAY, TAKE FIVE.
COOL SHOTGUN, DUDE.
YEAH.
I LIKE TO KEEP IT HANDY...

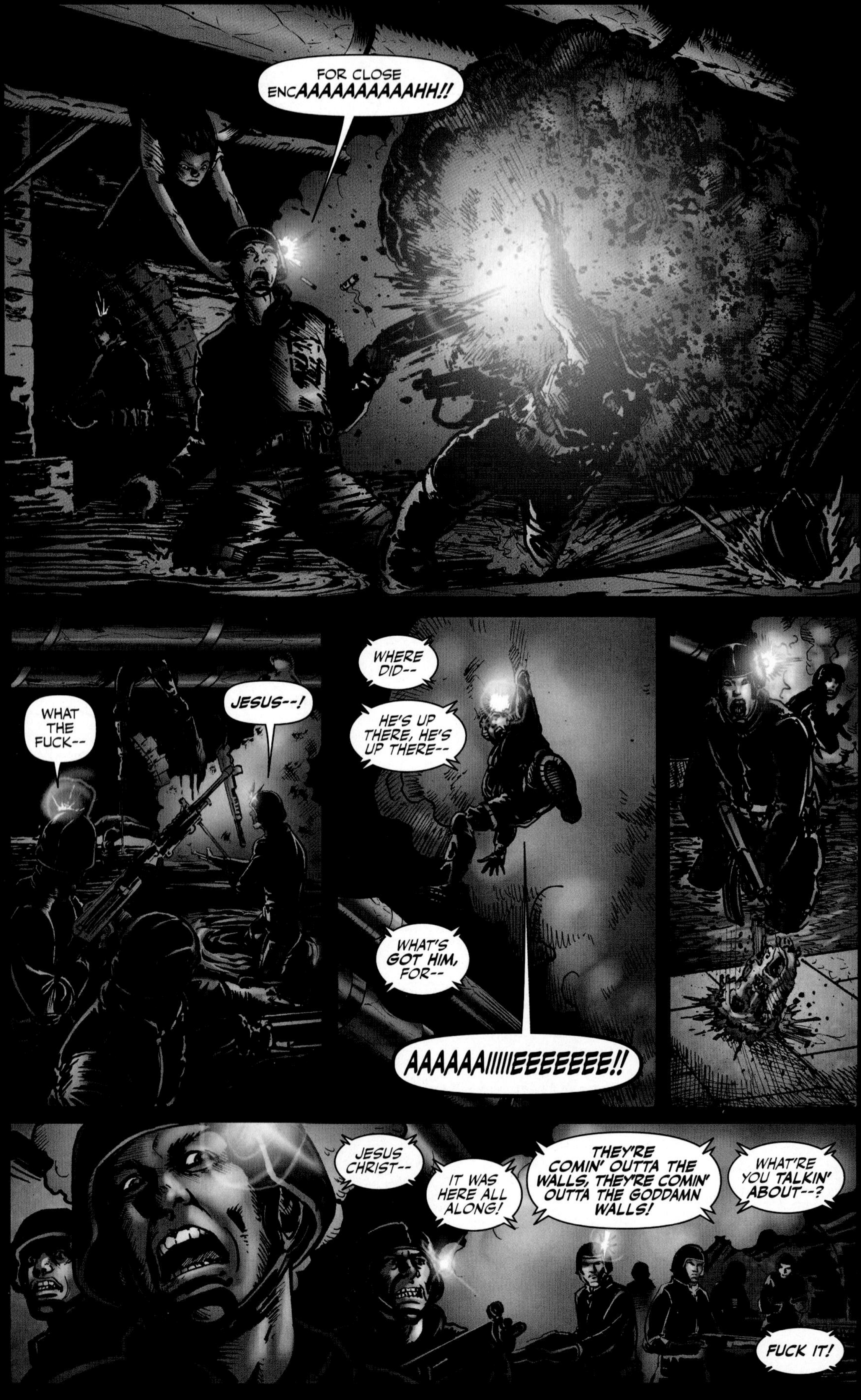
FOR CLOSE ENCAAAAAAAAAAAHH!!
WHAT THE FUCK--
JESUS--!
WHERE DID--
HE'S UP THERE, HE'S UP THERE--
WHAT'S GOT HIM, FOR--
AAAAAAIIIIIIEEEEEEE!!
JESUS CHRIST--
IT WAS HERE ALL ALONG!
THEY'RE COMIN' OUTTA THE WALLS, THEY'RE COMIN' OUTTA THE GODDAMN WALLS!
WHAT'RE YOU TALKIN' ABOUT--?
FUCK IT!

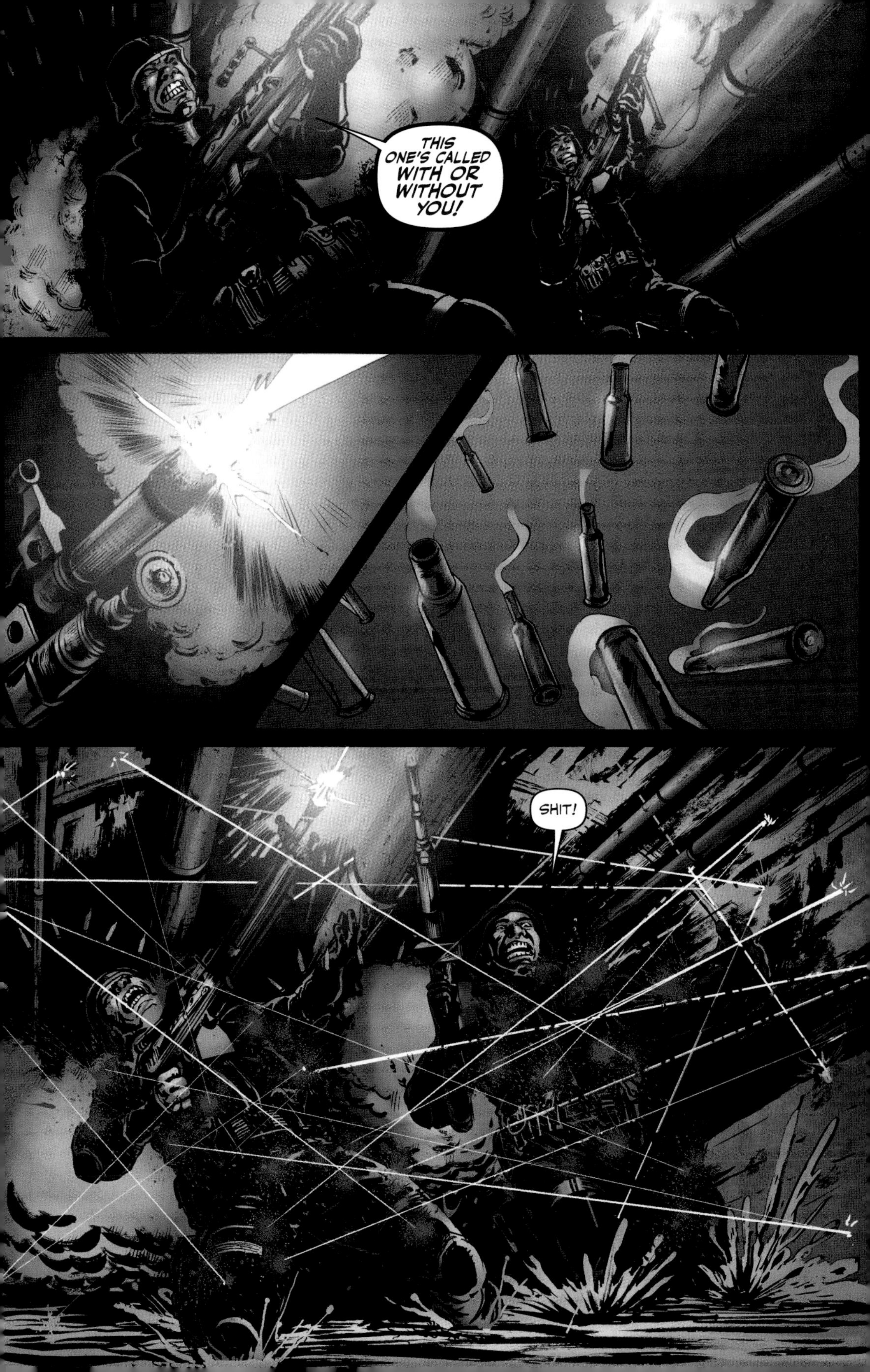
THIS ONE'S CALLED WITH OR WITHOUT YOU!
SHIT!

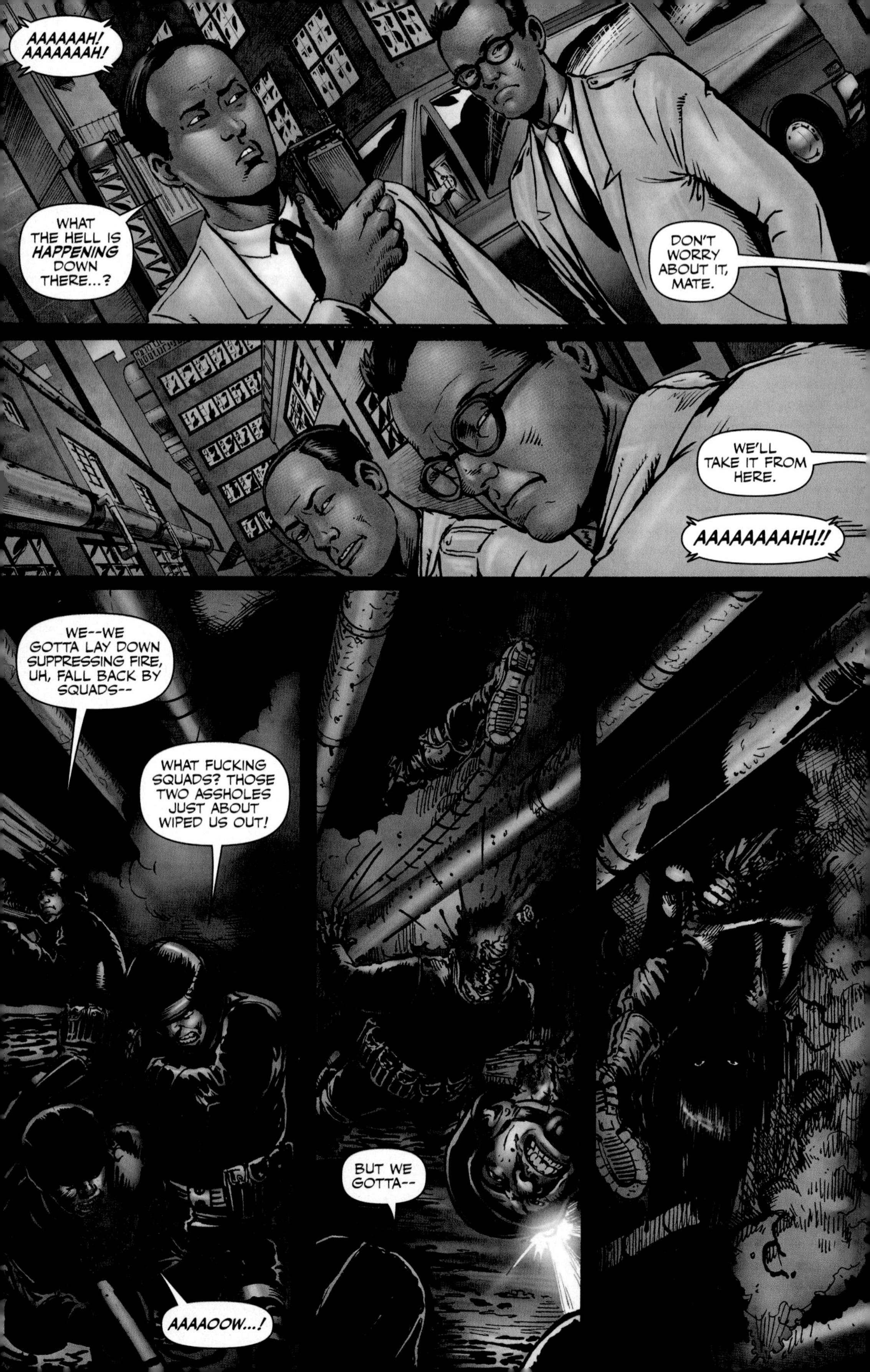
AAAAAAH! AAAAAAAH!
WHAT THE HELL IS HAPPENING DOWN THERE...?
DON'T WORRY ABOUT IT, MATE.
WE'LL TAKE IT FROM HERE.
AAAAAAAAHH!!
WE--WE GOTTA LAY DOWN SUPPRESSING FIRE, UH, FALL BACK BY SQUADS--
WHAT FUCKING SQUADS? THOSE TWO ASSHOLES JUST ABOUT WIPED US OUT!
AAAAOOW...!
BUT WE GOTTA--

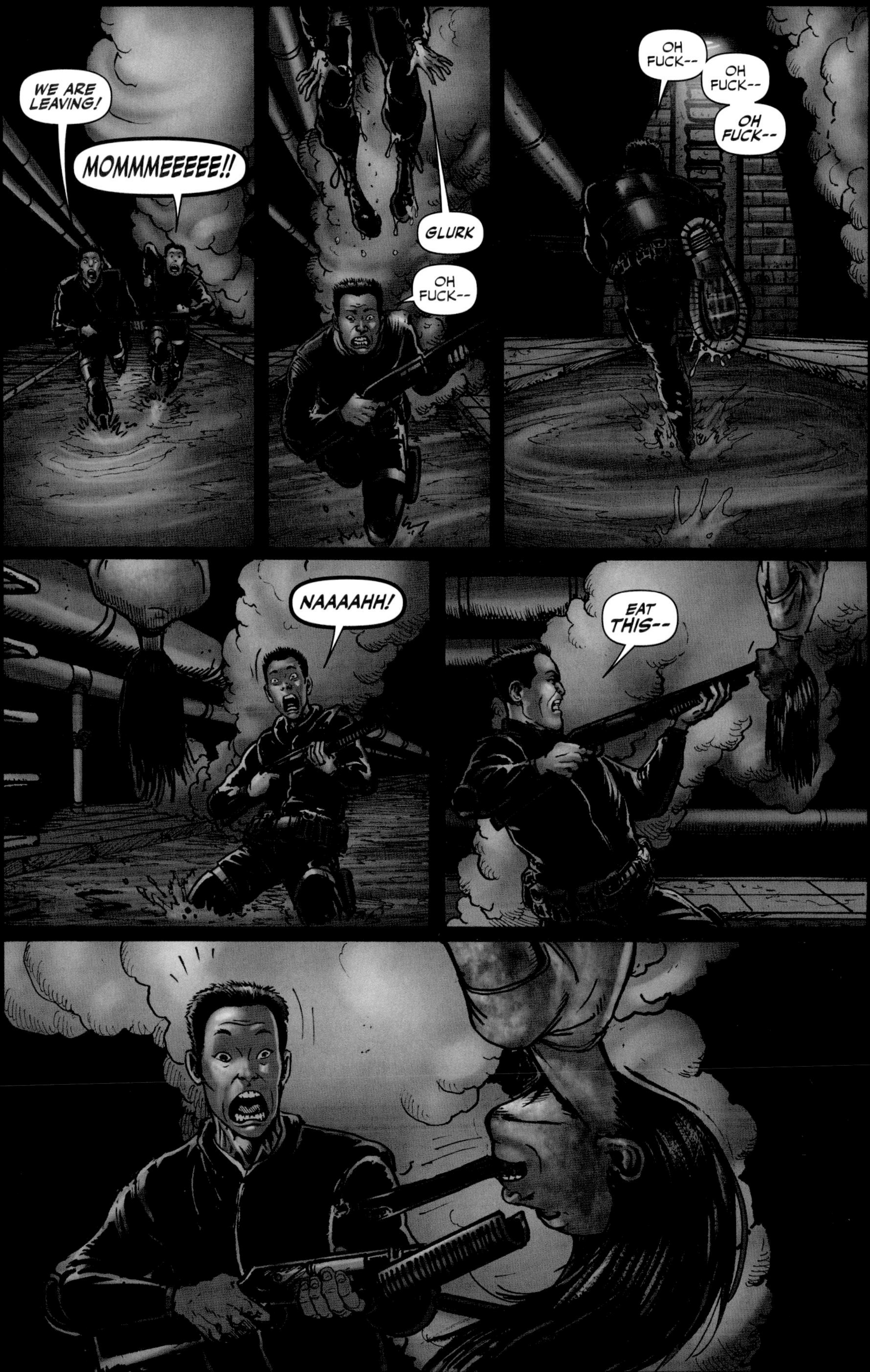
WE ARE LEAVING!
MOMMMEEEEE!!
GLURK
OH FUCK--
OH FUCK--
OH FUCK--
OH FUCK--
NAAAAHH!
EAT THIS--

NNOOOOOO...!

THAT DON'T SOUND TOO CLEVER.

AAAAAH--!

AAH--

HHHHHHHHHH

SSSHHHHHHHH

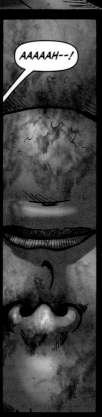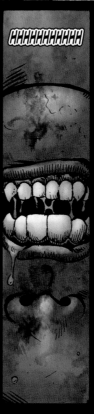

HOW COME THEY DIDN'T USE GAS FIRST, THEN GO IN SHOOTIN'?

'COS THEY'RE ARSEHOLES.

AAAAK!!

THAT'S THE TROUBLE WITH THESE MACHO BERKS, THEY THINK GUNS'RE THE ANSWER TO EVERYTHING.

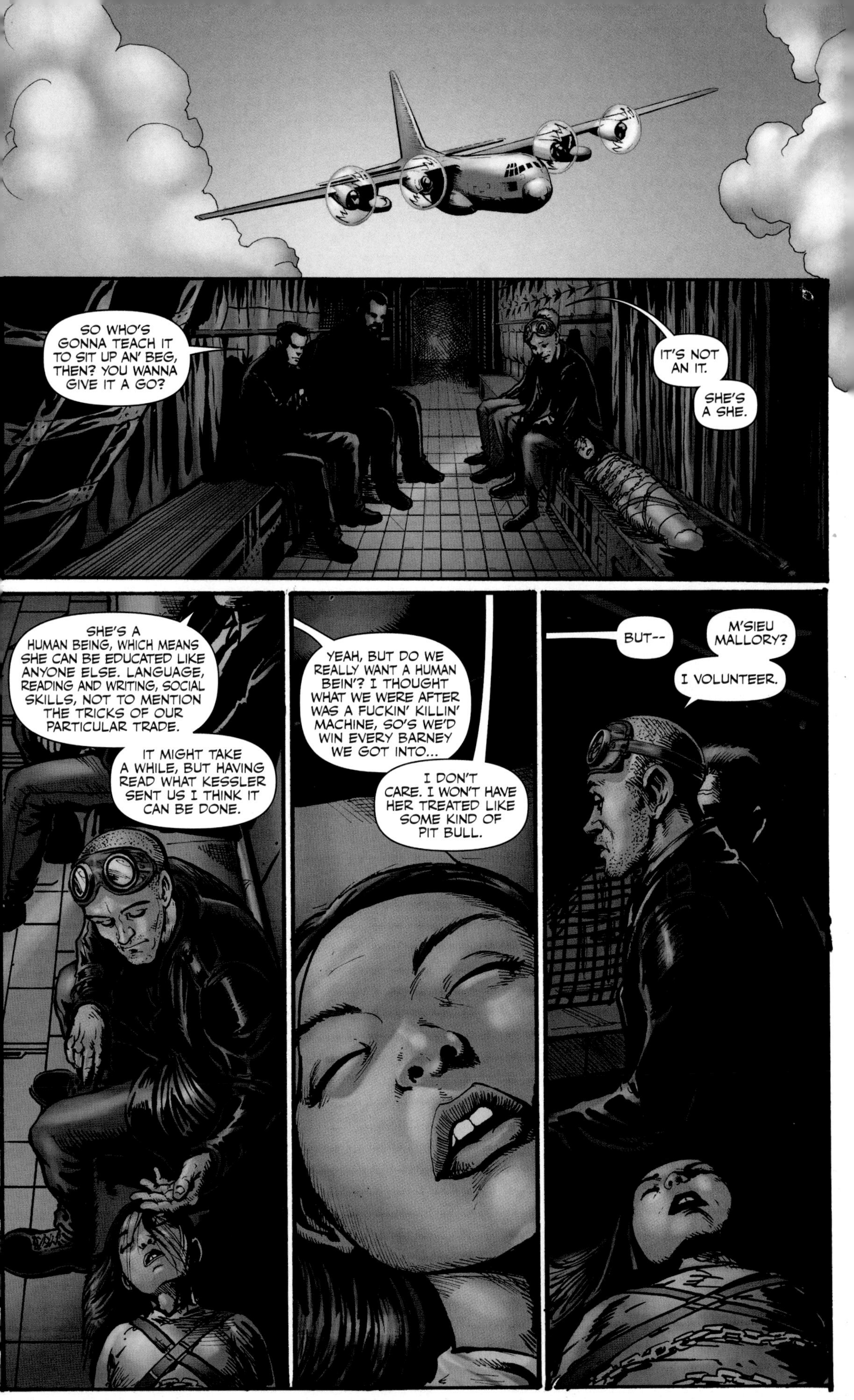
SO WHO'S GONNA TEACH IT TO SIT UP AN' BEG, THEN? YOU WANNA GIVE IT A GO?
IT'S NOT AN IT.
SHE'S A SHE.
SHE'S A HUMAN BEING, WHICH MEANS SHE CAN BE EDUCATED LIKE ANYONE ELSE. LANGUAGE, READING AND WRITING, SOCIAL SKILLS, NOT TO MENTION THE TRICKS OF OUR PARTICULAR TRADE.
IT MIGHT TAKE A WHILE, BUT HAVING READ WHAT KESSLER SENT US I THINK IT CAN BE DONE.
YEAH, BUT DO WE REALLY WANT A HUMAN BEIN'? I THOUGHT WHAT WE WERE AFTER WAS A FUCKIN' KILLIN' MACHINE, SO'S WE'D WIN EVERY BARNEY WE GOT INTO...
I DON'T CARE. I WON'T HAVE HER TREATED LIKE SOME KIND OF PIT BULL.
BUT--
M'SIEU MALLORY?
I VOLUNTEER.

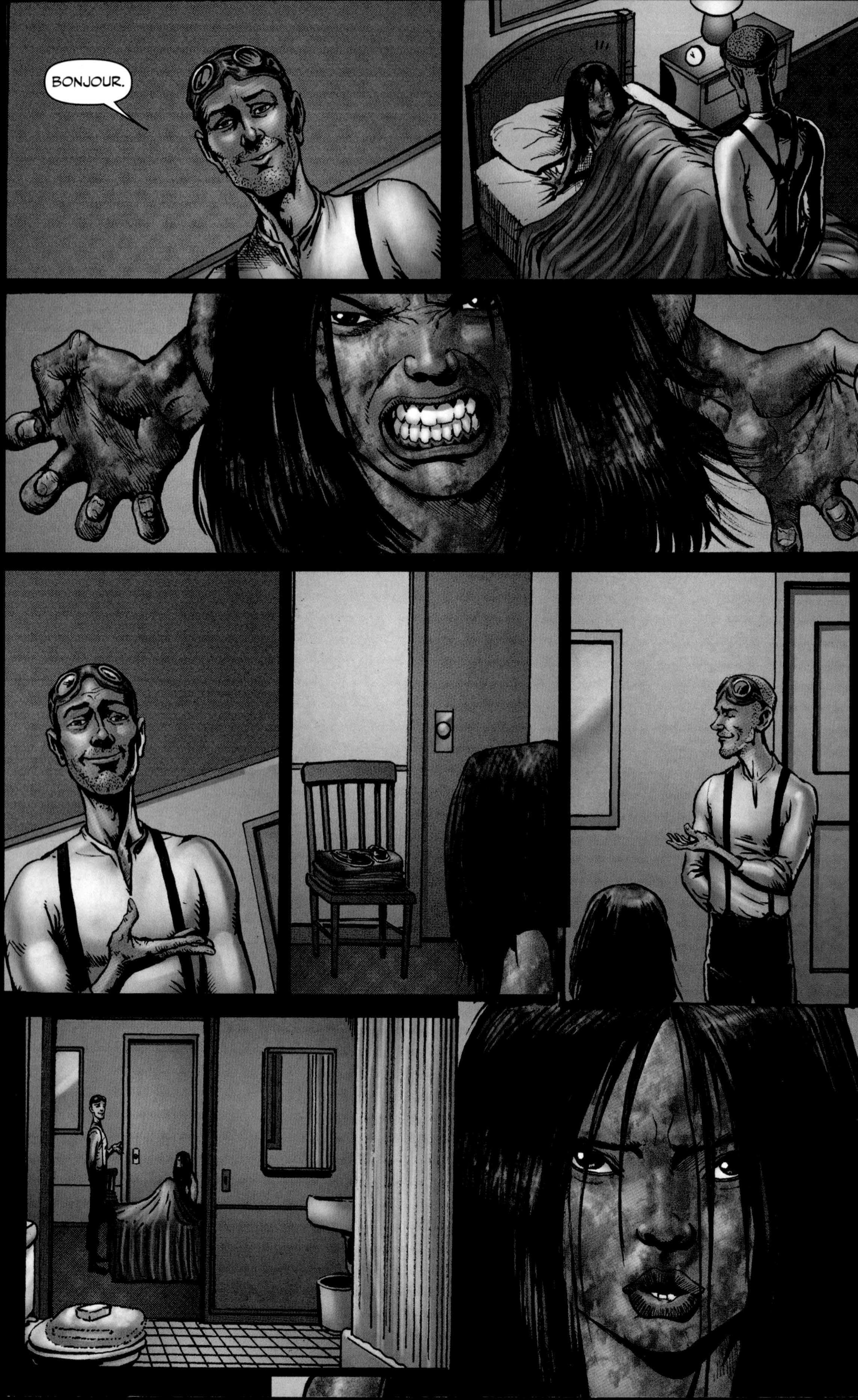
BONJOUR.

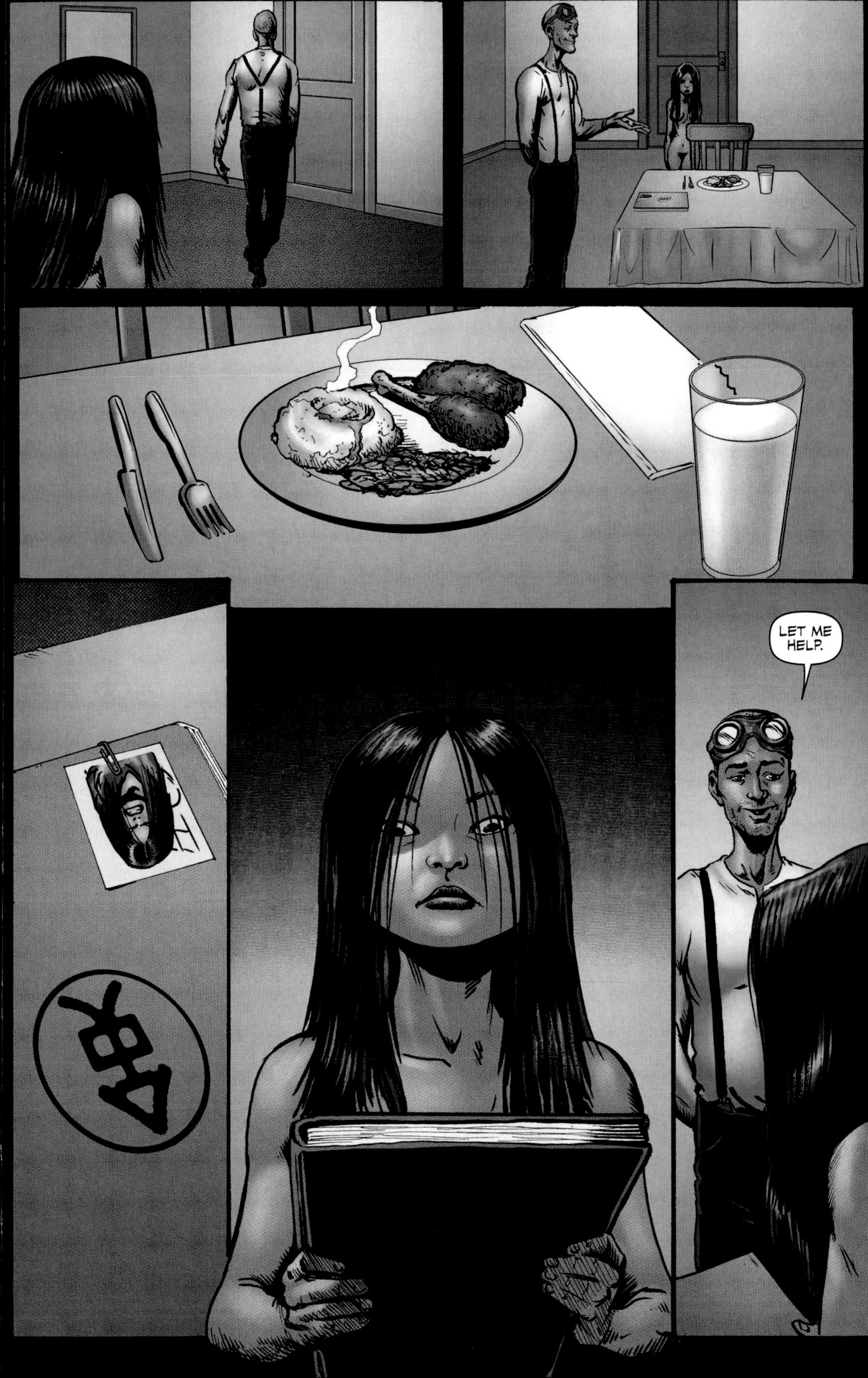
LET ME HELP.

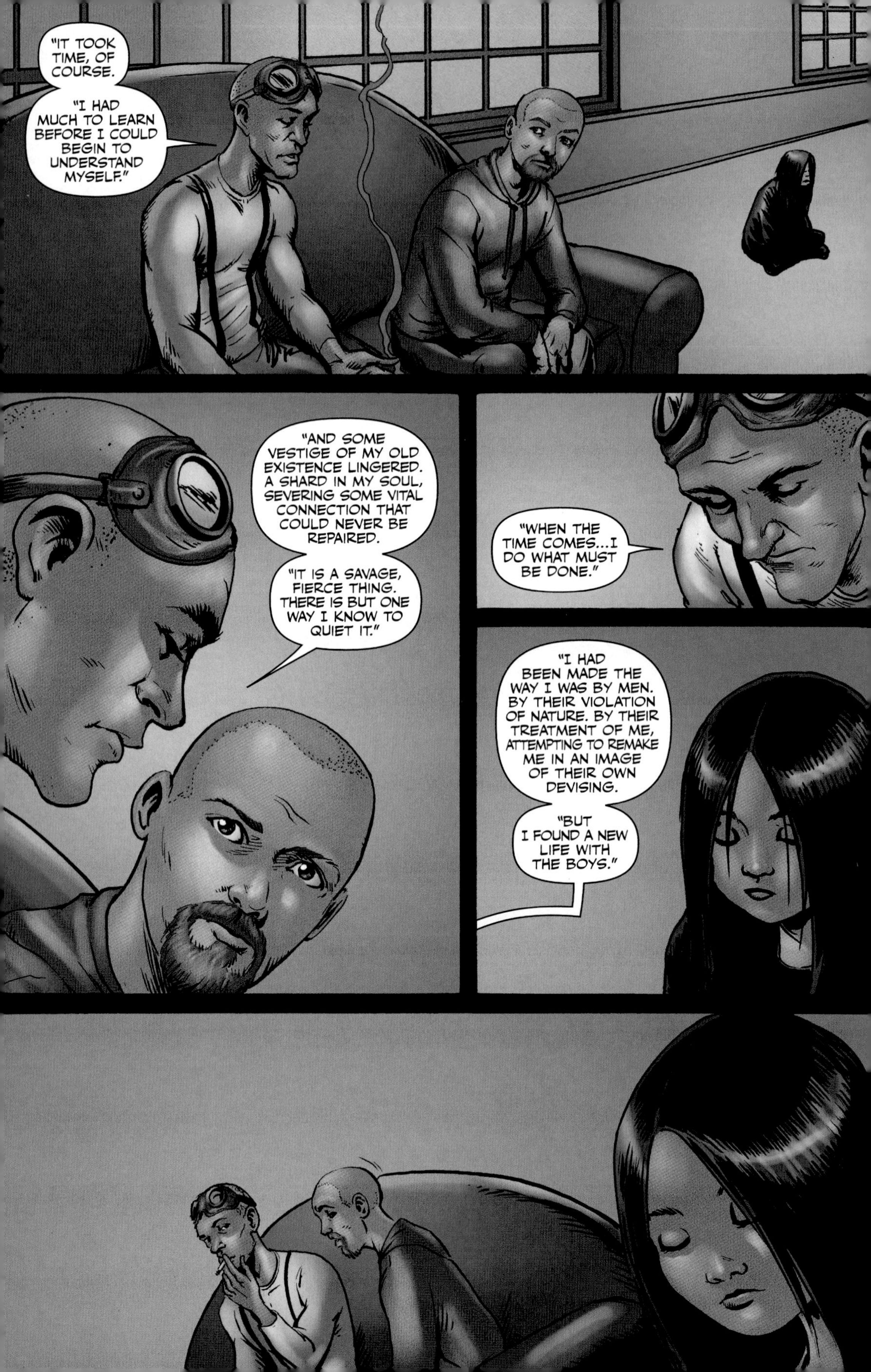
"IT TOOK TIME, OF COURSE.
"I HAD MUCH TO LEARN BEFORE I COULD BEGIN TO UNDERSTAND MYSELF."
"AND SOME VESTIGE OF MY OLD EXISTENCE LINGERED. A SHARD IN MY SOUL, SEVERING SOME VITAL CONNECTION THAT COULD NEVER BE REPAIRED.
"IT IS A SAVAGE, FIERCE THING. THERE IS BUT ONE WAY I KNOW TO QUIET IT."
"WHEN THE TIME COMES...I DO WHAT MUST BE DONE."
"I HAD BEEN MADE THE WAY I WAS BY MEN. BY THEIR VIOLATION OF NATURE. BY THEIR TREATMENT OF ME, ATTEMPTING TO REMAKE ME IN AN IMAGE OF THEIR OWN DEVISING.
"BUT I FOUND A NEW LIFE WITH THE BOYS."

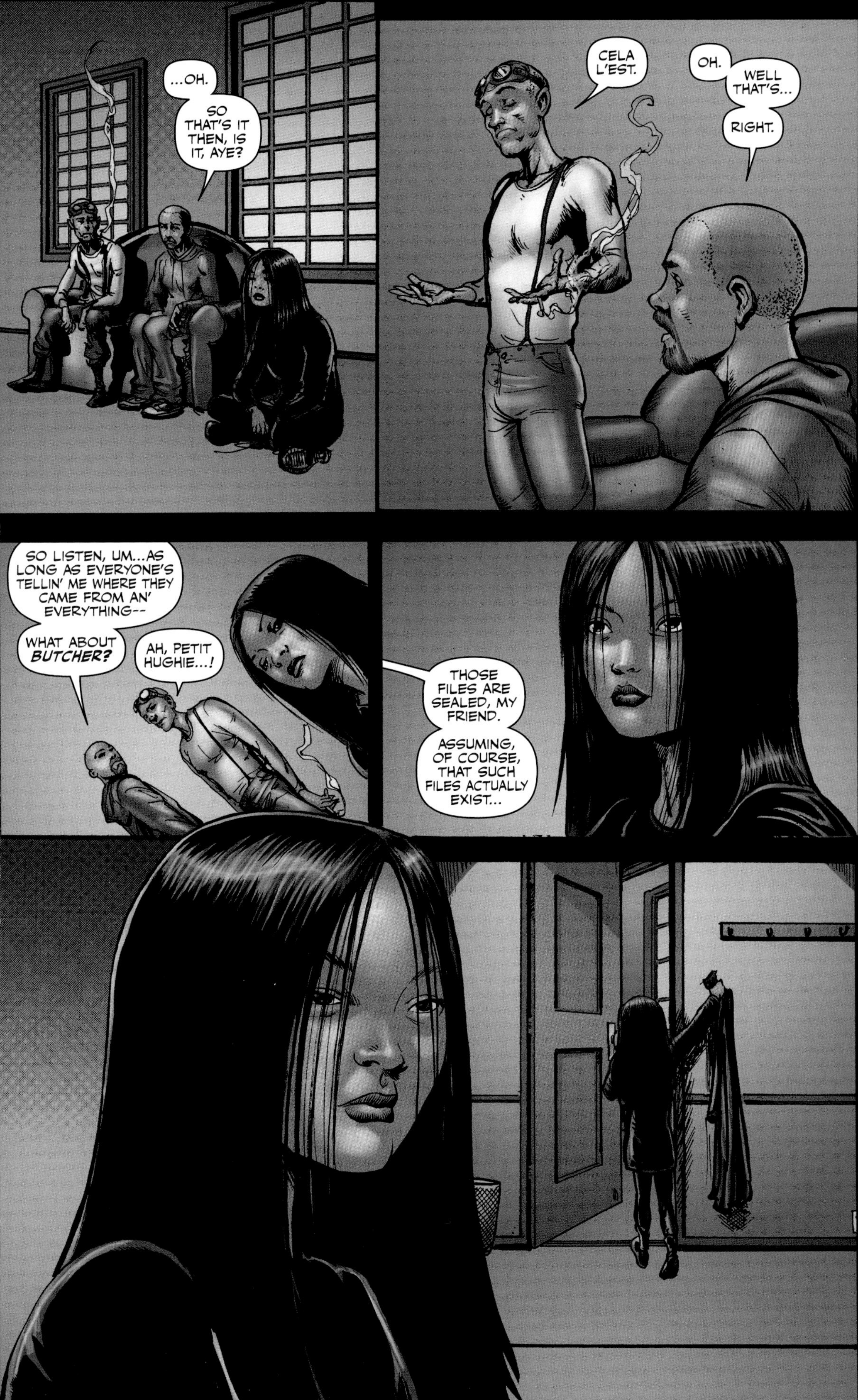
...OH.
SO THAT'S IT THEN, IS IT, AYE?
CELA L'EST.
OH.
WELL THAT'S...
RIGHT.
SO LISTEN, UM...AS LONG AS EVERYONE'S TELLIN' ME WHERE THEY CAME FROM AN' EVERYTHING--
WHAT ABOUT *BUTCHER?*
AH, PETIT HUGHIE...!
THOSE FILES ARE SEALED, MY FRIEND.
ASSUMING, OF COURSE, THAT SUCH FILES ACTUALLY EXIST...

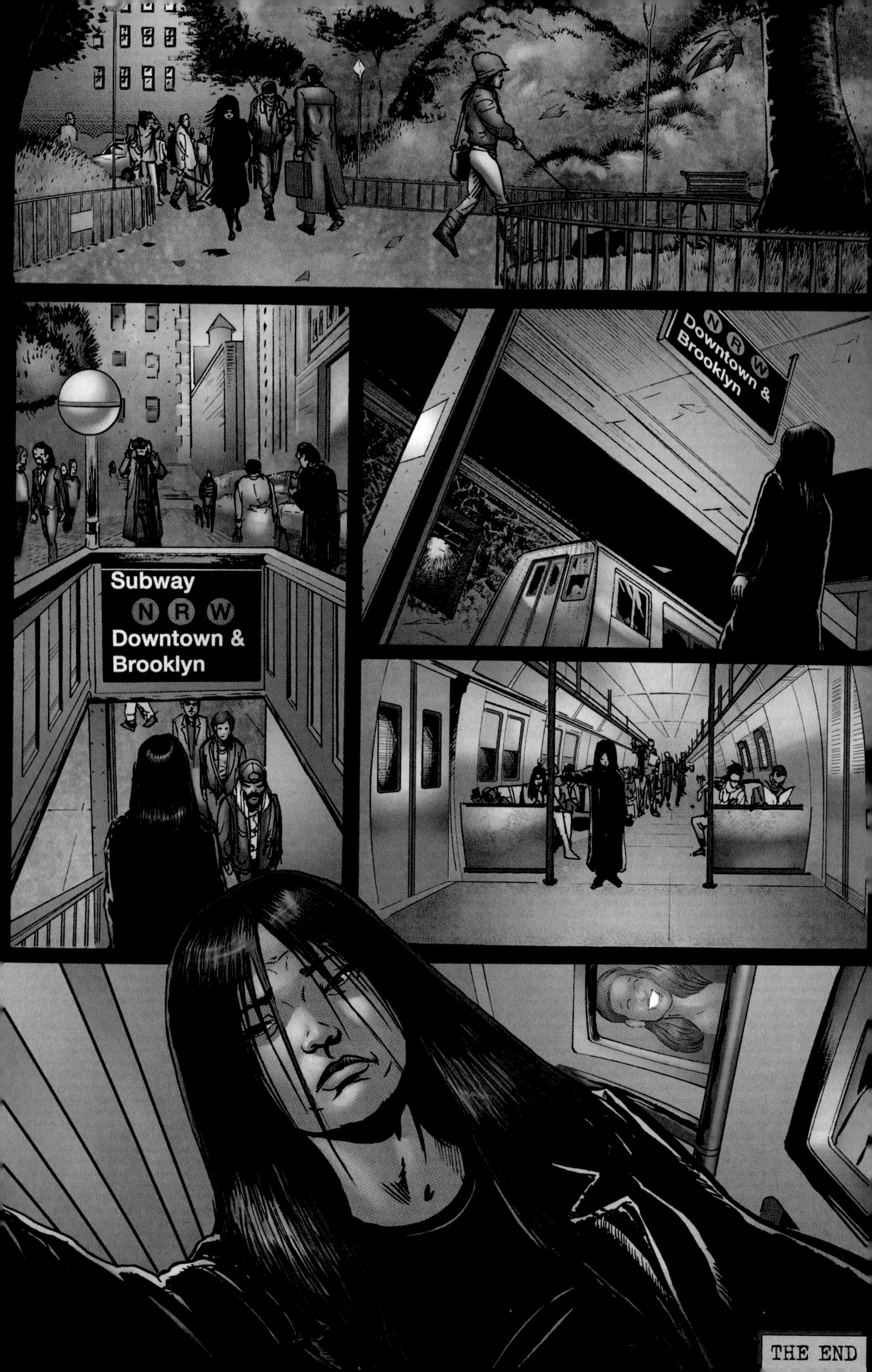

Subway
N R W
Downtown &
Brooklyn
N R W
Downtown &
Brooklyn
THE END

OMNIBUS
BONUS MATERIAL

Faithful Readers,

The following story is reprinted from the Comic Book Legal Defense Fund's "Liberty Comics Annual, 2010."

"The Comic That Got the Legend Fired"
Written by Garth Ennis
Art by Rob Steen
Colors by Rob Steen
Lettering by Rob Steen

For more information regarding the Comic Book Legal Defense Fund, go to: http://cbldf.org/

Regards,
The Editor

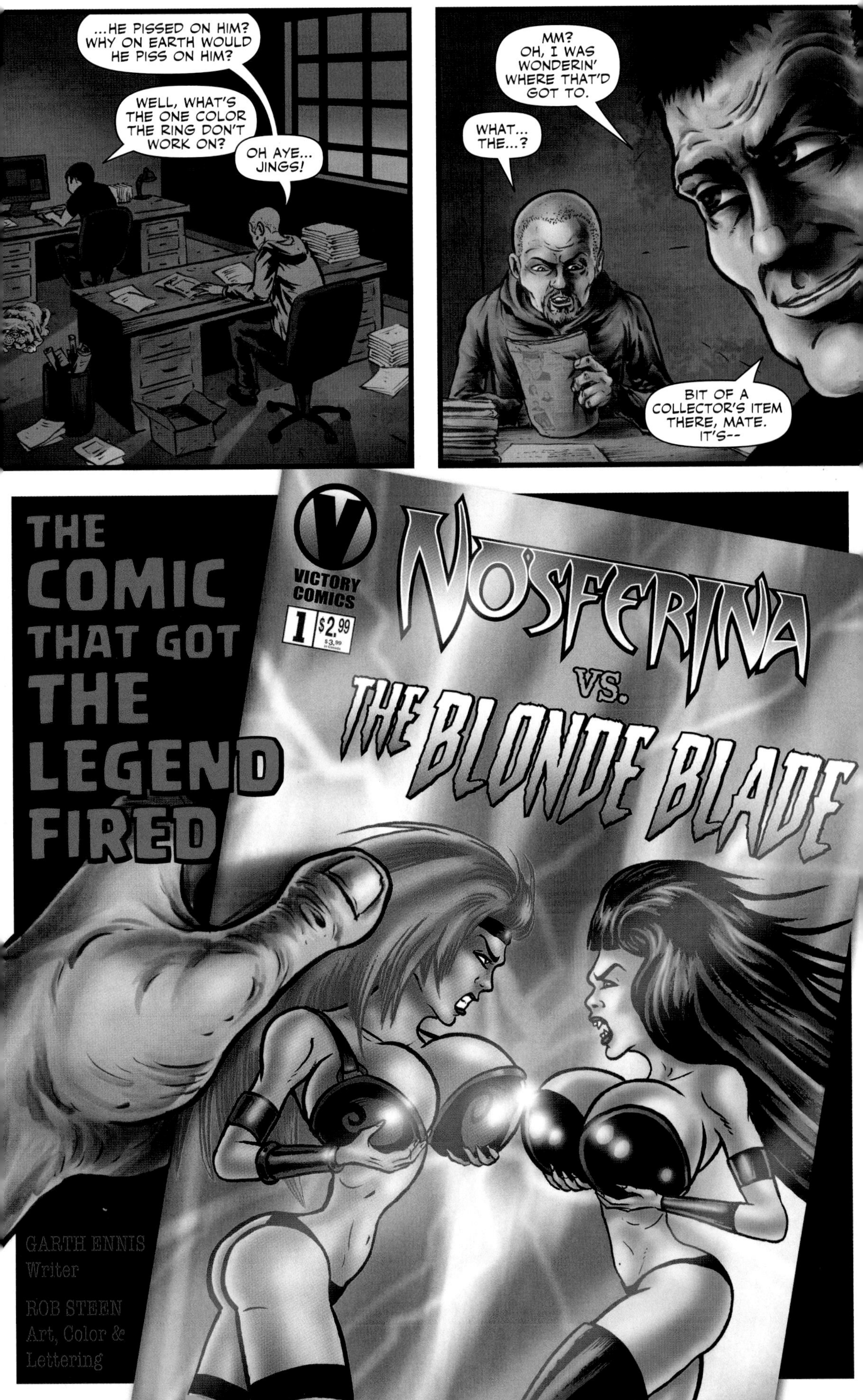
...HE PISSED ON HIM? WHY ON EARTH WOULD HE PISS ON HIM?
WELL, WHAT'S THE ONE COLOR THE RING DON'T WORK ON?
OH AYE... JINGS!
MM? OH, I WAS WONDERIN' WHERE THAT'D GOT TO.
WHAT... THE...?
BIT OF A COLLECTOR'S ITEM THERE, MATE. IT'S--
THE COMIC THAT GOT THE LEGEND FIRED
VICTORY COMICS
1 $2.99 $3.99 in Canada
NOSFERINA VS. THE BLONDE BLADE
GARTH ENNIS
Writer
ROB STEEN
Art, Color & Lettering

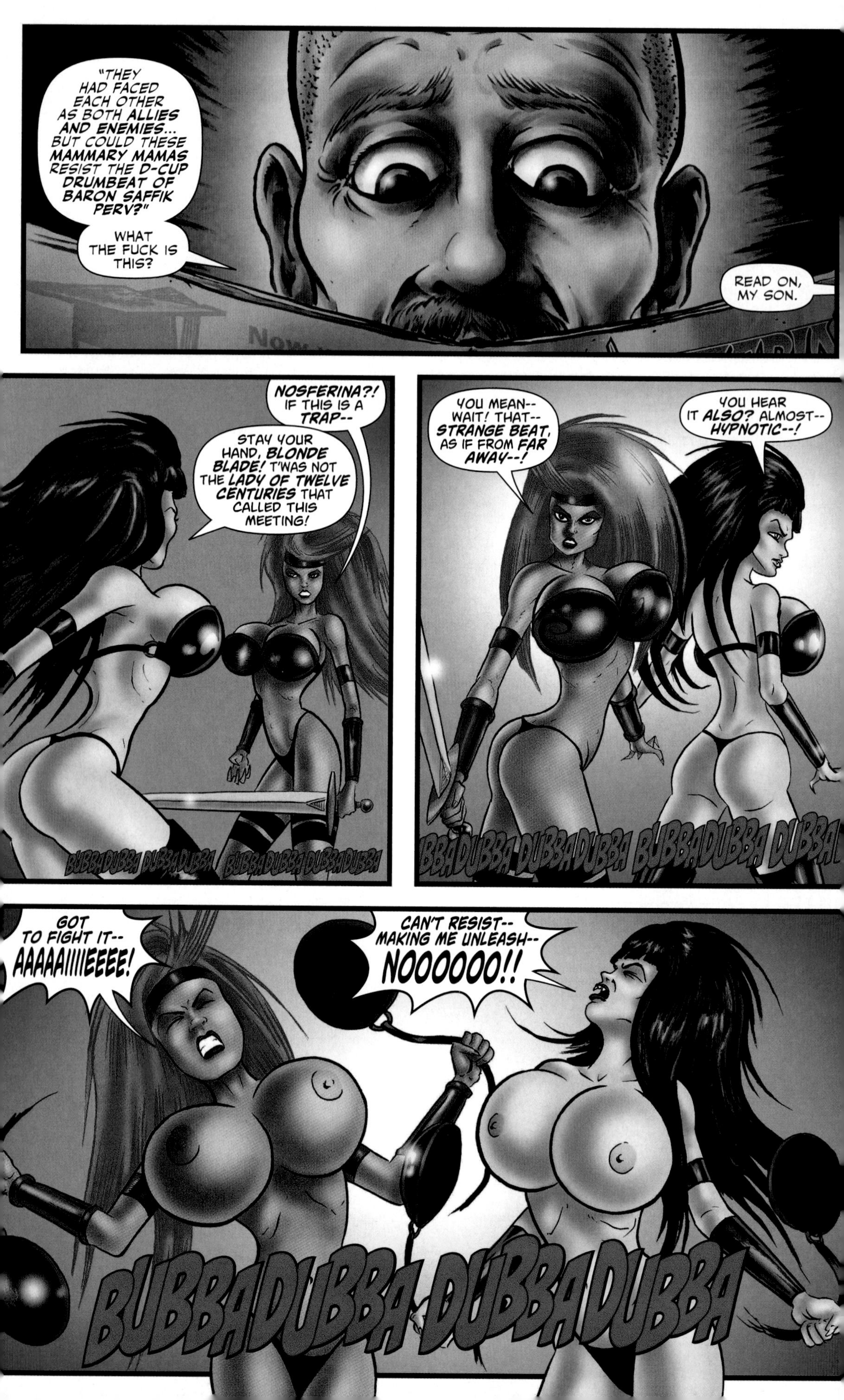
"THEY HAD FACED EACH OTHER AS BOTH ALLIES AND ENEMIES... BUT COULD THESE MAMMARY MAMAS RESIST THE D-CUP DRUMBEAT OF BARON SAFFIK PERV?"
WHAT THE FUCK IS THIS?
READ ON, MY SON.
NOSFERINA?! IF THIS IS A TRAP--
STAY YOUR HAND, BLONDE BLADE! T'WAS NOT THE LADY OF TWELVE CENTURIES THAT CALLED THIS MEETING!
BUBBADUBBA DUBBADUBBA BUBBADUBBA DUBBADUBBA
YOU MEAN-- WAIT! THAT-- STRANGE BEAT, AS IF FROM FAR AWAY--!
YOU HEAR IT ALSO? ALMOST-- HYPNOTIC--!
BBADUBBA DUBBADUBBA BUBBADUBBA DUBBA
GOT TO FIGHT IT-- AAAAAIIIIIEEEE!
CAN'T RESIST-- MAKING ME UNLEASH-- NOOOOOO!!
BUBBADUBBA DUBBADUBBA

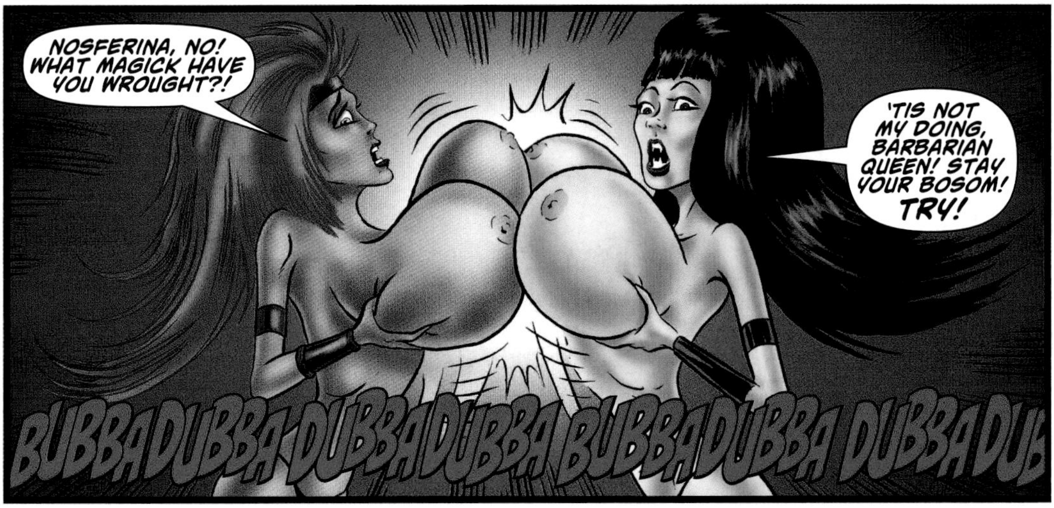
NOSFERINA, NO! WHAT MAGICK HAVE YOU WROUGHT?!
'TIS NOT MY DOING, BARBARIAN QUEEN! STAY YOUR BOSOM! TRY!
BUBBADUBBA DUBBADUBBA BUBBADUBBA DUBBADUB

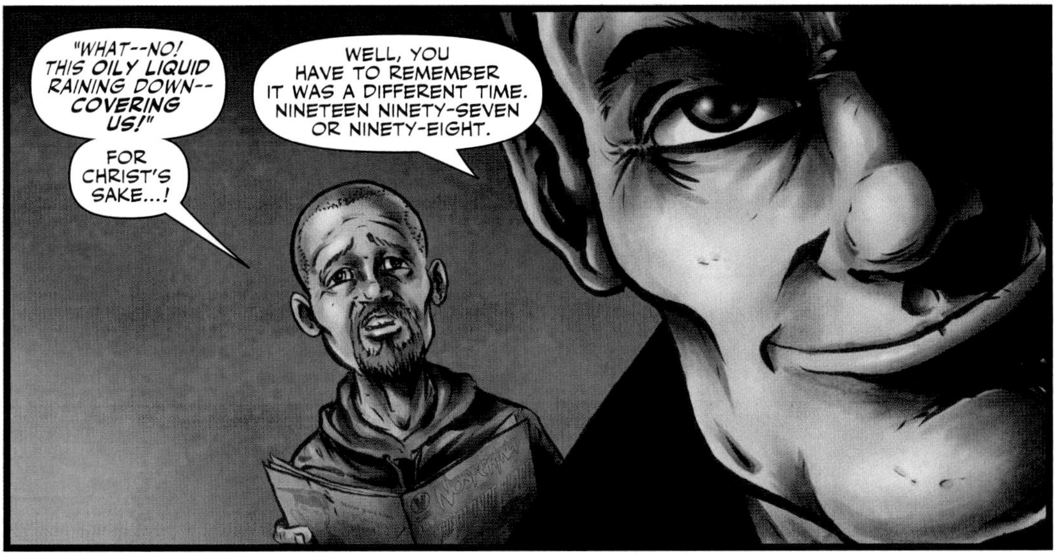
"WHAT--NO! THIS OILY LIQUID RAINING DOWN-- COVERING US!"
FOR CHRIST'S SAKE...!
WELL, YOU HAVE TO REMEMBER IT WAS A DIFFERENT TIME. NINETEEN NINETY-SEVEN OR NINETY-EIGHT.

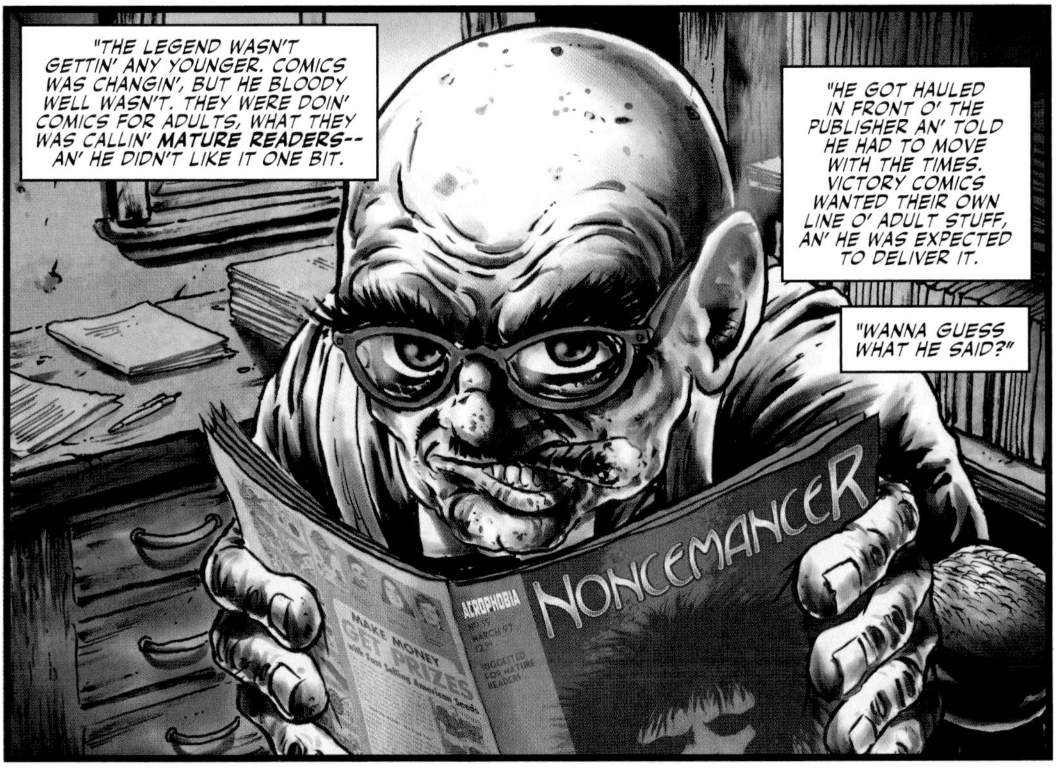
"THE LEGEND WASN'T GETTIN' ANY YOUNGER. COMICS WAS CHANGIN', BUT HE BLOODY WELL WASN'T. THEY WERE DOIN' COMICS FOR ADULTS, WHAT THEY WAS CALLIN' MATURE READERS-- AN' HE DIDN'T LIKE IT ONE BIT.
"HE GOT HAULED IN FRONT O' THE PUBLISHER AN' TOLD HE HAD TO MOVE WITH THE TIMES. VICTORY COMICS WANTED THEIR OWN LINE O' ADULT STUFF, AN' HE WAS EXPECTED TO DELIVER IT.
"WANNA GUESS WHAT HE SAID?"
AEROPHOBIA
NONCEMANCER
MAKE MONEY
GET PRIZES

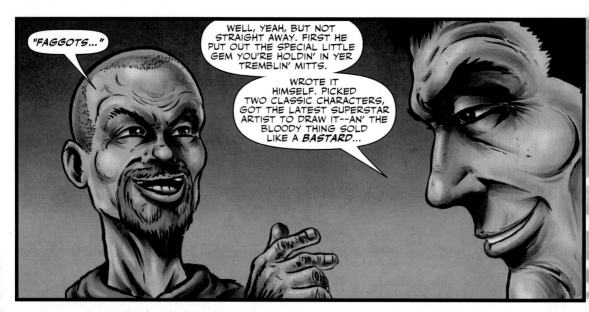

"FAGGOTS..."

WELL, YEAH, BUT NOT STRAIGHT AWAY. FIRST HE PUT OUT THE SPECIAL LITTLE GEM YOU'RE HOLDIN' IN YER TREMBLIN' MITTS.

WROTE IT HIMSELF. PICKED TWO CLASSIC CHARACTERS, GOT THE LATEST SUPERSTAR ARTIST TO DRAW IT--AN' THE BLOODY THING SOLD LIKE A *BASTARD*...

IS IT... DYING AWAY...?

ARE WE-- *FREE*--?

BUBBADUBBA, DUBBA DUBBA
BUBBADUBBA, DUBBA DUBBA

BUBBA DUBBA DUBBA

STARTING UP AGAIN! NO! NO!

NOOOOOOO!!!

BUBBADUBBA DUBBA DUBB

THE LEGEND SAID THAT IF THEY WANTED ADULT READERS-- WELL, STUFF LIKE NOSFERINA AN' THE BLONDE BLADE'D *ALWAYS* HAD ADULT READERS. DIFFERENT SORT, MAYBE, AN' NOT THE KIND YOU WANNA OWN UP TO, BUT THEY WERE THERE.

HE WAS RIGHT, TOO, THAT ONE ISSUE OUTSOLD *REVEREND SWEAR* AN' *BUSYDICK* AN' *BALDY DOME*, *3D GLASSES* ALL PUT TOGETHER.

SO... THEY FIRED HIM?

ON THE FUCKIN' SPOT.

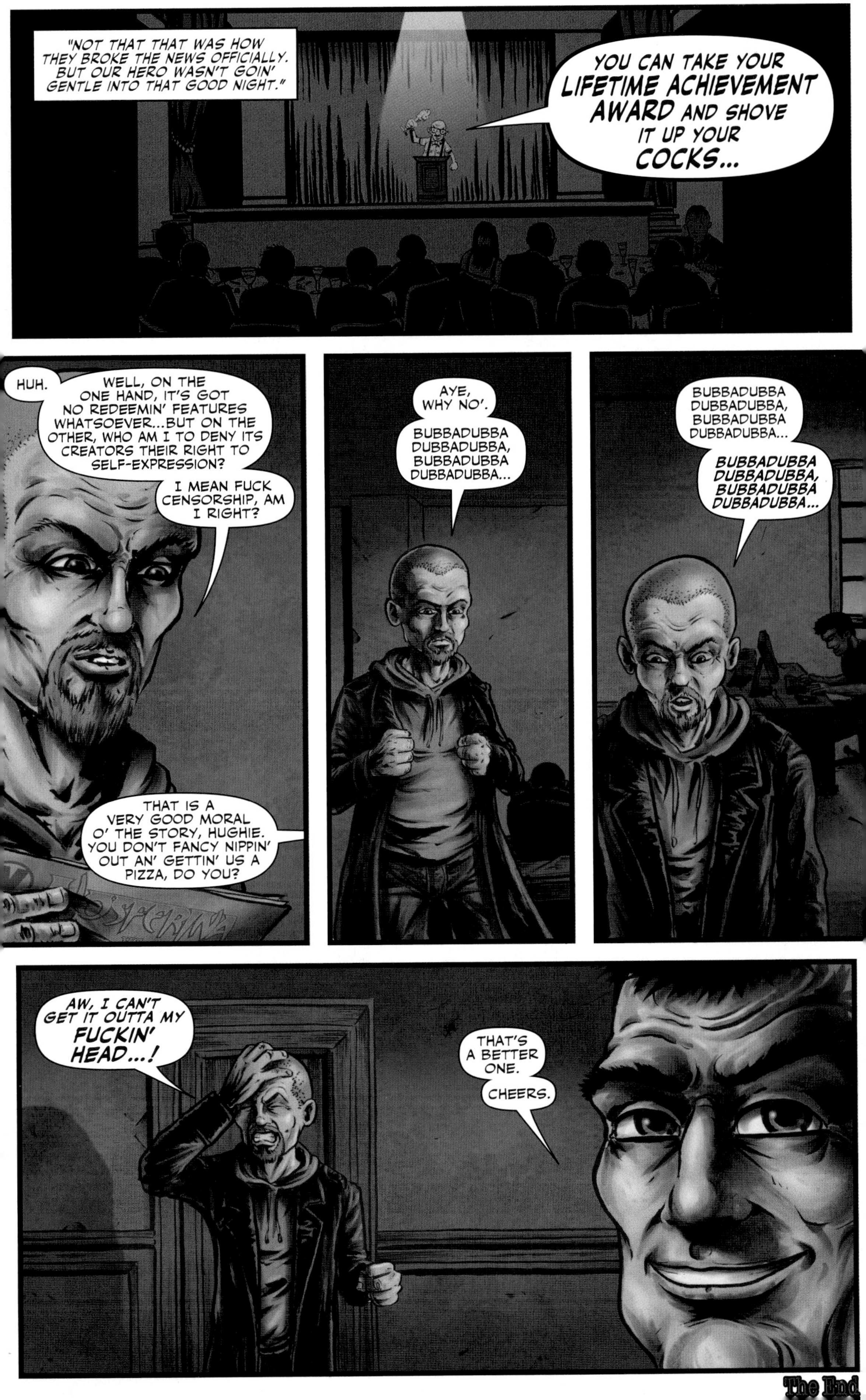
"NOT THAT THAT WAS HOW THEY BROKE THE NEWS OFFICIALLY. BUT OUR HERO WASN'T GOIN' GENTLE INTO THAT GOOD NIGHT."
YOU CAN TAKE YOUR LIFETIME ACHIEVEMENT AWARD AND SHOVE IT UP YOUR COCKS...
HUH.
WELL, ON THE ONE HAND, IT'S GOT NO REDEEMIN' FEATURES WHATSOEVER...BUT ON THE OTHER, WHO AM I TO DENY ITS CREATORS THEIR RIGHT TO SELF-EXPRESSION?
I MEAN FUCK CENSORSHIP, AM I RIGHT?
THAT IS A VERY GOOD MORAL O' THE STORY, HUGHIE. YOU DON'T FANCY NIPPIN' OUT AN' GETTIN' US A PIZZA, DO YOU?
AYE, WHY NO'.
BUBBADUBBA DUBBADUBBA, BUBBADUBBA DUBBADUBBA...
BUBBADUBBA DUBBADUBBA, BUBBADUBBA DUBBADUBBA...
BUBBADUBBA DUBBADUBBA, BUBBADUBBA DUBBADUBBA...
AW, I CAN'T GET IT OUTTA MY FUCKIN' HEAD...!
THAT'S A BETTER ONE.
CHEERS.
The End

THE BOYS 37
GARTH ENNIS

PAGE ONE

1.

The Boys' office. Hughie and MM are at their desks, tapping at their computers. Butcher has fallen asleep at his, newspaper he was reading fallen across his face, obscuring him from view. Terror dozes at his feet. The Female sits further back, reading. No Sign of Frenchie. Everyone relaxes with coats off, cups of coffee, whatever. MM and Hughie still have their arms in plaster.

2.

Close in. View past Hughie as he taps at the computer. On screen is a website for something called BELIEVE, with a big Christian cross and headshot on the Homelander, smiling kindly, at his most wholesome. Few paragraphs of text too, too small to read.

3.

Same angle as Hughie looks down to make a note, doesn't see Frenchie appear above the screen- just from the eyes up, peering intently at Hughie.

4.

Back a little. Frenchie gently raises his head and Hughie looks up and shits himself, gasping in shot. Biggish shot.

Frenchie: C'EST L'HEURE.

Hughie: **GAHH!!**

5.

MM glances round, not particularly worried, as Hughie struggles to recover from his heart attach. Frenchie stands up as if nothing is amiss, completely relaxed. Nearest us the Female doesn't even look up from her book- she's reading a graphic novel, a ROBO-HUNTER collection called PLAY IT AGAIN, SAM

Hughie: JESUS CHRIST, FRENCHIE, I
                     NEARLY FUCKIN' SHAT
                     MYSELF THERE--!

Frenchie;   IN FRANCE WE HAVE A
                     SAYING: "C'EST L'HEURE."

PAGE TWO

1.

Hughie peers up at Frenchie, bewildered. Frenchie's in his usual state of semi-ennui, little bit bleak, not really bothered with anything.

Frenchie:　　　WHICH IS TO SAY, THE TIME HAS COME.

"　　　"　　　TODAY, PETIT HUGHIE, C'EST L'HEURE HAS COME FOR YOU

　　　　　　　TO KNOW MY STORY.

2.

Hughie turns to MM, who smiles to himself nearest, not looking round. Frenchie raises a finger for dramatic effect.

Hughie:　　　SO—IS EVERYONE JUST GONNA START TELLIN' ME—

Frenchie:　　　**ECOUTE!**

3.

Hughie stares at Frenchie, who narrows his eyes a little as if trying to pin something down. Keeps the finger up for attention.

Frenchie:　　　CAN YOU HEAR IT, PETIT HUGHIE? THE STRAINING MELODY
　　　　　　　OF THE ACCORDION?

"　　　"　　　**NYEEEHH, NYEH-NYEH-NYEH, NYYEEEEEEEEHH**, IT SEEMS
　　　　　　　TO CARRY US FAR AWAY…

"　　　"　　　IT SEEMS TO WELCOME US…

4.

Headshot on Frenchie, smiling with quiet joy, eyes closed.

Frenchie:　　　A LA **BELLE FRANCE**…!

5.

Hughie only, staring at us. Pure what-the-fuck?

Off:　　　　　AND, HIGH IN THE SUN-KISSED PYRENEES, TO THE LITTLE
　　　　　　　VILLAGE OF **FRANGLAIS**—WHERE AN ANCIENT AND UNIQUE
　　　　　　　DIALECT IS SPOKEN BY THE INHABITANTS.

"　　　"　　　**NYEEEHH, NYEH-NYEH-NYEH, NNYEEEEEEHHH**…

PAGE THREE

1.

A scene of rural bliss: the sun blazes down on a little country road that wends its way through the gentle green foothills of the Pyrenees. Songbirds sing, rabbits frolic, a fawn watches from a field next to the road. Frenchie (about 15 years younger, but not too different) strolls down the road with his kitbag over his shoulder, smiling happily, enormously at ease. With him is another guy, a tubby, cheerful fellow in

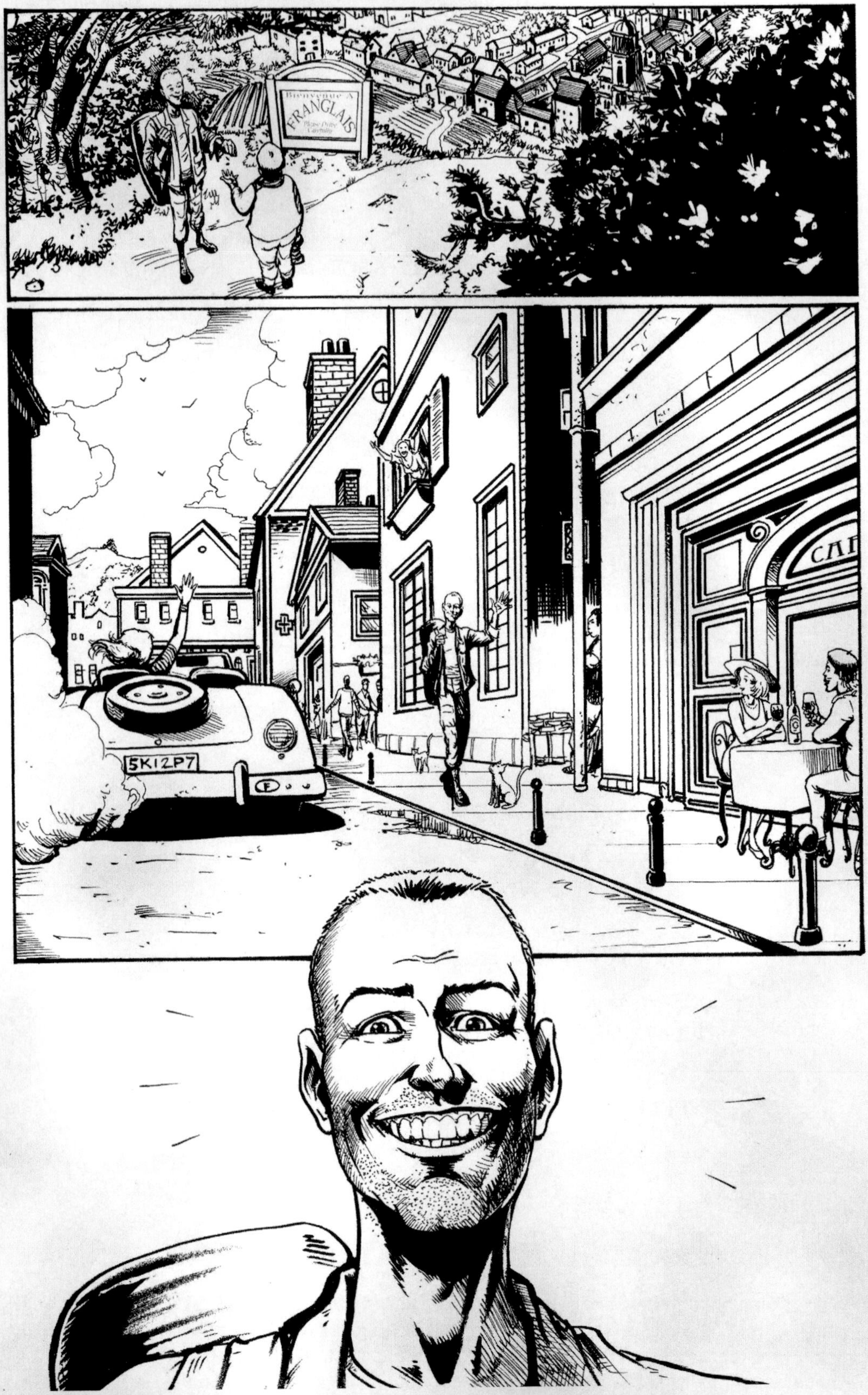
Bienvenue A
FRANGLAIS
5K12P7

a waistcoat and beret, playing the accordion and following a couple of yards behind Frenchie. Our hero wears nondescript camo fatigues and DM boots, no hat, no goggles. Same haircut.

Caption: "A YOUNG MAN HAS COME HOME FROM THE WARS."

Title: **LA PLUME DE MA TANTE EST SUR LA TABLE**

PAGE FOUR

1.

Frenchie has halted on the outskirts of an idyllic little mountain village, where the oldest buildings date back several hundred years. He drops a couple of coins in the accordionist's hand. Nearest us is a wooden sign mounted on a dry stone wall:

BIENVENUE A

FRANGLAIS

PLEASE DRIVE CAREFULLY

Frenchie: MERCI, PAUL.

Paul: MERCI, FRENCHIE.

"   "   WELCOME HOME, MON AMI.

2.

Big. Frenchie walks through the cobbled streets of the charming little town, smiling cheerfully, waving to the inhabitants. They wave back, from tables at cafes, from windows as they throw the shutters wide, from goofy little Renault Citroen cars. The women are all beautiful, the men all wear berets.

One: **BONJOUR, FRENCHIE!**

Frenchie: **BONJOUR, JEAN!**

Two: **WELCOME BACK, FRENCHIE!**

Frenchie: **BONJOUR, HELENE!**

Three: **FRENCHIE!!**

Frenchie: **BONJOUR, JACQUES!**

3.

Frenchie stops short, staring at us, smiling with quiet but intense joy.

Off(x2):   BONJOUR, FRENCHIE.

PAGE FIVE

1.

Frenchie has discarded his kitbag and is hugging his Mum and Dad outside their beautiful little cottage. He closes his eyes, home at last, smiling and trying not to cry. They hug back- his Mum is a plump little woman in her 50s, tears of happiness running down her cheeks, his Dad is a stocky, white-haired guy of 60 with a huge moustache, beret and big pipe, smiling with pride. Frenchie's taller than both of them.

Frenchie: BONJOUR, MUM.

"   "   BONJOUR, DAD.

2.

Inside, Frenchie sits at the old oak dining table with his Dad as his Mum hurries over with tray, on which rests a bottle of red wine and three glasses. Everyone's in good spirits, it's a happy atmosphere- but quietly so, a sense of relief that he's home rather than any wild celebration. He's taken his jacket off, just t-shirt, pants and boots now.

Frenchie: … NO, NO, I WILL NOT BE GOING BACK. MY BATTLES ARE
              FOUGHT AND MY SOUL IS AT PEACE, I AM DONE WITH LA GUERRE.

Mum: OH, MAY THE BLESSED VIRGIN BE PRAISED FOR HER MERCY!
              MUSIC TO MY EARS!

Dad: MAKE HASTE, CLAIRE. WE MUST DRINK A TOAST TO THIS
              HAPPY NEWS.

3.

Close in. Dad pours wine. All is still genial, but Frenchie has a puzzled smile on his face.

Mum: THE WHOLE VILLAGE IS OVERJOYED THAT YOU ARE HOME,
              FRENCHIE. EVERYONE HAS BEEN ASKING WHEN YOU WOULD
              COME HOME.

Frenchie: THAT IS GOOD, MUM—

Dad: AND SOON THE FESTIVAL OF LES SAINTES DE HAW-HAW
              WILL BEGIN! WE ARE ALL LOOKING FORWARD TO SEEING
              YOU COMPETE ONCE MORE!

Frenchie: THAT TOO IS GREAT, DAD. BUT…

4.

His p.o.v on Mum and Dad, both looking at each other, suddenly awkward. Dad stops pouring the wine.

Off: WHAT OF **MARIE?**

"   "   I HAD THOUGHT IF ANYONE WOULD COME TO WELCOME
              ME… IT WOULD BE HER.

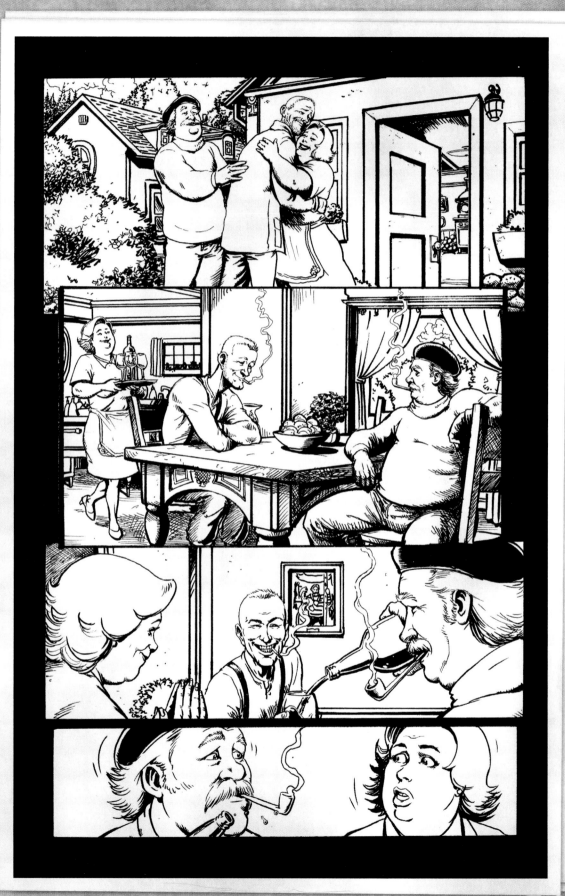

PAGE SIX

1.

Out of flashback, Frenchie remembering, faraway and melancholy. Hughie listens with the same bewildered look on his face, no idea what to think about this. Frenchie's nearer, gazing soulfully out the window.

Frenchie: MARIE… WITH HAIR LIKE SUNSHINE, LIPS LIKE BERRIES…

"   " BEFORE I LEFT, OUR HEARTS HAD BEEN AS ONE…

2.

Idyllic montage of Frenchie and Marie in love- fucking on top of a haystack with his pants pulled down and hairy arse exposed, Marie's ankles behind her ears… her wanking him off in the back of a Renault… fucking doggy-style, her howling at the moon, him roaring like a lunatic and slapping her vigorously on the arse… big headshots on the two of them swapping a good deal of spit, tongues flashing, chewing the faces off each other.

Play this for laughs, but don't show anything hardcore. Both about 18, Frenchie (when dressed) in jeans and t-shirt, Marie a staggeringly beautiful blonde with a sweet, kind look about her. Simple flower print dress, all very wholesome (when she's dressed).

Caption: "IT WAS A FIRST LOVE FOR US BOTH—ONE ENDLESS
SUMMER LONG BEFORE, WHEN INNOCENCE GAVE WAY TO
THE GREATER PURITY OF PASSION…

"   " "WE SWORE THAT WHEN I FINALLY CAME HOME, **NEVER**
WOULD WE PART AGAIN."

3.

Back in the cottage, frenchie looks puzzled- not worried yet- as Mum and Dad turn away, unable to face him. Dad tries to be brisk, but Mum bites her lip, anxious.

Dad: OH, SON, YOU SHOULD NOT CONCERN YOURSELF WITH SUCH
THINGS…!

Frenchie: BUT DAD, MARIE IS MY ONE AND ONLY LOVE. I PROMISED I
WOULD TAKE HER AS MY WIFE, WE ARE TO MARRY IN THE
VILLAGE CHURCH.

Mum: **FRENCHIE--!**

"   " MARIE IS NOT—SHE—OH, MON DIEU!

4.

Frenchie turns suddenly, attention caught. Further back Mum buries her face in her hands.

Mum: SHE IS NOT WHO YOU THOUGHT SHE WAS, SHE HAS GONE
TO—

Off: **FRENCHIE! COME OUT OF THERE, YOU FOOL!**

PAGE SEVEN

1.

Frenchie rushes outside, freezes, Mum and Dad anxiously following. Nearest us, twenty yards from Frenchie, a biker-booted foot rests on the ground next to a bicycle wheel.

Dad: WAIT, MY SON! DON'T—

Mum: **NO--!**

Frenchie: M-M-M-**MARIE?**

"   "   MARIE—ET—

2.

Big. Black Pierre sits astride his bicycle, sneering horribly at us, with Marie perched on the pillion seat behind him. He's a greasy, swarthy-looking complete bastard, with lank hair slicked back under his beret, biker jacket over his French person's stripey sweater, gold earring, five o'clock shadow. His bicycle is the same kind all French people have, an old-fashioned black thing from about 1920. Marie doesn't even bother to look at us- tons of make-up, bored expression, slutty heels with fishnet stockings, miniskirt and tight red sweater. Hair cut in a bob under the beret. Behind them, a cloud slides across the sun.

Off: **BLACK PIERRE?!**

Pierre;   **HA, HA-HA-HA-HA-HA, YOU PATHETIC BASTERRD!**

3.

Montage of Frenchie's childhood rivalry with Black Pierre- both aged 6, Frenchie (same haircut thoughout) busting a wine bottle over Pierre's head… both aged 10, Frenchie holding Pierre's head under the water in the village stream, the villagers cheering from the bank… both aged 15, the screaming Frenchie chasing the terrified Pierre down the street with a meat cleaver. Pierre was a bit of a fat kid (but no longer). Shorts and t-shirts thoughout.

Caption: "BLACK PIERRE. MY CHILDHOOD RIVAL.

"   "   "WHAT A **WANKER** HE WAS."

PAGE EIGHT

1.

Wide view. Frenchie steps towards them, aghast- has the look of a man in a dream, can't believe what he's seeing. Dad holds Mum tight, both miserable, can't face the terrible scene. Pierre leers nastily at Frenchie, Marie ignores everyone. Concerned citizens watch from the background.

Frenchie: BUT—BUT **WHY**, BELOVED?

"   "   WHAT ARE YOU DOING WITH… **HIM?**

Pierre: DID YOU EXPECT HER TO WAIT FOREVER, FRENCHIE?

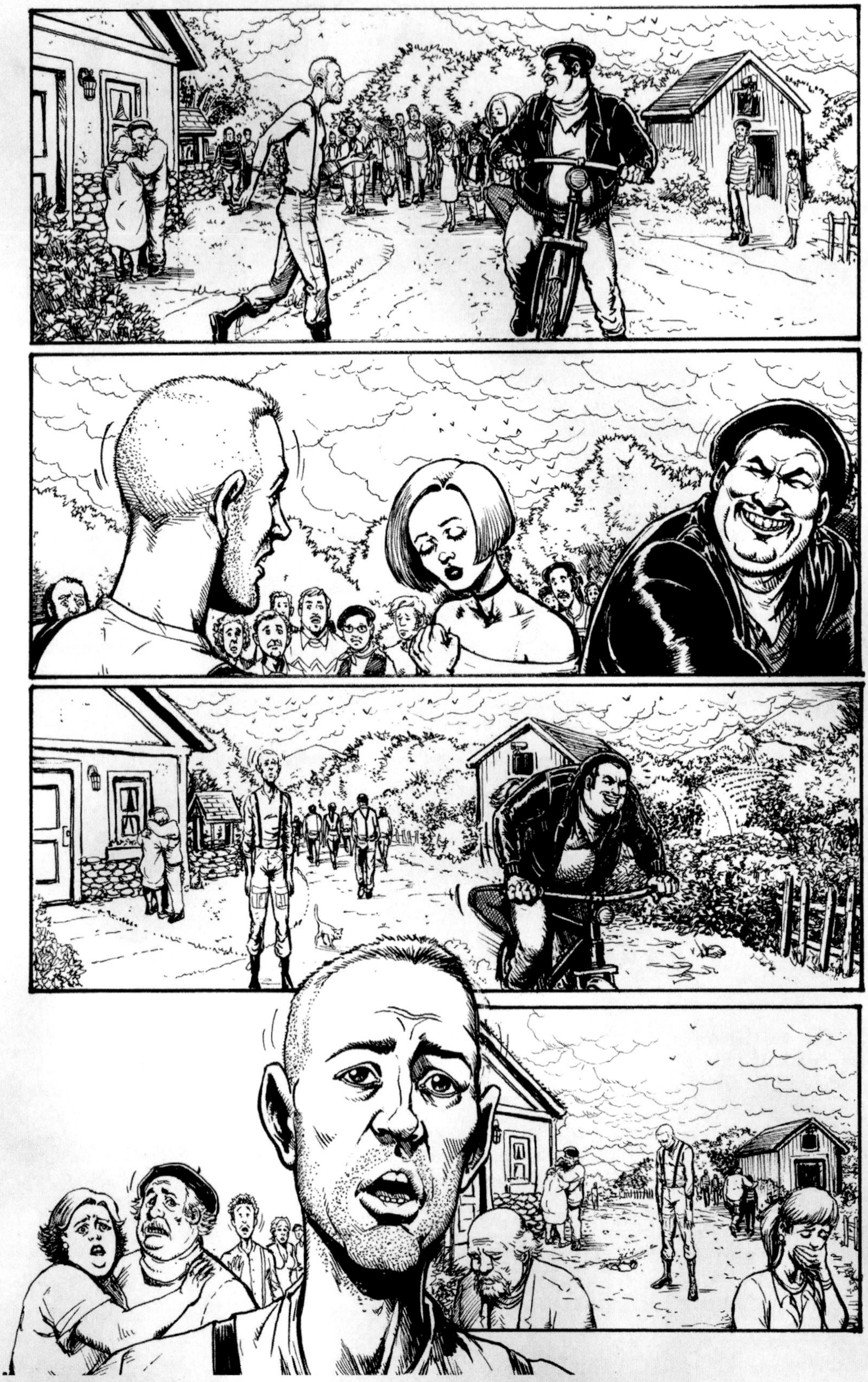

2.

Close in. Frenchie gazes pathetically at Marie, who coolly examines her fingernails. Black Pierre smiles horribly.

Pierre: YOU TOOK YOUR EYE OFF THE BALL, AS THE HATED AMERICANS SAY. NOW, THE PRIZE IS MINE.

"   "   AND HE WHO LAUGHS LAST, LAUGHS LONGEST… **EH?**

3.

View past the wretched Frenchie as Pierre pedals furiously off down the street, roaring with laughter, neither he nor Marie looking back.

Pierre: **HA HA HA HA HA HA HA HA <u>HA!!</u>**

4.

Frenchie gazes past us, wretched, pathetic, silent. A beaten man. Mum and Dad watch with great trepidation. The villagers keep their distance.

5.

Wide view. Frenchie slowly lowers his gaze. Dad holds Mum tight as she starts to sob. The villagers can't look at the tragic scene, slowly turning to go. The sky is clouding over, a general sense of gloom is replacing the earlier euphoria.

Frenchie: …OU EST PAUL?

PAGE NINE

1.

Night. Frenchie sits at an outside table in front of a café, gazing dully at the ground, not really eating the plate of snails in front of him or drinking his glass of wine. Quietly but totally miserable. Paul, the accordionist from page three, stands a couple of yards behind Frenchie, playing the violin this time- tragic expression on his face, making a show of playing great, long, slow strokes. The waiter and what few other customers are present avoid Frenchie's eye, bleak, awkward.

Frenchie: MERCI, MON AMI.

2.

Paul stops playing, Frenchie drops more coins into his hand.

Paul: MERCI, FRENCHIE.

"   "   DOES IT HELP…?

Frenchie: IT HELPS, PAUL.

3.

Frenchie only, morosely poking at the snails on his plate with his fork, not really interested. They still have their shells on, of course.

Frenchie:	IT HELPS… TO BREAK MY HEART…
Off:	**FRENCHIE…!**

4.

Pull back. He doesn't look up as his Dad appears, stricken.

Dad:	MY SON, MY SON, HOW IT TEARS AT ME TO SEE YOU LIKE THIS!
" "	YOU MUST **FACE** BLACK PIERRE, FRENCHIE! FACE HIM—AND **FIGHT** FOR WHAT IS YOURS!
Frenchie:	I WILL NOT TAKE THAT PATH, DAD.

5.

Frenchie only, raising his head to look offshot with a slightly tragic air about him. A haunted look flickers across his face, a bad memory.

Frenchie:	THE URGE TO FIGHT, TO MAUL, TO MURDER: IT IS THE GREATEST CANCER THAT AFFLICTS MANKIND. IT OBLITERATES THE BODY OF THE VICTIM, AND THE SPIRIT OF THE ONE WHO STRIKES THE BLOW.
" "	I HAVE SEEN IT…

PAGE TEN

1.

Big. Flashback to Frenchie's time in combat, as he roars with fury and fires his SAW offshot from the hip, one handed, using his other hand to drag a horribly wounded comrade to safety. Explosions burst further back, smoke fills the sky, dead bodies litter the ground around a burning Puma helicopter behind Frenchie. Bullets whizz past him, he's taken a couple of flesh wounds and is bleeding badly, not that he notices. He wears camo fatigues and flakvest, but has lost his helmet- by his shaven head shall we know him, as ever. This should be unpleasantly realistic in contrast to the rest of the story- maybe we're looking up at him slightly as the muzzle flash from his SAW lights the scene and dozens of empties tumble from the breech.

Frenchie:	**A MOI LA LEGION!!**

2.

Frenchie lowers his gaze again, quiet, giving up. Dad buries his face in his hands. Pull back a bit here.

Frenchie:	AND NEVER AGAIN WILL I RAISE MY HAND AGAINST MY FELLOW MAN.

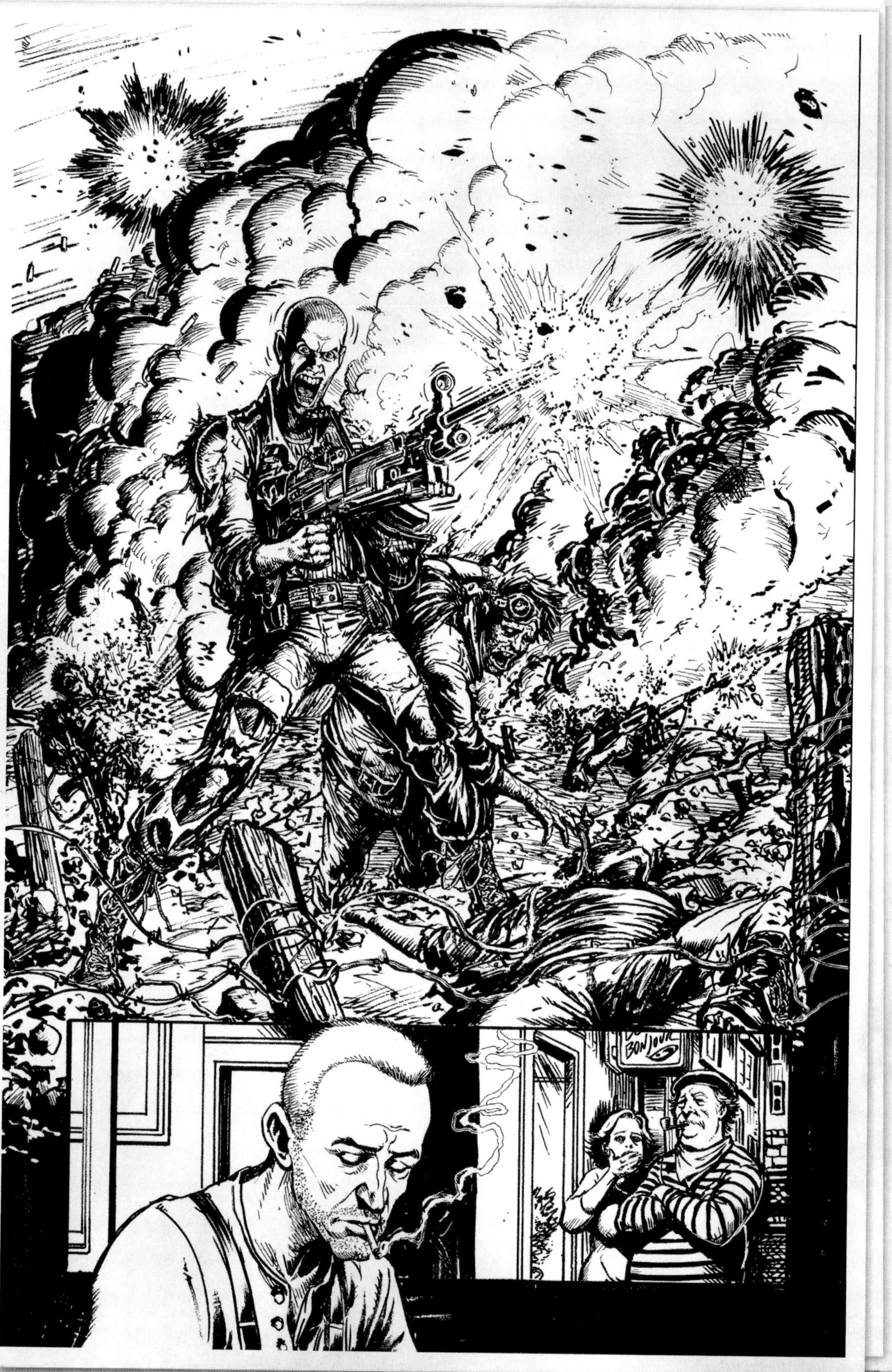

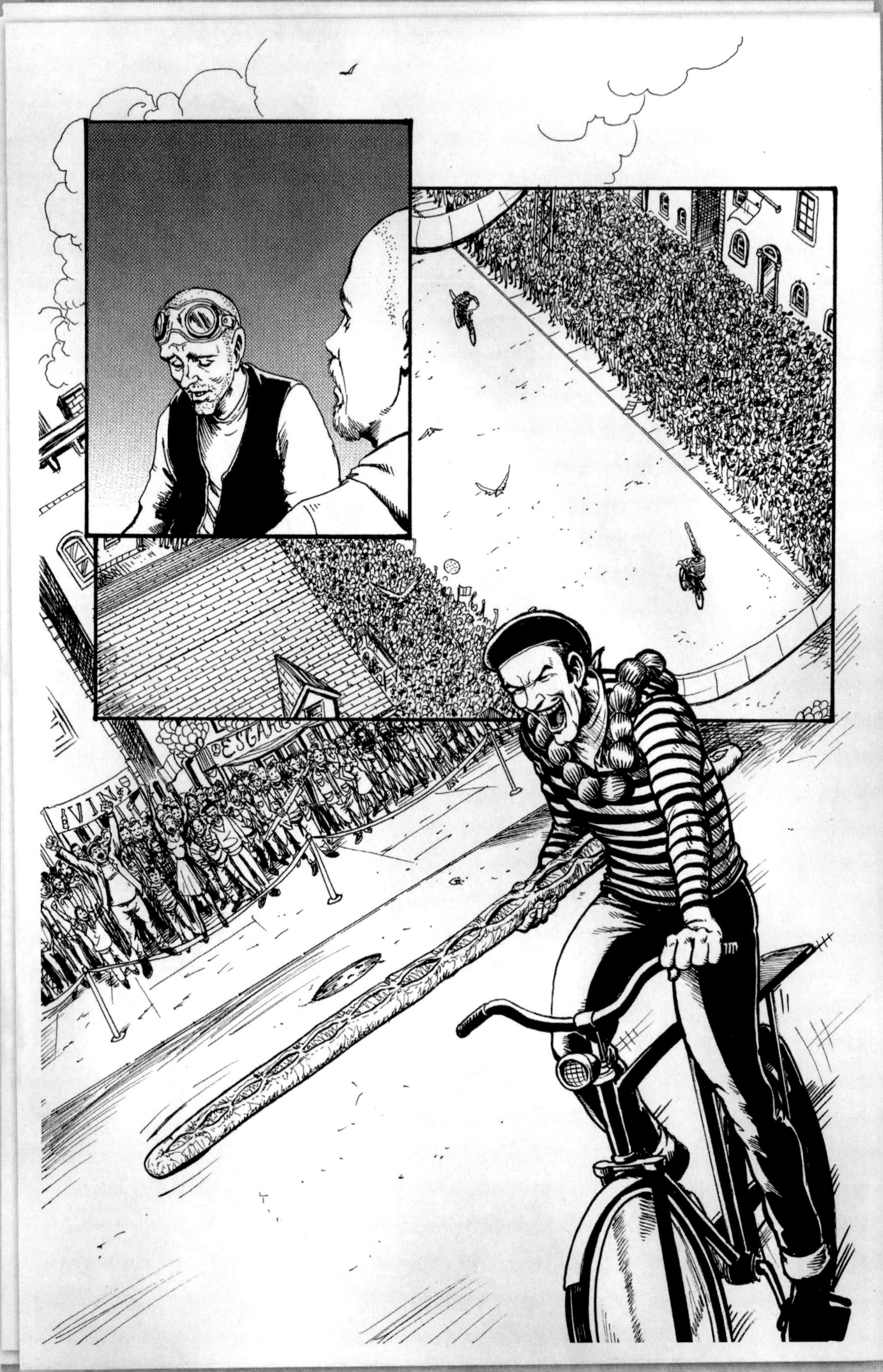

PAGE ELEVEN

1.

Hughie watches warily as Frenchie sits slumped in a chair, glum.

Frenchie: THE DAYS TURNED INTO WEEKS. MIDSUMMER CAME, AND
    THE GOLDEN CORNFIELDS RIPENED EVERYWHERE BUT IN
    MY HEART.

" " I WAS A MAN IN A DREAM, PETIT HUGHIE. BEFORE I KNEW IT,
    LES SAINTES DE HAW-HAW HAD ARRIVED.

2.

Wide view of the village square on a glorious summer's day. The streets and cafes are lined with people,
French tricolors fly from the telegraph poles, red, white and blue bunting hangs from the phone wires.
Stalls have been set up along the edges of the square, selling wine, baguettes, pastries, croissants and
snails. Everyone's in good form, glasses clinking in toasts or being swiftly refilled, pretty girls in
flowery dresses, guys in berets, Paul wandering around playing his accordion. The square itself has been
kept clear, and two cyclists face each other about a hundred yards apart. Not much detail on them yet. A
judge stands in the middle, chequered flag raised.

Caption: "IT IS A FESTIVAL THAT HAS BEEN HELD IN MY VILLAGE
    SINCE ANCIENT TIMES: IN WHICH WE CELEBRATE OUR LIFE
    AMIDST THE GREEN HILLS OF FRANCE, AND GIVE THANKS
    FOR THE BOUNTY GLEANED FROM HER RICH EARTH.

" " "IT IS ALSO A TIME WHEN SLIGHTS AND GRIEVANCES ARE
    SWEPT AWAY, ALL SUCH DISPUTES RESOLVED ACCORDING
    TO AN HONORABLE AND ANCIENT CUSTOM…"

Judge: **TROIS… DEUX… UN…!**

3.

One of the cyclists comes charging towards us, yelling dramatically. He wears a black beret and classic
black and white striped sweater, and a long string of onions hangs around his neck. Held out in front of
him like a knight's lance is an eight-foot long baguette.

Off: **ALLEZ!**

Cyclist: **AH-HAW-HEE-HAW-HEE-HAW-HEE-HAW-HEE-HAW!!**

PAGE TWELVE

1.

Wide view as the two cyclists race towards each other, baguettes extended in the manner of a medieval
joust. The crowd watch in amazed delight, unbelievably tense as the two warriors lock in combat.

Cyclist: **AH-HAW-HEE-HAW-HEE-HAW-HEE-HAW-HEE-HAW!**

Cyclist 2: **AH-HAW-HEE-HAW-HEE-HAW-HEE-HAW-HEE-HAW!**

2.

Big. One of the cyclists ducks under the other's lancing baguette and rams his own into the guy's chest. It surprises him but does no harm whatsoever, the baguette snaps like a twig. Both men are dressed identically, by the way.

Other: **MON DIEU--!**

One: **HAW-HAW!**

3.

The crows go wild with delight. The judge raises the winner's hand high.

Judge: **LE VAINQUEUR... RAYMOND DUPERIER!**

No bln: **HAW-HAW! HAW-HAW! HAW-HAW!**

4.

The two cyclists shake hands, smiling warmly, no ill-feeling between them at all.

Loser: WELL DONE, M'SIEU!

Winner: HONOR IS SATISFIED! MERCI, M'SIEU!

PAGE THIRTEEN

1.

Frenchie sits alone outside the café, as before- we can see it's down some side street, so the crowd in the village square can only be glimpsed further back. Mum watches sadly as Dad appeals to Frenchie, slightly desperate now- but Frenchie won't even look up, preoccupied with his bottle and glass of wine, bleak as ever.

Dad: ... FRENCHIE, BLACK PIERRE IS OUT THERE EVEN NOW! HE
                PREENS HIMSELF IN THE VILLAGE SQUARE, IN THE MANNER
                OF A STRUTTING PEACOCK!

Frenchie: IT IS NONE OF MY AFFAIR, DAD.

Dad: YOU **MUST** CONFRONT HIM, SON! IF ONLY FOR THE HONOR OF
                OUR FAMILY!

Frenchie: I CANNOT.

2.

Frenchie merely shrugs. Dad throws up his arms in torment, temper snapping.

Frenchie: MARIE IS GONE. THERE IS NOTHING MORE TO BE SAID.

"   "   WE MUST MAKE THE BEST OF IT; TOUT EST POUR LE MIEUX
                DANS LE MEILLEUR DES MONDES POSSIBLES...

Dad: **NNAAAAAHH, NOT VOLTAIRE--!**

3.

Pull back as Dad storms off, followed by the anxious Mum. Frenchie doesn't look up.

Dad: ENOUGH! ENOUGH, I SAY! YOU ARE NOT MY SON!

Mum: **GEORGES!**

Dad: I WASH MY HANDS OF YOU, YOU **COWARD!**

4.

In the square, the jousting has finished and the crowd wait in good-natured silence as the judge makes a little speech. Black Pierre stands nearest, sneering, not even bothering to listen as he swills red wine. One arm around the ever-bored Marie.

Judge;   GOOD PEOPLE OF FRANGLAIS, THE LAST CONTEST HAS BEEN DECIDED! LET US CELEBRATE ANOTHER PEACEFUL LES SAINTES DE HAW-HAW.

"   "   SO FILL UP YOUR GLASSES—

Off: **NON!!**

5.

Everyone turns, bewildered, not least of all Pierre himself.

Off: **I CHALLENGE BLACK PIERRE!**

PAGE FOURTEEN

1.

Frenchie's Dad sits astride a black bicycle- he's changed into the regulation costume, with beret and stripey sweater, onions round the neck, pipe discarded. He holds his baguette vertically like a spear, glares grimly at us, old but proud. Mum is appalled.

Off: **OLD GEORGES--?**

Mum: NON, MY HUSBAND, NON! THIS IS FOLLY!

Dad: SILENCE, WOMAN.

"   "   **C'EST UNE QUESTION D'HONNEUR.**

2.

Wide view. Everyone's astonished, riveted, you could cut the tension with a knife. Muttered conversations, nervous glances exchanged. Nearest us Marie glances curiously at Pierre, who all of a sudden isn't quite so sure of himself.

Bln: MON DIEU…

Bln 2:   OLD GEORGES IS TO FACE BLACK PIERRE…

Bln 3:   IT IS AS CHUCK BERRY SAYS, YOU NEVER CAN TELL…

Marie: PIERRE?

3.

Out of flashback. Frenchie frowns slightly, musing thoughtfully on this important point. Hughie's no less bemused.

Frenchie: WELL MIGHT THIS GIVE THE VILLAIN PAUSE. THE MEN OF MY
                         FAMILY HAD TRIUMPHED IN THE CONTEST AS LONG AS
                         ANYONE COULD REMEMBER: TO REFUSE MEANT ABSOLUTE
                         HUMILIATION, BUT TO TAKE HIS CHANCES WITH A CHAMPION
                         WAS TO RISK THE VERY SAME.

"   "   MUM RUSHED TO FIND ME. AT FIRST I COULD NOT BELIEVE
                         WHAT SHE WAS TELLING ME, THE VERY NOTION SEEMED

                         INSANE…

4.

Frenchie races down the street, desperate, his terrified Mum running along behind.

Frenchie: DAD! NO! YOU ARE TOO OLD, YOUR HEART WILL NEVER
                         STAND THE STRAIN!

Mum: OH, MERCIFUL SAVIOR--!

Off: **TROIS! DEUX! UN!**

5.

View past the appalled Frenchie as he bursts through the riveted crowd, sees the judge drop his flag, the cyclists race towards each other. (NB- Pierre hasn't changed clothes).

Judge: **ALLEZ!**

Frenchie: **NON!**

PAGE FIFTEEN

1.

Dad races towards us on his bike, baguette thrust straight forward, roaring, grim as hell.

Dad: **AH-HAW-HEE-HAW-HEE-HAW-HEE-HAW-HEE-HAW!**

2.

Black Pierre does likewise, nowhere near as confident, sweat lashing off him.

Pierre: AH-HAW-HEE-HAW-HEE—

"   "   **ULP--!**

3.

Frenchie remembers, grimacing with torment, eyes closed. Hughie can only stare at him.

Frenchie: BUT THEN…

"   "   IN THAT LAST, TERRIBLE INSTANT…

"   "   WEEKS OLD, STALE, AS HARD AS THE GRANITE OF THE PYRENEES BENEATH OUR FEET…

4.

Frenchie and the guys near him gape as a little kid nearest yells, points offshot, horrified.

Kid: **CROISSANT!!**

5.

Close. Pierre lets go of his baguette, ducks under Frenchie's Dad's, and slams a rock-hard croissant into the spokes of his opponent's bike's front wheel nearest us. Pierre has a look of savage desperation on his face, knows this is his only chance.

Off: QUE LE--?

PAGE SIXTEEN

1.

The bike stops instantly and Frenchie's Dad goes over the handlebars like a bullet, only his feet still in shot. Even Pierre is amazed as he sees the old man go past.

Off: **NON!!**

2.

Big. Frenchie flings himself at us in one of those exaggerated perspective shots we know so well, outstretched hand nearest, eyes bulging, screaming in unbelievable desperation.

Frenchie: **NNOOOOOOOOOOOOONNN!!!**

3.

Rear view, long shot on Black Pierre, racing off down a side street at maximum speed.

Pierre: **HA! HA! HA! HA! HA! HA! HA! HA! HA!**

4.

View past the horrified, frozen crowd, some people turning away in despair, as Frenchie and his Mum race towards the little figure sprawled ten yards from the twisted bicycle.

Bln: MERE DE DIEU—

Bln 2:   I CANNOT LOOK—

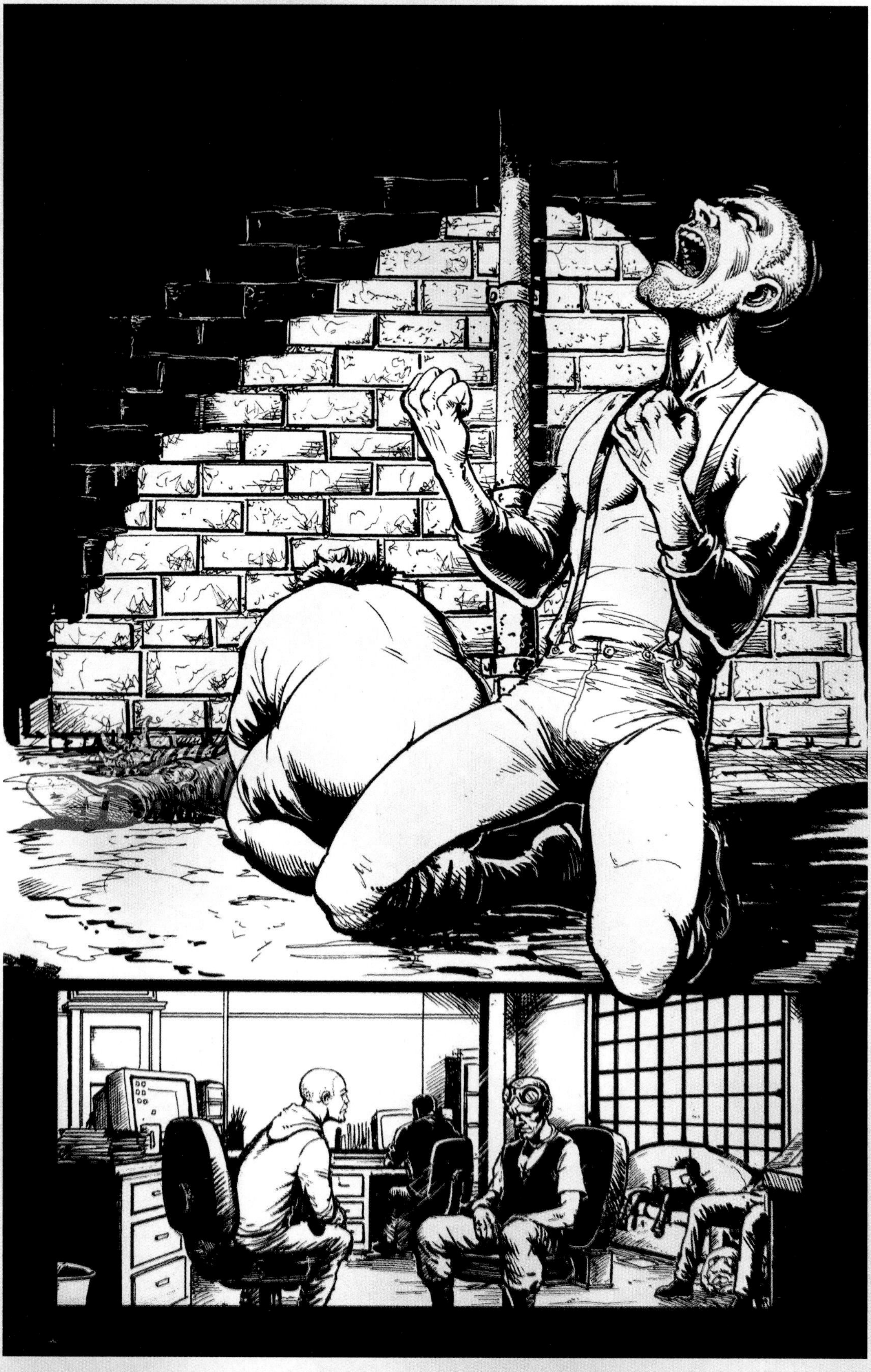

Bln 3:   THE **HORROR—**

5.

Frenchie stops short, staring down at us in utter horror. Nearest us a twisted, bloody hand sprawls from offshot. Mum sees it too, grabbing Frenchie's arm for support, slamming a hand across her mouth.

Caption: "IT WAS THE END OF EVERYTHING, PETIT HUGHIE."

PAGE SEVENTEEN

1.

Big. Mum kneels with her back to us, bent over Dad's body- which we never get a decent look at, just sprawled limbs- and weeps, face hidden from sight. Frenchie knees nearest, turned away from his parents, and howls his torment to the heavens like an animal driven mad by pain. Eyes tight shut, tears pouring down his cheeks, fists raised and clenched.

Caption: "IT WAS GOLGOTHA."

Frenchie: **MON DAAAAAAAAAAAAD!!**

2.

Wide view of the Boys' office. MM taps at his computer, the Female reads her book, Butcher and Terror doze. Hughie watches Frenchie, who sits slumped in his seat, gazing lifelessly at the floor. Even Hughie seems saddened by this.

PAGE EIGHTEEN

1.

Close in. Frenchie doesn't look up. Hughie seems slightly stricken.

Frenchie: MUM DIED SOON AFTER.

"   "   OF DESPAIR.

2.

The gloomy Frenchie stands over the graves of his parents in the village cemetery, ignoring the rain as it pours from a sky of black thunderclouds. No one else here. This isn't the funeral, it'd be some time later.

Caption: "BUT I KNEW IN MY HEART THAT I KILLED HER. JUST AS I
                  KILLED MY POOR OLD DAD.

"   "   "WITH MY PRIDE, WITH MY PACIFISM…WITH THAT CRIPPLING
                  CURSE THAT HAUNTS MY NATION: MY HATEFUL,
                  ALL-CONSUMING ENNUI."

3.

Big. Frenchie strides towards us out of the darkness- could be anywhere here- with his face set and grim, full of cold, ruthless intent. Wears an overcoat over his fatigues, but not the black leather one we're used to. No goggles, either. His bleak misery is gone now, but so is his earlier joie de vivre.

Caption:　　　　　"AND SO I LEFT FRANGLAIS BEHIND FOREVER, AND WANDERED OUT INTO THE WORLD: A MAN WITHOUT A HOME…

"　　　"　　　"WITHOUT HEART OR SOUL…

"　　　"　　　"WITHOUT A HOPE OF EVER KNOWING REDEMPTION."

PAGE NINETEEN

1.

Big. Black Pierre hangs dead, naked except for his beret, hands behind his back and legs bent back so his wrists are tied to his ankles. Seems to have had an extra-long string of onions forced through his body- one bulges unpleasantly from his mouth so he looks like a suckling pig with an apple, another presumably emerges from his arse, but we don't see the details. The onions form a loop by which the body is hung from a hook. Amazed expression frozen on his face.

Caption:　　　　　"OF BLACK PIERRE AND HIS EVENTUAL FATE, I WILL NOT

SPEAK."

2.

Big. Marie gazes in wretched amazement as Frenchie's hand comes into shot nearest, giving her the finger- make it big in shot. She's a mess, hair tousled, mascara running through her tears, hands clasped for forgiveness. Obviously having a nervous breakdown.

Caption:　　　　　"NOR OF THE TREACHEROUS MARIE, AND HER SICKENING PLEAS FOR ME TO TAKE HER BACK."

3.

Frenchie remembering, bleak. Hughie's intrigued in spite of himself.

Frenchie:　　　　SUCH THINGS WERE MEANINGLESS.

"　　　"　　　GUILT BURNED INSIDE ME WITH A DULL BROWN FLAME. SELF-PITY HOVERED ROUND IT LIKE A FART.

"　　　"　　　MY LIFE BEGAN TO BLUR…

4.

Exterior a shitty little Parisian bar in a side street, Eiffel tower in the distance. Lousy day.

Caption:　　　　　"I DRANK, OF COURSE. TO FILL THE BOTTOMLESS CHASM IN MY SOUL.

"　　　"　　　"WHEN THAT WAS NOT ENOUGH, I LEARNED TO QUENCH MY THIRST WITH TROUBLE."

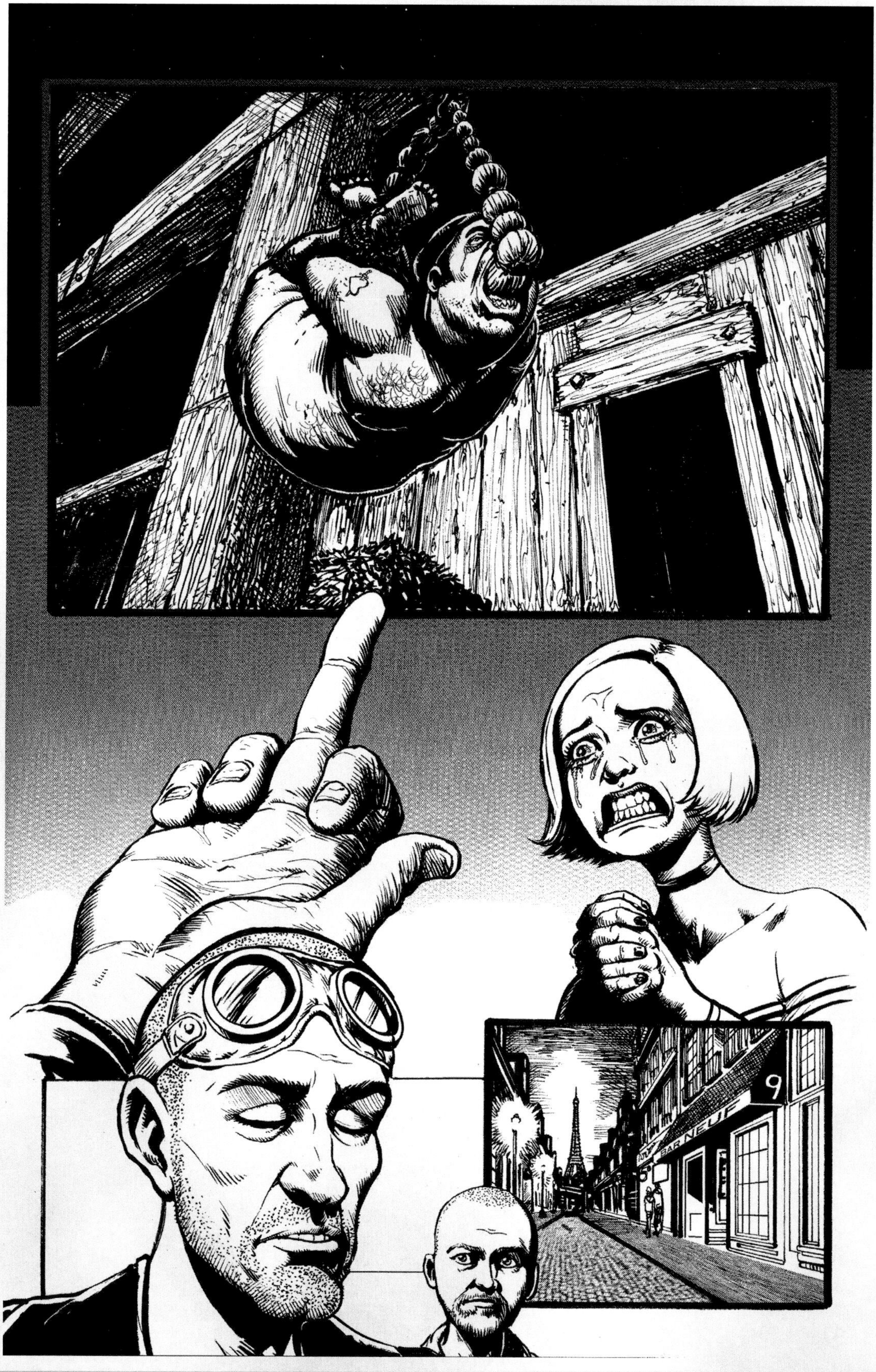
9
BAR NEUF

From in: YOU SPILLED MY DRINK.

PAGE TWENTY

1.

Inside, Frenchie- scruffy and dirty, looks like a vagrant- sits at the bar and looks calmly down at his overturned wine glass, wine pooling beside it. The largest and most obnoxious of a bunch of asshole tourists turns to look at him, puzzled- a dozen college jocks, all drunk enough to be trouble. This one's obviously been a bit careless with his brawny elbow. Meanwhile the locals stay well clear. Place is a complete shithole- this is real France, not Franglais.

Jock: WHAT'D YOU SAY, FROGGY?

Frenchie; I SAID YOU SPILLED MY DRINK.

"   " I WOULD LIKE YOU TO REPLACE IT.

2.

The bartender hurries forward with the bottle, knows what's coming, but Frenchie gently raises an index finger to stop him. The Jock sneers, his pals laugh.

Bartender; NE VOUS INQUIETEZ PAS, C'EST A MOI—

Frenchie: NO, IT IS ON HIM.

Jock: TELL YOU WHAT, WHY DON'T WE JUST CALL IT PAYBACK FOR SAVIN' YOUR ASS FROM THE NAZIS? YOU KNOW, THAT WHOLE THING WHERE YOU DIDN'T GROW UP SPEAKIN' **GERMAN?**

3.

Frenchie turns to look at him for the first time, calm and polite. The guy sneers at him, bewildered.

Frenchie: THAT WAS YOU PERSONALLY?

Jock: WHAT?

Frenchie: YOU SEEM SO YOUNG. WERE YOU WITH PATTON OR WITH HODGES?

Jock: WHAT THE FUCK'RE YOU **TALKIN' ABOUT--?**

4.

Frenchie only, facing us evenly, very polite. No sense of challenge whatsoever.

Frenchie: YOU STUPID, WORTHLESS, KNUCKLEDRAGGING LUMP OF DOGSHIT. YOU SEEK TO INVOKE MY COUNTRY'S HISTORY, BUT YOU DO NOT EVEN KNOW YOUR OWN.

"   " YOU ARE A DISGRACE TO THE UNITED STATES. FUCK YOU.

5.

Close up. A hand sets a file down on a corner table, next to a glass of water. Stamped on the front, next to a paperclipped headshot photo of Frenchie, is

LEGION ETRANGERE

PREMIER SECRET

Off: **I'LL KICK YOUR FUCKIN' <u>AAAAAAAAAAAHH!</u>**

Off 2:   HMMM.

"   "   WHAT I NEED NOW...

PAGE TWENTY-ONE

1.

It's Butcher, sitting calmly in the corner, smiling a dark little smile as he gazes thoughtfully offshot. This would be about a year before he found MM. No Terror.

Butcher: IS A MAD CUNT.

Off: **GET THE LITTLE FUCKER!**

"   "   **<u>UUUUNNGHH!!</u>**

2.

View past Butcher in the corner- we don't see his face- as he clasps his fingers behind his head and sits back to enjoy the fun. Frenchie goes down fighting under impossible odds. He's taken out two of the guys, both twice his size, but the rest are on him now and the result will be inevitable.

Caption: "AND THAT, I SUPPOSE, IS THE END OF MY TALE.

"   "   "A U.S. AIR FORCE FLIGHT TO WASHINGTON, A SHOT OF
                COMPOUND V, A STYLISH LEATHER OVERCOAT..."

3.

Hughie smiles at Frenchie, still not sure what to make of this. Frenchie smiles too, glancing at the Female as she reads nearest us, oblivious.

Frenchie: A NEW HOME.

Hughie: AN' YOU'VE BEEN WITH THE BOYS EVER SINCE, EH?

4.

Frenchie looks round at us, smiles warmly, genuine. Knowing look to him, eyes narrowed slightly.

Frenchie: WITH THE BOYS **A L'OUTRANCE**, PETIT HUGHIE.

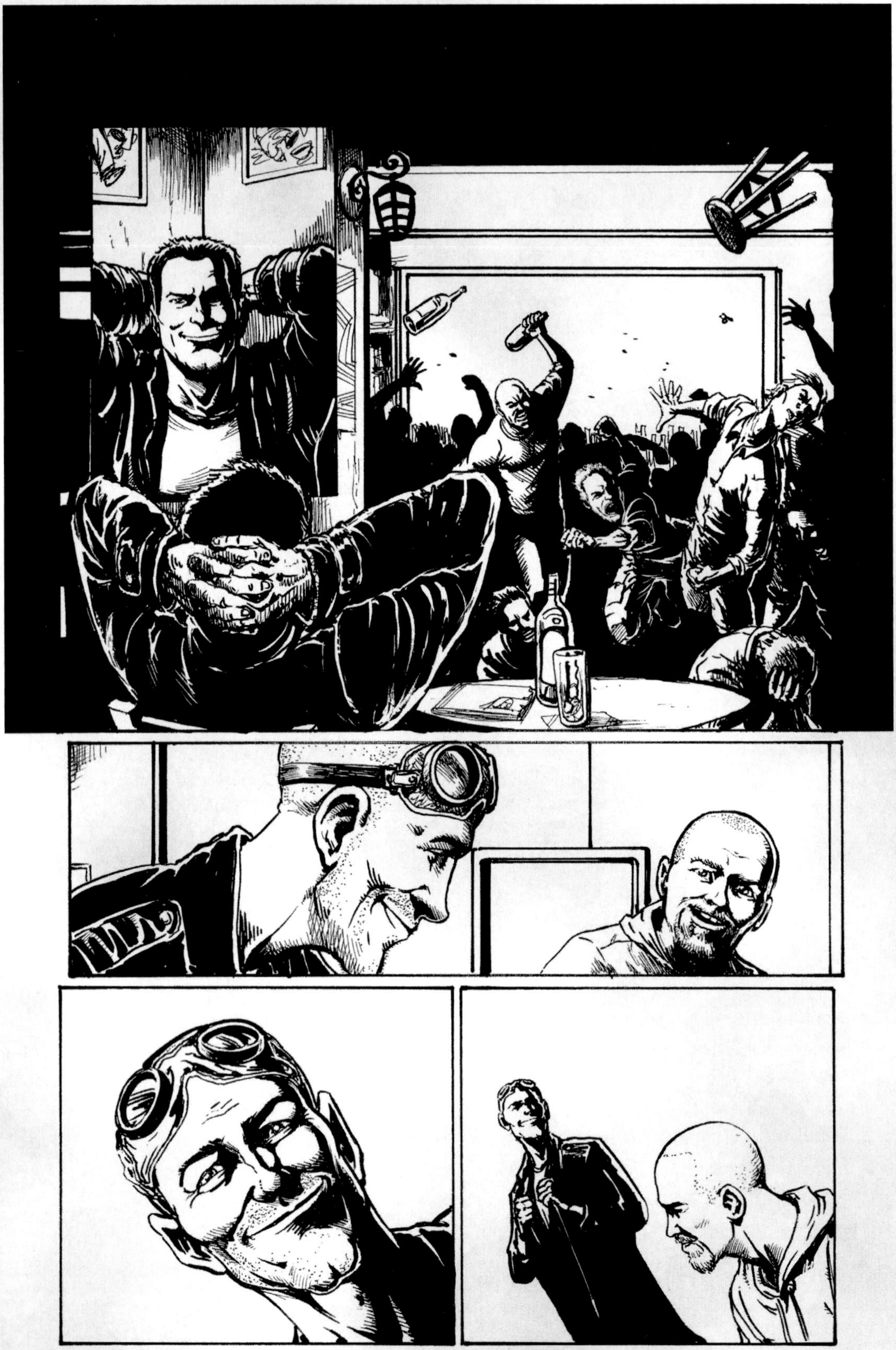

5.

Frenchie gets to his feet, smiling at the puzzled Hughie.

Hughie: WH—

Frenchie: "TO THE BITTER END."

PAGE TWENTY-TWO

1.

Hughie stares in confusion and alarm as Frenchie suddenly races across the room, sprinting flat out for the window. MM glances round, not all that surprised. The Female doesn't even look up from her book.

2.

Wide view as Frenchie leaps out the open window. Hughie stands up, stares, but MM has gone back to his computer. NB- this shouldn't look like a superhero launching himself into the air, just a mad bastard jumping out a window.

3.

View past Hughie at the window, watching the tiny figure of Frenchie sprinting across Madison Square Park.

Hughie: JESUS!

"   "   YOU KNOW, THAT'S THE MADDEST FUCKING THING I'VE EVER HEARD IN MY LIFE. D'YOU THINK IT'S **TRUE?**

4.

View past Hughie as he turns, curious. Butcher hasn't moved, newspaper still covering his face.

Butcher: LAST LINE'S THE BIT THAT COUNTS, MATE.

5.

Switch around so Butcher's nearest us, still not moving. Hughie stares at him, waiting for more, but nothing's coming.

6.

Wide now. Hughie turns away again. Everyone else carries on doing what they were doing. Peace, perfect peace.

Hughie: JINGS.

THE END

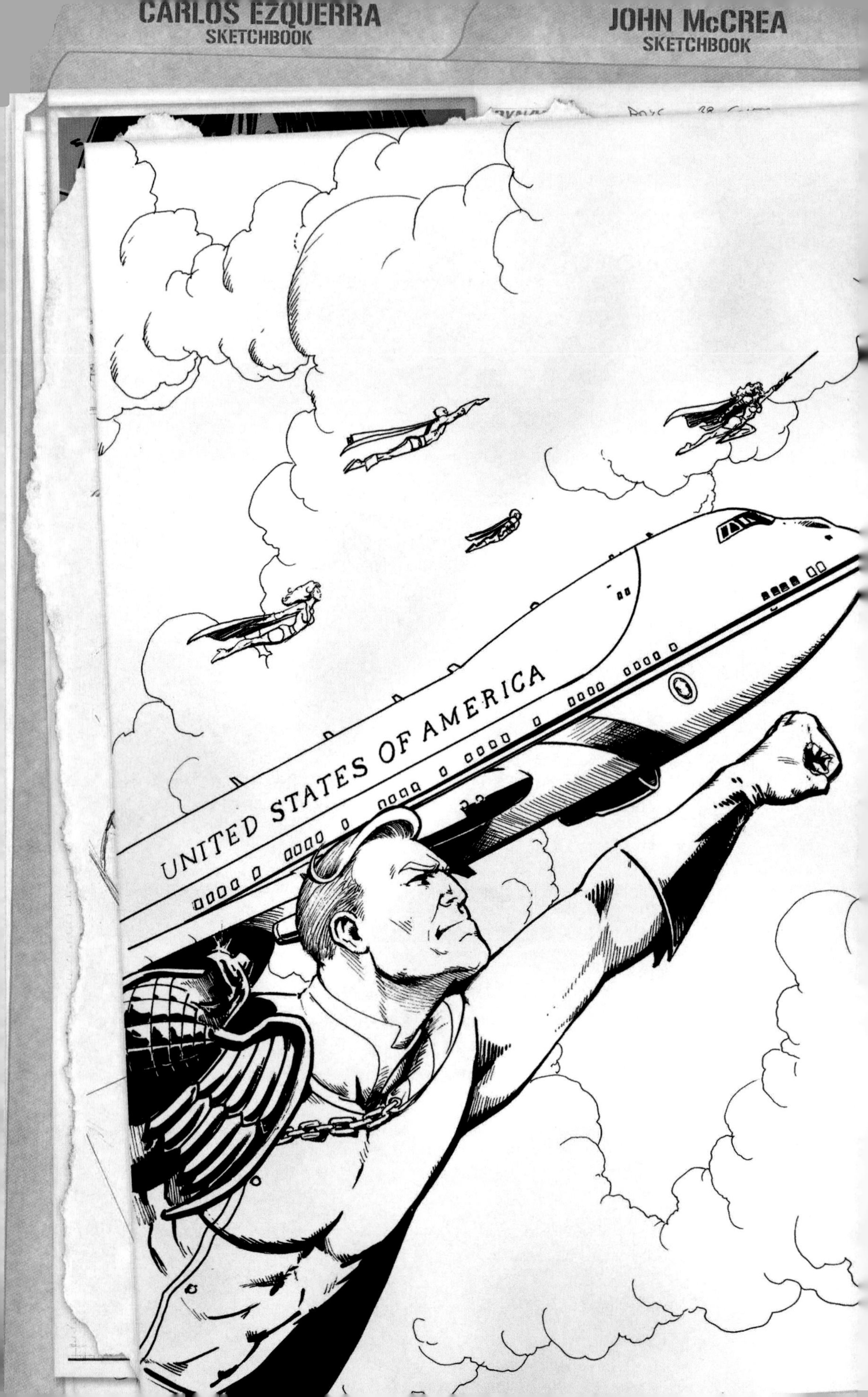
CARLOS EZQUERRA
SKETCHBOOK
JOHN McCREA
SKETCHBOOK
UNITED STATES OF AMERICA

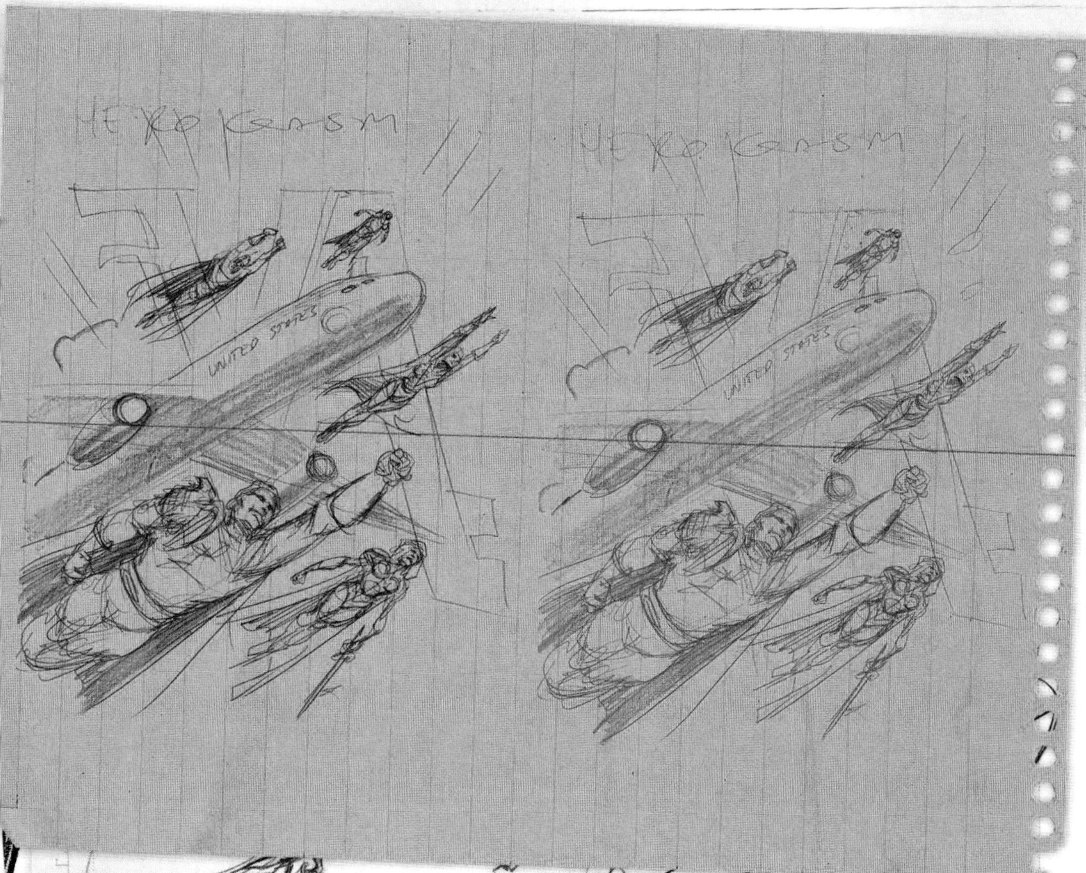
HEROGASM
UNITED STATES
HEROGASM
UNITED STATES

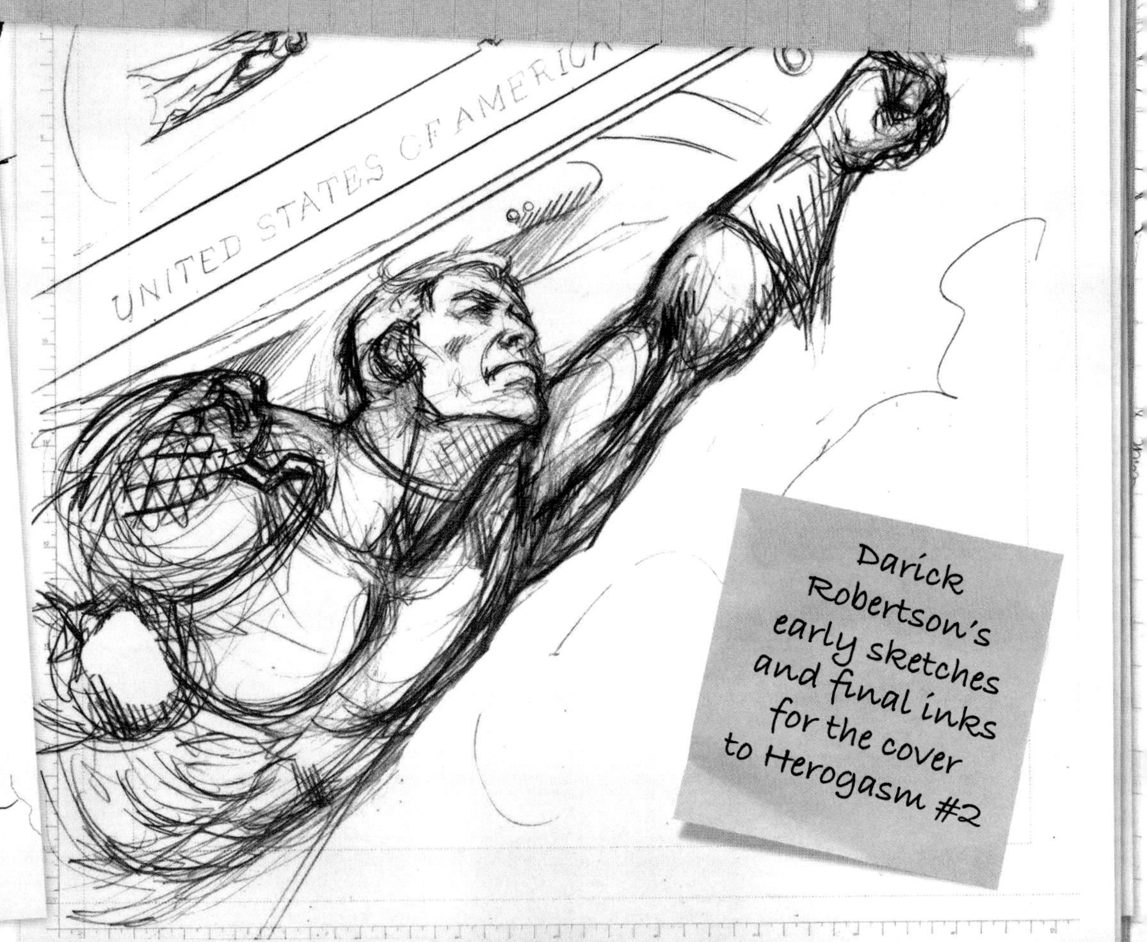
UNITED STATES OF AMERIC

Darick Robertson's early sketches and final inks for the cover to Herogasm #2

CARLOS EZQUERRA
SKETCHBOOK

JOHN McCREA
SKETCHBOOK

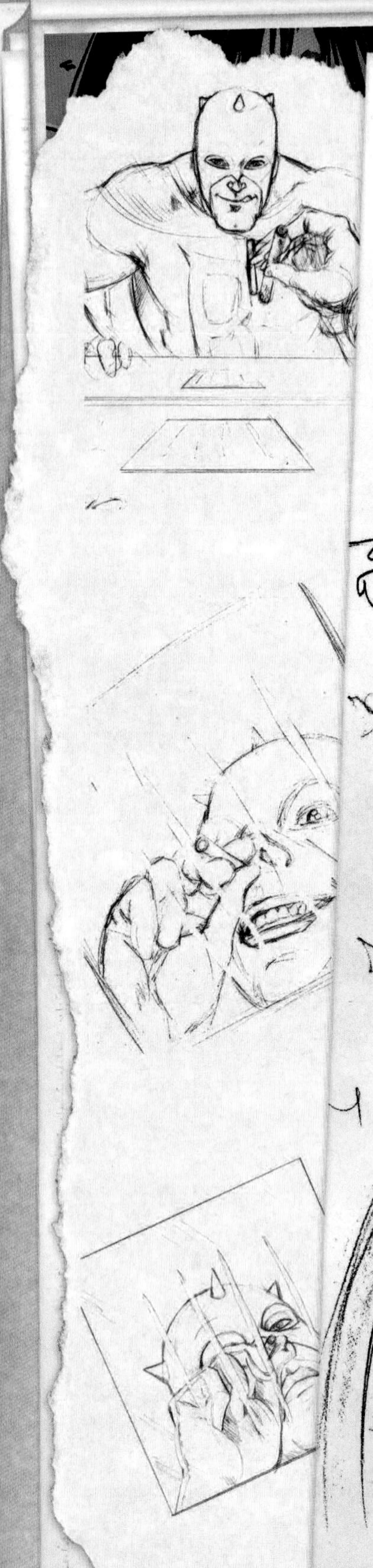

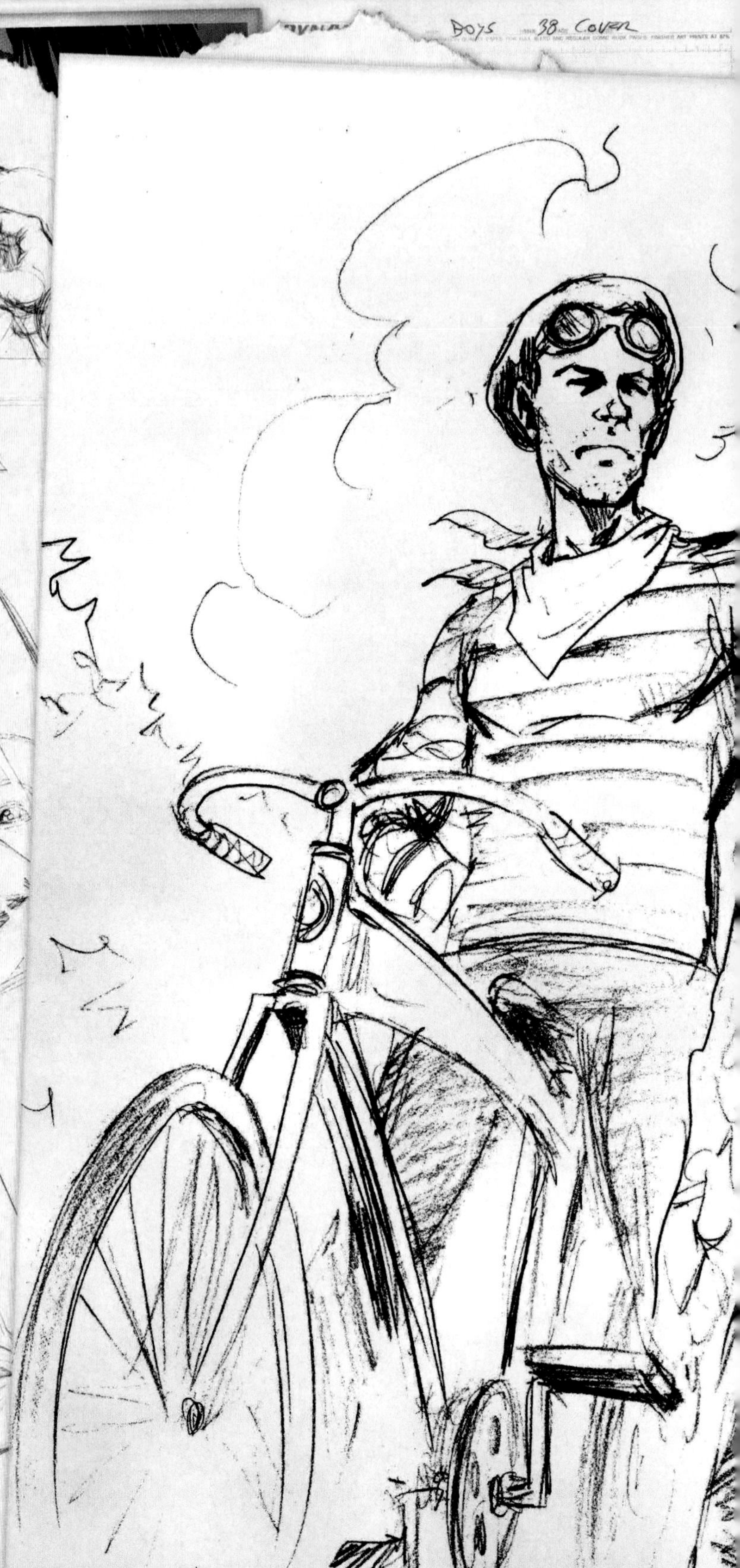
BOYS 38 COVER

DARICK ROBERTSON
SKETCHBOOK

BOYS #37 SCRIPT

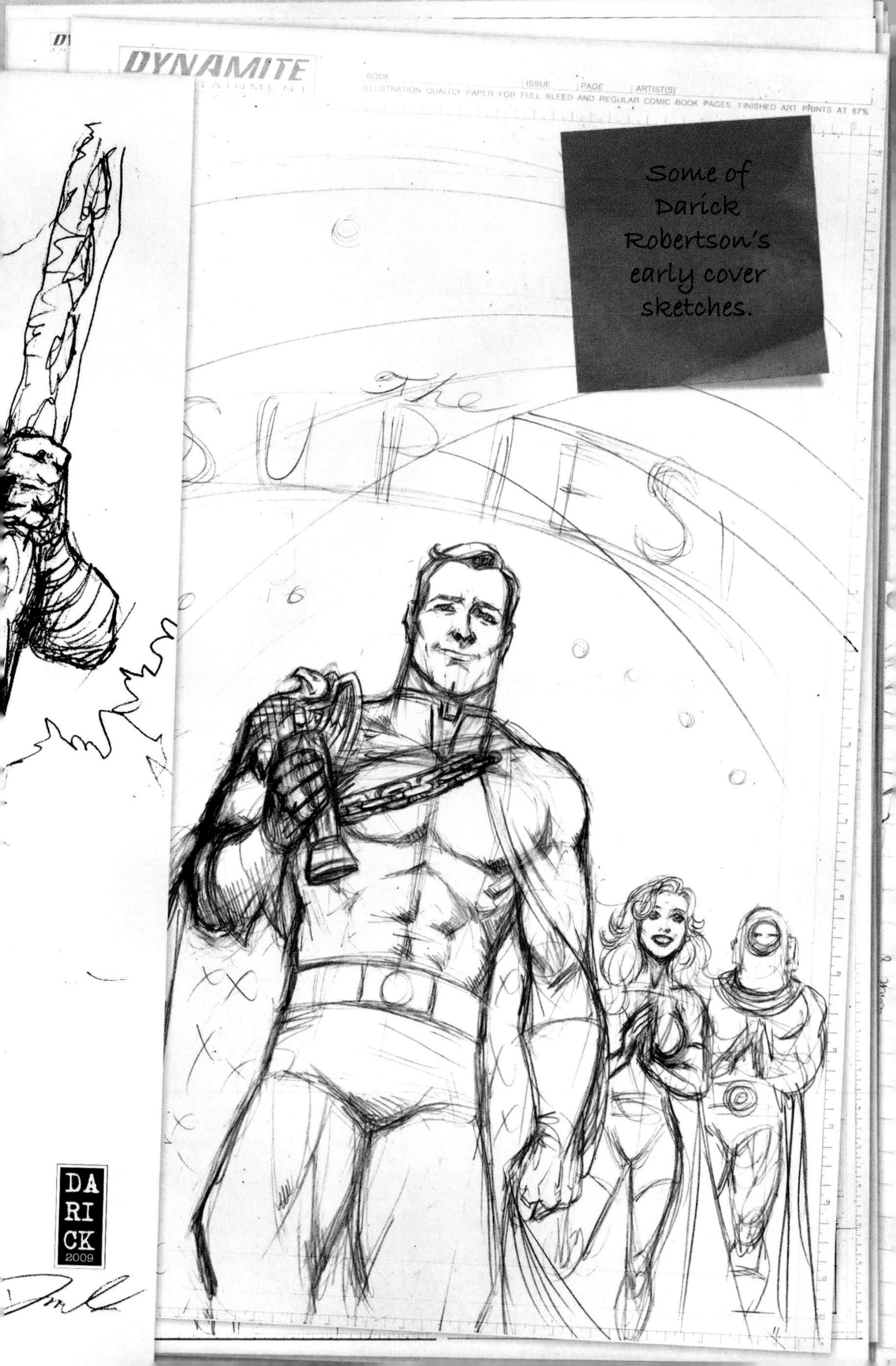
DYNAMITE
BOOK
ISSUE
PAGE
ARTIST(S)
ILLUSTRATION QUALITY PAPER FOR FULL BLEED AND REGULAR COMIC BOOK PAGES. FINISHED ART PRINTS AT 67%
DA
RI
CK
2009

Some of Darick Robertson's early cover sketches.

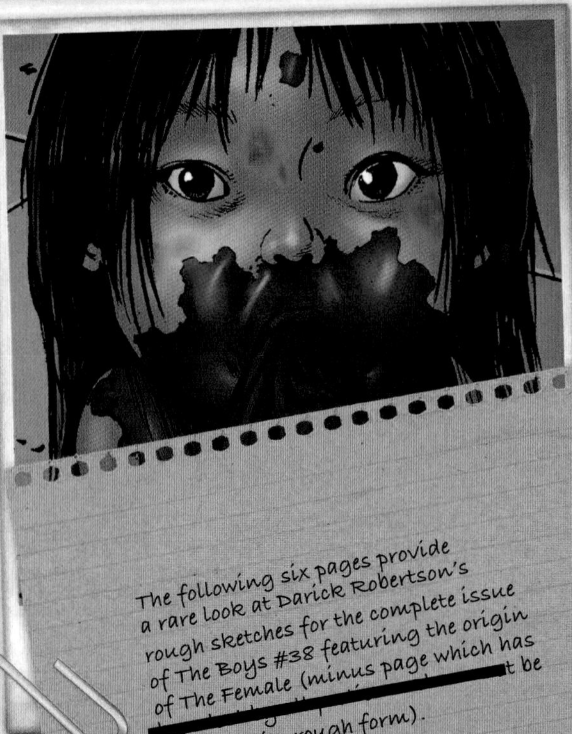

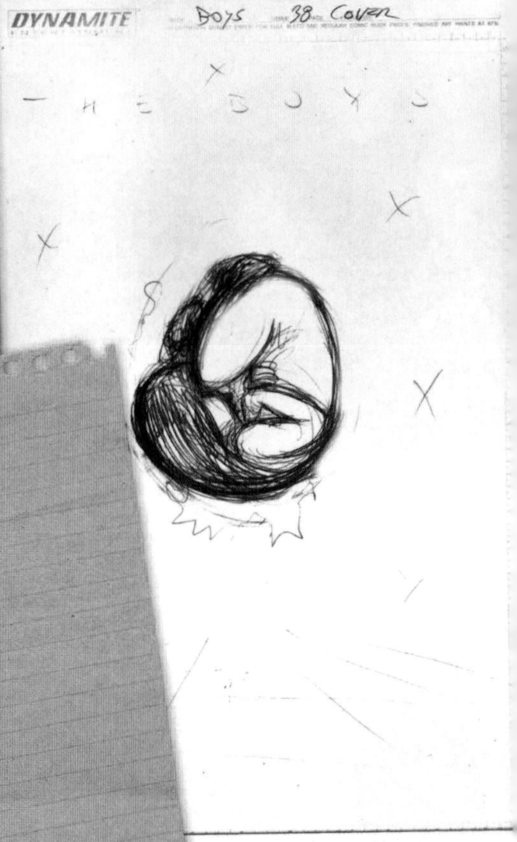
DYNAMITE
BOYS 38 COVER
THE BOYS

The following six pages provide a rare look at Darick Robertson's rough sketches for the complete issue of The Boys #38 featuring the origin of The Female (minus page which has [redacted] be shown in its rough form).

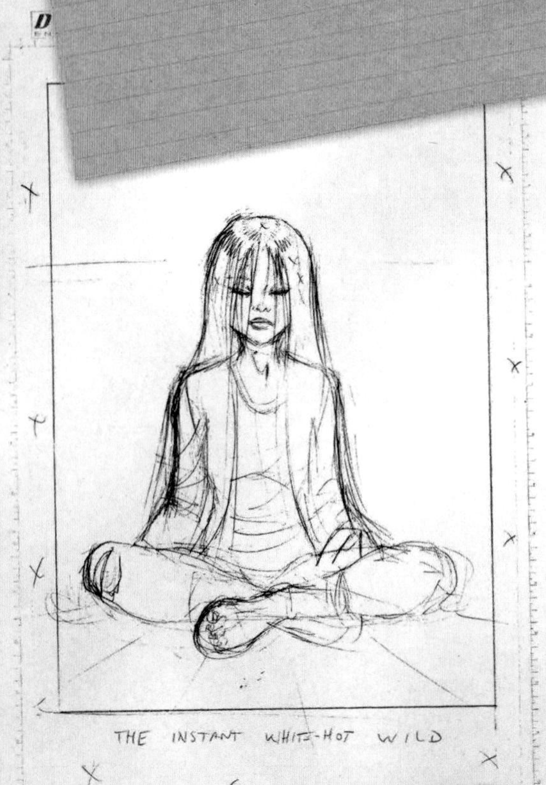
THE INSTANT WHITE-HOT WILD

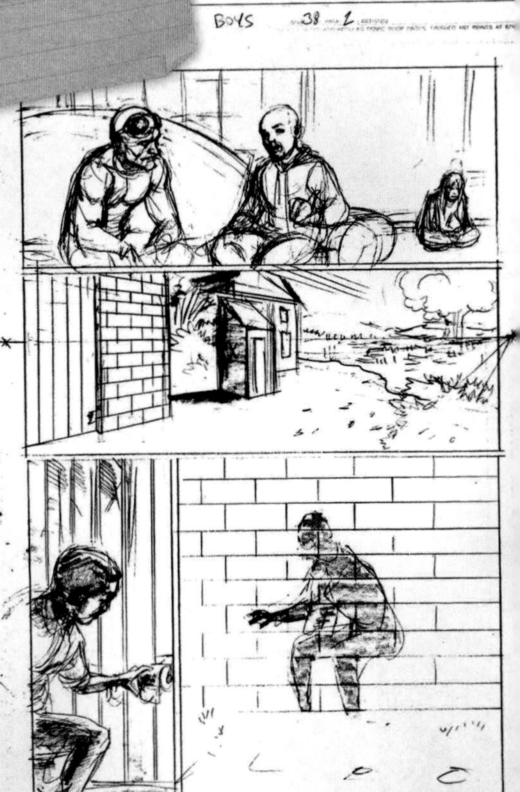
BOYS 38 1

DARICK ROBERTSON
SKETCHBOOK

BOYS #37 SCRIPT

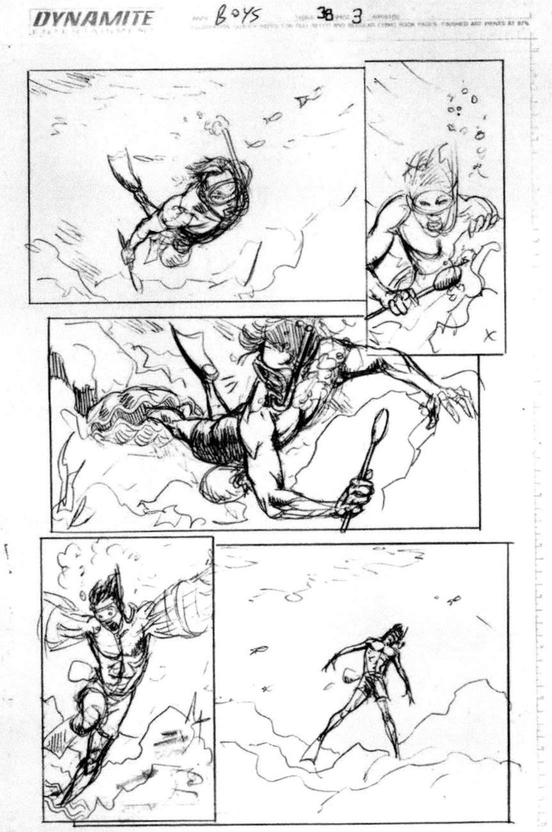
DYNAMITE
ENTERTAINMENT
BOYS 38 3

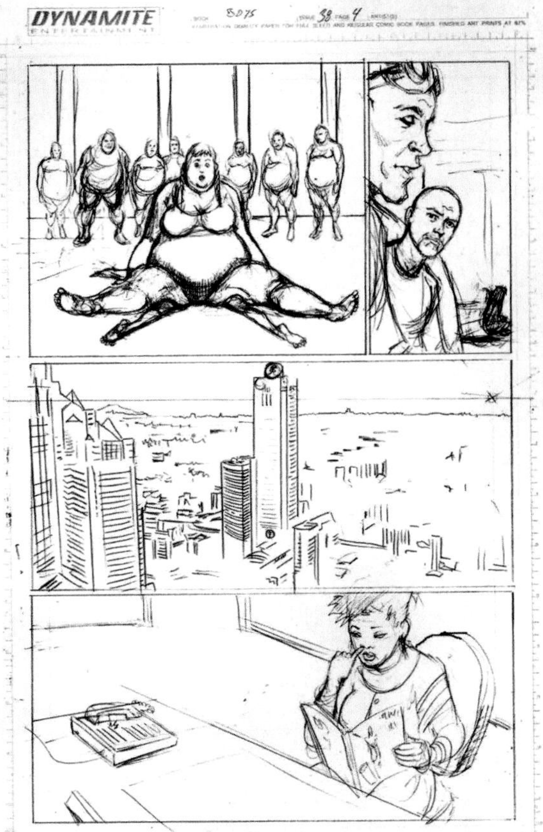
DYNAMITE
ENTERTAINMENT
BOYS 38 4

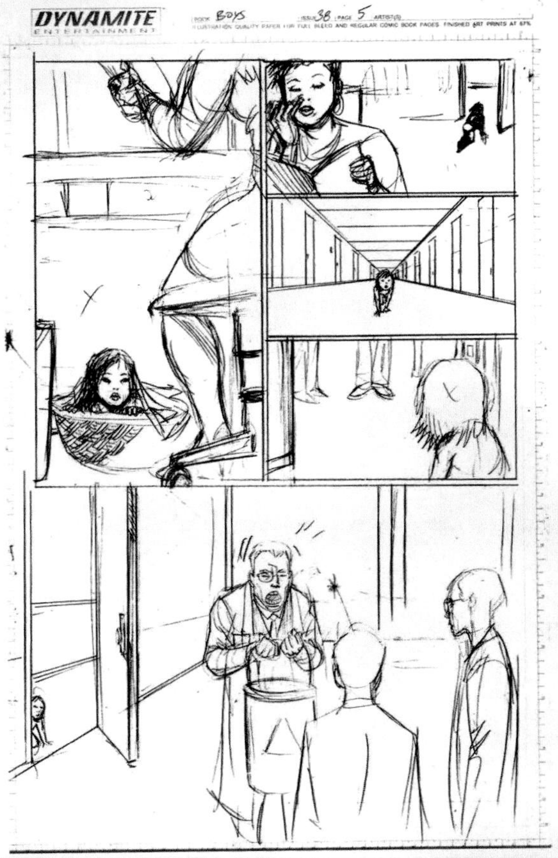
DYNAMITE
ENTERTAINMENT
BOYS 38 5

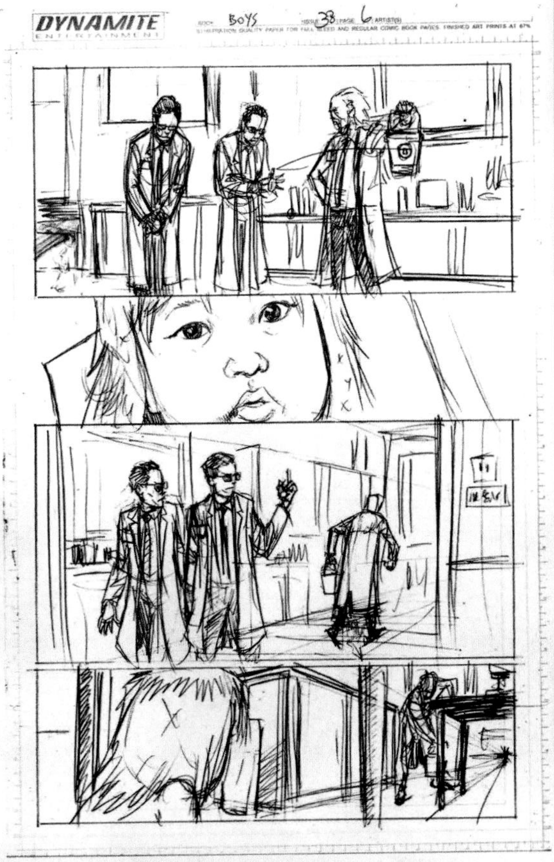
DYNAMITE
ENTERTAINMENT
BOYS 38 6

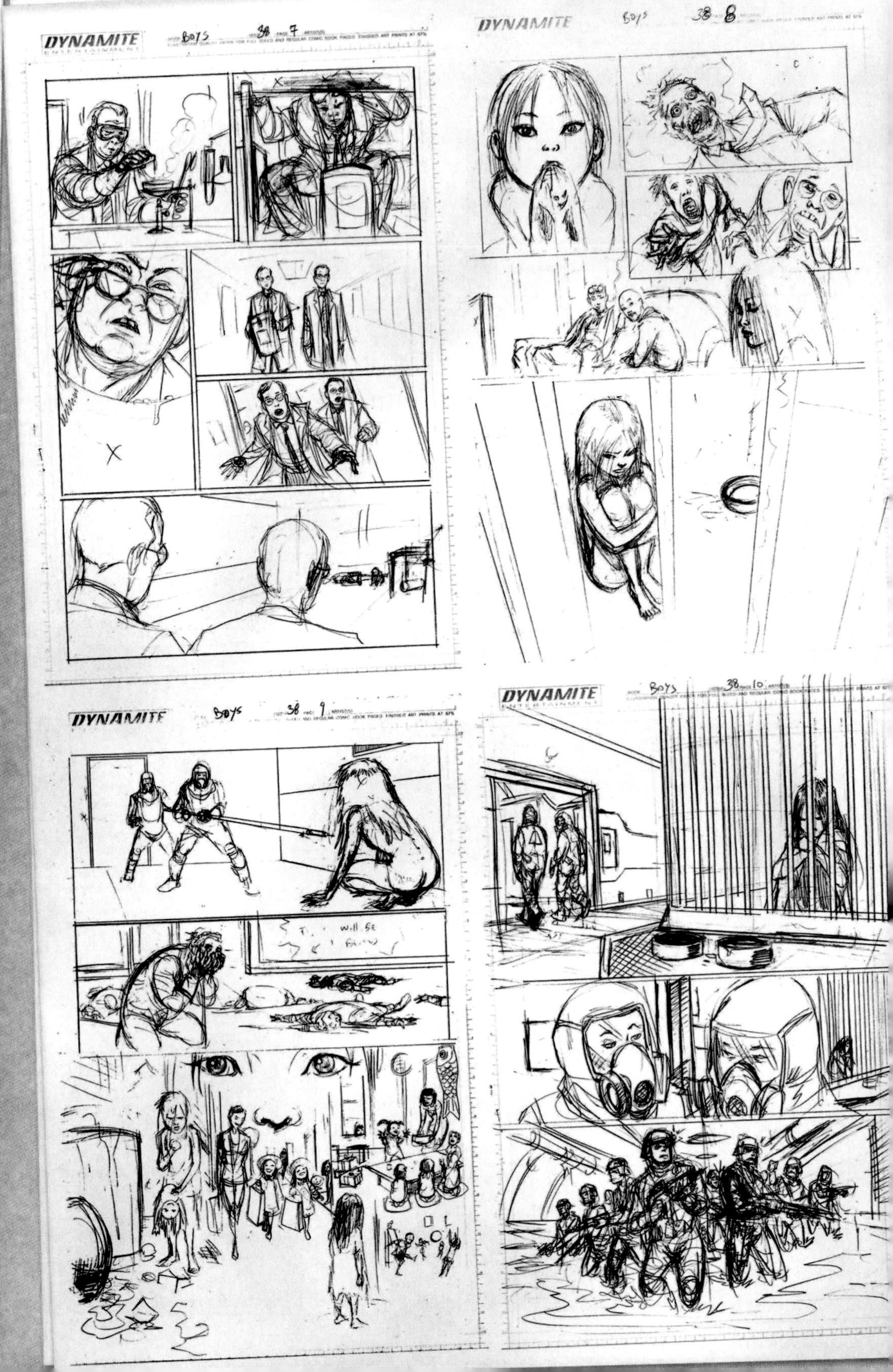
DYNAMITE
Boys 38 7
DYNAMITE
Boys 38 8
DYNAMITE
Boys 38 9
DYNAMITE
Boys 38 10

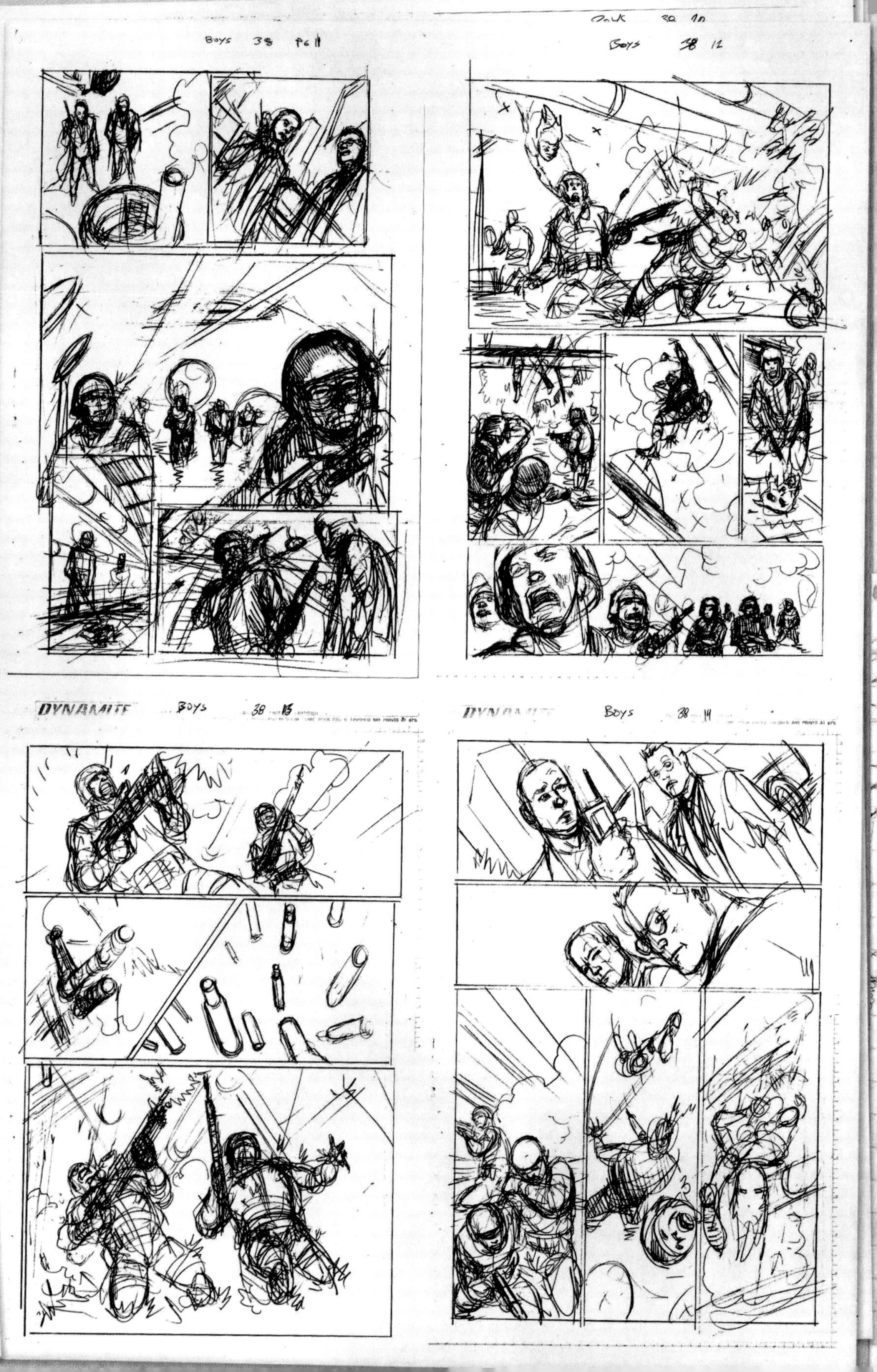
Boys 38 PG 11
Boys 38 12
DYNAMITE
Boys 38 13
DYNAMITE
Boys 38 14

CARLOS EZQUERRA
SKETCHBOOK

JOHN McCREA
SKETCHBOOK

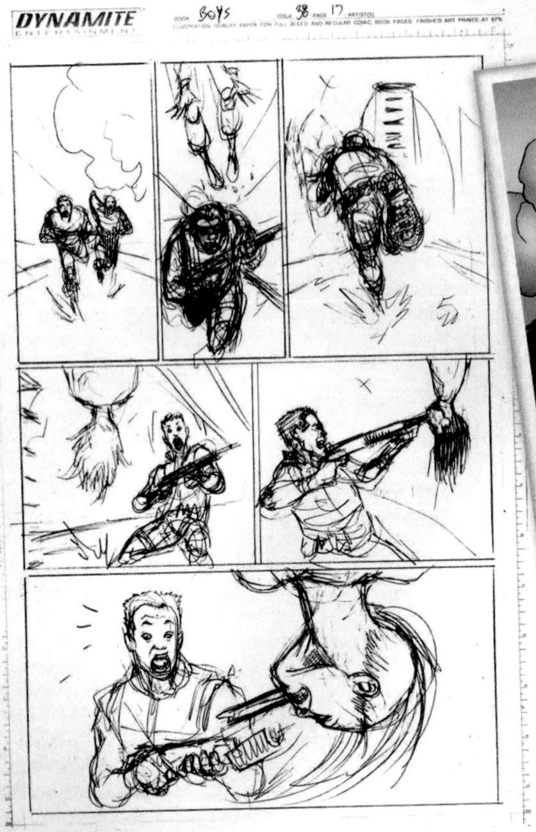

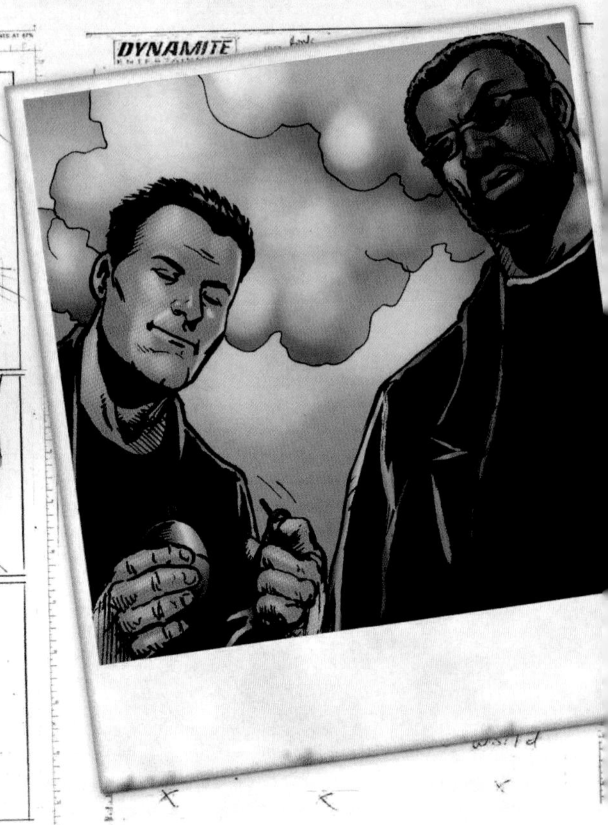

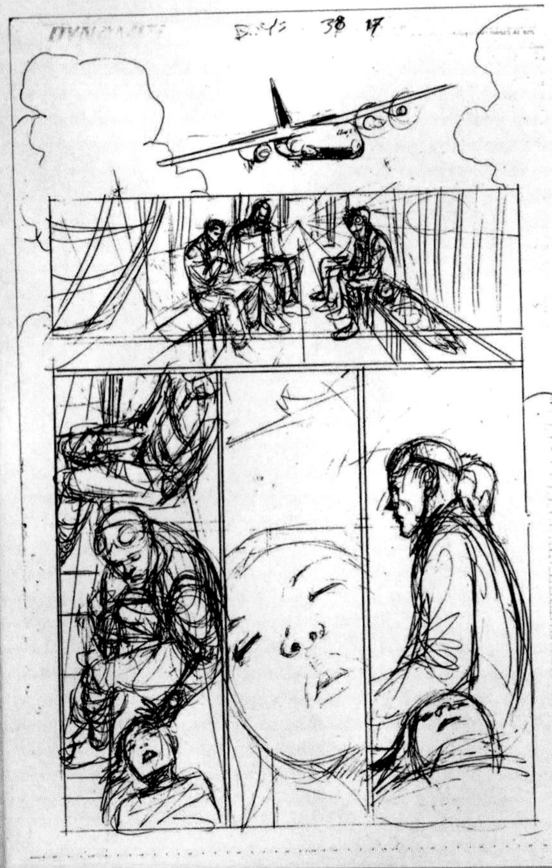

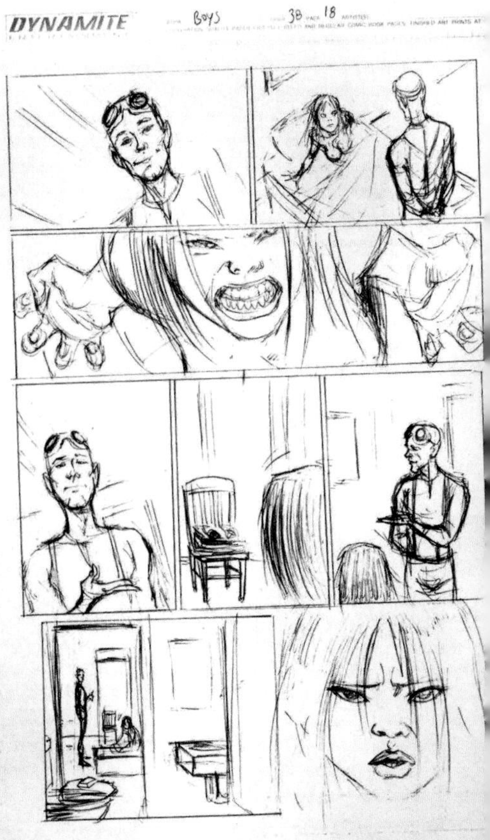

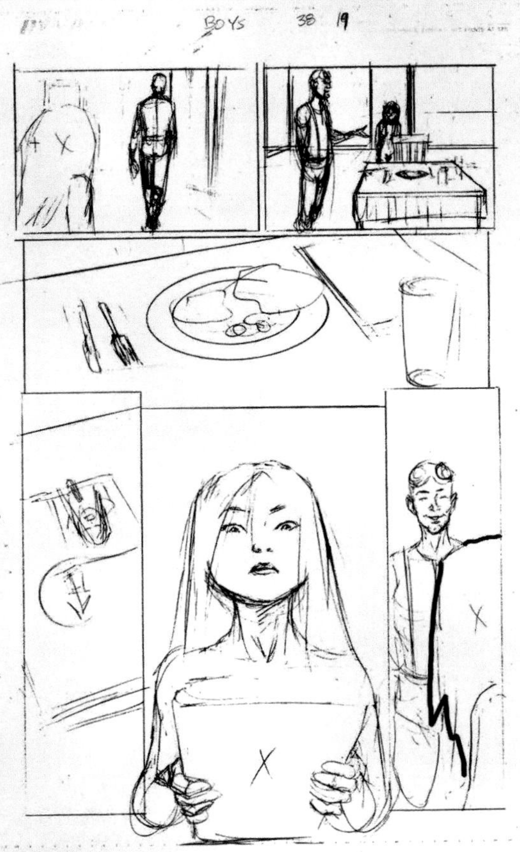
BOYS 38 19

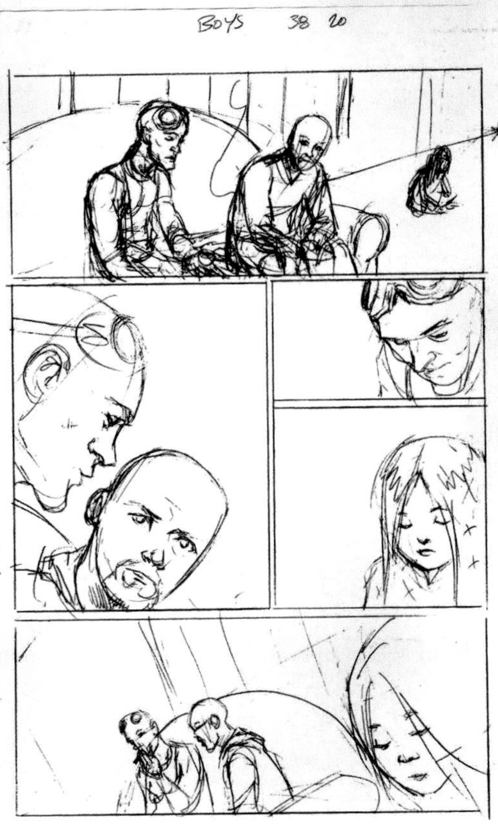
BOYS 38 20

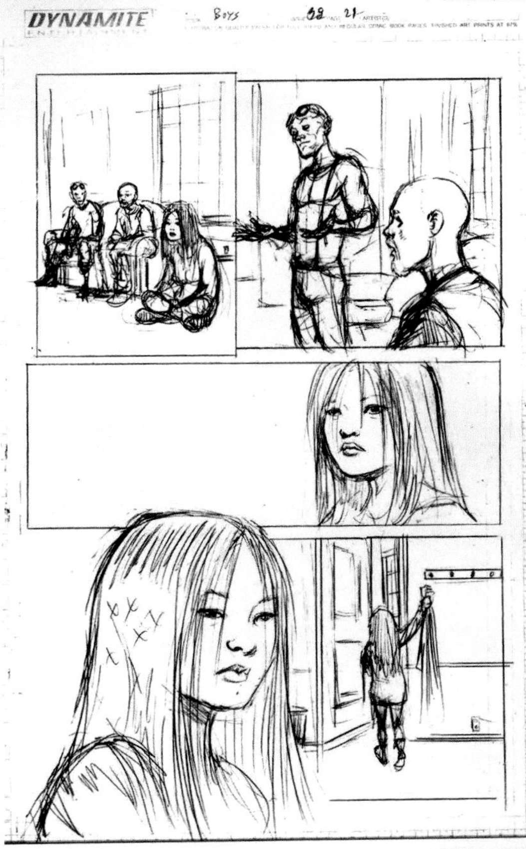
DYNAMITE
BOYS
21

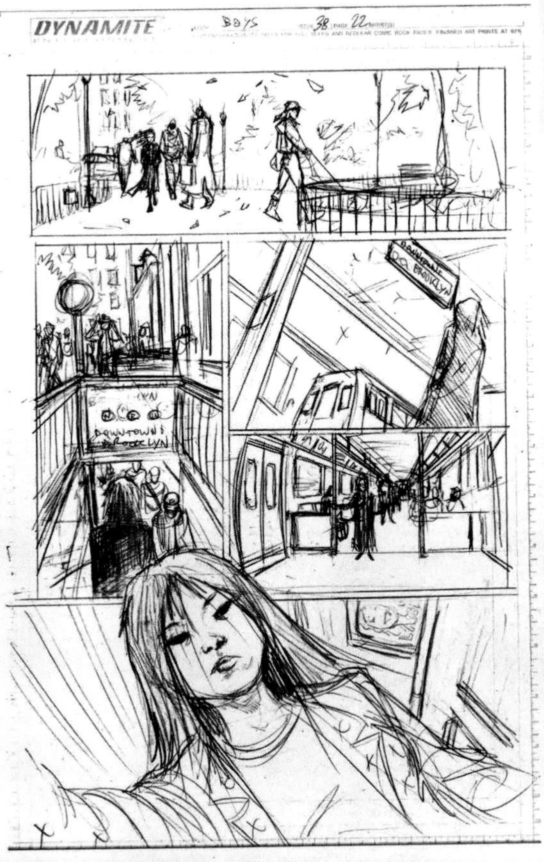
DYNAMITE
BOYS 38 22
DOWNTOWN & BROOKLYN

HEROGASM
PAGES 10-11 ROUGHS
by JOHN McCREA

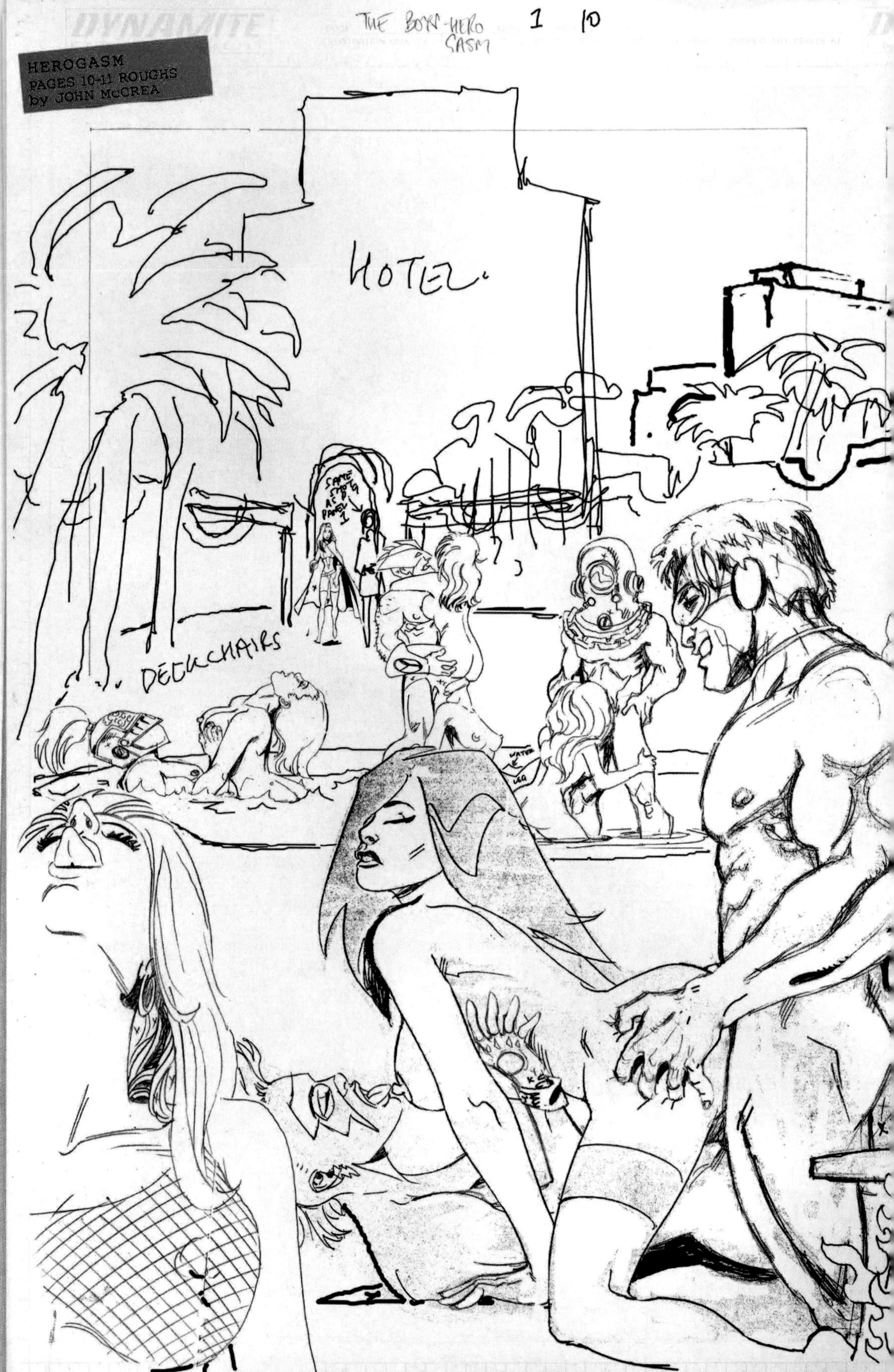
THE BOYS-HERO GASM 1 10
HOTEL
DECKCHAIRS
WATER
LEG

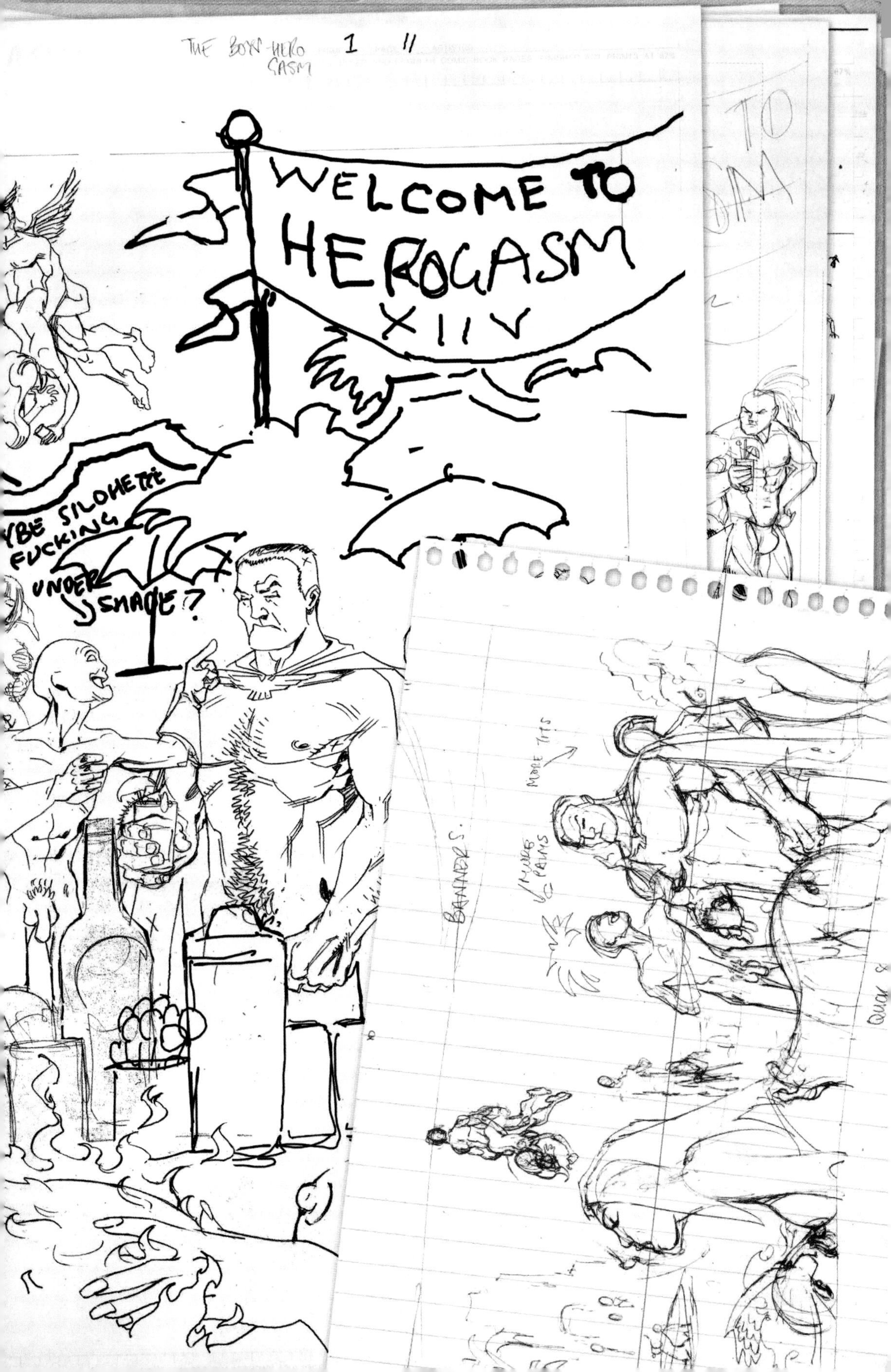
THE BOYS-HERO GASM 1 11
WELCOME TO HEROGASM XIIV
YBE SILOHETTE FUCKING UNDER SHADE?
MORE TITS
MORE PALMS
BANNERS

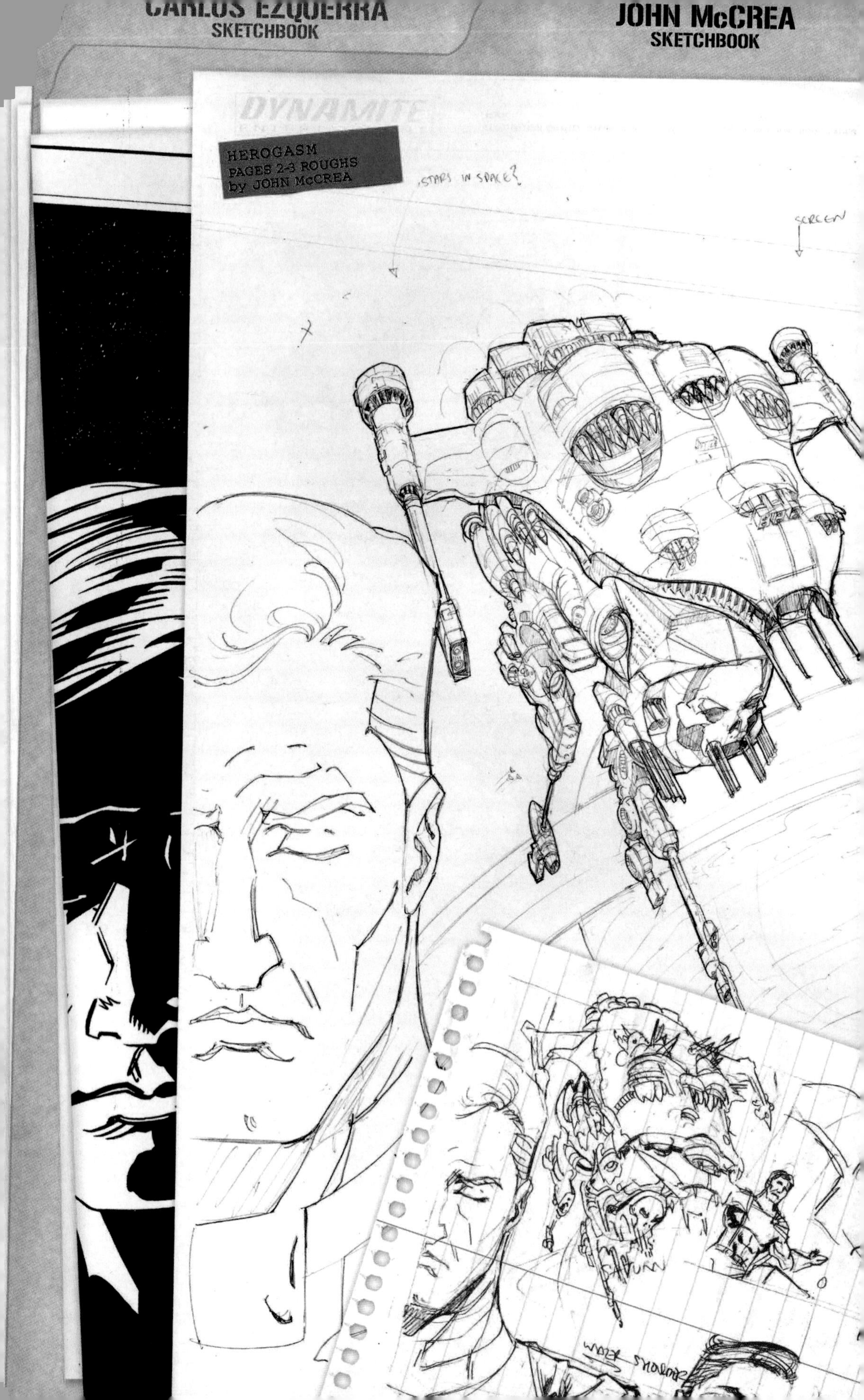
CARLOS EZQUERRA
SKETCHBOOK
JOHN McCREA
SKETCHBOOK
HEROGASM
PAGES 2-3 ROUGHS
by JOHN McCREA
STARS IN SPACE?
SCREEN
SATURN

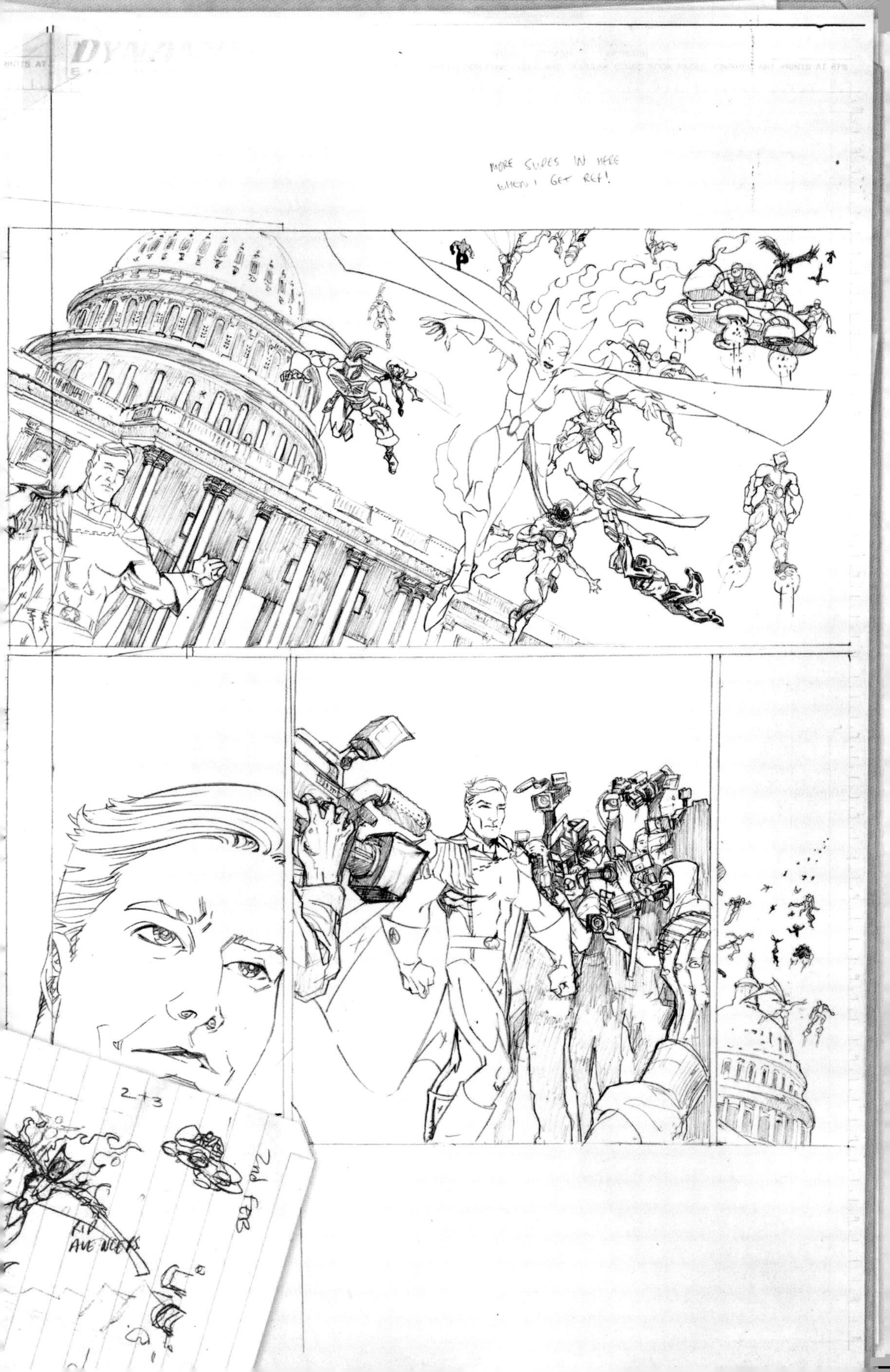
MORE SUPES IN HERE WHEN I GET REF!
2+3
2nd FEB
AVENGERS

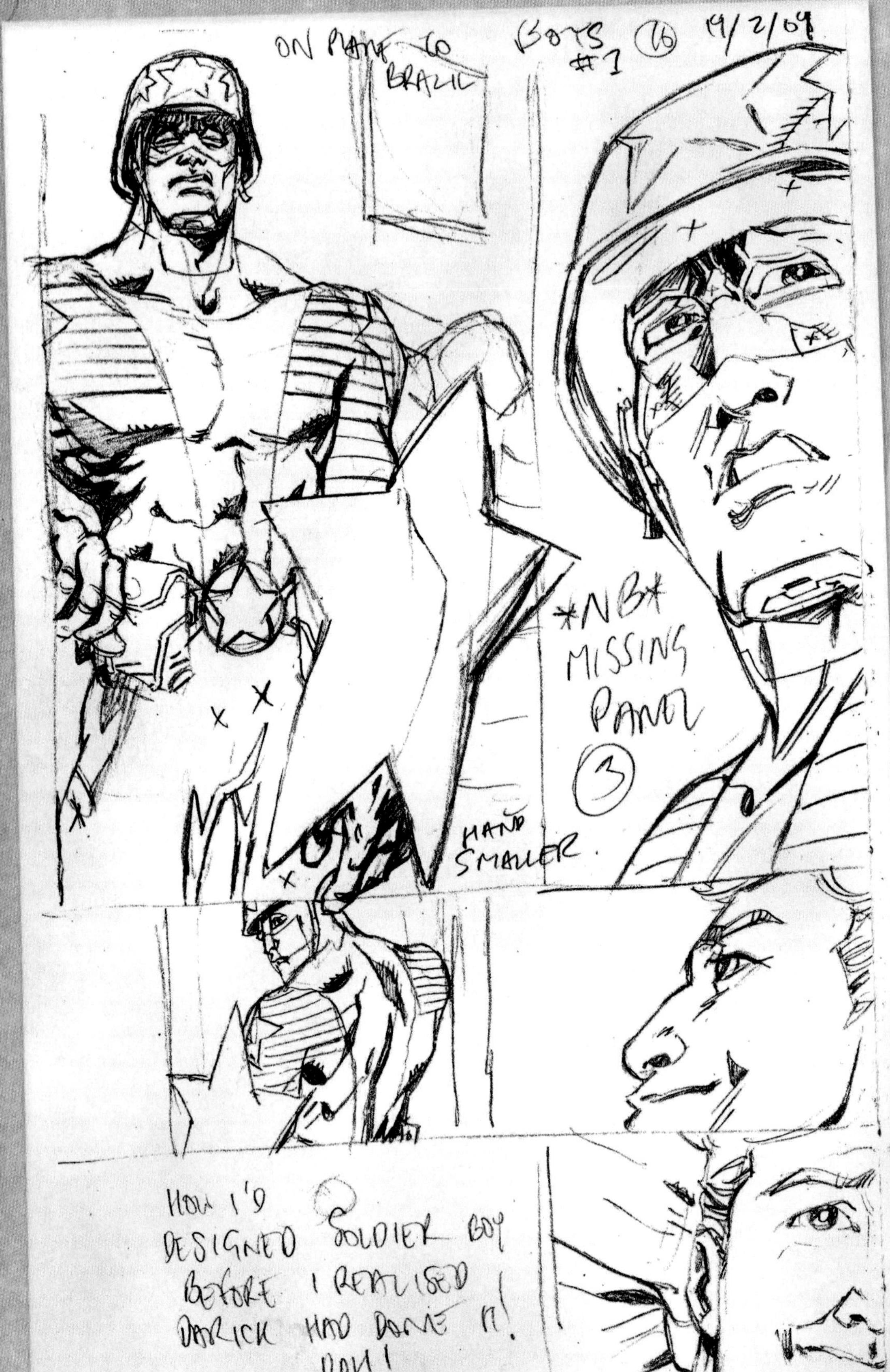
ON PLANE TO BRAZIL
BOYS #7
16
19/2/09
NB MISSING PANEL 3
HAND SMALLER
HOW I'D DESIGNED SOLDIER BOY BEFORE I REALISED DARICK HAD DONE IT! DOH!

DARICK ROBERTSON SKETCHBOOK

BOYS #37 SCRIPT

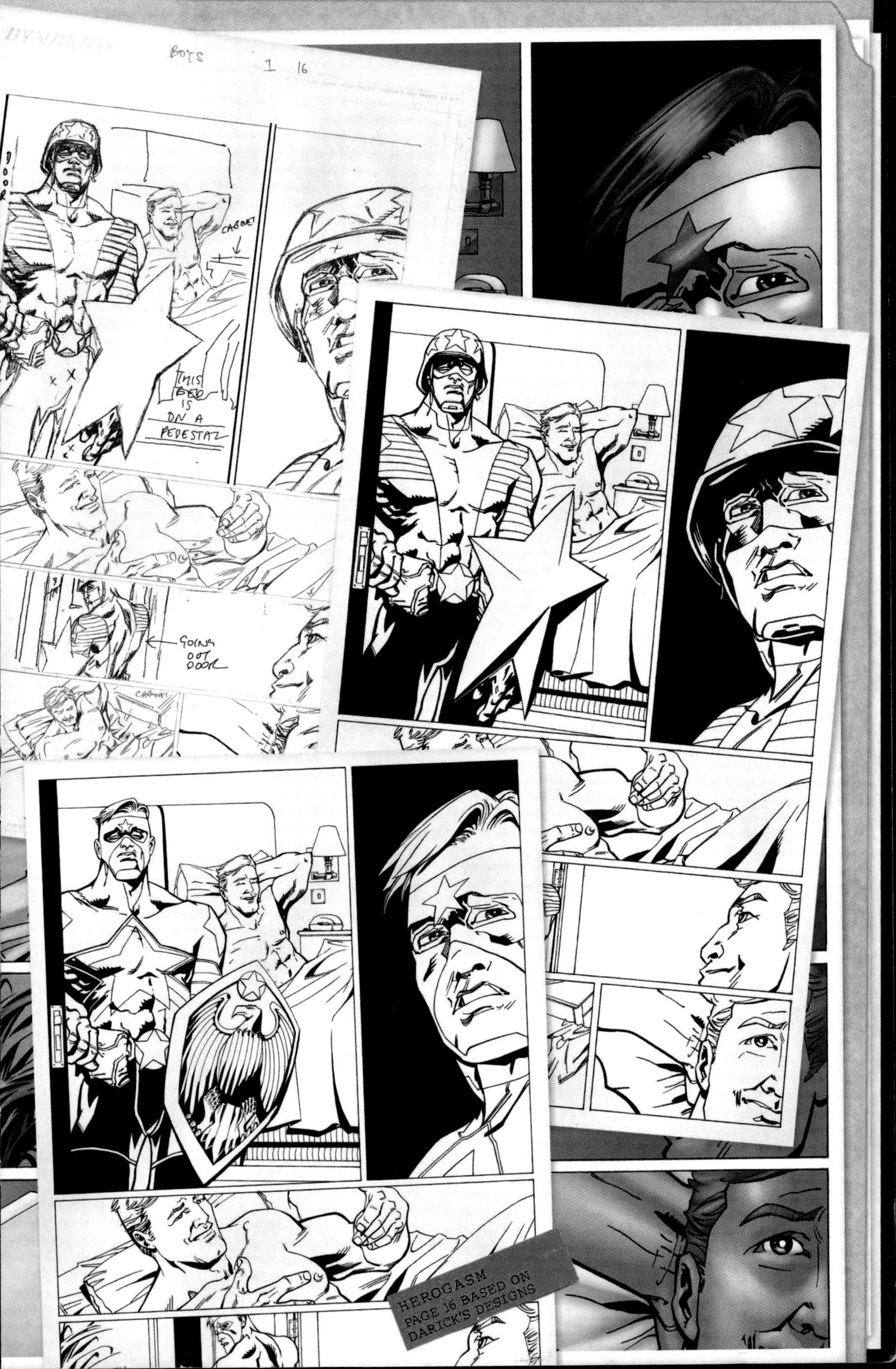
BOYS 1 16
DOOR
CABINET
THIS BED IS ON A PEDESTAL
GOING OUT DOOR
CABINET
HEROGASM
PAGE 16 BASED ON
DARICK'S DESIGNS

CARLOS EZQUERRA
SKETCHBOOK

JOHN McCREA
SKETCHBOOK

Carlos Ezquerra's roughs for The Boys' battle with Stormfront in The Boys #34

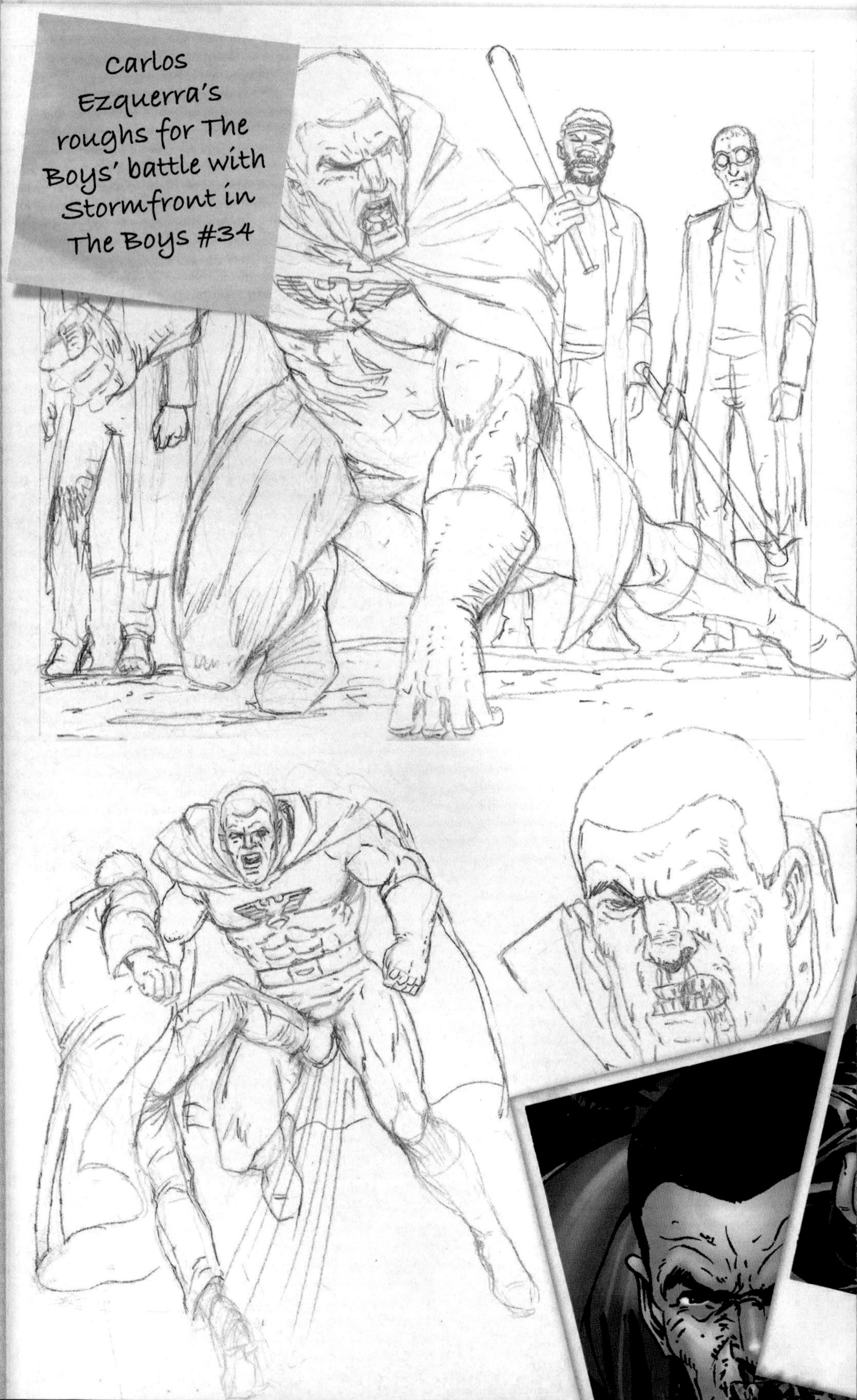

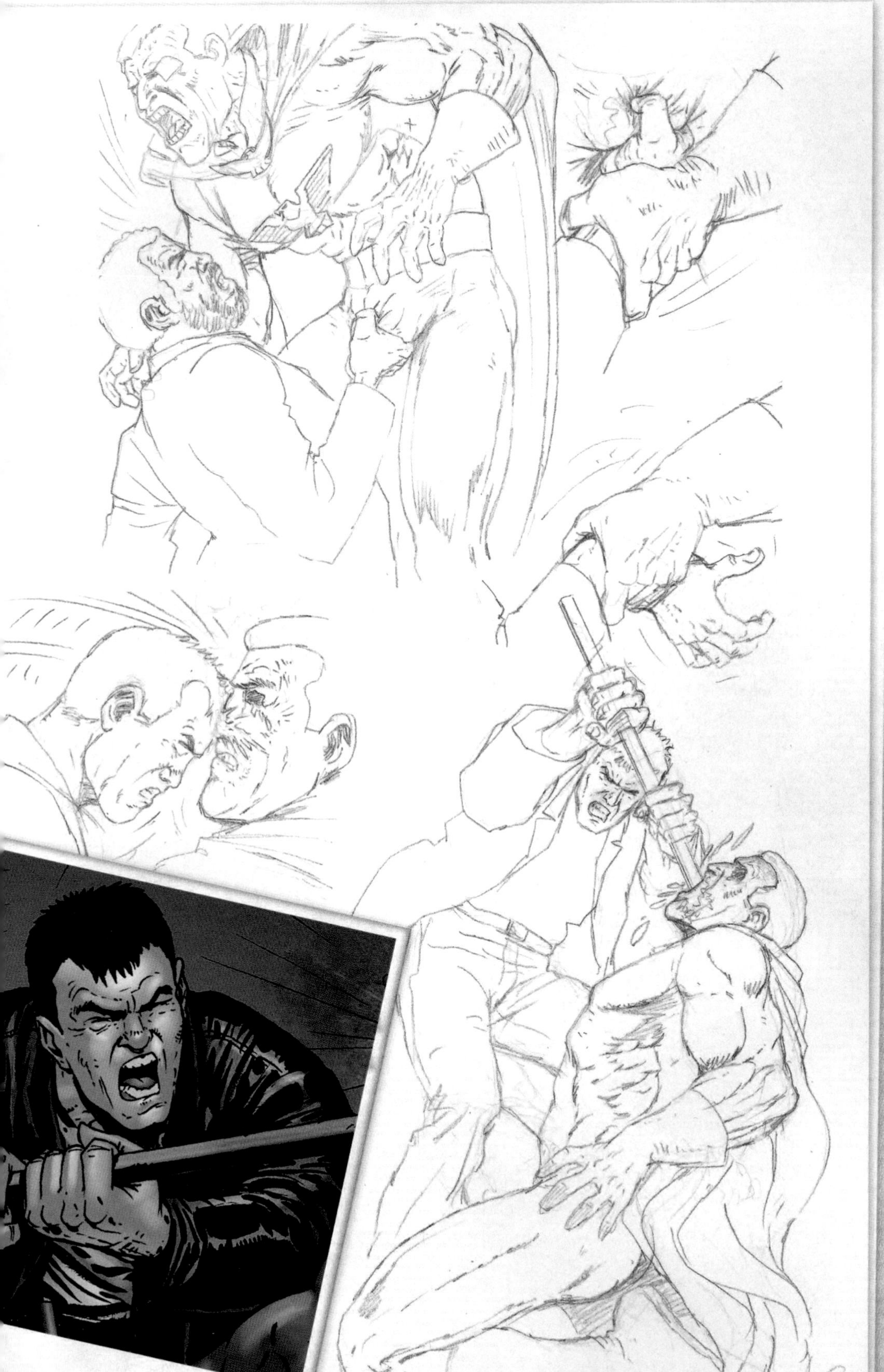

GARTH ENNIS

Garth Ennis has been writing comics since 1989. Credits include *Preacher*, *Hitman*, *Crossed*, *Rover Red Charlie*, *Code Pru*, *Caliban*, *War Stories*, *A Walk Through Hell* and *Sara*, and successful runs on *The Punisher* and *Fury* for Marvel Comics. Originally from Northern Ireland, Ennis now resides in New York City with his wife, Ruth.

DARICK ROBERTSON

Darick Robertson is an American comic book artist, writer and creator with a decades long career in the industry. Born and raised in the Northern California Bay Area and self trained as an artist, his notable works include co-creating the award winning *Transmetropolitan*, *The Boys*, *Happy!*, and *Oliver* with Gary Whitta for Image Comics, debuting in January 2019. Darick has illustrated for both Marvel and DC Comics on characters including Batman, The Justice League, Wolverine, The Punisher, and Spider-man.

JOHN McCREA

Artist John McCrea was born in Belfast, and has worked extensively in the British and American comic book industries. He previously worked with writer Garth Ennis on *Troubled Souls*, *For a Few Troubles More*, *Judge Dredd*, *The Demon*, *Hitman*, *Dicks*, *Chopper*, and *All Star Section Eight*. He can be found online at www.johnmccrea.com

KEITH BURNS

Keith Burns has drawn the war comics *Castles in the Sky* and *Out of the Blue*, as well as the successful revival of classic British character *Johnny Red*. He is a member of the Guild of Aviation Artists. Originally from Dublin, Ireland, Burns now resides in England.

CARLOS EZQUERRA

An industry veteran of countless stories and perhaps most famously known as the co-creator of *Judge Dredd*, Carlos Ezquerra has frequently been a collaborator with Ennis on such comics as *Bloody Mary*, *War Stories*, *The Authority*, *World of Tanks*, *Hitman*, *Preacher* and *The Boys* along with Ennis' *Battlefields* from Dynamite. Sadly, Ezquerra passed away in October 2018.

TONY AVIÑA

Tony Aviña got his start as an in-house colorist at WIldwtorm. His credits include *Sleeper*, *Stormwatch: Team Achilles*, *Authority: Prime*, *Battlefields*, *The Boys*, *Sherlock Holmes*, *Green Lantern*, *Justice League, Batman '66, Wonder Woman '77,* and *Suicide Squad: Hell to Pay*. He currently lives in St. Louis, which, contrary to popular belief, isn't one big farm (it's actually three or four moderately sized farms).

SIMON BOWLAND

Simon Bowland has been lettering comics since 2004, and in that time has worked for all of the mainstream publishers. Born and bred in the UK, Simon still lives there today alongside Pippa, his partner, and Jess, their tabby cat.

COLLECT THE COMPLETE SERIES!

**THE BOYS
OMNIBUS VOL. 1 TP**

978-1-5241-0859-5

Ennis, Robertson,
Snejbjerg

**THE BOYS
OMNIBUS VOL. 2 TP**

978-1-5241-0970-7

Ennis, Robertson,
Higgins

**THE BOYS
OMNIBUS VOL. 3 TP**

978-1-5241-1003-1

Ennis, Robertson
McCrea, Ezquerra

**THE BOYS
OMNIBUS VOL. 4 TP**

978-1-5241-1140-3

Ennis, Braun, McCrea,
Burns, Clark, Robertson

**THE BOYS
OMNIBUS VOL. 5 TP**

978-1-5241-1334-6

Ennis. Braun, McCrea,
Burns, Robertson

**THE BOYS
OMNIBUS VOL. 6 TP**

978-1-5241-1337-7

Ennis, Braun, McCrea,
Burns, Clark, Robertson

ALSO AVAILABLE FROM GARTH ENNIS & DYNAMITE:

THE COMPLETE BATTLEFIELDS VOL. 1 TP 978-1-60690-0255-4
THE COMPLETE BATTLEFIELDS VOL. 2 TP 978-1-5241-0385-9
THE COMPLETE BATTLEFIELDS VOL. 3 TP 978-1-5241-0474-0

RED TEAM VOL. 1 TP 978-1-6069-0443-5
RED TEAM VOL. 2: DOUBLE TAP, CENTER MASS TP 978-1-5241-0395-8

A TRAIN CALLED LOVE TP 978-1-5241-0168-8
JENNIFER BLOOD VOL. 1: A WOMEN'S WORK IS NEVER DONE TP 978-1-6069-0261-5

VISIT WWW.DYNAMITE.COM FOR A FULL LIST!